William M. Baker

A History

of the Tennessee

Supreme Court

A History of the Tennessee Supreme Court

JAMES W. ELY JR.
EDITOR

with

Theodore Brown Jr.
Timothy S. Huebner
R. Ben Brown
Ruth Anne Thompson
John R. Vile
Carl A. Pierce

Sponsored by Tennessee Supreme Court
Historical Society, Inc.

The University of Tennessee Press
Knoxville

First Edition.

This book is printed on acid-free paper.

Library of Congress Cataloging-in-Publication Data

A history of the Tennessee Supreme Court / editor, James W. Ely, Jr. ; with Theodore Brown, Jr. [et al.].
p. cm.
Includes bibliographical references and index.
ISBN 1-57233-178-X (cl.: alk. paper)
1. Tennessee. Supreme Court—History. I. Ely, James W., 1938– .
II. Brown, Theodore, Jr.
KFT512 .H57 2002
347.768'035'09–dc21 2001006534

TO VALERIUS SANFORD, whose leadership made the grand idea of a history of the Tennessee Supreme Court into a fine reality. Val has been a lawyer for more than fifty years and deems it a high honor to be one. He is dedicated to his clients and their causes, but he is also dedicated to the law itself as an important part of the civilized world. He is deeply interested in how the law began and how it evolved. It was not surprising, therefore, that he answered with an enthusiastic yes when asked to lead the effort to form the Tennessee Supreme Court Historical Society. Val brought the society into being, persuading many lawyers and other persons to be founding members, and he served as the society's first president. He followed through in every way to see that this history was written.

The first major project of the society is the publication of this history of the Tennessee Supreme Court. It is an important task. To quote Val, "Thus to understand, appreciate, or evaluate the law of any state, it is necessary to know something of the history of the law and of the people who shaped it. Lawyers, particularly, but, as well, all who take seriously their role as citizens, should foster that sense of the history of the law." Thanks to Val's leadership, the history of the Tennessee Supreme Court is now available to all citizens. It is a proud story and one that is well told in this book.

SO ORDERED by the Board of the Society.

CONTENTS

FIGURES

PREFACE

The history of the Supreme Court of the United States has been well chronicled. Few scholars, however, have explored the experience of state supreme courts. This omission threatens to distort our understanding of the evolution of legal doctrine and the importance of state law in the federal system. Over time state supreme courts have played a pivotal role in the growth of law. Before the adoption of the Fourteenth Amendment in 1868 state courts enjoyed substantial freedom to formulate legal doctrine. Despite the centralizing forces of the twentieth century and the growth of overriding federal constitutional law, state courts remain largely free to set their own agenda respecting private law, such as torts, contracts, and property. Moreover, state supreme courts have often been called upon to grapple with thorny legal issues long before they reached the Supreme Court of the United States. Indeed, developments at the state level frequently foreshadowed subsequent federal action. The decisions of state supreme courts, therefore, provide a unique window through which to glimpse how law functioned to meet the needs of society. Clearly the history of state supreme courts is a rich vein for historians to mine.

The scholarly neglect of state supreme courts is slowly changing, with the recent publication of volumes on the history of the high courts in Florida,[1] Missouri,[2] Massachusetts,[3] Virginia[4] and Washington.[5] The early history of the Pennsylvania Supreme Court has received attention.[6] Aspects of the history of the other state supreme courts have also been studied.[7] Likewise, historians have examined the work of southern high courts during the Civil War.[8] Projects dealing with the California Supreme Court, the Supreme Court of Delaware, the Supreme Court of Louisiana, and the Texas Supreme Court are well underway. Further, scholars have begun to provide collective portraits of state supreme court judges, and to analyze the caseload, dissent rate, and decisional patterns of state high courts.[9]

Additionally, there is a sizable literature on the political dimensions of state supreme court behavior. Scholars have studied policy making and judicial activism by state high courts.[10] Others have probed judicial selection and the issues raised by popular elections of judges.[11] But much remains to be done. Greater attention to the vital place of state courts in American legal history is essential to gain a better understanding of these important tribunals.

In common with most of its counterparts, the story of the Tennessee Supreme Court has never been told. To be sure, some scattered articles and sections in books consider aspects of the Court's history. But this book is the first attempt to treat systematically the development of the Tennessee Supreme Court, and to assess its place in the state's polity. The purpose of this volume is to provide a scholarly history of the Tennessee Supreme Court, and its predecessor, the Superior Court of Law and Equity, from statehood in 1796 through the judicial election of 1998. The book examines the role of the Court in the development of Tennessee and analyzes its decisions within the larger context of the legal history of the South. Sponsored by the Tennessee Supreme Court Historical Society, the work should enhance the general understanding of the Court's crucial part in shaping Tennessee jurisprudence.

The volume treats a number of issues, including the evolution and organization of the Supreme Court, biographical information about the judges, the changing nature of the Court's case load, judicial review, issues pertaining to judicial selection and tenure, the relationship between the Court's work and the social and intellectual climate of the state, and governance of the bar. The Court was often at the center of major political and economic controversies. Coverage encompasses diverse substantive areas of both public and private law, such as state constitutional law, property law, slavery, economic rights, criminal justice, family law, regulation of business enterprise, and race and gender relations. The book also addresses such contested issues as the Court's role in Reconstruction.

Several themes bulk large. Federalism has been a persistent concern. The book therefore gives careful attention to the interaction between the Tennessee Supreme Court and the Supreme Court of the United States. Although defiant on occasion, the Tennessee Supreme Court generally sought to accommodate its views to the decisions of the national tribunal. Another recurring theme is judicial deference to legislative decision making. The judges on Tennessee's high court early established the principle of judicial review, but rarely blocked legislative steps to address perceived social and economic problems. By and large, the members of the Court left policy determination to the political branches of government. Still, at times during the antebellum era, and particularly in the late twentieth century, the Supreme Court assumed a more activist role in asserting individual rights.

A third theme which runs throughout the Supreme Court's history is the struggle to secure judicial independence. This issue is closely related to the question of popular accountability of judges in a democratic society. In the early decades of the nineteenth century the Court, lacking a constitutional base, was repeatedly revamped by the legislature in ways that threatened to compromise judicial integrity. Not until adoption of the Constitution of 1834 was the Supreme Court established as a separate branch of government. Following a national trend, the Tennessee Constitution was amended in 1853 to provide for the popular election of Supreme Court justices. This set the stage for periodic battles over the composition of the bench and the direction of the Court. The rise of more intense two-party political competition in the late twentieth century heightened the conflict over how judges should be selected. Over time, therefore, Supreme Court justices had to balance their commitment to judicial independence with the notion, enshrined in the elective process, that judges should be limited in their discretion and reflect the values of the community they served.

Moreover, the work of the Tennessee Supreme Court casts light on the interplay between regionalism and national norms in shaping the legal culture of the state.[12] The Court was often called upon to mediate between traditional southern values and the economic and social forces which increasingly pulled Tennessee into closer ties with institutions outside the state. Although rarely an innovator in national legal developments, the Tennessee Supreme Court has generally, if sometimes belatedly, adopted emerging national standards in most areas of law.

Given the paucity of state supreme court histories, it is difficult to contrast the work of the Tennessee Supreme Court with the experience of similar bodies in other states. Comparative analysis of judicial behavior and perception of state high courts is a relatively undeveloped field.[13] Yet one study suggests that in some jurisdictions state courts have been more willing to define public policy and less inclined to defer to political institutions than has traditionally been the case in Tennessee.[14] Still other studies maintain that some state high courts have occasionally sought to circumvent decisions of the Supreme Court of the United States,[15] a practice not usually followed by Tennessee courts. In recent years commentators have urged greater judicial attention to state constitutional provisions as a basis for safeguarding individual rights. It remains to be seen how far the Tennessee Supreme Court will follow this course.

Some comment about the scope of this volume is in order. A work of synthesis, the book moves rapidly over many issues that warrant more comprehensive treatment. The authors have necessarily had to pick and choose topics from the Supreme Court's past. We hope, however, that we have represented the Court's history in a balanced and interesting way. Mindful that judges do not function in a vacuum, the authors have also sought to place the work of the Supreme Court in a broad context. They have been careful to take account of the political and intellectual currents of both Tennessee and the nation in piecing together the history of the Court.

Likewise, the career and attitudes of the judges who served on the Tennessee Supreme Court could not be treated in detail. Indeed, the available biographical information about many of the judges is skimpy. Several of these jurists, such as John Overton, John Catron, Nathan Green, and Horace H. Lurton, warrant a full biography.

There has been no attempt to impose a uniform voice or outlook on the several authors of this book. Rather, the authors have been encouraged to develop their own interpretative perspectives on the work of the Supreme Court.

Although this volume provides the most comprehensive treatment of the evolution of the Supreme Court of Tennessee available, it does not purport to resolve every question or establish a definitive interpretation. Rather, this is in the nature of an introduction to a vital but overlooked aspect of Tennessee history. Hopefully this book will stimulate other scholars to explore the work of Tennessee's high court.

In addition to the contribution by the authors, this book reflects generous assistance from many quarters. The Tennessee Supreme Court Historical Society, Inc. deserves special mention. The Society provided the impetus for a scholarly study of the Supreme Court and sponsored this volume. The members of the Society's publication committee, and especially Valerius Sanford, have been unstinting in their support and encouragement. Without this help the book would not have been possible.

James W. Ely Jr.
Nashville, Tennessee
February 2001

ACKNOWLEDGMENTS

Cecil V. Crowson Jr., Clerk of the Supreme Court of Tennessee, Nashville, and Frankie Lewis, Chief Deputy Clerk of the Supreme Court of Tennessee, Knoxville;

William B. Eigelsbach, Manuscripts, University and Special Collections, University of Tennessee, Knoxville;

Dr. Edwin S. Gleaves, State Librarian and Archivist, and staff, Tennessee State Library and Archives, Nashville;

Charles A. Sherrill, Director, Public Services, and staff, Tennessee State Library and Archives, Nashville;

Steve Cotham, Manager, McClung Historical Collection, Knoxville, Tennessee;

Harold D. Moser, Editor-Director, The Papers of Andrew Jackson, Knoxville, Tennessee;

Dr. Carroll Van West, Editor, *Tennessee Historical Quarterly*, Murfreesboro, Tennessee;

Edwin Peck Jr., Daytona Beach Shores, Florida, and John G. Peck Jr., Kingston, New Jersey;

Elizabeth B. Dunn, Women's Studies Reference Archivist, Duke University Rare Book, Manuscript, and Special Collections Library, Durham, North Carolina;

Richard A. Shrader, Manuscripts Department, Wilson Library, University of North Carolina at Chapel Hill, Chapel Hill, North Carolina;

Vaughan Stanley, Special Collections Librarian, Leyburn Library, Washington and Lee University, Lexington, Virginia;

Christie Speir Cameron, Clerk of Court, and Louise Stafford, Librarian, North Carolina Supreme Court Library, Raleigh, North Carolina;

Franz Jantzen, Office of the Curator, Supreme Court of the United States, Washington, D.C.;

Doris R. Martinson, Head, Knox County Archives, East Tennessee Historical Center, Knoxville;

Don C. Skemer, Curator of Manuscripts, Princeton University Library, Princeton, New Jersey;

Christopher M. Rooney, University of Pennsylvania Archives and Records Center, Philadelphia;

Joseph-James Ahern, Library of the American Philosophical Society, Philadelphia;

Rex Moses, President, McMinn County Chapter, East Tennessee Historical Society, Athens;

Hon. Carroll L. Ross, Circuit Court Judge, Tenth Judicial District, Athens, Tennessee;

Hon. Frank V. Williams III, Chancellor, Chancery Court, Ninth Judicial District, Kingston, Tennessee;

James B. Lloyd, Director of University Archives and Special Collections, University of Tennessee, Knoxville;

John Dobson, former Director of University Archives and Special Collections, University of Tennessee, Knoxville;

Sheila Devaney, Reference Librarian, University of Georgia Library, Athens, Georgia;

Dr. Stephen Wick, Knoxville Museum of Art, Knoxville, Tennessee;

Kathy Smith, The Jean and Alexander Heard Library Special Collections and University Archives, Nashville, Tennessee;

Thomas E. Vanderloo, Frank W. Wilson Library of the U.S. Courts, Chattanooga, Tennessee;

Shirley Wilson, C.G., Hendersonville, Tennessee;

Linda Sellars, Chapel Hill, North Carolina;

Thomas P. Keating, Nashville, Tennessee;

Michael Williford, Atlanta, Georgia;

Long, Aldridge & Norman, LLP, Atlanta, Georgia and Washington, D.C.;

Tom Ford, Houghton Library of the Harvard College Library, Harvard University, Cambridge, Massachusetts;

William Robert Ellis Jr., Civil & Military Branch, National Archives and Records Administration, Washington, D.C.;

Fred Romanski, Textual Reference Branch, National Archives and Records Administration, Archives II, College Park, Maryland;

Mary Ann Hawkins, National Archives and Records Administration, Southeast Region, College Park, Georgia;

Chapman A. Roane, Grenada, Mississippi;

Martin Cerjan, Associate Director of Public Services, Vanderbilt University Law Library;

Janet Hirt, Reference Librarian, Vanderbilt University Law Library;

Stephen Jordan, Reference Librarian, Vanderbilt University Law Library.

The following persons should be recognized as founders of the Tennessee Supreme Court Historical Society, whose contributions made this publication possible:

Alfred T. Adams
Jerry V. Adams
Honorable E. Riley Anderson
Foster D. Arnett
R. A. Ashley
T. Maxfield Bahner
Robert L. Ballow
H. Lee Barfield II
Joseph N. Barker
Leo Bearman Jr.
Margaret L. Behm
Julian L. Bibb
Honorable Adolpho A. Birch Jr.
Thomas C. Binkley
David T. Black
Martha S.L. Black
Charles W. Bone
Cyrus L. Booker
Phillip Larry Boyd
Martha B. Brasfield
Charles W. Burson
Michael E. Callaway
Gilbert R. Campbell Jr.
Robert R. Campbell
Honorable Ben Cantrell
Davis H. Carr
Jac Chambliss
John R. Cheadle Jr.
Honorable Cornelia A. Clark
W.J. Michael Cody
Charles L. Cornelius Jr.
Patricia Cottrell
Robert L. Crossley
Cecil Crowson Jr.
Wayne Culbertson
Sheila Jordan Cunningham
Honorable Martha Craig Daughtery
Ed R. Davies
Ames Davis
Maclin P. Davis Jr.
Ward DeWitt Jr.
Lewis R. Donelson
Honorable Frank F. Drowota III
James T. DuBois Sr.
Douglas L. Dutton
Thomas Dyer
Jim Emison
David Steele Ewing
Douglas Fisher
Honorable William H. D. Fones
William T. Gamble
Hugh P. Garner
C. J. Gideon Jr.
Honorable Ronald Lee Gilman

James C. Gooch
J. Houston Gordon
James M. Haley IV
William L. Harbison
F. Evans Harvill
Albert C. Harvey
Aubrey B. Harwell Jr.
Senator Douglas Henry
Joseph W. Henry Jr.
David B. Herbert
John J. Hollins
J. Fraser Humphreys Jr.
Billy C. Jack
Claudia S. Jack
Honorable Victor S. Johnson III
Thomas S. Kale
Paul D. Kelly Jr.
Frank S. King Jr.
Honorable William C. Koch Jr.
John M. Lannom
Lewis L. Laska
Joseph Martin Jr.
Donna Simpson Massa
Fred McClure
Burkett C. McInturff
Robert McMurray
Honorable Gilbert Merritt
Phillip H. Miller
Marlene Eskind Moses
Paul Neely
Honorable Charles H. O'Brien
Donald F. Paine
Mary A. Parker
Donald J. Polden
Thomas R. Prewitt Sr.
Allan F. Ramsaur
Mark A. Rassas
Pamela L. Reeves
Barney B. Regen
Honorable Lyle Reid
Janet Leach Richards
Michael Richards
Jack W. Robinson Sr.
Walter M. Robinson Jr.
Tom H. Rogan
John T. Milburn Rogers
Frank J. Runyon
Valerius Sanford
J. Nolan Sharbel Sr.
Honorable Marietta M. Shipley
Wilson Sims
Robert L. Smith
Robert D. Tuke
Honorable John A. Turnbull
William Landis Turner
Honorable Shirley Underwood
Howard H. Vogel
Honorable Gary Wade
Robert J. Walker
Robert Kirk Walker
Charles H. Warfield
John B. Waters Jr.
Alexander W. Wellford Jr.
Julia West
Lacy West
Jack Wheeler
Thomas V. White
Ed E. Williams III
John Lee Williams
Marianna Williams
W. Fred Williams
Louis C. Wolf
Robert F. Worthington Jr.
Kathryn Huff Yett

1

THE FORMATIVE PERIOD IN THE HISTORY OF THE SUPREME COURT OF TENNESSEE, 1796–1835

Theodore Brown Jr.

The formative first four decades of the Supreme Court of Tennessee began with the admission of Tennessee into the Union during the final year of George Washington's presidency and ended with little more than a year remaining of Andrew Jackson's tenure in the White House. For the nation, the period was one of exceptional growth, political diversification, and economic development. The new Republic's population more than doubled between 1800 and 1830. Between 1796 and 1835, a series of new political alignments emerged. The first was cultivated in the waning years of the eighteenth century by Thomas Jefferson and James Madison as an alternative to the Federalist Party but was eclipsed in the 1820s, initially by the National Republicans and then by another movement that came to be symbolized by and named for Jackson. By the early 1830s, however, Jacksonian Democracy in turn had generated the formation of an opposition Whig Party. Of even greater long-term significance, the nation's largely subsistence economy underwent transition to a market economy, at a price of becoming subject to the fluctuations of foreign markets, while the South (and to an extent Tennessee) continued to struggle with an economic system that was based on slave labor and that lagged behind the national trend, and the country began to come to terms with the inherently contradictory existence of human slavery in a land that professed to be free.[1]

At roughly the midpoint between 1796 and 1835 came the War of 1812 and Jackson's military victory over the British at New Orleans in early 1815. Jackson's triumph triggered what George Dangerfield called the awakening of American nationalism. Differences soon arose, however, about the direction in which that postwar nationalism was to be channeled. The "ultimate, crude, and controlling test," Dangerfield suggested, was between economic nationalism and democratic nationalism; "[t]he question was, in whose favor was this economy to be modified? And to what extent?" Whereas slavery and states' rights were the primary issues producing the shifting political coalitions that developed during the years immediately preceding the Civil War, the dramatic transformation of the nation's political landscape during the initial decades of the nineteenth century resulted in large part from different approaches to the issue of how best to deal with economic change. The economic nationalists expanded upon the views of Alexander Hamilton and many other Federalists and, though there were important exceptions, came to be identified first with the National Republicans and later with the Whigs. Proponents of economic nationalism such as Henry Clay and John C. Calhoun, at least in his early years, advocated federal subsidies of the nation's economic development in the form of federally funded internal improvements, protective tariffs, and a centralized national bank chartered by Congress to provide much-needed uniformity to the country's financial system. A necessary component of the economic nationalists' program was a strong federal government, the laws and policies of which were to prevail over those of the states, an ingredient that was provided by a series of decisions by the Supreme Court of the United States, which also reserved for itself the right to review federal and state laws for compliance with the federal Constitution, under the leadership of Chief Justice John Marshall.

Proponents of democratic nationalism, on the other hand, rallied around Jackson. Although they offered no systematic plan to compete with that espoused by the economic nationalists, the democratic nationalists—and Jacksonians in general—shared the nationalist outlook of their economic counterparts, held views that were anything but provincial, and, at least on economic issues, disagreed with their opponents less about ends than about means. They supported, for instance, a different kind of federal subsidy in the form of cheap public land, preferably to be made available on credit, to encourage the settlement of the trans-Appalachian region (even at the expense of the Cherokee Nation, whose landholdings were under the tenuous protection of a succession of federal treaties) and urged newly settled frontier states such as Tennessee to resolve conflicting land claims in favor of the squatter in possession. In their rhetoric, which bore a distinctly moral tone, they advocated a form of egalitarianism that favored the curbing of privilege and the conquest of elites and professed a "special solicitude" for American workers: they supported debtor-relief laws, zealously denounced (and ultimately destroyed) the "Monster" national bank, and insisted that the growing number of state-chartered banks honor their obligations with the hard metal of specie, not with paper notes; opposed the economic monopolies that they feared would result from special corporate charters; and were suspicious of public enterprise and public debt. As president, Jackson championed the Union, but he had little use for the strong, centralized form of federal supremacy—presided over by an independent judiciary—that was espoused by Chief Justice Marshall. Though some of Jackson's supporters, such as northern editors William Cullen Bryant and William Leggett and the political economist Theodore Sedgwick, advocated the abolition of slavery, most of those in the South (including Jackson himself) were slave owners who had no interest in withdrawing slavery from the full protection of the law, and the Jacksonians gave little or no attention to the plight of another group whose members were subject to a different kind of legal bondage: married women. Jacksonian egalitarianism was largely limited to Caucasian males.[2]

Tennessee during the first four decades of statehood was in many respects a microcosm of the nation at large, although an imperfect one. Originally formed as the federal Territory South of the River Ohio in 1790 from the westernmost counties of North Carolina, the state came into being under the watchful eye of Territorial Governor William Blount. Blount, a Federalist businessman and land speculator, subsequently became one of the leaders, with John Overton, of the Blount-Overton banking and political faction in Tennessee. The state's first four decades of statehood were dominated by the lengthy tenures of two governors, John Sevier and William Carroll. Sevier, who served six terms, initially appointed Jackson to the Court,[3] but the two subsequently became engaged in a bitter personal and political feud that lasted until Sevier's death in 1815. Carroll, an early "champion of 'the people' against entrenched interests" who emerged in the aftermath of the economic crisis known as the Panic of 1819 to defeat the Blount-Overton candidate in 1821, eventually held the office longer than any other person in the state's history but fell victim to the state's first Whig governor, Newton Cannon, in 1835. On the eve of joining the Union, the state was inhabited by 77,262 persons (including 10,613 slaves). By 1830, largely as a result of settlement encouraged by the availability of cheap public land, the population had grown to 681,903 inhabitants (including 141,603 slaves). During the initial four decades of statehood, most of the state's white inhabitants were subsistence farmers. Economic and industrial development was slow to come to Tennessee. Although the state's slave population increased by more than 227.8 percent between 1800 and 1810, the percentage of increase dropped noticeably during the ensuing decades, to 29.27 percent between 1830 and 1840. Far from immune from the growing criticism that was directed at the institution of slavery, Tennessee became an early, albeit limited and ultimately unsuccessful, source of abolitionist activity. In 1820 at Jonesboro in eastern Tennessee, Quaker Elihu Embree began publishing the *Emancipator,* the first newspaper in the United States devoted solely to the abolition of slavery. By 1827, twenty-five manumission societies had been formed in the state. With some regularity beginning as early as 1817, these groups petitioned the General Assembly to enact legislation providing for gradual abolition, and in 1825, the *Nashville Republican* published a plan authored by Frances Wright, one of the founders of the biracial community of Nashoba near Memphis, for gradual abolition.[4]

It was in this environment that the Court functioned between 1796 and 1835 and achieved a well-deserved reputation as one of the most progressive of southern antebellum appellate courts. The intervening four decades brought some twenty-two judges to its bench, several of whom—including Jackson himself—were leaders, both locally and at the national level, in the political movement that bore his name. All of the judges were immigrants from the eastern side of the Appalachians or, in the case of Robert Whyte (a native of Scotland), beyond. Most had little or no formal education. Each had acquired his knowledge of the law through the prevailing method of reading law with an established member of the bar and through the practice of law. With the exceptions of John McNairy and John Haywood, none had any prior judicial experience. The legal disputes that came before the Court reflected, and to some extent were a by-product of, the great policy issues of the time. Arguments on all sides of each of these issues were driven by conflicting interests, and the Court's decisions were not, of course, rendered within a vacuum. The political affiliations and views of most of the Court's members during the period remain largely conjectural (other than those of Jackson himself and John Overton, one of Jackson's closest friends and allies, but both had left the bench before the Jacksonian movement began in earnest). However, one of the judges, John Catron, was one of Jackson's most partisan and outspoken supporters, and an impressive number of decisions by the Court between 1796 and 1835 were consistent with policies advocated by many Jacksonians. The Court, for instance, curbed the exercise of arbitrary governmental powers by liberally, albeit selectively, construing a potentially significant provision of the state's Constitution that protected all free men from being deprived of life, liberty, or property except by "the law of the land"; adopted the rule of adverse possession that many of the Jacksonians favored; refused to alter the traditional common-law rule of strict liability for common carriers; upheld expansion of the state's jurisdiction into the Cherokee Nation in defiance of the Supreme Court of the United States; and fashioned egalitarian rules applicable to married women, apprentices, and the poor that actually went further than most Jacksonians were willing to go. Other equally significant decisions by the Court were altogether contrary to the views and interests espoused by the Jacksonians: the Court established itself as an independent branch of state government and exercised the right to review the constitutionality of legislative enactments; invalidated a significant debtor-relief measure adopted in the aftermath of the Panic of 1819; struck down the state's sale of common-school lands as unlawful under the federal compact governing such lands; upheld the land claims of Cherokees against those of white settlers; and, most notably, upheld and facilitated the right of private emancipation and required that the property interest of the slave owner at least share space in the scales of justice with the slave's rights as a human being.

THE COURT AS A DEVELOPING INSTITUTION

The drafters of Tennessee's Constitution of 1796 chose not to include an independent judicial branch in the new state's form of government. Instead, all judicial power was vested in "such superior and inferior courts of law and equity, as the legislature shall, from time to time, direct and establish." The courts' judges were to be elected by joint ballot of the General Assembly and were to serve during good behavior. Throughout the first four decades of statehood, Tennessee's highest court existed entirely at the discretion of the state's General Assembly, and the resulting uneasy relationship between the legislature and that court was a source of continual conflict.[5]

The first Tennessee legislature in 1796 carried forward the three-judge Superior Court that had existed under the North Carolina and territorial governments. The legislature also continued the existing three districts of Washington, Hamilton, and Mero until 1806, when the number of districts was increased to five. The two new districts, Robertson and Winchester, were carved out of the Mero District, which was continued as a smaller unit.

The county courts that had existed under the earlier governments continued as the state's only inferior courts through 1809.[6]

Through 1809, the Superior Court exercised original jurisdiction over all but the most minor of civil and criminal matters and heard appeals from the county courts. Typically, there were far more original actions on the Court's docket than appeals. Appeals were tried de novo and thus were time consuming for both the Court and litigants.[7]

The Superior Court functioned as a court of law and equity. Its judges maintained the traditional distinction between law and equity, although both law and equity cases were argued before the same bench. The Court typically began hearing equity matters during the second week of each term, often splitting each day's calendar thereafter between law and equity business, but clearly gave the most attention to civil and criminal proceedings on the law side, perhaps reflecting the infrequent use of juries in equity deliberations and the substantial number of continuances and dismissals of equity proceedings by the parties.

In the common-law courts of both England and the United States, there were certain prescribed forms of action to which a party was required to resort for the remedy of an alleged wrong. When there was no prescribed form to reach the facts in a particular case (facts that, for example, indicated fraud or warranted requiring another party to do or to refrain from doing certain things), the party was without a remedy—at law. Equity intervened when, in the words of the future jurist Joseph Story, "a plain, adequate, and complete remedy" could not be had in the courts of common law. By the time of the American Revolution, English equity jurisprudence had evolved into "an accepted and mature body of principles," and by the early nineteenth century, Story had become perhaps the leading advocate for an infusion of equity into American law as a means of softening the often harsh results mandated by the common law. His efforts were successful, and the eventual incorporation of equity into the mainstream of American law by the antebellum period was a result Jacksonian America found hard to resist.[8]

The early history of the Tennessee Court reveals the extent to which, consistent with the national trend, equity was becoming an integral part of Tennessee's law. Equity was a significant component of the early Court's jurisdiction. Indeed, during the period ending in 1827, when the full Court or its individual judges exercised original equity jurisdiction, the equity docket significantly hampered the Court's ability to function effectively. Bills to enjoin the enforcement of judgments obtained in a court of law were by far the most common type of equity litigation in the Court. Prior to the legislative reorganization of the Court in 1809, the law judgment that was the subject of such a proceeding was one that had been obtained by a jury verdict in the Superior

Court itself; after 1809, such law judgments were based on jury verdicts rendered in the circuit courts. This type of equitable relief had originated in England and was recognized in North Carolina's Court of Chancery throughout the colonial period. An injunction against enforcement of a judgment at law was granted only under limited circumstances, that is, when the defendant at law had a valid defense on the merits and was prevented from asserting that defense by fraud or accident, when the defendant at law had a valid defense on the merits that was unavailable in law, or when the defendant at law was subject to a void decree such as one vitiated by fraud, mistake, or lack of jurisdiction. The power to enjoin judgments at law was a supplemental aspect of the legal system and was employed sparingly.[9]

The Court exercised equity jurisdiction over all matters concerning fraud, over the foreclosure of mortgages and the exercise by debtors of their right of equitable redemption, and over the partition of land. Indeed, one of the cases that remained on the Court's docket for the longest period of time, *Williams v. Henderson & Co.* (1791–1802), was initiated by a petition for the partition of a two-hundred-thousand-acre tract of land located in eastern Tennessee.[10]

There was growing dissatisfaction, however, with the cost and length of time that litigation required during the first decade of the Court's existence. Occasional increases in the number of members of the Court did little to lessen demands for a complete overhaul of the state's judicial system. In a series of essays written under the pen name of "Sir John Oldcastle" for Nashville's *Impartial Review and Cumberland Repository* in 1808, for instance, a young Thomas Hart Benton, who later achieved fame as a U.S. senator from Missouri, articulated growing public sentiment against the Court and the entire judicial system. Benton suggested replacing the Court with six circuit courts and a one-man supreme court that would be perpetually in session, that would meet alternately in Nashville and Knoxville, and that would have no original jurisdiction but would be "limited to the supervision and correction of the law proceedings of the circuit courts."[11]

Transforming the Court into an exclusively appellate court and divesting it of all original jurisdiction was a significant proposal. Appellate courts were viewed at the time as necessary both to correct unintentional errors by lower courts and to ensure uniformity in the law. Both of those objectives, not to mention the similarly important goal of providing reasonably expeditious and inexpensive justice, were frustrated when the same tribunal exercised both appellate and original jurisdiction.[12]

When Benton was elected to the state senate in 1809, he introduced and passed legislation that effected the first major reorganization of the Court since statehood. The measure abolished the Superior Court, effective January 1,

1810, replaced it with a Supreme Court of Errors and Appeals, and created an intermediate system of circuit courts between the county courts and the new Supreme Court. The statute also divided the state into five judicial circuits and provided that the circuit courts were to exercise original jurisdiction over "all matters and causes at common law and in equity" over which the Superior Court had had jurisdiction; were to exercise exclusive jurisdiction over all criminal actions; were to have concurrent jurisdiction with the county courts over all civil causes; and were to have appellate jurisdiction over actions from the county courts "subject to the same rules, conditions and regulations now in use in appeals from the said [county] courts to the" Superior Court. The new Supreme Court thus was not to be a trial court but was to decide only those cases that came before the new tribunal on writs of error from the circuit courts or by agreement of the parties. The new Court was to be comprised of two judges, who were to be elected by a joint ballot of the General Assembly, and one circuit judge. Cases were to come before the Supreme Court by writs of error from the circuit courts. The new Court was to sit twice annually in each of the five circuits. Specific circuit judges were designated to sit with the Court in circuits other than their own. For the first time, the Court's judges were required to file written opinions with the record in each action.[13]

The success of the General Assembly's effort in 1809 to make of the new Supreme Court an exclusively appellate court of last resort was short-lived. In 1811, the General Assembly passed significant legislation revesting the Court with exclusive equity jurisdiction and divesting the circuit courts of such jurisdiction. All undetermined equity proceedings then pending in any circuit court were to be transferred to the Supreme Court and were to be heard by the Court when sitting in the circuit in which such proceedings had been pending.[14]

The General Assembly added confusion in equity cases, however, when it passed legislation in 1813 granting the circuit courts concurrent jurisdiction in all causes in equity over which the Court then exercised jurisdiction. An 1819 measure clarified the matter by providing that dissatisfied parties to equity proceedings before the circuit courts were entitled to appeal circuit equity decisions to the Supreme Court for de novo review of all questions of fact and law.[15]

In 1822, the General Assembly directed each of the Court's judges to conduct a Court of Equity, vested with original equity jurisdiction to be exercised concurrently with the circuit courts, once a year in each of the circuits and provided that the full Court was to meet only once, rather than twice, annually in each circuit. The same statute declared that the full Court should not have any original jurisdiction, "either in law or equity" but should possess only appellate jurisdiction over appeals and writs of error "from the courts of law and equity holden within the circuits where said Supreme Courts are holden." In a supplemental statute passed two days after enactment of the act creating the Court of Equity, the General Assembly clarified that appeals from the single-judge Court of Equity were to be taken to the full Court. The new Court of Equity, by implication, was not to hear equity appeals from the circuit courts, because the supplemental act also provided that all equity appeals from the circuit courts were to be heard by the full Supreme Court rather than the Court of Equity.[16]

Two years later, the legislature attempted to streamline the Court's schedule by limiting the places where the Court met to three, but at its next session, the General Assembly directed the Court to meet in Reynoldsburg, in Humphreys County, where all appeals from the Fifth, Eighth, and Ninth Circuits were to be heard.[17] The decision to add Reynoldsburg to the lengthening list of places where the Court was required to meet probably was a purely political move designed as an accommodation to legislators from the western part of the state. Reynoldsburg lay some seventy-three miles west of Nashville, situated "immediately on the east bank of the Tennessee river," scarcely fifteen feet above the river's water level. By the end of the decade, the hamlet had only 108 inhabitants, 28 dwelling houses, 2 taverns, and 3 stores. When sitting in Reynoldsburg, Judge Peck once noted in his typically caustic manner, the Court conducted its business "in a cyprus swamp, without lawyers, books or court-house."[18]

In still another effort to reorganize the state's judiciary, the General Assembly in 1827 divested the Court of Equity of its original equity jurisdiction and provided for the legislative election of two statewide chancellors who were to have "the same powers, privileges and jurisdiction in all respects that the judges of the supreme court now have when setting as chancellors." Legislation was passed three years later, however, which authorized the litigants to any equity action pending in any chancery court in the state that had been continued for two terms "by reason of the chancellor being incompetent to try the same" to transfer the action to the Supreme Court, "who shall try and dispose thereof." Exacerbating the confusion generated by the seemingly endless string of statutes that changed the structure, make-up, and jurisdiction of the Court as well as the places where the Court was to sit were the frequent changes made by the legislature in the times when the Court was to sit in certain places. The most egregious example of changes of the latter type occurred concerning the times when the Court was to sit in Sparta. Between 1824 and 1833, the months when the Court was to sit for its annual term in Sparta was changed legislatively no less than five times.[19]

In his letter of resignation from the Court in 1816, Judge Overton suggested to Governor McMinn that the legislature's decision in 1811 to revest the Court with exclusive equity jurisdiction had been a mistake. "[S]ince the time of giving the supreme courts original equity jurisdiction," Overton observed, "business of the most important nature has accumulated in several of them to a great extent." A complicating, and perhaps even more significant, factor was the number of places throughout the state where the Court was required to sit. According to the retiring jurist, who prided himself on having missed only two terms of court in more than eleven years of service,

> In the dispersed situation of the courts (to attend which, it is necessary to ride upward of fifteen hundred miles a year,) and state of business in them, I have learned by experience that a tolerably correct discharge of the duties of the office will be found unattainable, without the employment of every moment of time, in riding, sitting in court, and writing opinions, leaving no time for rest. A task, which it is candidly confessed, I am not capable of discharging with credit to myself, honor to my country, and above all, with a conviction at all times under the pressure of fatigue, that decisions will be founded on correct principles.[20]

Regrettably, the full force of Judge Overton's private observations, which only reiterated similar views that appeared to have been fairly widespread, was not realized until more than a decade later when, after the death of Judge Haywood as a result of the ordeal of performing his duties as chancellor at Franklin, the General Assembly in 1827 divested the Court of all original equity jurisdiction. The problems identified by Overton, however, were not effectively addressed until, with the adoption of a new Constitution for the state in 1835, the Supreme Court was limited to exercising only appellate jurisdiction and to sitting in three locations.[21]

Despite allegations throughout the period to the contrary, the Court's judges on balance appear to have performed their arduous duties diligently and conscientiously. During Jackson's tenure, for example, the Court was required to sit twice a year in three places throughout the state, and the length of court terms fluctuated between twelve and fifteen days. When in session, the Court met six days a week, including Saturdays. Administrative duties occupied the judges for the entirety of the opening day of each term. On the following day and for the remainder of the term, the judges, sitting en banc, heard original actions and appeals from the county courts, which were tried de novo. The judges and jurors typically heard several cases each day. Jackson on one hectic day sat on seven jury trials, and it was not unusual for trials to extend well into the night. Theodorick Bland, a young Virginia lawyer (and future chancellor of Maryland's High Court of Chancery) practicing with his cousin in the Court's Washington and Hamilton Districts in eastern Tennessee between March 1799 and March 1801, described one such trial as "the most lengthy and irksome I have known in this Country." The jury was seated at ten o'clock in the morning, the witnesses for the prosecution and defendant were heard "until candles were lit," the arguments of counsel on both sides were not completed until four o'clock the next morning, and the jury returned with a verdict of not guilty "a little before day." Given the relative frequency with which several lawyers represented each party throughout the period ending in 1835 and the difficult legal issues that the Court was routinely called upon to decide, often without any apparent controlling authority, Bland's courtroom experience probably was the rule rather than the exception.[22]

Because relatively few of the dockets and minute books have survived for each of the places in which the Court met during the period 1796–1835, it has not been possible to reconstruct a complete and accurate profile of the Court's case load either by term or for the entire thirty-nine-year period, to distinguish between the number of trials, appeals, and equity matters that were heard, or to determine the average number of cases that were disposed of each term. An analysis of the first sixteen volumes of the Tennessee *Reports* shows that the Court issued 1,425 reported decisions from 1796 through the end of 1835 and that the individual judges penned 1,447 opinions (including concurring and dissenting opinions) during that period. Although there were frequent terms when only one decision was reported, it was not at all unusual for the Court to render between 12 and 20 reported decisions per term, and during the early 1830s, the number occasionally ranged between 30 and 50 per term. At its March Term 1834 (Nashville), the Court rendered 52 reported decisions, and the number reached 56 at the March Term 1835 (Nashville). The high point occurred at the March Term 1833 (Nashville), when the Court issued 102 reported decisions.[23]

There were, of course, recurring complaints about the Court, especially during the 1820s. Most were based on alleged backlogs of the Court's docket, and dissatisfaction eventually led to the legislative crisis of 1831, discussed below. As will be seen from that discussion, however, such complaints appear to have disguised the actual reason for disaffection with the Court—namely, the Court's increasing exercise of its power to declare legislative acts unconstitutional. In his report to the state house of representatives on the "bold if not desperate" legislative proposals to abolish the Court that were introduced during that session of the General Assembly, the respected chairman of the House Judiciary Committee (and future governor) Aaron V. Brown concluded that there was actually no backlog of cases on the Supreme Court's docket at the time, except for Nashville; that the unusual accumulation of cases on the Nashville docket was largely attributable to Judges Whyte and Peck having been indisposed for much of the last term of court; and that, regardless of the difficulties caused by the age and infirmities of the Court's judges, the judicial decision-making process was by its very nature a methodical, deliberative, and thus typically slow process that was rendered even more so by difficult and complex legal issues.[24]

THE COURT'S JUDGES

Between 1796 and the end of 1809, the Court experienced a fairly rapid rate of turnover among its judges. A total of eleven men served as members of the Court during that initial phase in the Court's history. Short tenures on the bench, however, were the practice throughout Tennessee's early years as a state and were attributable, at least in part, to the salaries the Court's judges were paid. Describing judicial salaries as "inadequate," Samuel Cole Williams concluded that "[r]esignations in order to return to practice at the bar or to accept more lucrative positions in public life led to frequent changes in personnel." Indeed, after leaving the Court to practice law, Samuel Powel reported that he was earning nearly twice what his salary had been as a member of the Court. Initially, the problem was a constitutional one. The state's Constitution limited judicial salaries to a maximum of $600 per year until 1804, when the limitation expired. Each of the Court's first judges received a salary of $83.33 ⅓ per term of court, with a deduction therefrom made in proportion to the time he failed to attend court. Even the most faithful of judges who attended each day of each of the Court's biannual sessions could earn only $500 per year. In 1798, Judge Archibald Roane protested that the attendance requirement violated the state's Constitution, which referred to "annual salaries" for governmental officials. Moreover, Roane noted, "there are a number of official duties required of the Judges in Vacation for which no compensation [is] provided" by the statute. He urged the legislature to establish a salary level that would "best tend to secure the Independence of the Judges which Independence the Laws contemplate to be one of the best securities for the rights and privileges of the People." Beginning in 1806, two years after expiration of the constitutional maximum salary of $600 a year, the General Assembly authorized the judges to be paid annual salaries of $1,000, which were paid quarterly.[25] Each judge's annual salary was increased to $1,500 in 1809 and to $1,800 in 1819.

The state's first General Assembly elected John McNairy, Archibald Roane, and Willie Blount as the Court's first judges in April 1796. McNairy

(1762–1837), at the age of twenty-five, had been elected by the North Carolina legislature in December 1787 as the first judge of the new district Superior Court of Davidson County and had served as one of the three judges of the territorial Superior Court. McNairy resigned in 1797 to accept President Washington's appointment as judge of the United States District Court for the District of Tennessee.[26]

Roane (1759–1819), a native of Pennsylvania, was the first of the Court's judges to serve nonconsecutive terms (1796–1801; 1815–19). With the possible exception of Robert Whyte, Roane (A.B., Liberty Hall Academy, 1789) had received more formal education than any of the Court's other judges during the first four decades of statehood. He also had served as clerk and master in equity for the territorial Washington District Superior Court and as Hamilton District's attorney general from 1794 until his election to the Court in 1796. His initial term as a member of the Court ended in 1801, when he resigned to succeed John Sevier as the state's second governor. Defeated for reelection by Sevier in 1803, Roane returned to the private practice of law. Elected to represent Knox County in the state senate in 1811, he resigned his seat to accept the position as judge of the Second Circuit Court in November of that year, where he remained until returning to the Supreme Court in October 1815. He held the latter position until his death in January 1819.[27]

Blount, William Blount's half-brother, resigned within six months after his election. Governor Sevier appointed William Charles Cole Claiborne to Blount's seat in September 1796, but within a year, Claiborne, too, had resigned to accept election to the U.S. House of Representatives. As Claiborne's successor, the General Assembly in the autumn of 1797 elected David Campbell, who had served with McNairy as one of the judges of the territorial Superior Court. After surviving two impeachment trials, in 1798 and 1803, Campbell resigned from the Court in 1807.[28] To fill the vacancy left by McNairy's resignation in 1797, Governor Sevier chose Howell Tatum, but Tatum also soon resigned from the bench. In September 1798, Governor Sevier commissioned Andrew Jackson as Tatum's successor, and three months later the General Assembly confirmed Sevier's action by formally electing Jackson to the Court.[29]

Jackson (1767–1845) had followed McNairy to Nashville from North Carolina in 1788. The two had become friends while clerking for Spruce Macay, a prominent lawyer in Salisbury, North Carolina. McNairy appointed Jackson as prosecutor for the state, a position which he held from November 1788 until November 1789, when the North Carolina General Assembly elected him attorney general for the Mero District. He later served as attorney

Compiler of the first Tennessee Reports, John Overton served two nonconsecutive terms on Tennessee's Superior Court and Supreme Court of Errors and Appeals between 1804 and 1816. Portrait by Ralph E. W. Earl, courtesy of Travellers Rest Historic House Museum, Inc.

general under the territorial government. At the same time, Jackson was cultivating an expanding private practice. During the period 1788–96, he handled the second heaviest volume of cases and represented more clients than any other lawyer in the Mero District. He was elected by the legislature to the U.S. House of Representatives in October 1796 and to the U.S. Senate in September of the following year. Jackson's appointment to the Court came only months after his resignation from the Senate. He resigned from the bench in July 1804.[30]

The General Assembly unanimously elected John Overton to Jackson's seat on the Court in August of that year. He served until January 1810 and again from November 1811 until his resignation from the bench in 1816.[31] Overton (1766–1833), one of Jackson's few lifelong friends, was a native Virginian who had begun his career in the law in present-day Kentucky. He occasionally practiced law with Jackson and served as supervisor and district inspector of revenue in Tennessee. Between 1803 and 1806, Overton acted as the state's agent in negotiating a settlement with North Carolina concerning the latter's right to dispose of land located within the new state. Ratified by Congress in April 1806, Overton's settlement became known as the Compact of 1806 and provided the basis for several of the Court's most significant decisions between 1796 and 1835.

Along with his successor, Judge Robert Whyte, Overton was one of the foremost advocates for relying upon English law as the starting point for the Court's decisions. "In discussing the points of jurisdiction and relief," Judge Overton announced shortly after succeeding to Jackson's seat, "it will be necessary to consider, first, the case upon the ground of the English authorities; secondly, under the alteration introduced by our own government; and, thirdly, with a view to the shape in which the subject presents

Elected to Tennessee's Superior Court in 1801, Hugh Lawson White later served on the Supreme Court of Errors and Appeals and then became a United States senator. Library of Congress.

itself to the Court." Overton's analytical approach was that which was typically followed by the Court during the first four decades of statehood except when specific statutes of North Carolina, Tennessee, or the territorial government clearly governed.[32]

Overton devoted himself to a lifelong study of the law. He owned a substantial law library (in 1808, his collection contained some 160 volumes; an inventory that was filed with his will in 1835 lists more than 260 volumes) and appears to have served as an agent for eastern publishers of law treatises. Cumberland College awarded him an honorary doctor of laws degree in 1825.[33]

To one historian of the period, requiring state appellate judges to file written opinions and the publication of those opinions was "perhaps, the most significant achievement of the legal profession in the post-Revolutionary period: the beginning of the establishment of an American code of law." Overton echoed that sentiment by emphasizing the need for written opinions by the Court's judges "to serve as guides and lights, not only to the courts, but citizens at large." He penned at least 155 signed, published opinions of his own during his tenure on the bench (of a total of 1,447 signed opinions by all the judges, 1796–1835). In collaboration with Judge Thomas Emmerson, he published a collection of the Court's previously unreported decisions in the initial two volumes of the Tennessee *Reports* (1813–17). After his resignation from the Court, Overton returned to the practice of law and to tutoring young would-be lawyers at his home, Travellers Rest. He also turned his attention to his substantial business interests and to promoting Jackson's political career. Reportedly one of the wealthiest men in early-nineteenth-century Tennessee, Overton by 1819 had become the leader of the Blount-Overton political/banking organization. One of the founders of Memphis (1819) on land that he owned with Jackson and General James Winchester, he devoted a substantial portion of his later years to promoting the new town's growth and development.[34]

To the seat vacated by Judge Roane in 1801, the legislature elected Hugh Lawson White. A native North Carolinian, White (1773–1840) was the son of Gen. James White, the founder of Knoxville. After having been tutored by Roane, White read law with James Hopkins in Lancaster, Pennsylvania, and, upon returning to Knoxville, served as private secretary to territorial Governor Blount. Five years later, he served as one of three defense attorneys during Judge Campbell's first impeachment trial.[35]

Like Roane, White served nonconsecutive terms as a member of the Court. He resigned from the bench in 1807 to represent Knox County in the state senate. In March 1808, he accepted an appointment by President Jefferson as U.S. attorney for the Eastern Division of Tennessee, a position that he held until his election, at the age of twenty-eight, to one of the two seats on the new Supreme Court. White's resignation from the Court in late 1815 became effective in April of the following year. Declining opportunities to return to the Court in 1822 and 1824, White was elected to succeed Jackson in the U.S. Senate in 1825.[36]

In 1807, the legislature increased the number of the Court's judges to four and elected Samuel Powel to the new seat. Parry W. Humphreys was selected to fill the vacancy left by the resignation of Judge Campbell. Each appears to have served until the new Supreme Court was elected pursuant to the 1809 reorganization statute.[37] To the new Court the legislature elected former Judge White and George Washington Campbell. When Judge Campbell resigned in 1811, former Judge Overton was elected to fill the vacancy. Upon Judge White's resignation in December 1815, William Wilcox Cooke was appointed, and subsequently elected by the legislature, to White's seat.[38]

Between 1815 and 1823, the General Assembly increased the number of Supreme Court judges from two to four and increased the number of circuits from five to eight.[39] Former Judge Roane was elected to the first new seat in 1815. The death of Cooke in July 1816 left a vacancy on the Court that Governor Joseph McMinn filled by issuing a temporary commission to John Haywood, whose appointment the General Assembly confirmed in October 1817. Judge Overton's resignation in 1816 left still another vacancy on the Court, which Governor McMinn filled by appointing Robert Whyte. Whyte narrowly won election by the General Assembly to fill the seat in October 1817.[40]

John Haywood (1762–1826) was a native of North Carolina. The beneficiary of little formal education, he nonetheless had served as a member of the state's highest court before moving to Tennessee in 1807. He settled on a site a few miles southeast of Nashville, where he built a house called Tusculum and two log offices, one for use as his office and the other for young would-be lawyers who chose to study under his tutelage. He practiced law for nine years before his appointment to the Court. A huge man who weighed about 350 pounds, Haywood came to be known as "the Lord Mansfield of the South-west." "[J]ustly esteemed as profoundly read in the common law," Judge Peck once recalled, Haywood "had grown up with the practice in North Carolina, and has generally assisted in making the practice for us in this country." During his tenure on the Court, Haywood wrote more than 125 opinions (of a total of 1,447 signed opinions by all the judges, 1796–1835), of which perhaps the most significant was *Townsend v. Townsend* (1821), the first decision in which the Court invalidated an act of the General Assembly as unconstitutional. He also published two volumes of the decisions of North Carolina's highest court, three of the Tennessee

John Haywood was a member of the Tennessee Supreme Court from 1816 to 1826 and authored several legal and nonlegal works, including two early histories of Tennessee. Courtesy of the North Carolina Division of Archives and History, Raleigh, North Carolina.

Court's decisions, and several additional compilations and commentaries on the laws of the two states. His subjects were not confined to the law; he also published *The Civil and Political History of Tennessee* (1823), a history of his adopted state to 1796, *The Natural and Aboriginal History of Tennessee* (1823), and a strange little volume, published under the pseudonym "A Tennessean," entitled *The Christian Advocate* (1819), a work he characterized as "philosophical theology" in which he attempts to reconcile mankind's "highest intellectual attainments" with the precepts of religion. Then, in the mid-1820s—while performing his duties as a sitting member of the Court—he published a two-volume revision of the laws of his adopted state with Robert L. Cobbs. In the chill of a December's day in 1826, Judge Haywood set out from Tusculum, bound for Franklin to sit as chancellor in the Court of Equity. Either because of inclement weather or due to stubborn horses, or perhaps both, Haywood was compelled to walk a portion of the distance over wet and muddy ground. He reached his destination late in the evening in a state of exhaustion. Before the close of court, he had taken on all of the symptoms of pneumonia and returned home, where he died on December 22.[41]

Robert Whyte (1767–1844) served as a member of the Court for more than eighteen years, longer than any other of the Court's judges during the first four decades of statehood, and authored several of the Court's most important decisions between 1796 and 1835. Yet this important early Tennessee jurist remains a figure of mystery. A native of Scotland, he was reported to have attended either Edinburgh University or the University of Glasgow. When he emigrated to the New World is unknown, but it appears that he settled at least for a time in Virginia and might have begun reading law there. He has erroneously been credited with having been a member of the faculty of the College of William and Mary as a professor of languages (that institution has no record of his having been affiliated with the college in any capacity). When Whyte moved to Tennessee also is not known, but he was licensed to practice law in the Tennessee courts in September 1802. Whyte served as one of three defense lawyers for Judge David Campbell during the latter's second impeachment proceedings in October 1803. Whyte's abilities as a lawyer were such that he was engaged by fellow lawyers Jackson and Overton and by Return Jonathan Meigs, the U.S. War Department's military agent and agent to the Cherokee Nation, to represent them in legal matters. Whyte also attracted out-of-state commercial clients, whose dealings with Tennessee merchants and businessmen were a recurring source of litigation. With Overton, Judge Whyte was one of the Court's foremost advocates of English law as providing guidance for the Court. A jurist of quiet erudition, Judge Whyte authored some 134 signed opinions during his tenure on the bench (of a total of 1,447 signed opinions by all the judges, 1796–1835), thus joining Overton, John Catron, Peck, and Nathan Green as the five authors of more opinions for the Court than any of its other judges during the period. Almost always deferential and uniformly unpretentious, Whyte nonetheless never allowed himself to be intimidated by those colleagues whose views differed from his own; the power of his opinions consisted of solid research and logic.[42]

Upon Judge Roane's death in early 1819, Governor McMinn appointed Thomas Emmerson to the Court, an appointment the General Assembly confirmed in October of that year. Jacob Peck was elected to fill the vacancy left by the resignation of Judge Emmerson in 1822. Peck (1779–1869), a native Virginian, was licensed to practice law in Tennessee in 1808. He was representing the eastern Tennessee counties of Jefferson and Greene in the state senate when elected to fill Judge Emmerson's seat on the Court in August 1822. Nothing is known of his educational background. A man of

John Catron, an ardent political ally of Andrew Jackson, was a member of the Supreme Court from 1824 to 1835 and subsequently named by Jackson to the Supreme Court of the United States. Photograph by Handy Studios, Collection of the Supreme Court of the United States.

eclectic tastes, however, Peck was described by those who knew him as a "refined and cultivated" man with a fondness for poetry, painting, and music who "ever entertained the most liberal and enlightened views on all subjects." Peck authored 276 published opinions during his tenure on the Court (of a total of 1,447 signed opinions by all the judges, 1796–1835), ranking behind only Catron in terms of signed opinions during the period 1796–1835. He edited and published volume 7 of the Tennessee *Reports.*[43]

William L. Brown was elected to a new seat that was added to the Court in 1822. His resignation the following year left a vacancy that remained unfilled for a full year, the result of the first major standoff between the Court and the General Assembly. The dispute was triggered by an order of the Court, issued in 1823, that would have required students of the law to pursue a particular course of reading as a prerequisite to admission to the bar. The Court's order was unpopular—an "*unhallowed* decree" resulting from an "aristocratic stretch of power," as one prospective lawyer described it. In November 1823, therefore, the legislature passed a resolution suspending the order indefinitely. The hostility did not end there, however. When Governor William Carroll notified the legislature of Judge Brown's resignation, which had been tendered in October 1823, the legislators refused to fill the vacancy, thus leaving the Court with one less judge but with the new duties of conducting the business of the Court of Equity that had been created in 1822.[44]

The consequences of the General Assembly's inaction were addressed by Governor Carroll in his legislative message in 1824. "[T]he burden imposed upon the Judges of the Supreme Court," he warned the legislators, "is greater than can be borne by men who have arrived to those years that best qualify them for the faithful and correct discharge of the duties of that high station; and the consequence is, a delay of justice injurious to the people at large, and almost ruinous to suitors." The governor recommended increasing the number of the Court's judges and limiting the places where they were required to sit.[45]

The legislature responded by increasing the number of the Court's judges to six and by reducing to three the number of places where the Court was required to meet (Knoxville, Sparta, and Nashville). The Court's judges who presided over the Court of Equity, however, were to conduct the business of that tribunal twice annually in Greeneville, Rogersville, Kingston, Carthage, McMinnville, Franklin, Columbia, Charlotte, and Jackson.[46] To fill the two new positions on the Court, the legislators elected John Catron and former Judge White. When Judge White declined the opportunity to return to the Court, Governor Carroll appears to have appointed Thomas Williams to his seat. The governor appointed Henry Crabb to succeed Haywood after the latter's death in December 1826.[47]

In 1827, the General Assembly reduced the number of judges comprising the Court from six to three. Legislation passed in 1831 increased the number to four, with the fourth judge to serve as the Court's chief justice, as a result of which Nathan Green was elected to the Court, and Catron was named chief justice.[48]

The legislature's choice of Catron (1781/6?–1865) was a significant event in the Court's history. Reported to have been born in various counties in Virginia and Pennsylvania and in different years, Catron by early 1812 had begun reading law in Sparta, Tennessee, and was admitted to the bar in 1815. He served as solicitor general for the Third Circuit, 1815–17, and in 1818 moved to Nashville, where he practiced law until his election to the Court.[49]

During his tenure on the Court, Catron authored nearly 350 signed opinions (of a total of 1,447 signed opinions by all the judges, 1796–1835), more than any of his colleagues. His opinions occasionally revealed glimpses of remarkable native intelligence, if not brilliance. At other times, he used his rhetoric to espouse the political views held by his fellow Jacksonians or the prevailing moral standards and prejudices of the time, often relying upon moral principles when the law failed him. As a consequence, Catron exemplified a result-driven jurisprudence in the sense that his decisions frequently appear to have come from a man who had made up his mind as to the result that he wished to achieve and who had supplied supporting authorities for the desired result almost as an afterthought. His decision in *State v. Foreman* (1835) at the very end of his tenure on the Court, for instance, resulted from turning a blind eye to the logic and precedent of his own earlier decisions, and in upholding the authority of the circuit court to strike from its rolls a lawyer who had been indicted for killing a man in a duel, Catron in *State v. Smith* (1829) devoted more attention to the evils of dueling than to the law. Those who argue that dueling is the only honorable redress for a personal injury, he wrote, are "not very deeply read in the moral code. . . . [T]hey tell us wicked vengeance and murderous crime is *redress?* This is not the precept our Saviour taught, our religion inculcates, and our laws enjoin; malice, vengeance, and crime, have no place but in the catalogue of iniquity." Could any rational person believe, he asked, that a man who engaged in such morally reprehensible conduct "is a fit person to be an aider and adviser in the sanctuaries of justice!" In answer to his own rhetorical question, Catron issued a stern warning to the state's lawyers:

> Let it be once understood that the bar of Tennessee *dare* not fight, and it will be deemed cowardly to challenge a member of it; and this court solemnly warns every lawyer, that if he violates the laws made to suppress dueling, we will strike him from the rolls of the court. . . . The truth is, such men are too often insolent and impudent bullies, who tyrannise over, and impose upon, all orderly men about them; who literally dragoon society, by fear of personal violence, into silence and seeming acquiescence, with respect to their conduct. That such a counsellor is a disgrace, and serious encumbrance to any court where he is permitted to practice all will admit; those who engage in duels, the statutes deem, and we will treat, as of this description.[50]

Catron rarely seemed satisfied as a detached jurist; playing the part of the clever politician was more to his liking. For much of his adult life he labored tirelessly, both behind the scenes and publicly, to promote Jackson's career and policies. As a member of the Tennessee Supreme Court (and later as Tennessee's first member of the Supreme Court of the United States), he was intensely partisan, regularly offered political advice and favors to friends such as Jackson, his kinsman-in-law James K. Polk, and Martin Van Buren, and participated in public discussions of political issues. Shortly after Jackson had assumed the presidency in 1829, for instance, Judge Catron, apparently without any qualms about the propriety of engaging in such a public political debate while occupying his judicial post, "opened the president's war on the Bank of the United States" by publishing in the Nashville and Knoxville newspapers a series of attacks on the bank's local branch, denouncing what he termed the institution's excessive loans and interest rates. On another occasion after his appointment by Jackson to the U.S. Supreme Court, he allowed Polk, then a presidential candidate, to set up political shop in the Catrons' home in Nashville and arranged private political interviews for him during his stay there. Dismissing any concerns about the propriety of such conduct by a sitting member of the Supreme Court, Catron assured Polk, "Don't believe that I have any squeamishness on the Judgeship score. . . . I'll make it work like the old clock, and with less noise."[51]

THE COURT AND DEVELOPING AREAS OF THE LAW

Real Property Law

Adverse Possession

As one modern commentator has noted, there is not much land in Tennessee that "does not depend on adverse possession at some point for the demonstration of its title." Because title to significant amounts of land was at stake, the concept of adverse possession, or the possession of land adverse to other claimants, was an important one in early Tennessee law. As a result of defects in the grant system, many settlers claimed boundary lines for their lands that did not correspond with the descriptions contained in the patents upon which their grants had been issued. Others were not in possession of their entire tracts. There also were those who were in possession of lands as mere trespassing squatters or under deeds that could not be traced back to valid original grants. The resulting uncertainty in land titles was widespread and assumed a political aspect in the minds of some settlers who thought that many out-of-possession claimants who could found their titles on original grants were nonresidents who were not entitled to priority over those who had cleared the land and endured the hardships of frontier existence. In addition, for several years after Tennessee became a state, North Carolina retained the right to issue military warrants for lands located within the new state. The problem was exacerbated by an 1805 statute that validated champertous deeds and encouraged some to become "'landgrabbers' by buying cheap titles from claimants out of possession, some of whom were indeed nonresidents."[52]

One of the recurring issues that consumed much of the Court's time for nearly three decades was whether adverse possession for seven years was sufficient in itself under Tennessee law to establish valid title or whether possession had to be based upon "a connected title, either legal or equitable," derived from a grant. The issue, one Tennessee lawyer recalled, "engendered a controversy in Tennessee, from the excitement of which . . . very few persons of any consideration in society were entirely exempt [and which] continued, and raged with increasing intensity and bitterness, for a space of about twenty-five years; during the different vicissitudes and doubtful issues of which, it agitated our legislative councils and judicial tribunals to an extent that was both unexampled and alarming."[53] Each of the state and federal courts issued several inconsistent decisions that addressed (or appeared to address) the question, with the anomalous result that, for several years, the federal courts' construction of the statute was in direct conflict with that of the Tennessee Court.

The issue involved the interpretation of two statutes. The first was a confusing measure that had been enacted by the North Carolina Assembly in 1715 and that was subsequently adopted by Tennessee. The second was passed by the Tennessee General Assembly in 1797 for the purpose of clarifying the 1715 measure. The earlier statute appeared to afford protection to persons in actual possession of land, without any legal right to do so, by requiring that any other person holding any right or title to such land must enter into possession of or otherwise claim such land "within seven years after his, her or their right or title shall descent or accrue" or suffer "a perpetual bar" from doing so. In the autumn of 1796, prior to the convening of the First Tennessee General Assembly, the Superior Court was called upon for the first time to construe the 1715 act when it heard *Kerr v. Porter* (1796). The defendant in *Kerr* had been in possession for seven years, but a portion of that time had occurred before he obtained his grant, and he claimed that mere "naked possession" was sufficient in order for the protections of the 1715 statute to apply. Judge Overton, who had served as counsel in the case, later recalled "the public excitement occasioned" by the argument on behalf of the defendant that "the possession of any trespasser on the lands of the State or an individual might acquire a title by seven years' continuance, a doctrine which was thought to be iniquitous and unjust." The Court in *Kerr* actually avoided resolving the issue decisively, and it was for the purpose of precluding subsequent reliance upon "this evil [doctrine]," according to Overton, that the 1797 measure had been enacted by the state's first legislature.[54]

The 1797 statute protected any person who had been in peaceable physical possession of any land "by virtue of a grant or deed of conveyance founded upon a grant." Although the holdings are not entirely clear, the Court's initial construction of the measure appeared not to require a regular, unbroken chain of title from a grant as a prerequisite to the statute's applicability.[55]

In the ensuing years, however, the Court heard a number of appeals in which the issue was raised and issued opinions contrary to its earlier decisions. In *Weatherhead v. Bledsoe's Heirs* (1815), for instance, Judge Roane weighed in on the side of requiring a regular chain of title between the grant and the deed of the party seeking the protection of the statute. "[T]here must be some kind of connection shown," he concluded, "between the claim of the person wishing to avail himself of the statute of limitations and the grant from the State." Moreover, Roane continued, although such a connection need not be established "by a regular chain of valid deeds of conveyance," the defendant must introduce "such evidence as would satisfy a jury that each individual through whose hands the lands had passed acquired it lawfully by right, and not by wrong."[56]

Although the first decisions by the federal Circuit Court in Tennessee on the issue followed the Tennessee Court's earlier cases, the Supreme Court of the United States in *Patton's Lessee v. Easton* (1816) noted that the later Tennessee decisions required that the possessor's "deed must be connected with the grant."[57]

The Tennessee cases ultimately culminated in *Gray v. Darby's Lessee* (1825), in which the Court, in a decision by its newest member, Judge Catron, concluded that the drafters of the 1797 statute had "never contemplated the introduction of equitable, or apparent equitable title, for the purpose of forming a connection."[58] The Court's decision in *Gray* settled the matter, and the conflict between the state and federal courts on the issue ultimately was resolved in 1832, when the Supreme Court of the United States overruled one of its earlier decisions construing the 1797 statute to require a connection of title. Applying the revised interpretation of the act in *Gray,* it held as being the settled law of Tennessee that adverse possession of seven years was sufficient to give the occupant a valid title without showing any such connection.[59]

Damages for Breach of Warranty of Title

One of the most vexing problems facing early-nineteenth-century lawmakers was the proper measure of damages for breach of warranty in the sale of land. Most deeds included a warranty by the seller that he had seizin, or good title, in the land that he sold and often included a covenant guaranteeing the purchaser quiet enjoyment of his land. If such a purchaser subsequently was evicted by one holding superior title, the issue arose whether he was entitled to recover from his seller any increase in the value of the land, either because of improvements or due to rising prices, or was limited to a recovery of the purchase price that he had paid. The well-established rule at common law had been that the purchaser was entitled to recover only the original purchase price, but a number of states in the early nineteenth century enacted statutes that enabled evicted purchasers to recover the higher value of the land at the time of eviction.[60]

The Tennessee Supreme Court was one of the first western courts to rule on the issue. In *Talbot v. Bedford's Heirs* (1813), the Court declined to abandon the common-law measure of damages and held that, in the absence of a showing of fraud, the proper measure of damages was the lower, original purchase price plus interest. The Court, in a decision by Judge Overton, reasoned that, given the unsettled nature of many land titles, it would be an intolerable burden to require sellers to pay for any increase in the value of land.[61]

Right to the Value of Improvements in Ejectment Actions

For the purpose of promoting improvements by ensuring that developers reaped the benefits of their investments, a number of states during the first half of the nineteenth century adopted statutes that permitted a bona fide purchaser of land to recover the value of improvements from one who had superior title and had evicted him from possession. These so-called occupying claimant statutes were controversial because they abrogated the common-law rule that one who cleared or improved another's land without the owner's request or consent was not only entitled to no compensation therefore, but also was liable to the owner in an action of trespass.[62]

Tennessee's legislature passed a number of such statutes, including an 1809 measure which declared that when "any person in possession of any land under patent grant or lawful entry was dispossessed by due course of law," he was entitled, upon notice to the owner, to recover the value of his improvements. The 1809 act came under almost immediate attack as being unconstitutional. In *Townsend v. Shipp's Heirs* (1813), however, the Court sustained the act's constitutionality by construing the measure as merely affording the occupant a remedy at law that he previously had had in equity.[63]

In *Nelson v. Allen* (1830), however, Judge Whyte went out of his way to suggest that the state's occupant claimant statutes were unconstitutional and to reaffirm the common-law rule. Judge Whyte's decision was noted by New York's Chancellor James Kent as providing support for the common-law view. As Judge Catron explained in a lengthy footnote to the Court's reported decision, however, the constitutionality of the 1813 statute had not been an issue before the Court; the only question had been whether the owner was entitled to recover mesne profits from the occupant and whether the amount of such mesne profits should be set off against the occupant's judgment.[64]

The Law of Slavery

Emancipation Cases

During the first forty years of statehood, the Tennessee Court recognized that when the freedom of slaves was at issue, there was an interplay between what Judge Catron once referred to as "the rights of humanity" and "the rights of property." One of the "rights of humanity" that the Court recognized was emancipation, which in turn involved three different sets of interests: the property rights of the owner, the slave's right to receive freedom once it had been granted, and the state's interest in regulating the manner in which "new members may be introduced into its free community." In choosing this approach, the Court maintained a course of independence not only from the legislature of its own state but also from the highest courts of the other southern states and went further than any other of those courts to provide an analytical framework that facilitated rather than obstructed the slave's path to freedom.

Tennessee law gave a significant amount of latitude to owners with respect to the means by which they chose to emancipate their slaves. Manumission could be effected by will, by deed, or "'by any species of instrument' that would 'completely evince' the master's 'intent and volition' to free the slave." Slave owners also had a great deal of flexibility in the timing of emancipation and could condition freedom upon the occurrence of some future event, a method that caused particularly difficult conceptual problems when the slave was female and had children during the gap period between the time when the owner's statement of intention to emancipate had been made and the occurrence of the event upon which liberty was contingent.[65]

In the view that the Court ultimately adopted, the owner had "complete control over the question of emancipation" and could "free his chattel at pleasure." The Court required only that the owner demonstrate his clear intention to emancipate. As early as 1817, the Court recognized that a testator in his will could direct the executors of his estate to liberate his slaves.[66] Less than a decade later, in *Hope v. Johnson* (1826), the Court upheld testamentary instructions that the testator's slaves be freed, that the testator's plantation be sold, that the proceeds from the sale be used by the executors to purchase land in the Indiana Territory, and that title to such land be vested in the emancipated slaves.[67]

The Court also consistently upheld the use of the judicial system to ensure that an owner's intention to emancipate was fully effectuated. This judicial attitude was made clear when the legislature in 1831 attempted to transfer to the county courts all suits then pending in the district chancery courts under an 1829 statute which permitted a slave who had been emancipated by will but whose testator's executor had failed to effect the slave's freedom to file a "by-next-friend" bill for freedom in equity. In *Fisher's Negroes v. Dabbs* (1834), the Court invalidated the 1831 act as an unconstitutional attempt to interfere with the jurisdiction of the chancery court.[68]

Because of the prevailing presumption that any African American and anyone resembling an African American was a slave, the claimant in a suit for freedom was at a distinct disadvantage in terms of the kinds of evidence that were admissible to prove the contrary. Although the presumption was not an irrebuttable one, documentary evidence such as a deed of manumission or an emancipating will was rarely available. In *Vaughan v. Phebe* (1827), the Court held that reputation evidence was properly admissible in a suit for freedom to show the claimant's Indian ancestry, which was conclusive on the issue of freedom, and to show that within her community the claimant had always been considered to be free. *Phebe* represented an effort on the Court's part to address, though not to eliminate, the presumption by establishing an exception to the prohibition against the use of hearsay evidence in the limited context of suits seeking freedom. After *Phebe,* therefore, there was a significant evidentiary tool that had not been available before with which claimants of whatever race could prove their status as free persons.[69]

While the Court was increasingly willing to facilitate manumission during the first four decades of statehood, the General Assembly's record on the subject of emancipation was a mixed one. In contrast to the wide latitude that the Court was willing to give owners who desired to free their slaves, the legislature throughout the period attempted to impose an effective check on emancipation. Even though an owner, through whatever means, might have expressed an unequivocal intention to free a slave, the slave's freedom was not fully effectuated until the state had granted its consent. Between 1796 and 1802, the process for approving emancipation petitions was that which had been prescribed by a 1777 North Carolina statute that had been adopted by Tennessee. Such petitions were required to be approved by the General Assembly, and legislative approval was to be granted only upon a showing that the slave whose freedom was at issue had demonstrated "meritorious services." Under the provisions of legislation enacted in 1801, the authority to grant the state's consent to emancipation was delegated to the county court for the county where the slave owner resided. The county courts were authorized to approve manumission petitions when the owner had provided satisfactory assurance, in the form of a bond, that the freed slave would not become an economic burden to the county. Thirty years later, however, the legislature restricted the county courts' granting of consent to those cases in which the freed slave would leave the state. Moreover, although a judgment granting consent could be appealed, a freed slave whose petition had been denied by the county court was not permitted to appeal the adverse judgment.[70]

The policy goals of the consent statute appear to have been to protect the state from the economic burden that freed slaves might cause and from the discord that they might incite among the slave population. Ultimately, of course, in terms of accomplishing those objectives, the statute was ineffectual, because the result of a denial of consent was not to return the freed slave into a state of involuntary servitude. Rather, the freed slave who had failed to obtain the state's consent to his freedom merely existed in an intermediate state between slavery and freedom as a kind of quasi-slave who was likely to pose even more of a threat than would have been the case had consent been granted.[71]

The Court was never willing to act as a judicial legislator for the purpose of remedying the shortcomings of the state's manumission statute. Indeed, in at least one reported case, *Hope v. Johnson* (1826), the Court demonstrated not only its unwavering adherence to the legality of testamentary emancipation (*i.e.*, by will), but also its willingness to accommodate the efforts of a creative executor who was determined to circumvent the consent statute.[72]

Even the right that opponents of emancipation petitions had to appeal consent judgments proved to be an ineffective one, especially when the grounds for overturning such judgments were procedural or technical in nature. "Those who tried to void a judgment of freedom upon the basis of irregularities in the county court proceedings or in the record of those proceedings," it has been observed, "never received a sympathetic hearing from the Supreme Court."[73]

The Court was similarly unsympathetic to the argument that emancipation was invalid when former slaves had been taken out of the state, allegedly for the purpose of circumventing Tennessee's statutory manumission scheme. In *Blackmore v. Negro Phill* (1835), an elderly owner had attempted to emancipate several of his slaves but had failed to secure the requisite consent. The owner then sold the slaves on condition that the purchaser take them to Illinois, where slavery was prohibited by that state's

Constitution, and emancipate them there. This the purchaser did. When the freed slaves returned to Tennessee, the Court, speaking through Judge Peck, upheld the validity of the emancipation in Illinois.[74]

Throughout the antebellum period, the Tennessee Court consistently ruled that an owner's act of emancipation "conferred upon the slave 'a moral right to freedom'" that converted the owner's property right into an immediate, vested "right to liberty . . . which the Court then would protect on its own merits."[75] At times, however, the owner conditioned the emancipated slave's enjoyment of freedom upon the occurrence of some future contingency. One of the most difficult conceptual issues to face the Court was whether the children of a female slave who had been granted "a moral right to freedom" that was to take effect at some time in the future were entitled to their freedom when born during the gap between the grant of the mother's freedom and its effective date. Virginia's Supreme Court of Appeals had wrestled with the problem since 1799 and had issued inconsistent decisions on the issue. The highest courts of Kentucky, Delaware, and Louisiana also had confronted the dilemma and had, for various reasons, held that children born during the gap period were slaves.[76]

The Tennessee Court's first decision on the issue was unreported. In *Crenshaw v. Matilda* (1827), according to Judge Peck's notes on the case and the case file, the testator in a deed executed in Virginia in 1794 had liberated several of his slaves, including Matilda's mother, Delpha, "& their issue." The language of the deed was "do set free," but the owner had retained the right of guardianship with respect to those slaves who were then underage until they reached the age of maturity. Delpha was one of the latter class and did not come of age until 1806. Matilda was born in Tennessee in 1804. The defendant, the son of the original owner of Delpha and Matilda who had obtained ownership of Matilda from his father, argued that the instrument had been a "deed in futuro" and that because no right to freedom had accrued to the mother until 1806, none had accrued to Matilda at the time of her birth. The Court, Peck noted, concluded that the "deed of emancipation was in presenti" and that "this was an emancipation" of the mother and her unborn children in 1794 that was merely to take effect in 1806.[77]

In an extraordinary subsequent action, *Matilda v. Crenshaw* (1833), the victorious Matilda again sued her purported owner, who had retained possession of her and whom she had continued to serve during the pendency of the suit to establish her freedom. In the second action, Matilda sought to recover the value of her services between the date in 1825 when she had initiated her first suit and the date in 1827 when the Court affirmed the circuit court's judgment, plus the costs of prosecuting the first suit. This action was also successful. "[T]he first [suit] for freedom tries the title," Chief Justice Catron declared, "as an ejectment in cases of land; slave or no slave is the issue, which has never been holden in this state to involve the question of hire." Upon entry of the judgment in the first action, Catron continued, Crenshaw thereafter was "estopped to controvert the freedom of Matilda, or to say he rightfully held her to service from and after the commencement of the suit for title." The Court proceeded to grant Matilda an award of the value of her services between June 1825 and April 1827 at the agreed-upon rate of twenty dollars per annum plus the "fifty dollars in prosecuting her suit for freedom."[78]

The Court reached a similar result in two decisions reported as *Harris v. Clarissa* (1833, 1834), holding that the gap children born to a slave woman granted freedom upon reaching the age of twenty-five were also free. The Court's decisions in *Clarissa* were not, of course, libertarian in the modern sense; they were based "squarely on the law of property." Moreover, the Court undertook "no effort to undermine the notion of slaves as disposable chattels."[79]

This does not mean that there was no justifiable reason for the Court's choice not to use *Clarissa* as an opportunity to undertake an open assault against the institution of slavery. The initial decision in *Clarissa* in March 1833, it must be remembered, came at a time when the Court was not, constitutionally, an equal and independent branch of Tennessee's government. Indeed, the opinion was announced less than two years after Catron had felt it necessary to offer up his resignation in order to fend off the very real legislative threat in 1831 to abolish the Court altogether.[80] The Court, its judges surely understood, was a creature of the legislature and could be reined in or eliminated altogether at the whim of a legislative majority. Indeed, before it was recognized as a distinct branch of state government by the Constitution of 1835, the Court had never really operated in a political vacuum. Beginning with the Court's initial exercise of judicial review in 1821 and especially in 1830 and 1831, the Court had pursued a risky, albeit cautious, course of independence by overturning an increasing number of legislative enactments when the legislature was found to have ventured beyond constitutional limits. That course had resulted in the near-fatal legislative crisis of 1831. Catron and his colleagues no doubt had little desire to stir up another threat to the Court's continuing development as an institution by challenging the legislature not over the constitutionality of one of its enactments, which was a legal issue that really could not be avoided by the Court, but over the continued legal viability of the institution of slavery, especially when the issue before them could be resolved without reaching the larger policy question.

As creatures of politics who understood just how far they could go without arousing the legislature's ire, the judges also surely recognized that slavery served as the source of economic well-being for most members of the legislature. Not surprisingly, an overwhelming majority of Tennessee's legislators at the time were slave owners,[81] and to have led an assault against slavery would no doubt have been viewed as the equivalent of leading an assault upon the legislature. This the Court's judges were unwilling to do and understandably so, especially when, in *Clarissa,* another course was open to them which, although perhaps not going far enough from the modern vantage point, would nonetheless achieve the same equitable result within the structure of existing legal principles of property law.

Criminal Cases

Throughout this period in the Court's history, individual members of each county court in Tennessee exercised essentially exclusive jurisdiction over a wide variety of minor offenses alleged to have been committed by slaves. Special local slave courts consisting of three justices of the county court and four slave owners were vested with similarly exclusive jurisdiction over slaves who had been accused of crimes too serious to be handled by a single magistrate.[82] In 1815, the General Assembly increased the number of slaveholders from four to nine and four years later increased the number to twelve. The twelve slave owners were to serve as a jury; the role of the three magistrates was relegated to presiding over such so-called slave trials and imposing sentences upon convicted slaves.[83] There was no right of appeal from the decisions of Tennessee's special slave courts until the Supreme Court rendered its decision in *Bob, a Slave v. State* (1825).[84]

The slave in *Bob* had been convicted of murder and condemned to death. Bob's owner petitioned the circuit court for a writ of *certiorari* on the grounds of insufficient evidence and irregularity in the proceedings, but the petition was denied. On review, the Supreme Court reversed. Although acknowledging that the decision to grant or deny an application for *certiorari* was a discretionary one on the part of the circuit judge, the Court was of the view that such discretion must not be exercised arbitrarily and that the denial of *certiorari* was an error that could be appealed by writ of error to the Supreme Court.[85]

Judge Peck's appeal in a concurring opinion to the economic interests of slave owners not only preempted any legislative rebuke of the Court, but probably was responsible for the legislative sanction of *Bob* that followed within months of the announcement of the decision. When the General Assembly convened in October 1825, it approved the Court's decision in *Bob* by passing legislation authorizing appeals of convictions by slave courts to the circuit courts "in like manner as in cases of the conviction of white persons for similar offense" and granting slave defendants the same access to the Supreme Court "as in prosecutions against free white persons." The statute thus not only afforded protection to slave owners of their property interests, but also extended to slave defendants one of the most important procedural protections that were available to white defendants in criminal prosecutions.[86]

The ultimate fate of Bob before the slave court on remand in this particular case remains unknown. It is possible that Bob was not spared conviction, thus leaving the Court's creation of a right of appeal in slave criminal cases subject to criticism as having provided the slave defendant with little in the way of actual protection.[87] The same argument can be made, however, in virtually every case in which a criminal defendant, for any number of reasons, does not enjoy the benefit of an important new criminal procedural protection that is announced by the court in his or her case. The actual result for the defendant in such a case does not lessen the prospective significance of the new protection for future criminal defendants. The procedural protection created by the Court in *Bob* and thereafter endorsed by the General Assembly was a very significant one and remained inviolate until the slave courts were abolished: slave defendants and their owners were entitled to appeals from adverse decisions rendered by the state's slave courts. The ultimate significance of *Bob* lay in the declaration by Tennessee's highest court that, thenceforth, it "would read the laws governing criminal trials as [being] applicable to slaves as well as to whites."[88]

Tennessee statutory law provided for the prosecution and punishment of whites who killed or committed physical violence against slaves. In 1813, the Tennessee General Assembly enacted legislation providing that any person, owners excepted, who "wantonly and without sufficient cause" beat or abused the slave "of another person" was subject to indictment and the same punishment as those prescribed for similar offenses against whites. The Supreme Court heard no appeals of convictions under the statute during the first four decades of statehood.[89]

A 1799 statute, however, declared that any person who "wilfully and maliciously, with malice aforethought" killed a negro or mulatto slave and was convicted of such offense "shall be deemed guilty of murder, as if such person so killed had been a free man, and shall suffer death without benefit of clergy, any law, usage or custom to the contrary notwithstanding." The Tennessee statute was similar to those that had been adopted in other southern states. One of the most vexing problems for southern antebellum appellate courts arose when white defendants were found guilty of killing slaves but were convicted for a category of homicide less serious than murder. The appellate courts were faced with the dilemma of deciding whether other penal statutes or the law of common-law crimes might apply. The issue of whether such convictions for what later came to be known as lesser-included offenses might be permissible under the common law was one on which the Tennessee Court took an early and important stand.[90] In *Fields v. State* (1829), the Court ruled that common-law principles applied and that a white defendant could be found guilty of manslaughter for the killing of a slave. The decision established the terms of a debate within the southern appellate courts that raged on for the next thirty years.[91]

The decision in *Fields* has been seen as a "major exception" to the decisions of most other southern antebellum appellate courts on the same issue.[92] This approach, of course, was not without its critics. Judge Eugenius A. Nisbet of Georgia's Supreme Court, for instance, was of the opinion that the legal basis for *Fields* had been "wholly untenable" and that the decision had resulted from a "fervid zeal in behalf of humanity to the slave."[93] When the same issue came before the Supreme Court of Mississippi in 1859, Justice William L. Harris ruled that the common law was not applicable to slaves. Harris dismissed *Fields* and its progeny as aberrant cases that had been founded upon "unmeaning twaddle, in which some humane judges and law writers have indulged, as to the influence of the 'natural law,' 'civilization and Christian enlightenment,' in amending, proprio vigore, the rigor of the common law, and on a supposed analogy between villanage in England and slavery here."[94]

Notwithstanding such criticism, the Court's decision in *Fields* was important. By applying the substantive common law of crimes to Tennessee's slaves, the judges refined and expanded the kinds of acts that were encompassed within the definition of the killing another human being and increased the likelihood that those who engaged in such conduct would suffer some degree of punishment rather than none at all.

The Enigma of the Court's Slavery Decisions

Although not "libertarian" in the modern sense, the Tennessee Court through 1835 was significantly more sensitive to the "rights of humanity" of slaves than any of the other antebellum southern high courts.[95] Why the Tennessee Court's slavery decisions during this period differed so dramatically from those of the other southern high courts is a question to which, unfortunately, the surviving evidence suggests only speculative rather than definitive answers. For instance, it is true that Tennessee's slave population, both in terms of real numbers and in terms of a percentage of total population, during both the territorial period and the first four decades of statehood was lower than that of the other southern states. Between 1791 and 1795, the territory's slave population increased from 3,417 to 10,613 in total populations of 35,691 and 77,262 (approximately 10 percent and 14 percent), respectively. By 1800, the state's population of 105,602 included 13,584 slaves (approximately 13 percent). Ten years later, the state's slave population was 44,535 in a total population of 261,727 (approximately 17 percent). In 1820, Tennessee's total population of 422,813 included 80,097 slaves (approximately 19 percent). In 1830, the state's total population of 681,903 included 141,603 slaves (approximately 21 percent).[96] It might seem logical, therefore, that the economic stake of the state's white population between 1796 and 1835 in ensuring proslavery rulings from its highest court would have been less than that of white populations in the other southern states and that the Tennessee Court's judges thus were taking less a risk of generating negative reactions to their slavery decisions from the state's white population than would have been the case had Tennessee's population statistics been comparable to those of the other southern states. Even so, it should be remembered that the tenures of the Tennessee Court's judges did not depend upon the population at large, but rather upon the General Assembly, the overwhelming majority of whom, as has been noted, were slaveholders whose economic stake in perpetuating slavery was clear.[97] Moreover, the Court rendered several of its most far-reaching decisions after the slave uprising in 1831 in southeastern Virginia led by Nat Turner and, because Tennessee was not immune to the inevitable rumors that came in its wake, thus risked a negative reaction against itself and its opinions by legislators and the public at large generated by fears of similar slave insurrections in their own state.[98]

Similarly, the personal slaveholdings of the Court's judges did not appear to have been a factor in their decision to vote one way or another in slave cases. Of the judges who sat on the Court's most significant slavery cases through 1835, only one (Haywood) would have been considered a large slaveholder, that is, the owner of twenty or more slaves. In 1820, Judge Haywood owned twenty-one slaves, although at the time of his death six years later, he owned only six. Judge Whyte owned seventeen slaves in 1820 but only four in 1830. In 1830, Judges Catron and Green owned six slaves each, and Judge Peck owned three.[99] Although it is tempting to conclude from these numbers that most of the Court's judges had little economic stake in rendering their slavery decisions, historians and economists have noted that even one slave cost a great deal of money to purchase and maintain and thus was a significant financial investment. Any decision by the Court's judges that eroded the protections afforded the institution of slavery by the law thus would have potentially jeopardized their own economic interests.[100]

One can, of course, take the rhetoric found in certain of the Court's slavery decisions at face value and conclude that the judges voting to sustain emancipation or to afford procedural fairness to slave defendants were motivated by genuinely held antislavery sentiments. As G. Edward White has cautioned, however, each case in the American judicial system is decided by applying certain legal principles and terms to a specific set of facts, the resolution of each such case has conclusive significance only for the specific factual situation presented or one similar to it, and the judge's role in the process is defined as one of an informed and impartial arbiter of the dispute at hand "whose decision is allegedly based on the legal 'merits' of a case rather than on any personal inclinations of his own." An appellate judge's decision thus "may conceal rather than reveal the social attitudes of an individual judge. . . . Indeed, a historian's sense of the ideological currents of a particular time period may encourage him to impose a characterization on legal materials that they will not bear." Moreover, it is especially difficult, if not impossible, to determine the true state of a southern antebellum judge's mind on the issue of slavery from the public declarations contained in his judicial decisions without reconciling those statements with the judge's personal views on the subject as expressed in his private papers or nonjudicial writings. In the case of the Court's early judges, even less enlightenment is possible because few of their personal papers survive, and in them, the subject rarely is addressed.[101]

The opinions of four of the Tennessee Court's judges between 1796 and 1835—Haywood, Peck, Crabb, and Catron—contain statements that can be characterized as critical of the institution of slavery. It was Judge Catron's eloquent description of the competing interests of slave ("the rights of humanity") and master ("the rights of property") in 1833, for instance, that has frequently attracted the attention of legal historians, and in awarding damages to the free woman in *Matilda,* Catron observed that "a person held as a slave is controlled and compelled to act by the will of another, and is in fact and law imprisoned, although not within the four walls of a jail."[102] Unfortunately, virtually none of Catron's private papers has survived, and those that do remain contain no indication of the judge's private views on slavery. One hesitates to read too much into the opinions expressed by the result-driven Catron in any of his decisions. The often eloquent rhetoric in Judge Catron's early Cherokee reserve decisions, for instance, provided no hint of his illogical decision in *Foreman* scarcely five years later. Reading too much into the similarly eloquent rhetoric used by Catron in certain of his slavery decisions thus is a perilous course at best.

Judge Crabb was equally eloquent in his opinion for the Court in *Vaughan v. Phebe* (1827). "[I]t is no light matter to be a freeman in these United States," he declared. "Freedom in this country is not a mere name. . . . It is something substantial. It embraces within its comprehensive grasp all the useful rights of man; and it makes itself manifest by many privileges, immunities, [and] external public acts. It is not confined in its operations to privacy, or to the domestic circle. It walks abroad in its operations,—transfers its possessor, even if he be black, or mulatto, or copper-colored, from the kitchen and the cotton-field to the court-house and the election ground; makes him talk of Magna Charta and the Constitution." Regrettably, however, because none of Crabb's personal papers appears to have survived, it has not been possible to determine whether the views expressed in *Phebe* were actual expressions of his personal views on the subject of slavery.[103]

What is known is that two of the Court's judges—Peck, the author of *Negro Phill* and the strong concurring opinion in *Fields* who voted consistently to uphold emancipation, and Haywood, who with Peck authored the principal opinions in *Bob*—personally held strong antislavery views. As a member of the state senate, Peck had chaired that body's Committee on Slavery. In 1821, less than a year before his election to the Court, Peck issued a committee report refuting the frequently heard argument that emancipation would result in large numbers of freed former slaves' becoming an economic burden on the state's counties and recommending an amendment of the law to allow masters to emancipate "healthy, young slave[s]" who were not likely to become such a burden. "[V]ery few cases have occurred," Peck reported, "where slaves freed, in the state of Tennessee, have become a county charge." More significantly, Peck also urged the senate to consider legislation for gradual emancipation, to be effected by declaring that the "yet unborn" children of slaves were to be free. "[L]iberty to the slave," he observed in his report, "has occupied the research of the moral, philosophical, and statesmen of our own and other countries; a research into this principle extends wide into an evil, whose root is perhaps dangerously entwined with the liberty of the only free government."[104]

The reference by Peck to research by American statesmen into the subject of gradual emancipation suggests that he almost certainly was familiar with similar proposals that had been made since the late eighteenth century by public figures such as the young Jefferson and St. George Tucker (1752–1827), the respected Virginia jurist and professor of law at William and Mary, and that he might well have been aware of the economic arguments against slavery that were made by nineteenth-century political economist George Tucker (1775–1861), the elder Tucker's nephew and student who served as a member of Congress from Virginia, 1819–25. Jefferson had advocated gradual abolition in Virginia since the early days of the Revolution. Tucker had outlined his proposal in classroom lectures and in a pamphlet published in 1796, which also was included as an appendix to his widely used edition of

Blackstone's *Commentaries* (1803). "Whilst we were offering up vows at the shrine of Liberty," Tucker argued, "we were imposing upon our fellow men, who differ in complexion from us, a *slavery,* ten thousand times more cruel than the utmost extremity of those grievances and oppressions, of which we complained." The younger Tucker expanded the attack on slavery into the economic realm, arguing, for instance, in his *Letters from Virginia* (1816) that the institution was an impediment to the South's economic development and, in a noted speech in Congress in 1820 against the extension of slavery into Missouri, predicting the eventual abolition of the slave system based on the Malthusian doctrine of population.[105]

Although Peck's judicial decisions frequently included caustic observations on "the horrors of slavery" that were consistent with his personal views about the institution, it was in his concurring opinion in *Fields* that he expressed his outrage at the categorical argument that the slave was "on a footing with the live stock on a farm" and argued that the slave was *"a reasonable creature"* whose death at the hands of another with malice aforethought ought to be punished, like similar offenses at common law, as murder. "It is well said," Peck concluded, "that the master has the right to exact the labor of the slave—that far, the rights of the slave are suspended; but this gives the master no right over the life of the slave. . . . [T]hat law which says thou shalt not kill, protects the slave; and he is within its very letter. Law, reason, christianity and common humanity, all point out one way."[106]

Peck's opposition to slavery did not end with the conclusion of his service on the Court. In retirement, he befriended a northern abolitionist residing in Tennessee, Ezekiel Birdseye, and in the early 1840s, the two planned to establish a self-sustaining community in upper eastern Tennessee and western North Carolina that relied solely on free labor. Two decades after having publishing his committee report, in a letter seeking financial assistance for their project from the abolitionist-philanthropist Gerrit Smith of New York, Peck reiterated his long-standing view that slavery was an evil on both moral and economic grounds. "It is not every man who has been born and raised in a slave state," he wrote, "that could remain blind to the inhumanity of it—or who could view it any other wise than as impolitic on the Ground of Economy—And tho I do not aspire to the rank of a philosopher I am sure that to any community slavery is an evil."[107]

Haywood similarly made it clear in his *The Christian Advocate* that he considered slavery, in all of its forms, as one of the enduring evils of human history. Although the "abolition of slavery from the face of the earth," he lamented, was not expected to occur until the biblical millennium, mankind was nevertheless taking unmistakable steps toward that end, which he believed was consistent with "science and the genuine doctrines of true religion." Singled out by Haywood as two of the most praiseworthy examples of such progress were the part taken by Charles James Fox in the British Parliament's abolition of "the disgraceful slave trade" in 1807 and the treaty entered into by England and Spain in 1817 prohibiting the slave trade.[108]

Although Haywood died before the Court's most important slavery decisions were rendered, he authored the opinion in *Hope v. Johnson* (1826), in which the Court went out of its way to accommodate the efforts of a creative and determined executor to circumvent the consent statute. Haywood also joined Peck in authoring the primary opinions in *Bob,* in which the Court held that an appeal of a criminal conviction of a slave could be brought to the circuit court, and concluded by asking rhetorically:

> And in all conscience and justice, is not this in itself right and proper? Shall it be said that a human being shall be condemned to death by a wrongful sentence, and that there is no power residing in the law to rescue him from it? Does the law delight in cruelty? Will it inflict punishment where it is not deserved? Will it give no power to avoid the unjust sentence? Then where is the justice of the law, and where is its boasted humanity? . . . After so many ages of experience and of improvement, has no provision been made to obviate an evil so distressing to humanity?[109]

It is important to remember that it is not unusual to find sentiments against slavery expressed publicly and privately by southerners from the time of the Revolution through the 1830s. During the early days of the Republic, many southerners made it, in Professor Sellers's words, "painfully explicit" that they were at least subconsciously aware of the paradox of "'our everyday sentiments of liberty' while holding human beings in slavery." It is also important to avoid the mistake of concluding that such public expressions of antislavery sentiment always resulted in actions that were consistent with those views. "That the existence of slavery among us is a moral evil," observed the editor of a Nashville newspaper in October 1825, "is a proposition, the abstract truth of which, few will question; but then the assent to a proposition is not always followed by acting in conformity to its spirit."[110] It is fair to say, however, that the actions of Judges Peck and Haywood as members of the Court were consistently in conformity to the spirit of their personal antislavery views; that those actions were all the more notable because, conceptually at least, they were contrary to their own economic interests (both were slave owners); and that the strong moral tone of the expression of their views (especially those articulated by the respected Haywood) might well have been a significant factor in persuading their colleagues to join them in issuing the slavery rulings that set the Tennessee Court apart from all of the other highest courts of the antebellum South.

The Law of Domestic Relations

During the first four decades of statehood, the Tennessee legislature and the Court, largely through the exercise of its equity powers, mitigated in significant ways the rigid restrictions that the common law had imposed on married women. In the eyes of the common law, husband and wife were merged into one person, and that person was the husband. Marriage transformed the single woman, or *femme sole,* into a wife, or *femme covert,* whose "very being and existence," in Blackstone's words, was "suspended during the coverture." The legal result of the common-law fictional unity of husband and wife was that the husband acquired absolute ownership of all his wife's personal property, control of her real property during her lifetime, and under the doctrine of curtesy, a continuing life estate in all lands owned by his wife at the time of her death if a living child had resulted from the marriage.[111] By the end of the eighteenth century and the beginning of the nineteenth, however, American legislatures and courts of equity had begun to adopt substantial modifications of the husband's common-law power over the wife's person and property, and Tennessee was at the forefront of the reform movement.

Tennessee's Divorce Laws

Legislative divorces, a legacy from English law, remained the most commonly available method of severing the bonds of matrimony in the United States well into the nineteenth century. The new trans-Appalachian states, however, abandoned the legislative prerogative to grant absolute divorces and entrusted their courts with divorce jurisdiction.[112] Moreover, although innovative divorce laws were embraced by legislatures and courts in both the North and the South during the post-revolutionary era, those adopted by the new trans-Appalachian states generally were more progressive than elsewhere.[113] Tennessee's were more so than most.

Early Tennessee law recognized two forms of divorce: a bed-and-board divorce *(a mensa et thoro),* which was similar to a modern marital separation, and an absolute divorce *(a vinculo matrimonii),* in which the marital bonds were legally severed and as a result of which the wife was returned to the unmarried status of a *femme sole.*[114]

Tennessee's first divorce statute vested the Superior Court with jurisdiction over divorce actions and permitted absolute divorces to be granted for a number of reasons, including adultery, impotence, bigamy, and willful and malicious desertion or "absence without a reasonable cause, for the space of two years." In order to be eligible for an absolute divorce, the petitioner was required to be a citizen of the state and to have resided in Tennessee at least one year prior to filing his or her petition. The Court was authorized to grant a bed-and-board divorce to a woman whose husband had maliciously abandoned her or had turned her "out of doors" or had endangered her life "by cruel or barbarous treatment" or had forced her to withdraw by inflicting "such indignities to her person as to render her condition intolerable." Moreover, because the wife was without independent financial means under the common law's system of female coverture, the Court was authorized to make an award of alimony to the wife in a bed-and-board divorce in an amount up to one-third of the husband's annual income. The statute provided that alimony payments were to continue until a reconciliation of the parties had occurred or until the husband, by petition to the Court, offered to cohabit with the wife again "and use her as a good husband ought to do." In addition, the Court's divorce decrees were required to include provisions effecting a property division and awarding such part of the marital real and personal property as the Court deemed proper.[115] Although married women throughout the period could petition for divorce only through a "next friend" and were required to post a bond for costs incurred in actions that were not prosecuted, the General Assembly in 1831 enacted legislation that authorized aggrieved married women to obtain absolute divorces without incurring court costs.[116]

In the few reported divorce decisions by the Supreme Court between 1799 and 1835, the Court reinforced Tennessee's progressive legislative policy by vigorously enforcing the state's divorce statutes. In *Jones v. Jones* (1804), for instance, an action in which adultery committed prior to enactment of the 1799 measure was alleged as the ground for the wife's request for a divorce, the Court upheld the constitutionality of the statute and rejected the husband's argument that the act had been intended to operate prospectively only.[117]

In *Richardson v. Wilson* (1835), the Court upheld an alimony award in the context of an absolute divorce, even though such awards were not clearly authorized by the 1799 statute. Typically, alimony was awarded in the context of bed-and-board divorces to provide the separated wife, who had no independent means of financial support other than that provided by her husband, with a source of support during the pendency of the separation, whereas after entry of a decree of absolute divorce, the husband's duty of maintenance normally was viewed as having terminated. The Court appears to have concluded that the award was necessary in this case, however, in the light of evidence in the record indicating that the complainant was either insolvent or nearly so. The decision also seems to have been consistent with a trend in other jurisdictions to erase the distinction between alimony awards in bed-and-board divorces and property divisions in absolute divorces and to require the former husband in absolute divorces requested by the wife to provide some means of continuing economic support for the divorced female. Indeed, in its 1836 divorce statute, Tennessee's General Assembly allowed alimony awards in absolute divorces as well as in bed-and-board divorces when the complainant was the wife.[118]

Property Rights of Married Women

At the same time that it was enforcing the state's progressive divorce laws, the Court, primarily through the exercise of its equitable powers, imposed significant limitations on the husband's common-law rights with respect to the wife's property during the pendency of the marital relationship.[119]

Tennessee entered the Union at a time when courts of equity in both England and the new American Republic permitted the husband's common-law rights to be circumvented through the use of prenuptial contracts or marriage settlement agreements. Typically such contracts were three-party trust agreements among the prospective husband and wife and a trustee (usually the woman's father). The terms normally specified that all of the prospective wife's premarital real and personal property was to be transferred to the trustee to be held in trust during the woman's coverture and was to be deemed the wife's separate estate. Such agreements allowed the wife to dispose of her separate estate at death by will and often authorized the trustee to sell or invest the trust corpus at the wife's request, thus reserving for the wife some control over the disposition of her property. The income from the trust corpus normally was used for the support of the wife and her husband. The wife's separate estate thus was placed beyond the husband's control and beyond the claims of the husband's creditors. In cases such as *Morgan v. Elam* (1833), the Tennessee Court reiterated not only the validity and enforceability of such prenuptial agreements, but also the extent to which they effectively insulated the wife's property from the claims of the husband's creditors.[120]

The Poor

In 1797, Tennessee's legislature enacted a statute "making provision for the poor." Based on the English model, Tennessee's poor law vested responsibility for poor relief in the state's counties. Tennessee modified the method of support that had been prevalent during the colonial period, outrelief (providing assistance to paupers at home), by permitting direct cash payments to the poor. The statute authorized each county court to impose a tax on the taxable property and polls in the county for use in supporting the poor and directed each county trustee to distribute such funds to those persons designated by the court as "proper to be supported at the charge of the county." Although the state during the antebellum period permitted certain counties to construct poorhouses, experiments with institutionalization for the most part failed. Tennessee never adopted the policy of imposing legal liability on family members to support destitute relatives.[121]

During the period 1796–1835, the Court considered only a few cases in which the interests of the poor were at issue, and typically it was the interest of counties in managing the burden of supporting the poor, more than the interests of the poor themselves, that occupied the Court's attention. For example, one of the long-standing concerns in Anglo-American law was to prevent localities from being compelled to support illegitimate children. Southern legislatures thus adopted streamlined measures for locating unwed mothers and determining paternity. Tennessee initially operated under a 1741 North Carolina statute that mandated the issuance of a decree adjudging an accused male of being the father of an illegitimate child and rendering the accused responsible for such child's maintenance merely upon the making of a charge of paternity against the defendant under oath by the child's mother. Under the statute, the evidence of the mother was conclusive; the accused father was not allowed to dispute the charge. Although the Tennessee legislature subsequently amended the statute to modify the conclusiveness of the mother's accusation and to permit the accused father to obtain a hearing on the charge, the Court enforced the strict mandate of the act in *State v. Ingram* (1816). The Court recognized the potential for unfairness, as when the reputed father himself was a pauper or when, as in *Ingram,* the mother had married a third party before the child had been born but concluded that "[t]he indemnity of the public would be completely superseded by a rule of the common law" that was inconsistent with the rigid dictates of the statute.[122]

Apprenticeship was another method by which county resources were protected against an increase in the burden of supporting illegitimate children. Several states vested local authorities with sweeping authority to bind out illegitimate children regardless of their financial circumstances. An 1822 Tennessee statute, for instance, appeared to mandate the apprenticeship by the county courts of illegitimate children to their reputed fathers upon reaching the age of three. The Court in *Lawson v. Scott* (1826), however, rejected the argument that the statute was mandatory and limited the county courts' power to apprentice illegitimate children to cases in which the child was a pauper.[123]

The interests of the poor were directly at issue in two cases in which the issue was the access afforded the poor to the judicial system. In *Philips v. Rudle*

& Carmichael (1826) and *Brumley v. Hayworth* (1832), the Court construed the state's *in forma pauperis* statute as applying not only to trials, but also to the prosecution of appeals to the circuit courts and to the Supreme Court.[124]

Economic Development

To the continuing scholarly debate about whether antebellum southern legislators and judges fostered economic development in the South, the Court's record during the first four decades of statehood offers little in the way of clear contributions on one side or the other. For instance, although the Court's decisions generally reflected the growing incorporation of the doctrine of competition into early-nineteenth-century American law as the surest route to economic development, that was not always the case. Moreover, the Court during this period manifested an ambivalent attitude toward the construction of mills and consistently adhered to the ancient common-law rule imposing strict liability on common carriers for the safe transit of goods.[125]

In 1807, the Tennessee legislature empowered the county courts to allow "the owner or owners of ferry landings, or owners of land on each side of rivers where ferries have been established, or hereafter shall be, to erect a ferry or ferries . . . and the said ferry keepers are hereby authorized to land their boats on the opposite banks of the rivers." In both *Corporation of Memphis v. Overton* (1832) and *Blair v. Carmichael* (1829), the Court construed the 1807 statute in favor of the efforts of new, competitive ferry keepers to establish competing ferries, over the Mississippi River at Memphis and across the Tennessee River near the present site of Loudon in eastern Tennessee, respectively. Such decisions represented a departure from the English common-law rule and the "monopolizing spirit" of early North Carolina law. Then, near the end of the period, in *Allen v. Farnsworth* (1833), the Court narrowly construed the statute in favor of a ferry keeper on the Nolichucky River in the northeastern part of the state who had never been authorized by the county court to operate her ferry and actually had not operated her ferry for a period of several months. The Court held, in an opinion framed in language reminiscent of the old English common-law rule, that under the language of the statute, the prior ferry operator was entitled "to keep the ferry in preference to any other person" because she technically was the owner of the ferry landings on both sides of the river.[126]

The Court's decision in *Philips v. Stocket* (1806) provides an indication of the ambivalence with which the Court viewed the construction of mills on the state's streams. A 1777 North Carolina statute, which was adopted by Tennessee, had declared that "every water grist-mill which shall hereafter be built, that shall at any time grind for toll, shall be held and deemed, and is hereby declared to be a public mill." In *Stocket,* the complainant sought to enjoin the construction of a mill by the defendant, who owned the land on both sides of the stream that would have supplied the power for operating the mill, on the ground that construction of the mill would flood the complainant's lands. Reflecting Judge Overton's observation that "mills are a public benefit, and we should not therefore discourage the building [of] them," the Court ultimately denied the requested injunction. Three years later, however, when the complainant returned to the Court with evidence that his lands had indeed been flooded as a result of the mill-dam, the Court ordered the defendant to reduce the height of his dam "so as to permit the water within the bounds of the plaintiff's land to run without obstruction in its usual course."[127]

The 1777 statute by which gristmills were declared to be public mills included a provision allowing the condemnation of private property for the construction of such mills unless houses, orchards, gardens, or other "immediate conveniences" were to be taken. The Court refused to extend the definition of "public mill" beyond gristmills to include sawmills and paper mills in *Harding v. Goodlett* (1832), concluding that "[t]he saw-mill and paper-mill have no public character; the erection of these mills would be wholly for the private use of these petitioners." To take the objecting landowner's land for such use, in the Court's view, would have been an unconstitutional exercise of the power of eminent domain for the benefit of an individual rather than for the benefit of the public at large.[128]

The Tennessee Supreme Court in Corporation of Memphis v. Overton (1832) sanctioned the operation of competitive ferries across the Mississippi River at Memphis, the waterfront of which is shown here in a contemporary view. J. H. B. Latrobe, The Memphis Waterfront, *1832. © Collection of the New-York Historical Society.*

For centuries, the English common-law rule had been that common carriers were strictly liable for the safe transit of goods unless they could show that damage had been caused by "'the act of God or the public enemies.'" Beginning in the 1830s, however, many American courts began to allow carriers to limit their common-law strict liability by contract. The Tennessee Court did not join the trend. Beginning with *Craig v. Childress* (1823) and continuing in a series of cases throughout the period, the Court consistently adhered to the old common-law rule of strict liability.[129]

Criminal Law

The Court during the first four decades of statehood established a long-lasting precedent in the area of criminal law. Judge Catron's opinion in *Grainger v. State* (1830) introduced the concept of self-defense into the criminal law of Tennessee. Regrettably, Catron failed to draft his statement of the law with care. "If the jury had believed that Grainger [the defendant] was in danger of great bodily harm from Broach [the decedent]," Catron wrote, "*or thought himself so,* then the killing would have been in self defence [*sic*]." The judge's failure to qualify the phrase "or thought himself so" by requiring proof of sufficient grounds for such a belief led to subsequent abuses of the doctrine and allowed future defendants in homicide prosecutions to cite *Grainger* as precedent for establishing self-defense as a ground for acquittal by proving only the defendant's fearful state of mind without also establishing any reasonable basis therefor. At least one commentator has concluded that Catron's carelessly worded opinion in *Grainger* represented a significant erosion of the strict common-law rules as to homicide and encouraged violence and disorder in antebellum Tennessee.[130]

The Court also rendered a major decision dealing with criminal procedure in *State v. Doherty* (1806), in which it ruled, apparently for the first time in Tennessee, that a coerced confession was inadmissible in murder trials.[131]

THE COURT'S MOVEMENT TO INDEPENDENCE

The Cherokee Reserve Cases

The impetus for the assertion by the Court of its independence as a separate and equal branch of state government came from an unexpected source: the Cherokee Nation. By 1819, the only portion of the Cherokee Nation that remained within the present boundaries of Tennessee was confined to the southeastern corner of the state. After the Nation's cession of the land within what was called the Hiwassee District to the United States under the Treaty of 1819 (title to which vested automatically in Tennessee under the terms of the Compact of 1806), the boundary between Tennessee and the Nation was pushed farther southward, roughly to the Hiwassee River. The Hiwassee District consisted of an area that lay between the Hiwassee River on the south and the Little Tennessee River on the north.

The Treaty of 1819 and the earlier Treaty of 1817 set aside a 640-acre reserve for the head of each Cherokee family, provided that the procedures prescribed by the treaties were followed for claiming and locating each reserve and that the reserve was not subsequently abandoned. In *Cornet v. Winton's Lessee* (1826), the Court held that title to land located within the Hiwassee District which had been reserved to a Cherokee under the terms of the treaties prevailed over that granted to an individual by the state of North Carolina in 1800. The Court reasoned that the grant had been made subject to the Cherokee title, which was characterized as "a usufructuary right." Relying in part upon provisions of the Treaty of Holston (1791) and other treaties entered into with the Cherokee Nation between 1785 and 1798 in which the United States guaranteed to the nation "all their lands not hereby ceded," Judge Catron held that the Cherokees' possessory right "has long been considered in the nature of a *property* [right] over the soil, and subject to any of the Indian natives, when the sovereignty of any part of the Indian country was ceded to the United States."[132]

The decision resulted in a legislative firestorm. Although *Winton* had dealt with a grant issued by the state of North Carolina and not to purchases of land within the Hiwassee District from the state of Tennessee, it was apparent that the analysis followed by the Court in *Winton* would also apply to lands purchased from Tennessee that included Indian reserves guaranteed under the treaties. In the wake of *Winton,* moreover, several other cases were pending in the circuit courts that raised the issue of the validity of such Tennessee titles. Anticipating a ruling by the Court that would extend the *Winton* holding to invalidate Tennessee titles within the Hiwassee District, the General Assembly in 1826 appointed former Judge White, who at the time was serving as one of Tennessee's U.S. senators, to represent the state as counsel in all pending and future actions by Cherokees holding reserves under the treaties against any purchasers of land from Tennessee that lay within the Hiwassee District.[133] White was directed to review all testimony, and to collect any additional evidence, regarding the claims of the Cherokee reserve claimants in all such pending actions and to report back to the legislature the following year. When the legislature reconvened in 1827, it passed three resolutions authorizing the state to appeal any adverse rulings by the Court in the so-called reservation cases arising under the treaties to the Supreme Court of the United States and pledging the full faith and credit of the state to indemnify White "against any reasonable expense or liability which he may incur" in exercising the authority granted to him under the resolutions.[134]

During the 1820s and 1830s, the Tennessee Supreme Court decided several cases of significance to both Tennessee and the Cherokee Nation. Between 1819 and 1838, the portion of the Cherokee Nation that was located within the present boundaries of Tennessee was confined to an area south of the Hiwassee River in the southeastern corner of the state, roughly corresponding to the area depicted in this detail from an 1829 map of Tennessee. The state's Hiwassee District, shown here as McMinn and Monroe Counties, lay immediately to the north, between the Little Tennessee and Hiwassee Rivers. Courtesy Robert A. McGaw Collection/Special Collections, Vanderbilt University.

Four years after having decided *Winton,* in *Blair v. Pathkiller's Lessee* (1830) and in three related cases, the Court applied its holding in *Winton* to land titles within the Hiwassee District that had been issued by the state of Tennessee. At the conclusion of his opinion in *Pathkiller,* Catron could not resist referring to the three resolutions passed by the General Assembly and used the occasion both to reject the legislature's none-too-subtle effort to persuade the Court to reconsider its decision in *Winton* and to assert the Court's independence. "That the resolutions were intended to dictate to this court the course of future decision, we will not suppose," he wrote, "as this would be an attack upon the independence of the judiciary."[135]

The Court's Exercise of Its Power of Judicial Review

At its December term following announcement of the *Pathkiller* decision, the Court further asserted its independence and its authority to review legislative enactments. Although the Court on numerous earlier occasions had articulated its theoretical power to review the constitutionality of legislative acts, the Court on only one prior occasion had invalidated a legislative enactment as unconstitutional. That decision came nearly a decade earlier, when the state was in the throes of its first major economic depression.[136]

The Panic of 1819 revealed how vulnerable the United States had become to fluctuations in foreign markets. The end of the Napoleonic Wars freed up a storehouse of European goods to compete with those produced by the young American nation. By 1816, American producers were in trouble. Many American entrepreneurs had responded to the postwar boom by borrowing heavily to expand production. A corresponding boom in land speculation in the South had come in the aftermath of the War of 1812 and had led to the establishment of a plethora of state banks. Between 1807 and 1817, Tennessee's legislature chartered fourteen banks, each of which issued paper money in the form of notes that were backed only by the credit worthiness of the bank itself but that were redeemable on demand in specie (gold or silver coins). The banks, however, including those in Tennessee, failed to retain adequate reserves of specie for the redemption of their notes and, as 1819 approached, were ultimately forced to suspend specie payments, thus depreciating the value of the notes. They also began to demand payment of their loans.

Borrowers had gambled on the "indefinite continuance of high commodity prices and speculative profits" to enable them to retire their bank loans. It was a gamble that failed. Initially, the postwar price of American cotton soared, but by 1818, the British market had begun to dry up due to an influx of cheaper cotton from the East Indies. Cotton prices plummeted, and the effect reverberated throughout the nation. Then, in the spring of 1819, world commodity prices collapsed. The nation's—and Tennessee's—first major economic depression, the Panic of 1819, followed.

With prices falling, businesses failing, and an increase in mortgage foreclosures, debtors in Tennessee turned to the General Assembly for assistance. The legislature adopted its first major debtor-relief measure at the 1819 session. Under the Endorsement Act, judgment creditors were prohibited from executing on their judgments for a period of two years unless they agreed, by placing an endorsement upon each such judgment, to accept the state banks' depreciated paper money in satisfaction thereof.[137]

The Court invalidated the Endorsement Act in *Townsend v. Townsend* (1821). In an opinion by Judge Haywood, the Court held that the statutory restriction violated several provisions of the state and federal constitutions, including the prohibition against the impairment of contracts and the federal constitutional mandate that the states make nothing but gold and silver coin a legal tender in payment of debts. Significantly, in terms of the development of Tennessee constitutional law, one of the grounds for the Court's decision was the provision in the state's declaration of rights that "no freeman shall be . . . deprived of his . . . property but by judgment of his peers, or the law of the land": "Property in possession by this clause is secured to the owner, so that it can not be taken from him but by due course of law in a court regularly constituted and proceeding by the standing rules of law; not by act of assembly depriving the owner of it for the benefit of some other individual."[138] It was the first ruling by which the Court invalidated a legislative enactment as having been contrary to the state's Constitution.

Five years later, Haywood elaborated on both the law-of-the-land provision and the right of Tennessee's courts to review the constitutionality of legislative acts in an unreported opinion in *Toka Will v. Nelson* (1826). The opinion was not by the Court but was only an advisory opinion given in support of Judge Peck's decision in his capacity as chancellor to enjoin the state's scheduled sale of common-school lands under the authority of an 1825 statute (see discussion below). Haywood concluded that the statute was invalid on several grounds, including the law-of-the-land provision. His opinion included a vigorous assertion of the Court's right to review legislative acts. Either the statute was void, he proclaimed, or the Constitution's law-of-the-land clause was void. Responding to the argument that it was not within the power of the judiciary to invalidate legislative acts, Haywood asserted, "My answer is, that *all power assumed and not granted by the people in their constitution, is void, as to all the world, and as to every individual in this community*." Avoiding judicial review, he wrote, was a simple matter: "[L]et no acts be passed but such as the constitution does not forbid. Let not the rights of the people be invaded, and no one will dare to make opposition to constitutional acts. . . . It is . . . unorthodox to assert, that the judges are to obey all the acts of the legislature. They are the judges of the people and not of the legislature; servants of the people and not servants of their servants."[139] More than two years after Haywood's death, Judge Catron explained the law-of-the-land provision in *Vanzant v. Waddel* (1829), although in a passage that was only dicta, as the Court ultimately upheld the validity of the debtor-relief measure at issue:

> That a partial law, tending directly or indirectly to deprive a corporation or an individual of rights to property, or to the equal benefits of the general and public laws of the land, is unconstitutional and void, we do not doubt. . . . Our constitution . . . declares, "that no free man shall be deprived of his life, liberty or property, but by the judgment of his peers, or *the law of the land*." The clause, "LAW OF THE LAND," means a general and public law, equally binding upon every member of the community. . . . The right to life, liberty and property, of every individual must stand or fall by the same rule or law that governs every other member of the body politic . . . and every partial or private law, which directly proposes to destroy or affect individual rights, or does the same

> thing by affording remedies leading to similar consequences, is unconstitutional and void. Were this otherwise, odious individuals and corporate bodies would be governed by one rule, and the mass of the community who made the law, by another. . . . Such abuses resulted in the adoption of Magna Charta in England, . . . which is, and for centuries has been, the foundation of English liberty. Its infraction was a leading cause why we separated from that country, and its value as a fundamental rule for the protection of the citizen against legislative usurpation was the reason of its adoption as part of our constitution.[140]

The Court's decisions in *Townsend* and *Vanzant* and Judge Haywood's *Toka Will* opinion were significant for a number of reasons. First, of course, the actual exercise in *Townsend* of the Court's frequently asserted and vigorously articulated right to review legislative enactments and the resulting invalidation of a statute as unconstitutional was a bold and controversial step. The concept of judicial review in antebellum America was still in "an embryonic stage and a subject of controversy," with the result that the exercise of judicial review by state courts occurred relatively infrequently before the Civil War.[141] Second, the emergence of judicial review during the antebellum period evidenced a new and growing reaction in the states against legislative supremacy,[142] and *Townsend, Toka Will,* and Judge Catron's lengthy discourse in *Vanzant*—which was at once dicta and a warning to the legislature—on the meaning of the Constitution's law-of-the-land clause clearly indicated that such a reaction was well under way in Tennessee. Finally, and perhaps most important from a constitutional perspective, the Court's reliance on the Constitution's law-of-the-land clause revealed a willingness to equate that provision with due process and to interpret due process not only as restraining arbitrary legislation depriving citizens of their property, but also as mandating general, not special, laws that were to be applied equally to all. Catron's discussion of the clause's meaning in *Vanzant* reflected "the central tenet of Jacksonian Democracy—equal rights for all, special privileges for none" and articulated a theme of equal treatment that was echoed repeatedly (and widely quoted) in the decisions of state courts throughout the United States during the ensuing decades.[143]

When the Court convened in December 1830, after having issued its decisions in the *Pathkiller* cases in July of that year, it invalidated two additional statutes and initiated a series of decisions, issued in rapid succession over the next seven months, that prompted the most serious confrontation between the legislature and the Court in more than twenty years. In *Marr v. Enloe* (1830), the Court struck down two statutes that had authorized the county courts to levy property taxes as unconstitutional delegations by the General Assembly of its exclusive taxation authority and as violations of the Constitution's equal-and-uniform taxation requirement.[144]

A month later, in January, came *State Bank v. Cooper* (1831), in which Judge Peck and two other judges, sitting as a special court, invalidated an 1829 statute that had created the tribunal for the purpose of determining, with no right of appeal, certain claims asserted by the Bank of the State of Tennessee. Although the court invalidated the statute on several grounds, the most significant was that the measure violated the Constitution's law-of-the-land provision:

> By *"law of the land"* is meant a general and public law, operating equally on every individual in the community. . . . This provision was introduced to secure the citizens against the abuse of power by the government. . . . Legislation is always exercised by the majority. Majorities have nothing to fear, for the power is in their hands. *They* need no written constitutions, defining and circumscribing the powers of the government. Constitutions are only intended to secure the rights of the minority. . . . If the law be general in its operation, affecting all alike, the minority are safe, because the majority, who make the law, are operated on by it equally with the others. Here is the importance of the provision and the great security it affords.[145]

Cooper was followed in July by *Wally's Heirs v. Kennedy* (1831), in which the Court invalidated legislation mandating the dismissal of any ejectment action in which the land in question was a Cherokee reserve when the defendant could prove that the suit had been brought or prosecuted "upon any contingent interest, or in trust for any other person than the one in whose name the suit was brought." The statute, the Court held, was peculiarly a partial law that applied only to ejectment actions brought in the name of Cherokee reservees to recover lands under the provisions of the treaties of 1817 and 1819 and thus was invalid under the Constitution's law-of-the-land clause.[146]

Also announced in July was the Court's decision in *Lowry v. Francis* (1831), an opinion that ended a six-year period of confusion and uncertainty concerning the legislature's authority to sell the so-called common-school lands. The Compact of 1806 provided that the cession of lands by the United States to Tennessee was subject to several conditions, including a requirement that the state locate and appropriate one 640-acre tract of land per each six square miles within the ceded territory "for the use of schools for the instruction of children forever" and a stipulation that title to the lands was subject to Cherokee title to lands lying within the ceded territory.[147] Upon the subsequent cession by the Cherokees of their lands lying within the Hiwassee District, Tennessee (and its grantees) became vested with title to the former Cherokee lands subject to the conditions specified by the Compact of 1806 and by the reserve provisions of the Treaties of 1817 and 1819.

Although the lands within the Hiwassee District that had been acquired by the state in 1819 were subsequently surveyed and school lands duly designated therein, numerous disputes arose when the school-land tracts overlapped with the reserves set aside under the treaties for the heads of Cherokee families. The seriousness of the problem escalated significantly when the General Assembly enacted legislation in 1825 directing the treasurer for East Tennessee to sell the school-land tracts and to appropriate and earmark the proceeds from such sales for the maintenance of common schools, not just within each six-square-mile area of the territory ceded by the Compact of 1806 but throughout the state.[148]

These issues first appear to have been presented in *Toka Will v. Nelson* (1826), a case that originated before the Court of Equity sitting in Kingston in Roane County in the eastern part of the state. Toka Will was a Cherokee reservee, and a portion of his reserve was claimed by the state as a school-land tract in apparent violation of the stipulation agreed to in the Compact of 1806. When the state initiated proceedings to sell the tract pursuant to the 1825 act, Toka Will's agent presented Judge Peck, the Court of Equity's presiding chancellor in Kingston, with a petition to enjoin the sale. Judge Peck, apparently after having consulted with Judge Haywood and perhaps other members of the Court on the issue, granted the injunction in July 1826. Thereafter, a petition signed by members of the Supreme Court's bar was addressed to Peck, as the member of the Court who, while sitting as chancellor, had granted the injunction. Characterizing the *Toka Will* case as "embrac[ing] principles that are of vital importance to many of the best interests of our country, in relation to which there is and may be, considerable popular excitement," the petitioners alluded to Peck's having consulted with his "brother Judges" before issuing the injunction and requested "that their opinions and advice in this case, so far as expressed, may be made public." Peck responded by furnishing the petitioners with the opinion by Judge Haywood that has been discussed above. Haywood's opinion, although never officially reported, was privately printed and distributed. Haywood supported Peck's decision to enjoin the sale on the grounds that the state's claimed right to sell the school lands impermissibly conflicted with the provisions of the federal Compact of 1806 and that, by depriving the reservees of their claims to the extent that they overlapped the school lands without proper legal proceedings, the 1825 statute was unconstitutional under the law-of-the-land provision of the state's Constitution.[149]

Despite the opinions of Judges Peck and Haywood (which were, after all, not the opinions of the Court), the General Assembly passed a resolution when it convened for its 1829 session requesting the Court to issue a definitive ruling on whether the state was authorized to sell the school lands. Stating that "doubt exists as to the power of the state, to sell and dispose of the school tracts of land in this state," the legislators referred the matter to the Court, which was "directed and required to examine the subject thoroughly, and report their opinion thereon, to the next General Assembly." The resolution concluded with a mandate that "no further measures shall be taken in regard to the sale or rents of said lands by the state until the opinion of said court can be had relative to said lands."[150]

Recognizing that its opinion on the matter "was requested . . . by resolution [of the General Assembly] at the last session, which we will comply with," the Court decided the issue in *Lowry* in July 1831. The decision was against the state. Echoing Judge Haywood's 1826 opinion in *Toka Will,* the Court concluded that the Compact of 1806 required the state to appropriate and hold the specified 640-acre tracts of land, not the proceeds from the sale of such tracts, in trust for the perpetual use of schools. The 1825 statute "clearly violates the obligations of the compact of 1806 imposed upon the state of Tennessee," the Court held. "[T]he act, so far as it orders the school sections to be divided, sold and granted to purchasers, is unconstitutional and void."[151]

When it reconvened in September 1831, the General Assembly responded to the Court's decision in *Lowry* by defying it. A new measure was cleverly drafted and enacted which technically repealed all prior acts regulating school lands within the Hiwassee District (including the 1825 measure directing the sale of such tracts) but also provided that there were to be up to four common schools located in every township within the Hiwassee District, governed by a five-member board of trustees, "supported by the rents and profits of the school land therein," and "located wherever in said township the trustees may think proper." To avoid the Court's proscription against any sale of school lands, the new statute directed the trustees to lease the school land in each township for terms of up to five years for "the erection of water works or other valuable improvement[s], or for the purpose of improving said land by cultivating the same in small grain." For the purpose of dealing with the overlapping claims of Cherokee reservees, Section 15 of the act authorized the state to initiate and prosecute ejectment actions against any persons holding possession of any of the school-land tracts. The 1831 legislation was only a stop-gap measure, however. Twelve years later, in 1843, Congress authorized the sale of school lands with the consent of the local inhabitants, thus achieving the result that had been sought by the General Assembly in its 1825 act. Despite the Court's ruling in *Lowry,*

TO THE HON. ROBERT WHYTE, JACOB PECK & JOHN CATRON,

JUDGES OF THE SUPREME COURT OF ERRORS AND APPEALS.

WE take the liberty of addressing your Honors in relation to the despatch of business in the Courts over which you preside. The subject is one of great importance to yourselves, to us, and to our country. In a new and flourishing community, the delay of justice amounts, in most instances, to a denial of it. After a full experiment, it is evident that suitors are not only delayed, but that the causes in the Supreme Court cannot be determined in any definite or reasonable time.

It is entirely an error in the Legislature to compel your Honors to hold the sessions of the Court at so many different places; yet, we assure your Honors, that our best judgments, and the voice of the people, attribute the delay of business to other causes. That an independent judiciary is the bulwark of freedom, is an admitted maxim; and that the Judges in a republican government should possess the confidence of the people, and be able to discharge efficiently the important duties assigned to them, is no less true. When those duties are not or cannot be performed, there is reason to apprehend that the Legislature, sustained by the great mass of the people, will disregard the means in eagerness to attain the end, and, under the pretext of a change of system, by an act of legislation, will remove the Judges without a hearing or the form of trial.—This course would, in our opinion, be of evil example, and productive of mischiefs inferior only to the present absolute suspension of business.

Under these circumstances, we, as individuals and Counsel for Plaintiffs and Defendants in causes depending in your Courts, appeal to the patriotism of your Honors, and suggest that you would accelerate justice, advance the interests of our clients, vindicate your own honor, and aid in securing the independence of the judiciary, by resigning your commissions into the hands of the Legislature at the commencement of the next session. By this measure you will manifest your disinterested devotion to the true interests of the country, and impose upon the Legislature the necessity of making every reasonable improvement in our judiciary system, or will fix upon that body the public discontent which now rests solely upon the Judges. The names hereto subscribed will satisfy your Honors that this address is dictated by an anxious desire to elevate the character of our Courts; and upon our success depends in a great measure our own respectability and usefulness, which can only be ensured by the adoption of some system whereby the business of the country can be transacted.

We beg leave also to assure your Honors, which we do in perfect sincerity, that it is not from any motive of personal hostility or dislike towards either of you, that we have presumed to take this step; but, we feel conscious, that in thus addressing you, we have consulted, as well your own feelings and character, as our interests and that of the public.

We are, very respectfully, your obedient servants,

The above is the form of address adopted by us. If you approve of it, you can write one of a similar nature, or one more suitable to your views of the subject. Make a copy for each of the Judges, direct each to all of them, sign them not as a society but as individuals, & enclose them to Jacob S. Yerger our clerk; we will retain them until we shall have heard from every County in the State, & then deliver all of them, our own included, at the same time. —

In 1831, widespread dissatisfaction with the Supreme Court of Errors and Appeals caused Nashville lawyers to call upon its judges to resign. This form petition, addressed to the judges and urging them to resign, was adopted and circulated for signatures by the newly formed Nashville Bar Association. Robert Looney Caruthers Papers, Southern Historical Collection, Wilson Library, University of North Carolina at Chapel Hill.

therefore, the requirements of the Compact of 1806 relating to school lands within the Hiwassee District were never complied with.[152]

That was not the end of the matter, however. Dissatisfaction with the state's judicial system—and with the Court in particular—had prompted Nashville lawyers in early 1831 to organize the Nashville Bar Association, which circulated form petitions among attorneys in Davidson and neighboring counties, urging the Court's judges to resign.[153]

Removal of the Court's incumbents also became one of the paramount issues during the legislative elections during the summer of 1831,[154] and when the new General Assembly convened in September of that year, legislation was introduced with the objective either of forcing the incumbent judges to resign or of abolishing the Court altogether. The severity of the threat was such that Judge Catron tendered his resignation from the Court.[155]

A report by House Judiciary Committee in early October, however, concluded that, except for Nashville, there was actually no backlog of cases on the Supreme Court's docket and hinted that ulterior motives lay behind the effort to abolish the Court. One legislator identified legislative dissatisfaction with the Court's invalidation of unconstitutional statutes as the primary motivating factor for the attack on the Court and its judges. "We do not always hear the true cause of offence avowed by those who urge the repeal of judges out of office," the speaker observed on the floor of the House. "Men who from any motive take the lead in any measure of an unconstitutional character never forgive the judges who declare it so."[156]

Ultimately, the state's judicial system was amended rather than repealed. Compromise legislation passed on December 15 which, among other things, increased the number of the Court's judges from three to four, with the fourth judge to be known as the Court's chief justice, but made no reduction in the number of places where the Court was required to meet. Four days later, the legislature in joint session elected Nathan Green to the Court and named Catron to the post of chief justice.[157]

Although for the most part state supreme courts in the South during the Jacksonian period were relatively secure from legislative coercion and reprisal, there were exceptions, as Don Fehrenbacher has shown, notably in Kentucky and South Carolina. "The fiercest legislative attacks upon the judiciary," Fehrenbacher concluded from the episodes in those two states, "were directed not merely at punishing individual judges but at controlling the decisions of the supreme court or putting it out of business altogether." Tennessee in 1831 came close to providing a further exception. Instead, the Court emerged from the legislative crisis that year to continue its path to independence, although it would not achieve full constitutional status as a separate and equal branch of state government until adoption of a new Constitution in 1835.[158]

The Court's Defiance of *Worcester*

When the Court convened in Knoxville for its July Term in 1835, it noted that news of the death of Chief Justice John Marshall had been received, ordered a suspension of its session until the following Monday, and reported that each member of the bench and bar had agreed to wear crepe on his left arm for thirty days "as a mark of respect for the memory of one to whom the people of the United states are deeply indebted, as the greatest expounder of the Constitutional Law of the nation, whom the *Bench and Bar* recognize as a faithful instructor and guide in jurisprudence; and whose death is felt by *all* as a national calamity."[159]

At the same time that the Tennessee Court was honoring the memory of Chief Justice Marshall, it had under consideration a case that would result in a decision that defied Marshall's declaration of the supremacy of federal treaties over inconsistent state statutes in the landmark decision in *Worcester v. Georgia* (1832).[160] In *Worcester,* the Supreme Court of the United States invalidated certain Georgia statutes that had attempted to extend the state's jurisdiction into portions of the Cherokee Nation. Marshall's *Worcester* decision characterized the Nation as "a distinctive community, occupying its own territory, with boundaries . . . which the citizens of Georgia have no right to enter" and held that the measures impermissibly conflicted with treaties between the United States and the Nation, which, under the federal Constitution, were part of the law of the land.[161]

In November 1833, Tennessee's legislature passed similar legislation, the effect of which extended the criminal jurisdiction of five counties located in the southeastern corner of the state into that portion of the Nation that lay south of the Hiwassee District.[162] In *State v. Foreman* (1835), the Tennessee Supreme Court upheld the constitutionality of the 1833 statute, despite *Worcester,* by a vote of two to one. In a rambling, rhetorical opinion, Chief Justice Catron averred that any preexisting territorial rights and any right of self-government that native Americans might have held had been supplanted by the laws of the conquering colonists. Referring to native Americans as "savage beasts" and infidels and to their lands as "heathen lands," Catron declared that "the principle declared in the fifteenth century as the law of Christendom—that discovery gave title to assume sovereignty over, and to govern, the unconverted natives . . . —has been recognized as a part of the national law for nearly four centuries" and that "[o]ur claim is based on the right to coerce obedience." "The truth is," Catron concluded, "neither our theory nor practice has ever allowed to the Indians any political right extending beyond our pleasure." To the extent that *Worcester* had construed the applicable treaties as having acknowledged the Cherokee Nation as a separate entity within which the laws of Tennessee had no force or effect, Catron maintained, such a holding was "a principle that it is impossible for the states to abide by." Embracing a states' rights analysis, Catron characterized the treaties themselves as unconstitutional in the sense that they violated the federal Constitution's prohibition against the creation of a state within a state, thereby illegally infringing upon the sovereignty of the states, and concluded that the states were under no obligation to recognize unconstitutional treaties as the law of the land.[163]

Judge Green concurred with Catron, disagreeing with him as to the nature and extent of his by-right-of-conquest theory but concluding that when even a separate, self-governing people "become so impotent as to be incapable of self-government" and of preserving order, the government of the surrounding country may, as a matter of necessity, subject them to its jurisdiction as a means of protecting itself and its inhabitants to the extent necessary to maintain law and order.[164]

Peck vigorously dissented. "When a treaty is made and ratified," Peck reminded his colleagues, "it becomes, by the express letter of the federal Constitution, as much a supreme law of the land as the Constitution itself . . . and all judges are commanded to obey it." Dismissing Catron's by-right-of-conquest theory as irrelevant and characterizing Green's doctrine of necessity as the "tyrant's plea" and a dangerous legal principle, Peck viewed the states' rights approach as a troubling one with sinister implications. When the federal Constitution was framed, warned Peck, "there existed no spirit abroad to stir up conflict between single states and the general government. Then the bonds of union were more strong . . . and men were willing to sacrifice much of opinion for the sake of that harmony among sister communities which ought to be our pride and boast so long as we wish to exist as a nation acknowledging one general head." Peck also argued that the 1833 statute was partial and unequal in its operation and effect and thus unconstitutional under the law-of-the-land clause of the state's Constitution, in that Cherokees who lived in that portion of the Nation over which the state claimed jurisdiction were required to obey certain of the state's laws and to suffer the consequences of failing to do so but were afforded none of the benefits of state citizenship. "So long as we, as a people, profess to be governed by written compacts rather than by the sword or the strong arm of power," he wrote, "it will be a matter of pride . . . that we are just even to the weak."[165]

The views of the Cherokees that Catron articulated in *Foreman* certainly were at odds with those that he had expressed nine years earlier in *Cornet v. Winton's Lessee* (1826). "I hold that the early notions of the Spaniards and others, '*that the Indians were mere savage beasts without rights of any kind,*'" he wrote then, "have long since been exploded. . . . The Cherokees are, in point of fact, a conquered people . . . with acknowledged rights; which rights, I am proud to say, have for the last thirty years been respected with that good faith on our part that became us as honest men and christians, and which the courts of justice are bound to regard." More important, Catron's opinion in *Foreman* that the applicable treaties were unconstitutional was in direct contradiction of his own unquestioning reliance upon the same treaties as one of the underlying bases for upholding Cherokee claims in *Winton* and in *Blair v. Pathkiller's Lessee* (1830). His opinion also was at odds with the Court's decision in *Holland v. Pack* (1823), in which Judge Haywood had declared, "The Cherokees, though living within the limits of Tennessee, and upon lands the dominion of which belongs to this State, . . . are yet an independent nation, subject to laws, both civil and criminal, made by themselves for the regulation of their internal affairs." Moreover, in his own more recent decision in *State v. Ross* (1834), Catron had articulated concerns almost identical to those that Judge Peck expressed in his dissent in *Foreman* about partial and unequal laws. Catron was, of course, aware of these inconsistencies; the explanations that he offered for them were uncharacteristically short but entirely unconvincing.[166]

How then is Catron's position in *Foreman* to be explained? Certainly, something had caused the chief justice to abandon the analysis that he had followed in his earlier decisions, and it was neither the logic nor the compelling mandate of the Court's precedent. There are several possible explanations, but the surviving evidence does not point to any definitive answers. The most likely is that Catron viewed the case as providing an opportunity to facilitate the success of President Jackson's popular removal policy at a crucial time during pending treaty negotiations with the Cherokees. Jackson had first proposed the removal of all Indian tribes from the eastern United States in his First Annual Message to Congress in December 1829. Congress responded by enacting the Indian Removal Act of 1830, which authorized the president to exchange public land west of the Mississippi River for Indian land in the east. The land vacated by the Indians then was to be opened for white settlement. *Worcester* threatened the success of removal negotiations with the Cherokees, but the Treaty of New Echota, which provided for removal of the Cherokees, was signed in less than two months after *Foreman.* Catron sent a printed copy of the Court's decision to Jackson's hand-picked successor, Vice President Van Buren, shortly after it was announced, under cover of a letter advising the vice president that *Foreman* had been appealed to the Supreme Court of the United States and claiming that his opinion had been drafted as an attempt "to disencumber this cause of the authority . . . of Worcester" and "to place Foreman's case in an attitude to be decided . . . on the side of state sovereignty." Whatever the motivation of its author, Catron's opinion, one commentator has concluded, "seems less one of law than of the rationalization of power."[167]

The appeal of the Tennessee Court's decision in *Foreman* apparently was never docketed, and the ultimate fate of that appeal and of the *Foreman* case on remand in the circuit court remains a mystery.[168]

One commentator recently has concluded of *Foreman* and a similar decision by the Supreme Court of Alabama that "[t]he blatant refusal of the southern judiciary to follow the precedent set down by the United States Supreme Court [in *Worcester*] represented the final and fatal strike against the idea of Native American sovereignty in the East." When read in the light of the larger context of Jacksonian politics, however, the decision in *Foreman* acquires a more ominous significance. To paraphrase what one scholar has said about the effect of Jacksonian politics on the law generally, the decision in *Foreman* contributed to the "victory for southern constitutionalism [over John] Marshall's constitutional nationalism."[169]

Independence Achieved and the End of an Era

Foreman was the Court's last major decision before a new, reorganized Supreme Court, elected in December, assumed power in early 1836 under the state's recently ratified new Constitution. As the final years of the Court's first four decades of existence came to a close, so, too, came an end to the post-revolutionary era of legislative supremacy in Tennessee. The new Constitution placed the Supreme Court at the head of an equal, independent branch of state government. Perhaps more important, however, the Court already had firmly established—and exercised—its right to review legislative enactments to ensure that they comported with the basic law of the land.

The election of a new Court in December 1835 also brought to a conclusion a period of judicial activity that, on the whole, was remarkably progressive for a southern antebellum court. Each of the retiring jurists (and most of their colleagues who had served for any length of time on the Court) brought to the bench not only exceptional measures of perseverance and courage, but also a keen, if individualized, sense of fairness and a determination to ensure that the new state's experiment with self-government succeeded, and those qualities were reflected in most, if not all, of the Court's decisions during the first four decades of statehood.

2

JUDICIAL INDEPENDENCE IN AN AGE OF DEMOCRACY, SECTIONALISM, AND WAR, 1835–1865

Timothy S. Huebner

By 1835 Tennessee had come of age. No longer a frontier, the state had experienced huge population increases during the previous decade. A high birthrate and growing numbers of migrants from the East had kept the population steadily climbing, and many new residents had settled in the western portion of the state, though Middle Tennessee accounted for about half the state's total population. Small farmers—who constituted the overwhelmingly majority of whites—continued to raise corn, wheat, tobacco, and livestock, though cotton production had increased the most in recent years. To provide the labor necessary to cultivate crops, especially cash crops such as cotton, white Tennesseans held black slaves. While less than a fourth of white families in the state owned bondspersons, slaves made up about 20 percent of the population in 1835 and lived mostly in Middle and West Tennessee. The state's navigable rivers—the Mississippi, the Cumberland, and the Tennessee—provided opportunities for transportation and trade, especially with the advent of the steamboat. And although most Tennesseans lived the lives of simple yeomen farmers with modest amounts of property, they entered the two and a half decades before the Civil War with optimism. The spread of evangelical

Protestantism and the expansion of suffrage rights to all white males lent an air of hopeful egalitarianism to Tennessee society.[1]

While Tennessee expanded, American law and legal institutions also came into their own. The three or four decades prior to the Civil War were in many ways "the golden age of American law." During this period, state appellate courts across the country began to assert the power to overturn legislative acts. Judges became important policy makers, especially at the state level, and this was no exception in Tennessee.[2] Some of the most influential jurists in the state's history sat on the Supreme Court of Tennessee during this period, and the judges crafted law to accommodate Tennessee's changing society. During this period of judicial innovation, however, many state courts struggled for their very survival. As reformers nationwide sought to make courts accountable for their decisions, judges often found themselves submitting to popular election or other controls originating in the legislature. During the two and a half decades before the Civil War, Tennesseeans continually debated these issues of judicial independence and accountability, and in 1853 voters amended the state Constitution to mandate the popular election of judges. In an era marked by expanding political participation, even the judiciary was not immune from popular influence.

The sectional conflict and Civil War brought to a halt both Tennessee's uninterrupted expansion and the national trend of legal innovation. Debates over the expansion of slavery in new western territories after the Mexican-American War led to increased sectional polarization and the breakdown of national political parties during the 1850s. The conflict culminated with the southern bombardment of Fort Sumter in South Carolina in April 1861, which caused Tennessee and three other Upper South states to join the seven other slaveholding states that had already left the Union. The Civil War devastated Tennessee and its judiciary. For almost the duration of the war the Court ceased operation, and the reconstituted Court of 1865 garnered little of the respect that the antebellum tribunal had earned. In the chaotic aftermath of war, the Court again faced a challenge to its independence, this time from a controversial and overbearing governor who insisted on filling judicial vacancies by appointment. The story of the Tennessee Supreme Court during these years was thus a tale of achievement and failure—the Court experienced a golden age of judicial leadership and innovation, but it also waged a continual struggle for independence and survival.

THE JUDICIARY IN CRISIS, 1829–1834

When the sixty delegates to the Tennessee Constitutional Convention convened in Nashville on May 19, 1834, the future of the state's highest court—and of the judicial system as a whole—remained uncertain. For four decades, Tennessee had been operating under a Constitution that had not even mentioned a supreme court. The state's founding document of 1796 had simply stated that the "judicial power of the state shall be vested in such superior and inferior courts . . . as the legislature shall from time to time direct and establish." The legislature appointed all the state's judges by "joint ballot of both houses," and all judges served "during good behavior"—meaning for life, unless impeached. Whatever independence the judiciary gained from lifetime appointments they lost with the Constitution's placement of the courts under the dominion of the legislature. The results of this arrangement proved problematic: lawyers solicited judicial appointments, unsuccessful litigants pleaded for legislative redress, and the Supreme Court's very existence hung precariously in the balance.[3]

The period 1829–31 marked the high point of political struggle over the judiciary. In 1829, legislators began the process of impeaching two circuit judges, largely for political reasons, and during the same session lawmakers examined legislator Adam Huntsman's lengthy report on the judiciary, which described the state's court system as "the most expensive and least efficient of any in the United States." Indeed, the heavy burden of circuit riding and large volume of cases caused innumerable delays in the administration of justice. On the heels of Huntsman's report, in 1831 the Judiciary Committee of the Tennessee House of Representatives inquired specifically into the Supreme Court's inability to keep up with its business. Judge John Catron's reaction only aroused further suspicion of the judiciary. In response to the committee, he contended that it was "impossible" under the existing system to conduct all the business of the Court. "I feel very safe in saying," Catron wrote, "that were not another cause placed on the docket, except such as were left undecided at the last term, it would take the court three years to do the business on it, and that it would be badly done at that." Even if the Court were to stop riding the circuit and begin conducting all its business in one place, he contended, the judges still would not be able to cover the entire docket within a reasonable length of time. After sending this frank appraisal of the judicial system to the legislature, Catron, who had begun his career on the court in 1824, tendered his resignation.[4]

Catron's critique sparked three months of debate in the legislature over the future of the state Supreme Court. Lawmakers discussed how to reform the Court, or whether to abolish the tribunal altogether. They considered various proposals for making the judiciary more accountable and efficient, including abolishing tenure during good behavior, providing for the official publication of the Court's written opinions, alleviating circuit riding, and creating the position of chief justice. After considering such issues, in December 1831 the legislature passed a compromise reform measure. The law added a fourth member to the Court, who was to be the chief justice;

penalized judges for being absent from court with a fine of twelve dollars per day and required each judge to file an affidavit certifying how many days he had been absent in order to receive his salary; and provided that if the four members of the Court were equally divided in opinion, the inferior court's ruling stood. The statute also created the position of supreme court reporter, who was to furnish the public printer with a manuscript copy of the Court's decisions.[5] By enacting such legislation, lawmakers placated those calling for more accountability from the state judiciary while at the same time refusing to accede to those who favored abolition of the Court. Catron, whose candor had initiated much of the debate, won the praise of legislators for his "patriotism and virtue." In December 1831, under the provisions of the new law, the legislature elected the recently resigned Catron as Tennessee's first chief justice.[6]

Despite the 1831 reforms, when Tennesseans assembled nearly two and a half years later to write a new constitution—largely because they hoped to change the state's outmoded tax system—the role of the judiciary remained a source of contention. During the Age of Jackson, many Americans distrusted power concentrated in the hands of a few. For a decade and a half or so before Jackson's election, new states coming into the Union, as well as the older members of the Republic, including Tennessee in 1834, repealed laws and state constitutional provisions mandating property qualifications for voting. In the same way that reformers sought to sweep away these impediments to democracy, advocates of more democratic government favored greater accountability on the part of the judiciary. Suspicious of the Court becoming an entrenched aristocracy that operated outside the public's watchful eye, these reformers sought to hold judges accountable for their decision making. Moreover, many lawyers and judges also favored a more accountable judiciary. They viewed limitations on lifetime judicial service as a moderate and pragmatic way to increase the prestige and popular support of the judiciary by eliminating the influence of party and patronage. Thus, many delegates at the constitutional convention favored limiting judicial terms of service, and some even favored outright popular election of jurists. In 1832, Mississippi had became the first state in the Union to establish an elected appellate judiciary, although by 1834 no state had yet followed suit.[7]

Within the first week and a half of Tennessee's convention, no less than seven different proposals arose to eliminate judicial service "during good behavior," and one delegate subsequently proposed to allow voters to elect outright the members of the Court. West H. Humphreys, a prosperous Fayette County lawyer and later federal court judge, suggested that the voters in each of the three grand divisions of the state elect a Supreme Court judge. Humphreys believed that an "independent judiciary" that served during good behavior ran counter to American constitutional principles. "The theory of judicial independence," he argued, ". . . is a dangerous and delusive notion . . . in direct contradiction to the first principles of free government.—What is a judge but an agent to try and determine disputes between citizens? Render him independent and he is a master, a despot, anything but the agent of a free people." Humphreys criticized moderate attempts to institute periodic election by lawmakers as a "half-way ground" that would "make the judges the vassals of the legislature." Popular election, in contrast, ensured that legislators could not exert their influence over the administration of justice. "The three great departments," Humphreys concluded, "should spring directly from the people, and be wholly independent of each other." Although Humphreys offered a more radical proposal to achieve judicial accountability than those who proposed term limitations, all of these reformers agreed that allowing Supreme Court judges to serve during "good behavior" was no longer acceptable.[8]

Despite Humphreys's suggestion, momentum at the 1834 convention favored moderate change. In early July, two delegates introduced resolutions to retain the constitutional provisions regarding service during good behavior. One of the two, John J. White, a Sumner County lawyer, spoke passionately about the subject. Judges serving a series of short, successive terms, he believed, would contaminate the process of judicial decision making. "The ermine of justice," White proclaimed in debate, "should not be soiled with the strifes and conflicts and passions of party. . . . Of all curses, that ever were inflicted upon any people, one of the greatest is that of a dependent, time serving, electioneering, political judiciary." Yet even White acknowledged the need for some limits on judicial power. He proposed that both supreme and inferior court judges "hold their offices during good behavior, but not beyond the age of sixty years."[9] Age, he reasoned, constituted a more appropriate limitation on judicial service than popular opinion.

Over time, a consensus about the Supreme Court began to emerge, and on July 25, Newton Cannon, the chair of the Committee of the Whole, presented a tentative draft of a new constitution. The proposed document reduced the size of the Court to three members, one from each of the three divisions of the state; the legislature would continue to select the members of the Court by "joint vote of both houses." Moreover, judges would have to be at least thirty-five years of age, would serve twelve-year terms, and would "be re-eligible."[10] Delegates immediately began the process of considering the report of the Committee of the Whole, and on August 4 the convention took up those provisions relating to the judiciary.

Two extreme proposals for revision went down to defeat. First, Chairman Cannon introduced an amendment to adopt the original language from the 1796 Constitution regarding the judiciary, which would have in effect canceled all of the work of the committee relating to the judicial branch and again placed the court system under the control of the legislature. Despite support from notables such as Adam Huntsman, whose 1829 report had given birth to judicial reform in Tennessee, the assembly defeated the proposal thirty-six to twenty. Second, George Marr of Henry County introduced an amendment providing that "the qualified voters for members of the General Assembly" elect the judges of the Supreme Court. Delegates scuttled this last-ditch attempt at popular election by a vote of forty-eight to eight.[11]

Most of the proposed amendments pertained to the question of judicial terms of service. As they had when the convention first assembled, delegates again introduced a variety of limitations on judicial service. White reintroduced his amendment to retain terms of good behavior "but not beyond the age of sixty years." Others proposed terms of eighteen, fourteen, and ten years, while another delegate suggested eight years and reeligibility. None of these motions passed. Later, when the convention considered the proposed constitution with amendments (none of which pertained to the judiciary), delegate James Fulton, a lawyer from Lincoln County, proposed that the words "and re-eligible" be stricken from the clause providing for twelve-year judicial terms. His motion prevailed.[12]

In its final form, Section 1 of Article 6 of the Constitution of 1834 vested the judicial power of the state "in one Supreme Court, in such Inferior Courts as the Legislature shall from time to time ordain and establish, and the Judges thereof and in Justices of the Peace." Section 2 provided that the Court be composed of three judges, "one of whom shall reside in each of the three grand divisions of the State," and that the Court hold session at one place in each of the three regions. The Constitution did not provide for the position of chief justice. The Court's jurisdiction was to be strictly appellate, and the concurrence of two judges was required for any decision. According to Section 3, the General Assembly, "by joint vote of both houses," would appoint the judges, who were required to be thirty-five years of age and would serve terms of twelve years. Subsequent sections spelled out other details regarding the Court, including regulations about judicial salaries, cases in which a judge had a personal stake, and the appointment of Supreme Court clerks.[13]

On August 30, 1834, the convention delegates adjourned, and during the spring of 1835 Tennesseans voted to ratify the new Constitution by an overwhelming margin. In the end, the crowning achievement of the convention with regard to the judiciary was the establishment of a Supreme

Court which the legislature could neither create nor abolish. Tennessee conferred on its high court a significant degree of independence relative to other southern states. By the 1830s, Georgia still languished without a supreme court, and its Superior Court judges operated under the shadow of a censure imposed by the legislature in 1815. The South Carolina legislature, moreover, abolished that state's high court in 1835 because of a controversial ruling during the Nullification Crisis. Thus, the Tennessee Supreme Court's success in overcoming its troubled history during the early 1830s and achieving constitutional recognition was a significant accomplishment.[14]

That winter the Tennessee legislature passed a series of measures, pursuant to the new Constitution, that pertained to the Supreme Court. On December 1, 1835, lawmakers enacted legislation that officially created the Court, established the boundaries for the three divisions of the state for purposes of the Court's composition and jurisdiction, and provided that the Court hold two sessions a year in Nashville (March and December), and one each in Knoxville (June) and Jackson (April). The law also set the judges' salaries at eighteen hundred dollars per year.[15] In February 1836, the legislature passed three separate measures relating to the new Court. These laws mandated the publication of the Supreme Court's decisions, provided for an attorney general elected by the legislature whose duty was to "attend to all business of the State both civil and criminal in the Supreme Court," and delineated the degree of relationship between a judge and a party to a case that would disqualify the jurist from service. With the passage of these measures, a half decade of legislative debate over the role of the judiciary came to a close.[16]

JUDICIAL APPOINTMENTS AND CHEROKEE REMOVAL, 1835

With the ratification of a new Constitution and the passage of legislation officially creating the Supreme Court, Tennessee lawmakers elected members of the new tribunal in accordance with these legal provisions. Judges Robert Whyte and Jacob Peck retired voluntarily upon ratification of the Constitution and thus were not up for reelection in 1835. With their departure, the legislature unanimously elected William B. Turley as Supreme Court judge from the Western Division of the state and William B. Reese as judge from the Eastern Division.[17] Selecting the representative from Middle Tennessee would prove more controversial. Because the Constitution required that one of the three judges of the Supreme Court "reside in each of the three grand divisions of the State" and because John Catron and Nathan Green both resided in Middle Tennessee, only one of them could continue to serve on the Court.[18]

Catron's political loyalty to Andrew Jackson ultimately led to his defeat. Of humble birth and meager education, Catron had long benefited from his ties to Tennessee's hero of the War of 1812. After Catron joined Jackson on expeditions against the Creek Indians in central Alabama during the 1810s, Jackson recommended that Catron and his well-born wife settle in Nashville, where she had connections. Catron's law practice flourished there, and the legislature elected him to the Supreme Court in 1824.[19] In the meantime, Jackson became president and remained popular in Tennessee throughout most of his two terms in office. Toward the end of his tenure, however, Tennesseans reacted unfavorably to his attempt to make Vice President Martin Van Buren of New York the next occupant of the White House.[20]

Ever loyal to Jackson, Catron became one of the state's leading champions of Van Buren's candidacy by the end of 1835, and the judge suffered the consequences of his political preference. Most in the state supported favorite son Hugh Lawson White, a former member of the Court and a U.S. senator, and in October 1835 the state house of representatives openly indicated their enthusiasm by passing a resolution endorsing White's candidacy. Two months later, under the terms of the new Constitution, legislators elected the new members of the Court. Lawmakers chose Green, Catron's less experienced colleague on the Court, by a vote of seventy-one to twenty-seven. Catron spent the next year directing Van Buren's campaign in Tennessee, and despite the New Yorker's overwhelmingly defeat in the Volunteer State, he won the national election. On Jackson's last day in office, the outgoing president appointed his loyal friend Catron to one of two newly created vacancies on the United States Supreme Court. The *Nashville Union* viewed the selection as the perfect postscript to Catron's removal from the state bench. His ouster had occurred "because he would not abandon his old principles and become an humble supporter of Judge White," the Democratic paper claimed. Catron, the *Union* happily concluded, had "received the just reward of [his] independence and integrity."[21] For the next twenty-eight years, until his death in 1865, Catron served on the United States Supreme Court.

A few months before his departure, during the Tennessee Supreme Court's Summer Term of 1835, Catron delivered his last significant opinion as a state judge. *State v. Foreman* (1835) involved an 1833 law that extended the state's legal jurisdiction over the Cherokee, who resided on several hundred thousand acres in eastern Tennessee. The alleged murder of John Walker, a Cherokee, by another Cherokee man, James Foreman, led to a test of the law. Indicted in a county court, Foreman claimed that the alleged offense occurred outside the jurisdiction of the courts of Tennessee and within the Cherokee Nation. Thus, Foreman challenged the constitutionality of the 1833 act.[22]

Catron and his colleagues' decisions proved significant not only for the fate of Tennessee's Cherokee population but also for the larger issues of slavery, states' rights, and sectionalism that would later plague Tennessee and the nation. By upholding Tennessee's extension of jurisdiction over the Cherokee, Catron implicitly supported President Jackson's policy of Indian removal and overtly challenged U.S. Chief Justice John Marshall's recognition of the Cherokee's status as an independent nation in *Worcester v. Georgia* (1832). Writing in the midst of the forcible relocation of thousands of Cherokee and other Native Americans from the southeastern United States, Catron offered an extensive argument against the sovereign claims of any Native tribe that drew upon contemporary historical and legal theories regarding the relationship between Native Americans and European "discoverers."

The underlying assumption of the doctrine of discovery, as enunciated by Catron, was that all Native Americans were heathen "savages" who possessed inferior customs and culture. Because they possessed an inferior culture, Catron reasoned, they held no claims to the land upon the arrival of Europeans. "We maintain," he asserted, "that the principles declared in the fifteenth century as the law of Christendom—that discovery gave title to assume sovereignty over, and to govern, the unconverted natives of Africa, Asia, and North and South America—has been recognized as a part of the national law for nearly four centuries." Although Catron expressed apparent doubts about the morality of such a position, he nevertheless asserted that law and experience validated white European dominance. "To abandon the principle now is to assert that [our ancestors] were unjust usurpers," he wrote, "and that we, succeeding to their usurped authority and void claims . . . should in honesty abandon it, return to Europe, and let the subdued parts again become a wilderness and hunting ground."[23] Despite some misgivings, Catron firmly positioned the Court on the side of settlers of European origin.

Catron, who had consistently supported the land claims of Cherokees in a series of previous decisions, thus completely reversed his position on Native American rights.[24] By doing so, Catron came to the aid of his friend and mentor at a time when Jackson needed his support more than ever. By the middle of the 1830s, Whig political opponents and South Carolina nullifiers simultaneously attacked the president. Whigs assailed him for his vetoes of the Maysville Road bill and the National Bank's recharter, while the president's personal falling out with Vice President Calhoun and the continuing showdown with South Carolina over nullification of the federal tariff only compounded the president's political troubles. When *Worcester v. Georgia* came before the U.S. Supreme Court in the midst of this turmoil, Jackson's opponents gleefully seized upon the opportunity to obstruct the chief executive's policy regarding Native Americans. Chief Justice John Marshall's decision in *Worcester* favoring Cherokee rights in opposition to Jackson's removal policy thus pushed Catron closer to his mentor.[25] Knowing that Jackson needed him, Catron thus abandoned his support for the Cherokee.

While Catron's personal loyalty partially accounted for the judge's change of heart on Cherokee rights, the issue of slavery exerted a deciding influence. The discovery doctrine "comes in conflict with our religion and with our best convictions of a refined and sound morality," Catron bluntly admitted in *Foreman*. But, he continued, "our individual titles to lands from the Atlantic to the western Missouri line depend upon its firm and unquailing support. . . . The title of every slave in America, North and South, rests on no better or different foundation." In *Foreman,* Catron thus made the connection between the right of European discoverers to conquer the land and the authority of white southerners to own slaves.[26] If the white descendants of Europeans did not possess the right to take the land upon which they lived from the Cherokee, southern whites certainly lacked the right to enslave Africans—an unacceptable proposition to Catron. In the aftermath of Nat Turner's 1831 slave revolt in Virginia, Tennessee lawmakers had prohibited the immigration of free blacks into the state, banned emancipation without removal from the state's borders, and disfranchised free blacks in the 1834 Constitution. Catron's defensiveness about slavery thus reflected the attitudes of most white Tennesseans at the time.[27]

In Catron's mind, moreover, states needed to retain sovereignty within the Union in order to protect the land claims of white settlers, as well as the rights of slaveholders. Referring in *Foreman* to the power of the federal government to make treaties, Catron wrote, "It cannot, in times of peace, cede away to a people independent of the state a part of its territory and sovereignty. . . . The states are emphatically the basis of the Union and federal Constitution; to extinguish them is to extinguish the Constitution—to leave it nothing to operate upon." Even though Catron opposed nullification, later fought secession, and had never before expressed support for the idea that states retained their sovereignty within the Union, during the 1830s he realized the potential utility of asserting this doctrine when it came to controlling Native American lands and slave property.[28]

The case of *State v. Foreman* in the summer of 1835 marked a significant turning point in the history of Tennessee and its Supreme Court. Although the case was subsequently appealed and scheduled to be argued before the United States Supreme Court, the death of Foreman prevented the litigation from continuing, and the Tennessee decision stood as a judicial justification of Jackson's removal policy.[29] The case in some respects culminated the years of litigation involving land claims that had occupied much the Supreme Court's efforts in its early history. At the same time, the dispute foreshadowed the conflicts over race, slavery, and sovereignty that still lay ahead of both the state and the nation. Finally, *State v. Foreman* marked the changes in the Court's personnel. Of the three judges who wrote opinions in the case, only one, Nathan Green, would still be serving when the Court began its March 1836 term.

Green stood poised to lead the Court after Catron's departure. Born in Amelia County, Virginia, in 1792 to a respectable family but orphaned at a young age, Green gained "little more than meagre" education in a "common country school" in Virginia and served in the War of 1812.[30] Afterward he took up the study of law, married Mary Field, and began his practice in Virginia. After several months, the couple decided to move to Tennessee, where they settled in Winchester in Franklin County. Green had a gambling problem at the time, and one night at a hotel in Winchester he reportedly lost "a very large part of his fine estate, including what had come by his wife." Green promptly confessed his losses to his wife, informed her of the obligations he had made, and told her of the financial hardship they would have to endure in order to settle his debts. After relating all the details of this horrible incident, Green promised her that he would never gamble again. Without scolding him, his wife Mary reportedly said simply, "Then I am happy."[31]

After his decision to stop gambling, Green experienced a religious conversion that profoundly affected his personal and professional life. A Cumberland Presbyterian and a Whig, Green joined the temperance crusade in Tennessee and made speeches against the evils of strong drink. In the absence of his church's regular minister, moreover, he "often took the pulpit and expounded the Scriptures."[32] And as a lawyer, he saw professional ethics as closely linked to Christian character. "All are aware that their conduct, be it good or bad," he noted to a group of aspiring lawyers many years later, "must soon be known, and that in this virtuous community, a wholesome public opinion will frown on the vicious. And this knowledge must necessarily counteract the force of temptations to vice, and enable young gentlemen to preserve that purity of character which so much adorns the gentleman." He concluded, "A lawyer must be a gentlemen, which implies that he is honest, true, and just."[33]

During the 1820s, Green rose to prominence in political and legal circles. He and his wife moved to Lebanon in Wilson County, where in 1826 Green won election to the state senate. During the 1827 term the legislature created the courts of chancery and provided for the election of two chancellors. Having impressed his legislative colleagues, Green became chancellor for the Eastern Division of the state. Along with his colleague from the Western Division, William A. Cooke, Green compiled the rules of chancery practice for Tennessee and gained a seat on the Supreme Court four year later.[34]

Green earned a reputation as a stern and rational jurist. Though physically imposing at six feet, six inches tall, on the bench Green was "as impassive as a block of wood." He "put his whole soul in the fulfillment of his duty," wrote lawyer William Frierson Cooper, but was "slow in his conclusions and not quick in apprehension." According to a later judicial colleague, A. W. O. Totten, Green was at his best in conference, where he and his fellow judges met to decide the outcome of cases. "His strong and retentive memory, his logical and orderly arrangement of facts, his clear and distinct views of legal principles, and sound judgement, were there most conspicuous," Totten observed. Green often dealt with broad principles rather than technical issues in his opinions, which, despite lacking scholarly qualities, were "always clear, discriminating, and logical."[35]

William B. Turley joined Green as a judge of the Supreme Court representing West Tennessee. Born in Alexandria, Virginia in 1800, Turley spent much of his childhood in Loudon County, Virginia, and Davidson County, Tennessee, before his family moved to Hopkinsville, Kentucky, in 1816. An "industrious student," Turley entered Cumberland College (later called the University of Nashville) and graduated with high honors at the age of sixteen. He then read law under William L. Brown and opened a law office in Clarksville, where he practiced in the small surrounding towns in Kentucky and Tennessee for the next several years. In 1821 he married Annie C. Payne of Russellville, Kentucky.[36]

Turley rose rapidly within the Tennessee legal community. In 1829, he received an appointment as judge of the Eleventh Judicial Circuit of Tennessee, which included Wayne, Hardin, McNairy, Hardeman, Fayette, and Shelby Counties. After moving to Bolivar in 1830 to assume his duties, Turley soon earned a reputation for intelligent and fair dealings as a judge, as well as "cordiality" and grace in conversation. "With the members of the bar he seemed a great favorite," remarked Henry S. Foote, "all of whom spoke of him as decidedly the most rising man in the state."[37] As a judge, Turley decided cases with "readiness and despatch" and by 1835 had gained the attention of the legislature, perhaps because of this reputation for efficient decision making. After the state constitutional revision, he gained a seat on the Supreme Court at the age of thirty-five, whereupon he and his family moved to Jackson.[38]

In contrast to Green, Judge Turley was known for hasty decision making and a short attention span. Frequently when in conference with his fellow judges, according to one source, he would state his views to his colleagues, walk out, and leave the decision to them. While listening to counsel's arguments he seemed equally inattentive. "Judge Turley is exceedingly quick and ready—which sometimes leads to hasty conclusions," wrote a lawyer of that day. "He is impatient, fidgety. Listens with reluctance, and is apt to relax his attention." Another observer noted that, "as a man of full habit," Judge Turley "now and then after a hearty meal was known to be somewhat drowsy on the bench."[39] In spite of such behavior, Turley won wide acclaim for the style and substance of his opinions. He deeply admired Coke, the great English jurist, and rarely relied on precedents from other state courts.[40] Indeed, he viewed the indiscriminate acceptance of other reports as "the great evil of the day," which threatened to create a generation of "case lawyers, who accept anything as law they find in a book" and are "unable to detect a sophism from sound argument."[41] Turley's strong views and impulsive ways often put him at odds with Judge Green.

William B. Reese, the third member of the Court elected in 1835, represented the Eastern Division of the state. Born in Jefferson County, Tennessee, in 1793, Reese grew up in a prominent East Tennessee family. His father, one of Tennessee's first settlers and a member of the legislature of the failed state of Franklin, sent his son to a classical school in Cave Spring in his native county. Afterward, Reese attended Blount College and later graduated from Greeneville College with "first honors." After studying law, Reese gained admission to the bar, opened an office in Knoxville, and married Sarah Cocke in 1821. While attaining success as a lawyer, Reese also advocated various projects for improvement. He championed the building of a canal to the South Atlantic coast, helped organize and served as president of the East Tennessee Historical Society, and even worked for the abolition of slavery. In 1831, he replaced Nathan Green as chancellor for the Eastern Division of the state and four years later gained a seat on the Supreme Court. He was the first native Tennessean to serve on the Court.[42]

Reese's judicial work reflected his scholarly achievements. A man "of scholastic and literary culture of a very high grade," he viewed law as a science not be altered by the circumstances or hardships of a particular case.[43] Comparing him to his judicial colleagues, a contemporary observed, "He seems to reason well and methodically—with some of Turley's clearness, and with more than Green's precision in the application of cases." After his twelve years on the Court, he served as president of East Tennessee University (later called the University of Tennessee) until failing health forced him to retire. A Whig and an Episcopalian, of the three great judges of the antebellum era, Reese would prove to be the most careful and least colorful.[44]

By the end of 1835, the Tennessee Supreme Court emerged stronger than it had ever been. Not only had the Court gained legitimacy with the ratification of the new Constitution, the departing Judge Catron had rendered a popular decision supporting Indian removal and white settlement, and the new members of the Court had ascended to the bench with neither opposition from the public nor division within the legislature. Elected to twelve-year terms, Judges Green, Turley, and Reese would thus dominate the Tennessee Supreme Court for much of its pre–Civil War history.

CREATING AN EXPANDING ECONOMY AND A MORAL ORDER, 1835–1860

During the two and a half decades before the Civil War, the Tennessee Supreme Court devoted much of its attention to regulation of the state's economic and moral life. The vast majority of cases on the Court's docket involved the private economic transactions arising out of an agricultural and commercial economy: cases involving contracts, debts, land, and slaves. But the Court also played an important role in matters of public law: deciding upon the proper powers of the state under the Constitution and interpreting procedural and substantive fairness in criminal cases. Tennessee's antebellum judiciary took an active role in making policy within the bounds prescribed by the legislature. Increasingly during this period, judges perceived themselves as champions of progress, guardians of virtue, defenders of life, and protectors of the oppressed. Particularly in cases involving economic policy, morality and family, and homicide, the Tennessee Supreme Court took an active role in trying to transform society.

Economic Policy

During the 1830s, the Tennessee General Assembly passed legislation creating a comprehensive system of transportation. In addition to seeking federal aid, the state appropriated money for improvements to rivers, as well as the building of new turnpikes and railroads. Lawmakers chartered six railroad companies in 1831 and more in the years that followed. However, the Panic of 1837 drained many of the financial resources that were to be used on such projects, and eventually all the chartered railroad companies went bankrupt. Not until the 1840s did Tennesseans regain their enthusiasm for railroad building, and not until the 1850s did railroads begin operating in the state.[45]

The Court supported these efforts to build and expand railroads. In *Nichol v. Mayor and Alderman of Nashville* (1848), the judges took up the issue of whether the legislature had violated the state Constitution by authorizing Nashville to take stock in the building of a Nashville to Chattanooga railroad. At a meeting called by the Board of Mayor and Aldermen of the city, citizens overwhelmingly approved the purchase of stock in the railroad venture. Afterward, a disgruntled group of Nashville residents filed in bill in Chancery Court to halt the city's investment in the project, because, as taxpayers there, they had "faith that the corporation [of Nashville] taxes would be confined to legitimate corporation purposes, and would not be levied for speculation purposes." In the opinion of the Court, Judge Turley refused to speculate whether the railroad project would be beneficial to the state, but he nonetheless upheld the legislature's actions: "If the corporation had money, as it might well have, there can be no good reason why it should not be permitted to vest it in such stocks as might be supposed would be profitable; individuals so vest their money, and why should not a corporation be permitted to do so? . . . Is there any wrong in this. Is there anything against the public good in this?"[46] Ruling that a corporation was "the creature of the legislative department of government," the Court gave its approval to the legislature's authorization of the stock purchase.[47]

In *Woodfolk v. Nashville and Chattanooga Railroad Company* (1852), an eminent-domain case involving the same railroad company, the Court again aided the legislature's railroad-building program. Judge Robert L. Caruthers, elected to the Court in 1847, noted that many cases would be coming to the judges relating to the issue of compensation for land taken by the legislature, "as the spirit of public improvement has now taken possession of the minds of the people, and guides the public councils in our state." Noting the need to "guard the rights of citizens, on the one hand, and not improperly impede the cause of public improvement on the other," Caruthers attempted to define how fair compensation ought to be determined. The value of any land taken, he ruled, needed to be determined by a judicial tribunal, and the property owner was to be compensated in cash. "Here the constitutional provision ends; its inhibition on the government goes no farther. The Legislature may make any regulations it thinks right and proper for an account or estimate of incidental loss or damage or injuries to the landowner." Thus, the legislature had the power to determine compensation for any changes made to a person's property, including the building of fences or removal of buildings. Such matters were "separate and distinct" from "ascertaining the compensation required by the Constitution," he wrote.[48]

By the mid-1850s enthusiasm for railroad building spread across Tennessee. As the first railroad lines connecting the state to cities around the nation began operating, the Court demonstrated a more overtly positive attitude toward continued expansion of rail lines. In *Louisville & Nashville Railroad Company v. County Court of Davidson* (1854), Judge Caruthers reviewed the history of Tennessee's involvement with internal improvements. "It was discovered," he wrote, "that wherever a good system of railroads had been adopted prosperity had crowned the efforts of the people in every branch of business, and comparative darkness and inertia seemed to be settling down upon every section in which it had been neglected." Associating railroads with progress and comparing Tennessee's advances in the area to developments in other states, Judge Caruthers dismissed bills filed in three counties against acts of the legislature that had authorized county subscription of stock in the Louisville and Nashville Railroad Company. Again, as in previous cases, the Court upheld legislative attempts to foster construction of railroads.[49]

The Court's role in formulating economic policy proved significant. With the aid of such decisions, twelve hundred miles of railroad tracks were built in Tennessee during the 1850s, and an extensive network of roads, railroads, and navigable rivers thus spanned the state. This cheap and effective system of long-distance transportation allowed farmers to grow surpluses for export and connected the state's major cities to larger markets and ports throughout the country.[50]

Morality and Family

In addition to contributing to the state's economic development, the Tennessee Supreme Court also played a role in matters relating to morality and family. Much of the moral code of the Old South rested on the principles of evangelical Christianity. As revivals spread across the South during the early nineteenth century, huge numbers of Tennesseans began attending camp meetings and joining churches. These Evangelicals stressed the need for personal conversion and holy living, as many anticipated the Second Coming and sought to reform society in order to prepare the way. Even those disinclined to engage in social reforms such as temperance displayed an enthusiastic faith that demanded adherence to Christian moral principles. By 1860, the three largest Protestant denominations in Tennessee—Methodists, Baptists, and Cumberland Presbyterians—accounted for 83 percent of the state's churches. Evangelical Christianity informed Tennesseans' understanding of the institutions of marriage and the family, while religion also found expression in legal regulations of dueling, drinking, gambling, and prostitution. Familial and moral issues thus formed an important part of the fabric of nineteenth-century law, as legislatures and courts enacted and interpreted a variety of measures pertaining to both public and private morality.[51]

Like courts all over the country, the Tennessee Supreme Court took an increasing interest in the law of marriage and domestic relations during this period. As the growth of a market economy gradually contributed to the separation of the workplace from the household, women assumed new autonomy over the domestic sphere as well as moral guardianship of the home. The rise of this "republican family" included the ideal of companionate marriage—nineteenth-century writers on the family urged men to forge closer emotional ties with their wives and children. Because many judges viewed the family as the foundation of national morality, they saw themselves as obliged to protect the family ideal from the perils of the marketplace and the threat of adulterous or abusive husbands. Although Judge Turley once commented that domestic relations "are of so sacred a character, and involve to so great an extent the peace and happiness of mankind in general, that it cannot be otherwise than a source of deep mortification . . . to investigate and determine conflicting rights arising out of feuds existing between them," the Tennessee Supreme Court played a significant role in settling such disputes.[52] Judicial decisions, though usually paternalistic in tone, nevertheless helped women who sought assistance from the courts.

In divorce cases, for example, judges attempted to protect victimized wives who embodied the virtues of antebellum womanhood. A liberal 1842 amendment to Tennessee's divorce statute of 1836 prompted a sharp increase in the number of divorce cases heard by the Court.[53] While society generally frowned upon the legal dissolution of a marriage during this era, both the legislature and the Court saw adulterous husbands as a much greater threat to the family ideal than litigious wives. In *Richmond v. Richmond* (1837), for example, the judges sustained a lower court decision granting a divorce to a woman whose husband openly cohabitated with a slave woman at a house in Nashville. Judge Green found it "barely possible" that the man could be innocent of the charge of adultery, given that witnesses had seen him and the slave paramour in various compromising positions: once, for instance, "he buttoning up his pantaloons, and she brushing down her disordered and rumpled dress."[54] In *Payne v. Payne* (1844), a case of cruel conduct on the part of a husband, who regularly slapped and choked his wife and was "in the habit of using language to her which a gentleman will not employ to his slaves," Judge Green again sided with the wife. A devoted member of the Methodist Church, according to witnesses, the woman was a model of Christian character.[55] In cases pitting cruel husbands against virtuous wives, the Court unequivocally sided with virtue.

The Court also attempted to alleviate the economic victimization of wives. In *Chunn v. Chunn* (1838) the judges refused to allow an adulterous husband to claim the extensive wealth that his wife had brought to the marriage, in order to satisfy the claims of creditors. "Shall a man, who has violated his matrimonial vows, in every disgusting form, and, by harsh and unkind treatment, force his wife to seek protection in a recision of her nuptial contract, be heard, when he asks a support out of her estate?" Judge Turley asked. "It is mockery, worse than mockery." The Court also helped destitute wives by allowing them to sue for divorce *in forma pauperis*—as a poor person unable to pay court fees. In *Hawkins v. Hawkins* (1856), Judge Caruthers held that a woman needed to be able to "enter the courts of justice" no matter her economic status. "A *feme covert* having wrongs to redress," he wrote, "above all other needs the benefit of such a provision, because, by the marital right of the husband, her property goes, with herself, under his dominion and control." Continuing, Caruthers summarized the paternalistic perspective of the Court: "The law delights in the protection of the weak against the strong; and in no proper case will it withhold the hand of relief because of the inability of the injured party. Surely there are not cases to which an act to aid the weak in the assertion of their rights could be more fitly applied."[56] Finally, alimony became a standard part of divorce settlements during the period, and the judges upheld this right in a number of instances.[57]

When it was unclear whether women had in fact been maltreated in some way, the Court hesitated to decide in their favor, especially during the late 1850s. By that time, judges began to worry that the increasing number of divorce petitions posed a threat to the institutions of marriage and family. In *Rutledge v. Rutledge* (1858), for example, Judge Caruthers held that to be a good cause for divorce, desertion needed to "wilful and malicious" and "without reasonable cause." Caruthers believed that the liberal expansion of the divorce statutes had "been very much abused by the latitudinous construction given to them by the courts," and he thought the Court "would be derelict in duty to sanction the loose administration of the law of divorces, which has obtained in the some of the courts." A year later, Judge Robert McKinney, elected to the Court in 1847, echoed some of Caruthers's concerns. He held in *Thompson v. Thompson* (1859) that a wife could only receive alimony and court costs from her husband in a divorce case if she was "prosecuting or defending the suit in good faith." "If it be apparent, that her suit is without any just or reasonable foundation," McKinney wrote, "and that her cause is prompted by motives of malice or oppression towards her husband," no allowance should be made to her.[58]

Thus, the Court believed it had a moral obligation to uphold the family ideal. Tensions grew out of this position, as the judges sought to protect victimized wives by granting divorces without going so far as to undermine the institution of marriage. The Court experienced a similar conflict in the area of relations between parents and children. Judge Turley put it best when he noted once that "the right of parents to chastise their refractory and disobedient children is so necessary to the government of families, to the good order of society, that no moralist or lawgiver has ever thought of interfering with its existence." Still, he observed, "in chastising a child, the parent must be careful that he does not exceed the bounds of moderation and inflict cruel and merciless punishment."[59] In all of these early- and mid-nineteenth-century cases, the judges of the Tennessee Supreme Court increasingly took on the role of "custodians of the family."[60]

Outside the realm of family, the Court also assumed a more significant role in regulating public morality. During this period, one historian writes, a "concern for order, ethics, good manners, respectable habits, and standards of decency were principal objects of police." Because the categories of "criminal law, moral reform, and police regulation" often overlapped in antebellum America, state legislatures and judges—informed by evangelical Christianity in particular in Tennessee—played an important role in regulating such activities as liquor sales, gambling, and prostitution.[61]

Alcohol sales came under the scrutiny of the Court in several instances. In 1838, the state repealed all laws authorizing a license to retail liquor, thus making all retailing of alcohol a misdemeanor punishable by the state. The Court subsequently upheld this measure in *Dyer v. State* (1838), in which Judge Turley defined "retailing" as selling liquor in quantities smaller than a quart, as well as selling alcohol in larger quantities than a quart "to be drank at the place where sold."[62] In subsequent cases the Court proceeded to sustain indictments under the law, despite technical inadequacies, because, as Judge Green concluded, "in a misdemeanor, . . . so much strictness is not required."[63] Moreover, the Court also upheld those provisions of the 1838 law banning all liquor sales, in any quantity, on Sundays.[64]

In addition to liquor sales, cockfighting and prostitution also fell under the government's power to regulate. In *Johnson v. State* (1857), the judges took up the case of a Williamson County man who had charged spectators a dollar each to attend a cockfight he had advertised and organized. Judge Caruthers came down hard on the alleged criminal, who argued that his actions did not fall under the state's 1799 antigaming law, which covered "any game or match of hazard or address for money or other valuable thing." Caruthers not only held that the man's actions as indictable, he also strongly condemned gaming of all sorts. "All men should keep at a distance from such degrading practices," he wrote. "[Gambling] is prohibited by law and visited with penalties because of its destructive effects upon the moral character and social habits of individuals. It leads to idleness, dissipation, bankruptcy and wretchedness. Its victims are almost invariably converted into cold, selfish, reckless harpies."[65] The Court exhibited a similar willingness to uphold a Nashville ordinance prohibiting the renting or letting of a house to be kept as "house of ill fame." "A bawdy house is a common nuisance," Judge McKinney explained in *Childress v. Mayor and Aldermen of Nashville* (1855), "because it not only tends to corrupt the public morals by an open profession of prostitution, but it likewise endangers the public peace and good order, by drawing together profligate and disorderly persons."[66]

As evangelical Christianity swept across the South, the Tennessee Supreme Court decided an increasing number of cases that involved moral offenses. Judges hoped to create a well-ordered society of morally responsible individuals who looked out for the common good. For this reason, the Court condemned the adulterous and the profligate, the drunk and the disorderly. Although few cases came before the Court that explicitly involved religion, the religious and moralistic spirit of the age found expression in these legislative and judicial regulations of private and public morality. Perhaps the zealous spirit of many of the judges was most evident in a case involving an alleged violation of the state's 1815 statute prohibiting the disturbance of public worship. After the close of worship services, a group of Methodists met for the trial of a church member charged with "evil speaking." The defendant in the church trial, "by his violent language and demeanor" reportedly disturbed the meeting, and was convicted under the state law. On appeal, the Tennessee Supreme Court had no sympathy. The Court "for the suppression of these offences," rendered "a broader and more liberal construction" than the statute banning disturbance of worship literally required. "These 'wicked and disorderly persons,' . . . who trifle with sacred things, and show contempt for the rules of the church and the rights of conscience," Judge Caruthers concluded, "deserve no favor, and should be visited with the full measure of punishment authorized by the law."[67]

Violence and Homicide

The greatest moral threat to society, of course, was rampant fighting and killing. Like the rest of the Old South, early-nineteenth-century Tennessee was an unruly place. Hard drinking, horse racing, and cockfighting served as community rituals and forms of entertainment for many. Such activities, combined with the power and domination inherently associated with slavery, made the South a violent place. White southerners placed a premium on their personal liberty, independence, and reputation; the slightest injury or insult at times led to a brawl or duel. Memphis, a rough, young river town during the first half of the nineteenth century, gained a particular reputation for raucousness, as daily accounts of fighting filled local court dockets. In such a climate, homicide occurred with some frequency. Local courts and juries sometimes allowed such acts of violence to go virtually unpunished, for many white southerners accepted violence as a legitimate means of resolving conflict.[68]

Still, when juries did issue guilty verdicts in homicide cases, the Tennessee Supreme Court usually upheld convictions and did all in its power to stem the tide of lawlessness. During this period, Tennessee lawyers often attempted to free their clients and widen the legal definition of self-defense by relying upon *Grainger v. State* (1830), a case in which Chief Justice John Catron had excused Grainger for killing another man. Though the facts of the case clearly revealed that Grainger had acted in defense of his own life, Catron's carelessly written opinion led to some confusion in the interpretation of the law of homicide in Tennessee. "If the jury had believed that Grainger was in danger of great bodily harm from Broach, or thought himself so, then the killing would have been in self-defense," Catron wrote. By omitting the words "upon sufficient grounds" after "thought himself so," Catron unintentionally expanded opportunities for defendants to claim they had acted in self-defense.[69]

In subsequent cases the Court attempted to clarify the *Grainger* holding and the concept of self-defense. One such case, *Copeland v. State* (1846), involved a wife who had killed her husband's lover. Mary Copeland, "upon strong grounds of suspicion" that her husband had been carrying on an adulterous affair with Ruth Dougherty, continually watched Dougherty's house and threatened to take her life. Dougherty, meanwhile, fully aware of Copeland's feelings for her, similarly spoke of killing her rival. Persuaded by neighbors, Copeland "desisted from her threats and determined to bear the wrong." However, Dougherty apparently attacked Copeland when they met in a road one day, by striking her adversary with a three-and-a-half-foot-long hickory stick. Resisting the attack with a knife she was carrying, Copeland killed Dougherty. Convicted of second-degree murder, Copeland appealed to the Supreme Court.[70]

Judge Turley proved sympathetic to Copeland's claims and held that the peculiar circumstances of the case warranted a new trial. In writing his opinion, Turley openly expressed his bias in favor of Copeland. "We do not deem it necessary to disguise that our sympathies are enlisted in her favor, and that we have examined this record with the view of ascertaining if there were any legal grounds upon which we could be justified in giving her a new trial, and with an anxious desire that they might be found," he wrote. Acknowledging that no error existed in the judge's charge to the jury, Turley argued that only if the facts and evidence in the case did not justify the verdict could a new trial be ordered. To Turley, the case hinged on the point "at which the prisoner and deceased met, and as to which commenced the assault." Through a detailed examination of the evidence and testimony, Turley concluded that Dougherty had met Copeland on the road "with a determination to inflict severe punishment upon her" and that Copeland had merely "determined to resist and protect herself."[71] Definitively stating that the killing was not murder, Turley ordered a new trial.

A decade later, the case of *Morgan v. State* (1856) presented two significant issues involving the law of homicide: the meaning of double jeopardy and the definition of self-defense. Arraigned upon an indictment for "malicious shooting," the jury in Morgan's trial could not agree, whereupon one of the jurors withdrew from the case and a mistrial was declared. The case was continued during the next term of the court with the consent of Morgan, who appeared accordingly at his second trial. When the jury found him guilty as charged, he was sentenced to two years imprisonment in the penitentiary. In his appeal to the Supreme Court, Morgan argued that the dismissal of the jury during his first trial discharged him as well and that he could not be tried again for the same crime.[72]

Judge McKinney held that Morgan had not been tried twice in violation of the Tennessee Constitution. McKinney noted that American courts differed as to whether or not the protection against double jeopardy applied only after a jury verdict had been rendered in a case or simply once a jury had been empaneled and charged. Still, citing the Tennessee case of *Mahala v. State* (1837), McKinney argued that because the defendant had consented to the discharge of the jury, his second trial did not constitute double jeopardy. "[N]either at the time when the prisoner was again put upon trial, nor at any stage of the proceedings in the court below, was this objection made in any form," McKinney wrote. Morgan's failure to object to the discharge of the jury "in the proper time and in the proper form" constituted "a waiver of the supposed irregularity."[73] Therefore he could not claim this as grounds for reversing the verdict.

McKinney similarly dismissed Morgan's argument that the trial judge had improperly instructed the jury about the rules of self-defense. Here Morgan's counsel had relied upon *Grainger v. State,* that controversial case many attorneys argued had expanded the common-law doctrine of self-defense to allow any person who felt himself in danger to kill his opponent. McKinney bluntly stated that the trial judge had not erred in charging the jury that "the proof ought to show that [the prisoner's] fears were founded on some reasonable ground; that the law would not excuse the criminal act of the defendant, though under the influence of fear, if his fears were baseless and the phantoms of the imagination." These instructions, McKinney concluded, were "in accordance with the well-established doctrine of the common law."[74]

A few years later, in *Rippy v. State* (1858), the Court continued its crusade against armed violence and dangerous attempts to expand the definition of self-defense. The case involved James Ripley (his name was apparently misspelled in the title of the official report of the case), who was convicted for the second-degree murder of Houston Porter and sentenced to twenty-one years in the penitentiary.[75] In his opinion in the case, Judge Caruthers described the verdict as "well sustained by the testimony," and the only error in the trial, Ripley argued, was in the judge's definition of self-defense in his charge to the jury. "[T]o excuse the defendant, and therefore acquit him," the trial judge had stated, "the evidence ought to be such as to have reasonably satisfied the defendant that the deceased, at the time of the killing, was doing some overt act, or making some demonstration showing a present intention to carry such threats into execution."[76]

Caruthers found no error in this charge. Indeed, he lashed out at defendants such as Ripley who attempted to use the Grainger precedent to expand their right to kill in self-defense. "[N]o case has been more perverted and misapplied by advocates and juries," he wrote. "We have had one case before us in the last few years, in which [the argument that knowledge of violent threats against the life of the defendant gave him the right to kill his foe on sight] was charged as law. But for this, and the indications that it has obtained to some limited extent in the legal profession, it would scarcely be deemed necessary to notice it. There is no authority for such a position. It would be monstrous. No court should for a moment entertain or countenance it. The criminal code of no country ever has, nor, as we presume, ever will, give place to so bloody a principle." Caruthers reiterated that the danger of bodily harm needed to be "real, or honestly believed to be so at the time," "upon sufficient grounds," and "apparent and imminent."[77] The Court thus finally put to rest the meaning of self-defense in Tennessee.

The Tennessee Supreme Court did all within its power to end the widespread violence and killing that characterized antebellum southern society. In addition to formulating a strict notion of self-defense, judges upheld the constitutionality of a law banning the carrying of a concealed bowie knife, despite a defendant's claims that such a law violated the Tennessee Constitution's provision regarding the right to keep and bear arms. And in a subsequent case the Court broadly construed the meaning of this statute and upheld the conviction of a man who had been arrested for fighting and carrying a large knife similar to a bowie knife. The wearing of knives, Judge Turley wrote in support of the statute, "had proven to be extremely dangerous and destructive to human life; the carrying of which by truculent and evil disposed persons but too often ended in assassination."[78] Though they faced an uphill battle, the judges thus sought to end murder and mayhem in Tennessee.

NEW JUDGES AND JUDICIAL ELECTION, 1847–1854

During the late 1840s and early 1850s, the Tennessee Supreme Court entered a period of transition. Judges Green, Turley, and Reese retired from the bench to engage in other pursuits, so that by the end of 1852 none of these judicial giants remained on the Court. At the same time, Tennesseans debated the method of selecting their judiciary. Successive legislatures and governors expressed support for turning the process over to the voters of the state, and in 1853 Tennesseans ratified an amendment requiring popular election of all Supreme Court and inferior court judges. Thus, both the composition of the Court and the constitutional method of judicial selection underwent significant changes.

In 1847, the twelve-year judicial terms of Green, Turley, and Reese expired, and legislative elections for all three seats were held. Green, the longest serving and still the most popular of the three, had little difficulty winning a second term. With only token opposition, Green won on the first ballot with ninety-six of the ninety-seven votes cast in both houses of the General Assembly. On November 1, 1847, the senate declared him duly elected to the Supreme Court. Turley too won reelection, but he faced some opposition. Milton Brown and George W. Gibbs garnered enough support to prevent Turley from winning a majority of votes until the fourteenth ballot. On November 3, after two days of maneuvering and voting, the senate declared Turley the victor with fifty-one votes, compared to Brown's thirty-nine and Gibbs's eleven.[79]

Hoping to win a seat in the United States Senate, Judge Reese declined to run for election to another term on the bench, thus leaving the Eastern Division seat open. Spencer Jarnigan, whose term in the U.S. Senate had just expired, Robert H. Hynds, Thomas C. Lyon, and William H. Sneed were immediately nominated for the vacant judicial post. Robert J. McKinney, a Knoxville lawyer and partner of Sneed, although not formally nominated, received two votes on the first ballot, including that of the eminent lawyer Return J. Meigs. McKinney had already written a letter in support of Sneed's candidacy and even informed Meigs that he was not interested in the judgeship. Ignoring McKinney's wishes, Meigs persisted in pushing him for the position, and after the fifth ballot Meigs officially placed McKinney's name in nomination. After Sneed's name was withdrawn after the eighth ballot, McKinney's candidacy gained momentum, and by the twelfth ballot he finished second only to Lyon. No candidate having yet received a majority, lawmakers prepared for a thirteenth ballot, during which time Landon C. Haynes, the legislator who had initially nominated Lyon, dramatically announced that he was withdrawing Lyon's name from the race. This prompted many members of the legislature to switch their votes to McKinney, who won with fifty-three of ninety-five votes cast.[80]

McKinney took his seat on the Supreme Court during the December Term 1847. Born in County Coleraine, Ireland, in 1803, McKinney and his family came to the United States in 1809, settling initially in Philadelphia and later migrating to Rogersville in Hawkins County, Tennessee. There the young McKinney grew up in humble circumstances, worked on the family farm, and gained limited schooling during the winter months. He attended Greeneville College for a short time, although never graduated, and later studied law with his uncle, John A. McKinney, in Rogersville. Licensed to practice in 1824, McKinney was too poor to own a horse and ride the entire First Judicial Circuit, so early in his career he attended court sessions only in Hawkins, Greene, and Washington Counties. In 1826 he settled in Greeneville and became known as a lawyer for his logical and precise arguments, "occasionally tinctured with something approaching to sarcasm and irony."[81] He served as the delegate from Greene County to the Constitutional Convention of 1834 and also as an elector for Hugh Lawson White from the state at large in the presidential election of 1836. McKinney later moved to Knoxville, where he entered into partnership with Sneed, became an elder in the Presbyterian Church, and earned a professional reputation that led to his election to the Court. Serious and methodical as a judge, McKinney often dealt sternly and severely with members of the bar. Himself shy, he thought attorneys should "avoid everything at all approaching to a superfluity of illustration" and proved "diligent, painstaking, and unrelaxing" in his duties.[82] McKinney, Green, and Turley thus made up the Court from 1847 to 1850.

During the same session at which legislators elected the new Supreme Court, the issue of the method of judicial selection arose. Not since the Constitutional Convention of 1834 had Tennesseans seriously debated this question, but in 1847 David W. Ballew, a representative from McMinn County, proposed an amendment to the state Constitution that provided that "the qualified voters of the state" elect "the Judges of such inferior Courts as the Legislature may establish." Ballew's amendment passed in the house but failed to receive enough votes in the senate to move forward.[83] Although the proposed amendment did not apply to Supreme Court judges, Ballew's proposal sparked renewed debate over judicial selection that ultimately included the method of selecting members of the state's high court.

Tennessee newspapers in particular kept the issue of judicial reform alive during the next few years. In the spring of 1849, the Democratic *Nashville Union* pointed out, for example, that the experience of other states with popular judicial election had demonstrated how well such a practice worked. Tennessee's system of election by the legislature seemed corrupt in comparison. "We can conceive of no spectacle more humiliating than that of a candidate for Judge lounging for months about the lobbies of the Legislature, dogging members in their seats and in their rooms, seeking to make arrangements and combinations, and resorting to all the usual appliances and intrigues which mark the Legislative elections," the *Union* announced. Describing the whole process as having "degenerated into a species of log-rolling and bargaining," the paper proclaimed its support for popularly elected state judges in order to preserve republican principles. An independent judiciary, the *Union* reasoned, was necessary only in a monarchy, in order to protect the interests of the people: "But in a republic, the people themselves rule, and therefore do not need an independent judiciary to protect themselves." The voters, this Democratic newspaper concluded, were perfectly capable of choosing the state's judges.[84]

By the fall of 1849, political momentum in Tennessee sped rapidly toward mandating popular election of all state judges. The *Union* continued its push in an editorial just before the opening of the 1849 legislative session. The newspaper argued that "no person should be allowed to hold an office contrary to the wishes of those upon whom the power is to operate" and criticized Whig newspapers for keeping relatively silent on the issue.[85] Despite the *Union*'s condemnation of Whig inaction, support for popular judicial election arose from both parties. Little more than a week into the session, on October 9, 1849, Whig senator Abraham Tipton and Democratic representative Jacob Adcock proposed nearly identical amendments in their respective houses of the legislature that would mandate popular election of all inferior court judges and attorneys general for the state. The House Judiciary Committee, chaired by Democrat Edwin Polk, promptly reported favorably on the idea of popular election. The committee report criticized the existing system of legislative election of judges and attorneys general as "the worst possible mode of electing those officers." "The electing body is small," the report stated, "and there is great inducement for combination and influence to operate, and that, too, with the best intention, frequently at war with what should be the true tests in such elections—the merit and qualifications of the aspirant." The report of the judiciary committee dismissed the notion that popular election would politicize the court system. To the contrary, the report hailed popular election as the best means of institutionalizing selection based on merit. "We have no fear of the purity of the ermine being contaminated by popular contact," the report read. "The minds of the people would be tuned to those persons best qualified to fill those stations, and party influences . . . would become to be disregarded in a great degree where the dearest interests of the people would be involved." A week after the issuance of the committee report, in his message to the legislature, Democratic governor William Trousdale added his support to the movement toward popular election of judges.[86]

As discussion of the proposed amendment continued over the following weeks, Whig representative Edmund Cooper of Bedford County moved to alter the proposed amendment by adding Supreme Court judges to the list of those subject to election by the voters. Although house members twice postponed consideration of Cooper's addendum, on November 30, 1849, House Judiciary Committee chair Polk introduced a similar amendment providing that "the judges of the supreme court shall be elected by the qualified voters of the state at large." In addition, Polk's amendment reduced the length of supreme court judges' terms from twelve years to eight. This measure passed. As amended, the house accepted the proposed constitutional amendment on December 3, 1849, and the senate gave its approval on February 1, 1850.[87] Under the amending process spelled out in the Tennessee Constitution, all amendments needed to win approval by two-thirds vote in the next legislative session before submission to the voters. Accordingly, in November 1851 the resolution to amend the Constitution passed by a vote of seventy-two to one in the house and unanimously in the senate. In its final form, the amendment promised to make the state judiciary more responsive to public opinion: "The Judges of the Supreme Court shall be elected by the qualified voters of the State at large, and the Judges of such inferior courts as the Legislature may establish, shall be elected by the qualified voters residing within the bounds of any district or circuit. . . . Judges of the Supreme Court . . . shall be elected for the term of eight years." Having at last received the approval of the legislature, the proposed amendment then went before the people of the state.[88]

By the summer of 1853, popular election of the state's judiciary seemed a foregone conclusion. Because the amendments had received such widespread support in the legislature and because voters were more interested in the governor's race, the state's newspapers devoted little attention to the upcoming vote on the amendment. In a few brief editorials, the *Nashville Union* expressed its strong support and again accused Whig newspapers of timidly backing the measure.[89] In the meantime, the nonpartisan, "independent" *Nashville Gazette* provided the most extensive and enthusiastic coverage of the vote. Again citing other states' successes with an elected judiciary, the *Gazette* argued popular election would produce the most qualified judiciary and would "infuse a high confidence in the tribunal among the people." Labeling the few opponents of the amendment as "bitter and disappointed politicians, the old anti-progressives, and the leaches that hung fast to high emoluments and small services," the *Gazette* urged approval of the measure and lashed out against the existing judicial selection process for: "Let every man, then, come forward today, and record his vote in favor of the election of Judges by the people, and let tonight's sun go down, for the last time, upon this relic of by-gone days, and oppressive monarchy, and tomorrow's sun rise upon our State regenerated and redeemed."[90] On August 4, 1853, Tennessee voters approved the amendment by a wide margin. During the next legislative session, in January 1854, the General Assembly provided for the election of Supreme Court judges to occur on the fourth Thursday of May 1854.[91]

By the time the legislature and the voters had approved the judicial election amendment, the Supreme Court had already undergone more changes in its personnel. Judges McKinney, Green, and Turley had served together since 1847, but in April 1850 Turley resigned from the Court. Owing in part to his conflict with Green and also to his desire to settle in West Tennessee, after fifteen years on the Supreme Court Turley accepted the position of judge of the Common Law and Chancery Court at Memphis. According to Albert Marks, the impatient Turley was perhaps better suited to the work of a trial judge, for "it was irksome to him to go over in consultation the same ground over which his rapidly moving mind had carried him during the argument of a case." Turley served in this position for a short period until his accidental death. In May 1851, the *Memphis Daily Appeal* reported that, "stepping from the door of the hotel at Raleigh, he fell, and his cane, being broken, pierced his left side near the region of the heart, inflicting a terrible wound of which he died."[92] To fill the Western Division position on the Court, in 1850 the legislature elected A. W. O. Totten, a native of Overton County, Tennessee, who had lived much of his life in Trenton before settling in Jackson.[93]

After Turley's departure, it was not long before the last of the three great antebellum jurists of Tennessee retired as well. In 1852, Nathan Green, a member of the Court for twenty-one years, stepped down to accept a professorship in the Law Department of Cumberland University at Lebanon. Fearing that age would impair his usefulness on the bench, the sixty-year-old Green began devoting his efforts to educating the next generation of lawyers. Joining with the school's founder, Abraham Caruthers, as well as fellow professor Bromfield L. Ridley, Green helped to build the law school during these early years of its history and his reputation helped attract students from throughout Tennessee and the South.[94] Despite his renown as a jurist, many Tennesseans harshly criticized him in 1858 for publicly announcing his belief that Congress had the Constitutional authority to prohibit slavery in the territories and the District of Columbia. A few years later he opposed secession, but he nevertheless supported the South when the Civil War began, and he even unsuccessfully sought a seat in the Confederate Congress. After the war, in the spring of 1866, Green began efforts to resuscitate the law school, which had ceased operation in wartime, but he died on March 30, 1866.[95] Upon Green's retirement, Governor William B. Campbell appointed Robert L. Caruthers to serve from the Middle Division on the Court, and the legislature officially elected him on November 11, 1853.[96]

Caruthers took his seat on the Court during the September Term, 1852. Born in 1800 in Smith County, Tennessee, Caruthers grew up in humble circumstances. His mother died when he was two years old, and his father later became an invalid before his death in 1813. The young Caruthers then lived with his uncle for a few years before working as a day laborer and store clerk. In 1820 he entered Greeneville College, where he completed a year of study before reading law in the office of Judge Samuel Powell, a circuit judge in Greeneville. Caruthers began his law practice in Carthage but later moved to Lebanon in Wilson County. In 1823 he became clerk of the state house of representatives, briefly edited a newspaper in Carthage and in 1827 began serving as attorney general for the circuit, which included Lebanon. His professional career thus established, Caruthers compiled an impressive public record. He represented Wilson County in the legislature in 1835, published a compilation of state statutes with A. O. P. Nicholson in 1836, and served a term in the United States Congress from 1841 to 1843. In 1842 Caruthers took a leading role in founding Cumberland University in Lebanon, and in 1847 he joined with his brother Abraham in establishing the law school there.[97] Renowned as a lawyer, Caruthers was by most accounts "almost invincible before a jury."[98] His reputation as an advocate, social standing as a Cumberland Presbyterian elder, and distinguished record of public service made him a strong choice for the Court upon Green's retirement.

By 1854 the Tennessee Supreme Court had undergone dramatic changes. That year the legislature increased the salary of Supreme Court judges from eighteen hundred to twenty-five hundred per year.[99] The original members of the Court under the 1835 Constitution had all retired, and the Court as an institution had become subject to popular election. Judges Reese, Turley, and Green had lent stability to the Court by dominating its early history, and Judges McKinney and Caruthers would play similar roles until 1861. Judicial leadership, of course, would prove essential in the stormy years that lay ahead.

SLAVERY AND SECTIONALISM, 1835–1860

Slavery and the sectional conflict dominated much of the political and legal debate in antebellum Tennessee. The institution of slavery had played a role in the state's history from the beginning, although not until the opening of West Tennessee during the 1810s did the slave population experience rapid growth. On the eve of the Civil War, slaves constituted about one-fourth of the state's total population, a moderate proportion compared to the percentage of slaves in other southern states. The demographics of slavery varied widely in Tennessee: in the eastern part of the state slaves constituted only about 9 percent of the population; in West Tennessee slaves made up 34 percent of the population, and in some counties slaves outnumbered whites; in Middle Tennessee slaves accounted for 29 percent of the population, but two-thirds of slave owners there had fewer than ten slaves each. As the issue of slavery and its expansion into new western territories entered national political debate during the 1840s and 1850s, most white Tennesseans joined their fellow southerners in defending slavery as essential to the region's economy and way of life. At the same time, conflict within Tennessee—among the state's three distinct regions—became more pronounced. The cotton-producing plantation counties of the Mississippi Delta, as well as the rich basin counties and tobacco producing areas of Middle Tennessee, took a strongly "pro-southern" position during the sectional conflict and secession crisis. In contrast, East Tennessee—dominated by nonslaveholding yeomen—took issue with the rest of the state on the issues of slavery and disunion. The eastern portion of the state served as home to twenty-five antislavery societies totaling a thousand members as late as 1827, and most East Tennesseans vehemently opposed secession in 1861.[100]

Tennessee had enjoyed a liberal reputation with regard to the legal treatment of slaves, but events during the early 1830s intensified white Tennesseans' fears of insurrection and led to tighter legal controls. On January 1, 1831, William Lloyd Garrison, a Baptist minister in Massachusetts, published the first issue of his abolitionist newspaper, the *Liberator.* Garrison attacked slavery as a moral evil that needed to be eradicated immediately and soon formed the American Anti-Slavery Society to accomplish this end. That August, a literate and deeply religious slave named Nat Turner led an unsuccessful slave revolt in Southampton County, Virginia, that claimed the lives of fifty-five whites. These two episodes prompted states across the South to formulate new regulations regarding slavery and emancipation. In 1831, the Tennessee General Assembly enacted laws establishing procedures for local slave patrols, providing penalties for conspiracy to rebel, banning migration of free blacks into the state, and prohibiting emancipation of slaves except upon their removal from the state. Finally, an 1835 incident prompted further action on the part of the legislature. Amos Dresser, an Ohioan and a member of the American Anti-Slavery Society, arrived in Nashville to "sell Bibles" to support his seminary education. When authorities discovered that he was carrying abolitionist literature, he was arrested and interrogated by a local vigilance committee before being whipped and banished from the city. The following year, the Tennessee legislature attempted to halt abolitionist activity by banning "the publication or circulation . . . of seditious pamphlets and papers."[101]

A few years later, the Tennessee Supreme Court upheld the state's restrictions on migration of free blacks into the state, and, in the process, ruled that free blacks were not citizens within the meaning of the U.S. Constitution. In *State v. Claiborne* (1838), Judge Green concluded that free blacks "have always been a degraded race in the United States." Foreshadowing the United States Supreme Court's decision in *Dred Scott v. Sandford* almost twenty years later, Green concluded that though free blacks enjoyed "the fruits of their own labor," they had been "deprived of almost every other privilege of the free citizen, and constituting an inferior caste in society, with whom public opinion has never permitted the white population to associate on terms of equality." Similarly, he held, the Tennessee Constitution's guarantees of the rights of "freeman" did not include free blacks. Green viewed the restrictive law as wise policy, for he noted the potential problem of such individuals coming into the state "whose characters are unknown, and from whom there may be greater dangers."[102]

Although the Court never revisited the issue of the ban on free black migration into the state, during the 1840s, as fears of slave uprising subsided, both the legislature and the Court took steps to loosen restrictions regarding emancipation of Tennessee slaves. In 1842 lawmakers essentially reversed the 1831 law banning emancipation without removal by giving a county court the power to allow a slave manumitted by his owner to remain in Tennessee. The Court in many instances during the 1840s upheld the slaves' right to freedom in such cases. Always respectful of the desires of masters and the work of these local courts, the Supreme Court often gave eloquent testimony to slaves' right to sue for their freedom. The Court, however, effectuated manumission only if the master intended to free a slave and only if the local court had acted positively to support emancipation.[103]

One case in particular demonstrated the Court's willingness to interpret the master's wishes in support of emancipation. In *Elias v. Smith* (1845), the Court granted freedom to slaves even in the absence of written or oral declarations of a slave owner's intention because "the acts and conduct of the master" indicated such a desire. Elias, a free black man, was married to Tenor, a slave belonging to Phelps Read. Elias and Read had agreed that Elias could live with his wife and child until the child reached the age of ten, at which time the boy would be returned to his owner. Upon Read's death, the administrators of his estate assured Elias that he would be able to purchase his wife and infant son for a small amount, and Elias subsequently bought them for ten dollars. Some time later a creditor attempted to force Elias to sell his wife and child to satisfy a debt owed by Elias, but Elias asked the courts to prevent the sale "on the ground that the title to the slaves was vested in him for the purpose of emancipating them, and that they were entitled to their freedom, and not subject to his debts." In rendering the decision, Judge Reese saw the issue as a moral one. Had Elias been "a barbarian and monster" and sold his wife and child for his advantage, "is there a chancery court in Christendom, having jurisdiction over such a trust, which would not have promptly interposed . . . and enjoined him from perpetrating against them so flagrant a wrong?" As the creditor sought the same result "in a case little short in its enormity of that supposed," Reese sided with Elias to prevent the sale.[104]

By the end of the decade, a series of national events altered the political landscape in Tennessee and the nation. During the presidential administration of Tennessean James K. Polk, just after the start of the Mexican-American War in 1846, David Wilmot, a Pennsylvania congressman, had offered an amendment to a house appropriations bill that would have banned the introduction of slavery into any territory acquired from Mexico. The Wilmot Proviso, as it was called, ignited the flames of sectional tension. Although it never passed, for nearly four year after its introduction the amendment polarized Congress and the country along sectional lines. By 1850, fears that the proviso might pass and be signed into law by President Zachary Taylor prompted worried southerners to call a meeting of representatives from southern states in Nashville. By the time the delegates from nine states had assembled, however, a resolution to the sectional crisis was in the works. The Compromise of 1850—which provided concessions acceptable to northern and southern interests on such issues as fugitive slaves and slavery in the territories—eventually passed, and sectional conflict faded temporarily from the national stage.[105]

Tennessee again tightened its emancipation laws in the midst of this crisis. In 1849 the legislature reimplemented the 1831 restriction that a slave could only be emancipated upon leaving Tennessee. The Court, therefore, again had to adjust its decision making to the new policy. "It is a vexed and perplexing question, upon which public opinion, acting upon the representatives of the people," Judge Caruthers noted in an 1853 case, "has been subject to much vibration between sympathy and humanity for the slave and the safety and well being of society. Hence the frequent changes in our legislation on the subject."[106]

With the passage of the 1849 restrictions, the Supreme Court struggled to fulfill testators' aims of granting freedom for their slaves while upholding state policy mandating removal from Tennessee. Many testators granted freedom to their slaves without specific regard to where they would go upon emancipation. When provisions of a will conflicted with the policies of the state, the Court held that the testator's primary purpose—granting freedom for slaves—needed to be affirmed, despite legislative restrictions preventing emancipation within the state. Where a will discharged a person from all obligations to the heirs or distributees of the testator, the slave was free. As Judge Turley proclaimed in one case, "A devise of freedom is a substantive thing, whether it be recognized by the state or not." Such decisions ameliorated the legislature's strict policy and sanctioned "a kind of intermediate state, between freedom and slavery, which it is difficult to manage and regulate," according to Judge Caruthers. These decisions thus created a class of "nominal slaves" in Tennessee—a group of individuals who were free from the perspective of their masters but not in the eyes of the law.[107]

In 1854, a few years after the publication of the abolitionist novel *Uncle Tom's Cabin,* Tennessee lawmakers attempted to solve this problem once and for all by making freedom conditional on emigration to Liberia, a stance many southern states took during the 1850s. Judge Caruthers praised the new policy in *Boone v. Lancaster* (1854), another case where a testator's desires to free his slaves conflicted with the policy of the state.[108] "By the act of the last session these difficulties are mostly removed, and our laws made consistent and sensible on this subject," he wrote. "The struggle has been to devise some plan which would be just to the slave, and not inconsistent with the interests of society—that would sustain his right to liberty, and at the same time save the community from the evils of a free negro population." This "wise and judicious plan," he noted, superseded all other legislation on the subject and "took from the owners and the courts all discretion on the subject." The only way the slave in the case could attain his freedom, in short, was by removal to Africa. "There is no alternative," Caruthers wrote.[109] The Court thus joined the legislature in terminating the existence of an intermediate state between slavery and freedom. All subsequently emancipated slaves would have to be removed to Liberia.

The Tennessee Supreme Court earned a reputation among contemporaries and, lately, among historians, for judicial liberality and humanitarianism in its treatment of slaves. This is understandable. The Court consistently upheld the procedural rights of slaves in criminal cases and joined only the North Carolina court in ruling that the homicide of a white man by a slave could be reduced to manslaughter.[110] Moreover, in emancipation cases, Tennessee's judges exhibited a rhetorical commitment to liberty unequaled in the supreme courts of the Old South. Tennessee judges frequently acknowledged the slave's humanity, and Judge Green in particular gained a reputation for eloquence. "A slave is not in the condition of a horse or an ox. . . . [H]e is made after the image of the Creator," Green wrote in *Ford v. Ford*

(1846). "He has mental capacities and an immortal principle in his nature that constitute him equal to his owner but for the accidental position in which fortune has placed him."[111] Despite such lofty expressions, the Court—as all southern supreme courts—had the difficult task of reconciling a variety of competing moral impulses and external pressures. The desires of masters, the spirit of humanitarianism, the interests of white society, and the policy of the legislature all entered into the decision-making process. For these reasons, judicial rhetoric only went so far in ameliorating the conditions of slaves.

By 1860–61 the political situation in the United States and Tennessee reached a breaking point. In 1859, abolitionist John Brown led a raid on a federal arsenal in Harper's Ferry, Virginia, in an attempt to begin the violent overthrow of slavery. Brown's actions struck fear in the hearts of white southerners, who worried that such radical idealism would spread throughout the North. The political expression of such radicalism—to wary white southerners—was the new Republican Party, represented in the 1860 presidential campaign by Abraham Lincoln. Lincoln and his party pledged not to interfere with slavery where it already existed, but many southerners viewed Republican opposition to the extension of slavery and the U.S. Supreme Court's recent decision in *Dred Scott v. Sandford* as evidence of their opposition to slavery and the southern way of life. So hated and feared in the South were Lincoln and his party that the candidate's name did not even appear on the ballot in the southern states. Tennesseans had a choice of voting for any of the other three candidates: northern Democrat Stephen Douglas, southern Democrat John Breckinridge, or fellow Tennessean and Constitutional Union candidate John Bell. Although Bell carried Tennessee by a slight margin over Breckinridge, the moderate Constitutional Unionist won only three states nationwide—all Upper South or border slave states. With 39 percent of the popular vote, Lincoln won the election by winning the electoral votes of every free state.[112]

Despite Lincoln's election and the subsequent secession of seven Deep South states, Tennesseans generally hoped for compromise and conciliation. In a February 1861 secession referendum, voters opposed the calling of a secession convention by 55 to 45 percent. But these overall numbers masked the sharp divisions within the state on this subject. Almost three-quarters of West Tennesseans voted *for* a secession convention, while East Tennesseans cast 81 percent of their votes *against* a convention. Voters in the middle portion of the state were almost evenly divided, as 51 percent opposed secession.[113]

The judges of the Supreme Court were also divided on the issue of secession. Judge McKinney, from East Tennessee, initially opposed secession and received an appointment from Governor Isham G. Harris to attend the Peace Conference in Washington in February 1861 to attempt to resolve the sectional crisis.[114] Judge Caruthers, from Middle Tennessee, also served as a delegate to the Peace Conference in 1861, but he took a more pro-southern position by arguing there for the right of southerners to "go into all the Territories with our southern property."[115] Archibald Wright, the West Tennessee judge who had taken his seat on the Court in 1858, avidly supported secession from the start.[116] Not until after the Battle of Fort Sumter and Lincoln's call for troops to suppress the rebellion did Tennessee opt for secession from the Union. Even then, the vote in favor of seceding continued to reflect the divisions within the state, as East Tennesseans overwhelmingly supported remaining in the federal Union. When Tennessee cast its lot with the South, McKinney became a reluctant backer of the Confederacy, thus joining his colleagues in support of the southern cause.

THE WAR AND THE COURT, 1861–1865

During the Civil War, the experience of the Tennessee Supreme Court reflected the chaos and disorder that so characterized the state's history during the conflict. Secession from the Union, the clash of armies, and a succession of governors all took their toll on a tribunal that had accomplished so much in achieving recognition and respect before the war. The personnel of the Court changed continually, and the judges failed to meet at all from spring 1862 to fall 1865. Not since three decades earlier, when legislators had debated whether a court should even exist, had the Court experienced such a low point.

The Court's troubles began immediately after secession. Judge Robert Caruthers resigned his seat on the bench to accept a position in the new Confederate Congress, where he became the first Tennessean to take his seat. In the meantime, Governor Harris appointed Edwin H. Ewing to fill the vacancy until a statewide election could be held in October 1861. Ewing's tenure was brief. He served only during the September Term before being replaced by William F. Cooper of Nashville, who won election to the Middle Tennessee seat. Cooper served on the Court only during its December 1861 Term, the last term during which all the judges were present until after the war.[117]

Unlike in other states in the South, where civilian courts continued to operate during the war, military conflict brought the operation of the state Supreme Court to a halt in Tennessee. Because the state stretched from the Appalachians to the Mississippi and lay just south of Unionist-leaning Kentucky, Tennessee became a principal battleground of the war. Albert Sydney Johnston, chosen as "General Commanding the Western Department of the Confederate States of America" in 1861, attempted to establish a "Line of the Cumberland" to defend the state and all of the western Confederacy. However, inadequate weapons and supplies, as well as a lack of coordination in the production of gunpowder and transportation of foodstuffs, weakened Johnston's already thin defensive line of troops. Vulnerable to Union attack, Tennessee and the Confederacy suffered crushing defeats in February 1862 at the Battles of Forts Henry and Donelson, thus allowing federal troops to take over Nashville and plan further attacks to the west and south. A few months later, Confederates lost another key battle at Shiloh, where General Johnston died, and in June 1862 federal troops occupied Memphis, by then the state's largest city. By the middle of 1862 all of Middle and West Tennessee had fallen under Union control, and Governor Isham Harris and other state officials fled to the safety of Confederate lines in Mississippi.[118] Despite these federal victories, the fate of East Tennessee remained in doubt. For the next two years, Unionists and Confederates battled for control of the mountainous, pro-Union portion of the state, with the Confederates having the upper hand.

Despite a strong Confederate military presence in East Tennessee, by the first Monday in March 1862 only Judge McKinney showed up for a special term of the Supreme Court in Knoxville. He continued to appear each day that week in anticipation of his colleagues' appearance, but after five days as the sole judge present, McKinney adjourned the Court. Judge Wright, by that time, had already taken to the battlefield. "Too old to carry a musket," a eulogist later noted, "he spent the four years of the war with the armies in the field, seeking to infuse his strong spirit of resistance into all who came within his reach." With two sons fighting for the Confederacy, Wright wanted to be in the middle of the action. "There was no better figure in the Army of Tennessee than that of Judge Wright, mounted on a large gray mule, wearing his red bandanna in his mouth, and always found near the thunder of his son's battery," one contemporary noted.[119] Judge Cooper, the other absent member of the Court, perhaps had difficulty making his way from Union-occupied Middle Tennessee to Knoxville. No judges appeared for the April Term 1862 in Jackson, nor did any show up for the September Term in Knoxville. The clerk of the Court having died, a deputy clerk opened and closed the Knoxville session daily from September 8 to September 13. Finally, "being fully satisfied that a quorum of said Judges cannot be had at this term," the clerk declared the Court adjourned. The Tennessee Supreme Court officially ceased operation at that point, and the state's pro-Confederate government teetered on the verge of collapse.[120]

Rather than allow federal troops to rule the state, in March 1862 President Abraham Lincoln appointed Unionist Democrat and U.S. senator Andrew Johnson military governor of Tennessee. Johnson's effectiveness hinged on Union military success in the state, but his main concern throughout his stormy tenure was with restoring civil authority. Controversies surrounding suffrage rights and loyalty oaths, in addition to open hostility from secessionist elements and the Confederate army, hindered Johnson's ability to make progress toward this end.[121] Some county and circuits courts in Middle Tennessee began operating in the spring of 1862, and the U.S. Circuit Court reopened under the leadership of Unionist U.S. Supreme Court Justice John Catron (formerly of the Tennessee Supreme Court) in May of that year. Still, the restoration of civil authority proved difficult. Confederate forces retained control of East Tennessee until the fall of 1863, and Confederate General John B. Hood threatened Nashville—from which Johnson tried to govern—through much of 1864. Moreover, during this period civil courts often competed with military courts that operated under the direct control of Union generals, and the jurisdictional lines between these courts often overlapped.[122]

After the final defeat of Confederate forces in Tennessee at the Battles of Franklin and Nashville at the end of 1864, Johnson moved to reconstitute all civil authority in the state. With Johnson's approval, in January 1865 some five hundred Unionist Tennesseans—most from East Tennessee—assembled in Nashville. The convention, although originally called as a preliminary body to lay the groundwork for postwar Tennessee, ended up assuming authority over the state's new government. Delegates approved a state constitutional amendment abolishing slavery, as well as a "schedule to the amendments" that included several matters of policy. This schedule basically voided secession and the acts of the legislature during the war, approved the civil and military appointments of Governor Johnson, and granted to the first General Assembly to meet under the revised Constitution the power to determine "the qualifications of voters and the limits of the elective franchise."[123] As one of his last acts as military governor before assuming the vice presidency under Abraham Lincoln, Johnson attempted to reestablish nearly all civil courts in the state, including the Supreme Court. On January 25, 1865, he commissioned three new judges of the Tennessee Supreme Court. However, this court never met, nor did its judges render any decisions.[124]

Not until a new governor took office did the Court again begin functioning. After statewide elections in March, Parson William Brownlow assumed the governorship of the state on April 5, 1865, just days before the final surrender of the Confederacy. A Methodist minister and Whig newspaper editor from Knoxville, Brownlow was known for his vituperative partisanship and devotion to the Union. A longtime political enemy of Johnson, Brownlow had set aside his political differences with the Democrat during the war in order to promote the cause of the Union. Johnson, in turn, had lent support to Brownlow's gubernatorial candidacy.[125] Upon assuming office, Brownlow declared the supreme bench vacant and appointed new judges, although he did retain one of Johnson's nominees, Sam Milligan. James O. Shackelford and Alvin Hawkins also received appointments from Brownlow.[126] All of these men, of course, had staunchly supported the Union during the War. Milligan, a Democrat and chief political lieutenant of Johnson's, had himself worked as an newspaper editor in East Tennessee and served as a delegate to the Peace Conference of 1861. Shackelford, a former Whig from Middle Tennessee, had played an important role in the constitutional convention earlier that year. Hawkins, a native of West Tennessee and also a former Whig, had served as U.S. district attorney in Tennessee under Governor Johnson.[127] The war and the new political order it created had revolutionized the Court.

The period stretching from the 1830s through the end of the American Civil War was one of the most significant in Tennessee history. White Tennesseans had entered the era with great optimism. The hero of the Battle of New Orleans and favorite son of Tennessee, Andrew Jackson, occupied the White House when the period began, and by the end of Old Hickory's presidency, a majority of the state's population—white, agricultural, rural, evangelical, and politically aware—looked forward to many prosperous days ahead in the young Republic. During this era, the Court opened new lands to white settlement by sanctioning President Jackson's and Tennessee's Cherokee removal policy, while it attempted to further economic expansion and create a moral order by promoting the development of railroads and regulating public and private morality.

By 1865, another Tennessean—the tailor from Greeneville, Andrew Johnson—was president and the nation had endured a bloody civil war. Despite the Court's record in affording a relatively high degree of legal protection to slaves, the national debate over slavery and secession thrust Tennessee's divided populace into war. When the fighting ceased, more than 150,000 Tennesseans had taken up arms, including 31,000 who had fought for the Union cause. Union victory vindicated East Tennesseans' political loyalties, gave hope and freedom to 275,000 slaves, and brought about a revolution in state government. Throughout this period of great change, the Tennessee Supreme Court worked to establish itself as a significant and autonomous institution within the state's legal and political order. The struggle to maintain judicial independence, however, was far from over.

3

THE TENNESSEE SUPREME COURT DURING RECONSTRUCTION AND REDEMPTION

R. Ben Brown

Tennessee's experience during the Civil War was unique. Eastern Tennessee remained heavily Unionist in its sympathies, so much so that the Confederate government never firmly established itself in that region. Both Middle and West Tennessee were sympathetic to the Confederacy, but large portions of these sections were under Federal occupation for much of the war. Even in those parts of Tennessee that were not under Federal occupation, the Confederate hold on Tennessee was never secure. Tennessee was second only to Virginia in the number of major battles fought on her land. From General Ulysses Grant's invasion of northern Tennessee in 1862 until the Battle of Nashville in December 1864, Tennesseans were never quite sure which regime they were living under.

The meaning of the chaos of war for the Tennessee legal system was that it basically ceased to exist during these three years. Civil courts stopped operating, and in many cases courthouses and legal documents were destroyed. Much of Tennessee was under martial law during these years, and even that law functioned only sporadically. Tennesseans learned to live in chaotic conditions. The authorities of one side or the other regularly authorized acts that would ordinarily be illegal, such as the confiscation of stock, foodstuffs, and weapons. Sometimes criminal depredations were committed by groups claiming martial authority, but the groups were actually taking advantage of the chaos of the war to loot and plunder for their own selfish ends. By the end of the war, the state was facing widespread devastation and pervasive poverty, material conditions that shaped the political and legal history of the state during Reconstruction.[1]

After the defeat of Gen. John B. Hood's forces in the Battle of Nashville, the federal government secured its hold on Tennessee. Military Governor Andrew Johnson was preparing to take his new position as vice president of United States. William G. Brownlow, his successor as governor, became the most important political figure in Tennessee for the next five years as the leader of the Radical Party. The political parties of the antebellum years, the Whigs and Democrats, were destroyed by the war. Although by the 1870s the Democrats and Republicans had established a new two-party system, during Reconstruction in Tennessee, the two loosely organized political parties were the Radicals, usually ex-Unionists who embraced the changes the war had brought, and the Conservatives, usually ex-Confederates who wanted to return to antebellum ways.

The Radicals took the initial step in reconstructing Tennessee by holding a Unionist convention in January 1865 to reestablish the state government and the legal system. The convention declared void the Act of Secession and all acts passed by the Tennessee legislature since that act. The convention gave the first General Assembly meeting after the convention the power to determine who would have the franchise. The convention also voted to hold a referendum allowing the voters to abolish slavery on February 22, 1865. The convention set March 4, 1865, as the date for an election for governor and the legislature. The low turnouts for this referendum, approximately 21,000, and the general election, approximately 23,000, indicated that the new government did not have widespread support. Both of these totals were fewer then the number of Union votes against secession in 1861 and far lower then the 145,000 votes cast in the 1860 presidential election. The government further limited its popular base when the new assembly met in April 1865 and denied the franchise to those who had supported the Confederacy. With neither African Americans nor former Confederates voting, the new government had a very narrow base of support.[2]

Despite the limited support for the government, the Tennessee Supreme Court began sitting again. The Court was reorganized as a three-member panel that Brownlow appointed. Not surprisingly, the Reconstruction Supreme Court was committed to the Radical cause. The judges saw their function as recreating Tennessee law, politics, economics, and society along Radical lines. As a result the role of the Supreme Court during the years of Reconstruction, and also during years following redemption, became heavily politicized. Throughout the United States in the nineteenth century, lawyers and judges were committed to the project of creating a separate sphere for law outside of and resistant to political impulses.[3] However, in the aftermath of the Civil War, Tennessee judges did not have the luxury of even pretending to pursue an objective rule of law. The result was a strongly politicized jurisprudence in which ordinary judicial virtues, such as a reverence for precedents, had no place.

The history of the Tennessee Supreme Court for the twenty years following the Civil War has two main phases, each phase ending with the Tennessee Supreme Court intervening in the major political issue of the day. The first period, from 1865 to 1870, saw a Radical Court protecting Unionists and freedmen from Conservative Rebel sympathizers. This phase ended, ironically, when a repudiated Court changed the franchise rules so as to allow the previously disfranchised ex-Confederates to vote in the 1869 election. The Conservatives rapidly consolidated their power and adopted a new Constitution in 1870. This Constitution restructured the Tennessee Supreme Court and allowed a Conservative panel to be elected to the bench in 1870.

This panel rapidly repudiated the Radical jurisprudence of the previous five years. Additionally, the Conservative judges cooperated with the politicians to begin creating a racist social system and the semi-serfdom of a crop-lien system. However, economic issues, especially the issue of taxation to pay off the burdensome state debt, split the Conservatives, now formed into a revitalized Democratic Party, and allowed a limited Republican revival. Twelve years after the Conservative Court was established, it too became embroiled in the major political issue of redemption politics, the question of adjusting the Tennessee state debt. The Court's rejection of the Republican compromise on this issue paved the way for a return to conservative Democratic rule in the 1880s.[4] In the judicial election of 1886, the Tennessee electorate replaced four of the five members of this Court. The electorate was no longer entranced by the older judges' strong ties to the Confederacy and instead desired a younger, more vital Court, that would turn away from issues of the past and begin structuring a new Tennessee, for a New South.

THE RADICAL COURT

Before examining some decisions of the Radical Supreme Court and its effects on Tennessee society, we should first look at the personnel of this Court. Because the line between politics and law grew especially thin during this period, the biographies, and especially the political backgrounds, of the justices are important to understanding the Supreme Court's rulings and its role in Tennessee government. Even though the 1853 amendment to the

Constitution of 1834 required that Tennessee Supreme Court justices be elected, only one election was held between 1865 and 1870.[5] Governor Brownlow took it upon himself to appoint the members of the Supreme Court with the exception of those elected in May 1869.

During the first years of Radical rule, from 1865 until 1867, the same three men sat on the Court. However, a period of turmoil began in 1868, during which year all three justices resigned. Governor Brownlow struggled to find men to sit on the Court. The September 1868 session had to be canceled because the personnel turnover left the Court without any judges. Finally, an election in May 1869 seated the last Radical panel. In August 1869 the voters elected a Conservative legislature that authorized a constitutional convention. The new Constitution restructured the Court and mandated elections in August 1870 at which time the enfranchised Conservative electorate voted in a Conservative Court.

The first Radical panel that sat after the Civil War consisted of Sam Milligan, Alvin Hawkins, and James O. Shackelford. None of these men had roots in the upper reaches of southern society before the war. In fact, two of them rose from decidedly humble beginnings. Sam Milligan[6] came from a very poor background. He only managed to go to school with the help of a benefactor. He read law with an attorney who later became a Supreme Court judge, Robert J. McKinney. After passing the bar he practiced law in Greeneville, Tennessee. In addition to practicing law, Milligan was elected to the legislature and was a major in the U.S. Army during the Mexican War.

In 1860 Milligan was a delegate to the Democratic convention in Charleston, South Carolina. During the 1860 election, he aligned himself with the southern wing and supported John C. Breckinridge. But when the question of secession arose, he remained a Unionist and joined forces with Andrew Johnson. Milligan made enemies among committed secessionists, and he eventually fled to Nashville to avoid being arrested by the Confederacy. In 1864 he became a clerk in the office of Andrew Johnson, the military governor, and in January 1865, Johnson appointed him to the Tennessee Supreme Court. Milligan served under this appointment until March 1867, when he resigned and was promptly reappointed by Governor Brownlow. Milligan remained close to President Andrew Johnson, who offered him different federal positions. In July 1868, President Johnson appointed Milligan to the United States Court of Claims. Milligan resigned from the Tennessee Supreme Court and moved to Washington until his death in 1874.[7]

Sitting on the bench with Milligan was Alvin Hawkins, who also came from poor circumstances. Born on December 2, 1821, in Carroll County, Hawkins worked as a blacksmith, a farmer, and a schoolteacher before he read for the law. Although he never attended college, he got his license and opened a practice in 1843. He became active in Whig politics and, ten years later, was elected to the state legislature. Opposed to secession, he was an elector for Bell, the Unionist, in the 1860 election. With the death of the Whig Party, Hawkins became a Republican.

In 1864, President Abraham Lincoln appointed Hawkins U.S. attorney for western Tennessee, but in 1865 Hawkins resigned his federal position to accept Governor Brownlow's appointment to the Supreme Court. Hawkins left the Court in 1868 to accept an appointment as consul to Cuba. He soon resigned that commission due to a yellow fever scare and returned to Tennessee, where he was reelected to the Supreme Court in the 1869 election. Hawkins was elected governor in 1881, and his attempt to readjust the state debt led to the second crucial intervention of the Supreme Court in Tennessee politics during this 1865–85 period, as we shall see in greater detail later.[8]

The third member of this first Radical panel was James O. Shackelford. Shackelford came from a somewhat higher social class than the other two justices, having been born to a Virginia family with a grandfather who had served under George Washington. After attending Transylvania University, he obtained a law license and began practicing in Dover, Tennessee. In the late 1830s he moved to Clarksville, where he practiced law until his appointment to the Supreme Court in 1865. He was also involved in Whig politics and later joined the Republican Party. Still, Shackleford remained loosely tied to the Southern cause and had one son killed at Gettysburg wearing Confederate gray. Brownlow appointed him to the bench in August 1865. Shackelford resigned from the Supreme Court to became chancellor of the Nashville District from February 1867 until December 1867. He was reappointed to the Supreme Court in late 1868.

The reasons for Shackelford's move to the chancery division are unclear but probably have to do with the chaotic politics of Reconstruction. The mayor of Nashville during this time was a northerner. He was under attack from the Conservatives, who, of course, accused him of being a carpetbagger and claimed that he was raiding the city treasury. One of the tactics the Conservatives used to try to oust the mayor was to request the Nashville Chancery Court to appoint a receiver for the city. Perhaps Brownlow appointed Shackelford to the chancellorship in order to forestall this attack. In any event, during Shackelford's term as chancellor he did rule on such a bill and denied the relief the Conservatives requested. However, the Conservatives made an end run around the Nashville chancellor and got the chancellor of Gallatin, Tennessee, to issue an injunction and place the city in the hands of receiver.[9]

When Shackelford left the bench to become chancellor, Shackelford's position was taken by Horace Harrison. Harrison had been the chancellor for the

Nashville District before he and Shackelford swapped jobs. Harrison was young, having been born in 1829. His father died when he was fifteen, forcing him to take a job in the county clerk's office of Warren County. He later became the deputy clerk and master of the McMinnville Chancery Court for seven years. He joined the Whigs and was elected clerk of the state senate by the Whig Party in 1851. In 1855 he was admitted to the bar. In 1859, at the age of thirty, he moved to Nashville. He opposed secession and remained loyal to the Union. Lincoln appointed him U.S. attorney for the Middle Division of Tennessee, and in 1866 he became the chancellor of the Nashville District. He took Shackelford's seat in 1867 but then resigned in September 1868 to pursue a presidential elector position in the 1868 election.[10]

In 1868 all three sitting justices resigned. The result was that there were no judges to hold the September 1868 session. Brownlow scrambled to find replacements. He reappointed Shackelford and appointed Horace Maynard, a Radical congressman. Maynard may have the distinction of being the only appointee of the Tennessee Supreme Court to never take his seat. He served out his congressional term and apparently won a third term and so never sat on the Supreme Court.[11]

Brownlow finally found two more men to join Shackelford and restaff the Supreme Court in time for the 1869 December Term. Henry G. Smith had been born in 1807 and raised in Connecticut. He moved to Tennessee in 1832 and finally to Memphis in 1842. He had been a staunch Unionist during the war. Although he had no prior political or judicial experience, he was probably the most respected lawyer appointed to the Court during Radical Reconstruction.[12] He had a solid reputation among the Memphis bar. Smith was joined by George Andrews, a Michigan lawyer who had moved to Knoxville in 1865. That Brownlow had to appoint someone who had lived in the state such a short time, and was obviously open to the charge of being a carpetbagger, indicates the difficulty he had finding a qualified appointee who also was a reliable Radical.[13]

This panel was short-lived. They were appointed in late 1868 and only one of them was reelected in the summer 1869 elections. However, as we will see in more detail below, the panel had tremendous significance in Tennessee history because of their ruling allowing the de facto enfranchisement of former Confederates—a ruling that led directly to the end of Reconstruction in Tennessee.

The final Radical panel in Tennessee was elected in the summer of 1869. Only Andrews of the sitting judges was reelected. Alvin Hawkins, who had returned from Cuba, was also reelected to the Supreme Court. One new member was added, Andrew McLain from Smith County, Tennessee. A member of the Republican Party, McLain had practiced law in Carthage, Tennessee. He was elected a circuit judge for the circuit embracing Smith County in 1864.[14]

The members of the Tennessee Supreme Court during the era of Radical Reconstruction reflected the politics of the times. Few of them had judicial experience prior to the war. Nor were they, with the possible exception of Henry G. Smith, recognized as leaders of the Tennessee Bar. Although many of them had had Whig political experience, none of them had been an outstanding politician. In short, the Reconstruction Supreme Court was staffed by non-elite second-tier lawyers and politicians. What these judges did have was a commitment to Radical politics and disdain for those who had thrown in their lot with the Confederacy. Their jurisprudence would reflect their politics.

THE JURISPRUDENCE OF RADICAL RECONSTRUCTION

The politics of the Radical Supreme Court justices expressed itself most forcefully in the Radical Court's decisions that denied any aspect of sovereignty to the Confederate government. The Court was determined to ratify judicially the military defeat of the Rebel government. In a series of contract decisions, the Radical Court took delight in refusing to enforce contracts that agents of the Confederacy had made in order to facilitate the functioning of the Confederate government or the Confederate army. The Court went even further in cases involving Confederate money, holding that such notes were invalid as consideration for contracts because any trafficking in Confederate currency aided and abetted the rebellion. The Court's failure to cite to precedents and its openly instrumentalist reasoning further evidences the political nature of these opinions.

In the 1865 December Term, the Court, sitting in Nashville, began to implement its Radical jurisprudence. Judge Milligan established the basic stance of the Radical Court in the case of *Wright and Cantrel v. Overall* (1865). The Confederacy, Judge Milligan proclaimed, had not even been a de facto government; therefore, the Confederacy had no power to issue bonds or treasury notes. The purpose of the war was to determine whether the Confederacy would be able to establish itself as a sovereign nation. The Federal victory had decided this question and courts of the United States should do nothing to undermine this victory. As Judge Milligan put it, to give any validity to Confederate money would "settle by judicial determination what the Confederate States failed to achieve by arms."[15] As the Confederacy had been unable to force the political departments of the United States to recognize its sovereignty, the courts must follow the lead of the political branches and deny that the Confederacy had any aspects of sovereignty.

Furthermore, Judge Milligan argued that if the Court acknowledged a de facto sovereignty in the Confederacy, this acknowledgment would lead to injustice. State courts were not bound to "execute the laws of an extinct insurgent power, enacted against the policy and authority of the United States, and expressly for its overthrow."[16] If the courts gave such recognition to the laws of the Confederacy, they would only be advantaging the insurgents themselves.

Milligan applied these principles to a simple legal problem. A plaintiff had sued for recovery on an eight-hundred-dollar promissory note. The defendants had paid only three hundred dollars on the note and that payment was in Confederate money. Milligan cited commercial law that held that payment of genuine bank notes, which both parties think are good, will bind the acceptor even if the bank notes turn out to be worthless. However, a payment in forged paper was worthless and the payer of the forged notes received no credit. Confederate money was even worse than forged money, because it was issued to further the overthrow of the United States, and therefore the payer should receive no credit for paying Confederate notes. Milligan, however, realized that this doctrine, if taken too far, could lead to commercial chaos. So he tempered his holding by announcing an "executed contract" exception: if the payment of Confederate notes had completely settled the contract obligation of the parties so that the rights of the parties have vested, then "for the repose of society" the Court would not disturb that transaction. Later cases would explore the gray area surrounding this doctrine.

The Radical Supreme Court also refused to give a legal remedy to those who did business with the Confederacy. In *Wood v. Stone* (1865), a Confederate captain purchased a rifle from Stone, giving a note for the price. After the war, Stone sued for the price of the rifle. The Circuit Court instructed the jury that both parties were living in an area controlled by the Confederacy and that because the United States had recognized the Confederacy as the belligerent power, military occupation was lawful. Therefore, a contract made under these conditions would be enforced even if Stone bought the rifle to use in the Rebel army.

Judge Milligan declared these instructions incorrect. The Confederacy was "an unlawful combination of insurgent states."[17] Open war had broken out between them and the legitimate government. The seller knew that Tennessee was in rebellion, and yet after the war was over he was attempting to use Tennessee courts, a state of the United States, to enforce a contract aimed at destroying the United States. Because this contract was made against the public policy of the United States and with an agent of the Confederacy, the contract was illegal. Milligan rejected the argument that because the Confederate States had been granted belligerent status, the contract was enforceable. Belligerent status conferred some rights on other nations dealing with the Confederacy. However, the status did nothing to protect individuals whose allegiance should had been to the United States. To extend belligerent status rights any further would be to recognize the Confederacy as a sovereign and independent nation, which the war had decided the Confederacy was not. Stone could not recover for the rifle he sold to further this illegal conspiracy.

With these two 1865 cases, Judge Milligan set forth the Radical Court's basic stance toward the Confederacy. The Confederate states had been a traitorous conspiracy. Anyone who acted toward the Confederacy as if it was a legitimate government, either by contracting with its agents or using its money, would be left to their own devices. They certainly could not now come to the courts of a reconstructed state and seek relief for acts that had undermined the war effort of the United States. The Court reaffirmed its position that transactions involving Confederate notes would not be enforced in each of the next two sessions.[18]

In the September Term of 1866, Judge Shackelford took the opportunity of another promissory note case to refuse to enforce executory contracts based on Confederate currency. He ruled in *Thornberg v. Harris* (1866) that this attempt to issue currency violated the first article of the United States Constitution, which forbids states from entering into a confederation or emitting bills of credit. The Confederate states had violated this article in two ways. First, they had created a confederacy, and second, they had issued money. Because the issuance of Confederacy treasury notes violated the United States Constitution, the issuance was illegal.

But what of innocent subsequent holders of the notes? Ordinarily, after an illegal contract is consummated, later contracts wholly unconnected with the illegal contract are not tainted. However, in *Thornberg* Shackelford argued that the act of receiving and circulating Confederacy notes aided the Confederacy. Because all uses of Confederate notes supported the insurrection, the notes were illegal consideration for any contract. Shackelford also rejected the argument that the Confederacy had belligerent status, and that this status protected the users of Confederate notes. He maintained that because European nations refused to respect the Confederacy as an independent nation, the belligerent status did not give the Confederacy the sovereign power to issue money.

The Court's dislike of contracts based on Confederate money even extended to upsetting one executed contract. In *Shurer v. Green* (1866) a widow authorized her father, to whom she gave a power of attorney, to lend eight thousand dollars from her deceased husband's estate to A. L. P. Green. At the beginning of the war, shortly before the fall of Fort Donelson, the debtor sent an agent to redeem the note with Confederate currency. At first the father resisted the attempt to pay off the loan. The agent insisted that the money was good, and eventually persuaded the father to accept the money, and turn over the promissory note. The widow told her father that he should not have accepted the money, and that she would not have done so. She never received the Confederate money from her father. The Court interpreted her action as a failure to ratify the redemption of the promissory notes.

The Court refused to view this case as an executed contract. It felt that the debtor used superior knowledge as to the direction of the war to impose upon an eighty-year-old man. Under ordinary agency law principles, because the father had his daughter's power of attorney, his act would have been binding on his daughter. But the Court ran roughshod over these principles of agency law and found that this transaction, instead of being an executed contract, was a fraudulent imposition on an old man. Because the widow had done nothing to ratify this fraud by receiving the Confederate money, the executed contract doctrine did not apply.

The Radical Court was treading on dangerous ground with this opinion. This decision invited everyone who had accepted Confederate money, for any transaction, to rush to court and attempt to prove "fraud." Fraud, according to this opinion, amounted to little more than a stated reluctance to take Confederate money. Some plaintiffs took the Court up on this invitation. In *Jones v. Thomas* (1868), the Court found itself having to "clarify" the *Shurer* opinion. It ruled that Tennessee courts would not enforce executory or unsettled contracts, if the consideration was Confederate money, because Confederate money was circulated for the purpose of maintaining the rebellion. However, once a debt was settled, it should not be disturbed, except for such fraud, mistake or duress as would set aside payments not made with the tainted currency. "Something more than an unwillingness must exist" in the mind of the receiver.[19] Although the Court did not succeed in defining this "something more," this decision backtracked from the potential chaos that the *Shurer* opinion had portended.

One last hurdle arose to the Radical Court's attempt to condemn Confederate currency. The United States Supreme Court upheld a contract made in Alabama for the payment of Confederate treasury notes in *Thorington v. Smith* (1868). It ruled that the debtor could recover the actual value of the notes at the time and place of the contract. The Tennessee Supreme Court reacted to *Thorington* by reiterating that the problem with the Confederate currency was its use to aid the rebellion. In *Robertson v. Shores* (1869), the Court dealt with the *Thorington* decision by ratifying its prior condemnation of Confederate money: "This currency was the lifeblood of the Confederacy, and the war could not have been carried on for any considerable length of time without the support furnished by it."[20] The U.S. Supreme Court decision did not control the rulings of the Tennessee Supreme Court, as the U.S. Supreme Court was applying general principles of commercial law in a diversity case, not deciding a binding federal constitutional question. Therefore, the Radical Tennessee Court was free to follow its line of decisions and impose a more extreme penalty on using Confederate notes than did the national court.

The Tennessee Supreme Court ratified one contract that supported the Confederacy. A man agreed to rent his house to the Confederate army for use as a hospital. The homeowner sued to recover two hundred dollars in rent, even though he had known the house would be used to attend to wounded Rebels. The Circuit Court judge, following the lead of the earlier Supreme Court decisions, instructed the jury that if the rental was in aid of the rebellion, the homeowner could not collect the rent. The Supreme Court, in *Fottrell v. German* (1866), overruled this instruction and drew the distinction that if the homeowner was acting out of humanitarian motives, then he could recover. The Court remanded the case for the jury to decide this question.

Similarly, the Radical Court confirmed the wartime acts of local legal officials, such as judges, clerks, and sheriffs. As long as the officers were acting under laws that were valid prior to May 16, 1861, the date of secession, their acts were lawful. The Court ratified these official acts, even if at the time of the act, the area was under de facto Confederate control. For instance, in *Ward v. State* (1866) a man was prosecuted for selling liquor without a license. In fact, he had a license, but it had been issued by a clerk who had sworn his oath to the Confederacy, not the United States. The lower court charged, in what was surely a case of political prosecution of a Rebel, that a license issued by this clerk was a nullity. The Supreme Court overruled this holding, stating that to overturn all the official acts taken during the war would cause grave problems.

THEFT AND CONVERSION DURING THE WAR

The Radical Court used the Confederate currency cases to proclaim the traitorous and illegal nature of the entire Confederacy. In tort cases, however, the Court narrowed its focus to examine the actions of individuals. Again, the Court had to choose between limiting the number of complaints—after all, every minute of every battle saw hundreds of torts committed—and allowing Union supporters to recover for the wrongful acts of the Confederate forces. If the Court allowed the military uniform to protect all soldiers, then the Union sympathizers would have no recourse for the items taken or the imprisonments suffered at the hands of their Confederate neighbors. However, if the war conditions were completely ignored, innumerable court claims would arise. The usual parties to these suits seemed to have been people from the same neighborhood, complaining about very personal acts. Perhaps the parties were using the courts and the chaos of war to renew old feuds or jockey for current local power.

Even the Radical Court knew it could not allow Confederate soldiers to be prosecuted for acts committed against other soldiers. Thus the Court, in *Hammond v. State* (1866), reversed the robbery conviction of a Confederate soldier who was part of a squad that arrested a man who was dressed as a Union soldier. Although it turned out that the man had been discharged from the Union army, the Court held that the Union man's dress and his proximity to the fighting made him a combatant at the time. Furthermore, the Court found that the defendant's mere presence as a member of the arresting squad at the time that someone took a pistol from the victim did not meet the definition of robbery. The facts seemed to show that the defendant merely stood silently six to eight feet from the victim while the patrol commander took the pistol from the victim. The Court noted that the belligerent status of the Confederate army protected Rebel soldiers in their dealings with Union soldiers.

However, if a Confederate soldier used the chaos of war to further his own personal interest, he lost the protection of his uniform. In *Barnhill v. Phillips* (1867), a Confederate soldier took a horse from a Union soldier and claimed protection under the belligerency doctrine. The Court noted that the Rebel soldier sold the horse and kept the money for his own personal use. This taking was, therefore, a conversion, and the Union soldier could recover.

Once the Court had established that soldiers could not be sued or prosecuted for their acts against other combatants, it then drew a sharp line between combatants and civilians. Civilians could recover for torts Rebel soldiers committed against them even if the torts occurred under military direction. In *Davidson v. Manlove* (1865), a group of Rebel soldiers took a horse from a man named Manlove for the use of the Confederate army. The next day the defendant was riding the horse when it was killed. The Court ruled that the defendant's two acts, being in the party that confiscated the horse and then later riding the horse, amounted to a conversion or illegal taking of the animal. Similarly, in *Cochran and Thompson v.*

Tucker (1866), a group of Rebel soldiers imprisoned a former Union soldier who had returned from the fighting. The trial court instructed that enlistment in the Confederate army was no defense against wrongs committed against civilians. This plaintiff had been discharged from the Union army and was not involved in the fighting, so he was a civilian whose rights must be respected. The Court affirmed a five-thousand-dollar verdict for a plaintiff who sued for false imprisonment.

Confederate agents who were not in the military had no protection, even if they were acting pursuant to Confederate statutes. A. E. Smith was appointed to enforce a Confederate law that required the seizure of all guns in Cocke County, Tennessee. In *Smith v. Ishenhour* (1866), the Court held him personally liable for one of the guns he seized. The legal basis for this holding was that the constitutional amendment adopted on February 22, 1865, declared that all acts of the Tennessee legislature passed since May 6, 1861, while the legislature was acting for a Confederate state, were null and void. The amendment also declared that all acts made in pursuant in such statutes were null and void. Therefore, the defendant had no valid governmental cloak, and he was a simple tortfeasor. Moreover, the Court also expressed its disgust at this Confederate-era statute. It noted that this law was "the first attempt in the history of the Anglo-Saxon race . . . to disarm the people by legislation."[21]

THE RADICAL COURT AND THE FREEDMEN

Just as close to the Radical Court's heart, or at least its politics, as condemning the Confederacy as a traitorous conspiracy, was the project of protecting the freedmen. The Union-controlled areas of Tennessee had been specifically exempted from the Emancipation Proclamation. Tennessee slaves had been freed by the emancipation amendment that the Tennessee voters adopted by referendum in February 1865. Emancipation raised legal problems that the Radical Court found itself addressing.

The Supreme Court addressed cases in which attempted manumissions, usually by will, were overtaken by emancipation. The Court also considered changes in the criminal law as the African Americans were no longer subject to the slave code. Finally, the Court was called upon to decide who bore the financial loss when slaves were freed and executory contracts for their sale or hire were still pending. The Radical Court attempted to recognize the newly won citizenship of freedpersons in all of these situations.

By 1869, the Radical Court had worked out a jurisprudence that respected that humanity of the freed people. Illustrative of that jurisprudence was Judge Andrew's interpretation of a manumission and bequest in a will against the claims of the other legatees in *Armstrong v. Pearre* (1869). The will had attempted to provide money to allow a group of slaves to immigrate to Liberia. This immigration was a necessary part of any manumission because Tennessee antebellum law required that freed slaves leave the state. The will freed all slaves that were under age twenty-five as of the testator's death but required that these slaves be "hired out" until January 1, 1854, at which time they had the choice of being sold or immigrating to Liberia. Unfortunately, the estate was insolvent, so even though the slaves expressed their desire to go to Liberia in 1854, the Court ordered that they continue to be hired out to make up the deficit. The slaves were hired out through 1861 because the administrator of the estate reported that he still did not have enough money to send them to Liberia. In 1867 the estate held $3,107.43, all the funds coming from the hiring out of the never-emancipated slaves.

In 1867, the now-freed African Americans petitioned for the money the estate had accumulated from hiring them out. The widow and children counterclaimed for a share of this fund in order to pay certain legacies. The chancellor ruled that the legatees should get their money ahead of the freed slaves. Reversing this judgment, Judge Andrews denied the claims of the prior slave owners. In a striking rejection of the central premise of antebellum slave law, where the material interest of the masters was paramount, Andrews ruled that a "bequest of freedom is of a higher nature than a pecuniary legacy."[22] The Court refused to assume that these slaves had continued in slavery for an indefinite term merely to pay the legacies of the widow and children of their ex-master. Andrews could not give the slaves back their extra decade of servitude, but he awarded them the money their hire had earned in those years.

The Radical Court likewise bent the letter and violated the spirit of antebellum slave law in ruling on another will. In *Bedford v. Williams* (1867), a slave owner lived with his slave as if they were married. She bore him a daughter. In 1847 the slave owner established a trust for his would-be wife and daughter. The trust consisted of four slaves, two for each woman, with a right of survivorship between the women. The trustee had the power to sell the slaves, and continue the trust with any money derived from the sale. After the war, Emily, the daughter, sued her father's estate for the price of one slave the administrator had sold, and the hire of the other three. The legal impediment to Emily's claim was that under antebellum slave law, no slave could hold property. Therefore, a slave could not legally be a beneficiary of a trust.

Judge Milligan surmounted this problem by claiming that the girl's father, through his acts, had by implication manumitted the girl. However, even if the facts established a manumission by implication, Tennessee statutes forbade manumission without state approval. In this case, no one had ever applied for Emily's freedom because the slave owner had never explicitly freed her. Milligan jumped this hurdle by claiming that Emily was in an "intermediate state between freedom and slavery."[23] In this legal condition, no one but the state of Tennessee could deny her freedom. She had the right to enjoy the fruits of her labor, though she could only collect those fruits after the state had recognized her manumission. Because Emily was now freed by the emancipation amendment, she had the right to collect her property. Milligan's lively and successful attempt to stretch Emily's emancipation back almost two decades shows the great desire of the Radical bench to interpret expansively the rights of the freed slaves in the new social order.

Milligan had used the doctrine of "inchoate freedom" in an earlier case where the slaveholder's intent was much clearer. In *Porter v. Blakemore* (1865), one George Porter had managed to purchase himself out of slavery. Porter worked hard, and purchased his wife and several of his children. When his former master died, Porter was able to borrow eighteen hundred to purchase from his ex-master's estate those of his children still enslaved. A few years later, Porter died, not yet having paid off the note, and not having formally emancipated his children. The holders of Porter's note applied to the administrators of his estate to sell the still-enslaved children in order to pay off the debt. The chancellor ordered the sale. By the time the issue came up on appeal, emancipation made the selling of the children moot. However, Milligan took the opportunity to announce that the children had actually been quasi-free based on the father's words and evident intent. The Radical Court desired to strike at slavery, even in retrospect, and to declare somewhat-free as many slaves as possible.

The Radical Court also protected the property of ex-slaves against whites. When a white cousin appeared to contest a will granting freedom and devising property to the slaves of a pair of maiden sisters, the Court rejected this attempt to intercept the slaves' legacy. The will freed the slaves, and bequeathed all of the ladies' property to the slaves, provided they moved to Liberia. The cousin argued that because the now-freed slaves had not moved to Liberia, they were not eligible for the bequest and it should pass to him as the women's heir. The Court, in *Banks v. Banks* (1865), protected the ex-slaves rights, and granted them the property. The Court found that the condition that the slaves move to Liberia was only included in the sisters' wills because Tennessee law required all manumitted slaves to be transported to Liberia at the time the wills were drawn. However, the wills showed that the women desired to provide for the slaves. Because the slaves were now free without the need to transport themselves, the sisters' intent would be fulfilled if the ex-slaves got all the property.

As these cases illustrate, the Radical Court was very sensitive to the rights, both past and present, of the freedpeople. In every case, the Radical Court found a way to rule in favor of the African American claimants, and against their former owners' heirs. The Court ruled in favor of the African Americans even when so ruling required ignoring explicit conditions in a will. The Radical Court expanded this appreciation for the rights of freedpeople into criminal law.

In criminal cases, the Court had to determine the effect of the provisions in the 1865 Constitutional amendments that stated that freed people should not be subject to a different punishment for an offense than a white person. This amendment repealed all laws in conflict with this requirement. In *Wharton v. State* (1867), the Court was confronted with an appeal from a slave who had been convicted of the rape of a white woman, and condemned to death. A white man would not have been subject to the death penalty for the rape of a white woman. The Court held that the 1865 amendments repealed the penal statute that condemned a slave to death for the rape of a white woman because it imposed a different penalty on black men then on white men. This repeal acted as a pardon. Because the amendment did not contain a savings clause, there was no law under which this ex-slave could now be punished.[24] These cases indicate that the Radical Court showed no respect for the antebellum slave laws, and would insist that freedmen be treated as free men in the new legal regime.

Still, the Court punished criminals where it could do so consistent with these principles. For instance, in *Boyd v. State* (1869) a free man of color was convicted of first-degree murder. The Court let the conviction stand because the penalty—hanging—was the same for whites and blacks. Similarly, a freed man charged with bigamy raised the defense that his first marriage was not binding because he entered into it as a slave. The Court reasoned, in *McReynolds v. State* (1867), that even if antebellum law did not recognize the slave marriage, because the parties continued living together after emancipation, postbellum law recognized the marriage. The defendant had lived with his slave wife until January 1867, two years after emancipation, thereby ratifying the slave marriage. It followed that his second marriage was bigamous. In so ruling, the Court took seriously the meaning of emancipation, and required proof that the defendant's actions as a free man, not as a slave, invoked the legal consequences.

The Radical Court only split over one issue regarding the emancipation of slaves, and that was the matter of hiring slaves during the war. In *Gholson v. Blackman* (1867), an estate administrator, Gholson, hired out a slave named Ellen to Blackman. Blackman paid the hire for 1861, 1862, and 1863 to the estate. In 1864, Ellen's husband informed Blackman that he should pay the hire directly to Ellen. Blackman did so. Blackman and Ellen lived in

Clarksville, which was safely under Federal control by 1864. However, Ellen had not been officially emancipated because Lincoln's Emancipation Proclamation only applied to areas under Rebel control. Despite the lack of formal emancipation, by 1864 African Americans in Clarksville generally had begun to demand pay for their labor and the white citizens who wanted laborers found they had to deal with them as if they were free, despite the technicalities of the law.

After the war, Gholson sued Blackman for the hire of Ellen from January 1864 to February 25, 1865, when Tennessee officially emancipated the slaves. Despite the prevailing conditions in Clarksville, the Supreme Court ruled that under the law Ellen was still considered a slave, and Blackman had a legal obligation to pay the owner. Neither the various federal confiscation acts nor the Emancipation Proclamation freed Ellen before Tennessee emancipation. Because no law had freed Ellen, Blackman still owed her hire to the estate. Perhaps the Court had an easier time applying formal law here because the freed woman herself would not lose from this opinion.

Judge Shackelford, however, could not go along with this limitation on the African Americans' claim to freedom. He looked to the practices of the time and place. Slavery had been practically abolished by 1864. International law had superseded local law by that date. The laws of antebellum Tennessee no longer applied, but new civilian laws had yet to be adopted. Because slavery could only exist by positive law, and international law had never recognized slavery, all persons were free. In his view, when Ellen served out her hire in 1863 and stayed in Clarksville, she became a free woman.

THE SUFFRAGE DECISION

Governor Brownlow lost political strength as his administration became more Radical. In 1866 he arrested Conservative legislators and held them captive in the Capitol in order to get a quorum for the ratification of the Fourteenth Amendment. These acts succeeded in having the state readmitted to the Union and avoided congressional Reconstruction. Though the Conservatives were thus spared federal Reconstruction, which lasted in some states until 1876, kidnapping Conservative legislators did not win Brownlow the gratitude of that party. In fact, a Davidson County sheriff led a posse and stormed the Capitol in order to free the captive Conservatives. If Brownlow was going to keep control of the state, he needed new voters.[25]

The obvious place for Radicals to look for votes was among the freedmen. Although Brownlow had gone on record as opposing African American suffrage, the changing times combined with the need for more Radical votes in the August 1867 elections, led him to reverse his position. On February 26, 1867, he signed a bill giving the vote to all African American men. African Americans were, however, still excluded from jury duty and office holding.

Brownlow further entrenched Radical rule with two measures that gave him extralegal control of the voting process. One bill created a military force, the Tennessee State Guard, to oversee elections and prevent violence and intimidation directed at Radical voters. Second, the legislature gave the governor the power to set aside the registration of voters in any county where he disagreed with the decision of the local commissioner of registration. This act gave him a veto power over any local registrars who might become too lenient in allowing ex-Confederates and other Conservative supporters to get back onto the voting rolls. Brownlow's control over the registration apparatus assured the Radicals of an elective landslide.

The Radical Court had participated in establishing the legal framework for this overwhelming victory in *Ridley v. Sherbrook* (1866). In the 1866 December term, the Court turned back a possible end-run around the state suffrage laws. Bromfield Ridley attempted to register to vote despite his Rebel past. He had been an upstanding citizen and voter before the war, and had received one of President Andrew Johnson's pardons in July 1865. Despite the presidential pardon, the local commissioner of voters refused to give Ridley a certificate to vote because he did not meet the requirements of the voting act.

Ridley appealed this decision to the Supreme Court. The Court analyzed the 1865 Constitutional amendments that authorized the next General Assembly to pass new suffrage laws. The Court held that the franchise was not an inalienable right but a political one, which could be conferred or withheld by the state. The presidential pardon, while it reestablished Ridley's rights to national citizenship, did not control Tennessee's decision whether to grant or deny Ridley the political right to vote. Because the constitutional convention of 1865 legitimately authorized the 1865 General Assembly to pass legislation that limited the suffrage of former Rebels, the Court rejected this attempt to force the registrar to enroll a pardoned voter. This opinion assured the Radicals that they would continue to control the registration rolls, as long as Governor Brownlow could control the local commissioner of registration.

Political domination in Tennessee thus rested in control over the local county officials who actually made decisions about registering individual voters. As with much of Reconstruction politics, events at the national or state level merely established the rules, or the lack of rules, under which local political battles were fought.[26] The linchpin in the battle for Tennessee's political future became control over the local commissioners of registration.

Governor Brownlow had to rely upon the Supreme Court to support the act that gave him the right to set aside the registration of counties that did not follow the Radical line. Unfortunately for the Radical Party, 1868 was the year that the Court fell into chaos. As noted earlier, all members of the Court resigned during the year, and Brownlow had to search hard to find replacements. The 1868 September Term was canceled for lack of judges. When the Court personnel finally stabilized for the December Term, no one knew what to expect from this new bench. To add to this chaos, this entirely new panel would, for the first time since the war, face elections.

Brownlow's appointees would only sit for the December Term and part of the March Term before a new bench would be elected in May 1869. The entire Radical Party knew of the importance of a favorable Court to Radical rule. However, personal ambition led to opposition to the sitting members. This opposition was especially potent because the incumbents could not claim any legitimacy due to longevity of service.[27] In order to avoid splitting the Radical Party over who should sit on the Supreme Court, the Radicals called a nominating convention for Nashville in April 1869. Events conspired against this attempt to smooth over the rifts in the Radical Party. The night before the convention, a flood washed away two spans of the railroad bridge on the route from Memphis to Nashville, and a train bringing sixty-two West Tennessee delegates to the Radical convention ran completely off the tracks.[28]

Despite the absence of these delegates, the convention met in Nashville on April 20. Andrews, who was currently sitting, was unanimously nominated from the Eastern Division. Shackelford, the sitting judge from the Middle Division, had four opponents. Although he got the most votes on the first ballot, he did not get a majority. By the fourth ballot, Andrew McClain won the nomination. Henry G. Smith, the sitting judge from the Western Division, lost the nomination to Alvin Hawkins by one vote.[29]

The combination of the close vote and the absence of the West Tennessee delegation meant that, far from unifying the party, the controversy over the fairness of the convention sundered the party. Judge Shackelford announced on April 23 that he would not be bound by the result of the convention. According to Shackelford, the western delegates were instructed to vote for the current judges. These sixty-two votes would have allowed him to win on the first ballot and, of course, would have let Smith beat Hawkins, as Hawkins won by only one vote. Shackelford announced that because the true will of the people was for these votes to count, he would continue to run for his seat.[30] Shackelford went so far as to ally himself with T. A. R. Nelson, a leading Conservative lawyer and politician who would later sit on the bench after the Conservative victory. The two men agreed to support each other in their respective regions.[31] The Radical Party was beginning to fall apart, and a Supreme Court decision, rendered by this lame-duck Court, struck the final blow that hastened the process.

On May 24, 1869, the voters elected the bench that the Radical convention had nominated.[32] The sitting Court, however, had already unanimously decided the crucial disfranchisement case of *State v. Staten* (1869) and rendered its opinion on May 29. The press immediately recognized the political implications of this decision and newspapers across the state predicted the political triumph of the Conservatives.[33] Such coverage of a Supreme Court decision was quite an event, as Supreme Court opinions were rarely reported at all. The Conservative press loudly proclaimed that only the power of the commissioners of voters had kept the Radicals in office. Because this decision freed these commissioners from Radical control, the press foresaw that it would end Radical rule.

By June 13, Governor Brownlow officially announced his position on the case and the suffrage question. He defended the franchise law as having been necessary to protect loyal people from the leaders of the rebellion. He estimated that the *Staten* decision would give the vote to about twenty thousand Rebels. Furthermore, President Ulysses S. Grant and the northern Republican Party had come out in favor of universal suffrage. Therefore, Brownlow concluded, "the safely of the state, the welfare of its people and the protection of loyal citizen do not demand the perpetuation of existing disabilities."[34]

By this time Brownlow had been appointed to the senate. His appointee to the governorship, DeWitt Clinton Senter, was running against another Radical, William B. Stokes, for the governorship. Governor Senter saw the way the wind was blowing and he came out in favor of universal suffrage.[35] Senter began replacing any commission of registration who refused to register ex-Rebels. Stokes made one last appeal to the Supreme Court to stop Senter from replacing the Radical commissioners, but the Court upheld Senter's power in *Williams v. Boughner* (1869). Between these two Supreme Court decisions, the August 1869 election was held under de facto universal suffrage. Open suffrage spelled the end of Radicalism in Tennessee. The Conservatives dominated the general assembly elected in August, and they solidified their victory by getting voter approval for a constitutional convention.[36]

So what was this decision that effectively ended Tennessee Reconstruction? On its face, the decision in *State v. Staten* (1869) did not seem so portentous. William Staten applied to the commissioner of registration of Gibson County on December 10, 1867, to register to vote. The commissioner found him qualified and issued him a certificate. As mentioned earlier, the governor had the power to set aside the registration in any county if the governor was satisfied that "frauds and irregularities" tainted the registration. Using this power, Governor Brownlow set aside the registration of Gibson County on February 25, 1868, and declared the registration void. Despite the governor's act, Staten used his certificate to vote in a March 8, 1868, election for sheriff.

Staten was arrested and charged with a misdemeanor for voting with an invalid certificate. Both sides agreed to these facts, so if the statute authorizing the governor to set aside the registration was valid, then Staten was guilty.

Smith wrote the opinion of the Court, although Shackelford and Andrews both wrote separate concurring opinions. Smith based his opinion on what a modern constitutional scholar would call substantive due process grounds.[37] He declared that the franchise holder had a property right in his vote. Consequently, suffrage could only be taken away by due process of law. He quoted the Tennessee bill of rights for the proposition that "no freeman shall be . . . dissiezed of his freehold, liberties or property . . . or deprived of his life, liberty or property, but by judgement of his peers, or the law of the land."[38] The "law of the land," Smith noted, is merely another expression for due process of law. This legislative act did not provide sufficient due process. Instead, the "law of the land" requires an impartial hearing and a right to raise a defense before the state can take property, or in this case the vote, away from a citizen.

Under Tennessee registration laws, the franchise was granted in a judicial-like proceeding. Unlike other states, where a registrar functioned more like a clerk, in Tennessee the commissioner judged whether the applicant bore arms against the United States or otherwise aided the Confederacy. The statute authorized the commissioner to hear witnesses both for and against the applicant and determine the correct result. Because the legislation gave this responsibility to the commissioner, it could not empower the governor to set aside these decisions and strip franchise holders of their adjudged rights.

Smith's reasoning that suffrage was the equivalent of a property right contradicted the Court's earlier holding in *Ridley v Sherbrook*. If the right to vote was a vested right, arguably the Rebel soldiers and sympathizers who voted before the war should have had a vested right in maintaining the vote. Smith ducked this issue by simply noting that his analysis decided the current case, so he did not need to reach the issue of whether the 1866 franchise act was constitutional. Although Smith included a disclaimer that the state had the right to prescribe qualifications for the franchise and that the state could take the franchise away if it acted in a constitutional manner, his reasoning suggested that the 1866 franchise act was unconstitutional.

In his concurrence, Judge Andrews tried to walk a fine line between Smith's reasoning and the 1866 franchise act. Andrews agreed that voting was a property right, but it was also a trust. The legislature had a right to regulate this important trust, but the regulation must not arbitrarily deny any given individual of the right to vote. Therefore, this statute allowing the governor to set aside any county's registration was unconstitutional, not because it violated vested rights, but because it authorized the governor to arbitrarily deny the vote to those the commissioner had already found to meet the legislative criteria.

Shackelford, the author of the *Sherbrook* opinion, felt the need to defend his original stance on the franchise question. He especially noted that the 1796 Constitution gave the vote to African American free men. The 1834 Constitution, however, was adopted at a time of increased sectional conflict and removed the suffrage from free men of color. From this episode, Shackelford deduced that the franchise was "a political right or privilege and not a natural or inherent right."[39] Because the franchise was a political right, the sovereign had the right to restrict it. Restricting the franchise already granted would be unconstitutional if the franchise was a vested right. However, the franchise was merely a "trust or privilege," which the sovereign power grants and has the right to recall at any time "without the violation of any vested right."[40] Even though the sovereign has the right to revoke the franchise, it must follow appropriate procedures. This statute, thus, raised procedural due process, not substantive due process problem. The sovereign people acting in a constitutional convention could divest citizens of the franchise, but the legislature could not divest the citizen of this right, nor authorize the governor to do so. In particular, the act violated the separation of powers by giving the governor the ability to overrule the judiciary.

Whether the Court's reasoning overruled *Sherbrook* soon became moot. The politics of Reconstruction over took and superseded these judicial niceties. To Stokes's consternation, Governor Senter began removing any commissioner who refused to certify ex-Rebels. Stokes tried to counterattack through the judiciary and within a month of the *Staten* decision, the Radical Court found itself once again the Radicals' last line of defense. And once again, this lame-duck Court had its revenge on the convention that had repudiated two of its three members.

On June 19, 1869, six days after Brownlow announced in favor of universal suffrage, Senter removed the commissioner of registration for Shelby County, the county that included Memphis. The chancellor sitting at Memphis enjoined the removal of the commissioner, ruling unconstitutional the statute that gave the governor power to remove the commissioner. Senter's appointee immediately applied to the Court, still sitting in Brownsville, to supersede this injunction. In *Williams v. Boughner* (1869), Shackelford found that the statute that established the commissioner of registration in the various counties failed to fix the tenure for the commission. The governor was given unfettered power to appoint them. Shackelford relied on a United States Supreme Court precedent for the proposition that the power of appointment combined with no limitation on tenure in office implies the power to remove. Governor Senter's removal of this commissioner was, therefore, constitutional.

The Radical Court's decision in *Staten,* which added up to twenty thousand Rebel voters to the electorate, doomed Radicalism. In order to secure these votes, Senter came out for universal suffrage and replaced the commissioners who would not follow this program. Shackelford's opinion in *Williams v. Boughner* paved the way for Senter to remove any commissioner who refused to register former Confederates. Senter's acts, impelled by and enabled by the Supreme Court, led to his immediate victory in the governor's race against Stokes. However, his strategy lost the greater battle. The General Assembly elected as a result of these events was overwhelming Conservative.[41]

The Conservative General Assembly immediately began to rescind Radical laws, including the Tennessee State Guard Act, which gave the governor a military force to oppose the Ku Klux Klan. Most important, the General Assembly authorized a referendum for a new constitutional convention, which convention the voters approved by a five-to-one margin.

The constitutional convention met in January 1870. Although Radicals appealed to Washington to place the state under congressional Reconstruction, the Conservative convention forestalled this move by writing African American suffrage into the new constitution. The new Constitution diluted this promise, however, by including a poll tax provision.[42] For the history of the Tennessee Supreme Court, the most important constitutional change was the enlarging of the Court to five justices, with no more than two from any of the state's three grand divisions. The voters were to staff this new Court with an election in August 1870. To forestall squabbling about the initial makeup of the Court, a schedule to the Constitution provided that the Court should at first be composed of six judges, two from each grand division. The first judge to resign after January 1st, 1873 would not be replaced. This schedule left to chance the choice of which division would be underrepresented.[43] The voters approved this new Constitution 98,128 to 33,972. Senter lost his hard-won gubernatorial position in November 1870. The Radical Court did not last even that long. In August 1870 the new six-judge panel was elected. All six were Conservatives.[44]

THE CONSERVATIVE COURT

Unlike the Radical Court judges, the judges of the Conservative Court elected in August 1870 had been important antebellum politicians and lawyers or high-ranking Confederate officers. The Conservative judges brought much more prestige to the bench then the relatively obscure Radical judges. The two most impressive Conservative judges were A. O. P.

Nicholson and T. A. R. Nelson. The presence of these two men on the bench gave the Supreme Court more weight within the Tennessee political system.

A. O. P. Nicholson was born in 1808 and his family settled in Columbia, Tennessee. His family background was wealthy enough to allow him to attend University of North Carolina. He began to study law in 1829. By 1844 he had become an important Democratic supporter and also the editor of the *Nashville Union.* In 1845 Nicholson formed a prestigious law firm in Nashville. His stature was such that he was offered, but refused, cabinet positions in several national Democratic administrations. In 1857 he was elected to the U.S. Senate from Tennessee. When the war came, he supported the South. He was arrested and imprisoned by the Federal government, but Andrew Johnson intervened and had him released and sent

A chief architect of the Tennessee Constitution of 1870, A. O. P. Nicholson was elected to the Tennessee Supreme Court in that year and served as chief justice until his death in 1876. Tennessee State Library and Archives.

behind Confederate lines. He returned to Nashville when General Hood's army invaded in 1864. The Union forces again arrested him and put him in the Tennessee State Penitentiary. After the war he was left destitute, with only one cow and a small plot of land to his name. His reputation, however, remained intact, and Andrew Johnson called him to Washington to participate in defending Johnson against the impeachment charges. When it became clear that the Conservatives would elect their panel to the Supreme Court in 1870, his presence added the weight of the antebellum Democratic legal and political establishment to the bench. Nicholson became the chief justice of the new Court.[45]

Just as a Nicholson represented the cream of antebellum Democratic legal talent, T. A. R. Nelson provided a connection with Tennessee's antebellum Whig hierarchy. Nelson was also a college graduate, having graduated from the precursor to the University of Tennessee. He was admitted to the bar in 1832 and practiced in Carter County. He was elected attorney general for the first circuit and was a presidential Whig elector for Clay and Taylor. Nelson was elected to Congress in 1858 and 1860. In Congress, he made a celebrated speech in favor of the Union that was reprinted in the *London Times.* During the war, he was arrested by the Confederates and, upon his release, sat out the war in East Tennessee. Nelson's prominence as an orator and as a pro-Union East Tennessee Whig balanced Nicholson's Democratic and Middle Tennessee roots.[46]

In addition to the antebellum political reputation of these two leaders of the Conservative bench, the other members of the panel brought military prestige. John Sneed came from a family of Tennessee lawyers. He had represented Shelby County in the state legislature in 1845. He had been a district attorney general from 1851 to 1854, and the state attorney general from 1854 to 1857. Besides these solid legal credentials, he had served as a captain in the United States Army in the Mexican War and risen to the rank of brigadier general in the Confederate army.[47]

Two other judges also added military luster to the Conservative Court. Peter Turney was the son of a successful politician. In 1860, Turney supported secession and raised a regiment for the Confederacy, becoming its colonel. He was wounded at Fredericksburg.[48] Similarly, Thomas J. Freeman was elected colonel of a Confederate regiment and wounded at Shiloh. In addition to his military exploits he was recognized as one of the preeminent West Tennessee lawyers.[49] The last member of the bench, James Deaderick, had a solid antebellum career. He had been elected state senator from Washington County, been appointed an Indian agent by President Tyler, and was a presidential elector for John Bell in the 1860 election.[50]

This Court found itself called on to use its legal, political and military prestige to salvage the reputation of the Tennessee Supreme Court. The Radical Court had, of course, been portrayed as enacting Radical politics into Tennessee constitutional law. The first order of business for the new Conservative panel was to reverse this trend and instead enact Conservative political ideas into law. Only after the Radical precedents had been overturned could the Court turn its attention to creating a more judicious and legal, as opposed to political, reputation.

The other problem that the Radical Court had bequeathed to its Conservative successors was a huge backlog of cases that the Radicals had not resolved. This backlog rose from several sources. For one thing, the virtual closure of many courts during the Civil War had engendered much legal activity at the trial court level in the immediate postwar years. Second, the Radical Court was only composed of three judges and, as we have seen, turnover of personnel during the Reconstruction years meant that often these three judges were not available to hear cases. In fact, one entire session had to be canceled because of lack of judges. Third, the chaos of the war and the events of the postwar period raised a variety of legal problems that had not existed prior to the war. For instance, emancipation gave the newly freed slaves access to the courts, which added to the docket.

The first solution to the problem of the Court's backlog was the schedule of the 1870 constitution. This schedule provided that the Court would initially be staffed by six judges, two from each of the grand divisions of the state. This extra judge allowed the Court to divide itself into two divisions of three judges each. The backlog also forced the Court into undertaking other extraordinary measures to clear its docket. For instance, in 1873 Chief Justice Nicholson broke his leg. His doctor ordered him to remain bedridden in Nashville. The legislature passed a special resolution that allowed Nicholson to sit with two special judges and hear any cases pending before the Supreme Court in the Middle Division if the attorneys agreed. Although in theory these were not cases of the Supreme Court, they were later reported in the *Supreme Court Reports*.[51]

RESURRECTING THE CONFEDERACY

The Conservative Court set out to roll back Radical jurisprudence. The Court's most important objective in the beginning was to reject the Radical Court's refusal to treat the Confederacy as anything other than a large, traitorous conspiracy. Because half of the Conservative Court had served in the Confederate army and all the others except for Nelson were strong Rebel sympathizers, it was a matter of personal pride with these judges to resurrect the Confederacy and reshape its legal image as that of a proud and sovereign government.

The Conservative Court began immediately to reverse the anti-Confederate opinions of the Radical Court. Fittingly, Judge Nelson, a strong Conservative but not a Confederate sympathizer, authored the leading case reestablishing the Confederate government's legitimacy. In the first session after the Conservative Court was elected, Nelson decided *Smith v. Brazelton* (1870). In that case, neighboring landowners found themselves divided by the Civil War. Smith was a Confederate soldier; Brazelton joined the Union army. When the Confederate army camped on lands in their neighborhood, Smith directed the Rebels to use Brazelton's land. The Confederate army cut acres of timber and took five hundred bushels of corn from Brazelton's fields, and after the war, he sued Smith for this trespass and received a judgment for five hundred dollars.

Nelson reversed the lower court's judgment. Nelson ruled that the Rebel soldiers had the same right as Federal soldiers to take what they needed to prosecute the war. The war had been a civil war, and each side had belligerent status. He pointed out that Lincoln began the war by treating all Confederate soldiers as traitors but that he later agreed to treat them as prisoners of war. Nelson went further than was necessary to decide this particular case. He asserted the opinion that the Confederacy was at least a de facto government and probably had been a sovereign nation. He specifically overturned the holding in *Wright and Cantrel v. Overall* that the Confederacy had not been a de facto government. He ended the opinion with a ringing litany of the accomplishments of the Confederacy.

Chief Justice Nicholson followed up on Nelson's opinion by ruling in favor of a Confederate colonel that a jury had found liable for the value of five rifles his soldiers confiscated from the home of a Federal soldier. In *Cummings v. Diggs* (1870) Nicholson stressed that the war had been a civil war with each side entitled to exercise belligerent rights. These rights included the right to confiscate any property belonging to the enemy within the control of the Confederacy. For these reasons, the Circuit Court should have admitted evidence that the defendant was a Confederate colonel acting within a territory controlled by the Confederacy.

The Conservative bench also found itself having to police trial courts quite actively. Because much of its early caseload consisted of appeals from county courts controlled by Radical judges, the Court often disagreed with the rulings of the lower-court judges. For instance, in one case the plaintiff had been forced to leave home for two years in order to avoid capture for deserting the Confederate army. At the end of the war, he sued a local Rebel soldier who had attempted to arrest him. On appeal, the Court ruled that if the Rebel soldier had pled that he was acting under Confederate authority, this plea would have been a full defense. Of course, under the Radical decisions this plea had not been recognized as a defense at all, so the attorney had not raised this defense. The Conservative Court still managed to overturn the verdict, in *Ellis v. Spurgin* (1870), on the grounds that the Circuit Court judge had gone too far in commenting on the evidence.

The overtly political nature of the Conservative Court's opinions is also evidenced by the Court's treatment of Union defendants. Just as Confederates could do no wrong, or at least the evidence always failed to prove that they had done wrong, Union defendants were invariably liable. So while Confederates could seize rifles and horses, even if not under direct military orders, Federal agents acting under direct statutory authority were found to be acting wrongfully. Congress passed a statute that authorized Federal agents to seize abandoned Rebel property. A woman with Rebel sympathies had moved from her home out of fear when the Union forces overtook her town. An authorized federal agent seized her personal property. After the war she sued for damages. Predictably, the Reconstruction jury found against her. The Conservative Court, reviewing this decision in *Hart v. Reynolds* (1870), gave her every protection possible. It struck the defendant's pleadings; overturned the verdict on the grounds that certain evidence should not have been admitted and corrected the judge's instructions.

In *Branner v. Felkner* (1870), a Union soldier confiscated a horse that had been used by the Rebel army. Finding numerous errors, the Supreme Court overturned the verdict for the defendant. The defendant failed to prove he was a Union soldier and the Circuit Court judge's instructions were too broad because private soldiers were not allowed to confiscate contraband.[52] This last ruling directly contradicted the Conservative Court's rulings that Confederate soldiers could seize Union sympathizer's property without direct orders.

When the United States Supreme Court had the opportunity to review the Conservative Court's decisions toward Union agents, it found error in the Conservative Court's treatment of those acting under Federal orders. In *Burts v. Beard* (1872), a landowner sued to recover for 155 cords of wood that the defendant had taken from his land. The defense, which the Court cavalierly overruled, was that the woodcutter was acting under the authority of the United States Military Railroads. The United States Supreme Court held, in *Beard v. Burts* (1877), that because the woodcutter harvested the wood under the orders of, and for the direct benefit of, the United States military, his act was protected against civil suit. The U.S. Supreme Court ordered the suit dismissed.

The politicization of the judiciary was not, of course, all on the side of the Conservative Supreme Court. The Radical Circuit Court judges in the

Reconstruction era, as well as those who remained on the bench during Conservative rule, acted with equal prejudice against former Rebels and present Conservatives. One Radical judge attempted to use the "Act to preserve public peace," otherwise known as the Ku Klux Klan Act, to bar Conservative attorneys from practicing. The act required judges to have all court officers take oaths that they would not support any secret organization. The Radical judge, in *Ingersoll v. Howard* (1870), interpreted this phrase "court officers" to include attorneys who were "officers of the court." One attorney, Ingersoll, refused to take the oath prescribed by the court. Ingersoll stated that he opposed the Ku Klux Klan but he objected to taking the oath and he wanted a Supreme Court ruling that this statute actually required attorneys to take this oath. The Radical judge found Ingersoll in contempt. Ingersoll persuaded an attorney who had taken the oath to renew the objection. The judge refused this motion and additionally refused to make a record of the court proceedings that would allow an appeal of his ruling. Ingersoll petitioned the Supreme Court for a mandamus to require the court to create a record. The judge provided a record before the mandamus was issued, but Nicholson ruled that the mandamus would have been justified. Nicholson further declared that the Radical judge's interpretation that the Ku Klux Klan Act was meant to cover attorneys was "palpably absurd." This statute only applied to those employees that worked directly under the control of the court.

Given the heavily politicized atmosphere in Tennessee courts, much of the Conservative Court's first year was given over to consolidating its pro-Confederacy jurisprudence. In *Gunter v. Patton* (1870), a Confederate soldier was held liable for converting a horse. The Radical trial judge suggested in his jury instructions that any Confederate conscript who failed to try to desert could be liable for the torts of any of his companions. The Conservative judges had no trouble in rejecting this instruction. No one, the Court reasoned, should be put under a duty to desert: "If caught in the act of desertion, no fantastic or quixotic notions of sublimate patriotism would save him from . . . a ignominious death."[53]

Once the Conservative Court had succeeded in retroactively elevating the Confederacy to sovereign status, the Court began to rehabilitate Confederate currency and invest it with value. The Radical Court, as discussed above, had ruled that Confederate currency was not only valueless, but that agreeing to accept the currency was aiding and abetting a traitorous conspiracy. Therefore, under a Radical jurisprudence any contracts that involved paying or receiving Confederate notes that had not been fully executed before the war ended, would not be enforced.

The Conservative Court rejected these holdings. The Court used various substitutes for consideration, such as reliance of the parties or a very strict construction of the executed contract doctrine in order to rule in favor of parties who had used Confederate currency. For instance, in *Williams v. Elkins* (1870), the plaintiff had agreed to take two hundred dollars in Confederate money for a mill. When the fortunes of war changed, the plaintiff refused to accept the Confederate money and after the war sued for a return of the mill. The Court ruled that the plaintiff had made a bad bargain and would have to live with his contract. The Court rejected the plaintiff's argument that since the contract was to pay Confederate money it was void in the first instance. However, in these cases, the Court fell short of ruling that Confederate money was a valuable consideration.

The Conservative Court was gradually working its way to declaring Confederate currency valuable. Finally, Judge Freeman refuted the Radical doctrine that the mere use of Confederate notes voided a contract because the use supported treason in *Naff v. Crawford* (1870). A debtor owed three hundred dollars in Confederate currency based on a promissory note. In contested circumstances, the debtor exchanged the original note for one that was due in "a current bank notes." When the creditor attempted to collect the notes after the war, the debtor claimed that he was forced to exchange the notes by threats and that he owed nothing because the original note was for Confederate currency. Judge Freeman might have ducked the issue of the value of Confederate currency, but said that it was time to face the issue directly.

Judge Freeman noted that the Radical doctrine was that Confederate money was issued for an illegal purpose because it tended to support the Confederacy. Freeman pointed out that, while contracts that intend to violate public policy, such as renting a room for purposes of prostitution, are invalid, contracts that merely facilitate a prostitute's living, such as selling her provisions, are not themselves void. So the element that destroys a contract is the agreement to accomplish an illegal end. Users of Confederate notes were not primarily attempting to subvert the United States, they were just continuing to do their business under the prevailing conditions. The only money available in many parts of the country was Confederate currency.

Accordingly, Freeman determined that the mere use of Confederate notes was not illegal and the contracts that were based on them were not void. In order to present this opinion as based in law and not mere politics, Freeman relied heavily on Chief Justice Chase's opinion for the United States Supreme Court in *Thorington v. Smith* (1868). Chase said "while the war lasted, however, they [Confederate notes] had a certain contingent value, and were used as money in nearly all business transactions of many millions of people."[54] Freeman argued that Chase's holding meant that Confederate money could not be compared to counterfeit bills as the Radical Court had done. Instead they were genuine promises to pay on the condition specified, which was the establishment of Confederate independence. The failure of this condition was nothing more than an ordinary business risk. Because the notes had contingent value, they provided valuable legal consideration for any contracts. Freeman knew that the Radicals would view his ruling as a political decision and therefore ended with a plea that his opinion be accepted as a matter of law: "We have gone at greater length than we desired in to the reasons . . . [for] overruling decisions made by our predecessors, . . . [to] show that we have not done this on any mere theories of our own."[55]

Despite Freeman's plea, the underlying rationale of both the Radical and Conservative decisions about Confederate currency was political. For the Radicals, these notes facilitated a traitorous conspiracy and thus not only had no value, but also were actually evil in themselves. For Conservatives, the notes were proof that for years the Confederacy had succeeded as a sovereign nation, even pumping into the economy that essential lifeblood: a fiat money that millions accepted as legitimate. Neither side could prove the other "legally" incorrect. Given the two sides presuppositions the legal conclusions were both valid. Only the changing of the political guard could allow Conservative judges to overturn the Radical's base assumptions about the villainy of these notes.

Later cases confirmed the Freeman holding in *Naff.* In *Sherfy v. Argenbright* (1870), a special judge, that is a non–Supreme Court judge sitting by temporary appointment, also overruled the Radical rulings about Confederate currency. This judge similarly relied on *Thorington v. Smith,* the United States Supreme Court decision, an ironic call upon federalism to support a decision that celebrated the value of Confederate money. However, the judge argued that Chief Justice Chase did not go far enough, because Chase refused to acknowledge that the Confederacy was a de facto government. Shields, the special judge, spent four pages, completely unnecessary to the decision in this case, arguing that the Confederacy was a de facto government. The judge also devoted two pages to explaining why it was permissible to overrule the precedents of a Radical Court. Because these decisions were of recent origin, did not affect longstanding property rights, and were contrary to other authorities, it was permissible to disregard them. Furthermore, overruling these precedents did not destroy any vested interest, "at least not any that is bounded in justice or right," a comment on the illegitimacy of the Radical Court.[56]

By 1871, the circuit courts had begun to adopt the Conservative jurisprudence on Confederate notes. One court's instructions, which the Supreme Court validated, shows the scope of the validity of Confederate notes as valuable consideration. In that case the promissory note contained no limitation on the currency in which the note should be repaid. However, the loan had been for Confederate notes, which the debtor used to pay his taxes. The Circuit Court judge instructed that the Confederate money could be valid consideration if (1) the note was executed within Confederate lines, (2) Confederate money was passing as currency at the time the note was made, and (3) the loan was not made directly in aid of the Confederate war effort. The Supreme Court ratified this statement of law in *Bond v. Perkins* (1871) and added that a loan to pay Confederate taxes was not made directly in aid of the war effort.

The Supreme Court further limited the effect of the doctrine that loans were valid only if not made in direct aid of the war by recognizing as legal many of the business transactions that took place during the war. For instance in *Jones v. Planter's Bank* (1872), Planter's Bank loaned five thousand dollars to a debtor, after the debtor had discussed with several of the bank's directors that the purpose of the loan was to set up a manufacturing plant to produce arms for the Confederate army. The bank made the loan pursuant to a board of director's resolution that authorized loans to the Confederate states for military purposes. Furthermore, some of the members of the board of directors of the bank informed the debtor that he would not have received the loan for any other purpose. The Court held that despite this evidence, as long as the loan was a private loan to a private party, the individual knowledge of the directors did not turn this loan into an official act in aid of the Confederacy. If loans made to pay taxes to the states of the Confederacy or manufacture arms for the Confederacy were not made in direct aid of the Confederacy, few loans to an individual or company would violate the third strand of the Court's test.

This line of Conservative jurisprudence reached its high watermark in *Bank of Tennessee v. Cummings* (1872). In that case the bank made a loan to an individual to manufacture saltpeter to sell to the Confederate government in order to make gunpowder. The officers of the bank knew the purpose of the loan and approved of the loan because they favored this purpose. The Court affirmed the validity of this note because the Confederacy, as a belligerent, had a right to defend itself. Therefore, during the war Confederate citizens could aid in the defense of the Confederacy. With this ruling, Judge Turney seemed to have validated almost any contract that occurred behind Confederate lines.

In later years, the Court found it necessary to back down from this position that a party had to intend to enter into an illegal contract, not merely know that the other contracting party was attempting an illegal act. This distinction, while beneficial to parties dealing with Rebels, threatened the Court's ability to control other types of contracts where the Court wanted to limit the parties' ability to contract for illegal purposes. In *Henderson v. Waggoner* (1878), the Planter's Bank had lent money to equip a Confederate military unit and sued to recover on the note. The defense maintained that the note was void because its purpose was to aid the military of the Confederacy. The defense introduced evidence that the bank's board of directors were aware of this purpose. Judge Deaderick stated that the Court should adopt the rule that if the seller knew that an article, innocent itself, was to be used for any illegal or immoral purpose then the sale would be void. Deaderick went further, limiting the holding in *Jones v. Planter's Bank* to those exact facts.

As the passions associated with Reconstruction subsided, the Court revisited some of the political decisions it made in those years. For instance, the sharp division that the Court made between "innocent" Confederate money and treasonous activity no longer served the purpose that it once had. By the late 1870s the Court was more interested in asserting control over market activities. Thus, we get opinions such as Judge Deaderick's in *Henderson,* which emphasized the Court's police power over dubious market practices even at the expense of validating the Confederacy. As time passed, the Conservative Court had to turn its attention from its initial task of rejecting Radicalism to the more difficult one of creating a legal structure for a postbellum society and economy. This new society and economy was one in which old attitudes toward African Americans and the market had to be reanalyzed.

ESTABLISHING THE NEW ORDER

In one area of the law, both the Radical and Conservative court agreed: the family was the basic unit of society. Tennessee statutes during this period allowed courts to grant a divorce as long as one marriage partner could prove that the other spouse had destroyed the marriage by committing certain specified actions. The most common grounds were adultery and desertion without support for over two years. Where a party could prove these acts, the Court affirmed grants of divorce. But neither the Radical nor the Conservative Court hesitated to apply the statute strictly and enforce technical rules in refusing to grant divorces.

Adultery was only a ground for divorce if the spouse seeking the divorce was blameless. In *Cameron v. Cameron* (1865), the wife refused to move from Pennsylvania to Tennessee with her husband and was shown to be living in an adulterous relationship. Even though the wife did not defend against this action, the chancellor dismissed the suit because the husband did not prove that he had been chaste since the separation. The Court affirmed, noting that a contrary decision would allow parties to seek a collusive divorce. Similarly, the Court refused to grant a divorce in *Lishey v. Lishey* (1880), because the wife only suspected that her husband had two children by an African American woman who had been his slave. The wife could present no proof other than her husband's solicitude toward his ex-slave and her children. Finding this insufficient, the Court affirmed the dismissal of the suit.

The Court also took a stand against collusive out-of-state divorces in *Gettys v. Gettys* (1879). The Court refused to recognize a Utah divorce when the evidence showed that the husband went to Utah for just a few weeks and was never a bona fide citizen of Utah. When the parties complied with the statute, however, the Court would, with misgivings, allow a divorce. In *Lanier v. Lanier* (1871) the husband proved that his wife had either poisoned him, or, at least, abandoned him when he was deathly ill. "Doubting, as we do, the policy of our statutes in allowing so many causes of divorce not prescribed by the great Author of Marriage," the Court reluctantly granted the divorce.[57] Judge Turney wrote a forceful dissent arguing that divorce contradicted biblical injunction and natural law and that courts should not enforce the statute. The Court displayed similar reluctance in *Thomas v. Thomas* (1865), where a wife successfully proved adultery, but the husband pointed out that she had allowed him to return to the marriage bed. The Court only granted her a divorce from bed and board, in effect a legal separation. In only one case, *Willard v. Willard* (1873), did the Court allow a divorce without proof of the statutory requirements. In that case the wife's brother had threatened the groom with a gun to force him to the altar, a classic shotgun wedding. The Court found that a marriage must have the consent of both parties and lack of such consent due to coercion would make the marriage voidable. Because the husband had done nothing to ratify the marriage, the Court allowed him to prove his lack of consent.

The Court also showed respect for the institution of marriage by allowing women to sue for breach of promise to marry. In *Coover v. Davenport* (1870) the Court permitted a woman to pursue her breach of promise case against a married man even though she had continued to see him after she learned that he was married. The Court held that the defendant had deceived her by insisting that he was getting a divorce. Similarly, in *Williams v. Hollingsworth* (1873), the Court allowed a woman to prove both breach of promise and seduction but instructed that the defendant could introduce evidence of her prior sexual conduct to mitigate damages.

While marriage remained the bedrock of society, emancipation had ended slavery and thus changed the legal, political and social relations between the races. The Conservatives accepted political equality between the races as the price of avoiding congressional reconstruction. The 1870 Constitution secured African American suffrage, but only because the drafters were afraid that failure to include the provision would lead to federal intervention. However, the Conservatives were not willing to accept any trace of social equality. In particular, the races could not be allowed to intermarry. One of the first acts of the Conservative legislature was to pass a miscegenation law.[58] The Tennessee Supreme Court was soon called upon to test the constitutionality of this act in *Lonas v. State* (1871). An African American man was convicted and sentenced to two and a half years in prison for his marriage to a white woman. When he could not find an attorney to represent him, the Court appointed J. Scott Payne as his counsel. Based on the published report of this attorney's argument, he did a good job. Payne argued that the miscegenation law violated his client's right to make contracts as guaranteed by the Fourteenth Amendment. He reasoned that the law regarded marriage as a type of civil contract, and that the Fourteenth Amendment provided that all citizens, black and white, had the right to contract. He also argued that this measure acted as an ex post facto law because the marriage had existed before the legislature enacted this law.

The state attorney general argued that the rights of citizens of states were distinct from the rights of citizens of the United States. The rights protected by the U.S. Constitution were limited to those that belonged to the citizens of the United States. Marriage was an institution regulated by state, not federal, law. Therefore, marriage was not a privilege of a citizen of the United States. Citizens of other states did not have a right to come to Tennessee united in an interracial marriage and "to shock the public sense by a mixture of incongruous breeds."[59] Furthermore, the miscegenation law did not violate the right to contract because there cannot be a valid contract if the purpose of the arrangement is illegal. Like contracts for gaming or usury, a contract to enter into a interracial marriage was void. But most tellingly, the attorney general argued that both races do have an equal right to contract, or rather an equal disability. Just as a white citizen cannot marry an African American, so an African American cannot marry a white citizen. "This is the substance of our law, to prevent the production of a hybrid race."[60]

The Tennessee Supreme Court supported the legislature's attempt to prevent the social equality of the races. The Court admitted that the United States Constitution and its new amendments did have some authority over the states. However, states retained substantial rights. The Court reasoned that only if the Thirteenth or Fourteenth Amendments or the civil rights acts gave Africans social equality could the United States Constitution forbid a miscegenation statute. The Court first ruled that the ability to enter a marriage was not a privilege or immunity as defined by the Fourteenth Amendment. Neither was it a contract; instead, marriage was a domestic relation. "The laws of civilization demand that the races be kept apart in this country."[61] For this reason the statute was constitutional and the conviction upheld.

In *State v. Bell* (1872), another prosecution under the miscegenation act came to the Court. Since Mississippi was still under Reconstruction, Mississippi law allowed interracial marriages. A couple who had married in Mississippi moved to Tennessee. The husband was prosecuted under the miscegenation statute. His defense was that Tennessee was required by the full faith and credit clause of the Constitution to respect marriages that were legal in the state in which the marriage took place. The Supreme Court held that Tennessee courts were not bound to respect this marriage because it contravened the morals of the state. The Court stated that just as Tennessee would not be required to recognize the marriage of a father to his daughter or a polygamous marriage, the state did not have to validate interracial marriages.

Although the Tennessee Supreme Court was quick to support laws that denied "social" equality to African Americans, the Court protected the rights of the African American in economic settings. For instance, in *Norris v. Stephens* (1877), a widow with five children had hired out her eldest son to a man named Stephens to help support the family. In September 1870 the mother and son had a fight and the boy left home. On September 5, 1870, the county court bound the boy to Stephens as an apprentice. Neither the mother nor the son was a party to this apprenticing, and the mother received no notice of the proceedings. The boy worked for two years and ten months until he came of age. He sued for back pay and Stephens's defense was that the boy was apprenticed. The trial court supported the alleged master.

The Supreme Court, pointing to a number of procedural errors, reversed this case and ordered a new trial. The Circuit Court had never made a formal finding that the boy had been abandoned. Furthermore, the boy seemed perfectly capable of taking care of himself, as he had been helping support his family. Hence, the court did not need to bind him out. Even if a need had existed, the court should have notified the mother and then made a finding as to whether or not she was able to maintain the boy. However, trial courts in the future could easily subvert this decision by merely making the necessary findings.

The Tennessee Supreme Court also enforced the 1865 act that had repealed all laws in support of slavery. In 1879 some white men were indicted for playing cards with African American men. This statute had been passed during slave years, primarily as a measure to control slaves. The law had never been specifically repealed. In *Wells v. State* (1879), the Court reversed these convictions and ruled that because this law was part of the fabric of slave law, the 1865 act had implicitly repealed it.

The Court also protected African Americans who had been the beneficiaries of their master's will during slavery. In *Deberry v. Hurt* (1874), a master had provided five hundred dollars to be held for the benefit of a slave who should be manumitted on the master's death. The trustee had provided the slave with a house and some farm land with part of the money. The slave had never been freed, probably because under Tennessee law he would have had to leave the state if he had been formally emancipated. So this slave lived by himself on the land. After the war the slave sued for his inheritance. The Court held that manumission was not a necessary prerequisite for the slave to enjoy the bequest. The trustee could get credit for providing the house and land, but he had to prove their value and pay the rest of the bequest.

This Conservative Court was in perfect agreement with the Conservative legislature that Tennessee law need not treat African American as the social equal of whites. The Court was quite willing to take a states' right stance that minimized the impact of the Reconstruction amendments. However, in cases that presented the question of whether African Americans should be treated equally under the law, the Tennessee Supreme Court protected the African American's legal rights. At the county level, the courts did not seem as sensitive to the legal equality of the newly freed citizens, but the Supreme Court reversed cases where prejudice seemed evident. The Supreme Court also supported the legislature's attempt to limit the violence that it been endemic during Reconstruction, another position which, at least initially, probably helped to secure the legal rights of African Americans.

In its first legislative session, the Conservative legislature passed an act limiting the right to carry arms. The act provided, "that it shall not be lawful for any person to publicly or privately carry a dirk, swordcane, Spanish stiletto, belt or pocket pistol or revolver."[62] This act immediately came under constitutional attack in *Andrews v. State* (1871). The Supreme Court heard three consolidated cases that raised the constitutional issues. Alvin Hawkins, the former Radical Supreme Court judge, represented two of the defendants charged with violating the statute. He argued that the statute violated the Second Amendment to the United States Constitution and that the 1870 Tennessee Constitution only gave the legislature the power to regulate, not the power to prohibit, the carrying of arms. Attorney General

Joseph Heiskell argued that the Second Amendment had no application to the states. He maintained that if the people of Tennessee chose to part with a portion of their liberty, that is, the right to carry guns, in order to create a more civil society, the voters had that right.

The Supreme Court found it easy to dismiss the Second Amendment argument. The United States Supreme Court in *Barron v. Baltimore* had ruled that the Bill of Rights did not apply to the states.[63] Therefore, the only issue was whether the Constitution of Tennessee limited the legislature's right to regulate the bearing of arms. The Constitution of 1834 had guaranteed all free white men the right to keep and bear arms. The Constitution of 1870 had added a section to the Constitution of 1834, which stated that "the citizens of this state have a right to keep and bear arms for their common defense. But the Legislature shall have power by law, to regulate the wearing the arms, with a view to prevent crime."[64]

A sharply divided Court interpreted the right to bear arms to encompass only those arms that would be appropriate for a soldier. Other types of arms could be regulated by the legislature. The Court held that the legislature did have the right to regulate dirks, sword canes, stilettos and belt or pocket pistols, as these were not the types of weapons that soldiers would ordinarily carry. As to the provisions regulating the carrying of revolvers, if the law intended to cover soldiers' revolvers, it was too broad. The Court added that a defendant could not avoid prosecution under this statute by declaring he was carrying the illegal weapon for self-defense. The entire policy behind this statute was to stifle violence that had been prevalent during and since the Civil War. In order for this law to be effective, all citizens must stop carrying the proscribed weapons.

Judge Nelson wrote a ringing dissent, a very unusual event in the early years of the Conservative Court. Nelson argued that the Constitution of 1870 and the statute only meant to give the legislature the power to regulate how arms were carried, not the power to prohibit carrying arms completely. He particularly argued that free citizens should have the right of self-defense. Judge Turney concurred in this dissent.

After ratifying the legislature's attempt to rein in the violence that had plagued Tennessee society since secession, the Court implemented this policy in later decisions that interpreted the carrying arms statute. In two cases, *Miller v. State* (1873) and *Gayle v. State* (1880), the Court ruled that magistrates who were usually not involved in arresting criminals could not carry arms. Once again the Conservative Court, although this time with some dissension, cooperated with the Conservative legislature to try to set Tennessee on a more stable course and reinstitute the rule of law in place of the rule of politics and armed gangs.

LIEN LAWS

Perhaps the most important role for the Supreme Court in the 1870s was to establish the legal rules under which Tennesseans could rejuvenate their agricultural production. Emancipation had fundamentally changed the relationship of landowners and black laborers.[65] In the postbellum society the two groups had to develop a way of working with each other. Landowners remained in control of the means of production: land, work animals, seed, and farming implements. The laborers succeeded in gaining control over their own and their family's labor. By the 1870s, the usual way of getting the labor and land together was some sort of share cropping arrangement. The landowner would provide the land and varying amounts of other provisions, such as seed, stock, implements and even provisions for the laborer's family; the laborer would provide the work, and the parties would share the crop. The essentially legal component of the evolution of the cropping system was the lien law. The lien law set out the various parties' interest in the crop. The lien law also dealt with third-party claims against the crop, usually creditors of either the landowner or the laborer.

The basic rule that the Conservative Court developed in the 1870s was that the landowner won. Given the background of this Court, the political era, and the widely shared agrarian values of Tennessee society, this bias of the Court in favor of landowners over laborers was perhaps inevitable. What sets Tennessee's jurisprudence apart from that of other southern states is the uniform preference for landowner rights over the rights of owners of capital.[66]

The Court moved to establish the rights of landowners over tenants in the first sessions after its election, even before the legislature changed the law. In *Hunt v. Wing* (1872), the Court interpreted a share agreement entered into under Mississippi law in favor of a landowner over laborers. A landowner rented out a plantation for four thousand dollars and retained an express lien on the crops and livestock to secure payment of the rent. The renter hired forty African Americans to work the land. The renter defaulted on the rent, and the landowner confiscated all the crop except twenty-four bales of cotton that an agent of the Freedmen's Bureau claimed was owed to the African American laborers. These twenty-four bales were set to Memphis to be sold. The landowner replevined, that is seized through legal process, these bales. The African American laborers, through their best friend, an agent of the Freedmen's Bureau, sued to recover the cotton, claiming a superior right in the crop for the laborers.

The Court first rejected the idea that a "best friend" could represent free citizens under no disability. However, the Court graciously, if with prejudicial comments, stated that it would not dismiss the case for this procedural irregularity. The Court went on to note that the common law favored the right of landowners to seize property without any process. Unless a statute changed that law, the Court must prefer the landowner's claim. The only way the laborers could prove a superior claim in this crop would be to show a specific statutory right. The laborers could not show this right. Some of the laborers were working for wages instead of a shares. The Court ruled that those laborers could only file a creditor's attachment that would attach to any surplus over the landowner's claim. As for those laborers who were working on shares, their interest in the crop was not localized in these particular bales of cotton. These laborers did not have an interest sufficient to justify intervention in this suit. The Court left the laborers to pursue the bankrupt renter.

Even in a case where the laborer managed to get away with the proceeds of a crop sale, the Court made a ruling that gave landowners a tremendous practical advantage in all future disputes. In *Philips v. Maxwell* (1872), a tenant, Maxwell, had agreed to pay $775 rent for ninety acres of farmland. His crop made nine bales of cotton. The landowner retained possession of the cotton after it was ginned. Maxwell removed three bales and sold them without the landowner's knowledge. Maxwell then went back for three more bales and the landowner stopped him from removing the cotton. Maxwell allegedly agreed to let the landowner keep the remaining six bales until the rent was paid. However, that night Maxwell took the cotton to Pulaski, Tennessee and sold it to a broker. Maxwell then absconded.

The landowner attached the cotton in the broker's possession. The broker raised the defense that he had bought the cotton in the ordinary course of business and without knowledge of any lien. The Court held that when a lien becomes fixed on a crop, the lien dates back to that date the parties entered into the contract. Additionally, the landowner could pursue the crop no matter who took possession of it. Because the landowners' lien "overreaches any title acquired by the purchaser of the crop from the tenant, although without notice of the lien,"[67] the landowner prevailed. This case gave landowners complete control over the crop. No broker could risk purchasing a crop from a tenant, because the landowner could always retake the crop based on his lien. All cautious brokers would insist that the landowner sign off on the purchase, thus leaving tenants subject to the sharp dealing of landowners.

Later decisions by the Court continued to put tenants in an inferior position. Even though the landlord had complete control over disposition of the crop, in *Magill v. Holston* (1873), the Court ruled that until the landlord took actual possession of part of the crop, the tenant bore the risk of the crop being destroyed. In that case the tenant and landlord were in the process of the dividing the crop when a flood destroyed the crop. The

Supreme Court declared that the tenant bore all the risk until the landlord's portion was physically delivered.

The legislature joined in this process of creating a landlord-friendly lien law. An 1875 amendment allowed landlords a lien for supplying food and clothing to their tenants, as long as the landlord kept an account of the supplies.[68] The previous law had only allowed a lien for seed, livestock, and farming implements and had required a written contract stating the consideration for the lien. The Court interpreted this new amendment in *Lewis v. Mahon & Goodloe* (1878), where a creditor of the tenant tried to levy against the crop. The landlord had failed to execute a written contract giving him a lien. The Court ruled that because the landlord had provided food and clothing to the tenant, the landlord's lien would be good based on the accounting for the supplies.

In *Dougherty v. Kellum* (1879), the Court further eased a landlord's ability to establish a crop lien. The landowner filed an affidavit in support of the attachment that claimed the tenant owed fifty-five dollars "more or less" for rent and supplies. This affidavit violated many aspects of the lien law. It did not provide a written contract memorializing the rent portion of the lien. Moreover, it did not have attached an accounting for the supplies provided to the tenant. Also, the "more or less" language indicated that the landowner was estimating the amount owed. Even after noting all of these procedural difficulties with the landlord's claim, the Court ruled that because the jury had given a verdict for the landowner, the improper attachment had no prejudicial effect and the landowner could collect from this crop. The practical result of this decision was to allow landowners who had good relations with the sheriff to have a crop attached and to circumvent any procedural safeguards as long as he later got a jury verdict in his favor.

In only one case, *Patterson v. Hawkins* (1879), decided during this period did a tenant win a partial victory. A tenant entered into a cropping contract for two-thirds of the crop. The tenant, allegedly through his own negligence, only grew enough cotton to make three bales. When the cotton was sold, the landowner received a judgment for all three bales. The trial court ruled that if the tenant had been a better farmer, he would have made nine bales of cotton. Therefore, the landowner could claim the whole crop. The Supreme Court reversed this ruling, holding that the landowner could only get the third he contracted for. The lower court did not have the right to speculate on the size the crop should have been.

The Supreme Court's preference for landowners is not at all surprising. The entire Conservative movement was aimed at reestablishing the political control of the more substantial white citizens. The primary asset that the war left these citizens was their land. No matter what sympathy these judges might feel toward the plight of the newly freed African American, the judge's political, social and economic interests lay in allowing white landowners to gain control of the new agricultural system. The Court not only preferred landowners to laborers, but consistently preferred landowners to creditors. The 1875 amendment to the lien law also reflected the legislature's preference that the landowner supply tenants with food and clothing, because only the landowner could take a lien in the crop for these items.

When the Court considered cases pitting landowners against creditors, landowners almost always won. For instance, in *Mann v. Taylor* (1871), a third party had sold some tenants supplies on credit. The lower court instructed that the landowners and laborers formed a partnership and therefore the entire crop was available to satisfy the creditor's claim. The Supreme Court reversed, ruling that the landlord and laborers were tenants in common, so that the creditors could not satisfy their demands from the landowner's portion of the crop. Recall that a year later the Court held that when a crop was destroyed the landowner had no interest in the crop until it was divided. So the landowner had enough interest to protect the crop against the tenant's creditors, but not enough to be harmed by disasters to the crop. The main consistency to the Court's jurisprudence was that landowners prevailed.

In another supplier versus landowner case, *Polk v. Foster* (1874), the Court went to great lengths to deny the supplier any rights in the crop. The landowner had bought the land for 500 bales of cotton. He agreed to deliver 125 bales every year for four years. The landowner then gave a lien on the land to a supplier to secure advances for supplies. The supplier took the crop when it was made and sold it. The landowner and the mortgage holder both sued the supplier for conversion of the crop. The lower court dismissed the lawsuit, holding that future crops cannot be mortgaged, so the claim of the mortgage holder must fail. The Supreme Court reversed and held that the mortgage holder had made a conditional sale and thus the mortgage was really a lease of the land for 125 bales of cotton. The court provided no authority for converting a conditional sale into a lease. However by doing so, the court was able to hold that the supply creditor was an inferior position to a landlord leasing the land. By this slight of hand, the Supreme Court was able to protect both the mortgage holder and the current landholder, those with landed interests, from the claims of the supplier, who only had a contractual interest.

The Conservative court, in conjunction with the Conservative-dominated legislature, succeeded in creating a lien law that protected the agrarian interests of landowners. If the Court's preference for landowners over tenants is quite understandable, if not laudable, Tennessee seemed unusually harsh on commercial creditors. In other states moneylenders contested strongly with landowners for lien superiority.[69] This tendency to be wary of the power of capital owners probably had its roots in the Jacksonian antibank battle of the 1830s. In establishing the rules for the postbellum economy, the Court consistently expressed a suspicion of the market forces, which were becoming stronger as Tennessee was drawn into the interregional economy.

RESISTING THE MARKET

The Conservative Court's relationship with the growth of national markets during this period reflected the agrarian fears of conservative white Tennesseans. Generally, the Court did not favor innovative market practices. For instance, in *Marshall v. Thruston* (1879), a bank sued to collect three notes for $860. The defendant had given these notes to settle transactions involving the buying and selling of Tennessee state bonds. These transactions were clearly future sales, meaning that a trader would agree to either buy or sell bonds at a future date. Essentially, the buyer was betting on which way the price of the bonds would fluctuate. The sales were leveraged in that the buyer only paid a fraction of the price, thus magnifying the gains or losses in comparison with the money actually paid for the contracts. On the date set by the contract, the parties would not actually buy or sell the bonds, but instead would settle up by paying the difference between the amount agreed and the market price on that date. The bank claimed that it was a mere agent, placing these contracts on the New York market and charging a commission. The debtor claimed the bank was a principal in buying and selling of futures contracts, or, if an agent, the bank knew full well that these contracts were a form of gambling. The defendant argued that because these contracts were essentially gaming contracts, they were void and he did not owe the note given to cover his losses.

The Supreme Court approved the trial court judge's instructions that these contracts were only valid if the parties actually meant to deliver the goods bargained for. If instead, the intent was to speculate on the price, then the whole transaction was void as nothing more than a wager. The Court thus held that futures contracts were against public policy.

However, the Court did give the bank some protection. If the bank could prove that it was a true agent who was merely brokering the sale of the bonds with a New York party, then the bank could collect on the notes. On the other hand, if the money was advanced to enable the debtor to speculate on the futures market, then the bank could not collect. The

Court was clearly not happy with these market innovations and was not eager to lend its aid in facilitating them by enforcing them.

The Court similarly looked with a baleful eye on an innovation in consumer credit in *Singer Manufacturing Co. v. Cole* (1880). The Singer Sewing Machine Company sent salesmen through Tennessee selling their sewing machines directly to consumers. The company required each salesman to use a contract that purported to be a lease of the machine to be paid 15 months after the sale. The intent was to retain title in the machine until the customer paid. The Supreme Court recognized the contract for what it was: a sale with reservation of title for security. "However reprehensible and calculated to excite suspicion of unfairness . . . with its verbiage expressing literally a different meaning from what was intended," the Court allowed the exact terms of the contract to be enforced but was clearly not happy about doing so.[70]

Interregional trade also allowed confidence men opportunities for defrauding Tennesseans. The Court had to determine when fraud moved from civil to criminal liability. In *Delaney v. State* (1872), a swindler established himself as a salesman for a New York bagging and rope company. He discussed business prospects with a bank president in order to establish his bona fides and then, later the same day, presented a printed check drawn on the New York firm. The bank cashed the check. Of course, the firm had never heard of the salesman and refused to honor the check. The defendant was arrested and charged with obtaining money under false pretenses. He argued that he had merely lied and that a conservative businessman would not have been fooled by his scheme. The antebellum rule in Tennessee had been that if "common prudence and caution" would have protected the victim, then a defendant had not committed the crime of obtaining money by false pretenses.

The Court, however, was quick to defend this naïve Tennessee banker. The Court held that the bank need not do business with such suspicion that it had to investigate the truth of every customer's claim of identity and connection. The Court, in short, rejected the defendant's somewhat audacious plea that the bank was so naïve that criminally innocent lies sufficed to bilk it.

Likewise, the Court held the line on Tennessee's 6 percent usury law, which the Conservatives had passed in their first legislative session. In *Richardson v. Brown* (1877), some parties tried to get around the usury law by stating on the face of a note that it had been executed in Jackson, Mississippi, where a 12 percent rate was legal. In fact, the note had been executed in Memphis. The Supreme Court observed that because the rate was not usurious on its face and because only by proof could the defendant establish that the note was executed in Memphis, the plaintiff could recover the initial amount plus the 6 percent statutory interest. The Court also rejected a bank's attempt to use an ambiguity in the usury law to avoid repaying a deposit in *Exchange & Deposit Bank v. Swepson* (1878). The bank's cashier had orally promised a 10 percent interest rate on the deposit. Under the usury statute, interest rates in excess of 6 percent but no more than 10 percent, had to be in writing for the rate to be effective. When the depositor attempted to withdraw his money, the bank refused to honor the request. On being sued for the return of the deposit without interest, the bank claimed that the entire transaction was void because the 10 percent interest rate was not in writing. The Supreme Court rejected this claim, explaining that although the depositor could not enforce the 10 percent rate orally promised, he did not lose his deposit just because the bank had made an unenforceable agreement.

Railroad accidents generated a significant amount of litigation in the years following the Civil War. The Court resisted the railroads' demands for protection from tort liability as the railroad net expanded throughout Tennessee and connected the state ever closer to the interregional market. Antebellum laws had placed very strict requirements on the railroad to avoid accidents that injured people or livestock. An 1856 statute required that every train keep an employee on duty to look for obstructions. If the lookout saw livestock, humans or any obstruction on the track, the engineer had the duty to blow the whistle, apply the brakes and "use all necessary means stop the train." The failure to take these steps would lead to strict liability for any injury done to livestock. Moreover, the railroad had the duty to demonstrate that the crew had taken all the required measures. The antebellum Supreme Court held the railroad stringently to these standards.[71]

The initial reaction of the Conservative Court was to follow antebellum practice and require that the railroads strictly observe the statutory requirements. The Court, in *Nashville & Chattanooga Railroad v. Thomas* (1871), held the railroad liable for failure to comply with the statutory measures when an animal suddenly appeared on the tracks, even if the crew did not have time to react and blow the whistle and brake. In a similar case, *Memphis and Charleston Railroad v. Smith* (1872), the railroad proved that when a mule ran in front of the train, the crew blew the whistle and applied one of the three brakes. Chief Justice Nicholson ruled that the company must prove that the crew applied all three brakes or the company would be liable. Even if the railroad proved that applying the other two brakes would not have avoided the accident, the statute imposed liability for not applying those brakes. The Court also noted that Tennessee did not recognize a defense of contributory negligence against the livestock owners for allowing the mule to run on the range: "Our statutes, in various ways, recognize the running out of stock on the commons or range as lawful."[72]

While many states protected livestock on the railroad tracks, Tennessee was unusual in having the same rules apply to people on the tracks.[73] The Court held railroads to the strict statutory standards in these situations as well. In *Hill v. Louisville and Nashville Railroad Co.* (1876), the Court found a railroad company liable for a wrongful death arising from a nighttime collision. With the aid of the headlights, the engineer saw a group of men on the track but did not ring his bell until within twenty-five feet of them. The engineer never blew the whistle or applied the brakes. He testified that he assumed the decedent would step off the tracks because he, the engineer, saw the other men do so. The decedent was too drunk, however, to take care of himself, and the train hit and killed him.

The railroad company argued contributory negligence under common law. The Court ruled that the common law did not control because the statute had superseded it. The statute required that when the engineers saw a person on the track, he must sound the whistle, apply the brakes, and take every means to prevent an accident. The engineer had no right to expect that the man would leave the tracks. "The *statute,*" the Court observed, "does not brook *the slightest speculation* upon things that are *probable or possible* either *by the court* or *by the company's agents;* but demands *an absolute obedience* to its provisions whether they seem necessary or not."[74] Because the engineer was under a positive duty to blow the whistle, the Court refused to ameliorate the strict requirement that the statute imposed on the railroad.

The Tennessee Court's attempt to protect its citizens from the many injuries that resulted from the proliferation of railroads after the war even extended to severely limiting the fellow-servant doctrine. Under this doctrine railroads were not liable to their workers for injuries suffered on the job due to their co-worker's negligence.[75] This rule saved railroads millions of dollars in damages for injuries to their workers and arguably subsidized the antebellum expansion of the railroads. Railroads did not have to pay for the injuries to their laborers nor incur the expense necessary to make railroad work safer.[76]

Southern courts had generally adhered to the fellow-servant rule, with the significant exception of not applying this doctrine to slaves. The underlying rationale behind the rule was that workers freely assumed the risks of co-worker negligence, and that high wages compensated them for this assumption of the risk. This contractual analysis could not be applied to slaves who had no choice but to work where ordered and received no wages. Moreover, planters were not anxious to give railroads a carte blanche to hire and then damage or destroy their valuable human property.[77]

The Conservative Court continued this tradition of limiting the fellow-servant rule even after emancipation. In *Louisville & Nashville Railroad v.*

Bowler (1872), the Court drew a distinction between the negligence of fellow servants of the same grade and the negligence of a supervisor. The Supreme Court reasoned that an ordinary worker had neither control over or the power to resist the orders of his foreman. The railroad was obligated to choose these managers with care, and was responsible if its choice was faulty and the foreman's decisions injured workers. Judge Turney even quoted approvingly from a Shackelford opinion, an acknowledgment of the Radical Court rarely seen in Conservative Court opinions. Turney also noted that the railroad's claim that a subordinate should disobey a foreman's orders and then seek redress in the courts if discharged for doing so, was unworkable in practice. In fact, railroads would never allow their employees to second-guess their supervisors.

As the years progressed, however, the Court began rethinking the obligations that railroads had toward both workers and animals. By 1885, the Court had restricted enforcement of the statutory requirements. In *East Tennessee, Virginia and Georgia Railroad v. Rush* (1885), a worker was ordered to set up a signal to a passenger train that the track ahead was blocked. The worker set up lights that should have been visible for a quarter mile. The worker then negligently fell asleep sitting on the tracks. Despite the lights, the engineer on the passenger train took no action to avoid the obstruction and hit the worker, injuring him severely.

The worker claimed that under the statute, the engineer had a strict duty to blow the whistle and apply the brakes when he saw the light. The railroad insisted that the worker's contributory negligence caused the injury. The Supreme Court curtailed the railroad's duty to comply with the statute. First, the railroad was only responsible for actual collisions, not secondary injuries cause by an accident. Second, the Court pointed to a string of cases that relieved the railroad of the statutory duties in train depots and yards. These cases held that the railroad had no duties to servants and employees of the railroad in these areas. Furthermore, the Court also relied on a string of cases that expanded the definition of which workers could be fellow servants. It had applied the fellow-servant rule to cases involving engineers and firemen, firemen and common laborers, engineers and assistant fireman, and engineers and brakeman, holding that all of these duos were fellow-servants despite the differences in grades. Therefore, the fellow-servant status of the engineer and this brakeman from another train overrode the statutory duty that the engineer would otherwise have had toward this worker.

The Court did not backtrack as far on the railroad's duty toward stock, because Tennessee had rejected the common-law duty to fence animals during the antebellum period. However, the Court did begin to place mild limits on the railroad's duty. In *East Tennessee, Virginia and Georgia Railroad v. Scales* (1879), a mule jumped in front of the train the as it approached a trestle. The train complied with some of the statutory requirements and avoided hitting the mule. The parties presented contradictory evidence as to whether the engineer sounded the whistle, but it was uncontroverted that the mule died by falling off the trestle rather than by being hit by the engine. The trial judge instructed that if the train had come to a halt and the mule died by jumping off the trestle, then the railroad was not liable, even if the engineer did not comply with the statute.

Judge Cooper affirmed, noting that the Court had previously held railroads liable for failure to meet all of the statutory requirements even when an animal jumped on the track suddenly making avoidance impossible. But Cooper noted that he considered the correct law to be that if the railroad did not comply with the statutory requirements, then the jury should decide whether compliance would have made a difference in avoiding the accident. Given Judge Cooper's desire to lessen the burden on the railroad, he had no trouble ruling that if no actual collision occurred, then the railroad would not be liable for this mule, even if the crew failed to comply with the statute.

The Conservative Court had to cope with changing economic conditions, both within and outside the state. These judges came from a social background that favored upper-class agrarian interests and their jurisprudence reflected this attitude. On liens, the court uniformly preferred landowner rights to those of both laborers and third-party creditors. The Court was unhappy with such innovations as consumer credit and futures contracts. On the issues raised by railroad accidents, the Conservative Court initially protected stock on the range and the interest of laborers. However, as railroads became more important to the commercial interests of the landowners who were producing for the market, the Court softened its attitude toward the railroad. The Court began to give the railroad strong protection against the claims of injured employees and some protection from the claims of livestock owners. This change in jurisprudence developed even though legislature stayed silent on these issues. The growing importance of interregional markets also drew the Court into one more highly politicized case. The Court was called upon to decide the rights of holders of Tennessee state bonds, most of whom were non-Tennesseans, and once again, the political control of the state hinged on the Court's decision.

READJUSTMENT

The most controversial issued raise by the penetration of the interregional market into Tennessee's economy and society was the issue of the refunding the state debt. Much of the controversy arose because the majority of the debt itself was incurred during the years of Radical rule. At the end of the Civil War the debt for public expenditures, such as building the State Capitol, was slightly less than $4 million. The greater part of the debt was owed on state bonds issued on behalf of railroad companies. These companies had not been able to pay off this debt, because the war had devastated their tracks and rolling stock. The state was still responsible for the debt and the accumulating interest.[78] Brownlow's administration had reacted to the devastation of the railroads by appropriating another $14 million in bond proceeds to rebuild the rail network. In 1879, a legislative investigation uncovered corruption and found that little of the money had ever been used for actual construction. Instead, most had been stolen. When the Conservatives took over the state government, the debt hovered near $43 million.[79]

The refunding of the state's debt might seem an unlikely issue to split the dominant Democratic Party. However, state tax burdens were anything but esoteric in the postbellum era. One southern historian has argued that postbellum state taxes, which seem mild by the standards of the early twenty-first century, were especially burdensome to the rural plain white folk because, in the antebellum period, their lives had been virtually tax-free. Southern legislatures in the antebellum period had derived most state revenue from taxes on slaves and land; after the war, the revenue from the slave tax had to be replaced with increased property taxes. Furthermore, the devastation of the war and the need to provide services to the freedpeople greatly increased the demand for public services. The increased tax rates of the postbellum era seemed unjust to large numbers of white southerners.[80]

In Tennessee, the question of funding the debt split the Democratic Party wide open. On the one hand, rural Tennesseans felt beleaguered by the tax burden that paying off the debt required. Because they saw little advantage to themselves of assuming this burden and blamed it on corrupt Radical officials, they wanted to repudiate the debt. Tennesseans involved in mercantile activities, however, and those who wanted the state to move forward and increase nonagrarian economic activity, realized that the price for acceptance in the national market would be funding the state debt. This faction of the Democratic Party was willing to pay this price. The battle between these two factions—called low-taxers, who wanted to repudiate all or some of the debt, and state-credit Democrats, who wanted to honor the debt—became so severe that it split the Democratic Party and allowed a brief Republican resurgence.

By 1878 the gulf between these two factions of the Democratic Party was so great that in order to nominate a candidate for governor, the party had to settle on an independent politician who refused to take the stand on the refunding issue. The Democrats elected Albert S. Marks, who tried to deal with the refunding issue by holding a referendum on a settlement that would pay off 50 percent of the debt at an annual interest rate of 4 percent and repudiate the rest of the debt. This proposal, known as a "50-4" settlement, was rejected by the voters.[81] The Democrats' inability to solve the refunding crisis led directly to the election of a Republican governor. In 1880 the Republicans nominated Alvin Hawkins, who had served on Radical Supreme Court. A coalition of Republicans and state-credit Democrats elected Hawkins on a platform that opposed any scaling back of the debt.

This Republican resurgence depended upon solving the readjustment crisis. After much political maneuvering in the legislature, and probably some bribery, the Hawkins administration finally passed a bill calling for the issuance of new bonds that would pay 100 percent of the debt at a 3 percent interest rate, a "100-3" solution. In order to steal this political victory away from the Republicans, and avoid paying the full debt, low-tax Democrats filed suit to attack the constitutionality of this law. The most important political question since restoring suffrage was now in the hands of the Tennessee Supreme Court.[82]

The arguments before the Court in the case of *Lynn v. Polk* (1882), commenced on January 17, 1882. Both the *Memphis Daily Appeal* and the *Nashville Banner* carried daily reports of the arguments. Each side had lined up an array of legal talent. The low-taxers had eight attorneys, including former governor Albert Marks. The refunders replied with six attorneys. Argument lasted for almost two weeks. On February 10, 1882, the Court issued its opinion. By a vote of three to two, the Court found the 100-3 refunding bill unconstitutional.

The importance of the decision led the each judge to issue his own opinion. Together the opinions take up over 150 pages of the Tennessee *Reports*. The case presented four main issues. First, did taxpayers have standing to bring a suit enjoining the funding board from issuing new bonds and exchanging them for the old? Second, could the funding board be enjoined because Tennessee had a statute forbidding suits against the state or its officers? Third, was the provision that required Tennessee tax collectors to accept as payment for taxes the matured coupons from these bonds constitutional? And last, could the Court look into the allegations of bribery and corruption in the legislature when deciding on the legality of the 100–3 bill?

The crucial issue was the constitutionality of the coupon provision, although the Court wrestled with the other issues at length. A statute forbade suits against the state, so the holders of the outstanding bonds could not force Tennessee to pay. The bondholders thus had insisted that the new bonds include coupons that necessarily had value because they were acceptable for taxes. The low-tax attorneys argued that the current state legislature did not have the power to force later legislatures in effect to allocate tax revenues first to the payment of the bonds. Without the redeemable coupons, a later legislature could decide that tax moneys should be spent on the other priorities. However, if the coupons were received in lieu of taxes, the legislature would lose the flexibility to make such a decision.

Furthermore, no doubt existed that by making the coupons redeemable for taxes the legislature would enter into a binding contract with the bondholders. If tax collectors refused to accept the coupons, the new bondholders would have the right to sue in federal court arguing that the refusal to accept the coupons impaired their binding contract rights. Tennessee judges and politicians well knew that the United States Supreme Court would invoke the contract clause of the U.S. Constitution to enforce the redemption of these coupons. In two cases after the Civil War, *Furman v. Nichol* (1868) and *Keith v. Clark* (1878), the United States Supreme Court had overturned Tennessee Supreme Court holdings that Bank of Tennessee bank notes did not have to be accepted for taxes. The federal court held that the contract clause required Tennessee to accept the notes since the 1838 legislation chartering the bank had included the provision that its notes would be redeemable for taxes. In *Keith,* the United States Supreme Court had even required that Tennessee tax collectors accept notes issued during the years of Confederate control, which notes were issued for the purpose of furthering the Confederate war effort. Consequently, the Tennessee Supreme Court was certain that these redeemable coupons would create a binding contract that the United States Supreme Court would enforce against later legislatures.

Three of the judges found this refunding bill unconstitutional because the redeemable coupons limited the ability of future legislatures to allocate state funds. Chief Justice Deaderick and a special judge dissented. All the judges recognized the political importance of this decision. For instance Judge McFarland said, "No case of greater importance, I suppose, has ever been presented to this court; and no case has probably ever been argued before it as thoroughly or with more learning and ability."[83] Despite the political importance of the case, the Tennessee Supreme Court was acting in a more legal and less political manner that it had been in the late 1860s and early 1870s. When these judges made disclaimers that they were making their decision based on their vision of the law rather than their political preferences, the disclaimers did not seem to be mere window dressing.

The Court's decision that the 100-3 plan was unconstitutional left the Republicans with both an opportunity and a quandary. The opportunity was that the Democrats would remain divided over the refunding issue. The quandary was that the Republicans needed to keep working at resolving this issue that the voters had elected them to solve. Governor Hawkins called a special session of the legislature to try to draft a politically acceptable measure that did not include the unconstitutional redeemable coupons. Hawkins had to accept partial repudiation of the debt, 40 percent of the par amount of the old bonds, in order to attract enough Democrats to pass such a measure. To make the plan somewhat palatable to the state-credit faction, Hawkins agreed to gradually increase the interest rate, in staggered steps implemented over six years, from 3 to 6 percent. This bill, awkwardly referred to as the "60 3-4-5-6" plan, passed on May 16, 1882.[84]

The low-tax Democrats wanted the state to repudiate even more of the debt and adopted that stance for the upcoming gubernatorial campaign. They closed ranks in favor of further repudiation. In a four-way race, the Democrats emerged with the governorship and a majority of both houses over the Republicans, Greenbacks and the state-credit Democratic minority. The Democrats used their majority to repudiate the 60 3-4-5-6 plan and replace it with a "50-3" plan that paid the bonds at 50 percent of par with a 3 percent interest rate. The Democrats excepted certain prewar debts from the repudiation and paid them at 100 percent.[85]

The Supreme Court remained tainted by its role in this controversy, even though its three-to-two decision in *Lynn v. Polk* probably helped the Democratic Party reestablish its control over the state. By early 1886, the Democratic press was calling for a wholesale repudiation of the bench. In a May 12, 1886, editorial, the *Nashville Banner* claimed that the men on the Supreme Court were not keeping up with the backlog of cases. Moreover, their decisions were not being accepted as authoritative. The underlying problem was the age of the men on the bench. They were not sufficiently active and energetic to deal with the docket and still write well-researched and soundly reasoned opinions that would command respect.[86]

In June 1886 the Democratic convention renominated only one sitting judge, Peter Turney, the most politically popular judge.[87] The other four nominees were younger men who had made their reputations since the Civil War. The other nominee from the Middle Division was Horace H. Lurton. Waller C. Caldwell and W. C. Folkes were the nominees from the Western Division. All four of these men were nominated on the first ballot of the convention.[88]

The final nominee was also the most controversial. David Snodgrass was only thirty-five, literally only weeks older than the constitutional minimum. He had spent his first thirty years in Sparta, Tennessee. Snodgrass had been a leading low-tax Democrat and had led the 1880 bolt from the convention that resulted in the Republicans' resurgence in that election.

The 1886 election marked a sea-change in Tennessee politics. No longer did the Civil War, and the issues it raised, dominate the political landscape. Instead, a new generation addressed fresh issues. Not only were the four new Democratic nominees for the Court younger men, but defection of the state-credit Democrats allowed more populist-oriented electioneering. Tennessee rejected the backward-looking politics of Reconstruction and redemption and turned to a new generation of leaders who had grown up in the postwar world.[89] The new Supreme Court reflected these political changes with their youth and reputations based on postwar activities. The bench that was seated in 1886 had its face turned toward New South realities and was ready to leave behind the political battles that had inflamed the passions, and molded the opinions, of jurists of the preceding generation.

4

THE TENNESSEE SUPREME COURT, 1886–1910

James W. Ely Jr.

As Tennessee approached the end of the nineteenth century, the polity was confronted with new challenges. Tensions aroused by the Civil War and Reconstruction gradually faded amid signs of improved business conditions and a mood of confidence. But this optimism masked economic and social tensions.

The majority of Tennesseans were still engaged in agriculture, with tobacco, wheat, and cotton as the principal cash crops. Sharecropping was a common arrangement across the state, and many croppers fell heavily into debt. During the early part of this period, moreover, farmers were plagued with a downward slide in farm prices. Growing out of this economic distress, the Farmers' Alliance was formed and became a significant force in state politics.[1] Although agriculture remained dominant, there were sustained efforts to encourage industrialization and to lure northern capital. Industrial enterprises included iron and steel production, railroading, lumber products, textile mills, and tobacco. In particular, the Louisville and Nashville Railroad wielded considerable economic and political power. Industrial employment, centered in urban areas, mounted steadily during this era. Many industrial employees, however, suffered poor wages and unsafe working conditions.[2]

Industrialization in turn encouraged the rapid growth of Tennessee cities. Out of a population of two million in 1900, only 16 percent of Tennesseans lived in cities. Although a predominantly rural state in outlook, Tennessee nonetheless experienced steady expansion in urban areas. Memphis was the largest city, followed by Nashville and Knoxville.[3] Significantly, the state attracted few immigrants following the Civil War, and the state's population was overwhelmingly native-born. Notwithstanding New South ideology and hopes for economic development, Tennessee, like other southern states, was burdened by lingering rural poverty and lagged behind the north in personal income.

The Democratic Party gained political ascendancy in the period from 1886 to 1910. But the party was hampered by persistent factionalism. Consequently, the Republicans, with a solid base in East Tennessee, were often able to mount effective competition and, unlike the situation elsewhere in the South, remained a potent factor in political life.[4]

One of the most painful issues facing Tennesseans was the relationship between whites and blacks. Approximately 24 percent of Tennessee's population was black. In Tennessee, as across the region, the rights of blacks steadily eroded during the late nineteenth century. An 1881 law, for instance, sanctioned segregation in railroad passenger transportation. Democrats were particularly determined to curtail the influence of black voters in state political life. A series of measures, culminating in the Dortch law of 1889, served to effectively disfranchise illiterate blacks in urban areas. This process of exclusion from the ballot was completed in 1890, when the legislature established a poll tax. These steps rendered blacks largely powerless in the political arena. Moreover, the imposition of formal racial segregation in public facilities isolated blacks from economic and educational opportunities. Separate schools for black students were inadequately funded.[5] It is a measure of their subordination that blacks rarely mounted legal attacks on discriminatory practices.

Several explosive issues tested the political fabric of the state. The first grew out of the practice of leasing state convicts for a profit to private employers. These convicts were used in a number of enterprises. The lease system gave rise to bitter conflicts and violent strikes in East Tennessee when mining companies used convict labor to replace free workers. The so-called convict war hastened the demise of the lease system. This problem was not finally resolved, however, until the lease between the state and the principal coal company expired in 1895 and the state resumed direct control over inmates.[6] In addition, the Prohibition movement gained strength at the start of the twentieth century. "Prohibition," one scholar has observed, "was the principal issue during the first decade of the century."[7] The four-mile law of 1877—forbidding the sale of alcoholic beverages within four miles of a chartered school outside towns—was expanded from time to time until it effectively outlawed liquor sales in all rural areas. After years of lobbying, prohibitionists secured a statewide ban on liquor in 1909.[8]

The first decade of the twentieth century saw the emergence of the Progressive movement in Tennessee and the nation. Advocating a broad cluster of economic and social changes, Tennessee Progressives urged a more active role for state government to improve public services and regulate business.[9]

Thus, change impacted many aspects of life in Tennessee. As industrial activity and urbanization started to transform the state, both legislators and the Supreme Court were called upon to accommodate the legal interests of contending groups. Fledgling regulation of the economy, the adjustment of industrial accidents, the exercise of eminent domain, and control of public morals were among the most dramatic issues presented to the Supreme Court in this era. Given the increasingly national character of the economy, state judges had to be mindful of federal constitutional constraints.

JUDICIAL PERSONNEL AND STRUCTURE

Under the Tennessee Constitution of 1870 the Supreme Court consisted of five judges, no more than two of whom could reside in any one of the grand divisions of the state. The judges were popularly elected and served for eight-year terms. They were authorized by the Constitution to designate a chief justice and to appoint the attorney general, who held office for eight years. The Constitution directed that the Supreme Court hear cases at Knoxville, Nashville, and Jackson.[10]

Thirteen persons served as judge of the Supreme Court between 1886 and 1910.[11] Reflecting the statewide dominance of the Democratic Party, all were white male Democrats. With the exception of William C. Folkes, who graduated from the University of Virginia Law School, each of the judges received his legal education in Tennessee. Five attended Cumberland Law School, a testament to the importance of that institution in shaping the legal culture of Tennessee at the end of the nineteenth century.[12] Four others had followed the time-honored practice of preparing for the bar by work in an attorney's office. No single judge served throughout the entire period, but several were on the bench for extended terms. First elected in 1870, Peter Turney was a judge for twenty-two years. Moreover, W. D. Beard was a member of the Court for seventeen years, and David L. Snodgrass, Waller C. Caldwell and John S. Wilkes each served for sixteen years. On the other hand, Aaron D. Bright, appointed to fill a vacancy in 1894, was on the Court for only six months and wrote just one opinion.

Two members of the Court resigned to accept other public office. Peter Turney, having been elected governor in 1892, left the chief justiceship in January 1893 upon his inauguration. Despite considerable criticism for seeking political office while a judge, Turney remained on the bench until he became governor.[13] This decision may have been influenced in part by his desire to appoint a family friend, Wilkes, to his seat. A few months later

A large number of Tennessee Supreme Court judges in the nineteenth and early twentieth centuries received their legal education at Cumberland Law School in Lebanon, Tennessee. Starting in 1878, law classes were conducted in Caruthers Hall. Courtesy Cumberland School of Law, Samford University.

Horace H. Lurton was appointed judge of the U.S. Circuit Court of Appeals by President Grover Cleveland. In 1909 President William Howard Taft nominated Lurton for a seat on the Supreme Court of the United States, a post he held until his death in 1914.

With the exception of Turney, who was reelected, the judicial election of 1886 produced an entirely new slate of Supreme Court judges. An ardent ex-Confederate, Turney had studied law in his father's office. He wrote few opinions for the Court, and did not demonstrate any outstanding ability as a jurist. One scholar declared that many of Turney's relatively few opinions were "so short and cryptic as to be not readily understood."[14] The new judges in 1886 were Waller C. Caldwell, David L. Snodgrass, William C. Folkes, and Lurton. Caldwell, a graduate of Cumberland School of Law, and Snodgrass, a former state legislator, were diligent judges who authored a number of important opinions and carried a large share of the Court's work. Both were reelected in 1894. Folkes's career on the Supreme Court was cut short by his death in May 1890. Serving less than four years, he did not leave much of a mark on Tennessee jurisprudence.

Lurton, a former soldier in the Confederate army and another Cumberland graduate, established the most distinguished record of this group of judges.[15] He soon emerged as the intellectual leader of the Court and wrote a number of leading opinions. Unafraid to tackle one of the major issues of the day, Lurton delivered a thoughtful address in 1891 on contracts in restraint of trade and early antitrust policy.[16] In 1893 the *Nashville Daily American* declared, "Judge Lurton has had a career on the Supreme Court bench that has made him famous. Many knotty points have been settled by him, and his opinions on corporation law points are cited all over the country as authorities."[17] While a member of the Sixth Circuit Court of Appeals Lurton also served as a part-time professor at Vanderbilt University Law School from 1898 to 1905, and as Dean between 1905 and 1910.

Horace Lurton, who served on the Tennessee Supreme Court from 1886 to 1893, was later appointed to the Supreme Court of the United States. Photograph by Harris and Ewing, Collection of the Supreme Court of the United States.

W. D. Beard was named by the governor to fill the vacancy created by the death of Folkes, and he served briefly in 1890. Thereafter, Benjamin J. Lea was elected to complete the expired term. He had previously served as the attorney general of Tennessee and as a member of the state senate. One historian pointed out that as a judge "Lea did not attempt to make a display of his learning, or to gain a reputation by the writing of long opinions."[18] Lea became chief justice when Lurton was appointed to the federal bench, but died in March 1894. The governor named Bright to replace Lea temporarily pending the upcoming election.

As noted above, Governor Turney named Wilkes to succeed him as a member of the Supreme Court in January 1893. Wilkes was an officer in the Confederate army and prepared for a legal career by study in a law office. He conducted a general practice of law in Pulaski.

The judicial election of 1894 saw the reelection of Caldwell, Snodgrass, and Wilkes. William K. McAlister Jr., who had been appointed by the governor to replace Lurton, was also elected. Although his formal legal education was sketchy, McAlister had served as the city attorney for Nashville and as a circuit judge. While on the Supreme Court he frequently wrote opinions and enjoyed an excellent reputation. After leaving the bench in 1910 McAlister joined the law faculty at Vanderbilt University.

Another new member of the Court elected in 1894 was W. D. Beard. After completing his legal education at Cumberland, Beard joined the Confederate army and was severely wounded. After interim service on the Supreme Court in 1890 he was appointed chancellor in Memphis. While on the Supreme Court, Beard authored a number of leading decisions and was the chief justice from 1902 and 1910.

There was a further turnover of Supreme Court membership in 1902. Wilkes, McAlister, and Beard were reelected that year, but both Caldwell and Snodgrass retired. John K. Shields, who trained for a legal career in his father's law office and served as a chancellor, was elected to one of the vacant spots on the bench. He would later be selected as a United States senator from Tennessee. The other newcomer was Matthew M. Neil. A Cumberland School of Law graduate, Neil had been president of the Tennessee Bar Association and a judge on the Court of Chancery Appeals. Neil was a prolific author of judicial opinions and was noted for his substantial contribution to the development of equity jurisprudence.[19]

The final change in the composition of the bench during this period occurred in 1908. Upon the death of Wilkes in February of that year, the governor appointed Bennett Douglas Bell to the Supreme Court. Having received his legal education at Cumberland, Bell served as district attorney general and as a Circuit Court judge before his elevation to the high court.

He was elected in 1908 to the balance of that unexpired term, but remained in office only until 1910. Bell apparently wrote just one published opinion for the Court.[20]

In addition to changing membership, significant modifications in Tennessee's judicial structure impacted the work of the Supreme Court. A steady increase in the number of appeals, fueled by a growing population and more robust business activity, produced a backlog in the disposition of cases. Like state courts elsewhere, the Tennessee Supreme Court had difficulty in keeping pace with the flood of legal business. By the 1880s it was evident that the overworked Supreme Court could not adequately dispose of its burgeoning docket. Accordingly, in 1883 Governor William B. Bate urged creation of intermediate courts of appeals. Instead, the legislature provided limited relief by empowering the judges of the Supreme Court to appoint three referees for each of the grand divisions of the state for a term of two years.[21] These referee commissions were to report on the law and facts of civil cases filed before 1885 and referred to them by the Supreme Court. The reports of the referees were final unless assignments of error were submitted. Several future Supreme Court judges, Caldwell, Snodgrass, and Bright, served as referees.[22]

The success of these commissions of referees paved the way for the establishment of a permanent intermediate appellate court to help handle the appellate docket. Shortly after he became governor in 1893, Turney renewed the call for an intermediate court to reduce the burden on the Supreme Court.[23] Two years later the state legislature heeded this request, declaring: "In view of the crowded condition and rapid increase of litigation in the Supreme Court, it is impossible for that court to keep its docket clear."[24] Decrying the resulting delay in hearing cases, lawmakers created a three-member Court of Chancery Appeals. The jurisdiction of this court extended to all equity cases that might be transferred to it by the Supreme Court. Findings of fact by the Court of Chancery Appeals were deemed conclusive, but legal questions could be appealed by writ of error. The efforts of this tribunal finally resolved many cases, and thus reduced the flow of appeals to the Supreme Court.

In 1907 the legislature granted even more substantial relief to the Supreme Court. The Court of Chancery Appeals was renamed the Court of Civil Appeals and expanded to consist of five judges.[25] Its jurisdiction was widened to embrace all equity and civil cases, with certain exceptions. Appeals from lower courts were to be taken directly to the Court of Civil Appeals. Judgments of this tribunal were final, but litigants could request Supreme Court review by writ of *certiorari.* Appeals involving the constitutionality of state statutes and questions concerning state revenue, however, continued to go to the Supreme Court.

Despite these improvements, the Supreme Court judges of this era shouldered a heavy work load. In the late 1880s, for instance, the Court disposed of more than one thousand appeals a year.[26] Inevitably a large number of decisions were rendered without written opinion. Still, the Tennessee Supreme Court issued between 100 and 150 opinions annually between 1886 and 1910. The volume of opinions declined slightly after 1900, reflecting the effect of the intermediate Court of Appeals.[27] By any standard the Supreme Court, if more selective in hearing cases, remained busy.

This overhaul of the Tennessee court system was part of a national pattern. Many states in the late nineteenth century sought to alleviate the burden on their supreme court by creating intermediate courts and giving the high court greater control over the docket. Discretionary review by writ of *certiorari* allowed a supreme court to focus on those cases deemed most important. Likewise, the Evarts Act of 1891 created new circuit courts of appeal in the federal system and curtailed the right of appeal to the Supreme Court of the United States.[28]

Together with a small number of other states, Tennessee provided for the designation of a chief justice by the members of the Supreme Court. This mode of selection may have hampered the emergence of strong judicial leadership. Two of the chief justices in this period, Lurton and Lea, served for less than a year and hardly had time to assert authority over their colleagues. But there is no evidence that any of the judges who were chief for longer times, such as Turney (1886–93), Caldwell (1894–1902), and Beard (1902–10), ever became a dominant intellectual force on the Court. Consistent with the pattern in other state courts at the turn of the twentieth century, the office of chief justice was not a powerful post.[29]

NATURE OF JUDICIAL WORKLOAD

It would be a mistake to attribute an elaborate judicial philosophy to the Tennessee Supreme Court in this era. Like their counterparts in other states at the start of the twentieth century, the Tennessee Court heard primarily private law disputes, many of which grew out of commercial transactions. A sizable number of appeals involved disputes over real property. Tort cases claimed an increasing share of the Court's time, with railroad accidents providing a fertile source of litigation. Compared to modern court dockets, criminal and constitutional law constituted a relatively small amount of the Supreme Court's business.

The burden of increased appeals, coupled with the largely private law nature of most cases, contributed to the infrequency of dissenting opinions. The dissent rate in this period was consistently low. The members of the Court achieved unanimity in most decisions. Another factor helping to explain this consensual norm was the shared political affiliation and common social attitudes of the judges. They reflected the views of the dominant political group in Tennessee public life. This pronounced tendency to produce unanimous opinions was consistent with the national pattern for state supreme courts.[30]

Unlike the role played by increasingly activist state courts in other jurisdictions,[31] the Tennessee Supreme Court did not take the lead in determining public policy. Indeed, the Court never directly challenged the legislative program and was content to let legislators set the policy agenda. In 1900 the Court declared that "the policy or impolicy for a given Act is a matter for the final decision of the General Assembly as an essential part of its exclusive power of legislation, and the judiciary is precluded from entering that domain."[32] Although the principle of judicial review was well established, the Supreme Court did not find any major statute unconstitutional. The Court appeared to conceive of its role as adjudicating private disputes by applying common-law rules and as enforcing legislative enactments.

One manifestation of this passive approach was a high regard for precedent, particularly with regard to decisions affecting land titles. In a revealing 1890 opinion the Court explained, "It is better that the law should be fixed and certain rather approximately perfect. The change of ruling on any point is more or less evil." Overruling of prior decisions, the Court observed, should be reserved for "exceptional cases."[33] Likewise, the Court declared in 1903 that it would adhere to long settled rules governing real property even if the question might be resolved differently were it presented for the first time. The Court was anxious to protect individuals who acquired land or entered contracts in reliance upon settled rules of law.[34]

In writing opinions, the Supreme Court was cognizant of decisions in other jurisdictions and the work of leading treatise writers. Approximately 40 percent of the cases cited in opinions were from other state or federal courts. Moreover, the Court relied heavily on legal treatises such as Thomas Cooley's influential *A Treatise on the Constitutional Limitations Which Rest Upon the Legislative Power of the States* (1868). English decisions, on the other hand, were rarely cited, although the Supreme Court occasionally mentioned William Blackstone's *Commentaries on the Laws of England (1765–1769).*[35]

REGULATORY AUTHORITY

The Tennessee Supreme Court in this era gave a consistently broad reading to state regulatory authority under the police power. In so doing it sustained virtually all of the economic legislation that regulated contractual dealings, payment of wages, and railroad operations.

During the late nineteenth century both state and federal courts affirmed the liberty of contract doctrine. Under this principle the right to make contracts was constitutionally protected against legislative abridgement.[36] Although the Tennessee Supreme Court recognized that parties were generally free to enter contracts, it maintained that the right of contracting was not unlimited. In *Dugger v. Insurance Company* (1895), for example, the Court upheld the constitutionality of a state statute requiring that insurance companies pay the full amount of loss caused by fire up to the amount of the policy, and voiding any contrary provisions in a fire insurance policy. The Court stressed the power of the state to control insurance contracts to safeguard policy holders.

Another limitation on the freedom of contract was upheld in the leading case of *Harbison v. Knoxville Iron Company* (1899). Many factories at the end of the nineteenth century paid their employees in scrip or merchandise orders rather than money. This practice was deeply unpopular with workers and generated considerable strife. Yet state laws which abolished scrip payment were assailed as infringements of the liberty of contract.[37] In *Harbison* the company effectively coerced its employees to accept payment in coal orders rather than cash. Pointing to an 1899 Tennessee statute that, upon request, employers must redeem scrip or merchandise orders in money, the plaintiff brought suit to recover cash payment.

The Tennessee Supreme Court ruled that a corporation was a person entitled to protection against deprivation of liberty or property without due process. It also insisted that liberty as contemplated in both state and federal constitutions encompassed the right "to pursue any lawful calling, vocation, trade, or profession, to make all proper contracts in relation thereto, and to enjoy the legitimate fruits thereof." Nonetheless, the judges ruled that liberty of contract was subject to legislative regulation and that the wage payment law was a legitimate exercise of the police power. They explained that the legislature sought to ameliorate the disadvantaged position of employees by placing employer and workers "upon equal ground in the matter of wages."[38] The judges emphasized that the statute imposed no great hardship on the employer and was calculated to promote improved employment relations. The United States Supreme Court, in a decision which quoted extensively from the Tennessee opinion, affirmed this judgment in 1901.[39] The *Harbison* litigation marked a major turning point in vindicating state legislative authority to supervise the manner of wage payments.

Similarly, the Tennessee Supreme Court in *State v. Co-Operative Store Company* (1910) validated a law which established a standard weight for a bushel of corn meal. Noting that this measure was designed to protect consumers against fraud and short weights, the Court quickly rejected the argument that the regulation infringed the liberty of contract.

The Court also found no constitutional objection to a statute establishing a mechanic's lien for subcontractors and materialmen. Admitting that the law increased the legal burden of the property owner, the judges concluded in *Cole Manufacturing Company v. Falls* (1891) that the lien provision protected mechanics who had done work and was made part of the owner's contract.

As in other states, Tennessee localities were prone to place heavy burdens on railroads to change existing facilities in order to accommodate street crossings. In *City of Harriman v. Southern Railway Company* (1903) the Supreme Court heard an application by the city to compel the railroad to construct a bridge over its track at an intersection with a street. The railroad pointed out that the track was in existence before the street was built or the city incorporated. Noting that the growth of the city's population raised safety concerns with respect to crossing the track, the Court held that the state, under its police power, could authorize a municipality to require a railroad to construct an overpass at its expense. This duty could be placed on the carrier regardless of the fact that the track was laid out first. Brushing aside an argument that this directive effectuated a taking of property, the Court declared that the cost incurred by the railroad was merely incidental to the exercise of the police power. This outcome contradicts the once fashionable image of a Court subservient to railroad interests.

Promoted ostensibly to protect public health and safety, occupational licensing burgeoned in the late nineteenth century.[40] At issue in *Haworth v. Montgomery* (1891) was a state statute which provided that no person could practice medicine without a certificate from a board of medical examiners. The Supreme Court readily accepted legislative authority to prevent "the carrying on of a profession, occupation, trade, or business, except in compliance with the statute."[41] Hence, a contract to provide medical services by an unlicensed doctor was void. Likewise, the Court affirmed the conviction of persons who engaged in the practice of medicine without a license. For example, a defendant who treated patients with electric rays was found in violation of the statute.[42]

One of the most important regulatory initiatives in the late nineteenth century was the enactment of antitrust laws. With the growth of large-scale corporate enterprise, many businesses sought to stabilize volatile markets through a variety of contractual or trust arrangements. These practices were seen as diminishing economic competition and raising prices, and they aroused widespread public hostility. As the Tennessee Supreme Court pointed out, contracts which unreasonably restrained trade had long been treated as void at common law.[43] To strengthen the common-law rule, Tennessee lawmakers enacted a series of statutes which culminated in the antitrust act of 1897. The act prohibited all agreements which lessened competition in the importation or sale of articles in Tennessee. This changed the common-law rule by making such contracts illegal and actionable. Remedial provisions were particularly significant. In addition to allowing the recovery of monetary damages by injured parties, the statute imposed criminal punishments and possible forfeiture of corporate charters on violators. By passing early antitrust measures, Tennessee joined with a number of other states that had adopted such measures by 1900.[44]

In a line of cases the Tennessee Supreme Court upheld the constitutionality of the antitrust act. The most complete analysis of the statute was in *State v. Schlitz Brewing Company* (1900). Noting that courts do not review the wisdom of legislative policy, the Supreme Court held that liberty of contract was subject to control. However, the judges could be strict in assessing the sufficiency of an indictment for violation of the antitrust law, insisting that the alleged conspiracy to restrain trade must be adequately described.[45]

In appropriate circumstances, however, the Supreme Court was prepared to enforce vigorously the Tennessee antitrust act. At issue in *State v. Standard Oil Company* (1907) was a suit to oust the defendant, a foreign corporation, and restrain it from doing business in the state. The Court, in a lengthy opinion, construed the revised 1903 antitrust law as applicable to articles in intrastate commerce and hence not an infringement of congressional power over commerce between the states. Finding evidence of a combination to restrain trade in oil, the Court enjoined Standard Oil from doing business, other than interstate commerce, in Tennessee. In 1910 the Supreme Court of the United States unanimously affirmed this decision by the Tennessee Supreme Court, ruling that the state antitrust law did not impermissibly regulate interstate trade.[46]

The Tennessee Supreme Court's record concerning economic regulations revealed a consistent pattern. The Court regularly deferred to the legislature's judgment and permitted lawmakers to curtail freedom of contract or impose cost on business enterprise in various contexts. Certainly the judges made no sustained effort to hamper legislative efforts to address economic issues.

TAKINGS JURISPRUDENCE

Closely allied to the scope of state regulatory authority was the exercise of eminent domain. Both the Fifth Amendment of the United States Constitution and the Declaration of Rights in the Tennessee Constitution of 1870 provided that private property could not be taken for public use without just compensation.[47] Moreover, in 1897 the United States Supreme Court ruled that the principle of just compensation was an essential element of due process applicable to the states through the Fourteenth Amendment.[48] Toward the end of the nineteenth century, state and local governments began to interact with property owners in more complex ways. Government, for example, utilized eminent domain to acquire land for a range of projects. Improvements in urban areas often inflicted injury on adjacent landowners. The Tennessee Supreme Court dealt regularly with litigation produced by governmental actions affecting privately owned land. The decisions of this era did much to shape takings jurisprudence in Tennessee.

The purpose of the takings clauses was to prevent the public from singling out one individual or a small group to carry an undue share of the burdens of government. Takings jurisprudence requires courts to balance the constitutional guarantees of private property with the need to accommodate economic and technological changes. At root is a basic question: Should individual owners or the general public bear the expense of providing social goods? Answering this inquiry, the Tennessee Supreme Court explained in 1893, "It is a plain dictate of justice that the public, not the individual citizen, should bear the burdens imposed upon private property for the public benefit." The Court added that the legislature had no power to authorize "the taking of private property for a public use without compensation."[49] This understanding of the protective function of the takings clauses influenced the Supreme Court's handling of the cases.

One crucial inquiry is whether property has been "taken" by the government or by an enterprise acting under governmental authority. A recurring problem was the extent to which governmental action, short of outright acquisition of title by formal eminent domain proceedings, effectuated a taking for which compensation was required. The physical invasion of land as a consequence of municipal improvement projects gave rise to considerable litigation. For instance, a change in the grade of a public street could impair access to adjacent lots or cause physical damage to neighboring land. In 1886 the Supreme Court held that grading of streets by city authorities, which threw surface water onto adjacent land causing damage, represented "a taking and application to public use" and was therefore compensable.[50] Likewise, the Court determined in *Hamilton County v. Rape* (1898) that the impairment of the right of access to an adjoining lot by a change of street grade constituted a taking of a property right for which the owner was entitled to compensation.

This line of cases concerning physical invasion or destruction of property interests was completed in the landmark case of *Barron v. City of*

Memphis (1904). The city enlarged a pier supporting a bridge, and thereby diverted a stream which overflowed Barron's land. This flooding destroyed part of the lot by erosion and undermined a house. Sustaining Barron's taking claim, the Supreme Court declared that under the Tennessee Constitution "it is not essential that there should be an actual appropriation of the property taken to the public use." Instead, the judges maintained that the Tennessee Constitution was "sufficiently liberal to protect owners from any direct or indirect invasion of their property rights."[51] In this situation, they reasoned, the city's public works caused "a practical destruction" of the property and was compensable.

An increased burden on a public roadway could also amount to a taking of property. In *Street Railway Company v. Doyle* (1890) the company operated a steam-engine train for passengers over streets in Memphis. An abutting landowner, who held title to the center of the road subject to the public right of way, argued that the railway constituted an additional burden on the servitude. Agreeing, the Supreme Court pointed out that the railway operations obstructed and rendered more dangerous ordinary street travel. It followed that the owner was entitled to compensation for the increased burden because the company could not avoid the constitutional obligation to pay for the appropriation of property.

On the other hand, public improvements did not represent a taking of property when they just impaired the value of an earlier franchise. When Davidson County constructed a free bridge over the Cumberland River, the natural consequence was to divert traffic from a nearby turnpike and ferry. The aggrieved turnpike company alleged that the county's action virtually confiscated its property by depriving it of tolls. Noting that absent the grant of an exclusive franchise the legislature was at liberty to authorize rival means of transportation, the Supreme Court in *Turnpike Company v. Davidson County* (1892) denied that there was a taking of the franchise. No part of the company's property was actually appropriated, and the Court refused to consider depreciation in the value of the franchise as a taking. In reaching this result the judges favored improved transportation based on competition over the monopoly claims of the prior turnpike company.

Another area of contention in taking law is the requirement that private property be taken for public use. Throughout the nineteenth century, legislators in Tennessee and elsewhere delegated the power of eminent domain to business corporations for the purpose of making improvements to serve the public. Railroad companies were routinely given the power to acquire land, and they instituted a number of condemnation proceedings in this era. The Supreme Court showed no inclination to challenge legislative findings that use of eminent domain by private corporations served the public interest. However, the judges strictly construed the right of eminent domain conferred by corporate charter or statute. Thus, in 1903 the Court pointed out that a water company was not authorized to condemn a supply of water which flowed over the land of third persons.[52]

Both the federal and Tennessee Constitutions mandated the payment of "just compensation" when property was taken by the government. This requirement vindicated the constitutional policy safeguarding individuals against confiscation of their property for public purpose. The Tennessee Supreme Court's most comprehensive discussion of the meaning of "just compensation" came in *Alloway v. City of Nashville* (1890). The city brought proceedings to appropriate certain land "for reservoir purposes." At issue was the correct standard for ascertaining the value of the property taken. Building on principles established in the antebellum era, the Supreme Court stressed that just compensation under the Tennessee Constitution meant "the fair cash value of the land taken." This was defined as "the market value." According to the Court, market value included "every element of usefulness and advantage in the property."[53] It was necessary, therefore, to consider location and capability for any useful purpose in estimating value. By the same token, market value of the property could not be determined by singling out its value for one special use. By insisting upon cash value as determined by general market conditions the Supreme Court seemingly adopted a balanced measure of compensation protective of individual property rights in the face of governmental action.

PROPERTY LAW

In addition to eminent domain cases, the Supreme Court heard numerous appeals dealing with a wide array of property law issues. For the most part these cases involved disputes between private parties. The Court typically resolved these matters by applying long-settled common-law principles. As interpreted by the Court, property law served to protect owners and facilitate land transfers, while at the same time retaining flexibility to adopt legal norms to new conditions.

The property issues that came to the Supreme Court were far-ranging in scope. They encompassed the rights and duties of co-tenants, adverse possession, the property rights of married women, easements, curtesy, trespass, homestead claims, the law governing landlord and tenant, and even an application of the Rule in Shelly's Case. Although litigation over land predominated, several appeals involved alleged gifts of personal property. Most of these cases did not implicate larger public policy concerns and do not warrant treatment here.

Although the Supreme Court ordinarily allowed parties wide latitude to negotiate land sales, there were situations in which the Court set aside purchase contracts or conveyances as fraudulent. In *Mann v. Russey* (1898), for example, the Court articulated the general rule: "Parties competent to contract have a right without legal interference to make their own agreement, and fix any price they see proper to receive or pay for property." Where, however, there was a great disparity between the value of the property and the contract price, the Court applied equitable principles and raised a rebuttable presumption of fraud. Thus, the Court set aside the contract of a person of "very infirm mental capacity" to purchase property at "a grossly exaggerated price."[54] In effect, the judges affirmed the traditional maxim that equity will not enforce an unconscionable bargain.

Similarly, the Supreme Court in 1895 canceled a deed where a wife, living in secret adultery with another man, persuaded her elderly husband to convey a house to her. The Court was unsparing in its condemnation of the wife's behavior: "Such a course of conduct constitutes the grossest and most outrageous fraud. . . . It would shock the conscience of mankind to allow a shameless woman to thus prostitute the most sacred of all earthy relations into a fraudulent devise and scheme to obtain the money of a confiding husband."[55]

In an era before the emergence of modern land-use controls, aggrieved individuals often turned to the law of nuisance to police offensive activities by neighboring landowners. Accordingly, the Supreme Court heard a number of cases in which parties were seeking redress from nuisances. A threshold inquiry was to determine what actions constituted nuisances. The Court pointed out that not every inconvenience resulting from business activity or urban life was unlawful. As the Court explained in 1905,

> The noise of paved streets and of street cars is a material discomfort to abutting owners. The smoke from factories, hotels, and manufacturing establishments may form a material discomfort and annoyance to persons living near by; but these are discomforts and annoyances that the individual must bear in deference to the convenience and comfort of the public.
>
> The noise of trains passing through the country districts and the dust of vehicles passing along the public highways may be a great annoyance to residents along the line of such roads; and the rumbling of carriages of belated revelers and of early market wagons along the paved highways may disturb the slumbers and harass the

> nerves of persons who desire to sleep in the cities; but it is not for such annoyances and discomforts that the law allows redress, but only where the discomfort and inconvenience proceeds to such an extent as to injure the usable and rental or permanent value of the property that the law will award damages. It must amount, to some extent, to the taking of the value of the property, either temporary or permanent, and depriving the owner there.[56]

Since each case turned upon the particular circumstances, the Court had considerable latitude in applying the nuisance doctrine.

Nuisance litigation was frequent and covered a variety of land-use disputes. In *Weakley v. Page* (1899) the Court affirmed its jurisdiction to abate a nuisance. An adjacent property owner in Nashville charged that the value of his land was sharply diminished by the existence of a brothel in the area. Finding that houses of ill fame constituted a nuisance, the Court readily granted an injunction to protect neighbors. On the other hand, in *Harvey v. Ice Company* (1900) the Court rejected a claim that a stable in Memphis was so offensive as to be a nuisance.

Railroad operations were often challenged as a nuisance. A few examples illustrate the range of the problems raised by railroading. One case involved dynamite blasting to construct a rail line, the noise of which rendered a nearby house unlivable and forced the occupants to leave. Another concerned the smoke, soot, and noise caused by trains entering a freight yard and roundhouses in Nashville.[57]

The Court also grappled with the elusive distinction between public and private nuisance. Generally individuals could only obtain relief from private nuisances. Public officials had the sole authority to seek abatement of public nuisances which affected large number of persons in a locality. Invoking the doctrine of public nuisance could sometimes defeat a private claim. Thus, in *Chattanooga v. Reid* (1899) the Court held that an owner who discharged garbage and kitchen water onto a street, providing offensive odors, created a public nuisance. But the failure of the city of Chattanooga to abate this nuisance did not give rise to a cause of action against the city by an injured landowner.

At the turn of the twentieth century, the Supreme Court confronted several appeals which raised the problem of industrial pollution and anticipated later environmental concerns. These cases required the Court to balance the dominion of private property owners against the desire for economic expansion. Judicial formulation of the nuisance doctrine had a direct impact on the viability of industrial enterprise. In *Nunnelly v. Southern*

Iron Company (1895), for instance, the judges dealt with an iron ore plant which deposited large amounts of dirt and waste materials into a river, thereby polluting the water and injuring plaintiff's land. They upheld an award of monetary damages as compensation for the nuisance.

Still, the Supreme Court was reluctant to grant injunctive relief where the societal benefit from the nuisance was seen as outweighing the injury to individual property owners. This was made clear in *Madison v. Ducktown Sulphur, Copper & Iron Company* (1904). Several owners of small farms complained that two companies emitted large volumes of smoke which rendered their homes less attractive and damaged their crops and timber. The Court had no difficulty in holding that the actions of the company constituted a nuisance for which the injured parties were entitled to a monetary sum. But the Court declined to enjoin the companies' operations. Rather, it pointed to a Tennessee statute which conferred discretion on the courts to determine whether a nuisance caused by "a work of public utility" should be abated. The Court stressed that the companies employed a large number of persons and paid substantial taxes. It further opined that injunctive relief would compel the two companies to cease operations. Somewhat rhetorically, the Court asked, "Shall the complainants be granted, in the way of damages, the full measure of relief to which their injuries entitled them, or shall we go further, and grant their request to blot out two great mining and manufacturing enterprises, destroy half of the taxable values of a county, and drive more than ten thousand people from their homes? We think there can be no doubt as to what the true answer to this question should be." Recognizing that this was a situation of conflicting rights, the Court declared that "the law must make the best arrangement it can between the contending parties" and ordered an assessment of damages.[58] In essence, the Court concluded that the copper industry was more important to the state's economy than a few farmers.

The Tennessee Supreme Court heard several disputes concerning ownership of church property.[59] Typically arising out of contests between factions of divided congregations, these cases put the judges in the awkward position of passing upon decisions of ecclesiastical bodies. The dilemma was best illustrated by *Landrith v. Hudgins* (1908), which grew out of the union between the Cumberland Presbyterian Church and the Presbyterian Church in the United States of America. A faction asserting allegiance to the united body filed a suit claiming church property in Fayetteville. The defendants denied the validity of the union and maintained their right to the property based on the conditions in an 1852 deed conveying the land to the Cumberland Presbyterian Church.[60]

Mindful of constitutional constraints on the resolution of religious questions by civil authorities, the Tennessee Supreme Court observed that the courts "have no power, under the constitutions by which they exist, in this country, to intermeddle with religious matters purely as such, or to assume to settle for contending parties in churches any question of doctrine, discipline or organization."[61] But property rights, according to the Court, were on a different footing and were governed by civil property law. When property was given in trust to propagate certain religious doctrine, the Court reasoned that it must ascertain whether a proposed new use constituted a diversion from the purpose of the trust. This necessitated an inquiry into which party represented "the true church." In making this assessment the civil courts were not bound by the decisions of church tribunals. After a lengthy review of the doctrines of the two Presbyterian Churches, the Supreme Court concluded that land in dispute should remain with the defendants, who were identified with the original Cumberland Presbyterians. As a result of this ruling, much of the Cumberland Presbyterian property in Tennessee was left in the hands of those opposed to the union.

Although the Court's willingness to adjudicate title to church property was consistent with the approach followed in some other jurisdictions, it was out of step with the decision of the United States Supreme Court in *Watson v. Jones* (1871). Decided under diversity jurisdiction, Watson held that civil courts should accept as conclusive the determination of ecclesiastical tribunals regarding the property rights of religious organizations.

PUBLIC MORALS AND HEALTH

Like judges elsewhere, the members of the Tennessee Supreme Court allowed legislators a wide rein to promote moral ends and safeguard public health. Sunday closing laws were repeatedly upheld by the Court. Affirming the conviction of a blacksmith for working on Sunday, the Court maintained in 1886 that such action tended "to corrupt public morals, and the example is pernicious and contrary to law and the well-being and good order of society."[62] Nor was the Court impressed with defendant's argument that he observed the seventh day of the week rather than Sunday as a Christian Sabbath. Other Sunday closing cases turned largely on whether the evidence sustained a conviction for illegal activity on that day. The Court tended to be strict in enforcing the closing laws. Hence, a grocer who sold goods on Saturday night but did not deliver them until Sunday was found in violation.[63] So settled were Sunday closing laws that they were not challenged on constitutional grounds.

Sunday laws were driven by other concerns than public morality. In *Breyer v. State* (1899) the Tennessee Supreme Court considered the validity of an 1891 statute making it a misdemeanor to engage in barbering on Sunday. Upholding a conviction, the Court observed,

> It is a notorious fact that, prior to the passage of the Act in 1891, barber shops all over the State were kept open on Sunday, and the former statute was wholly ignored and disregarded. Yet it is part of the history of this legislation that it was enacted at the urgent solicitation of the barbers themselves, acting individually and collectively through their organized associations. A day of rest was needed for this most industrious and overworked trade, and it was admitted that without the imposition of heavier penalties it could not be secured, for none were willing to close their shops on Sunday unless all were made to do so. The former law was found wholly ineffective.[64]

POLITICS OF THE FUTURE.

The Tennessee Campaign suggests some of the accomplishments which will be required in future political candidates.

As satirized in this 1906 cartoon, the Prohibition movement strongly influenced the political climate and judicial elections in early-twentieth-century Tennessee. From Frank Leslie's Illustrated Magazine.

Obviously the desire of many barbers for a shorter work week provided an instrumentalist rationale for this Sunday closing measure.

Gambling was also viewed with disfavor. The judges affirmed a number of convictions for unlawful gaming. In the same vein, the Supreme Court broadly sustained legislative authority over liquor. The drive for prohibition in Tennessee steadily gained ground during the late nineteenth and early twentieth centuries. The four-mile law, first enacted in 1877, prohibited the sale of liquor within four miles of a chartered school outside incorporated towns. Repeatedly amended and expanded in scope, the four-mile law became the vehicle for establishing prohibition in rural Tennessee.[65]

The constitutionality of the four-mile act and its progeny was repeatedly sustained by the Tennessee Supreme Court.[66] Noting the extensive scope of state authority to protect public morals and safety, the Court flatly declared in 1903, "The traffic in intoxicating liquors is universally recognized as a proper subject for police regulation, and may be controlled, restricted, or even totally prohibited, without violating any constitutional right under the police power."[67] It followed that regulation and prohibition of liquor sales was a matter for the legislature, and the Supreme Court would not review the exercise of legislative power in this area. Consequently, the Court regularly affirmed convictions for illegal liquor sales.

Although generally supportive of the state's prohibition drive, the Supreme Court was also mindful of federal authority over interstate commerce. This was demonstrated in *State v. J.W. Kelly & Company* (1910), which involved the shipment of whiskey from a Tennessee distillery to a customer in New York. The Supreme Court quashed an indictment of the distillery on grounds that a shipment out of state was within the protection of the commerce clause of the United States Constitution. Acknowledging that the state had the power to halt the sale of alcoholic beverages within its boundaries, the Court nonetheless ruled that the state could not prevent sales in interstate commerce. It brushed aside the state's argument that this result opened the door for fraudulent reshipment of liquor to Tennessee consumers. The Court explicitly ruled that state police power must yield to national commerce.

Perhaps the most striking use of state regulatory power to promote public health was the 1897 statute prohibiting the sale or disposition of cigarettes in Tennessee. At first blush it seems unlikely that Tennessee, a major tobacco growing state, would ban the sale of cigarettes. Anticigarette sentiment in the 1890s was fueled by a blend of health concerns, antagonism toward the monopolistic American Tobacco Company, and fear that cigarettes encouraged other social ills. Lawmakers were also animated by the goal of protecting the valuable cigar trade from competition with cigarettes, then an increasingly popular new way to smoke. Consequently, several states enacted cigarette prohibition laws.[68] In *Austin v. State* (1898) the defendant received a shipment of cigarettes from outside Tennessee. He challenged his conviction under the statute on grounds that the sale of an imported article in its original package was protected by the commerce clause of the United States Constitution.

Validating the statute, the Supreme Court developed two arguments. First, the Court stressed that cigarettes were deleterious to health. "Their use is always harmful," the judges said, "never beneficial. They possess no virtue, but are inherently bad, and bad only."[69] It followed that such a noxious product was not a legitimate article of commerce, and the state could ban its importation. Second, the Court reasoned that the sale of cigarettes in this case did not take place in the original package and was thus not protected by the federal Constitution.

The outcome in *Austin* was affirmed by a sharply divided United States Supreme Court, albeit on different grounds. Refusing to take judicial notice of the injurious effects of cigarette smoking, the Court emphasized that tobacco products had long been recognized as a legitimate article of commerce. The Court agreed that Tennessee could restrict the sale of goods determined by the legislature to be harmful to health, but held that the state could not prevent the importation of articles shipped in their original packages. In this case, however, the Court determined that small boxes of cigarettes were not original packages and hence unprotected by the commerce clause from state police power.[70] This important decision opened the door for additional legal restrictions on the use of cigarettes.

TORTS

Tort law emerged as a distinct body of law in the nineteenth century to govern liability for accidents. Like courts elsewhere, the Tennessee Supreme Court adopted the principle that liability for injury was generally predicated on fault. An injured party had to show both that the accident was caused by negligence and that the claimant had not contributed to infliction of the injury. The number of tort cases mushroomed in the late nineteenth century as the result of accidents in the industrial workplace.

The Tennessee Supreme Court followed the main currents of tort law based on fault, and in that regard recognized a cluster of defenses that hampered recovery by accident victims. The Court adhered to the doctrine of contributory negligence which barred an action if the plaintiff was in any degree responsible for causing the accident.[71] Allied to contributory negligence was the assumption of the risk rule. Under this doctrine an injured party could not recover when he performed work with full knowledge of hazardous conditions. The Court invoked this rule several times to reject claims by injured employees.[72] The consequences of the assumption of the risk doctrine could be harsh. For instance, in *Brown v. Electric Railway Co.* (1898) the widow of a man described as "an illiterate negro, an ordinary laborer," was denied any recovery when her husband was crushed in the collapse of an earth bank. The Court reasoned that the danger was obvious and therefore the deceased assumed the risk of excavation work.

Another barrier to suits by injured employees was the fellow servant rule. This doctrine held that an employee injured through the negligence of a co-worker could not recover from the employer. This doctrine rested on the notion that workers knew the ability of fellow employees and assumed the risk incident to each other's negligence. The Supreme Court applied the fellow servant rule throughout this period.[73]

But application of this doctrine required a determination of which employees were fellow servants. In a complex industry such as railroading, where employees commonly worked in different departments, this was a difficult question and one which generated a host of appeals. One could hardly be deemed to assume the risk of negligence by workers in separate units. In many cases the Tennessee Supreme Court found that the fellow servant rule was inapplicable where railroad employees were hurt by actions of workers in other departments, thereby permitting recovery against the employer. Thus, it held that a conductor and a telegraph operator, a car inspector and an engineer, and a conductor and a station agent were not fellow servants.[74] Even so, the concept of fellow servant was stretched to unrealistic limits. In 1904 the Court ruled that employees working on different trains at the time of an accident were fellow servants because they were engaged in the same kind of service.[75]

Another much litigated exception to the fellow servant rule involved orders given employees by supervisors. A person authorized by the employer to give orders to subordinates was treated as a vice principal. Negligence on the part of a vice principal was attributed to the employer. The vice principal exception, however, compelled the Supreme Court to make precise, and perhaps even contradictory, distinctions between classes of employees.[76] It also was evidence of the Court's willingness to restrict, yet not overrule, the fellow servant doctrine. In fact, the common-law liability rules were increasing inapposite in an industrial society. But the adoption of a worker's compensation scheme in Tennessee would not take place until after World War I.

In marked contrast to the law dealing with injured employees, owners of livestock killed on railroad tracks were likely to prevail in lawsuits. Claims for

Frequent railroad accidents produced many appeals to the Tennessee Supreme Court and were a major factor in shaping tort law at the turn of the twentieth century. This train wreck occurred in Washington County in 1904. Tennessee State Library and Archives.

livestock killed by trains flooded the courts. Following the lead of other states, the Tennessee legislature in 1891 enacted a statute subjecting railroads to strict liability for damage to livestock on unfenced track. The obvious purpose of this measure was to indirectly impose a duty on railroads to fence their track. The Supreme Court upheld the constitutionality of the fence statute against various objections. Viewing this legislation as a means to safeguard public safety, the Court declared in 1892, "The duty of fencing, and the resulting liability for failure to perform such duty, is imposed, not so much in the interest of the owners of animals which may go upon an unfenced road, as in the interest of the general public, who are concerned that accidents shall be avoided, and public travel be made as safe as the exigencies of that manner of transportation will permit."[77] The statute posed some interpretative problems concerning the extent of the duty to fence, but the Supreme Court applied the law forcefully. Railroads could not escape liability for accidents on unfenced track by showing their high degree of diligence in operating trains.[78]

Although the frequency of railroad accidents did much to shape Tennessee tort law at the turn of the twentieth century, the Supreme Court also heard several appeals which involved breach of a statutory duty by other business enterprises. In *Queen v. Dayton Coal & Iron Company* (1895) a boy of ten was injured while working in a mine. Pointing to a statute which made it a misdemeanor to allow a boy under twelve to enter any mine, the Supreme Court opined that violation of the statute constituted negligence per se and rendered the employer liable. Similarly, a 1906 appeal involved the failure of a hotel to comply with laws requiring fire escapes. The Court ruled that a boarder, injured as the result of a fire, could proceed in a negligence action. Holding that the obligation to erect fire escapes was a valid exercise of the police power, the Court stated, "The duty of the defendant to place the fire escapes upon its hotel was not a contractual obligation, and the doctrine of assumed risks has no application to this case. The ordinance is a police regulation, made for the protection of human life, and in the interest of that portion of the public occupying hotels and lodging houses. Public policy requires that duties of this kind be discharged, and that all consequences of a failure to do so shall follow."[79]

Some scholars have argued that the tort law of this period was tailored to shield fledgling enterprise from the financial burden of accidents, and thereby promote economic growth.[80] This is not the appropriate place to address that thesis in detail, but the record of the Tennessee Supreme Court does not support such a conclusion. Admittedly the judges reached some outcomes, especially with respect to injured employees, that seem problematic to modern eyes. Yet the Court was not one-sidedly sympathetic with business enterprise. For instance, it decided as many cases against as in favor of railroads and displayed no sympathy for violators of safety statutes. Rather than a scheme for assisting corporations, tort law in Tennessee reflected the widely shared and deep-seated belief that those responsible for losses should bear them. In most situations fault, not ability to pay, was seen as the only legitimate basis on which to base liability. In handing down decisions grounded on this premise, the judges were simply reflecting the dominant values of the age.

RACE RELATIONS

By the 1880s white Tennesseans, like their counterparts elsewhere in the region, were enacting laws to curtail social contact between whites and blacks. Coupled with the appearance of segregation laws was the disfranchisement of many black voters. Although some blacks, feeling powerless, acquiesced in the spread of segregation, others protested these developments and challenged them with lawsuits. Much of the debate over race relations in Tennessee centered on access to railroad passenger cars and tightened suffrage requirements.

As railroads became the principal means of travel in the Gilded Age, both races had to ride on the same trains. A particular source of controversy was the desire of black female passengers to ride in the first class "ladies' car," which was set aside for women and accompanying men, and in which smoking was prohibited.[81] Lawmakers responded to this pressure by mandating separate accommodations. An 1881 law provided that railroads must furnish separate cars or portions of cars "which all colored passengers who shall pay first-class rates of fare may have the privilege to enter." This ambiguous measure did not compel carriers to separate passengers, only to have distinct first-class accommodations available for blacks.[82] The compromise implicit in the legislation was negated by the Supreme Court's decision in *Chesapeake, Ohio & Southwestern Railroad Company v. Wells* (1887). A black female passenger was put off the train when she refused to sit in the second class coach and requested seating in the ladies' car. Engaging in the fiction that the accommodations were alike, the Court reversed a jury verdict in favor of the passenger. In effect the Court cast a blind eye on discriminatory practices and the absence of first class facilities for black passengers.[83]

As racial conflict over rail accommodations accelerated, the legislature in 1891 enacted a law requiring railroads to provide "equal, but separate accommodations for the white and colored races," and dictating that conductors assign passengers to cars by race. Failure to comply was made a misdemeanor. Sustaining this law, the Supreme Court held in *Smith v. Smith* (1898) that the act was not an impermissible state regulation of interstate commerce. Viewing racial segregation as an appropriate exercise of the police power to maintain social order, the Court commented:

> If it be true, as is sometimes said, that race prejudices exist here that make it uncomfortable or unsafe, or promotive of disorder, to mix the races in public conveyances, then both safety and good order are promoted, as well as comfort in their separation. The state is to judge of the necessity for such a regulation. Whether either or both should be uncomfortable, unsafe, or liable to the injury or annoyance of disorder by such intermixture in travel is not the question. The question is whether it, in fact, is so, or whether the state legislature reasonably deemed it so, and provided against the consequences. It is in these respects, therefore, entirely reasonable.[84]

The decision legitimized segregation laws in Tennessee and opened the door to additional segregationist moves.

In 1903 the legislature extended the policy of transit segregation to urban street railroads. The Memphis Street Railway Company was convicted and fined for failure to provide the mandated separate accommodations. The Supreme Court, in an unusual move, struck down the 1903 act as a violation of the provision in the Tennessee Constitution governing the caption of laws amending former statutes.[85] Commenting on this decision, the *Railroad Gazette* observed, "It appears that there has been strong opposition to the law, not alone from the negroes, but on account of the inconvenience of attempting to separate the two races without a partition, and because it is very uneconomical for the railroad companies."[86]

Of course, this ruling based on technical grounds did not long stem the segregationist drive. The lawmakers passed a new measure in 1905 requiring separate cars or spaces for white and black passengers. The refusal of a black customer to move from a section of a street car in Memphis reserved for whites set the stage for another constitutional challenge. In *Morrison v. State* (1906) the Supreme Court rejected a number of arguments, and held that the statute did not violate equal protection norms. Pointing to "the fixed and unchangeable relations and differences of the two races," the Court discussed at length the rationale behind segregation: "The propriety and necessity for the separation of the white and colored races in Tennessee and other states, where the two races are something like equally divided in numbers, for the material benefit of both of them, is now conceded by all persons conversant with the conditions existing in these states. . . . It violates the rights of no one. It deprives no one of any privileges or immunities to which they are entitled by virtue of any law. It does not discriminate against either race, but applies to both with equal force and effect."[87]

Although railroad segregation sparked persistent opposition and legal attacks, white Tennesseans at the end of the nineteenth century were resolved to restrict black participation in other aspects of public life as well. Confronted with growing black agitation for equal treatment and anxious to cripple the state Republican Party, Democrats in the legislature moved to overhaul the election laws in order to reduce black political influence. The centerpiece of this drive was the Dortch Act, passed in 1889 and revised a year later. This measure required a secret ballot in Memphis, Nashville, Knoxville, and Chattanooga, areas with high levels of black voter participation. It also banned assistance to illiterate voters in marking ballots. The act effectively prevented illiterate blacks from voting. Not as sweeping as disfranchisement measures elsewhere in the South, the Dortch Act, in tandem with the poll tax of 1890, nonetheless produced a sharp decline in black suffrage.[88]

The Dortch Act was challenged as a disguised attempt to impose an educational qualification on the right to vote in violation of the Tennessee Constitution. Unimpressed with this argument, the Supreme Court in *Cook v. State* (1891) upheld the validity of the act as a step to control illegal voting and to stop corruption at the polls. Ignoring the act's obvious racial dimensions, the Court viewed the measure simply as a reform aimed at preventing bribery or coercion of the ignorant.

Racial discrimination was also a factor in the administration of criminal justice. The Supreme Court heard several appeals in which black defendants, convicted of a crime, asserted that no blacks served on the grand jury or were in the pool of potential jurors from which the trial jury was selected. This racial exclusion, it was argued, violated the equal protection clause of the Fourteenth Amendment. The Court gave short shrift to this contention. Treating the objection to the composition of the grand jury as a question of procedure, the judges ruled in several cases that the argument was not raised in a timely manner.[89] Nor was the Court impressed with evidence that blacks had not been called as jurors in Davidson County for years.[90] Clearly the Court was disinclined to examine closely the systematic exclusion of blacks from service on juries.

The Supreme Court did not initiate the racial caste system in Tennessee, but its decisions reinforced the emerging segregationist order. In so doing, the judges reflected the social values of white Tennesseans. Indeed, there can be little doubt that the judges shared the prevalent racial outlook and were largely unconcerned about the deteriorating legal position of blacks. One must, in fairness, take account of the political climate which constrained an elected judiciary on this emotional issue. Moreover, the work of the Tennessee Supreme Court was in complete harmony with the contemporary civil rights jurisprudence of the Supreme Court of the United States. This was, after all, the age of *Plessy v. Ferguson* (1896).[91] The Tennessee Supreme Court's acquiescence in the coming of racial segregation could be seen as an accommodation to the realities of life in Tennessee at the turn of the twentieth century.

DOMESTIC RELATIONS

Attitudes about marriage and family relationships changed markedly in the course of the nineteenth century. There was a growing emphasis on mutual affection between husband and wife, and a widespread acceptance of the theory that women had a unique role as moral guardians of the home. These emerging views clashed with the more traditional patriarchal notion of marriage. Legislators and judges gradually formulated a body of domestic relations law governing such matters as marriage, divorce, sexual relations, and child custody.[92]

Several aspects of domestic relations law were protective of women. The tort of seduction, for example, allowed women seduced by a fraudulent promise of marriage or other inducements to recover monetary damages. Recovery was premised on the belief that seduced women were victims of male lust and suffered a loss of reputation. The Tennessee Supreme Court affirmed a number of jury verdicts awarding damages for seduction.[93] Suits for seduction were sometimes combined with actions for breach of promise of marriage.[94] In one 1897 case the Court sustained a sizable three-thousand-dollar award of damages for breach of marriage contract when the conduct of the defendant was egregious.[95]

With the rise of companionate marriage spouses were less willing to remain in unhappy unions. The Supreme Court did not hear a large number of divorce cases, but it upheld divorce decrees where the statutory grounds were satisfied. Thus, wives obtained divorces based on their husband's cruelty, adultery, and desertion.[96] Recognizing that sometimes divorce served a larger social interest, the Court declared in a 1900 appeal that "it is in the interest of well ordered society, of the wife and of the moral future of the children, that this marriage be dissolved."[97]

An increase in divorce raised the allied question of which former spouse should have custody of minor children.[98] At common law a father was deemed the natural guardian of his children, and thus the husband had the paramount right to custody in the event of marital dissolution. Reflecting the new social attitudes toward women and child nurturing, the Tennessee Supreme Court moved away from paternal custody. In awarding custody, courts began to stress the best interest of the child as the controlling standard. As the Tennessee Supreme Court explained in 1888: ". . . while ordinarily the father would be entitled to the custody, still the Court will look to see in whose custody the real interest and welfare of the child demand that it should be placed."[99] The Court then applied the emerging tender years doctrine, which held that minor children should be placed in the care of the mother. This rule proceeded directly from the belief that women were better suited than men for child raising.

While the tender years doctrine tended to favor the wife, its application was tempered by reliance on parental fault in awarding custody. Since wives instituted most divorce actions, the fault rule often worked to their benefit. But the rule could be wielded against mothers who acted improperly. Thus, in *Evans v. Evans* (1900) the Tennessee Supreme Court refused to give custody of two boys to an adulterous wife.

CRIMINAL LAW

Criminal law did not occupy a prominent spot on the Supreme Court's docket at the turn of the twentieth century. Since the rights of the accused set forth in the Bill of Rights of the United States Constitution were not deemed applicable to the states, fashioning a criminal justice system remained largely the task of state lawmakers and judges. Criminal appeals rarely raised issues of constitutional rights. Instead, they focused on the admission or exclusion of evidence, faulty instructions to the jury, and the sufficiency of procedures and pleadings. In an age when courts paid close attention to form and procedural regularity, judges were quick to reverse convictions because of technical errors in indictments.[100]

The Tennessee Supreme Court heard criminal appeals ranging from murder to minor statutory offenses. Although relatively few criminal cases were appealed, the Court reversed a number of convictions on procedural or evidentiary grounds. In *State v. Argo* (1906), for instance, the judges quashed a perjury indictment for failure to state the nature of the controversy in which the alleged false oath was made. Likewise, the Supreme Court in the same year reversed a murder conviction because the evidence did not support the verdict.[101] To be sure, the Court in a number of cases found that the evidence was sufficient to sustain a conviction for murder.[102]

The issue of self-defense was raised in several murder appeals. Rejecting a self-defense argument, the Supreme Court in *Hamilton v. State* (1898) noted that the armed defendant was not in imminent danger and the victim was shot while running away. The murder conviction was affirmed. On the other hand, the Court was more sympathetic where the defendant, a boy of sixteen, killed a man who was beating his crippled father. Although the son was illegally carrying a pistol, the Court reversed his conviction, declaring that "if the son really believed, on reasonable grounds, that a deadly assault was being made upon his father, and that, owing to the superior power of his antagonist, he would be killed or receive great bodily harm as the result of the assault, it was his legal right, as well as his filial duty, to interfere and prevent the killing or maiming of his father, and to use such means as were necessary, under all the circumstances, to effect this purpose."[103]

Insanity as a defense, however, was viewed skeptically by the Supreme Court. At issue in *Turner v. State* (1907) was a murder apparently committed as part of a bizarre agreement whereby the defendant was to kill his lover and then himself. After he failed to take his own life, the defendant was convicted and sentenced to hang. The Court brushed aside the contention that the defendant was insane. It found no evidence of an unbalanced mind, and refused to infer insanity based on the atrocity of his actions.

Capital punishment was regularly carried out in Tennessee until the mid-twentieth century. This execution of three murderers took place in Warren County in 1900. Tennessee State Library and Archives.

On occasion murder appeals provided a window through which to glimpse a larger social upheaval. *Gardner v. State* (1908) arose out of the "Black Patch war," which engulfed certain tobacco-growing counties of Tennessee and Kentucky between 1906 and 1909. Desperate to halt a steep decline in tobacco prices, tobacco growers organized the Planters' Protective Association. The plan was to authorize a committee to pool the tobacco crop of members and thus obtain a better price from the huge American Tobacco Company. When some growers refused to join the association, a secret band of tobacco night riders was formed. Their goal was to compel all farmers to cooperate by a campaign of terror. Night riders destroyed crops and plant beds, burned barns, and whipped and shot growers who refused to join. Anyone who criticized the association or sold tobacco independently was a target. Lawless conditions in the affected counties grew steadily worse.[104]

The intimidation tactics of the night riders aroused intense resentment. When calls for public officials to maintain order proved ineffective, those opposed to night riding took steps for self-protection and began to carry arms. There were frequent clashes between the different factions. This was the situation when the two defendants, together with others, set out at night from Clarksville to arrest certain night riders and help nearby residents. The defendants were posted at a crossroads when the fatal shooting of Vaughn Bennett took place. Bennett was masked and armed and was with a group of night riders. The evidence was conflicting as to whether the deceased was ambushed or whether the defendants fired in self-defense.

Convicted of second-degree murder after a trial in Montgomery County, the defendants appealed on grounds that the venue of the trial should have been changed to Davidson County. The Supreme Court reversed the conviction and directed a change of venue. It also ruled that the defendants should be able to introduce evidence showing the perilous situation in the Black Patch area. Emphasizing that the appearance of a band of armed

The Tennessee Supreme Court took a firm stand against night riders, a secret band of masked and armed men who engaged in a campaign of terror against independent tobacco growers during the "Black Patch War" of 1906–9. Violence erupted when the independent growers refused to join the Planters' Protective Association, whose goal it was to pool the tobacco crop of members and thus obtain a better price. These night riders came from Gibson County in 1908. Tennessee State Library and Archives.

men would arouse apprehension of bodily harm, the Court noted the inherently threatening nature of night riding:

> This is very evident from the consideration that, when men go out upon the public road masked and armed, and garbed like night riders, thus proclaiming themselves as members of an organization widely notorious for its use of the cudgel, the shotgun, and the torch against the person and the houses and the property of defenseless people, the very sight of them is a suggestion of danger, an indication of a lawless purpose, a ground and reason for instant and anxious alertness. The presence of a body of men so masked, garbed, and armed, or even of one man so accoutered, is an outrageous breach of law and order, and is an imminent and violent threat against all other persons who may encounter him or them, or against all other persons whom he or they may encounter.[105]

On the other hand, the Court displayed no hesitancy in *Rhinehart v. State* (1909) in upholding the death sentence for a night rider convicted of first-degree murder. One historian has contended that the Rhinehart conviction was a major step toward ending mob violence in the tobacco counties.[106]

Of course, most criminal appeals involved less dramatic incidents than murder and night riding. The Court heard relatively few cases dealing with sexual offenses. As explained by the Court, the purpose behind statutory rape "was to protect virtuous young women and to safeguard them against the wiles of the seducer."[107] Yet the judges were cautious in applying this law. In *Jamison v. State* (1906), for example, they reversed a conviction for sexual intercourse with a female under eighteen. They pointed to technical defects in the indictment and errors in the trial court's jury instructions as to whether the victim was a lewd women unprotected by the statute. Clearly the Court saw the virtuous character of the women as essential to establishing criminal behavior. By the end of the nineteenth century, Tennessee, like most states, had outlawed abortions.[108] Cases involving abortion were rare, but here as well the Court moved carefully. In 1906 it reversed the indictment of a man for procuring an abortion in North Carolina for a Tennessee resident. It reasoned that since the principal offense was committed in another jurisdiction the defendant could not be convicted in Tennessee as an accessory before the fact.[109]

The Court had little patience with wrongdoers who breached the public peace. The widespread practice of carrying arms contributed to a violent culture. Legislators sought to halt this practice by making it a criminal offense to publicly or privately carry any pistol, knife, or other weapon. The

Supreme Court construed this statute broadly to prohibit the practice of going armed, and ruled that a violation of the law did not require concealment about the defendant's person.[110] Similarly, the Court upheld the indictment of a group of rowdies who disturbed a Christmas tree celebration in a rural district. Expressing concern about the lack of police protection in rural communities, the Court sustained the indictment on grounds that disturbance of lawful public assemblies was a common-law misdemeanor.[111]

The Tennessee Supreme Court could be persnickety about pleadings and rules of evidence, but it was generally content to enforce the substantive criminal law as defined by the legislature and common law. The Court manifested no interest in protecting the rights of the accused by expansive interpretation of constitutional provisions or second-guessing law enforcement officials. This deferential attitude toward the administration of criminal justice mirrored the Court's support of state regulatory authority in civil cases.

STATE TAXATION

Although Tennessee, like most states, relied heavily on the property tax at the turn of the twentieth century, lawmakers experimented with new kinds of levies. In 1891 Tennessee adopted an inheritance tax. As revamped two years later, this measure taxed all property at death passing by will or intestacy to collateral relatives or strangers at 5 percent of value. Property going to spouses and descendants was exempt from levy. The Tennessee Supreme Court readily upheld the constitutionality of this modest inheritance tax in *State v. Alston* (1895). Noting the long history of inheritance taxation in England and the United States, the Court took the position that the disposition of property of death was governed by state law and subject to regulation. It insisted that the inheritance tax was "not upon the property, but the right or privilege of acquiring it by succession."[112] Nor did the Supreme Court find any constitutional infirmity in the more favorable treatment accorded direct descendants over collateral relatives and strangers. Such distinctions, the Court reasoned, were natural and not arbitrary. In a later case, however, the Supreme Court maintained that the inheritance tax statute should be strictly construed against the government.[113]

The taxation of railroad property was a recurring issue for the Court. Part of the problem was that railroads were an interstate business, and the Court had to devise a formula to ascertain what portion of the business was subject to state and local taxation. Moreover, some railroad companies continued to claim exemption from taxation under the terms of antebellum charters. They argued that attempts to levy state taxes constituted an unconstitutional impairment of the obligation of contract. In *Knoxville and Ohio Railroad Company v. Harris* (1897), however, the Supreme Court upheld the imposition of a privilege tax on a railroad whose charter granted an exemption from taxes on the capital stock and property of the company. "Taxes," the Court observed, "are the life-blood of civil government. The right of taxation is an attribute of sovereignty."[114] It followed that any grants of tax immunity should be strictly construed. The charter only provided for exemption from *ad valorem* taxation, and therefore the legislature was free to levy a tax for the privilege of doing business in Tennessee. Since the tax was based entirely on business within the state, the Court saw no interference with interstate commerce. This decision did a great deal to curtail the scope of old tax exemptions and require all enterprises to pay a share of the public tax burden.

PRACTICE OF LAW

The Tennessee Supreme Court took seriously its authority to police professional misconduct by attorneys. Since lawyers are officers of the Court, the judges maintained that they had inherent power, independent of any statute, to uphold the dignity of the legal profession and promote the orderly administration of justice. The Supreme Court explained in 1890: "Too much is staked upon the honesty and good conduct of lawyers for Courts to wink at flagrant misconduct."[115] Thus, it showed no hesitancy to disbar attorneys for intentionally deceiving a trial judge and for the misappropriation of client funds.[116]

Similarly, the Supreme Court looked with disfavor upon the solicitation of lawsuits by attorneys. A mine explosion in 1902 caused a number of lawyers to actively seek out claimants with possible causes of action against the company. In a later dispute over recovery of promised compensation to an attorney, the Court emphatically denied that "a spirit of commercialism has lowered the standard of the legal profession." Instead, it insisted that the practice of law was not a business and that attorneys "rushing to the scene of disaster in hot haste" and soliciting victims was inconsistent with the character of the legal profession.[117] The Court ruled that this improper conduct lowered the standards of the profession and could not constitute the basis for the recovery of any compensation.

The years between 1886 and 1910 produced enormous social and economic changes in Tennessee. The Supreme Court was confronted with a growing number of private disputes as well as cases which raised issues of public policy. Although the Court played an active role in resolving conflicts, it employed judicial review sparingly and deferred to legislative judgment in setting the state's economic and social agenda. The Tennessee Supreme Court was not an activist tribunal seeking to blaze new paths or second guessing the political process. Above all, the judges mirrored the sentiments of the age and rarely departed from prevailing social norms. Judicial attitudes in Tennessee during the late nineteenth century were in sharp contrast to developments at the national level. The United States Supreme Court began to wield judicial review forcefully and to assume a more prominent role in shaping policy.[118] That was not the path followed in Tennessee.

5

A FREE AND UNTRAMMELED JUDICIARY: THE TENNESSEE SUPREME COURT, 1910–1946

Ruth Anne Thompson

The years 1910 to 1946 were volatile ones in Tennessee's history, as competition between the state's rural interests and growing urban centers exacerbated tensions that already existed due to geography, agriculture, and history. The Supreme Court of Tennessee inevitably became involved in the early-twentieth-century's complex problems as commercial interests began to supplant agriculture, and as the legislature enacted reforms and regulations to meet new needs. Most members of the Court had rural roots but came of age during this time of urban growth. Thus, with backgrounds not unlike the state's governors and members of the General Assembly, the Supreme Court accepted both Progressive reforms and traditions of the past. It upheld a broad exercise of the legislature's police powers, while respecting the separation of powers and guarding its own prerogatives. Both dissenting and concurring opinions were rare, and a mostly unified Court generally accepted legislative and gubernatorial policies as long as they did not cross constitutional boundaries.

Along with courts across the United States, the Tennessee Supreme Court faced a new era of interpersonal relationships brought on by the rise of industrialism in the late nineteenth and early twentieth centuries. Many Progressives sought to redress the problems of the age through regulation and government reform. Southern Progressives in particular were interested in promoting modernization and the economic development of the nation's poorest region, while maintaining long cherished values and social systems. Industrialization came late to the South, and most of the region's Progressive reformers remained faithful to the agrarian past and traditional religious tenets. They were suspicious of labor unions and eastern financiers, and wedded to the white supremacist philosophy. Tennessee lawmakers, likewise, were influenced by the Progressive movement. Still primarily an agricultural state, by the turn of the century Tennessee could not ignore the inroads of industry and urbanization. Tennessee's reform spirit would continue well into the mid-twentieth century as proponents of change in the state called for prohibition of alcoholic beverages, increased support for public education, laws regulating the work environment and employer-employee relations, improved transportation, and electoral reform. The Court's opinions from the 1910s to the 1940s reflect these changes, involving litigation over the increased interaction between people thrown together in the workplace and forced to deal with each other in novel settings.[1]

The decisions of the Tennessee Supreme Court between 1910 and 1946 support recent studies concluding that the notion that Progressive-era courts were enemies of reform is largely a myth.[2] While the Tennessee Supreme Court occasionally invalidated legislation, it usually agreed with the legislature's initiatives in areas such as worker's compensation and other business regulation. Apart from economic legislation, however, the Court also heard lawsuits dealing with the Progressive-era reforms of the 1910s, the governmental restructuring introduced by the Peay administration in the 1920s, and the complex problems of the Depression era. The Tennessee Supreme Court neither led nor hindered the legislature's efforts to control behavior, regulate industry, and reorganize government. The Court accepted advances for women in areas of property law and electoral reform and sustained the state's segregationist policies even as the nation was feeling the first stirring of the modern civil rights movement. Although the legislature remained under the control of the state's rural delegations, legislators, governors, and judicial officers recognized the changes, for good or ill, brought by the new industrial age. Yet it was within the framework of southern values that Tennessee politicians and their constituents embraced the reform spirit of the age and in which the Tennessee Supreme Court settled disputes and interpreted the law.

This was also an era of political turmoil and transition. In 1910 a serious fracture in the state's ruling Democratic Party gave the minority Republican Party its first opportunity for political control since the 1880s. In the 1920s and 1930s, powerful politicians such as Luke Lea of Nashville and Edward

H. Crump of Memphis struggled for power. As the state became involved in the fight for democracy overseas during the Second World War, foes of Crump argued for an end to machine politics in Tennessee, and engaged in a battle that would eventually see the decline of the powerful boss. The Court normally stayed out of political maneuvering, although it often reviewed contested legislation or decided other issues dividing the antagonists. Occasionally, however, the Court's rulings or the actions of the judges themselves would become part of the controversy. Nonetheless, the Tennessee Supreme Court, and its judges, retained a reputation of honor and stability in the midst of changing, and sometimes contentious, times.

THE JUDGES, 1910–1946

Although eighteen judges would serve on the Tennessee high court between 1910 and 1945, their composite portrait changed little during these years. All of them were male, white, and had active careers as lawyers, jurists, or politicians in the Democratic Party prior to their elevation to the Supreme Court. Six, William D. Beard, Matthew Neil, Arthur S. Buchanan, Nathan Lynn Bachman, Alexander Wilds Chambliss, and Frank Hoyt Gailor, were the sons of clergy. Four, John K. Shields, Grafton Green, Francis Fentress, and William H. Swiggart, were the sons of lawyers. Their legal training ranged from studies in private law offices to Gailor's degree from Oxford University, but seven of the men had degrees from Cumberland University, with Chief Justices Green and A. B. Neil having especially close connections to that institution. Their average age was just below fifty at the time of their elections or appointments. The two youngest were Green and Swiggart, who each came to the Court at age thirty-seven. The eldest was A. B. Neil at age sixty-eight. They served an average of about thirteen years, ranging from Francis Fentress's nine months, to Green's thirty-six years. Justices McKinney and Chambliss also had lengthy terms of service on the Court, each remaining for twenty-four years. All had spent time in private practice, and all but M. M. Neil, Buchanan, and Green had served on a lower court bench before coming to the state high court. Buchanan, Hall, Chambliss, and A. B. Neil had spent a brief time in the state legislature, Buchanan in Mississippi, the others in Tennessee. Two men, Shields and Bachman, would serve in the United States Senate after resigning from the Court.[3]

Three men, Bennett D. Bell, William K. McAlister and William Dwight Beard, saw the end of their Supreme Court careers at the beginning of this period. McAlister had been a former Nashville city attorney and Circuit Court judge before his appointment to the Court in 1893, and was twice reelected. Bell served only a short time on the Court, from 1908 until 1910.

Both McAlister and Bell were defeated for reelection in a hotly contested judicial primary election in 1910. Chief Justice Beard, the last member of the Court to have been a member of the Confederate army, sat on the bench briefly in 1890, and was then elected in 1894, 1902, and 1910. He died of a heart attack in December of that year and Governor Malcolm R. Patterson appointed Arthur S. Buchanan to fill the vacancy. Buchanan, a Mississippi native, had been in private practice in Memphis, and despite his association with the discredited Patterson, he was unopposed when he went up for election in 1912. He resigned from the Court in 1917 because of ill health.[4]

John K. Shields was first elected to the Supreme Court in 1902, and won reelection in 1910. Shields was the leader when he and two other judges, Beard and Matthew M. Neil, broke with the Patterson administration and the Democratic Party to run as independent Democrats in the judicial election of 1910. He became chief justice that year, but resigned from the Court in 1913 to be the last Tennessean elected to the United States Senate by the General Assembly. He served twelve years in the Senate, and while there earned the enmity of President Woodrow Wilson when the Democrat Shields refused to support the Treaty of Versailles and the League of Nations. The issue was used against Shields in his next unsuccessful reelection bid.[5]

Three others elected in the 1910 contest were Matthew M. Neil, David L. Lansden, and Grafton Green. Neil served two terms on the Supreme Court, from 1902 until 1918. He had been a private attorney, president of the Tennessee Bar Association, and a judge of the Chancery Court before his election. Neil resigned from the Court in 1918 to return to private practice. David L. Lansden was a schoolteacher before he began his practice of law in Putnam County, later serving as chancellor of the Fourth Chancery Division. He was chief justice from 1918 until his retirement in 1923. Grafton Green, who served on the Court for the entire period, from 1910 until his death in 1946, was born and educated in Lebanon, Tennessee, and was in private practice in Nashville at the time of his election to the high court. Green, who became chief justice in 1923, was the grandson of Tennessee Supreme Court Justice Nathan Green, who also had a long tenure on the bench, sitting from 1831 until 1852. Grafton Green's father, Nathan Green Jr., was a longtime professor at Cumberland Law School.

In 1913, the legislature elected Justice Shields to the United States Senate, and Governor Ben W. Hooper appointed distinguished lawyer and historian Samuel Cole Williams to fill the opening. The justice won his seat in the August 1914 regular election with the support of the state's remaining "Fusion" coalition members, although the coalition would break apart by the November election that year. Williams, who would serve five years, began his career as an attorney in Humboldt, Tennessee, before commencing a successful practice in Johnson City. After resigning from the Court, Williams went on to become the first Dean of Emory University's Lamar Law School. In 1929 he was appointed to the Tennessee Code Commission and edited Williams's *Code Annotated,* published in 1934. He later published several well-received works on Tennessee history, including *The Lost State of Franklin* and *Early Travels in the Tennessee Country,* and a number of studies of the state's legal history, including a look at the Court upon which he had once served, *Phases of the History of the Supreme Court of Tennessee.*[6]

The year 1918 saw the elevation of four men to the Court. Francis Fentress served only nine months, filling out the term of Arthur Buchanan. Prior to his appointment, Fentress served as chancellor in Shelby County, and returned there to private practice after his resignation. Nathan Lynn Bachman of Chattanooga was a city attorney and Circuit Court judge before his election to the Supreme Court in 1918. In 1923, he resigned to campaign unsuccessfully for the United States Senate. In 1933, Governor Hill McAlister appointed Bachman to replace Cordell Hull in the United States Senate when the latter became secretary of state. Bachman won both the short-term election of 1934 and election to a full term in 1936, but he died less than a year later in April 1937. Frank P. Hall of Dresden was one of the first judicial candidates in 1910 to criticize the Patterson administration backed primary plan, and he ran successfully as an independent for the Court of Civil Appeals. In 1918 he was elected to the Supreme Court, and was preparing to run for a second term in 1926 when he died. Colin Pierson McKinney of Ripley served the longest tenure of these four men. Justice McKinney was serving as chancellor of the Ninth Chancery Division when elected to the Supreme Court in 1918, where he stayed until his retirement in 1942.[7]

Governor Peay appointed two judges in 1923, both of whom would also remain on the Court for many years. Alexander Wilds Chambliss was named in 1923, and became chief justice at the death of Grafton Green, serving less than a year until his own death in 1947. A Virginia native who made his home in Chattanooga, he served a term in the state senate before becoming mayor of Chattanooga from 1901 until 1905, and from 1919 until 1923 when Governor Austin Peay appointed him to the Supreme Court. Between his terms as mayor, he served for two years on the Court of Civil Appeals. William L. Cook of Hickman County had been a member of the General Assembly, and was a Circuit Court judge for the Ninth Judicial Circuit from 1908 until 1923, when Governor Peay appointed him to replace Justice Lansden.[8]

William H. Swiggart's father was an attorney and Circuit Court judge who occasionally served as a special judge for the Tennessee Supreme Court. Swiggart began his own law practice in his hometown of Union City before his appointment as assistant state attorney general, a position he held for twelve years. In 1926, Justice Hall was already on the ballot for reelection at the time of his death, and the Democratic Party's executive committee chose Swiggart to take Hall's place. Swiggart won the election and stayed on the Court until 1935, when he resigned to become general counsel for the Nashville, Chattanooga and St. Louis Railway. When Swiggart resigned, Governor McAlister appointed Memphis attorney and Chancery Court judge David W. DeHaven. DeHaven, former president of the Shelby County Bar Association, served on the Supreme Court from 1935 until his death in 1942.

A. B. Neil was born in Lewisberg, and attended Cumberland Law School, where he would later serve as professor and dean. His varied career included membership in the General Assembly and then service as a judge in the criminal and circuit courts while continuing his duties at Cumberland. Neil was a Democratic nominee for the Supreme Court in 1942, when Governor Cooper appointed him to the high bench upon the death of Justice Cook. In 1947, Neil became the chief justice of the Supreme Court, and he served until his retirement in 1960. While serving as chief justice he was named chairman of the Tennessee Code Commission. Alan Prewitt of Bolivar had been serving as a special judge on the Court in 1942, as he had earlier in 1937 and 1941, before running and winning a seat in 1942. In 1960 he was named chief justice, serving in that position until his death in February 1963.[9]

The last justice to join the Court during this period was Frank Hoyt Gailor, the son of Tennessee's Episcopal bishop, Thomas Frank Gailor. A Rhodes scholar, he attended the University of the South, Columbia University, and Oxford University. He served with both British and American forces in World War I, and after the war he moved to Memphis, where the became a private attorney. Following a stint in the legislature, he became Shelby County trustee and then circuit judge. In 1943 Governor Cooper appointed Gailor to the Supreme Court, an appointment that raised a minor controversy because of an ongoing battle over poll tax repeal and Justice Gailor's ties to the Crump organization in Memphis. Nonetheless, Gailor was a respected jurist who won a seat in at the next judicial election, and sat on the Court until his death in 1954.[10]

PROHIBITION AND POLITICS, 1910–1914

No reform, no regulatory scheme, was more controversial in Tennessee than was Prohibition in the early decades of the twentieth century. No other single issue created such bitter feuds and political realignment. The Court's review of this controversial reform revealed its acceptance of legislative regulation of social and economic activities. Further, the contentiousness that surrounded the issue would lead the Tennessee Supreme Court into the center of a political firestorm. Tennessee had lagged behind other states in the region in adopting statewide Prohibition, but by 1908, through a series of laws and local votes, most of the state's rural areas, cities, and towns were dry. Only Memphis, Nashville, Chattanooga, and LaFollette remained wet. In that year, Prohibition became a major campaign issue in the Democratic gubernatorial primary. The candidates were the colorful and contentious Edward Ward Carmack and the incumbent governor, Malcolm R. Patterson. After a spirited campaign, local option supporter Patterson defeated Prohibitionist Carmack, carrying Middle Tennessee as well as Shelby and Hamilton counties. Patterson's primary victory, as well as his solid win in November against the Republican challenger seemed to vindicate his position. The newly elected Democratic legislature, however, would be controlled by Prohibitionists.[11]

After his defeat, Carmack became the editor of the *Nashville Tennessean,* owned by Prohibitionist and future political power broker Luke Lea. Throughout the fall of 1908, Carmack used the paper to criticize the leaders of the Democratic Party and to promote the Prohibitionist cause. Among those Carmack singled out for criticism was Col. Duncan B. Cooper, a good friend and political ally to Malcolm Patterson, and a former friend of Carmack. On November 9, 1908, Carmack published yet another bitter editorial against Cooper, and on that afternoon, apparently by chance, Carmack met Colonel Cooper and his son Robin on Union Street in Nashville. Shots were exchanged, and within moments Carmack was dead. The Coopers were arrested and charged with first-degree murder, and Prohibitionists suddenly had a martyr in place of an advocate. Tennessee papers, led by the *Tennessean,* fueled the frenetic atmosphere, portraying Carmack as a fallen saint and the Coopers and the liquor interests as villainous co-conspirators. Carmack's death caused the Prohibitionist-controlled legislature to pass a series of laws to honor the slain hero, including laws prohibiting the sale and manufacture of alcohol. Nonetheless, bars stayed open in the state's four largest cities, with no consistent effort on the part of local officials to enforce the law, and Prohibitionists remained angry and distrustful. The tensions of the past decade were reaching a crisis point for the Democratic Party.[12]

After a two month trial in which Governor Patterson testified on behalf of his old friends, a jury convicted both Coopers of second-degree murder, despite the fact that the elder Cooper apparently never fired a shot. The Coopers appealed, and in the spring of 1910, interested parties waited for the Tennessee Supreme Court to release its decision. The ruling would turn out to have grave implications for the fall 1910 election, when all five members of the Supreme Court—Beard, Bell, McAlister, Neil, and Shields—were up for reelection. The Democratic state executive committee, controlled by Patterson's allies, met two weeks before the Court would announce its decision in *Cooper* and decided that the party would hold a county-unit primary for all state posts, including the judicial offices. Under this plan, the candidate who received a plurality of the vote in any county would then receive the votes of all county delegates at the state convention. Patterson's opponents charged that, while the delegates would be required to vote for their county's winner, the Patterson-dominated executive committee would choose the delegates, and therefore control the convention.[13]

Controversy also arose over using this method to choose candidates for the Supreme Court and Court of Civil Appeals. Prior to this, nominees to the high court had been chosen in a separate state convention, but one of the planks in the state Democratic Party platform of 1908 had provided that all nominees be chosen by vote of the people. Despite this, the debate over the method of judicial nomination turned out to be the most contentious issue of the executive committee meeting, and the unhappiness with the plan did not end with the committee's decision. On the day after the committee announced the plan, two members of the Supreme Court, Justices B. D. Bell and William K. McAlister, declared that they would take part in the primary. In a statement, Bell noted, "My choice is a primary. I have always preferred to submit my claims to the people for any office. This was well known to my associates and all others for months before the meeting of the committee."[14]

Bell's comments did not, however, reflect the opinion of other prominent judicial candidates in the state, including several of his colleagues on the Supreme Court. Frank P. Hall, a candidate for the Court of Civil Appeals, who would win election to the Supreme Court in 1918, charged that the committee's decision reversed longstanding traditions and that the purpose was "not to give the people the right to name their judges, but to make the judiciary an integral part of a political machine." Hall was soon joined by other jurists, including Beard, Shields and Neil of the Supreme Court, in announcing that they would not participate in the primary. The Supreme Court judges soon linked their actions to their opinion in the case of *Cooper v. State.*[15]

On April 13, 1910, the Tennessee Supreme Court issued a split decision that affirmed the twenty year prison sentence given to Colonel Duncan Cooper, while reversing and remanding Robin Cooper's conviction. The younger Cooper was ordered to receive a retrial on the grounds that the judge failed to instruct the jury as to his "purpose and intent" in the shooting, and because of some errors in the introduction of testimony and the examination of witnesses. Shields, Neil, and McAlister voted to sustain the conviction of Colonel Cooper. Beard, Bell, and McAlister voted to reverse Robin Cooper's conviction. Originally, Beard had written an opinion overturning both convictions, but, when the majority disagreed, Shields wrote the opinion that was eventually issued as that of the majority. Less than half an hour after the members of the Court left the bench, people learned that Governor Patterson had issued Colonel Cooper a full pardon. In so doing, Patterson effectively ended his chances for reelection in the fall and dealt a blow to his party that would take years to heal. The pardon emboldened Prohibition Democrats and other political enemies of the governor to break with him over the election of a new Supreme Court.[16]

Patterson's pardon of Duncan Cooper was soon linked to the controversy over the judicial election. Although Beard had voted to overturn both of the Cooper convictions, he joined publicly with Justices Shields and Neil in charging that the governor had tried to use the nomination process to influence their decision in the *Cooper* case, an allegation that Patterson hotly denied. The judges stated that when the time came for the state committee meeting that Patterson was so upset over the Court's failure to release its opinion that he approved, or perhaps suggested, the primary plan. Beard, Shields, and Neil regarded this as a threat, saying in a statement that they believed that they had been offered the alternative of reversing the Cooper convictions or having to submit to an open primary. Patterson admitted that he had expressed interest in the release of the *Cooper* opinion, but said that he did so as citizen who wished to see a quick resolution to the matter. He attacked the Supreme Court for waiting seventy-two days after the oral arguments to issue the decision, and he questioned the Court's timing in quickly releasing the opinion after criticism over the primary plan had erupted. Patterson especially singled out Judge Shields for criticism, charging that Shields had actively supported Carmack in 1908, and that it was the justice's refusal to consider any compromise that had led Beard and Neil to join him. Shields, in turn, was quite implacable in his opposition to the governor. According to Shields, the primary election plan "unquestionably was, part of a deliberate effort by Governor Patterson to invade and interfere with our solemn duties as Judges of the Supreme Court, to overawe that tribunal, and improperly influence its decision in a case then pending before it." On April 18, Beard, Shields, and Neil, along with David L. Lansden and Grafton Green, announced their decision to run for election to the Supreme Court without participating in the June Democratic primary. They were joined by the independent candidates for the Court of Civil Appeals, F. F. Wilson, J. C. Higgins, John M. Taylor, Frank P. Hall, and H. Y. Hughes.[17]

Despite Patterson's protests, when the Democratic Party's state executive committee met again on May 7, its members tried to appease the judges on several key points, including a promise of a separate judicial primary. The independent judges refused these overtures, and made plans for their own convention on May 18. The ten independent candidates for the Supreme Court and the Court of Civil Appeals issued a statement giving their reasons for refusing to negotiate with the state committee. Their first concern, they said, was the "integrity and independence of the judiciary" and the continued "purity of the courts." Patterson, according to the judges, had attempted to manipulate the Court: "We stand for an untrammeled judiciary, for absolute freedom of thought and action upon the part of the court for freedom from machine control and political manipulation, and for equality of all men before the law."[18]

Newspapers in the state championed the cause of the "free and untrammelled judiciary" candidates, cheering when anti-administration Democrats chose to hold their own judicial convention in May to nominate the independent slate of judges. The split in the Democratic Party inspired Tennessee's Republican leaders to back the independent judicial candidates rather than submit their own roster of candidates, allegedly after conferring with the party's national leaders, including President William Howard Taft. As the anti-Patterson, pro-Prohibition forces in both parties began rallying behind the independent ticket, worried regular Democrats nominated their own candidates, R. M. Barton, William K. McAlister, R. C. Cook, Bennett D. Bell, and R. E. Maiden, to run as their nominees for the Supreme Court for the August election.[19]

The regular Democratic campaign received little attention, with the state's major newspapers focusing on the speeches and appearances of their rivals

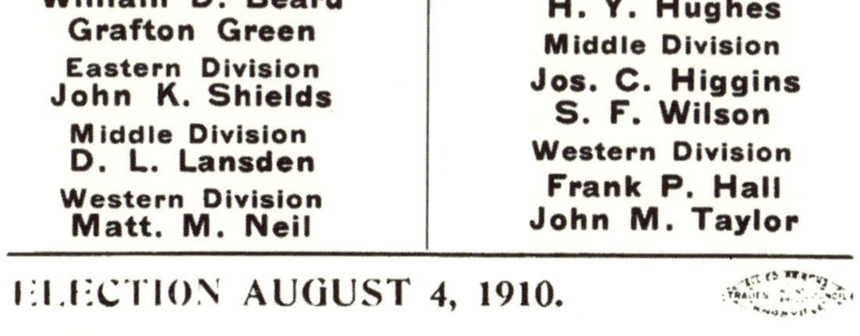

VOTE FOR A

"FREE AND UNTRAMMELLED JUDICIARY"

For SUPREME COURT	For COURT of CIVIL APPEALS
State at Large William D. Beard Grafton Green Eastern Division John K. Shields Middle Division D. L. Lansden Western Division Matt. M. Neil	Eastern Division H. Y. Hughes Middle Division Jos. C. Higgins S. F. Wilson Western Division Frank P. Hall John M. Taylor

ELECTION AUGUST 4, 1910.

This 1910 judicial election card anticipated the victory of an independent slate of judges to the Tennessee Supreme Court. John K. Shields Collection, University of Tennessee Special Collections Library.

in the independent camp. During the campaign, the independents did not openly criticize the regular Democrat judicial candidates. Rather, they lambasted Governor Patterson and the Patterson "machine," arguing that he was attempting to corrupt the purity of the judicial branch. The supporters of the independent ticket continually raised the pardon issue while tying the governor to the state's liquor interests, and they insinuated race into the fight. In earlier years, Prohibitionists had warned that there would be no end of the "negro problem" without an end to the liquor trade, and now they proclaimed that Patterson and his allies in the liquor industry were manipulating the state's African American voters. Allegations of the corruption of black Democratic votes would continue throughout the election.[20]

Patterson and the regular Democrats attempted to fight the independent onslaught. They charged that Shields, Neil, and Beard hoped to control the Court and distribute political favors. They alleged that it was the judges themselves who had attempted to use the *Cooper* opinion for political purposes. There were also charges that the three Supreme Court judges had banded together to control the appointment of the state attorney general, Charles T. Cates, and that there was some collusion in the choice of Court librarian. At least one regular Democratic candidate, Judge Cooke of Chattanooga, issued a statement denying that he was an "administration" candidate. Cooke insisted his candidacy was suggested by friends, and he defended the fairness of the primary plan. Patterson defended his pardon of Cooper, insisting that it was based upon his knowledge of the record of the case, and he called the independent judges "bolters without cause."[21]

In the end, the real issue set before the people on August 4, 1910, was simple. The election had become a referendum on Carmack, Patterson, and "machine politics." As stated by the *Knoxville Journal and Tribune,* "Those who believe the governor did wrong in pardoning the slayer of Carmack with the haste exhibited and in the manner he did, will support the independent ticket."[22] That sentiment prevailed, and election day saw the triumph of the "free judiciary," and the repudiation of the administration candidates. The independent ticket out polled the regulars by a large majority. The independents carried Republican east Tennessee and it was estimated that about fifty-five thousand Democrats defected to vote for the independents.[23]

Two of the major results of the 1910 election were the eventual withdrawal of Patterson from the gubernatorial race in November, and the subsequent election of Fusion candidate, Ben W. Hooper as the state's first Republican governor since the 1880s as the independents and Republicans remained united. Although regular Democrats nominated Patterson, the beleaguered governor soon realized the futility of his campaign, and he withdrew from the race. The effect of the August election on the Supreme Court itself was less dramatic as the judges returned their attention to their normal duties. Beard, who would die five months after the August election, stepped down as chief justice, and Shields was chosen to replace him. Beard's death gave Patterson the chance to appoint a judge who would sit until the next election. Perhaps wisely, he did not pick one of the candidates from the regular ticket, but instead chose Memphis attorney Arthur S. Buchanan to fill Beard's position. At the next election, in 1912, Buchanan was elected, and then reelected in 1918, apparently without suffering any ill effects from Patterson's taint. A major consequence was the election of both Justices Lansden and Green, who would each serve long tenures on the Court. In particular, Green would serve for the next thirty-six years, earning a reputation as one of the Court's most respected members.[24]

The Court could not, however, ignore the factionalism that continued to plague the state's political branches over the next few years, as disputes over new laws or legislative practices often ended up in the courts. Just as the controversy over Prohibition had not ended with the death of Edward Carmack, it did not end with the election of Hooper and the Fusion-controlled legislature.

Grafton Green was elected to the Tennessee Supreme Court in 1910 and served as chief justice from 1923 to 1947. Tennessee State Library and Archives.

Almost immediately, the Court was faced with another challenge of the Prohibition statute, and whether or not the Court was influenced by the Patterson battle, the Court gave a stirring endorsement of legislative prerogatives while upholding the constitutionality of the new law.

Motlow v. State (1912) involved Lem Motlow, operator of the famous Jack Daniels distillery in Lynchburg. Motlow was charged with illegally operating a whisky distillery and with the manufacture of intoxicating beverages for the purpose of sale. A jury found Motlow guilty, and the appeal tested the constitutionality of the 1909 law, which outlawed the manufacture of intoxicating liquor for the purposes of sale. Motlow argued on appeal that the law was unconstitutional because the legislation arbitrarily treated one class of persons different from another because the statute allowed the continued manufacture of 188-proof alcohol for medicinal purposes. In upholding the statute, Neil noted that while it would be infinitely more difficult to enforce Prohibition without ending the manufacture of alcohol, the legislature could reasonably make this distinction. The opinion defined the breadth of the legislature's police powers, and provided an explanation of the Court's view on substantive judicial review. The police power, Neil explained, was immense, was indefinite, and ever changing as new situations arose. The Court's role in reviewing the statute was not to decide whether the policy adopted by the legislature was either "wise or foolish." The opinion explained that the Court would simply determine whether a law was reasonable—if the law tended to protect the health, safety, or morals of the people, if the law focused on all the people rather than a particular class, and if the law was constitutional under the state or federal Constitutions, then it would be upheld.[25]

The Court continued to hear many appeals under the Prohibition statutes even as the lingering bitterness between the state's political factions spilled into other areas. One important case decided before eventual reconciliation of the state's Democrats was the controversial *Webb v. Carter* (1913). The Court was called on to determine the constitutionality of a revised election law that had been passed over the governor's veto after a bitter partisan struggle between regular Democrats and the Fusionists. The regulars had enough votes in the state house to override the governor's veto. However, they did so in the absence of a quorum, because a number of Fusionists had left the state in order to halt an override vote. Justice Buchanan's opinion concluded that not enough members were present to constitute a quorum. The Court noted the inherent difficulty it faced in overturning the action of one of the other branches of the government, but found that the override attempt was inconsistent with provisions of the state Constitution.

The importance of *Webb v. Carter* was underscored by the number of opinions it produced in an era when dissenting and concurring opinions were rare. Chief Justice Neil and Justice Williams wrote concurring opinions, and Justice Lansden wrote a dissenting opinion which Justice Green joined. The chief justice's lengthy opinion stressed the importance of insisting that the legislature follow the dictates of the Constitution, given that the document is the most important check on potential legislative corruption. Justice Lansden's dissent argued that the purpose of Article 3, Section 18 was to allow both houses of the legislature to reconsider a law once a governor had voiced objections. In his strongly worded dissent, Lansden argued that the legislature had the power to pass the law; and that allowing a mere procedural defect to defeat the bill also allowed procedure to take precedence over a constitutionally granted power. He ended his opinion by stating, "This case legalizes the filibuster. As its results are upheld and apparently approved by the court of last resort, it will become the trick of the politician and the resort of the spoilsman."[26] Thus, the filibuster was recognized as another tool to be used by members of the often contentious General Assembly. However, the rest of the decade proved to be much less turbulent than its opening years.

As for the Supreme Court, after the election of 1910 the "free and untrammeled" justices focused their attention on law and not on politics. Apart from their review of cases such as *Motlow* or *Webb,* they appear to have avoided any participation in the political wrangling between the Fusionists and the regulars. When the Democratic Party announced its approval of Prohibition in 1914, the wayward independents returned to the fold, after first supporting the election of Hooper's only Supreme Court appointee, Samuel Cole Williams, in the August election. Democrat Thomas C. Rye became the new governor, and regular Democrats regained control of the legislature. Democratic electoral dominance in the state meant that there would be little political drama or partisanship shown in the election of justices in the coming years. The slate of justices approved by the Democratic Party, with some of the candidates having already been appointed as interim justices by Democratic governors, were routinely elected. One exception to this generally noncontroversial process would come during the decade of the 1940s, when opponents of Edward H. Crump charged that the Memphis boss was attempting to pack the Court with his men.

THE COURT AND GENERAL ASSEMBLY IN AN AGE OF REFORM

In *Motlow v. State,* the Court stressed that the General Assembly's broad police powers—"the power that the people themselves have"—made it the state's primary policy-making body. Yet as shown by *Webb v. Carter,* the legislature's power in this area was not absolute, and the Supreme Court would overturn actions of the legislature that it felt overstepped other constitutional boundaries. Examples of this philosophy abound between 1910 and 1946, as the Court reviewed the cases that arose amid the increasing complexity of social and business relationships of the times.

The legislative changes were often small, affecting only a few. For example, the Court upheld laws regulating businesses performing public services, such as boardinghouses. In *Nance v. O.K. Houck Piano Co.* (1913) the Court ruled that the legislature could determine to protect owners of boardinghouses from the possible fraud of patrons by giving the former liens on the property of the latter for security purposes. In *State v. Anderson* (1920), the Court distinguished regulatory fees from fees designed to raise revenue, holding that the police power could be used to collect money. Justice Hall's majority opinion found that the purpose of a law that included payment of licensing fees by dog owners was permissible as it was imposed to regulate dog ownership, not to raise a revenue. Likewise, in *Athens Hosiery Mills v. Thomason* (1921) the Court found licensing fees imposed under the Bureau of Workshop and Factory Inspection Act a valid expression of the legislature's police power. The Court held that the legislature had the authority to impose reasonable fees to help pay for the cost of running the agency, even if more money was raised than spent.

One of the most comprehensive reforms enacted by the legislature during the 1910s, was the 1919 worker's compensation law, a statute providing new protections for employees injured in industrial accidents. Cases under the act would fill the Court's docket in the following decades. Under the common law, an injured employee's only remedy was to prove the employer's negligence and bring suit. This was a daunting task as the employer had a vast array of defenses, such as assumption of the risk, that limited any liability for industrial accidents. The Tennessee statute required that employers with ten or more employees carry compensation insurance for their employees. Certain groups were excepted from coverage, notably farm workers, coal mine operators, independent contractors, and common carriers engaging in interstate commerce. The statute was elective, but if an employer did not participate the law eliminated the common-law defenses of assumption of the risk, contributory negligence, and the fellow servant rule. Employees could elect not to pursue remedies under the act, but in that event the employer would be able to use the various common-law defenses.

The Tennessee statute did not create a commission to oversee the new law. When a dispute arose under the statute, the parties could adjudicate issues in the court system. Appeals went directly to the Supreme Court by writ of error, bypassing the Court of Civil Appeals (later the Court of Appeals).

In the decades following the passage of the act, a large number of worker's compensation cases worked their way up to the state's high court. The Court sustained the law against a variety of constitutional attacks in *Scott v. Nashville Bridge Company* (1920). Justice Hall's opinion dismissed charges that the law was discriminatory because it excluded coal mine operators, citing other regulations the state had imposed on the coal mining industry because of its risky nature. The Court denied that the law unconstitutionally deprived the parties of the right of trial by jury because of the elective nature of the law. Justice Hall wrote that the law did not unconstitutionally deprive an employee of a property right, and that the legislature could properly apply the law to minors. Justice Bachman dissented because he believed the law made an arbitrary and unreasonable classification due to its exemption of coal mine operators.

Over the next twenty-six years, the Tennessee Supreme Court would review dozens of worker's compensation cases. For example, in *Vantrease v. Smith* (1921), the defendant, who operated a sawmill, argued that the act did not apply to him because he had no more than six employees working at his mill at one time. He did, however, regularly employ workmen in different locations. The plaintiff's injury occurred at the sawmill. The Court held that act applied and that the legislature intended the statute to cover the number of employees, not the location of the accident. A more complex case, *Milne v. Sanders* (1921), involved the death of a sixteen year old worker who died from burn injuries at a chair company. The chair company insisted that the death was the result of a deliberate act of another employee, a young man who allegedly threw a lighted match into a highly flammable room in retaliation for an earlier disagreement with the deceased. The accused employee had been convicted of murder in a separate proceeding. Justice McKinney's opinion stated that there was nothing in the record in the worker's compensation case that showed that the other worker had intended to harm the deceased, and that the Court could not make that assumption. The Court then determined that the deceased's death arose out of the "course of his employment," and was therefore covered by the act.

While the Court recognized the importance of individual property rights, it did find that when balanced against the problems inherent in urban growth, property rights in land could be regulated through zoning. In the early twentieth century, municipalities throughout the country had begun to rely on zoning as an effort to control city growth. In *Euclid v. Ambler Realty* (1926), the United States Supreme Court had approved "use zoning,"—the creation of zones or districts within a municipalities in which only certain uses were allowed. The Tennessee Supreme Court upheld zoning in *Spencer-Sturla Co. v. City of Memphis* (1927). The defendant had been found guilty of unlawfully maintaining a mortuary in violation of the municipal zoning ordinance. Justice Swiggart's opinion stated that the statute did not deny persons use of their land, but merely regulated its use. He cited earlier opinions for the proposition that, "an exercise of the police power, otherwise valid and constitutional, cannot be defeated because property rights are taken or destroyed thereby without compensation." The Court then addressed the question of whether a statute granting the power of land use regulation was within the state's police power. Justice Swiggart's opinion found that the purpose of the statute—to prevent overcrowding and resulting health and safety concerns—justified a reasonable exercise of the state's power. The opinion examined the reasonableness of the statute, including provisions allowing preexisting, nonconforming businesses to remain, and pointed out that the purpose of zoning was not necessarily to change existing property uses, but to control future urban growth.[27]

The Court generally respected the police powers of the legislature and municipalities, but would overturn statutes if it found the law created an unreasonable classification among the people, or if it violated some other constitutional right. For example, in *State v. Nashville, Chattanooga & St. Louis Railway* (1911), the Court overturned a statute making it a misdemeanor for joint stock companies, associations, or corporations, to fire employees because of the employee's vote in an election. In effect, the act covered only corporations, because the state did not have either of the first two categories of businesses, and the law did not cover partnerships. Justice Shields, writing for the Court, could find no reasonable justification for the distinction, and held that it violated the equal protection rights of corporations under the Fourteenth Amendment.

The Court made its disapproval of legislative monopolies clear in *Noe v. Mayor and Alderman of Town of Morristown* (1913). After finding that the legislature had not given the town authority to grant a monopoly over the slaughter of animals to a local business, the Court went further and held that the legislature could not create a monopoly of any business or occupation that was a common right of the citizens. Chief Justice Matthew Neil's opinion distinguished the United States Supreme Court opinion in the *Slaughterhouse Cases* (1873) because the monopoly granted by Louisiana in that case concerned only the place where the slaughter of livestock would take place, and unlike the Morristown ordinance, allowed anyone to perform their own slaughtering at that location. Even so, the *Noe* Court warned the legislature that it doubted that such a monopoly would be allowed in any event. The opinion cited with approval language of Michigan jurist Thomas M. Cooley who expressed concern over a governing body granting monopolies, benefiting one group of citizens over another, and contracting away its powers to aid all citizens. Chief Justice Neil submitted that the legislature could authorize a municipality to obtain a location to be used as a slaughterhouse with municipal employees in charge, but such an authorization would have to allow for persons to do their own slaughtering or to have it done by persons they chose.

The Court dealt with a different kind of business relationship in *State ex rel. College of Bishops of Methodist Episcopal Church, South, v. Board of Trust of Vanderbilt University* (1914). The case arose out of several years of controversy between Methodist church officials and the Vanderbilt Board of Trust over who had the final right of governance over the university. This dispute had led to a 1906 report by the independent Vanderbilt Commission, which concluded that the university had been founded by the annual conferences of the Methodist Episcopal Church, South, and that their successor, the church's General Conference, was now the sole member of the corporation under Tennessee law. The commission report also cited an 1895 law that gave denominations the right to elect members of the boards of trustees of educational institutions that the denominations were "maintaining" and "patronizing." Further, the commission said that the charter granted the church bishops the rights of "visitors," a common-law term, meaning that the bishops would have the final interpretive say over the meaning of the corporation's laws.

Disagreement over the commission's report erupted into a lawsuit in 1910, after the Board of Trust had refused to seat three trustees that had been named to the board by the General Conference. The bishops asked the state courts to establish and enforce their rights under the charter. The Supreme Court's opinion resolved the issue, but found primarily in favor of the university, repudiating most of the findings of the 1906 Vanderbilt Commission. Justice Williams, a Vanderbilt graduate, recused himself from the case, and Knoxville judge William R. Turner sat in his place and wrote the opinion, with Justice Lansden concurring in the result, but not all of the reasoning. Turner's opinion noted the long relationship that had existed between the university and the church from the time of Vanderbilt's founding until the disagreements of 1910. The Court pointed out that in order for a denomination to have rights of governance under law it had to "establish," "maintain," and "patronize," the educational institution. Turner found that the Methodist Church had done none of these things with regard to Vanderbilt University. Cornelius Vanderbilt was the primary founder, according to the opinion, and the church had not maintained or patronized the university over the years through additional gifts. Turner's opinion also concluded that the original charter was not intended to grant the bishops the common-law right of visitors, and even if it had, such rights belonged only to a patron or founder. On the other hand, the Court stated that the university had an obligation, once it chose new members for the board, to submit those to the General Conference. This limited victory for the church was tempered by Turner's warning that if the General Conference refused to cooperate with the university, it would lose any role in university governance. The Court's ruling did not lead to a reconciliation between the parties; by the end of the year the church and Vanderbilt had severed their relationship.[28]

By the 1930s, of course, the Court was called upon to interpret and review legislation enacted on the state and national level to deal with the Depression crisis. Indeed, the economic distress brought about by the Depression raised questions involving employee grievances, insolvent banks, and creditor/lender disputes. While the Court continued to respect the legislature's police powers, it struck down several statutes that it found violated other constitutional strictures. In 1931, Governor Horton called two extraordinary sessions of the General Assembly to consider ways to pay the state's debts, and in the second session he specifically asked for an income tax law. A 1931 law permitted a graduated tax on certain types of income. The Tennessee Supreme Court in *Evans v. McCabe* (1932) invalidated the law on the grounds that the Tennessee Constitution limited the assembly's ability to tax income. Chief Justice Green stated that the language in Article 2, Section 28 giving the legislature the authority to tax "incomes derived from stocks and bonds that are not taxed ad valorem" prevented the legislature from taxing any other kind of income. Green also observed that the tax could not be considered a valid tax on property because Article 2, Section 28 required that property be taxed at an "equal and uniform" rate.[29]

Also during the 1930s, the Court heard several challenges to regulation of specific professions and found that the legislature had unconstitutionally interfered with the liberty of contract. For example, the Court ruled that a statute requiring certification of accountants was unconstitutional. The opinion in *Campbell v. McIntyre* (1932) quoted at length from cases decided by the United States Supreme Court that limited the government's right to interfere with a business or occupation. In sharp contrast to the words expressed in the 1912 *Motlow* decision, Justice Swiggart's words spoke of the limits of the legislature's police powers: "Current legislative history, both state and national, indicates that it is now more important to the preservation of constitutional government that emphasis be placed, in statement, upon the constitutional restraints on the police power of the legislature, rather than upon the extent to which that broad power may be exercised."[30]

The opinion cited the United States Supreme Court for the proposition that the right of persons to contract for employment could not be regulated merely by a legislative pronouncement that to do so was in the public interest. Justice Swiggart noted that the Fourteenth Amendment due process rights and the rights found under Article 1, Section 8 and Article 11, Section 8 of the Tennessee Constitution were "substantially the same." The standard of review was that stated in *Motlow,* namely, whether the purpose of the law was to protect the public as opposed to a particular group, and whether the act violated either the state or federal Constitution. However, here the Court found that rather than protecting the public, the statute merely protected the rights of licensed accountants, and infringed on the right of contract between private parties.

In the late 1930s, the Court also struck down two laws setting minimum wages. In *State ex rel. Bales v. Hamilton Co.* (1936), the Supreme Court invalidated a minimum wage law for Hamilton County schoolteachers on grounds that it deprived the county of its liberty of contract rights, as well as placing a burden on that county that was imposed on no others. Likewise, in *State v. Greeson* (1939), the Court invalidated a statute that allowed the state Board of Barber Examiners to establish minimum prices for barber services. The law was passed as a health and safety measure, one which would provide barbers with sufficient money to modernize their equipment. The Court reasoned that this interfered with the barbers' personal liberty and right to contract with respect to their labor.

In contrast, the Court upheld legislation that protected the right of a Knoxville teacher to her job in *City of Knoxville v. State ex rel. Hayward* (1939). During the Depression crisis, several municipalities adopted regulations limiting the rights of married women to work. The Knoxville school board fired a schoolteacher after her marriage. The Court overturned the board's action because it conflicted with a 1937 private act of the legislature that said that marriage did not provide grounds for dismissal. The Court distinguished *Bales,* and cited the 1927 *Scopes* decision, discussed below, in holding that the legislature had the power to define the terms of employment for state employees.

The minimum pricing law in *Greeson* was similar to other laws being enacted around the nation on the state and federal level in attempts to deal with the crisis caused by the Depression. In fact, the Court upheld several new laws passed in response to the needs of the Depression. For example, in order to take advantage of the new Social Security program, the legislature in 1936 enacted an unemployment compensation statute. As with the worker's compensation statute, the Court upheld the measure and reviewed many appeals under the new regulation. The Court also spent some time in the 1930s and 1940s ruling on New Deal legislation that affected Tennessee employers and employees. In *Rust v. Newby* (1937), a National Recovery Act case that was decided after the federal law had been found unconstitutional by the United States Supreme Court, the Tennessee Court held that employees who had conspired with their employer to evade the act could not recover money that they should have received if the law had been followed. According to Justice Cook, the fact that the law was later found to be unconstitutional made no difference. The Court in *Dye v. McIntyre Floral Co.* (1940) interpreted the Fair Labor Standards Act, exempting from its provisions a Davidson County nursery, finding that the company fell within the exception for those "employed in agriculture." Thus, during these years the Court approved of many of the legislative regulatory schemes enacted by the General Assembly, and worked within the national system in reviewing new federal laws.

WOMEN AND AFRICAN AMERICANS BEFORE THE COURT

As with business regulation, the Tennessee Supreme Court accepted the policies of the legislature in matters dealing with women and racial minorities. During these years, the legislature enacted significant reforms in the area of women's property and electoral rights. African Americans saw fewer advances in their legal status, continuing to live under the burden of the state's Jim Crow laws. In neither case did the Supreme Court take the lead; rather, it played the role of enforcer and interpreter. The Tennessee Supreme Court and its justices were products of their time. They recognized the changing role of women and the evolution of the state's property and family law, even if they did not always heartily embrace such changes. The justices did, however, endorse segregation. Tennessee was a southern state with regional sensibilities, and the white, male governors, legislators, local politicians, and members of the Supreme Court worked within those boundaries. By the 1940s, however, as the state's institutions, including the Supreme Court, grappled to uphold the policy of segregation, there were nonetheless hints of the changes to come.

In 1920, the Tennessee General Assembly provided the crucial thirty-sixth vote in favor of the woman suffrage amendment. The Court upheld the legality of the proceedings when several legislators attempted to enjoin the governor from certifying the ratification vote. Chief Justice Lansden dissolved the injunction and the full Court affirmed Lansden's action in *Clements v. Roberts* (1921) on separation of powers grounds, finding that a circuit court had no power to enjoin officials in the executive and legislative branches from performing their duties when those officials had the right to determine whether their acts were constitutional. In *Vertrees v. State Board of Elections* (1919) the Court had previously upheld the constitutionality of the Tennessee law that gave the state's women the right to vote in presidential and municipal elections. Another case, *State v. Bell* (1920), dealt with the refusal of the Davidson County trustee to accept poll taxes from female voters. The female voters and plaintiffs argued that the word "male" had been eliminated from the Tennessee Constitution's poll tax provision, and that they were required, as were men, to pay the tax for the year preceding the election. The Court declared that women in 1920 were in the same situation as men who reached voting age that year, and were not liable for the preceding year's poll tax in order to vote, and thus there was no reason for the trustee to accept their payment.

Tennessee's women were the focus of another major reform during this era, one that certainly generated more attention by the Supreme Court. In 1913, the General Assembly passed the Married Women's Emancipation Act. Although there had been married women's property statutes before this time, they had merely provided some exceptions to the common law. The 1913 law sought to eliminate "all" of the common-law "disability" of coverture. The Court sustained the constitutionality of the statute in *Parlow v. Turner* (1915), and held that a husband no longer had the right to collect rents from his wife's property. In the years following the passage of the 1913 act, the Court ruled on a number of issues regarding women's rights under the new law. While accepting the law, it tended to interpret the act narrowly when considering its effect on the common-law marital relationship. For example, stressing the importance of marriage, the Court held in *City of Chattanooga v. Carter* (1915) that the 1913 law did not alter that relationship and affected only the wife's rights to her own property. Hence, a husband could still recover damages for the personal injuries of his spouse. Nor did the act abrogate the common-law stricture against one spouse suing the other spouse for a tort committed during marriage. In *Lilienkamp v. Rippetoe* (1915), the Court again stressed the common-law unity of the husband and wife and the responsibilities and duties that unity imposed. Neither, said the Court in *Baker v. Dew* (1915), did the emancipation act alter the husband's right to his wife's personal property when she died intestate. The Court did rule that the law ended the common-law presumption that held a husband responsible for the crimes of his wife, and likewise the husband's common-law liability for the voluntary torts of his spouse.

Apart from continuing to uphold the common-law rule of spousal immunity, the Court occasionally sounded regretful over the changes that the emancipation statute, and the passing years, had brought with regard to family unity. The case of *Younger v. Gianotti* (1940) involved the question of whether the statutory removal of common-law disabilities affected the common-law rule that the domicile of a wife followed that of the husband. The Court's detailed opinion spoke of the tension between the reality of contemporary life and a public policy that strove to protect the family unit. After reviewing the law in several other jurisdictions, it held that a wife could acquire a domicile separate from that of her husband. Balancing the competing policies of promoting the sanctity of the marital relationship with that of allowing modern women to own property and enter into business relationships, the Court found that the latter policy triumphed. To hold otherwise would be "to close one's eyes to the reality of present conditions and to ignore the fundamental changes touching the status of married women, effected by modern legislation."

Tennessee's divorce laws also had an important impact on women as well as men during these years. Despite the Court's recognition of the importance of the marital bond in the decisions dealing with the women's emancipation acts, the main concern in the divorce cases tended to revolve around the continued support of the wife and the welfare of any minor children, not protection of the marriage relationship. In *Toncray v. Toncray* (1910), the defendant had obtained a divorce in Virginia without providing any notice to his wife, a resident of Tennessee, the state in which the married couple had also resided. The Supreme Court, in an opinion written by Justice Green, upheld the validity of the Virginia divorce, while allowing the wife to sue for alimony in the Tennessee. The Court noted that such a decision avoided bringing unwelcome social consequences to subsequent marriages and resulting children. However, this did not abrogate the husband's common-law responsibility to support his wife. Still, the *Toncray* Court modified the alimony decree, reducing it on the grounds that the defendant had a second wife and child to support and they would suffer if he was forced to turn over most of his money to the former wife. The Court was willing to abide by new statutory guidelines in determining fault in divorce actions. For example in 1919, the assembly passed a law that allowed a husband to divorce his wife on grounds of "cruel and inhuman treatment." The Court in *Parks v. Parks* (1928) found that the statute should be construed in a similar way as the law granting the same right to a wronged wife.

Other cases stressed the husband's duty to support his wife and children. In *Williams v. Williams* (1922), the judges said that a court did not have the discretion to deny alimony to a wife on the basis that she had resources to adequately support herself, but was required by the statutes to order the husband to provide for his spouse. Although the Court agreed with the practice of providing for alimony payments in lump sum, in *Taylor v. Taylor* (1921) it instead ordered that the wife receive monthly payments based on the husband's more considerable income. Justice McKinney's opinion emphasized the wrong done to the wife of twenty years in reaching this conclusion. In *Brown v. Brown* (1930), the Court held that because of the married women's property act, the only interest a husband had in his wife's real property was as a tenant in the entirety in jointly owned property, which would be converted to land held by tenants in common at the time of the divorce. Even where the divorce was granted to the husband, the Court pointed out that he had no further right to her property, and that Tennessee law made no provision for alimony to the husband.

In *Graham v. Graham* (1918) the judges looked at the issue of custody and support of children. In language that would be widely quoted by the Court in subsequent years, Justice Lansden wrote, "The cardinal inquiry in all such cases is: What is the best interest of the infant children?" At issue in *Graham* was a father's refusal to support two children as long as they remained in the custody of the mother, although he had made no effort to gain custody. Apart from pointing out the father's legal duty, the *Graham* Court noted the parent's natural duty, and expressed its inability to understand the father's willingness to avoid his responsibility. The opinion affirmed the decision of the Court of Civil Appeals that the father pay money to defray the expenses of the children. The Court continued over the years to stress the importance of parental responsibility to support minor children.

Regarding the status of the state's African American population, segregation was the law in the state, and the Court's published decisions reveal few legal challenges to this system. In fact, in *Shelton v. Chicago, Rock Island and Pacific Railroad* (1918) a railroad line was challenged for not maintaining segregated facilities, and the Court held for the plaintiff. A white passenger complained that the carrier had seated her for dinner while black passengers were seated at tables in the same car. The Court found the railroad line liable even though the applicable statutes did not mention dining cars. The railroad had tried to meet the general requirement of separation by first serving white passengers, and then blacks at a later time, but there had been a mixup on this particular occasion. The Court ruled that the plaintiff was entitled to receive damages because of the railroad's negligence.

Three years later, the Court tacitly accepted segregated school facilities in *Greenwood v. Rickman* (1921) when it upheld the constitutionality of a private act establishing a new school district in Putnam County. Three of the plaintiffs to the lawsuit were African American; they did not challenge the fact that African American children would be segregated under the law. They argued against the law on the grounds that it did not provide any benefit at all to the minority children, and was therefore unconstitutional class legislation under Article 11, Section 8 of the Tennessee Constitution. Justice Hall's opinion pointed out that the law directed the local board of education "to make suitable and proper provisions for the education" of African American children, and therefore did not unconstitutionally discriminate against them.

Twenty-one years later the judges heard a direct challenge to segregated higher education in *State ex rel. Michael v. Witham* (1942). The African American plaintiffs were seeking admittance to the University of Tennessee's professional and graduate studies programs. The university pointed to Tennessee's criminal code, which made it a misdemeanor to permit integrated schools or classes. After the filing of the various lawsuits, the legislature enacted a law authorizing the state board of education and the commissioner of education "to provide educational training and instruction for negro citizens of Tennessee equivalent to that provided at the University of Tennessee . . . for white citizens. . . . [P]rovided, that members of the negro race and white race shall not attend the same institution or place of learning." At the same time the legislature appropriated $220,000 for the state's primary African American college for the next two fiscal years, and the members of the state board of education met quickly to create a committee to plan for graduate training for African Americans at the Tennessee Agricultural and Industrial State College for Negroes. The haste with which the legislature and board of education acted was doubtless a recognition of the United States Supreme Court ruling four years earlier in *State of Missouri ex rel. Gaines v. Canada* (1938), where the Court had ordered the admittance of an African American plaintiff to a Missouri state law school in the absence of any comparable law school for the state's African American residents. The Tennessee Supreme Court's unanimous opinion in *Michael* found the state's new policy to be constitutionally adequate and refused to admit the plaintiffs to the University of Tennessee. The Court cited the mandatory nature of the law, saying that under its terms the board of education had to create facilities equal to those provided for the state's white graduate students: "The legislation of 1941 took no rights away from appellants; on the contrary the right to equality in education with white students was specifically recognized and the method by which those rights would be satisfied was set forth in the legislation. What more could be demanded?"[31] One thing that could be demanded was a change in the state's voting laws that would allow more of the state's poor white and African American citizens to exercise the franchise. But as will be seen below, when the legislature attempted that particular reform, the Court found it to be unconstitutional.

CRIME AND PUNISHMENT

In its criminal law decisions, the Tennessee Supreme Court remained mindful of the prerogatives of the legislature and law enforcement officials, while at the same time working to guarantee that defendants received the constitutional protections guaranteed by the Tennessee Constitution. The Court followed the accepted view that the Bill of Rights in the United States Constitution did not apply to the states. However, the guarantees of the state Constitution did apply, and the Court followed them, although it could not be considered a leader in procedural reform. The Court again reflected the sensibilities of the state and its officials and citizens, and attempted to balance their concerns with the rights of defendants.

There were several overhauls to the state's sentencing laws in the early decades of this period, and these, of course, came before the state's high court. In *Woods v. State* (1914) the Court upheld the 1913 indeterminate sentencing law that established a board of parole to determine when a convicted person would be released and to oversee the person during the period of parole. At an unspecified time the board of parole would be able to propose that the governor recommend a final discharge. The *Woods* Court upheld the statute against charges that it denied the defendant the right of trial by jury or due process of law, and against allegations that the legislature had unlawfully vested the parole board with judicial or legislative powers, or had interfered with the governor's right to pardon.

The Court in *Shipp v. State* (1914) looked at a 1913 revision in the state's death-penalty law. The defendant, convicted of first-degree murder, was automatically sentenced to death as required by the statute for that crime. After briefly stating that it found no mitigating factors in the record, the Supreme Court addressed the method of execution. The defendant had committed the act leading to his conviction on July 13, 1913. In September, the General Assembly repealed the portion of the death-penalty law that provided for death by hanging and replaced it with a law providing for death by electric chair, with the new act to take effect immediately. The Court ruled that the legislature intended that the new law apply to all cases where a defendant was sentenced to death whether the crime was committed before or after its passage. Justice Buchanan's opinion stated that the new law did not affect the offenses that were punishable by death, only the means of implementing the sentence.

The General Assembly later abolished capital punishment except in cases of rape and where a criminal serving a life sentence was convicted of another offense that would have been punishable by death under the old law. In

1919, the legislature reinstated the death penalty for convictions of first-degree murder unless the jury found mitigating circumstances, wherein the jury would then impose a sentence of twenty years to life. In two opinions—*Gohlston v. State* (1920) and *Mays v. State* (1920)—without ruling on the constitutionality of the death penalty itself, the Court held that the new statute gave the jury, not the trial judge, the exclusive power to fix punishment for a conviction of first-degree murder. The Court noted another problem with this statute five years later in *Winton v. State* (1925): that of juries convicting defendants of first-degree murder and imposing a minimum sentence when the facts did not support all of the elements of the crime. In *Winton,* the defendant had killed a deputy sheriff who was in the home of the defendant's father. The prosecution asserted that the defendant had learned of the planned arrest of his father, and had armed himself in order to keep the officers out of the home. The Supreme Court found no premeditation in the defendant's acts, and in reversing for a new trial, pointed out that it had reversed several such cases since the passage of the 1919 act where the facts did not justify a first-degree murder conviction but where the jury had apparently compromised by giving a lesser sentence. The Court, in fact, chastised prosecutors in fairly strong language: "If those charged with the enforcement of the criminal laws would not insist upon convictions for first degree murder when the facts do not justify it, the result would be more affirmances in this court, and the trouble and expense of new trials would, in many instances, be avoided."[32]

Although incorporation of the Bill of Rights was years in the future, the Supreme Court reviewed many cases involving state constitutional protections. A number of cases dealt with the stricture against unreasonable searches and seizures, often arising in arrests and convictions dealing with the state's Prohibition laws. The Court held on several occasions, such as *Hughes v. State* (1922), that the prosecution could not use illegally obtained evidence at trial. One 1926 case dealt with the state constitution's protection of "possessions" from unreasonable searches and seizures. Given that Section 7 already protected "houses," the Court held in *Welch v. State* (1926) that the extra word referred to other types of real or personal property that was in someone's possession. The defendant in *Welch* owned an acre of land about three hundred yards from his home. The lot was enclosed by a fence, and the sheriff, without a warrant, entered the lot and found a still in a dugout. The Court found that this area was covered by the term "possessions," and that the sheriff had conducted an unconstitutional search. Nonetheless, the Court also recognized that there were occasions when an officer would have sufficient probable cause to arrest and to search without a warrant. In *Hughes v. State* (1922), the judges upheld the validity of searches of the immediate premises incident to an arrest.

During these years the Supreme Court interpreted other rights guaranteed under Section 9, including the right "to demand the nature and cause of the accusation against him." In *Jordan v. State* (1928), the Court held that this section was not violated by an indictment which charged that the defendant had transported whisky from one point in the county to another, as this was not a material element of the offense. Section 9 also guarantees the right to a speedy trial. In *Arrowsmith v. State* (1915), the Court found that the trial court had denied this right when, without notifying the defendant or his attorney, the trial judge ordered that ten indictments "be retired from the docket" until the defendant served the sentence he had received after conviction on the first indictment. The Court could find no reason for this, holding that this had the effect of prolonging the process "needlessly and vexatiously."

Although the impact of the law was debatable, perhaps the most famous criminal appeal heard by the Court during the 1920s was that of schoolteacher John T. Scopes after his conviction for violating Tennessee's 1925 antievolution statute. Scopes's trial was one of the twentieth century's most memorable. The Supreme Court's role in the controversy was somewhat anticlimactic, although Chief Justice Green's opinion did successfully diffuse the issue. After an eight-day trial that garnered national publicity, the jury found Scopes—who admitted teaching evolution—guilty of violating the antievolution law. The judge fined him one hundred dollars, the minimum allowed under the statute. Scopes appealed to the Supreme Court, and in a fairly unusual development, three members of the four members of the Court who participated in the case filed an opinion. Justice Hall died on July 26, 1926, nearly two months after the oral argument, and his successor, Swiggart, did not participate in the appeal.[33]

Chief Justice Green and the majority reversed Scopes's guilty verdict and remanded the case for a new trial because the judge imposed the minimum fine of one hundred dollars in contravention of the Tennessee Constitution, which required that any fines in excess of fifty dollars must be levied by the jury. In addition, however, the different judges tried to define the meaning of the law. In his opinion, Chief Justice Green reviewed the statute and wrote that it was intended "to forbid teaching that man descended from a lower order of animals," but that other theories of the evolution of human beings would be allowed under the statute. The chief justice based this finding on his understanding of the common use of the word "evolution," and by the statute's explicit language. Thus, the statute was sufficiently

William Jennings Bryan (standing) assisting the prosecution in the famous 1925 Scopes trial in Dayton, Tennessee, dealing with the state's antievolution laws. Although the Tennessee Supreme Court played a secondary role in the controversy, it reversed the conviction of Scopes. Tennessee State Library and Archives.

definite, and was further narrowly restricted to apply to teachers in their roles as employees of the state. Green cited other opinions which found that the right and privilege to serve the state was limited by the conditions set by the state. Justice Chambliss concurred, agreeing that the legislature could proscribe the teaching of evolution. But he distinguished between *theistic* evolution and *materialistic* evolution, saying that the legislature only intended to forbid the latter. The first, according to Chambliss, taught that God created man. Materialistic evolution denied God's role. Thus, any teacher or school could properly teach a controversial theory regarding evolution, as long as the there was no denial of God's creation of man. In dissent, Justice McKinney found the evolution statute void because of uncertainty of meaning. He quoted the United States Supreme Court, saying "a statute which either forbids or requires the doing of an act in terms so vague that men of common intelligence must necessarily guess at its meaning and differ as to its application violates the first essential process of due process of law."

Justice McKinney's opinion may, indeed, have been the closest expression of the Court's true belief over the statute. Chief Justice Green's majority opinion ended by proposing that as the defendant was no longer employed by the state, "[w]e see nothing to be gained by prolonging the life of this bizarre case. On the contrary, we think the peace and dignity of the State, which all criminal prosecutions are brought to redress will be better conserved by the entry of a *nolle prosequi* herein. Such a course is suggested to the Attorney-General." The Court released its opinion in *Scopes* in January 1927. In December of that year Chief Justice Green spoke before the annual meeting of the American Association for the Advancement of Science. In his address, the chief justice commented that "the Supreme Court, that is, the majority of it, has never been able to agree as to what the evolution statute means."[34]

Search and seizure cases continued to be heard by the Court in large numbers. In one such case, *Massa v. State* (1929), it held that if an officer was aware of the commission of a criminal offense a warrantless arrest was proper. Nonetheless, where a warrant was needed, the Court ruled that it must be specific. For example, in *Parker v. State* (1941) the Court held the search of a person invalid when the warrant provided for the search of the defendant's vehicle.

The Court also protected other constitutional rights of criminal defendants. The decision of *Rounds v. State* (1937) dealt with the convictions of two African American men for the first-degree murder of a white store owner. Rounds, who received a sentence of death by electrocution, appealed to the Court arguing that the police unconstitutionally obtained his confession. At some point after the murder took place, the police targeted the defendant as a suspect. They took him into custody on Saturday and questioned him periodically over the next three days. On Monday night, police took the defendant to a room in the courthouse, and the defendant testified that from that point until his confession on Friday he was not allowed to lie down or sleep. The defendant also testified that the officers whipped him, and twisted and bent his arms and legs. The officers denied having physically mistreated Rounds or denying him sleep, but the Court found their testimony on the sleep question unconvincing. Further, there was also uncontradicted testimony stating that the defendant went into a "religious frenzy" after giving his confession, becoming so out of control that the police officers called a physician to treat the defendant. Chief Justice Green spoke for the Court in holding that "[t]o deprive a human of sleep for four days and nights is a form of torture not less severe than physical violence." Without discussing whether the officers had physically harmed the defendant, the Court ruled that the officer's refusal to allow the defendant to sleep rendered the confession inadmissible: "Resort to torture, in any form, by officers of the law, is not to be countenanced."[35]

Another basic right under the Tennessee's Constitution is the right to counsel, and the Supreme Court found a denial of this right in *Poindexter v.*

State (1946). The defendant was nineteen years old, accused of killing a young girl, and did not meet with his appointed counsel until moments before the trial began. On appeal, the state assistant attorney general recommended a reversal, and the Supreme Court agreed. Justice Chambliss spoke for the Court in saying that the right to counsel provision promised more than the right to an attorney's services at trial; rather, it guaranteed the advice of counsel in preparing a defense.

In the 1930s and 1940s, the Court ruled again on cases involving capital punishment. The death penalty continued to be imposed and carried out with little or no controversy. As in earlier decisions, the constitutionality of the death penalty itself was not an issue, and the Court upheld the jury's right to impose the punishment. In *Woodruff v. State* (1932), it refused to define what mitigating circumstances might be used to prevent a death sentence but held that "mere mental deficiency" was not recognized as such a circumstance. The defendants in *Porter v. State* (1941) were convicted of murdering a night watchman at a Coca Cola bottling plant in Jackson in order to rob the cash drawer containing the proceeds from the day's sales. The Supreme Court found no reason for interfering with the jury's verdict, and concluded that there no factors in the record that mitigated against imposition of the death penalty.

CONTINUED POLITICAL DIVISIVENESS

The reconciliation of the state's Democrats in 1914 did not bring about political harmony in the volunteer state. The state's Republican minority remained a viable force, and although unable to control elections, it was often able to influence them. The agrarian-controlled assembly watched as governors such as Austin Peay and urban political leaders such as Luke Lea and Edward H. Crump consolidated their power bases. These years would be punctuated with periodic spats and occasional legal wrangling between the various factions. For the most part, the Supreme Court stayed out of these disputes, but on several key occasions ruled on appeals involving the contending parties. In the midst of the Great Depression, for example, the Court was faced with a number of suits and prosecutions resulting from the failure of Luke Lea's partnership with businessman Rogers Caldwell, an association that cost the state millions of dollars and led to an out of state jail sentence for Lea.[36] More so than Lea, however, Crump brought controversies to the state and his allies and enemies into court. The state's foremost political presence by the early 1930s, Crump was a particularly polarizing figure. His feud with Governor Gordon Browning brought several cases before the Supreme Court in the late 1930s. In the early 1940s, the efforts of Crump's opponents would erupt in a major challenge to the constitutionality of a poll tax repeal law, and would drag the Supreme Court into another political controversy.

The Supreme Court first dealt with Crump in a 1916 appeal dealing with the Memphis mayor's ouster from office. The judges in *State ex rel. Thompson v. Crump* (1916) upheld Crump's removal due to his failure to enforce several of the state's vice laws, including those dealing with Prohibition. Still, the ouster proved to be but a temporary setback for the Memphis politician. By 1932 and Lea's downfall, Crump was fully in control of his city and a force to reckon with across the state. Crump endorsed candidates would have an edge in statewide elections over the next two decades. Crump used his influence to support several candidates for governor in the 1930s, including former congressman Gordon W. Browning in 1936. After Browning's election, a series of disagreements between the two men led to an open split. Browning sought to limit Crump's influence through a number of legislative enactments that would soon come before the Court for review.

In 1937, Browning called two extraordinary sessions of the General Assembly to push for laws he openly aimed at the Memphis mayor. The legislature passed an election reform bill that would have the effect of limiting the voting power of Shelby County in Democratic primary elections, a law that gave the governor the power to investigate alleged illegality in voting registration lists, and a law expanding the membership of the state election commission. The assembly also created a state crime commission, which would aid Browning in investigations of alleged corruption.[37] In February 1938, the Court dealt a blow to Browning's election law plan by invalidating the section of the act that limited the total vote in each county. In *Gates v. Long* (1938), Chief Justice Green noted that diluting voter participation in an election could not be justified as an exercise of the police power, nor could it be supported on the ground that an innocent activity might sometimes be regulated because of a potential for fraud or other wrongful end. The stated purpose of the law was to allow the "entire electorate" of a political party to participate in primary elections, and diminution of the vote could not be said to be reasonably related to that end. The Court in *Rushing v. Tennessee Crime Commission* (1938), however, sustained the expansion of the state elections board and the constitutionality of the crime commission.

By the early 1940s, Crump's opponents had begun to focus on another electoral reform: elimination of the poll tax as a prerequisite for voting. Poll tax reform had become a leading liberal cause in the South, with the tax's opponents charging that it contributed to the South's notoriously low voter turnout and that it was a tool of machine politicians such as Edward H. Crump. Indeed, Crump's strength was in his organization, and that organization made sure that voters, black and white, paid the tax. Attempts to eliminate the poll tax by federal action failed repeatedly throughout the 1930s and 1940s. In 1941, the Tennessee legislature failed to pass a state repeal, and the anti-Crump *Nashville Tennessean,* which had adopted the cause of poll tax reform as its own, blamed the Memphis politician. Crump responded that he opposed the repeal of the poll tax until the state adopted a voter registration system, arguing that otherwise there would be no way to properly identify voters. The *Tennessean* was not convinced. It blasted Governor Prentice Cooper, who was supported by Crump, but whose administration had backed the repeal, for "betraying his pledge to restore the vote to the people" by allowing the poll tax to remain a "weapon in the dictator's hand."[38]

When the Tennessee Supreme Court became involved in the controversy, the anti–poll tax, anti-Crump forces watched carefully. In 1943, Governor Cooper's administration again supported a poll tax repeal, and this time it passed. There was a great deal of rejoicing among the enemies of the poll tax. Now, at last, the Crump machine had been wounded. But the triumph did not last long. A lawsuit was filed challenging the law, and on July 3, 1943, the Tennessee Supreme Court in *Biggs v. Beeler* (1943) ruled, by a margin of three to two, that the legislative repeal of the poll tax was unconstitutional under Article 2, Section 28 and Article 1, Section 4 of the Tennessee Constitution. The majority, Chambliss, Prewitt, and Gailor, held that even though those sections had required legislative action to make the poll tax provisions effective—in this case, the 1890 act of the General Assembly making payment of a poll tax a prerequisite of voting—once the legislature had done so it could not turn around and invalidate a constitutional mandate. Justice Chambliss's opinion, quoting an unnamed member of the Court on the issue, said that "[t]o hold otherwise . . . would make [Article 2, Section 28] meaningless, while appellants freely concede that it is mandatory." The dissenting judges, Green and Neil found no authority to support the position that a constitutional provision that was not self-executing could become mandatory once the legislature had acted. Both men chastised the majority for ignoring the doctrine of separation of powers in overruling the legislature.[39]

Proponents of repeal were quick to express outrage. Anti-Crump newspapers announced their suspicions over the vote of the newest member of the high court, Frank Gailor. The *Biggs* decision was Gailor's first announced vote on the high court since Governor Cooper had appointed him on June 7, 1943. Gailor came to the Court with superb educational qualifications. He was a Rhodes scholar, with degrees from the University of the South and

Oxford, had served with both the British and American forces during World War I, and had a long career as a lawyer and public servant in Shelby County. The editor of the *Memphis Press Scimitar,* however, was critical of his appointment to the Court based on his long association with Crump. The *Nashville Tennessean* picked up on this criticism prior to the release of the *Biggs* opinion, but seemed to give him the benefit of the doubt after noting that the late Justice DeHaven had likewise been a friend of Crump's, but one who had "reportedly several times declined to subject the dignity of the high office to political pressure." On July 4, 1943, page one of the *Nashville Tennessean* included the headline "The People Be Crumped." The editorial that followed lambasted the three man majority who voted against the repeal. Gailor was singled out as one who Crump had "sent to wear the robes" of justice, and whose vote enabled the Court to deny the will of the legislature. These charges ignored both the fact that Crump ally Cooper had supported the repeal measure and Gailor's own fine reputation.[40]

Despite the outrage expressed by a few poll tax opponents, the *Biggs* decision did not harm the Court's nor Justice Gailor's reputation for honesty and integrity. Gailor was sitting as a special judge at the time of DeHaven's death, and was always considered to be a likely candidate for the vacancy. He won election to the Court in 1944 and 1950, and served on the bench until his death in 1954. Three years after the *Biggs* opinion, the Court issued a *per curiam* opinion, *Johnson v. Graham* (1946), reaffirming its ruling in *Biggs,* and finding that a trial court properly determined that the 1943 repeal statute had been found invalid. Chief Justice Green and Justice Neil concurred with the result in *Johnson,* while noting that they continued to dissent from *Biggs.*

As in 1910, the Court had been brought into a political battle, but the Court itself was respected for attempting to stay above the controversy. The *Nashville Banner* commended the Court for upholding the Constitution, arguing that the issue was not whether the tax was just, but whether it was constitutional. It pointed out that the Tennessee Supreme Court was "a court, not a legislature; an interpreter of law—not a political forum."[41]

BENCH AND BAR

This period of Tennessee history saw significant changes for the state's judges and attorneys. If the Court was deferential to the legislature on certain issues, it was also concerned with its own prerogatives. As the issues facing the bench became more complex, the judges of the Tennessee Supreme Court recognized the need for stiffer qualifications for bar membership, and watched as critics of the state's judicial structure called for reform of the court system. The legislature created a new Court of Appeals and approved the construction of a new building to house the state's judicial officers. During all of these changes, the members of the Supreme Court remained committed to their duties as officers of the judicial branch, mindful of the past, while hopeful for the future of the Tennessee courts.

Throughout these years the Supreme Court recognized that each of the three branches had its own duties under the Constitution, and it was reluctant to use its powers to overrule the decisions of the governor or the legislature. In *Webb v. Carter* (1913), where the Court had determined the validity of a veto override, Justice Buchanan's majority opinion noted the awesome responsibility of the Court in reviewing the actions of the other branches: "Delicate, indeed, is the duty, and important the power which rests upon this court whenever called on to pass judgment upon the validity of an act of a coordinate department of the State."[42] Other decisions, of course, sustained the prerogative of the other branches. In *Clements v. Roberts* (1921) the Court held that where the Constitution authorized the governor to perform a ministerial function, and the assembly a legislative function, the Court had no power to interfere with either action.

Still, the separation of powers also prohibited the political branches from interfering with the Court's constitutional duties. *In re Cameron* (1912) dealt with a disbarment proceeding. In appealing the judgment against him, the attorney raised several issues, including whether the trial judge ought to have been incompetent to preside over the disbarment because of prior dealings between the parties. Justice Matthew M. Neil's opinion noted the lack of such a statute in Tennessee and further doubted the policy implications of taking away a judge's own discretion to determine whether he could fairly rule over a proceeding. In 1937, the assembly passed a law making judges incompetent to try cases where the legal counsel for either party shared a blood relationship with the judge. The statute came before the Court after several lawyers challenged the decision of a Washington County chancellor who declared himself incompetent to hear a case in which his son was an associate of the firm representing a party before him. Justices Chambliss, McKinney, and Cook, whose sons were all practicing attorneys in Tennessee, did not hear the case, and Governor Browning appointed special judges to help hear the appeal. The Court held that the legislature did not have the have the power to decide when a particular judge was or was not competent to preside over a case unless they did so pursuant to authority granted by the Constitution: "We adhere to the fundamental principle of democratic constitutional government that, while the judiciary may not properly legislate nor determine the policy of legislation, in like measure the

Legislature may not invade the judicial sphere by limitations not directed or permitted by the charter of our liberties, the Constitution itself."[43]

As both life and law in the state became more complex, members of the bar and other observers called for more highly trained lawyers to meet the new challenges. Just before this period began, the General Assembly and the state bar association had adopted some important provisions regarding the profession's membership and conduct. In 1903, the General Assembly created a board of law examiners to test the qualifications of bar applicants, and then to present qualified persons to the Supreme Court for licensing. Then, in 1909, the Tennessee Bar Association adopted the Canons of Professional Ethics established by the American Bar Association controlling the conduct of attorneys. In 1938, the Supreme Court would adopt the Canons of Professional Ethics as rules of court.[44] The Court emphasized the importance of both standards and ethics in *In re Bowers* (1918). The board of law examiners reported to the Supreme Court that Bowers, an applicant for the bar, did not meet or understand the ethical standards required for bar admission. The Court ruled that the recommendation of the bar examiners as to the fitness of an applicant to the bar would be conclusive absent some allegation of corruption in the process. Further, Justice Lansden's opinion stressed "that the ideals of the legal profession must be kept to the highest mark, and that its members must have a proper conception of the ethics of the profession and must be required to live up to these standards."[45]

During these decades, the Supreme Court gradually raised the standards required for the education and training of the bar. Since the 1880s, the Tennessee Bar Association had been asking the General Assembly to require a two year course of legal study for all new attorneys. While the legislature itself did not mandate these minimum standards, in 1919, it authorized the Supreme Court "to prescribe rules to regulate the admission of persons to practice law." The Court chose to impose a minimum requirement of a high school education, or its equivalent, followed by one year of law school or study with a qualified attorney, followed by a bar examination. Supreme Court Rule 7 set forth the subjects covered on the bar exam, including constitutional law, criminal law, equity, real and personal property, and professional ethics. According to a later report of the bar association's Committee on Legal Education and Admission to the Bar, the chief justice told them that the judges felt a two-year requirement of study was too stringent given that many potential lawyers had joined the military during World War I. Nonetheless, these standards remained the same until the 1930s. It should be noted that the Cumberland School of Law, with whom several of the judges and the attorneys who practiced before them had close ties, offered the only one-year course of legal study in the country at this time. However, during the 1930s, the Court slowly responded to requests to raise the educational criteria. In 1932, the Court announced that it would require candidates to the state bar complete two years in a law school, and in 1935, the Court mandated that candidates for the bar examination must also attend a reputable law school. And, in 1938, the Court added the requirement that students have two years of pre-law study.[46]

Occasionally the authority to impose standards on the profession was challenged, but the Court upheld the legislature's right under its police powers to insist on such requirements. One issue raised by the defendant in *In re Hickey* (1924) was whether the grounds for disciplinary action against an attorney had to be found in the specific legislative provision governing the subject. Justice McKinney's opinion noted that the legislature could not forbid a court to exercise its inherent power to discipline an attorney, but found that the statute in question was broad enough to meet any cases meriting review. In *Gregory v. City of Memphis* (1928), Justice McKinney stated that the practice of law was a privilege granted by the legislature, not a right. The defendant in *Lamb v. Whitaker* (1937) was practicing law without a license, and argued that the law authorizing an injunction against him unconstitutionally deprived him of his property without just compensation under the state Constitution. Justice McKinney again addressed the subject, and held that the legislature's power to protect its citizens from harm provided the authority to mandate qualifications for certain professions, including law.

The Court also issued several opinions dealing with attorney misconduct and discipline, and was always mindful of the importance of maintaining standards of integrity and honor of both courts and judicial officers. For example, *In re Cameron* (1912) upheld the authority of a trial judge to begin disbarment proceedings based on his own knowledge, not predicated on a motion by another member of the bar. The Court reversed the judge's decision in the case, however, and called for a new trial because the record clearly revealed that the trial judge had determined the attorney's guilt before the beginning of the trial. Justice Neil wrote that the people of the state must believe that a judge's rulings are handed down in an impartial manner: "It is of lasting importance that the body of the public should have confidence in the fairness and uprightness of the judges created to serve as dispensers of justice." Four years later the judges stressed the importance of the bar's integrity, calling the legal profession "the great unbonded trustee of the human family."[47]

Professional disagreements between members of the bar sometimes spilled over into disciplinary proceedings. In looking at the occasionally contentious disputes between parties, the Supreme Court distinguished between an attorney's right to criticize a court, and the malicious filing of false charges against another member of the bar. The defendant in *Hickey* (1924) had criticized a trial judge in various conversations, and had published a newspaper article that was likewise critical of the judge, although not with respect to a pending case. The defendant in *State v. Bomer* (1942) had filed fraudulent charges seeking disbarment of two other members of the Shelby County Bar, allegedly in retaliation for his own one-year disbarment in 1937. While the Court felt that Hickey's criticisms were intemperate, he had a right to express them under the state Constitution's freedom of speech provision, and his suspension was reversed. Bomer's actions, on the other hand, led the Court to uphold his disbarment and to stress the seriousness of attempting to deprive a fellow attorney of his livelihood and reputation, while at the same time abusing the judicial process.

The Tennessee Supreme Court's composition and jurisdiction remained defined by Article 6 of the Constitution of 1870. The Court's size remained at five judges, with no more than two from any of the state's three grand divisions. Throughout these years, East Tennessee was the region underrepresented on the Court. However, under a unique provision in the Tennessee Constitution, the state's attorneys general are appointed by the Supreme Court, and although not required by Article 6, the men who served as state attorney general and reporter Charles T. Cates of Knoxville (1902–13), Frank M. Thompson of Chattanooga (1913–26), Leonidas D'entrecasteaux Smith of Knoxville (1926–32), and Roy H. Beeler of Knoxville (1932–54) all came from the eastern section of the state.[48]

Several groups and individuals criticized the state's appellate court system between 1910 and 1946, yet the Supreme Court remained essentially unchanged amid charges that it was inefficient and antiquated. One interesting cosmetic change did take place during these years, however. In his history of the state Supreme Court, historian and former justice Samuel Cole Williams pointed out that it was not until about 1923 that the court began the custom of wearing judicial robes, with Williams asserting that some of the justices saw such robing as undemocratic. Williams related a story of an unnamed dissenting justice, presumably Williams himself, whose refusal to wear the robes carried the day during a 1917 discussion over the issue. The justice declared to the other four, "You who favor robes may appear on the bench so attired. For my part, I shall sit in citizen's clothes."[49]

In a more significant reform, in 1925 the General Assembly passed a law restructuring the state's second highest court, the Court of Civil Appeals, in an effort to alleviate the Supreme Court's case load by further limiting appeals to that body. The assembly abolished the five-member Court of Civil Appeals that had been established in 1907 and replaced it with a new nine-member

Court of Appeals. The new court was to sit in rotating panels of three judges in each of the state's three grand divisions. The law attempted to minimize the Supreme Court's burden in equity cases by limiting review of facts to those cases where the chancellor and Court of Appeals disagreed on findings of fact. Other changes to the judiciary included a 1911 law creating a juvenile court system, which the Supreme Court upheld in *Childress v. State* (1915) as a measure providing for the protection and care of delinquent minors. The assembly also created the state's first courts of general sessions. Although the Constitution of 1870 forbade the abolition of the office of justice of the peace, the Supreme Court upheld the transfer of the powers of that office to new courts of general sessions in *Hancock v. Davidson County* (1937).

Perhaps the most important event for the judges themselves during the decade of the 1930s was the construction of the Supreme Court building in Nashville, the Court's first permanent home. In 1935, the legislature took advantage of funds offered by the Public Works Administration to build the structure, which initially housed not only the Supreme Court and Court of Appeals but also was the home for the state attorney general and the state law library. The law provided for the use of a state-owned lot adjacent to the Capitol and created the "Tennessee Court Building Commission"—Governor McAlister, Chief Justice Green, and Attorney General Beeler—to oversee the project. The finished building, an impressive structure of marble, granite and stone, was designed by

The Tennessee Supreme Court in 1927 (clockwise from left): William H Swiggart and Colin P. McKinney, standing, William L. Cook, Chief Justice Grafton Green, and Alexander W. Chambliss, seated. Tennessee State Library and Archives.

The Tennessee Supreme Court building in Nashville, opened in 1937, was the Court's first permanent home. Tennessee State Library and Archives.

the Nashville architecture firm of Marr and Hollman. The $750,000 cost was financed by approximately $195,000 of PWA funds and through the sale of state bonds. The first floor contained a courtroom on one side, and a new law library, open to all the state's lawyers, on the other. The second floor was given to the attorney general's office, and the third provided offices for the judges, as well as conference rooms for each court. As initially designed, two judges were to share each office.[50]

The building's dedication took place on December 4, 1937, with members of both courts, members of the state bar association, and other public officials attending. The role of the judiciary was on everyone's mind, given the recent battle in Washington over Franklin Roosevelt's "court packing plan," which Justice Green referred to in his remarks. All the speakers reflected upon the significant role played by the judicial branch of government, with the president of the bar association, Memphis attorney Charles N. Burch noting that "[a] free, independent, fearless judiciary is the cornerstone of a free government." Governor Browning spoke of the "friendly" relationship between the judicial and executive branches, and stated his belief that Tennessee citizens saw the Court as the "final refuge for liberty." Justice Green followed up on the theme of collegiality between the courts, bar, political branches and the people, and expressed his happiness in the belief that "the people of Tennessee share the respect for the courts that is manifest by the bar."[51]

Yet, as noted, the court system did have its critics, and calls for reform continued into the 1940s. Some observers decried the organization of Tennessee's judicial system, as well as the composition and jurisdiction of the Supreme Court. One suggestion made by members of the bar was for the formation of a judicial council to study and make recommendations on policy, rules, or needed legislation. In 1943, the General Assembly responded and created the council. It was composed of one member each of the Supreme Court and the Court of Appeals serving along with representatives of other courts in the state, the attorney general, members of the legislature, state law schools, the private bar, and two laymen. Justice A. B. Neil served as the Supreme Court's representative on the council, which would make suggestions on procedural reform to the General Assembly. While viewed as an important step toward court reform, calls for more substantive changes continued as this period ended.[52]

On November 29, 1946, Dean William Wicker of the University of Tennessee College of Law spoke of the Tennessee courts before Sixth Annual Southern Institute of Southern Government. Wicker praised the integrity and qualifications of Tennessee's Supreme Court judges, past and present, but he also submitted that reforms were needed in the area of judicial selection, in the Court's number of judges, and in the appeals process. He argued that judicial elections in Tennessee did not provide, in reality, a true elective process. Yet despite occasional comments such as this by attorneys and legal scholars, and occasional political controversies erupting over issues such as the 1910 election debate or the poll tax decision, the Tennessee Supreme Court remained an institution of honor and dignity. Criticism of the judges was rare. Perhaps none was as respected as Chief Justice Grafton Green, who served throughout all the years covered in this chapter, writing hundreds of opinions on all aspects of the law. On December 4, 1937, nine years before his death, Green spoke at the dedication ceremony of the new Supreme Court building facing the west side of the Capitol building in Nashville. The chief justice spoke with pride of the state's past judges, and optimistically about future jurists: "I believe judges of the future will be altogether capable of solving future problems which, as we view them in anticipation, seem so difficult. I believe that they will preserve the constitution although their interpretation of some sections of the constitution may not be our present interpretation. And I have no doubt but that those who succeed us on the bench will be as scrupulous to maintain the good name of the Tennessee courts as we have tried to be."[53]

6

THE TENNESSEE SUPREME COURT, 1946–1974: TRANQUILITY AMID A NATIONAL JUDICIAL REVOLUTION

John R. Vile

The year 1946 came one year after the end of World War II. America was quickly demobilizing many of its troops abroad, and former soldiers and their young families, whose children would soon be known as the "baby boomers," were anxious to resume civilian life. Thanks in part to the GI bill, many former soldiers returned to college campuses, and, as the demand for consumer goods took the place of the earlier demand for military hardware, America began riding a wave of prosperity and optimism, only partially dimmed by the emergence of a cold war and renewed fears of international communism. Not only had World War II successfully defeated tyranny abroad, but it, like American cold war rhetoric, also had stoked the aspirations of millions of African Americans. Within a decade, the United States Supreme Court's decision in *Brown v. Board of Education* (1954) awakened a movement that shook the southern system of racial segregation to its very foundation, while *Baker v. Carr* (1962), a case originating in Tennessee, opened the way for increased representation for growing urban and suburban areas. Later in the decade, the nation was further convulsed by controversy over the Vietnam War.

At the state level, the years from 1946 to 1974 began during the administration of Democratic governor Jim McCord and one year before the death of Chief Justice Grafton Green. Democrats Al Gore Sr. and Estes Kefauver served during much of this period (Gore from 1953 to 1971 and Kefauver from 1949 to 1963) as Tennessee's U.S. senators and shared aspirations for national office with Democrat governor Frank Clement who played gubernatorial leapfrog with fellow Democrat Buford Ellington from 1953 to 1971. By the end of the period, Republican senators Howard Baker Jr. (who served from 1967 to 1985) and Bill Brock (who served from 1971 to 1977) had replaced Gore and Kefauver.[1] In 1952 the state cast its first electoral votes for a Republican presidential candidate (Dwight D. Eisenhower) since 1928, continuing to vote Republican in presidential contests through 1972 excepting the election of 1964, when Tennessee voted for Democrat Lyndon Johnson over Republican Barry Goldwater. The period under review in this chapter ended with the election of a new Court in 1974, just four years after the election of Winfield Dunn, the state's first Republican governor in fifty years. At the national level, these years encompassed the presidencies from Harry Truman through Richard Nixon and the chief justiceships of Fred Vinson and Earl Warren as well as the first five years of Warren Burger's service as chief.

Although the Vinson years were relatively quiet, the Warren years were among the most judicially active and liberal in American history.[2] Not only did the United States Supreme Court mandate racial desegregation in the *Brown* case, but during these years it also completed the application of most provisions of the Bill of Rights to the states via the Fourteenth Amendment, intervened in state and congressional apportionment cases, liberalized freedom of speech and press, widened the scope of the Establishment Clause of the First Amendment, and developed a right of privacy. Moreover, the Burger Court's decisions in cases such as *Furman v. Georgia* (1972), striking down the death penalty as then exercised, and in *Roe v. Wade* (1973), voiding most state abortion laws, show that much of the activism of the Warren Court survived into its early years.

THE COURT'S CONTRASTING ROLE

Although Tennessee's highest Court often enforced decisions reached by the United States Supreme Court, it was little affected by the philosophy—prominent at the national level as well as in some of the states—that viewed the federal judiciary as being on a relatively equal policy-making level with the two elected branches.[3] With few exceptions, from 1946 to 1974 the Tennessee

The Tennessee Supreme Court in 1946 (left to right): Alan M. Prewitt, Alexander W. Chambliss, Chief Justice Grafton Green, A. B. Neil, and Frank H. Gailor. Tennessee State Library and Archives.

Supreme Court was highly deferential to the elected branches, and especially to the state legislature. At times when dissenting opinions were common among the nine members of the United States Supreme Court, including Abe Fortas (the only Tennessee-born United States Supreme Court justice who served during this period),[4] the five members of the Tennessee Supreme Court almost always spoke with a unanimous voice. Although the Tennessee Supreme Court eventually abandoned the notation "All concur" that followed most of its decisions early in the period under review, as in the period that preceded, there were never more than a handful of concurring and/or dissenting opinions in any term between 1946 and 1974.[5]

Whereas United States Supreme Court decisions during this time period are often lengthy, Tennessee Supreme Court opinions rarely cover more than three or four pages in the official reports, and most cases cited relatively few precedents.[6] Moreover, the unanimity of the Tennessee Supreme Court justices on most issues was in sharp contrast to the diverse points of view that were often reflected on decisions by the United States Supreme Court during the same time period. Mary Jean DeLozier's observation that there was "a paucity of that philosophic reasoning which has graced the opinions of the United States Supreme Court in decisions involving religious liberty"[7] was true of most areas of Tennessee Supreme Court decision making. Moreover, although the United States Supreme Court reversed numerous precedents from 1946 to 1974, the Tennessee Supreme Court almost always adhered to available precedents.[8] On a more disturbing note, a 1966 report observed that lawyers often failed to file briefs before the Court in a timely fashion, and justices seldom read legal arguments in advance;[9] as demonstrated in the chapter that follows, this became an issue in the Supreme Court electoral contest in 1973–74.

THE PERSONNEL

From 1946 to the election of 1974, sixteen men occupied regular seats on the Tennessee Supreme Court (a somewhat larger number who served as substitute "special justices" are not treated here). Two of the sixteen justices, Grafton Green and Alex Chambliss, left the Court in 1947 after more than sixty years of combined service. Of the remaining fourteen justices, five served from ten to twenty-two years with Hamilton Burnett sitting from 1947 to 1969, Alan M. Prewitt from 1942 to 1961, A. B. Neil from 1942 to 1960, Pride Tomlinson from 1947 to 1961, and Ross Dyer from 1961 to 1974. Chester B. Chattin and Larry B. Creson both served from 1965 to 1974; Frank H. Gailor served from 1943 to 1954, John E. Swepston from 1954 to 1961, Allison B. Humphreys from 1967 to 1974, Weldon B. White from 1961 to 1967, Sam L. Felts from 1960 to 1965, George McCanless (state attorney general from 1954 to 1969) from 1969 to 1974, and Andrew D. Holmes from 1963 to 1965.[10]

From 1946 to 1974, six different individuals, all selected by their peers for indefinite terms, served as chief justice. Grafton Green served his last year at the beginning of this period, and was followed by Alex Chambliss's brief tenure from February to September 1947. A. B. Neil, who served the longest term as chief during this period, followed from 1947 to 1960. Prewitt served from 1960 to 1963, Burnett from 1963 to 1969, and Dyer from 1969 to 1974.

Published information about the justices is available in various editions of the *Tennessee Blue Book*[11] and from obituaries and memorials, some of which are published in official Court reports. Although it is impossible to gain the detailed information about the state's highest justices that is available in the expansive biographies and papers of the justices of the United States Supreme Court, enough is known to account, at least in part, for the high degree of judicial unity during the period in review.

All sixteen Tennessee justices were white male Democrats, and they shared many other characteristics that derived from the selection process for appellate judges and gave the Tennessee Supreme Court, like other state courts, a distinct "institutional identity."[12] Scholars have observed that, although this process was "elective in theory," most members "reached the bench initially by gubernatorial appointment, ran unopposed in succeeding elections, and were rarely defeated."[13] Of the fourteen justices whose years of service fall largely into the 1946 to 1974 time period, the youngest came in office at age forty-nine with most being appointed at about age fifty-eight and retiring about age seventy. All but two of the fourteen justices had judicial experience prior to their elevation to the Supreme Court, and, of the two that did not, Pride Tomlinson had served as Maury County attorney from 1921 to 1947 and had chaired the Tennessee Code Commission from 1945 to 1946, and Ross Dyer had served as a delegate to the limited constitutional convention of 1953.

All fourteen justices were born in the South. Holmes was born in Mississippi, Chambliss in South Carolina, Swepston in Arkansas, White in Texas, and all the others in Tennessee. Over half of those on the bench from 1946 to 1974 had served in the military, three (Gailor, Neil, and White) had served in the Tennessee legislature, and most were active in church and civic affairs. All who are listed as being affiliated with churches were Protestants, and, judging from their obituaries, many were fairly devout. Chief Justice Hamilton S. Burnett even published an article entitled "The Lawyer as Christian" in which he argued "that the prosecution of the law" is "consistent with the sincere profession and practice of Christianity," and that, "in some particulars, the lawyer enjoys peculiar advantages for attaining eminent usefulness in the Christian life."[14] Most of the Tennessee Supreme Court justices were affiliated with one or more organizations such as the Elk, Masons, Kiwanis, American Legionnaires, and were members of state and local bar associations.

The similarities in legal educations help account for the great unity of the Court from 1946 to 1974. Five of the fourteen justices (Chattin, Felts, Humphreys, Neil, and White) earned law degrees from Cumberland University, and Justices Neil and Humphreys both taught there and served as deans. This school, which moved in 1961 from Lebanon, Tennessee, to Birmingham, Alabama, where it is now associated with Samford University, was known for its conservative curriculum that retained a one-year program long after other law schools had moved to two- and three-year curricula[15] and long eschewed the dominant case method of instruction for focus on the written law itself.[16] Cumberland appears to have had a remarkable influence, but other institutions also contributed to the education of the justices. Four of fourteen justices (Creson, Holmes, McCanless, and Prewitt) earned law degrees at Vanderbilt University in Nashville. Justices Burnett and Swepston graduated from the University of Virginia. Tomlinson earned his degree at George Washington University, Gailor, who had been a Rhodes Scholar and studied at Columbia University, received an honorary D.C.L. degree from Sewanee, and Dyer earned his degree at night from the YMCA

School, now the Nashville School of Law. Significantly, although there were several other night schools for lawyers in Tennessee during this time,[17] most of which offered questionable educations, no others produced Supreme Court justices during this period; neither did the state's leading public law school, the University of Tennessee.

By law, justices on the Supreme Court represent each of the three geographical divisions of the state. In assessing why so many Tennesseans have succeeded in national politics, scholars have observed that sensitivity to the state's political and geographical diversity may play a vital part, lending moderation and conservatism to the state's politics.[18] This is undoubtedly true of the justices who served on the state Supreme Court from 1946 to 1974.

Students of the Tennessee Supreme Court can gain considerable insight into this period of the Court's history from a revealing privately printed autobiography, written and published by Justice Albert Neil after his retirement.[19] Not only did Neil serve for eighteen of these years (thirteen as chief justice), but his fifty years of service on the Tennessee bench, which included service on the Criminal and Second Circuit Courts of Davidson County, is apparently a record.[20] Fellow justices may or may not have been as conservative as Neil, but, as was indicated earlier, most of the Tennessee Supreme Court decisions in which he had a part were unanimous.

It is tempting to cite Neil's mistaken claim in his foreword that his life, which began in 1873, "embraces the last half of the Eighteenth and the first half of the Nineteenth Centuries,"[21] as proof of his reactionary views, but, such errors aside, his opinions had a distinctly conservative cast. Neil, whose father fought for the Confederacy, noted that his views of the value of states' rights were shaped largely by what he knew about carpetbaggers and Reconstruction and that these events taught him "the right of the people to live in a free state unmolested by the overlordship of a centralized government at Washington."[22]

Neil's views were typical of a white Southern states' rights Democrat. He favored state and local government over the national government and followed his observation that "there is no place on the judiciary for willful men" by noting that "[i]f the Supreme Court at Washington can change the law at will as it affects our political institutions contrary to long existing precedents, we are not far removed from a tyrannical government."[23] Neil denied that federal constitutional limitations applied to the exercise of state police powers. In expressing his concern over the United States Supreme Court's decision in *Brown v. Board of Education* (1954), Neil wrote that "to say that judges can make the law at will, based alone upon sociology, and declare their decision to be 'the law of the land' is a complete abandonment of our system of constitutional government. The rights of the several states in relation to all matters, other than issues pertaining to that of National Defense, is of paramount importance."[24] Neil disagreed with the Supreme Court's decision on prayer in public schools;[25] could not understand African Americans' complaints with the legal system;[26] said that he had never expected "to contend at the Bar with a lawyer of the female sex;"[27] accused the National Association for the Advancement of Colored People (NAACP) of attempting "to inject the race problem into every controversy,"[28] and believed this and other civil rights organizations to be "infiltrated by Communists."[29]

Reflecting an emphasis on collegiality that has been observed in other state courts,[30] Neil described the work of the Court as being "most harmonious," and, dispelling any thought that justices might simply have assigned opinions and deferred to their colleagues, he noted that "every case, including all material questions, are considered by every member of the Supreme Court."[31] He also commented that when Attorney General Roy Beeler died in 1944, "[i]t was unanimously agreed that no one would be appointed who was not acceptable to every member of the Court."[32]

THE CASELOAD AND ACHIEVEMENTS

From 1946 to 1974, the Tennessee Supreme Court served exclusively as an appellate judicial body, reviewing a wide gamut of cases encompassing both civil and criminal law. Prior to 1967, when an intermediate Court of Criminal Appeals was created,[33] criminal appeals went directly to the Supreme Court. A Court of Civil Appeals for civil cases had previously been established in 1907. Scholars examining state supreme courts during this time period classified the Tennessee Supreme Court as one in a medium-sized state with "substantial control" over its caseload and "relatively light caseloads, measured by published opinions."[34]

In addition to cases that the Supreme Court accepted from lower appeals courts on writs of *certiorari,* the state legislature allowed for appeals from trial courts "(1) from judgments in cases when there is no testimonial conflict, such as judgments entered on demurrer; (2) from judgments in suits under the Workman's Compensation statute; and (3) from judgments involving constitutional questions and other public law questions." In 1970, one of the few years for which I have found such information, the Court's caseload was divided as follows: *certiorari,* 25 percent; direct workman's compensation cases, 25 percent; cases where there was no testimonial conflict, 26 percent; and cases involving constitutional questions, 24 percent.[35]

A study that relied on statistical samplings of eighteen cases per year concluded that in the period from 1940 to 1970, 14.3 percent of the caseload of the Tennessee Supreme Court was devoted to "Property, Contract,

Collection, & Corporate Law Cases," 50 percent to "Criminal & Public Law Cases," 7.9 percent to Private Torts (excluding workman's compensation), and 16.9 percent to "Constitutional Cases."[36] This same study found that the Tennessee Supreme Court reversed a relatively high number of lower court decisions—overall it ranked fourth highest among sixteen states in the percentage of cases it reversed; sixth of sixteen states in declarations of unconstitutionality in cases involving constitutional issues; and fifth among sixteen states in the percentage of cases favoring defendants.[37] The Tennessee Supreme Court's caseload of 205 for 1970 was slightly higher than in the two previous years[38] but apparently included unpublished or summarily decided opinions not covered in this essay.[39] It is noteworthy that, at a time when most other states had created commissions to do this work, approximately a fourth of the Tennessee Supreme Court's caseload during the period of this study was devoted to workers' compensation cases,[40] which could be directly appealed to the Supreme Court as a matter of right. The high volume of workers' compensation cases was a concern for years, but, as the next chapter demonstrates, the Court did not obtain relief until the Appellate Court Improvement Act of 1992 provided for such cases to be assigned to a special three-judge appeals panel.

Much of the Supreme Court's caseload would be familiar to students of today's Court. From 1946 to 1974, individuals were far more likely to be charged with the manufacture and possession of illegal whiskey, or "moonshine," than the possession or sale of marijuana and other drugs,[41] but other issues have not changed much. The Court served as a final interpreter of wills and insurance contracts and of disputes involving the property of those who died intestate. The Court had to decide whether governments had followed proper procedures in exercising their rights of eminent domain, whether such governments had adequately compensated property owners, and whether claims for compensation had been filed in timely fashion.

The Court reviewed the constitutionality of bond issues and tax laws, the latter suits most typically reaching the court from individuals who had paid their taxes under protest. The Court heard appeals in annexation cases, on the application of gaming laws, and on certificates of necessity and convenience issued by the Public Service Commission or the Railroad and Public Utilities Commission. The Court heard landlord-tenant controversies, settled electoral disputes, and resolved controversies over the proper allocation of funds between city and county governments. Developments in adoption and other areas of family law were also on the Court's docket. And, of course, the Court reviewed the adequacy of the evidence to support convictions and alleged denials of the rights of criminal defendants appealing convictions for larcenies, robberies, rapes, homicides, and incest.

Although the Tennessee Supreme Court eschewed judicial activism from 1946 to 1974, it played an important role during this time period. However reluctantly, the Court helped to interpret and enforce federal court decisions calling for desegregation of the schools, reapportionment of the state legislature, liberalized freedom of speech, and increasingly more formal criteria for assuring the rights of criminal defendants. Moreover, the Supreme Court upheld calls for state constitutional conventions that proposed the first successful changes in the state since the 1870s; gave its imprimatur to the Hall income tax on dividends, earnings from mutual funds, and certain interest on bonds;[42] approved the state sales tax; approved the consolidation of the Nashville City and Davidson County governments; upheld and enforced the state's right to work laws; permitted the nation's first slum clearance project in Nashville; adopted the Canons of Professional and Judicial Ethics in 1947; helped oversee the writing and enforcement of the Tennessee Code Annotated; oversaw the creation of the Tennessee Judicial Conference and the completion of a new Supreme Court building in Knoxville in 1953; enforced the Married Woman's Emancipation Act; added an executive secretary in 1964; accepted the state legislature's assignment of supervisory control over all lower courts in 1973; and, that same year, resolved a disputed judicial election that resulted from a new system of judicial selection.

The Tennessee Supreme Court in 1953 (seated, left to right): David Sousden, clerk, Hamilton S. Burnett, John E. Swepston, Chief Justice A. B. Neil, Alan M. Prewitt, Pride Tomlinson, Attorney General Roy Beeler. Also pictured is Burnes Miller, messenger, standing. Tennessee State Library and Archives.

THE COURT'S VIEW OF ITS FUNCTION

Most of the Tennessee Supreme Court's decisions relative to constitutional issues from 1946 to 1974 are best understood by examining the views that the justices shared on the function of the Court and its relation to the two elected branches. One theme dominates the Court's decisions. Scholars who have studied other state courts during this period have classified state supreme court justices according to whether they regarded themselves as "law-makers" or "law-interpreters."[43] The Tennessee justices clearly regarded themselves as the latter, consistently eschewing any role in making the law or in assessing the wisdom or utility of legislation, and, wherever possible, they sustained legislation through deferential interpretations or by eliding individual sections that were questionable. Although such cases are legion, those below are fairly representative.

In *Royal Jewelers Co. of Knoxville v. Hake* (1947) counsel informed the Court that its reading of a state tax law would lead to dire consequences. Noting that the lawyer should address this argument to the state legislature, Justice Gailor observed that "[t]he judicial function is to declare the law as we find it . . . , and it is for the Legislature to weigh the effect and consequences of legislation enacted."[44] In sustaining a law regulating bail bondsmen in that same year, Gailor noted that in "construing statutes and declaring their constitutionality," the Court "cannot debate or question the advisability, fairness or policy of the law makers. Such aspects of legislation are for the Legislature."[45] Similarly, in construing a sales tax in 1947, Justice Neil said that "when words are used in a statute defining the limits of an exception, we cannot, under the guise of interpretation, enlarge the scope of the exception."[46] Justice Prewitt agreed with his colleagues in a 1949 case in which a hapless individual discovered that the laws of Tennessee did not recognize his divorce (therefore making him a bigamist): "It does not lie within our province to make judicial amendments to statutes. This is a matter for the Legislature and not for this Court. The defendant's only recourse is to the Governor, who has the power to extend clemency."[47]

Such expressions of opinion continued in 1949. In upholding a Nashville zoning regulation, Tomlinson observed that the legislature had the sole power to weigh the effect of such zoning on individual rights.[48] Sustaining legislation regulating intoxicating liquors in this same year, Chief Justice Neil, whose autobiography proclaimed his personal belief in natural law,[49] noted that "we are not concerned in determining the constitutionality of an Act 'whether it was dictated by a wise or foolish policy, or whether it will ultimately redound to the public good, or whether it is contrary to natural justice and equity. These are considerations solely for the Legislature.'"[50]

In approving a plan for a limited constitutional convention in *Cummings v. Beller* (1949), Justice Burnett denied any concern "with the wisdom or policy of what the Legislature proposes."[51] Likewise, in 1952 Chief Justice Neil emphasized that "[t]he wisdom or unwisdom of the statute is a matter for the Legislature and not for the courts, which cannot legitimately question the policy or condemn the effects of any law consistent with the organic law of the State and the Nation."[52]

In his autobiography, Justice Neil took aim at the ideas of sociological jurisprudence, which he associated with the United States Supreme Court.[53] His successors likewise opposed the idea that they had the responsibility to interpret the Tennessee Constitution in light of the times. It addressed such an argument in a 1966 case where the Court was urged to alter the law so that a wife might sue a drug company that sold a product that had resulted in her husband's impotence, for loss of his consortium. Justice Creson observed that "this argument is rightly directed to the Legislature."[54] Similarly, in deciding that the state's prohibition of more than 10 percent interest per year did not apply to revolving charge accounts, Justice Humphreys noted that "this Court cannot even on valid economic and sociological grounds declare an act of the legislature unconstitutional."[55]

DECISIONS ON THE EXERCISES OF POLICE POWERS

Closely related to the Supreme Court's view of its relation to the elected branches of government was its broad conception of the police powers—a term used to describe a state's authority over matters involving public safety, health, and morals. Although the Court sometimes required the legislature to demonstrate that its legislation was directed toward a public—as opposed to a private, or personal—interest, it rarely questioned such legislation when the General Assembly cited such a purpose. Indeed, the Court's pronouncements about the breadth of state police powers were generally consistent with its comments on the distinction between law-making and judicial interpretations.

In 1948, the Court upheld a state prohibition on naturopaths (individuals not trained in medical school who used various "natural" means of healing) as "a valid exercise of the police power of the Legislature."[56] In a 1948 case sustaining the state's open shop law, Justice Prewitt commented that "the Constitution does not recognize an absolute and uncontrollable liberty, but a safeguarded liberty, in a social organization which requires the protection of law against the evils which menace the health, safety, morals, and welfare of the people."[57] Upholding state regulations of optometrists in 1949, Justice Gailor observed that "the policy of legislation and the question whether a statute is or is not beneficial to the public health or safety, and so a reasonable exercise of the state police power, is a question exclusively for the determination of the Legislature, and is not a subject for judicial review."[58]

The Supreme Court in *Nashville Housing v. Nashville* (1951) upheld a slum clearance ordinance that shaped the subsequent appearance of the area in front of the state capitol building. The Court observed that "[t]o remove health, crime and fire hazards by slum clearance, is clearly a proper and reasonable exercise of the police power."[59] Faced in 1957 with the legislature's right to mandate the use of Eastern Standard Time throughout the state, Justice Tomlinson observed, "The police power of the State is an inherent attribute of sovereignty and derives from the principle that such statutes are essential to the maintenance of public morals, public safety and public health."[60] In dealing in 1957 with a regulation of burial insurance, Justice Burnett observed, "With the Legislature rests determination of the reasonableness of regulations under the police power and a court will not exercise the question de novo and overrule such judgments by substituting its own, unless it clearly appears that those regulations are so 'beyond all reasonable relation to the subject to which they are applied as to amount to mere arbitrary usurpations of power.'"[61]

Although resisting the use of its own power to expand the Constitution, the Court was willing to allow the legislature to adopt legislation to meet perceived contemporary needs. In upholding most provisions of the Motor Vehicle Act in *Ford Motor Co. v. Pace* (1960), Justice Prewitt noted, "In considering the question, whether or not the Legislature has the right to enact such a statute under the police power, we must take into consideration and look at things in the light of the social and economic conditions existing at the present time rather than at the time our Constitution was adopted. Legislative power is not static and helpless but arises to adjust and face new conditions as they appear to affect the people of the State."[62]

In 1966, the Court reprimanded a trial judge for refusing to grant a beer license on the testimony of individuals—mostly local pastors—that beer was inherently harmful. Granting that courts could decide whether the granting of a particular permit could lead to a specific harm, Dyer said that "[t]he courts are without authority to determine if the sale of beer, in general, is harmful or immoral. This is a matter for the General Assembly."[63] Opponents of the state law requiring motorcycle riders to wear helmets claimed that it violated the principle of "private right to private harm." The Court upheld the law in 1969 and replied that "the test of constitutionality is not limited to the question whether the conduct of a member of the class will probably result in harm to others outside that class, the test includes, whether there is danger to the safety and well-being of the class members by the practice sought to be regulated, and whether the regulation is reasonably designed to guard against this danger."[64] Similarly, in a 1971 case, the Court sustained a Clarksville ordinance requiring the repair or removal of buildings under its power to prevent fire hazards.[65]

Tennessee Supreme Court decisions from 1946 to 1974 generally upheld state taxes. In *Hooten v. Carson* (1948), Chief Justice Neil validated the 1947 states sales tax of 2 percent: "Regardless of whether the right to buy or sell is a natural right, we think the Law is well settled that the State in the exercise of its sovereign power may impose a privilege tax upon any and all business transactions to the end that the general public be protected from unfair trade practices, and where the tax is not capricious or unreasonable."[66] In sustaining a franchise tax in this same year, the Court noted, "It is only when application of the formula results in allocating to the taxing state an amount of earnings or net worth palpably disproportionate to the business done or property owned in the taxing state that the 'due process clause' of the Federal Constitution may be successfully invoked by the corporation taxed."[67] In another case relative to railroad taxation decided in 1948, the Court granted "a very wide discretion" to the legislature in "[t]he assessment for taxes and the collection thereof."[68]

The Supreme Court's attitude toward school regulations generally exemplified its deferential view of state police powers. In *State v. Marion County Board of Education* (1957), the Court upheld a regulation excluding married students from attending public school during the term immediately following their marriage. Rather than questioning the board of education's claim that the presence of such newly married students had an adverse psychological impact on their peers, the Supreme Court said that "Boards of Education, rather than Courts, are charged with the important duty of operating the public schools. So, it is not a question of whether this or that individual judge or court considers a given regulation adopted by the Board as expedient. The Court's duty, regardless of its personal views, is to uphold the Board's regulation unless it is generally viewed as being arbitrary and unreasonable."[69]

In a second case from 1973, the Court upheld the firing of a teacher who refused to follow a school board's ban on the wearing of beards. The Court again deferred to "school experts," and saw social ramifications in individual grooming decisions: "But the grooming of one person is of concern not only to him but to all others with whom he comes into contact; we have to look at each other whether we like it or not. It is for this reason that society sets certain limits upon the freedom of the individual to choose his own grooming."[70]

If the central current of Supreme Court decision making recognized state police powers, there were occasional cross-currents where the Court ruled that the state had improperly infringed constitutional rights or violated provisions of the Constitution. Thus, in a 1948 case the Court invalidated a Johnson City regulation of taxis that it believed violated the antimonopoly provision of Article 1, Section 22, part of the state's Declaration of Rights.[71]

More commonly, the Tennessee Court denied that the state legislature had cited a valid purpose under its police powers. In 1956, for example, the Court struck down a law prohibiting gifts to gasoline customers by questioning whether the sale of gas was affected with a public interest and observing that "[t]o uphold the statute in question would be to allow a governmental agency of the State to exercise control over all private enterprises."[72] Similarly, the Court took a crabbed view of the public interest in a 1958 case striking down an ordinance prohibiting the fencing of front yards within restricted areas on the basis that aesthetic concerns were not part of a state's police powers.[73] In *Livesay v. Tennessee Board of Watchmaking* (1959), the Court voided a system regulating those engaged in watch repairs. Rejecting a professed state interest in prohibiting fraud, the Court argued from consequences. If such a rationale were accepted, the Court warned that the legislature could regulate any business enterprise.

Two other 1970 cases also show that the Court sometimes vindicated economic rights over state police powers. The judges struck down a law requiring that electricians working independently have greater credentials than those working with others as discriminatory.[74] Further, the Court invalidated a regulation of fortune-tellers that applied only in the populous Shelby County, declaring, "It is difficult, if not impossible, to perceive any reasonable relationship between population and whatever evils might accompany fortune-telling."[75]

EXERCISES OF JUDICIAL REVIEW TO VOID LEGISLATION

Although the Tennessee Supreme Court generally deferred to legislative judgments in the period from 1946 to 1974, there were some notable exceptions. Even opponents of activist judicial review will sometimes accept judicial invalidations of improperly adopted legislation.[76] There are probably not many such instances at the national level, but in the less formalized state legislature,[77] such mistakes certainly occur. On at least three occasions from 1946 to 1974 the Tennessee Supreme Court struck down legislation because of such improprieties.

In *City of Nashville v. Browning* (1951) the Court considered the constitutionality of that year's general education bill. Apparently, the bill that the Speakers of the legislature and the governor signed was not the same as the bill that one or both houses passed. Striking down the measure, the Court noted that "a bill signed by the Speakers when different from that passed by the Senate and House, is no law."[78] In *D.M.C. Corp. v. Shriver* (1970), the Court faced a somewhat different scenario relating to the provision that each bill must be read three times before its passage. Apparently, a "shell" bill, containing only a title, was read on the first two occasions, with the content not added until the third reading. Voiding this law, the Court observed, "It results and we so hold that a 'bill' introduced in the Legislature containing only a title is not a 'bill' within the meaning of the word as used in the first sentence of Section 18, Article 2, of the Constitution of Tennessee."[79] Similarly, in *Fuqua v. Davidson County* (1950) the Court invalidated a private act regulating primary elections where a bill passed by the house had been amended by the senate and signed by the governor but never returned to the house for a revote.

Related to these cases are those in which the Tennessee Supreme Court enforced Article 2, Section 17 of the state Constitution, which provides that "[n]o bill shall become a law which embraces more than one subject, that subject to be expressed in the title. All acts which repeal, revive or amend former laws, shall recite in their caption, or otherwise, the title or substance of the law repealed, revived or amended." Generally, the Court deferred when possible to the legislature. Thus, in a 1954 case, it sustained a private act labeled so as to authorize "two Justices of the Peace for the town of Erwin," even though the effect of the act—creating two new justices of the peace—resulted in a total of three.[80] Similarly, the Court generally did not interpret the caption clause of the Constitution to strike down laws the purpose of which was effected by corresponding enabling provisions.[81]

However, the Court did sometimes strike down legislation under Article 2, Section 17. In *Baxter v. Jenkins* (1956), for example, the Court invalidated a private act that did not cite the law it intended to amend, and in *Melvin v. Bradford Special School District* (1948), it voided an act on the basis that its purpose was broader than its caption.

RULINGS UNDER ARTICLE 11 AND THE DELEGATION DOCTRINE

Most of the laws that the Tennessee Supreme Court invalidated during the period under review here were voided under authority of two sections of the state Constitution that had special reference to private bills,[82] namely, Article 11, Section 8 and Article 11, Section 9. The first section provided that "[t]he Legislature shall have no power to suspend any general law for the benefit of any particular individual, nor to pass any law granting to any individual or individuals, rights, privileges, immunities, or exemptions other than such as may be, by the same law extended to any members of the community, who may be able to bring himself within the provisions of such law."

The second section specified:

> The General Assembly shall have no power to pass a special, local or private act having the effect of removing the incumbent from any municipal or county office or abridging the term or altering the salary prior to the end of the term for which such public officer was selected, and any act of the General Assembly private or local in form or effect applicable to a particular county or municipality either in its governmental or its proprietary capacity shall be void and of no effect unless the act by its terms either requires the approval of a two-thirds vote of the local legislative body of the municipality or county, or requires approval in an election by a majority of those voting in said election.

In 1946 the Supreme Court cited Article 11, Section 8 in voiding a private act suspending the poll tax in McMinnville[83] and in striking down a private act authorizing the County Court in Knoxville to issue bonds for the erection and repair of school buildings.[84] The Court thought the first conferred a special benefit on the residents of McMinnville, and the second conferred special benefits "upon particular school districts to the detriment of other districts in the same county."[85] In 1947, the Court invalidated a private act designed to penalize governmental officials in Sullivan County who overspent their budgets. The Court found no reason "why the overdrawing of a budget in Sullivan County constitutes a greater offense to the public welfare of that county than it would be to the remaining counties of the State."[86]

In 1950, the Court voided a private law appointing and paying for certain deputies both because the title of the law failed to indicate its scope and because it suspended a general law for the benefit of particular individuals.[87] That same year the Court invalidated a public law preventing the operation of theaters only in Mountain City on Sunday,[88] struck down a private act changing school funding in a single county,[89] and voided a beer option law applying only to counties of from 27,650 to 27,750 on the basis that each attempted without adequate reason to confer a special privilege or extend a general exemption from general laws.[90]

In 1952, the Court used Article 11, Section 8 to strike down a private act designed to allow a particular individual to practice dentistry without a license[91] as well as another permitting issuance of bonds in Campbell County without the voters' assent and in the teeth of an opposition petition signed by 20 percent of the population.[92] The Court found no reason for justifying such discrimination in either case. In 1955 the Court voided a private act abolishing the superintendent of public instruction in Hamilton County and vesting such duties in a director appointed by the board of education. The Court ruled that only the people or the county court could fill a county office created by the legislature.[93]

The Court sometimes applied Article 11, Sections 8 and 9 to zoning ordinances. Thus, in *Grant v. McCullough* (1954), it struck down an ordinance designed to change the zoning of a single lot in a residential neighborhood to a commercial classification as improperly designed to benefit a specific individual. Similarly, in *Shatz v. Phillips* (1971), the Court invalidated a zoning ordinance that established different standards for the storage of used and waste materials in different zones: "[N]o where in the record does it appear that the discrimination is a reasonable one—quite the contrary—it clearly appears that the petitioners' use of the property would not be such as to cause any result justifying the exercise of the police power under the municipality's zoning ordinance."[94]

Sometimes the results of the Court's rulings on Article 2, Sections 8 and 9 were quaint. Thus in 1959, the Court found that a city law outlawing pinball machines conflicted with general state laws exempting such machines from the state's gaming regulations.[95] In 1968, the Court likewise found that a private act regulating fire crackers in Fentress County was not provided for under the Home Rule Amendment and could not be justified by showing that "Fentress County is in any different circumstances or condition than any other county in the State of the same size and population."[96]

Such decisions continued into the 1970s. Thus, the Court invalidated an annexation law applicable to a single city,[97] and voided a private act providing for a special liquor privilege tax in Brentwood. The Court was unable find any "reasonable basis why a particular business in Williamson County should be subject to a different and higher tax than are similar businesses in all the counties of the State."[98]

Invocations of Article 2, Sections 8 and 9 were not always fatal. In a 1948 case, the Supreme Court upheld the validity of a tax on amusements in Knox County because it primarily effected individual relations rather than the county "in its governmental or political capacity."[99] In *Wallace v. Lewallen* (1955) the Court permitted an extension of voting times by private act in the Fourth Civil District of Anderson County that it thought was justified by increases in that district's population. Similarly, in 1962, the Court approved a law allowing consolidation of cities and counties in counties with populations over two hundred thousand and permitting the selection of members of charter commissions there: "The classification is reasonable because we all know that it is in these large counties that the problem of the large cities as to the ever increasing population just beyond the corporate limits becomes more acute, complex and confusing."[100]

A judiciary that generally defers to a legislature might still protect both the legislature and itself from improper delegations of power. Cases from 1946 to 1974 in which the Tennessee Supreme Court faced such issues are evenly split between those where the Court accepted such delegations and those where it did not. In the former category is a decision upholding the authority of the Nashville Traffic Commission against charges that it had improperly been delegated legislative powers.[101] The Court also confirmed the authority of the Department of Public Welfare to license child care[102] and allowed a county health board to require immunizations.[103]

By contrast, the Court ruled that a Railway and Public Utilities Commission had encroached on judicial powers in ordering a railroad to abandon certain "team tracks."[104] In addition, the Court ruled that the Juvenile and Domestic Relations Court of Nashville was illegal because it had no "fixed and determined" jurisdiction and "its existence results from the delegation of legislative authority to a municipality in plain violation of the Constitution of Tennessee."[105]

CONSTITUTIONAL CHANGE

Just as the Tennessee Supreme Court generally deferred to the legislature, so too, consistent with themes that date back to the Jacksonian era, it professed great deference to the people. This attitude showed itself from 1946 to 1974 both in the Court's decision to approve of constitutional conventions and the changes they enacted and in its decisions on the role of the people in participating in and making judgments as jurors.

The decisions in which the Tennessee Supreme Court legitimated constitutional change are among the most important in the twenty-eight-year period under review. The state Constitution had been adopted in 1870, and previous attempts to amend it had failed.[106] Fears that a constitutional convention might become a "runaway" body that would initiate unwanted changes posed a major stumbling block. The Tennessee Supreme Court helped surmount this obstacle when it ruled in *Cummings v. Beeler* (1949)—counter to a declaration by the state's attorney general—that the people could vote to limit a convention. Speaking through Justice Burnett, the Court squarely rested this judgment on its belief, expressed in Tennessee's Declaration of Rights, that "[t]he people are possessed with ultimate sovereignty and are the source of all State authority."[107] In a relatively rare concurring opinion, Justice Prewitt further justified the Court's stance by noting that whatever a convention did would be recommendatory only. Although voters did not approve the first call for a convention, "[a]gainst an eighty year background of frustrated constitutional reform, the narrow defeat was a psychological victory."[108] It prepared the way for the Convention of 1951, the work of which was ratified in 1953.

In *West v. Carr* (1963), the Court rejected claims that a convention called for 1965 was illegal because it was apportioned like the legislature, the system of which the United States Supreme Court had just invalidated. Similarly, in *Illustration Design Group v. McCanless* (1970), the Court sustained the people's right to call a convention on five questions, one of which classified property into three types. Again, the Court relied on the doctrine of popular sovereignty: "[T]he people, as the reservoir of all sovereign power of the State, have delegated to the Legislature the authority and power to initiate change in their Constitution, subject to their final adoption or rejection by popular vote." The Court further noted that "the people have not only delegated authority to the Legislature to propose the call for a convention, and thus limit and define the scope and action of such convention, but they have expressly limited the consideration and action of the convention to the proposals already approved by a vote of the people."[109]

In *Southern RR v. Dunn* (1972), the Court validated a convention's work by deciding that the constitutional provision limiting a constitutional convention to every six years applied to six years after the convening, rather than the adjourning, of the previous convention. Similarly, in 1973 the Court upheld the convention's authority to provide certain exemptions for property devoted to "religious, charitable, scientific, literary, or educational purposes."[110]

JURY VERDICTS

Another indication of the important role that popular sovereignty played in Tennessee politics was the Supreme Court's regard for the jury. The Court frequently sought to preserve the fairness of the jury system. Still, the Court did not hesitate to strike down jury verdicts that it did not believe were justified by the evidence.

Because the Supreme Court traced the right to a trial jury not only to the state Constitution but also to the common law, Tennessee Supreme Court decisions from 1946 to 1974 were actually more restrictive than current federal decisions regarding state jury trials.[111] Thus, although federal courts do not today require states to have a jury of twelve, the Tennessee Supreme Court did. Thus voiding a verdict in *Patten v. State* (1968) where the presence of an alternate juror raised the number of jurors to thirteen, the Court said that the right to a jury in a criminal case was "a trial by jury as it existed and was in force and use according to the course of the common law under the laws and constitution of North Carolina at the time of the adoption of the Tennessee Constitution of 1796."[112] In another case invalidating a jury composed of thirteen members, the Court noted that "[a] criminal conviction is just as invalid if tried by a jury of more than twelve members as it is when tried by a jury of less than twelve members."[113] On a related issue, the Court decided that common-law precedents voided a verdict where a judge had improperly charged a jury in the early morning hours of a Sunday.[114]

Article 6, Section 14 of the Tennessee Constitution specifies that only juries can impose fines of more than $50; this rule, it may be recalled, had led in an earlier period to the invalidation of the penalty imposed in the Scopes Trial. In the period covered by this chapter, the Court enforced this requirement in a number of cases where lower judges ignored it.[115] The Court did occasionally permit minor deviations in jury procedures that did not appear to affect the fairness of verdicts. It thus ruled that the omission of the name of a twelfth juror from a jury roll did not invalidate a sentence.[116]

When matters of fundamental fairness were at issue, however, the Court consistently stood its ground. Thus, at a time when the Court was otherwise upholding a system of racial segregation within the state, it remanded the conviction of an African American man for assault to commit murder upon a white man on the basis that a trial judge had struck a black juror after all peremptory challenges had been exhausted: "If the trial judge could, upon his own motion, and without stating any cause, discharge the juror he could arbitrarily discharge any number of venire-men who are qualified for service and by so doing add to the number of peremptory challenges by the State, in plain violation of law. The repetition and continuation of such a practice would result in a undisguised mockery of our system of jury trial."[117] In this same case, the Court classified the state counsel's use of the term "human fiend" to describe the defendant as prejudicial.[118] In yet another case written when racial segregation was state law and the justices were still referring to African Americans as "colored" people, the Court overturned a second-degree murder verdict where the district attorney had scorned the testimony of a white witness who had testified favorably as to the character of a black: "If white men who testify on behalf of a negro were to be thus held up to scorn, the inference followed that jurors who voted to acquit a negro were beneath consideration."[119] In a similar case, the Court voided a grand jury selection in a case where the jury cards were marked with a *C*, designating individuals as "colored," and thus presumably providing a mechanism to exclude them.[120]

On a related issue, then as now, although the Court agreed that purposeful exclusion of African American jurors was illegal, it did not think that the right to a jury guaranteed individuals the right to a jury composed in part, or in whole, by members of their own race.[121] In failing to overturn a case in which blacks had apparently been in the appropriate "pools" but had not actually served on either a grand or petit jury, the Court observed that "members of the Negro race have no constitutional right to trial by a mixed race jury. All they have is a right that their race not be discriminated against in the selection and drawing of grand juries."[122]

The Supreme Court affirmed that juries served as final judges of both law and fact,[123] and it voided jury judgments where it thought that a judge did not give proper instructions[124] or where the judge polled jurors in an inappropriate manner.[125] Consistent with modern United States Supreme Court decisions, the Court ruled that, although a defendant was entitled to a jury trial, such a defendant could waive this right, either explicitly, as in *Seale v. Luttrell* (1968), or implicitly, as where an attorney brought his client's criminal case on a day that he knew was devoted to nonjury matters.[126]

On a related issue, the Court upheld a state statute requiring that a defendant who testified be the first defense witness,[127] until the United States Supreme Court voided this practice in *Brooks v. State* (1972). Even then, the Court decided that the case should not apply retroactively to cases in which the defendant had still taken the stand and testified.[128]

THE RECOGNITION OF FEDERAL SUPREMACY

The Tennessee Supreme Court was rarely in sync with the philosophy or judgments about constitutional issues that the United States Supreme Court handed down from 1946 to 1974. However, at a time when other courts, particularly in the American South, often attempted to evade United States Supreme Court decisions,[129] the Tennessee Court repeatedly indicated its deference to such decisions, even when it found them disagreeable. Using a classification developed by Kenneth N. Vines in a study of southern state courts from May 1964 to December 1968, the Tennessee justices acted like "Federals," who accepted the authority of United States Supreme Court decisions, rather than "States Righters," who emphasized local conditions and needs, or "Compromisers," who wavered between the two views.[130]

In a 1948 case involving the legitimacy of picketing, the Court noted that "[t]he decision of the Supreme Court of the United States as to whether a certain act, degree of law violates the Constitution of the United States is binding upon the state courts."[131] Similarly, in *Roy v. Brittain* (1956) the Court noted that it was bound by the United States Supreme Court's desegregation decision in *Brown v. Board of Education* (1954). The justices opined, "We know of no case . . . in which the Courts of this State may enjoin the enforcement of a Federal District decree that is based upon the express mandate of the

Supreme Court of the United States."[132] Faced in *Campbell v. State* (1964) with a trial court that had said it was "not going to be bound by" federal court decisions on the right to counsel in a criminal case, the Court again sustained federal supremacy and reprimanded the trial judge: "[A] statement of this kind is rather unfortunate in a record, and should not have been made, because all of us know that in taking the oath of office to act as a judge we take the oath to abide by the Constitution of the United States as well as the Constitution of the State of Tennessee. We likewise know that the Constitution of the United States is superior in that when those acting under the Constitution of the United States, as the Supreme Court of the United States does on such a question, then we of the State courts are bound thereby."[133]

The Supreme Court might have fudged the issue in *Bowen v. State* (1972) where it responded to the United States Supreme Court's capital punishment decision in *Furman v. Georgia* (1972) by conceding "that the United States Supreme Court's opinions are binding on this Court," but denying that this decision "has the immediate effect of voiding judgments of this Court which are not involved in proceedings before it."[134] The Court was on firmer ground in a case later that year in which it ruled that the provision in the Tennessee Constitution seeking to require new elections before the state legislature could ratify the Twenty-sixth Amendment, allowing eighteen year olds to vote in state and federal elections, was an unconstitutional attempt to regulate a "federally derived power."[135]

RACIAL ISSUES

The United States Supreme Court had an important impact on racial relations during the period under review, and its decisions clearly upset a long-standing way of life that the Court had once approved in *Plessy v. Ferguson* (1896). Although before *Brown v. Board of Education* the Tennessee Supreme Court had attempted to guarantee that African American defendants were given fair criminal trials, it had clearly approved racial segregation. Thus, affirming a Memphis ban on a "talking motion picture" featuring "little negroes" in a 1949 case, Justice Neil observed that "the South does not permit negroes in white schools nor recognize social equality between the races even in children."[136]

When the United States Supreme Court invalidated racial segregation, most Tennessee leaders responded much more moderately than leaders in nearby states. Similarly, the Tennessee Supreme Court followed the lead of the United States Supreme Court, frequently ruling on behalf of minority litigants.[137] Thus, even though the state Constitution prohibited expenditures for racially integrated institutions, the Tennessee Supreme Court refused to allow counties to close, rather than to integrate, their schools. In sustaining the desegregation of Clinton High School, where Governor Clement had sent in the state guard to preserve order,[138] Chief Justice Neil observed that, if the Court were to enjoin spending on desegregated schools "the result would be the closing of Clinton High School until the State of Tennessee could either adopt a policy of operating its public school system contrary to the Supreme Court decision in Brown v. Board of Education, *supra,* or abandon the present system of public education. We are unwilling to enter a decree which would have the undoubted effect of closing Clinton High School and possibly other schools in Anderson County."[139] In rejecting a plea, filed ten years later, for students to be bused to the schools nearest their homes, the Supreme Court ruled that "[u]nequal treatment is no ground for the relief sought absent arbitrary, and unreasonable abuse of discretion, or the commission of some unconstitutional act over and beyond the authority of the School Board."[140]

A decision in the following year confirms that the Court took its obligation to follow federal constitutional rulings seriously. In this case, it ruled that an individual who sold land to blacks was not liable for claimed losses in property values. Justice Burnett found "no legal violation of any of the rights of others by the sale of this property."[141]

A ruling three years later was more problematic. There the Court refused to invalidate a procedure under which the all-white state Association of Funeral Directors submitted a list to the governor for appointments to the Board of Funeral Directors and Embalmers.[142] Although the judgment appears inconsistent with federal precedents, the board was not required to nominate white nominees, and the governor was "authorized" but not "required" to select from the list of nominees submitted to him. In a 1961 case, however, the state Court appears to have purposely closed its eyes to the motives behind a trumped up case convicting civil rights activist Myles Horton of selling beer and operating the Highlander Folk School for profit. The Court professed that Horton's conviction on these grounds made it unnecessary "to pass upon the constitutional question as to the mixing of white and colored, male and female in the same school."[143]

The Court was clearly uncomfortable with the demonstrations that accompanied the struggle for civil rights.[144] In *Ford v. State* (1962), the Court sustained a conviction for obstructing a religious assembly where a group of young blacks entered a municipal theater leased by an Assemblies of God Church and scattered throughout the assembly after being told that it was not open to them. Still, in sustaining the conviction, the Court commented that "this is not a suit to enjoin a discriminatory practice, nor is it a damage suit based upon the violation of civil rights, but rather a criminal action charging the defendants with willfully disturbing a religious assembly."[145] Moreover, in upholding a conviction for conspiracy to injure a business by blocking a cafeteria that did not serve "colored people," the Court assumed, for the sake of argument, "that discrimination based on race by a facility such as this cafeteria does violate the due process and equal protection clauses,"[146] but observed that "these questions are not presented here."[147]

In *Swain v. State* (1966) the Court sustained an extortion conviction against African American defendants engaged in a boycott while in *Humphreys v. Brown* (1969) it decided that state courts were not bound to accept federal civil rights actions. In the latter case, the Court ruled that it was illogical to require state courts to enforce "an alleged cause of action which owes its very existence to congressional recognition of reluctance or refusal of the State courts to act."[148]

Cases involving race and voting were not prominent in Tennessee Supreme Court decision making from 1946 to 1974. In *Town of McMinnville v. Curtis* (1946), the Tennessee Court struck down the poll tax exemption that had been granted by private act to McMinnville but not because of race but because it exempted a single city from a general constitutional requirement.[149] The Court later invalidated a challenge to Tennessee's ratification of the Twenty-sixth Amendment.[150] The Tennessee Supreme Court does not appear to have faced any cases during this time period questioning United States Supreme Court decisions invalidating the all-white primary[151] and

Racial demonstrations in early 1960, such as this sit-in at a lunch counter in Nashville in February, raised troublesome issues for the Tennessee Supreme Court. Photograph courtesy of the Nashville Tennessean.

sustaining the Voting Rights Act of 1965.[152] Excluding the apportionment decision in *Baker v. Carr* (1962), the best-known voting rights case originating from Tennessee during this period was the United States Supreme Court decision in *Dunn v. Blumstein* (1972) striking down the state's one-year state residency and three-year county residency requirement.

THE RIGHTS OF WOMEN

In his autobiography, Justice Neil noted that he had never expected to see the day when females would be lawyers.[153] Had he lived, there were undoubtedly many other developments in the field of women's rights, beginning with the United States Supreme Court decisions in *Reed v. Reed* and *Frontiero v. Richardson,* which would have surprised him. A number of decisions evidence the Tennessee Supreme Court's attitude toward women's rights prior to this time.

In a 1947 case, voiding a statutory rape conviction where there was evidence of the woman's questionable moral character, the Court noted that such laws were designed "to protect the purity of young women."[154] The Court did, however, enforce the Married Woman Emancipation Act, voiding, for example, convictions for possession of alcohol by husbands in cases where the wife was found to be guilty.[155]

Two decisions exemplify the Supreme Court's attitudes toward women's rights during this period. The first opinion, *State v. Silva* (1972), is especially noteworthy because it was written at a time when the United States Supreme Court had already begun to recognize the danger of sexual stereotypes. The case arose from an incident in which Silva, a twenty-nine-year-old married man, was charged with contributing to the delinquency of a minor. Silva, who was engaged in fund raising for the Mission Workers Association, had hired a fifteen-year-old girl to collect donations outside his establishment in Nashville. The defendant had picked her up from school on a day when students had been dismissed early because of snow, taken her to a combination motel-restaurant in Williamson County, parked outside and engaged in about thirty minutes of hugging and kissing in his car. This aroused the suspicions of an observer who called the police. They arrived to find that Silva had gone inside the motel to rent a room and fled when he saw the police. They subsequently caught, arrested, and jailed him. Although his wife testified on his behalf, Silva was convicted and sentenced to jail.

Although he upheld his conviction, Special Justice Erby Jenkins recommended that the lower court put Silva on probation. Jenkins's recommendation rested on Jenkins's stereotypical predictions about the future behavior of the defendant's wife. Jenkins speculated that "if the pattern of wifely conduct runs true to form, he will throughout his natural life be reminded of the time she saved him from jail." Jenkins observed that "it is a woman's right." Jenkins then speculated that the mental jail the defendant's wife would construct for her husband would be ever more painful than any prison term: "A convict stays in jail for a stated time, is released, and aside from the stigma of prison, he is free, but a convict husband must forever bear the shackles of guilt." Continuing his ruminations on the defendant's plight, Jenkins declared, "[H]e is forever and eternally on probation to his wife, who will be his wife, his warden and parole officer all wrapped up in one. What a sad fate for any poor mortal to face." Jenkins sealed his argument by quoting from Proverbs 20:19: "[I]t is better to dwell in a corner of a housetop than with a brawling woman in a wide house."[156] Jenkins underestimated the severity of the defendant's offenses and victimized the defendant's wife by attributing to her, with little if any apparent evidence, stereotypical attributes thought to be characteristic of her gender. This unanimous decision thus inadvertently highlighted the chauvinistic attitude of the all-male Court issuing it.

Jenkins's comments in another case involving interspousal immunity in a car accident are similarly revealing. Jenkins defended the doctrine of immunity by observing that "[w]hile modern attitudes toward marriage and the home and family and woman's liberation tend to disparage the relationship and its unity, in our opinion the rule is for the best good of the marital relationship and the 'classification' consequent thereto is not invalid." Even more telling was Jenkins's dour view of the consequences of extending equal protection and due process standards to domestic relations: "If the marital relationship and its common law consequences ever come to be considered as a suitable subject for the enforcement of the peculiar notions of a majority of a Supreme Court as to what would be 'fair play' between such parties . . . the present disorder and disarray in our society and in our courts will be as a monk's cell compared to an eighteenth century madhouse."[157] Other cases from this period also concerned sexual relations and gender. Thus, in 1947, the Court permitted a suit for "seduction and breach of promise of marriage" to go forward in a case where the woman involved had conceived a child.[158] The Court continued to accept judgments in "alienation of affection" cases.[159] On a number of occasions, the Court voided convictions of sexual offenders on the basis that the testimony against them (even in cases involving juveniles) had been inadequate because it involved the unsubstantiated testimony of the victims who were judged to be "accomplices" to the crimes.[160]

The closest the Court came to deciding a case of sexual harassment during this period occurred in 1972. It involved an accident precipitated when an employee disregarded his employer's instructions and "goosed" a fellow employee who lost control of a bottle, injuring the employee doing the "goosing." The Court decided that this accident did not arise in the course of his employment and was not therefore entitled to worker's compensation.[161]

ABORTION AND PRIVACY RIGHTS

Since the United States Supreme Court's decision in *Roe v. Wade* (1973), the right to an abortion has often been tied to the right of privacy, which the justices articulated in *Griswold v. Connecticut* (1965) striking down a Connecticut birth control statute. There is little Tennessee case law from 1946 to 1974 on abortion. Although the Tennessee Supreme Court generally upheld state antiabortion laws, cases confirm that the common law did not consider a fetus to be a "person" protected by the Fourteenth Amendment.

From 1947 to 1974, the Tennessee Supreme Court generally assumed the constitutionality of state laws regulating abortion. Thus, in 1949, it sustained an abortion conviction.[162] Similarly, in a 1966 case, the Court upheld a conviction for the felonious use of an instrument to procure abortions.[163] The Supreme Court did overturn the 1959 conviction of a pharmacist for attempting to procure a miscarriage, but it did so because the state had not proved an actual attempt to commit one.[164]

On several other occasions, the Tennessee Supreme Court ruled that a fetus was not a person who could collect damages, unless such a fetus was subsequently born alive. In 1958, the Court said that an unborn viable child was not a "person" within the compass of wrongful death statutes but "a part of its own mother's physical body."[165] Similarly, in a 1963 case, the Court denied recovery for an accident that resulted in a stillborn child.[166] A 1962 decision did permit recovery for the accidental death of triplets who had been viable and who were born alive—and were thus classified as "persons"—prior to succumbing to injuries from accidents received prior to birth.[167]

Other privacy decisions did not depart widely from modern precedents of the United States Supreme Court. Thus, the Tennessee Supreme Court ruled that one could not collect libel judgments against a newspaper that published information that was already available in the public record.[168] Similarly, the Court ruled in 1967 that a woman who had previously consented to the use of her photo—which, the Court observed, was not "immodest"—in a lounge's poster, could not object when the lounge used this picture for a public advertisement.[169] Likewise, in rejecting an argument for a right to privacy to ride motorcycles without a helmet, the Court observed that "the regulated right is not one exercised in private where it cannot affect the public."[170]

FIRST AMENDMENT RIGHTS OF RELIGION

From 1946 to 1974, the United States Supreme Court revolutionized thinking about First Amendment religious rights. Few of its decisions were more path-breaking or controversial than those in *Engel v. Vitale* (1962) and *Abington School District v. Schempp* (1963) invalidating the recitation of prayer and devotional Bible reading in public schools. These decisions were particularly unpopular in Tennessee, which did not repeal its antievolution law that had led to Dayton's historic Scopes Trial until 1967[171] and where schools continued to ignore or defy the United States Supreme Court on school-related religious issues. Thus, a school superintendent responded to a political scientist's survey about school Bible reading and prayer by saying, "I am at a loss to understand the necessity for this survey. I am of the opinion that 99% of the people of the United States feel as I do about the Supreme Court decision—that it was an outrage and that Congress should have it amended. The remaining 1% do not belong in the free world."[172]

The Tennessee Supreme Court was generally reluctant to advance *dicta* not directly relevant to a case. Chief Justice Neil's unanimous decision in *Carden v. Bland* (1956) provides a glaring exception. Because Neil wrote before the United States Supreme Court rendered its opinions on the same subjects, the Tennessee ruling did not constitute defiance of the United States Court's holdings in those cases. However, the decision in *Carden v. Bland* and Neil's autobiography[173] indicate that the Tennessee justices would have disagreed sharply with the United States Court's opinions.

Carden v. Bland involved a taxpayer suit against the Nashville city schools for providing for singing religious songs, reading a Bible verse, and the recitation of the Lord's Prayer. Although the practice had ceased, teachers in the school also had required their students to attend Sunday school and punished those who did not by making them copy passages from the Bible.

Neil acknowledged the potential establishment clause issues involved in this case. He thus observed that "it is beyond the scope and authority of School Boards and teachers in the public schools to conduct a program of education in the Bible and undertake to explain the meaning of any chapter or verse in either the Old or the New Testament." Neil, however, denied that such issues were involved here: "[T]he counsel . . . confused an hour, or a short period of reverence, or a simple act of spiritual devotion as being a form of worship that is being sponsored by an agency of the State to the prejudice of other religious groups."

As Neil viewed the situation, the Bible was "not a sectarian or denominational book," and attorneys who so argued in their otherwise "commendable zeal" had "overlooked the broader concept that religion *per se* is something which transcends all man-made creeds." Citing several United States Supreme

Court decisions regarding the doctrine of separation of church and state, Neil argued that the establishment clause should not be tortured into a meaning that was never intended by the "Founders of this Republic, with the result that the public school system of the several states is to be made a Godless institution as a matter of law." Neil further suggested that public school teachers were actually responsible for imparting faith in God to their students: "[T]he highest duty of those who are charged with the responsibility of training the young people of this State in the public schools is in teaching both by precept and example that in the conflicts of life they should not forget God."[174]

Harden v. State (1948) involved members of a Holiness Church who handled snakes as part of their worship services in contravention of state law. In this case, the Court reaffirmed its support for the exercise of state police powers designed to protect the public health and welfare. Justice Tomlinson thus noted that "the Court would usurp an exclusive prerogative of the legislature if it should presume by decree to write such exception into the statute."[175] Citing the United States Supreme Court's decision on polygamy in *Reynolds v. United States* (1879), the Tennessee Supreme Court distinguished the absolute rights of religious adherents to believe what they chose from their more limited rights to engage in harmful behavior. On a related matter, the Court cited its snake-handling precedent when it upheld a conviction in *Gaskin v. State* (1973) for the manufacture of marijuana against pleas that it interfered with the religious freedom and Ninth Amendment rights of a group headed by Stephen Gaskin. Gaskin had led about 350 to 360 followers from San Francisco in a bus caravan and settled in Lewis County where they grew marijuana to enhance their meditation.

In *McGowan v. Maryland* (1961), the United States Supreme Court validated Sunday closing laws that have a secular purpose. Although the Tennessee Supreme Court also upheld Sunday closing laws from 1946 to 1974, it rarely judged such cases harshly. In a 1948 case, the Court restricted the fine for violating the law to ten dollars because the offending establishment had only been charged with a single violation of the law.[176] In a 1957 case, the Court again upheld a Sunday-closing law, but opponents had challenged the law, not on establishment grounds but on the basis that the law illegally discriminated between goods that could be sold and those that could not.[177] Similarly, although upholding a Sunday closing law in 1958, the Court ruled that the offense caused no special injury that would enable it to issue an injunction against continuation of the practice.[178]

In *Walz v. Tax Commission* (1970), the United States Supreme Court confirmed the legitimacy of tax breaks for religious groups. On a number of occasions from 1946 to 1974, the Tennessee Supreme Court had to rule on the tax status of various religiously affiliated groups. In 1951, the Court upheld the tax-exempt status of the Sunday School Board of the Southern Baptist Convention in Davidson County.[179] The Court narrowed this ruling slightly in *Nashville v. State Board of Equalization* (1962) where it decided that the city of Nashville could tax the parking lot, cafeteria, and snack bar of this board, saying that "it can hardly be said that the Board's use of these parts of its real estate . . . for the operation of parking lots, cafeterias, and snack bar, is a use 'for purposes *purely religious*' as contemplated in our Constitution."[180] In a 1970 case involving the use of state bonds to help fund religiously affiliated hospitals, the Court ruled that allowing support to such hospitals on a "nondiscriminatory basis" was a way of securing equality for such hospitals rather than of providing "any 'preference' of a religious establishment."[181]

FREE SPEECH AND FREE PRESS RIGHTS

The United States Supreme Court liberalized protections for speech and press from 1946 to 1974 and beyond. Tennessee Supreme Court decisions from this period were consistent with general trends in United States Supreme Court reasoning. In cases involving symbolic speech, or speech connected to action, the United States Supreme Court widened protections while recognizing that certain place, time, and manner restrictions were still applicable. Although the previously cited Tennessee Supreme Court decisions dealing with civil rights demonstrations may have been more restrictive than the United States Supreme Court would have been, the Tennessee Supreme Court did recognize that the First Amendment permitted peaceful protests. The Supreme Court drew a similar line when faced with picketing. Thus, in two 1948 cases, the Court upheld the right to picket.[182] In the first of these cases, the Court upheld the union's right to picket even where such action might injure the business: "In the case at bar we are not justified in concluding that peaceful picketing of petitioner's place of business will result in irreparable injury to its business. Furthermore, if the union, in peaceful picketing, is in the exercise of its legal right and exercising that right in a legal manner, then it cannot be enjoined from such exercise of such right even though in so doing injury results to the employer."[183] In cases in which the Court enjoined picketing it did so because such picketing might result in violence[184] or involved too many people—so called "mass picketing."[185]

In the 1960s the United States Supreme Court liberalized obscenity standards. Although the Tennessee Supreme Court upheld obscenity laws in most of the cases it heard on the subject, it generally aligned itself with U.S. Supreme Court decisions. This was often difficult because that Court, which never extended constitutional protection to obscenity, constantly shifted its standards for categorizing such material, until finally arriving at a *modus vivendi* with the three standards established in *Miller v. California* (1973).

In 1957, just about the time the United States Supreme Court began to enter this field, the Tennessee Court heard a challenge to state obscenity laws alleging that they were a "hodge podge" of contradictions. Much as the United States Supreme Court would eventually do in *Miller*, the Tennessee Supreme Court defended the law by relying on community standards: "The common sense of the community as well as the sense of decency, propriety and morality, is sufficient to apply these statutes to each particular case and point out what particular conduct is rendered criminal by them." In this case, the Court upheld a conviction involving photographs and writings about "various unnatural sexual acts too reprehensible to put in print."[186]

A number of cases before the state's high court involved films. The Court generally sustained injunctions against movies specifically found to be obscene but protected wider free speech concerns. In upholding an injunction in 1967 against a film called *London Night Life*, the Court denied a more restrictive request to close the theater. The Court observed that "the statute clearly comprehends injunctions only against specific material. That is obscene material."[187] Similarly, it upheld restraint against a film entitled *Without a Stitch* in 1971[188] and *Cry Uncle* in 1973.[189]

A 1967 case upheld a two-day injunction that had been issued until a film's obscenity could be ascertained. Observing that "obscenity is excluded from constitutional protection since it is utterly without redeeming social importance," Justice Dyer extolled First Amendment freedoms: "The First Amendment to the Constitution of the United States, made applicable to the States by the Fourteenth, in effect guarantees to the people the right of free expression in order that there may be a full and unrestricted interchange of ideas for bringing about any political and social changes desired by the people. This amendment gives protection to all ideas, no matter how unorthodox or controversial, so long as they have the slightest redeeming social importance." As in previous cases, the Supreme Court previewed the film in question, *Mondo Freudo*. Agreeing that the film appealed "to a prurient interest," the Court observed that the movie did "inform people [that] sexual filth exists in the world," but that the film's effect was "just to add to the sexual filth already in the world."[190]

The United States Supreme Court held during this period that libel and slander were not protected by the First Amendment, but, in *New York Times v. Sullivan* (1964), it tightened the standard of proof in this area for public figures and allowed for free and open debate. Tennessee Supreme Court decisions from 1947 to 1974 reflected similar concerns. In a previously cited case, the Court ruled that a newspaper could not be sued for printing information available in the public record but permitted the jury to decide whether other information printed was false and malicious.[191] In *Smith v. Fielden* (1959), the Court decided that a newspaperman could not be sued for slander for words spoken during the course of a trial. Similarly, in a 1961 case, the Court ruled that an individual could not be sued for telling a legislative committee that stores that issued trading stamps tended to have higher prices than those that did not.[192] Finally, in *Applewhite v. Memphis State University* (1973), the Court ruled that the statute of limitations did not preclude a suit against Paul J. Underwood for allegedly libelous information in a book entitled *Night Riders of Reelfort Lake* and published by Memphis State University.

THE RIGHTS OF CRIMINAL DEFENDANTS

The Warren Court aggressively extended the protections of the Bill of Rights of the United States Constitution to those accused of, or convicted of, crimes.[193] The Tennessee Supreme Court generally acquiesced but rarely led the way to new protections. On occasion, however, the Supreme Court did articulate its shared concern for all citizens. After rejecting the testimony of a girl who had testified against her father in an incest case, Justice Gailor thus observed that "although we are convinced of the defendant's guilt of this abnormal and revolting crime, his conviction was obtained by unlawful means. 'Odious' individuals are not governed by one law and the rest of the citizens by another. But all are protected by the general law of the land."[194]

The Tennessee Court applied a standard of reasonableness in Fourth Amendment search cases that is arguably close to that of today's United States Supreme Court. In overturning an armed robbery conviction when it judged a search and seizure to be illegal, the Tennessee Court thus noted that "it is a factual question as to whether or not a search is reasonable or unreasonable. There is no definite formula . . . but each case is bottomed on its own facts."[195] Similarly, in accepting a search of packages found outside a house that was properly searched, the Court noted that only "unreasonable" searches were invalid.[196]

The Court frequently voided searches either that it judged to be unreasonable or where it decided that the warrants authorizing such searches were invalid. The Court thus voided searches that it considered to be mere "fishing expeditions."[197] It also invalidated searches and seizures initiated on the basis of mere suspicion[198] or conducted on the basis of inadequate information.[199]

In other instances, the Court voided searches and seizures where warrants were defective. For instance, it decided that police could not conduct a second search for illegal whiskey on the basis of an earlier warrant.[200] In 1958 the Supreme Court invalidated a search of a house that it did not consider to be incident to a lawful arrest.[201] At least twice, the Tennessee

Supreme Court voided searches conducted under warrants that allowed for the search of multiple rooms occupied by different persons.[202] On one occasion, the judges struck down a search involving an illegal one-hour detention of a car,[203] and, in another, it invalidated a search because the warrant contained neither the name of the officer who had requested it nor the hour or date that it had been issued.[204] Similarly, the Court invalidated a search and seizure of drugs based on an informant's testimony where the state offered no proof that it rested on the informant's personal knowledge.[205] Before the United States Supreme Court's historic decision in *Mapp v. Ohio* (1961) mandated state use of the exclusionary rule, the Tennessee Supreme Court acknowledged that its use of the exclusionary rule was not based on the Constitution per se, but was a judicially created rule "deemed necessary to prevent the flouting of the Constitution and the invasion of the constitutional rights of citizens."[206]

The Fifth Amendment of the United States Constitution protects individuals against compelled self-incrimination and guarantees the right to counsel in criminal prosecutions. The United States Supreme Court under Chief Justice Earl Warren mandated an increasing number of formal warnings designed to see that defendants knew these rights. The Tennessee Supreme Court expressed genuine regard for the "voluntariness" of confessions but delayed implementation of mandatory warnings to defendants until United States Supreme Court rulings made it obligatory.

Prior to the United States Supreme Court rulings in *Escobedo v. Illinois* (1964) and *Miranda v. Arizona* (1966), the Tennessee Court focused primarily on whether confessions were extracted by force but did not hesitate to void such confessions where such force had been employed. In a 1947 case voiding such a forced confession, Chief Justice Chambliss defined force to include both physical and psychological means: "This Court has repeatedly denounced the mistreatment by officers of a prisoner for purposes of forcing a confession, or for any other reason. And it has been the uniform practice of this Court to refuse to consider a confession obtained from one accused of crime by mistreatment, whether physical or mental."[207] Similarly, in *Williams v. State* (1948), the Court presumed that when one confession was extracted through the threat of violence, the second was also presumed to be invalid. That same year, the Court reversed a conviction where a judge improperly instructed jurors that they could draw a "presumption" rather than an "inference" from a defendant's failure to respond to a rape accusation.[208] In *Giles v. State* (1947), a case that preceded major United States Supreme Court precedents, the state Court tied its regard for the voluntariness of confessions to Article 1, Section 9 of the state Constitution (part of the Declaration of Rights) and voided a confession made voluntarily to a magistrate because he had not warned the defendant of his rights, and the defendant confided in him as a friend rather than as a judicial officer.[209]

The year 1966 evidences considerable confusion, if not outright resistance, on the part of the Tennessee Supreme Court to United States Supreme Court rulings. The United States Supreme Court might itself have had difficulty with *Beaver v. State* (1966), decided several months before *Miranda.* In *Beaver,* the Tennessee Supreme Court decided that a defendant who claimed, without being warned by the police, that he knew his rights, could give his confession. In so ruling, the Court continued to believe that its earlier standard was still acceptable: "The failure of officers to advise one arrested for a crime he is entitled to Counsel and to remain silent are circumstances to be considered by the trial judge in determining the voluntariness of a confession."[210] In a less ambiguous case from that same year, the Supreme Court decided that a statement made without a police warning had been given "freely and voluntarily" and was therefore acceptable: "The failure of the police or sheriff to so advise a defendant is merely a fact to consider in determining whether a confession was voluntary."[211] Similarly, in upholding a first-degree murder conviction that same year in a case where officers professed to have warned a defendant of his rights, the Court continued to rely on its earlier test of voluntariness: "If one charged with a crime freely and voluntarily confesses to the charge without inducement, coercion or fear, he has not been fundamentally prejudiced, and by voluntarily making a statement he has waived his right to counsel and to remain silent, although he has not been advised of these rights by the officer."[212] The Tennessee Supreme Court had retreated from this position by the end of 1966. Thus, in *Vandegriff v. State* (1966) it ruled that the state could not use an exculpatory statement that a defendant gave in an emergency room before being warned of his rights. Although it failed in the next year to apply either *Escobedo* or *Miranda* retroactively,[213] by 1968 the Court sent a clear signal to all criminal lawyers in the state by writing, in a *per curiam* opinion, "The sooner it is realized by all concerned that the *Miranda* guarantees must be afforded to an accused, in full good faith and with intention on the part of the interrogators to comply fully therewith, in the spirit in which these tests are laid down and required, the sooner the time will come when it will not be necessary for this Court to reverse as it must do in this case."[214]

From 1946 to 1974, the United States Supreme Court significantly expanded the Sixth Amendment right to counsel, most notably when it decided in *Gideon v. Wainwright* (1963) that states were obliged to supply counsel to indigent defendants in felony cases. This case overturned *Betts v. Brady* (1942) in which the Court had refused to extend a right to counsel in noncapital felony cases, absent exigent circumstances. In this area, at least for a time, the Tennessee Supreme Court may have established more protective rules than the United States Supreme Court.

Thus, in a 1955 case, the Court stated that "persons who are brought to trial upon an indictment for a felony are entitled to be represented by counsel."[215] The Tennessee Supreme Court was much less concerned about whether defendants had been informed of this right. In 1953, the Court sustained a gambling conviction when the record was silent, thus assuming that the police must have made the defendant aware of his right to such assistance.[216] Moreover, in a case that shows the condition of juvenile justice in the state prior to the United States Supreme Court's *In re Gault* decision (1967), the Tennessee Supreme Court ruled in *Jackson v. Bomar* (1964) that there was no error when counsel was not appointed for a juvenile charged with assault to commit murder and rape. Despite the serious charges, the Court observed that the hearing before the juvenile judge "was not a criminal proceeding" but one designed "to provide for the welfare of the child, and to remove him from unpropitious surroundings."[217] This same year, however, the Tennessee Court overturned a criminal conviction where police had not informed a defendant of his right to counsel: "There is no claim anywhere in this record that this boy was advised of his constitutional right to remain silent, or that he was warned that his answers might be used against him, or about his rights respecting a consultation with an attorney. The fact of this business is that his attorney was refused the right to see him on two occasions on the morning of the day after the arrest."[218] In a more problematic decision in *State v. Henderson* (1967), the Court ruled that a defendant who did not get his attorney until fifteen minutes before trial had not been deprived of adequate representation. The judgment is complicated by the fact that the appointed counsel had gotten the charges reduced, and the defendant had no witnesses to call on his behalf.

In another decision that has generated considerable controversy, the Tennessee Supreme Court denied James Earl Ray's request for a full trial after he pled guilty and accepted a life sentence from a judge for the assassination of Dr. Martin Luther King Jr. in Memphis.[219] The Court had previously ruled in a liquor case that, once tendered, a judge could refuse to allow a defendant to withdraw a guilty plea.[220] Special Justice Erby Jenkins was thus on solid ground in the *Ray* case when he described the Court's rationale: "[I]t is well settled in Tennessee that when a defendant pleads guilty and fully understands what he is doing, as we believe this defendant did, there can be no legal ground to justify the granting of a new trial. Otherwise, the doors of our state prisons would remain ajar to those who are incarcerated therein on pleas of guilty, and who becoming dissatisfied, seek relief on motions for new trial." Jenkins argued his point with remarkable passion and effectiveness:

> In Tennessee, as in all other liberty loving civilized countries, ambush killers are not looked upon with favor, to say the least. In a country where you do not shoot a sitting duck or a fowl unless in flight, where a rabbit or other game of the field is allowed a chance to run; and where one does not shoot down his fellow-man unless that man has committed an overt act that would justify the defendant in so doing; jurors are inclined to deal harshly with such defendants. The defendant and his attorney [Percy Foreman], with his years of experience, knew this, and in the light of this knowledge of human nature to react violently against those who have committed unprovoked violence, they made the decision to plead guilty and such plea, in the opinion of the Court, should stand.[221]

Although Ray's plea had been designed to avoid the death penalty, in *Furman v. Georgia* (1972), the United States Supreme Court decided that the death penalty, as then administered, was arbitrary and even freakish and thus constituted "cruel and unusual punishment" prohibited by the Eighth Amendment. The Court has subsequently accepted revised capital punishment laws providing for consideration of aggravating and mitigating circumstances and for a bifurcated trial separating the deliberations that decide on guilt or innocence from those imposing a penalty.[222]

Only after 1972 did the Tennessee Supreme Court give much attention to the Eighth Amendment. Indeed, in a 1969 case that looks shockingly like the famed Scottsboro case in Alabama, attorneys for eight of eleven black defendants, five of whom were sentenced to death by electrocution for a gang rape of two white girls, apparently attributed the cruel and unusual punishment clause to the Seventh rather than the Eighth Amendment.[223] Between July 13, 1915, and November 7, 1960 (Tennessee's last execution until February 2000), eighty-five blacks and thirty-nine whites were executed by electrocution in the state for convictions of first-degree murder, rape, and assault with attempt to rape.[224] In many rape cases, the Court specifically mentioned that blacks had perpetuated these crimes against whites, suggesting, like the comparative numbers of whites and blacks executed, that race influenced some juries in deciding on their penalties.[225]

In the early 1960s, the Supreme Court heard arguments in two cases tied to the United States Supreme Court decision on reapportionment in *Baker v. Carr* (1962). Litigants attempted to invalidate the death penalty on the basis that the state legislature, which had provided for it, had been malapportioned.[226] In rejecting these arguments, the Court observed that the state law providing the death penalty for rapists dated back to 1871 and had been continually reaffirmed since.

The *Furman* decision prompted a novel state response. In two cases from that year, the Tennessee Supreme Court allowed the governor to commute the death penalty to ninety-nine years in prison, thus trying to bypass retrials.[227] In upholding commutations that the defendants did not want, the Court argued that, although pardons were incomplete unless accepted, commutations did not require such acceptance.

Other Tennessee Supreme Court decisions adhered to standards of the United States Supreme Court regarding due process as articulated in the Fifth and Fourteenth Amendments. Thus, two rulings from 1973 recognized that hearings were essential to due process. In one, the Court ruled that the state did not have the right to revoke a license under the Tennessee Financial Responsibility Act without first providing a hearing.[228] Similarly, the Court decided that a tenured teacher could not be discharged without due notice and hearing.[229]

In two 1968 cases, the Tennessee Supreme Court invalidated classifications based on wealth. In *State v. Luttrell* the Court ruled that the state was discriminating against a petitioner forced to pay off debts of $173 by serving in prison at $2 a day. Similarly, in *Elliott v. State* the Court ruled that failure to provide an indigent defendant in a rape case with transcripts was a reversible error. The Court's decisions regarding the right of indigent defendants to counsel express a similar theme.

THE REAPPORTIONMENT DECISIONS

The year 1960 marked the first time in the state's history where the urban population outnumbered the rural,[230] and so it is appropriate that the period from 1946 to 1974 marks the emergence of significant cases dealing with state legislative apportionment. In *Baker v. Carr* (1962), in a case appealed through the federal courts, the United States Supreme Court concluded that Tennessee's system of apportionment, which—contrary to the state's constitution—had not been altered since 1901, constituted a justiciable political question under the equal protection clause of the Fourteenth Amendment.[231] Transcripts of the state's argument reveal that the attorney general had forcefully defended Tennessee's malapportioned legislature by making arguments from state sovereignty that were much more forceful than those typically made by the Tennessee Supreme Court, albeit similar to those found in Justice Neil's autobiography.[232] In *Baker,* the United States Supreme Court specifically noted that Tennessee had no system of initiative or referendum whereby its system of representation might be changed. In subsequent cases, the Court decided that the equal protection clause required "one-person, one-vote" or approximate equality of legislative districts.

The Tennessee Supreme Court had refused involvement in apportionment matters in *Kidd v. McCanless* (1956). Although it subsequently noted that "the question of reapportionment is not a judicial question,"[233] in *Kidd,* the Court seemed less concerned about the justiciability of legislative apportionment than about the consequences of declaring an existing legislature to be malapportioned. Responding to arguments that the existing body would continue to be the de facto legislature, the Court speculated that, instead, "we would not only not have any existing members of the General Assembly but we would have no apportionment act whatsoever under which a new election could be held for the election of members of the General Assembly." It concluded that "the effect of striking down an apportionment statute . . . would be to destroy the State Government,"[234] and, in a decision with serious implications for First Amendment free speech rights, even disbarred Z. Tommy Osborn, a prominent Nashville attorney who criticized the opinion, until he publicly apologized.[235]

In *West v. Carr* (1963), where the Court was still trying to assess the implications of *Baker v. Carr,* it decided that the differences between a state legislature and a state constitutional convention were so fundamental that malapportionment would not void the recommendations of the latter body. Moreover, by 1964, the Court denied that the decision in *Baker* had the effect that the Court had itself predicted in *Kidd v. McCanless.* Deciding that a felony prisoner had not been denied equal protection because the laws that had convicted him had been enacted by a malapportioned legislature, the Court said that "malapportionment notwithstanding, the acts of the Legislature were those of a *de facto* body, and, as such, valid." The Court further observed that "should the contention of the petitioner be sustained a state of chaos and confusion would result. This would have the ultimate effect of destroying all legislative enactments and eventually the State government." Not surprisingly, the Court decided it was obligated to avoid such chaos, "since to hold the acts of our Legislature since 1901 invalid because of malapportionment would cause a state of chaos and confusion to exist, we will balance the equities between the individual complaint in this case and the public at large and refuse to hold the acts of our malapportioned Legislature invalid, because to do so would destroy our State government."[236]

The Court tackled the reapportionment issue in other cases. In 1966 it upheld a provision in the Tennessee Constitution prohibiting counties from being split in apportioning the state senate and thus providing for multimember districts: "[T]he Federal decisions recognize that if the ratio between population and representation is preserved, the mere fact that multiple representatives to one house are elected from one district does not violate the equal protection clause of the Federal Constitution."[237]

SUPERVISION OVER LAWYERS

From 1946 to 1974, the Tennessee Bar Association lobbied assiduously for an integrated bar,[238] that is, one in which lawyers would be required to be members of state and local bar associations. The Tennessee Supreme Court twice refused to issue such a mandate. In 1955, the Court noted that, at a time when about 61 percent of the state's thirty-six hundred lawyers were members of the state bar association, approximately 23 percent of state lawyers favored such integration, an equal number opposed, and the state legislature—the wishes of which were "entitled to much consideration in acting upon this petition"—also was opposed. Reviewing similar requests from other states, the Court noted that "[n]o State Supreme Court, in so far as this Court can find, has required integration of the bar in the face of these facts."[239] In a *per curiam* opinion rejecting petitions for integration again in 1972, the Court observed that the situation was "not materially different from that presented in 1955."[240]

Other Supreme Court decisions did confirm the right to discipline members of the bar who engaged in unethical or illegal conduct. Thus, in *Ex parte Chattanooga Bar Association* (1959), the Supreme Court ruled that a Chancery Court had jurisdiction over a lawyer's unethical conduct. It noted that its own authority over such matters "has never been thought of as denying to trial courts their inherent authority to discipline members of the Bar, or to entertain a motion by any lawyer, or any Bar Association, to investigate the unethical and unlawful practice of law."[241] In *Schoolfield v. TN. Bar Association of Chattanooga* (1961) the Court ruled that a judge who had been convicted of moral turpitude in a Senate impeachment trial that grew out of congressional investigations of the Teamsters Union and was presided over by Chief Justice Neil,[242] could be permanently disbarred.

Supreme Court decisions on the requirements for judges were inconsistent. In *Kivett v. Mason* (1947), the Court decided that an individual otherwise "learned in the law" but not "a practicing attorney" could not be barred from serving as County judge of Claiborne County.[243] Similarly, in *State v. Freshour* (1967) the Court ruled that a layman who is qualified, but not licensed, in the law could serve as a judge of the Court of General Sessions of Cooke County. However, in *La Fever v. Ware* (1963), the Court found it was reasonable to require that judges of the General Sessions Court in White County be "licensed attorneys." Viewing existing constitutional requirements as a minimum only, the Court ruled that "the Legislature possesses the necessary power and authority to add to these qualifications provided it does so on a reasonable basis."[244] *Kivett v. Mason* and *State v. Freshour* have been overturned, and statutes now require all judges to have passed the bar.[245]

PRELUDE TO THE ELECTION OF 1974

One of the Supreme Court's most dramatic cases occurred in *State v. Dunn* (1973) when the Court confronted a suit by two individuals both claiming a seat on that body. This case arose when Justice Larry Creson died on June 19, 1972. Acting under the newly enacted merit selection plan of 1971, a plan that appears to have been highly favored by lawyers,[246] Governor Winfield Dunn notified the newly created nine-person Appellate Court Nominating Commission of the vacancy and asked it to submit three names. The governor announced that he had appointed the only Republican, namely, Thomas F. Turley Jr., from among the three nominees. Although the vacancy occurred more than thirty days before the election, the governor did not, as required by law, order a new election to fill the vacancy. Robert L. Taylor, a former appellate judge, subsequently announced that he would be a write-in candidate in an election to be held on August 3. The governor denied Taylor's eligibility. Only 4,030 of 668,000 voters participated, but a majority of their ballots (3,301) went to Taylor and only 555 to Turley. The secretary of state subsequently issued Taylor a certificate of election, and he took the oath of office, but the governor also issued a commission appointing Turley from September 1, 1972, until September 1974. Although neither individual had taken a seat on the bench, both duly claimed their rights.

The Tennessee Supreme Court held that neither candidate was eligible. It decided that constitutional requirements for an election were "not self-executing."[247] Moreover, the function of such elections was to confirm or reject a nominee, not to elect altogether different individuals. Although finding that the Appellate Nominating Commission was unconstitutional because it contained members of the state legislature, who the Court thought were barred from such offices, the Court, as it generally did in such cases, simply elided this section of the law and saved the rest.

This decision featured a rare dissent by Justice Humphreys, which is probably the strongest articulation of judicial equality during the entire period.[248] Humphreys doubted the validity of the new judicial selection plan because he did not consider the voters' yes or no choice to be a genuine "election" as mandated by the Constitution:

> [B]y turning over to the Legislature the right to say how Supreme Court Judges shall be chosen, this Supreme Court abdicates its place as a coequal part of our tripartite state government, and subordinates itself to the Legislature. Of this subordination, there can be no doubt. Where once the Constitution protected this Court, and preserved it, it must now take its chances with the Legislature. Today the Plan provides for recall by majority vote. But this is only statutory, so what is to

> keep the Legislature from providing for recall by a different percentage. For that matter, what is to keep it from saying that a judge must be approved by an affirmative vote of such a percentage as will empty the Bench of its presently serving judges? If all of this is truly within the power of the Legislature, there is nothing to save this Court.[249]

Addressing a petition to rehear (petitions which almost inevitably failed during the entire time period under review), Justice McCanless offered clearer direction to the governor by saying that because no election had been held as required for the term beginning on September 1, 1972, a vacancy existed. Thus, the governor could now notify the Appellate Court Nominating Commission of the vacancy, receive nominees, and make an appointment. The governor complied. Although many observers expected the commission to renominate Turley, he withdrew, and Dunn named Judge William Fones of Memphis (an independent) to the slot.[250]

Meanwhile, the Legislature had been reconsidering whether Supreme Court justices should be exempt from the operation of the recently adopted Missouri Plan—a reconsideration that stemmed largely from partisan fears that, with the election of Governor Winfield Dunn, Republicans were about to gain control of the Court.[251] Although the Tennessee Bar Association opposed and Governor Dunn vetoed this dual system, the General Assembly readopted it over his veto. In developments outlined in the chapter that follows, voters subsequently elected the Democratic slate of candidates to the Supreme Court in the 1974 elections, thus preserving for a few more years the all-white, all-male, all-Democratic (excepting one independent) club.[252]

From 1946 to 1974, the Tennessee Supreme Court rarely blazed new trails. Its rulings reflected the generally conservative sentiments of the voting majority that prevailed during this period and which, through most of this time, underrepresented urban areas and African Americans.[253] The Supreme Court frequently exercised its powers to review decisions of the lower courts, but it was extremely deferential to the elective branches. Far from riding on the tide of the more liberal and activist national judiciary, the Supreme Court probably viewed itself as being swept along by its undertow. Too cognizant of its subordinate status and its constitutional obligations to engage in resistance, the Tennessee Supreme Court also was too concerned about the perceived negative effects on state sovereignty to celebrate the creation, expansion, and protection of new individual rights during this era.

7

THE TENNESSEE SUPREME COURT AND THE STRUGGLE FOR INDEPENDENCE, ACCOUNTABILITY, AND MODERNIZATION, 1974–1998

Carl A. Pierce

Article VI, Section 3 of the Constitution of Tennessee provides that the five justices of the Supreme Court shall be elected by the qualified voters of the state for eight-year terms. The requirement that the justices be elected is to assure their ultimate accountability to the people. Each of the newly elected justices is required by law to take an oath to "support the constitutions of the United States and that of this state, and to administer justice without respect of persons, and impartially to discharge all the duties incumbent on a judge . . . , to the best of the judge's skill and ability." This chapter portrays the history of the Supreme Court of Tennessee during the last quarter of the twentieth century in terms of the effort of the justices to abide by their oath of office when deciding important and often controversial cases and the effort of the General Assembly and the voters to figure out how to hold the justices accountable to the people.

The story begins in 1973–74, with Tennessee awkwardly adjusting to a new political era in which a Republican had been elected governor, with the

General Assembly repealing a never-used nonpartisan method for the election of Supreme Court justices, and with the voters then electing a slate of five white male candidates nominated by the Democratic Party—William J. Harbison, Joe W. Henry, Robert E. Cooper, Ray L. Brock Jr., and incumbent Justice William H. D. Fones. It then turns to an examination of the effort of these justices, and their successors, to mold new law relating to a variety of new issues confronting Tennessee in a quarter century during which its citizens were adjusting to a more evenly balanced two-party political process, a diversifying population, an expanding and changing economy, changing social values, a startling increase in crime, and the demands of black and female Tennesseans for equal opportunity.[1] The story ends in 1998 with the voters retaining five incumbent justices—Chief Justice E. Riley Anderson and Justice Frank F. Drowota III, both white male Democrats elected to the Court as Democratic Party candidates; Adolpho A. Birch Jr., a black male Democrat appointed by a Democratic governor and retained by the voters in the first nonpartisan Tennessee Plan retention election; Janice M. Holder, a white female Independent appointed by a Republican governor; and William M. (Mickey) Barker, a white male Republican appointed by a Republican governor—for an eight-year term, during which they would lead the Court into the twenty-first century. It is a story of change: new justices, new methods for striking the constitutionally required balance between judicial independence and public accountability, and numerous changes in Tennessee law and the administration of justice in the Volunteer State.[2]

SELECTING A NEW COURT, 1973–1974

In 1973, Tennessee lawyers and politicians began to focus their attention on the expiration of the terms of office of Chief Justice Ross W. Dyer, Justices Chester C. Chattin, Allison B. Humphreys, George F. McCanless, and a fifth justice who would soon be appointed by Republican governor Winfield Dunn to complete the unexpired term of Justice Larry Creson, who had died in 1972. They were aware that the selection of the justices to serve on the Court from 1974 to 1982 would be governed by a 1971 law, called the "Modified Missouri Plan," pursuant to which the incumbent justices could declare their candidacy for reelection and have their names submitted to the electorate, without party designation, for a yes-no vote as to whether they should be retained in office for another eight-year term. There would be no opposing candidate. If, however, any of the justices chose not to seek reelection, Governor Dunn would fill the vacancy by appointing one of three persons certified to him by a nonpartisan nominating commission as the "best qualified and available nominees." The names of the governor's appointees would then be submitted to the electorate, without party designation, for a nonpartisan retention vote. Again, there would be no opposing candidate on the ballot—simply the question as to whether the recently appointed justice should be retained in office.

What was novel about this situation was that the Democratic Party no longer had a role to play in the election of the justices and that, as a result of political realignments in the 1960s, Tennessee had a Republican governor. Expecting the retirement of Justices Chattin, Humphreys, and McCanless, Democratic politicians became concerned that Governor Dunn would appoint three Republicans to the Court who would then stand for election without there being anyone on the ballot for whom a Democrat could vote. The Democrats assumed that this new Republican majority on the Court would replace the incumbent attorney general, Democrat David Pack, with a Republican. Principle as well as politics was involved, however, because there remained considerable disagreement across party lines about whether the Modified Missouri Plan was the best way to "elect" judges.

Democrats in the General Assembly secured passage of a bill that repealed the Modified Missouri Plan as applied to the Supreme Court. The vote had a decidedly Democratic tilt but cut across party lines. Governor Dunn vetoed the bill and stated that he approved of the plan and could see no reason to retain the system for intermediate appellate courts and return to partisan elections for the Supreme Court. The General Assembly, however, voted to override the veto. It would once again be up to the Democratic and Republican Parties to nominate candidates to run for election to the Court.

Attention immediately turned to the question of how the candidates for the upcoming election would be chosen. For the state Democratic Party, Chairman James Sasser announced a major innovation in the way it would select its candidates. The party's executive committee appointed a fifteen-member blue-ribbon Judicial Selection Commission to make recommendations to the committee with respect to possible nominees for the Supreme Court seats. The commission's charge was to submit the names of not more than ten possible candidates to the executive committee, which, in turn, would select the party's candidates for the Court. To reduce political partisanship, the commission did not ask candidates to discuss their political affiliations or voting record but simply asked them to state that they desired to be Democratic nominees for the Court. After holding hearings, the commission recommended eight candidates to the executive committee: Chief Justice Dyer, Justice Fones, Court of Appeals Judge Robert Cooper of Chattanooga, Court of Criminal Appeals Judge Charles O'Brien, Chancellor

Ray Brock of Chattanooga, Nashville lawyers William Harbison and Virginia (Bonnie) Cowan, and Joseph W. Henry from Pulaski.

Voting was close in the executive committee. When the dust settled, the committee had selected Justice Fones as its candidate for the West Tennessee seat over former Court of Appeals Judge Robert Taylor, a staunch Democrat who had questioned Justice Fones's bona fides as a Democrat and who, in spite of his failure to secure the recommendation of the Judicial Selection Commission, had still vigorously sought the nomination. Harbison was tapped for the Middle Tennessee seat on the Court over Cowan. Judge Cooper prevailed over Chancellor Brock and Judge O'Brien in the contest for the East Tennessee seat in an outcome that surprised those who expected that Judge O'Brien would fare better because he was married to Annabelle Clement, the politically powerful sister of the late Democratic governor, Frank Clement. Henry prevailed over Cowan for one of the at-large seats, ending her bid to become Tennessee's first woman to serve as a justice of the Supreme Court. Finally, in an outcome that seemed to surprise everyone, Chancellor Brock was selected over Chief Justice Dyer. Newspaper reports described the sixty-three-year-old Dyer as "visibly shaken by the defeat." Other observers, however, had predicted that the chief justice was in danger of not being renominated because he lacked support among blacks due to his conservatism and had rankled some Democrats by his "familiarity" with the Dunn administration.[3]

Meanwhile, after an equally innovative but ultimately unsuccessful attempt to put together a "bipartisan" ticket that would include Chief Justice Dyer, Justice Fones, Harbison, and two East Tennessee Republicans, the Republican executive committee nominated Donald Hildebrand of Nashville to run against Harbison for the Middle Tennessee seat and Erma Greenwood of Knoxville and Allen Shoffner of Shelbyville to run against Chancellor Brock and Joe Henry for the two at-large seats on the Court. With her nomination, Erma Greenwood gained the distinction of being the first woman ever to stand for election to the Tennessee Supreme Court. The Republicans did not nominate candidates to run against Justice Fones for the West Tennessee seat or Judge Cooper for the East Tennessee seat. Several independent candidates also qualified to stand for election. As no one qualified to run against Justice Fones for the West Tennessee seat, the sole incumbent on the Court was assured reelection.

The five Democratic candidates campaigned together and conducted a five-week statewide tour in which they met with interested community groups. They also announced a ten-point campaign commitment to the bench and bar and to the public. They responded to some criticisms of the Court they hoped to replace by committing to read briefs prior to oral argument, to use law clerks to help them be better prepared for oral argument, and to establish new procedures for assigning cases among the justices. The goal of these reforms was to "guard against one-judge opinions" and to ensure that "all opinions reflect the collective thinking of the entire court." The Democratic nominees also called for revision of the Court rules to provide for a more orderly and expeditious processing of appeals to the Court and the simplification of the state's rules of appellate procedure. They declared they would use the Court's authority to balance unequal caseloads in the various judicial districts throughout the state. To this was added a commitment to carefully consider the adoption in Tennessee of the American Bar Association's Code of Judicial Conduct and to support mandatory retirement of judges at age seventy. Finally, the Democrats promised a more open system for selecting the attorney general.[4]

Although careful not to comment about specific issues that might come before the Court, the Democratic slate was portrayed as likely to be a "reasonably liberal" Court in the sense that it would be protective of civil rights and willing to "modernize" Tennessee law. Henry, for example, was characterized in the *Nashville Tennessean* as projecting a "decidedly liberal image" with respect to civil rights, reapportionment, and women's rights. He also thought that the Supreme Court should exercise "proper and effective leadership" in modernizing Tennessee's judicial system.[5] Similarly, William Harbison was portrayed as "pretty much in agreement" with the United States Supreme Court's views on the rights of persons accused of crime, such as affording a right to counsel to persons under interrogation. Harbison was also quoted as thinking that the Court should be reasonably liberal in developing law that would be more favorable to plaintiffs in civil rights cases, but that most changes in the law would have to be made by the legislature.[6]

Unlike the Democrats, the Republican candidates did not work together to produce a coordinated campaign. Only Erma Greenwood made a systematic effort to raise campaign funds, and she was the only Republican whose campaign bore any resemblance to the statewide tour of the Democrats. Nor did the Republican party rally to the cause of the three candidates. Not surprisingly, then, all the Democratic candidates won handily in the August election. Justice Fones, of course, ran without opposition. Judge Cooper garnered 81 percent of the vote in the race for the East Tennessee seat. In the only head-to-head contest between a Democrat and a Republican, Democrat William Harbison garnered 60 percent of the votes to easily defeat his Republican opponent. In the race for the at-large seats, Chancellor Brock was the leading vote getter with 174,845, followed by Henry with 127,775. Republicans Greenwood and Shoffner each attracted about 80,000 votes—well behind Brock and Henry.

Thus ended a remarkable seven-month political process that had begun with a partisan legislative vote in the House and Senate to exempt Supreme Court elections from the Modified Missouri Plan but was then followed by conscientious efforts of both political parties to restrain their partisan political impulses as they worked to select "the best qualified" persons to stand for election. The campaign lacked partisan spark, as the Democratic candidates emphasized their credentials rather than their party affiliation, and the Republican Party failed to provide meaningful support for its candidates. With this said, however, party-line voting surely played a role in the outcome. Perhaps the most noticeable feature of the election was the passivity of the voters, many of whom simply chose not to vote for the Supreme Court seats. In the end, however, most agreed that the outcome of this political process was the election of five well-qualified justices who would make their mark on the law and administration of justice in Tennessee. Those who favored contested elections for the election of Supreme Court justices saw the outcome as vindication of their views. Those who favored the nonpartisan Modified Missouri Plan breathed a sigh of relief but remained convinced that party politics and Supreme Court elections were a dangerous mix.

THE JUSTICES, 1974–1990

When the victorious Democrats assembled in Nashville to take their oaths of office, it was clear that this was a new Court. Only Justice Fones was a carryover, and he had been on the Court only a year. Prior to his appointment to the Supreme Court by Governor Dunn, the fifty-six-year-old Fones had practiced law in Memphis from 1945 until 1971, when he was appointed to serve as a Circuit Court judge in Memphis. Of the four new justices, Justices Cooper and Brock brought with them the most judicial experience. The fifty-three-year-old Cooper began his legal career in private practice in Chattanooga but soon thereafter embarked on a career of public service, first as an assistant district attorney from 1951 to 1953, then as a Circuit Court judge from 1953 to 1960, and then as a Court of Appeals judge from 1960 until his election to the Supreme Court. Justice Brock, fifty-two, had practiced law in Chattanooga until 1963, when he was appointed to the Chancery Court bench by Democratic governor Frank Clement. He had been reelected for an eight-year term in 1966. Justice Harbison, fifty-one, came to the Court from a distinguished career in private practice in Nashville. Finally, Justice Henry, fifty-seven, added both variety and spice to the Court. The self-proclaimed "country lawyer" from Pulaski had served in the General Assembly from 1948 to 1950 and then served as the adjutant general of Tennessee from 1953 to 1959. Henry was well known for his wit and rhetorical flourish. The justices selected Justice Fones as chief justice but decided to rotate the position among themselves with each justice to serve as chief justice for approximately nineteen months.

Justices Fones, Cooper, Brock, Harbison, and Henry served together until Justice Henry's untimely death in 1980. Shortly thereafter, Republican governor Lamar Alexander made history when he appointed George H. Brown Jr., a forty-one-year-old Memphis attorney who had served as co-chairman of Alexander's 1978 gubernatorial campaign, to fill the vacancy created by Justice Henry's death. Although he lacked judicial experience, Brown had previously served in public office, both as a director of the Federal Equal Opportunity Commission and as a longtime member of the Memphis Board of Education. Of greater significance in a state that was still adjusting to the civil rights movement, however, was the fact that George Brown Jr. was one of the relatively few black attorneys in Tennessee and that, upon taking his oath of office, he became Tennessee's first black Supreme Court justice and the first Republican to sit on the Court since Reconstruction.

Still to be determined by statewide election in August, however, was whether Tennessee voters would let Justice Brown serve out the remaining two years of Henry's term. The executive committee of the Republican Party endorsed Justice Brown as the party's nominee. Just as quickly, the Democrats named a seventeen-member "blue-ribbon" committee of party leaders and attorneys to help the party's executive committee select a candidate to run against Justice Brown. In the end, the executive committee tapped Judge Frank F. Drowota III as the party's candidate to run against Justice Brown. Drowota, forty-two, had practiced law from 1965 to 1970, when he was appointed to the Davidson County Chancery Court. He was named to the Court of Appeals in 1974.

In the ensuing campaign, Governor Alexander threw the full weight of his administration behind Brown. Both Brown and the governor emphasized the state's need for diversity on its Supreme Court and downplayed Brown's lack of judicial experience. Democratic U.S. senator James Sasser and the Democratic leadership waded in on the side of Judge Drowota and emphasized his eight year's experience as a judge. Then, on August 7, the voters ended Justice Brown's short tenure on the Supreme Court. Judge Drowota captured approximately 50 percent of the votes cast in the Supreme Court race to prevail over Brown, with 38 percent of the votes, and anti-pornography crusader Larry Parrish of Memphis, who ran as an Independent and garnered 12 percent of the statewide vote.

Justice Drowota took his seat on the Court in September 1980, and in 1982, the Democratic Party's executive committee nominated all of the incumbent justices to stand for reelection to the Court. The incumbent justices easily prevailed over their Republican opponents, the most noticeable feature

William J. Harbison, then chief justice of the Tennessee Supreme Court, speaking on election night, August 5, 1982, when the entire Democratic Party slate was elected. Also pictured are (from left) Judges Robert E. Cooper, Ray L. Brock Jr., William H. D. Fones, and Frank F. Drowota III, accompanied by his wife, Claire. Courtesy of Frank F. Drowota III.

of the election being that almost half of those who went to the polls did not vote in the Supreme Court election.

Justices Fones, Harbison, Cooper, Brock, and Drowota worked together until 1987 when Justice Brock, then sixty-five years old and bothered by health problems, announced his resignation from the Court. Democratic governor Ned McWherter nominated Court of Criminal Appeals Judge Charles O'Brien to take Justice Brock's seat on the Court. O'Brien had practiced law in Memphis from 1948 to 1967 and in Crossville from 1967 to 1970. Active in the Democratic Party, he served in the Eighty-third and Eighty-fourth General Assemblies and in 1970 was elected as the party's candidate for a seat on Court of Criminal Appeals. In 1974, after his unsuccessful bid to be one of the party's nominees for the Supreme Court, he had been reelected for a full eight-year term on the Court of Criminal Appeals. He was again reelected in 1982. In 1988, as required by state law, Justice O'Brien stood for election as the Democratic Party's nominee to complete Justice Brock's unexpired term and easily won reelection.

Thus the history of the Tennessee Supreme Court from 1974 to 1990 was the work of just seven men—Justices Fones, Harbison, and Cooper serving two full terms, Justice Brock serving with them for thirteen of those sixteen years, Justice Henry serving for the first six years and Justice Drowota the remaining ten years, and Justice O'Brien finishing out the last three years of the 1982–90 term. All had been elected to the Court as nominees of the Democratic Party.

MODERNIZING THE LAW AND THE ADMINISTRATION OF JUSTICE, 1974–1990

A unique and recurrently controversial constitutional responsibility of the Court is to appoint the state's attorney general. The Court's role is singular because Tennessee is the only state in which the attorney general is appointed by the Supreme Court, and it has been controversial because of complaints that this method of selecting the state's top legal officer is "undemocratic." After soliciting applications and using a new screening process, the justices appointed Ray A. Ashley of Dyersburg to serve an eight-year term as attorney general. The Court would repeat this task in 1976, when it named Brooks McLemore to succeed Ashley, and in 1978, when it named William M. Leech Jr. to succeed McLemore. In 1984, the Court named W. J. Michael Cody to succeed Leech and in 1987 appointed Charles Burson to serve until the end of the Court's term in 1990.

Only a relatively small portion of the cases heard by the Court afforded the justices a significant opportunity to "modernize" Tennessee law. A considerable part of its work consisted of the disposition of appeals that the Court was required by various statutes to hear. In 1980 and 1989, for example, 59 percent of the cases reviewed came to the Court by direct appeal. A significant portion of these cases were appeals from trial court decisions awarding or denying worker's compensation claims for on-the-job injuries. Some of these cases on direct appeal raised important issues, but many did not. The balance of the Court's workload consisted of cases chosen for review by the Court pursuant to its discretion to review decisions of the intermediate appellate courts by issuance of a writ of *certiorari*. In determining what cases it would review, the justices looked for issues of public importance, issues about which the courts of appeals could not agree, and issues not previously addressed by the courts. Yet, even given these criteria, most of the cases selected for review did not present much opportunity for the Court to make major changes in Tennessee jurisprudence. Although it is not possible to fully chronicle or evaluate this aspect of the Court's work, it seems fair to say that the justices took these cases seriously and resolved them in accordance with their best understanding of the law.

In spite of its heavy routine workload, the Court never lost sight of its aspirations to modernize Tennessee law in accordance with sound public policy and to improve the administration of justice in the state's trial and appellate courts. As Justice Fones recollected in 1995, "Those of us on the '74 Court felt we had to make up for 100 years of not bringing the law up to date."[7] When afforded the opportunity, the Court demonstrated its willingness to resolve difficult and controversial legal issues that implicated important constitutional, political, and social values, and, within the scope of its constitutional authority, to reshape Tennessee law as the justices thought was in the best interest of the state. The justices also evidenced that they were not always of one mind either about what the law was, or should be, or, as would sometimes be the case, about whether it was appropriate for the Court, rather than the General Assembly, to make the change in question. With respect to the judicial system, for which it felt a special responsibility, the Court made a sustained effort to wield its constitutional authority and political influence to bring about seriously needed changes in the structure of the system and the rules by which the judicial process was governed. It is these cases and initiatives for which the 1974–90 Court will be remembered.

Guardian of the Constitution

One of the Court's most important and sometimes controversial roles was as the final interpreter of the Tennessee Constitution. With respect to freedom of religion, for example, the Court held in *State ex rel. Swann v. Pack* (1975) that the state could enjoin a religious group from handling poisonous snakes as part of its religious service on the ground that such action constituted a public nuisance. In connection with the election of a Baptist minister from Chattanooga as a delegate to the 1977 Constitutional Convention, the Court, over a dissent by Justice Brock, held in *Paty v. McDaniel* (1977) that Tennessee's constitutional prohibition against ministers and priests serving in the legislature did not abridge their freedom of religion in violation of the First Amendment of the United States Constitution. Writing for the majority, Justice Fones held that the prohibition against legislative service was justified by the state's compelling interest in preserving the separation between church and state. Justice Brock's dissent was ultimately vindicated, however, when the United States Supreme Court in *McDaniel v. Paty* (1978) unanimously invalidated Tennessee's constitutional prohibition against ministers and priests serving in the General Assembly.

As the General Assembly and Tennessee's police and prosecutors waged a legal war against pornography, the justices came face-to-face with the sexual revolution that was trying to establish a toehold in the state. The Court first sustained the constitutionality of an obscenity statute passed by the General Assembly in 1974 against claims that it was so vague as to violate Article I, Section 19 of the Tennessee Constitution and the First Amendment to the U.S. Constitution. In *Taylor v. Kirkpatrick* (1975), the Court specifically approved the statute's definition of "patently offensive" and "obscene." Having viewed the films in question, the justices had no hesitation in branding them "grossly obscene" and "hard core pornography." But

The practice of handling poisonous snakes as part of religious services posed constitutional questions for the Tennessee Supreme Court concerning the free exercise of religion. Photograph courtesy of the Nashville Tennessean.

in *News Mart Inc. v. State* (1978), the Court held that an injunction restraining the exhibition of obscene movies that did not name or specifically describe the movies that could not be exhibited was not authorized by the statute, but if it was, it would be an unconstitutional prior restraint on the freedom of expression. To avoid a chilling effect on legitimate speech, pornography would have to be prohibited with specificity.

Not satisfied with the legal vigor with which Tennessee's legal war against smut was being waged, the General Assembly passed the Tennessee Obscenity Act of 1978. Not long thereafter, the Court was asked to declare the act unconstitutional as an abridgment of the freedom of speech. Discussing what he called the "intractable obscenity problem," Justice Fones indicated in *Leech v. American Booksellers* (1979) that the Court could not permit the General Assembly to impose greater restrictions on freedom of speech than allowed by the United States Supreme Court and invalidated the 1978 act. Such was not the fate, however, of a Chattanooga ordinance that prohibited females from appearing in a public place so costumed that one or both breasts were wholly or substantially exposed to public view. In response to a claim that the statute was unconstitutionally overbroad, the Court in *City of Chattanooga v. McCoy* (1983) refused to invalidate the statute because its overbreadth was "minimal and insignificant." Although willing to protect artistic, socially redeeming expression of ideas that involved some nudity, Justice Fones insisted it was a "travesty to allow nude and crude public exhibitors of the human body the privilege of asserting the rights of persons who contribute to society's permanent values and are entitled to First Amendment protection and to read into a public indecency statute an intent to suppress free speech and oppression." The Court had reached the limits of its tolerance for use of the First Amendment to protect conduct that local legislators thought violated standards of decency in their community.

Tennesseans also challenged several other significant legislative initiatives as violating their freedom of speech. In *Dorrier v. Dark* (1976), the Court rejected a claim that Tennessee's new experiment with openness in government—the Open Meetings Act—had a chilling effect on the speech of those governmental officials who could no longer talk behind closed doors. Then in *Bemis Pentecostal Church v. State* (1987), it also turned back a First Amendment attack on the Campaign Financial Disclosure Act of 1980, holding that the state had a compelling interest in protecting the integrity of the electoral process and that the limited financial disclosure requirements were narrowly tailored to further that interest. On the other hand, the Court protected the free-speech rights of telephone solicitors and the charities on for which they were calling. In *WRG Enterprises v. Crowell* (1988), it declared unconstitutional those parts of Tennessee's Solicitation of Charitable Funds Act that prohibited all telephonic solicitation and limited solicitor's compensation to not more than 15 percent of the contributions. It also invalidated a provision in the state's sales tax that taxed mail order sales of magazine subscriptions but exempted mail order sales of subscriptions to newspapers that contained matters of general interest and reports of current events. The Court held in *Newsweek Inc. v. Celauro* (1990) that the differential application of the sales tax was a content-based burden on free speech. If the General Assembly wanted to tax mail order subscriptions for magazines, it would have to tax mail order subscriptions of newspapers as well. Then in its final opinion addressing free speech, the Court, over the dissent of Justice Fones in *Freeman v. Burson* (1990), invalidated a statute banning solicitation of voters within one hundred feet of a polling place. A suggestion in the majority's opinion that a ban limited to twenty-five feet might pass constitutional muster prompted Justice Fones to note the seventy-five-foot difference, to estimate that it would take about fifteen seconds to walk such a distance, and to observe that "if the electorate of Tennessee is dependent on the free speech available 15 seconds before they enter the polling place, to cast an informed ballot, God help us." Subsequently, in *Burson v. Freeman* (1992), the United States Supreme Court reversed the Court's decision and upheld the one-hundred-foot limit as necessary to secure a compelling state interest in preserving the secrecy of the ballot.

As the guardian of a Tennessean's right to be free from unreasonable searches and seizures, as stated in the Fourth Amendment to the U.S. Constitution and Article I, Section 7 of the Tennessee Constitution, the Court had a major role in Tennessee's war against the illegal drug trafficking that was at the root of an exploding crime rate in the state. Most of the Court's cases concerning search and seizure involved drugs. In one line of cases, the Court set forth the legal boundaries restricting the right of the police to conduct warrantless searches. Because there were "no exigent circumstances," the Court in *Fuqua v. Armour* (1976) would not permit a warrantless seizure and subsequent search of a vehicle car parked at the house where an alleged drug dealer was arrested, even though the automobile was subject to forfeiture under the provisions of the Drug Control Act of 1971. In *Drinkard v. State* (1979), the Court held that the police could not seize and subsequently inventory the contents of a car driven by a defendant who was stopped for drunk driving, but who was not suspected of any other crime and had authorized his passenger to drive the car home. While there was just cause to arrest the driver, there was not reasonable cause to take the car into custody, too. In yet another case involving marijuana, the Court in *Hughes v. State* (1979) applied the United States Supreme Court's "stop-and-frisk" doctrine to suppress evidence obtained after two college students were stopped by police officers who were not aware of any specific facts warranting the stop. As the police began to target Tennessee's marijuana farmers, the Court was asked to determine the limits imposed by the Constitution on warrantless entry onto a farmer's property. Although acknowledging "the difficulty police officers have in enforcing the law against clandestine illegal activity," the Court concluded in *State v. Lakin* (1979) that "obtaining a search warrant does not ordinarily impose insurmountable difficulties, particularly in the absence of an emergency." It adhered to prior Tennessee cases that the Court acknowledged imposed more restrictions on the police than were being imposed by the federal courts when they applied the Fourth Amendment in similar situations and held that normally a search warrant would be required for a search of occupied, fenced private property, as distinct from "wild and wasteland" that might be "roamed at will without a search warrant." Although conceding that the Fourth Amendment and Article I, Section 7 ordinarily should be construed alike, the Court did not think it appropriate to depart from settled Tennessee precedent unless that precedent was demonstrably in error. In *State v. Roode* (1982), on the other hand, the Court held that aerial surveillance of a marijuana field was not a search with the meaning of the Fourth Amendment because farmers do not generally expect that their cultivated fields will be shielded from aerial view, and there were exigent circumstances that justified the warrantless entry that followed after the pilot reported his discovery. In *State v. Hendrix* (1989), a divided Court ruled that a warrantless search and seizure could be justified by exigent circumstances caused by actions of police officers who had probable cause to secure a search warrant, but did not do so. Justices Fones, Harbison, Cooper, and O'Brien held that the seizure did not violate the constitutional rights of the defendants so long as none of the actions causing the exigent circumstances were illegal. Justice Drowota dissented, believing that the majority opinion "erodes the constitutional protections afforded by the Fourth Amendment" by allowing the police to circumvent the constitutional requirement that searches be conducted pursuant to warrants issued by a neutral judicial officer.

Other cases called into question the validity of search warrants that had been secured by the police in connection with their investigation of criminal activity. In *State v. Little* (1978), the Court held that an affidavit sufficient on its face to justify issuance of a warrant could be challenged if it contained any intentionally false information or a false statement that was essential to the establishment of probable cause. "To hold otherwise," the Court said, "would effectively destroy the protections against unreasonable searches and seizures." In *State v. Melson* (1982), on the other hand, the Court rejected a claim that the affidavit was insufficient because it did not establish the credibility or reliability of what several persons had told the police officer and that only one of those persons was identified as a reliable source. The Court differentiated between citizen witnesses and typical criminal informants or tipsters and did not require a specific showing of credibility when a police officer reported information obtained from ordinary citizens. Although it upheld the affidavit, the Court admonished law enforcement officials to take more care when drafting affidavits in the future. The final chapter in this part of the Court's history came, however, when the Court in *State v. Jacumin* (1989) declared that in cases involving police informants it would adhere as a matter of Tennessee constitutional law to what was known as the United States Supreme Court's "*Spinelli-Aguilar* test" for determining the sufficiency of an affidavit based on the statements of police informants. It did so even though the Supreme Court itself had rejected the test in favor of a more flexible inquiry into the "totality of circumstances." While supportive of Tennessee's war on crime, the Court took seriously its responsibility to define and enforce the constitutional rules by which the war had to be waged.

The Court also became a major player in Tennessee's economy by interpreting and enforcing Tennessee's constitutional limitation on the General Assembly's authority to legalize an interest rate in excess of 10 percent. This legal limit was creating problems in Tennessee's financial markets because inflationary pressures had caused market interest rates on a variety of loans to rise above the legal limit. Capital was flowing away from Tennessee, and this was retarding the state's economic growth. Not surprisingly, lenders and borrowers had begun looking for ways to avoid the 10 percent limit. In *Cumberland Capital Corporation v. Patty* (1977), the Court held that discounting practices and services and maintenance fees that were authorized by Tennessee's Industrial Loan and Thrift Companies Act, and had been used to generate a rate of return on loans in excess of 10 percent, would be unconstitutional if they resulted in an effective interest rate in excess of 10 percent. This holding not only invalidated one of the most commonly used techniques to evade the interest cap but also made it clear that the Court would not tolerate any more creative evasion of the Constitution. After noting that Article XI, Section 7 had been criticized for its "fixed rigidity," Justice Henry explained, "We do not test legislative enactments by our conception of morality or merit. Our sole duty is to ensure that legislation complies with mandates of our Constitution. Nor are we privileged to sit in judgment on the merits of constitutional provisions. We may only construe and abide them and mandate they be respected." Informed that the constitutional limit on interest rates would be enforced by the Court, those seeking higher interest rates took a leadership role in securing the adoption and ratification of an amendment to the Constitution that would allow the General Assembly to set the legal interest rate as it deemed appropriate. Ironically, in this instance it was the Court's insistence on adherence to the old law—the 1870 Constitution—that led to its modernization.

In 1989, the Court found itself in the middle of another controversial issue: charitable bingo. Bingo had become a major source of revenue for numerous churches and other charitable organizations. At the same time, however, many Tennesseans were opposed to gambling, even if for a good cause. In *Secretary of State v. St. Augustine Church* (1989), the Court held that bingo was a lottery within the meaning of Article XI, Section 5 of the Tennessee Constitution that deprives the General Assembly of power to authorize "lotteries for any purpose." Although acknowledging the political controversy over bingo, the Court expressed no opinion about the desirability of legalizing bingo or any other form of gambling. It was convinced, however, that bingo as traditionally played, no matter how defined or whether played for charitable purposes, was a lottery prohibited by the Tennessee Constitution. If Tennesseans wanted to legalize bingo, they would have to amend their Constitution.

Modernizing the Law

Between 1974 and 1990, the Court made major changes in Tennessee's common law. It was this body of judge-made law that many thought needed modernization in light of the numerous changes in Tennessee's social and economic circumstances. During the 1970s and 1980s, for example, Tennessee was experiencing rapid social change, particularly with respect to gender roles. When the justices took office, considerable gender bias could still be found in Tennessee law. The Court stuck its first blow for gender equality in *Robinson v. Trousdale* (1974) when it held that a husband's unilateral sale of property he owned jointly with his wife as tenants by the entirety was ineffective to convey his wife's interest. The case implicated Tennessee's Married Women's Property Act of 1913, which abolished the common-law doctrine of coverture that legally disabled the wife from acquiring or disposing of real property independently of the husband and enabled the husband to use and dispose of the property without the wife's consent. The statute had been amended in 1919 so that it would not abolish the common law tenancy by the entirety that conferred upon the husband the exclusive right to use or sell real property held in this form of ownership. Justice Henry, writing for a unanimous Court, completed the abolition of coverture. "We do not believe that the common law disability of coverture has any sanction in our jurisprudence or any relevance in our society," he wrote. "At best it is outmoded; at worst oppressive and degrading." Justices Henry and Brock wanted to hold that coverture was a sex-based classification that violated the equal protection clause of the United States Constitution and the "law of the land" provision of the Tennessee Constitution. Chief Justice Fones and Justices Harbison and Cooper, however, chose to abide by a traditional judicial policy of avoiding constitutional questions where their resolution was not necessary to decide the case before the Court.

The Court next spoke out in favor of gender equality when it unanimously held in *Dunn v. Palermo* (1975) that a woman is not required upon marriage to assume her husband's surname. Noting that the common law was not static and immutable but "in constant growth, going through mutations in adapting itself to changing conditions and in improving and refining doctrine . . . [in a quest for] . . . perfection in the achievement of justice," Justice Henry rejected the argument that continuing force of law should be given to the admittedly longstanding custom of women adopting their husbands' surnames. "We live in a new day," Justice Henry declared, and to rely on old customs as a source of legal obligations "would stifle and chill virtually all progress in the rapidly expanding field of human liberties."

Although clearly inclined toward legal equality of the sexes, the Court remained cognizant of its role as an appellate court and the need to base its decisions on an adequate record of the proceedings in the lower courts. Thus, lacking such a record in *Scharff v. State* (1977), a majority of the justices refused to resolve a constitutional challenge to Tennessee statutes that required judges to exempt from jury duty any woman who requested an exemption. Writing for the Court, however, Justice Fones was willing to say that the constitutionality of these statutes was "highly suspect." Justice Henry, however, saw no need for such caution. "The time has come," he said, "for us to stop whispering and whistling about the constitutionality of . . . [these statutes] . . . and to say flat-footedly that . . . [they] . . . are unconstitutional." Such statutes, he insisted, are "a throw-back to the now wholly discredited belief that a 'woman's place is in the home'" and only serve as "a subtle form of anti-feminism under which women are denied a portion of their rights as citizens."

The Court's push for gender equality in the common law or as a constitutional entitlement did not always redound to a woman's benefit. For example, it was a male who benefited when the Court held in *Davis v. Aetna Life and Casualty Co.* (1980) that the differing treatment of widows and widowers under the worker's compensation statute was unconstitutional. A widow was given the benefit of a conclusive presumption that she was dependent on her husband's earnings, but a widower was required to prove his dependence on his wife's earnings. As had the United States Supreme Court, the Court held that such discriminatory treatment could not be justified by the cost savings associated with a presumption that a wife would be dependent on her husband's wages. Rather than invalidate the presumption for widows, however, the Court approved the lower court's decision to extend the presumption of dependency to widowers. The Court's commitment to gender equality also led it to impose new duties upon married women. It declared in *Kilbourne v. Hanzelik* (1983) that the common-law rule that husbands, but not wives, could be held liable for necessaries provided to their spouses "defies logic and denies justice" and "cannot pass constitutional muster under the equal protection guarantees of the state and federal constitutions." With legal equality came duties as well as rights.

As Tennessee's population grew and became more concentrated in cities and suburbs, there was a comparable increase of the number of situations in which negligent conduct resulted in personal injury. Such injuries led to requests that the Court reject tort law precedent that barred recovery in what plaintiffs thought were meritorious cases. Such cases afforded the Court a number of opportunities to reevaluate and to make major changes in Tennessee tort law. The Court, for example, promptly indicated its dislike for immunities from liability for negligence. In *Johnson v. Oman Construction Company* (1975), the Court attacked the extension of the state's governmental immunity to local governments as "an anachronism and as at variance with modern concepts of justice." Because, however, the General Assembly had recently enacted legislation dealing with some aspects of governmental tort liability, the Court decided to afford the lawmakers some additional time to remedy what the Court saw as a serious flaw in Tennessee law. "We are reluctant," Justice Fones wrote, "to take judicial action in this area . . . without giving the General Assembly an opportunity to establish a comprehensive and uniform tort claims procedure governing suits against cities, counties, and other political subdivisions or their agencies in the duly constituted courts of the state." When the issue came up again in *Cooper v. Rutherford County* (1975), Justices Fones, Harbison, and Cooper noted that the General Assembly had made additional progress in addressing the problem and held once again that it "would be inappropriate for us to judicially accelerate the tort liability of counties in the present and prospective state of the law." Justices Henry and Brock, on the other hand, were unwilling to await further legislative action. Calling governmental immunity "a cankered, corroded and corrupted area of our law," Justice Henry thought the Court should "condemn this legal monstrosity to the oblivion which it so richly deserves." The majority's patience was rewarded when further legislative action in 1976 and 1980 made it unnecessary for the Court to modernize Tennessee's law in this regard.

The Court was also asked to reconsider the long-accepted principle of interspousal immunity that precludes husbands and wives from suing each other for negligence. After first cutting away at the doctrine, the Court "totally abolished" all interspousal tort immunity in *Davis v. Davis* (1983). Justice Brock, with the concurrence of Justices Drowota and Cooper, noted that the doctrine had been derived from the nineteenth-century concept that husband and wife were a unity. The Court held that "the legal abstraction of unity, now a historical oddity rather than a functioning concept of law, is no longer available to support retention of interspousal immunity." The majority also noted "the high cost exacted by the rule because of the absolute bar it places in the path of potentially meritorious claims." Justice Harbison and Special Justice Humphreys dissented in the belief that any changes in the law with respect to interspousal immunity should be made by the legislature and that the majority's decision would weaken the family unit.

In addition, the Court took action to liberalize the law with respect to statutes of limitation that required injured persons to file their claims within a specified period of time or be barred from doing so. In *Teeters v. Curry* (1974), for example, the Court held that the statute of limitations in a medical malpractice case begins to run only when the patients discover or should reasonably have discovered the injury suffered as the result of the malpractice. Prior decisions had held that the cause of action accrued when the negligent act occurred rather than when the injury was discovered. Subsequently, the General Assembly enacted the Medical Malpractice Review Board and Claims Act of 1975, which, among other things, provided that the statute of limitation would in certain circumstances run from the date on which the negligent act or omission occurred. The Court subsequently upheld the constitutionality of this statute in *Harrison v. Schrader* (1978). Although the Court clearly was willing to use its common-law powers to adjust legal rules, it deferred to the ultimate authority of the legislature to override the common law.

The Court also reshaped the law governing liability for intentional and or negligent conduct that causes injury to person or property. In *Street v. Calvert* (1976), the Court relegated to the "ash heap" Tennessee's "conflicting" case law with respect to "last clear chance," an exception to the rule that a person who is contributorily negligent cannot sue a person whose negligence was the primary cause of the injury. In its place, the Court adopted the modern formulation of the doctrine as set forth in the American Law Institute's Restatement of Torts. The Court also considered abolishing contributory negligence and replacing it with a rule of comparative negligence, as had been done in many other states. It chose not to do so, however, because it would be a major change in Tennessee law, and the issue had not been raised either at trial or in the Court of Appeals. Although wanting to modernize the law, the Court was unwilling to do so at the expense of an orderly judicial process through which the issues in question could be fully argued. Still committed to "the right of . . . innocent victims of wrongful conduct to seek recompense at the hands of the wrongdoer," however, it cut back on contributory negligence in several cases. In *Cole v. Woods* (1977), for example, the Court overruled prior case law that would impute a driver's contributory negligence to a passenger just because the passenger owned the car and was presumed to have the right to control the driver. Then in *Arnold v. Hayslett* (1983), the Court clarified that "remote contributory negligence" of the plaintiff would not bar all recovery, but would only result in a reduction in the damage award. A broader assault on contributory negligence, however, would have to await the 1990s.

The Court likewise rejected or revised other aspects of Tennessee's common law so as to increase the likelihood that persons injured by wrongful conduct would be able to secure compensation from the wrongdoer. In *Velsicol Chemical Corp. v. Chattanooga Coke & Chemicals Co.* (1976), the justices held that a person who had suffered an indivisible injury because of the concurrent, but independent, wrongful acts or omissions of two or more wrongdoers, could recover the full amount of the damages from any of the wrongdoers. The Court thought the new rule was "more consonant with modern legal thought and pragmatic concepts of justice." In *Olson v. Molzen* (1977), the Court adopted a new test to determine when public policy required the invalidation of a contract limiting one's liability for negligence and held that an exculpatory clause signed by a patient as a condition of receiving medical treatment was contrary to public policy. In *Hudson v. Gaitan* (1984), the Court also rejected a long-accepted common-law rule that a landowner was not liable for ordinary negligence that caused injury to licensees, such as social guests, as distinct from invitees, who come onto the premises for a business purpose. It held that the landowner must in all cases use such care as is reasonable under all the attendant circumstances, with foreseeability of the presence of the visitor and the likelihood of harm to him being the primary factors in assessing liability.

Although the Court made many changes in Tennessee tort law that expanded the rights of those injured by negligent conduct, a majority of Court could not always be mustered to do so. In *Cornpropst v. Sloan* (1975), for example, the Court, with Justice Henry dissenting, refused to impose a duty on the owners or operators of a shopping center to protect their customers against criminal acts of third persons, unless they knew or had reason to know that such acts were occurring or were about to occur. The majority thought that it would be unfair to impose upon the "shopkeepers and merchants" of Tennessee a vague duty to protect their customers against criminal acts of unknown and unidentified persons. They rejected the notion that a different rule should apply to shopping centers. Justice Henry, on the other hand, thought that the emergence of shopping centers had rightfully "opened a new vista into the concept of tort liability of the owners, occupiers and possessors of public business premises." Given that the goal of shopping centers is to attract large numbers of shoppers in relatively compact areas, Henry thought that the shopping center and store owners should be required to act reasonably to protect their customers against crimes likely to occur in such an environment.

In *Barranco v. Jackson* (1985), the Court could not agree about the propriety of departing from common-law precedent. When the Court's earlier decisions abolishing interspousal immunity spurred a challenge to the common-law rule granting parents immunity from suit by their children, Justice Harbison, with the concurrence of Justice Cooper and Special Justice F. Lloyd Tatum, tersely explained that "there are substantial differences between the parent-child relationship and that of spouses" and that "in the opinion of the majority, the rule . . . has continuing vitality and should be adhered to unless modified or changed by action of the General Assembly." Justices Drowota and Brock dissented. Unlike the terse opinion of the majority, Justice Drowota presented a comprehensive analysis of the reasons for parental immunity and the modern trend throughout the country to either limit or abolish the immunity. For the moment, and for this issue, anyway, the Tennessee Supreme Court would buck rather than embrace the modern trend.

The Court also refused to break new legal ground when, in *Smith v. Gore* (1987), it unanimously refused to permit a woman who had given birth after her doctor had negligently failed to effectuate her sterilization to recover the costs of rearing the child whose birth she had wanted to prevent. The Court applied traditional principles of tort law to hold that the doctor could be liable for the damages associated with the child's birth, including recovery for pain and suffering, emotional distress, lost wages, and punitive damages. The Court balked, however, at awarding as damages the costs of rearing the child because of the state's longstanding public policy, reflected in a variety of statutes and the state's common law, requiring parents to be responsible for the support of their children. Central to its holding was the Court's understanding of the limitations on its role in declaring public policy. Justice Drowota explained that the Court's role was not to declare what the state's public policy should be, but rather to decide whether there was any controlling public policy reflected in the state's Constitution, statutes, or the common law and, if there was, to apply that policy to the case before it. Where the Court could identify a controlling public policy or identify competing public policies pertinent to an issue before it, the Court would not create new law. To do so, the Court explained, was very different than finding that there was no public policy opposed to a proposed modification by the Court of a common-law rule in response to changing social circumstances. Mindful of the economic realities of raising a child and the hardship likely to result from its holding, the Court nonetheless insisted that the General Assembly was the proper body to reconcile the competing social policies. This case served as a major statement by the Court that it would not engage in "judicial legislation."

In addition to its decisions altering Tennessee's tort law, the Court also made a significant change in Tennessee's contract law. In *Dixon v. Mountain City Construction Company* (1982), for example, the Court noted the dramatic increase since World War II of the sales of newly constructed homes and the inability of the typical purchaser to ascertain defects in the construction. It then aligned itself with those states that had recognized that "the home buying public has a legitimate expectation that the workmanship and materials used by a builder-vendor in the construction of the dwelling will meet the standard of the trade for homes in comparable locations and price range and that such a warranty is implicit in the contract and survives the passing of title to the real estate and the taking of possession." Although such an implied warranty could be modified or eliminated in the contract of sale, the Court's decision made a major change in the law governing the purchase of new homes.

With respect to employment relationships, however, the Court was unwilling to change Tennessee's long-established common-law rule that an employee-at-will could be fired without cause unless there was a clear constitutional or legislative policy that warranted an exception to the rule. Still, in *Clanton v. Cain-Sloan Company* (1984), the Court recognized for the first time a cause of action for retaliatory discharge in a case in which an at-will employee was fired because she had filed a worker's compensation claim. The Court held that recognizing a cause of action for retaliatory discharge was necessary to effectuate the legislature's intent in adopting the worker's compensation statute. The Court did not, however, question the viability of the common-law rule. It merely saw itself as carrying out the clearly implied will of the General Assembly. The Court confirmed that it would not mount an assault on the employment-at-will doctrine when it noted in *Chism v. Mid-South Milling Company Inc.* (1988) that it could not permit exceptions to "consume" the rule and would only allow recovery for wrongful discharge if the employer had violated a "clear public policy" evidenced by "an unambiguous constitutional, statutory or regulatory provision" and the violation was a "substantial factor" in the discharge.

Many of the Court's significant decisions expanding the rights of women involved married women. Implicated in these decisions, of course, was the family—a social institution the state sought to protect through its "family law." Amid widespread social change affecting the family during the 1970s and 1980s, the Court was frequently asked to resolve disputes between parents, between parents and their children, and between parents and the state. Resolution of these disputes required the Court to reevaluate whether Tennessee law was consistent with modern thinking about how best to provide legal support for the state's most important social institution.

With more Tennesseans seeking divorces, the Court, as well as the General Assembly, was asked to reconsider Tennessee's law governing divorce, custody, alimony, and child support. For example, in two cases in 1977, a year in which the General Assembly first approved the granting of divorce on the grounds of "irreconcilable differences," the Court interpreted Tennessee's divorce laws with an awareness of the modern trend to make it easier for an unhappy couple to end a failed marriage. Rather than require a wife who had pleaded cruel and inhuman treatment to start over again and file for divorce specifically alleging adultery or desertion, the Court held in *Farrar v. Farrar* (1977) that the husband's adultery could constitute cruel and inhuman treatment. Accepting the traditional public policy of sheltering the institution of marriage, the Court also noted the "obverse side to the coin of public policy" and gave equal consideration to the fact that "society is ill-served by a legally commanded continuance of a marriage which exists in name only." Then, in *Chastain v. Chastain* (1977), the Court reversed a judgment denying a divorce on the grounds of abandonment to a wife who had engaged in an adulterous affair after her husband had left her. By a vote of three to two, the Court held that the wife's adultery did not bar her from obtaining a divorce on the grounds that her husband had abandoned her. The majority again noted the problems that could result by leaving a couple legally bound to each other when, as evidenced by the misconduct of both, the marriage was beyond salvage. Justices Harbison and Cooper dissented, believing that the principle of recrimination, whether or not socially desirable or practically sound, was deeply embedded in the jurisprudence of the state and that trial courts should have the equitable discretion to deny a divorce to an adulteress. This disagreement among the justices persisted into the 1980s, but the Court did rule in *Fisher v. Fisher* (1983) that the respective fault of the parties who were granted a divorce was not relevant to the division of their jointly owned property.

Just as Tennessee was experiencing a growth in the number of marriages that ended in divorce, it was also experiencing a dramatic increase in the number of children being born out of wedlock. Hence, the Court was called upon to address questions about the legal rights of the illegitimate children as well as the legal procedures used to determine paternity and to compel payment of child support. In *Allen v. Harvey* (1978), the Court rejected the last vestiges of the common-law rule that a child born out of wedlock could not inherit from either of the natural parents. Although indicating that a higher standard of proof of paternity could be demanded, the Court rejected the common-law ban and permitted inheritance from the father where the father acknowledged paternity or it could be established by clear and convincing evidence. While not condoning "irresponsible liaisons beyond the bonds of marriage," the Court was unwilling to penalize the innocent offspring for sins of the parents.

The judges were also drawn into the state's efforts to establish the paternity of illegitimate children and compel payment of support when it was asked to determine the constitutionality of a statute that provided that the alleged father in a paternity proceeding "shall not be compelled to give evidence." In *Department of Human Services v. Vaughn* (1980), a divided Court found the statute unconstitutional—a decision that prompted a vigorous dissent by Justices Harbison and Cooper. Justice Henry held that the statutes exempting the alleged father, but not the mother, from the obligation to testify in a paternity action violated the Equal Protection Clause of the Fourteenth Amendment of the United States Constitution and the "Law of the Land" provision of Article I, Section 8 of the Tennessee Constitution. He blasted the statute as "a blatant declaration of male supremacy, male chauvinism at its very worst, and a throwback to the days when laws were made by men and for men." Concurring, Justice Brock saw the rule as depriving the mother of procedural due process of law by denying her access to needed testimony without good cause. In dissent, Justices Harbison and Cooper did not think it was appropriate for the Court to resolve the constitutional question. Conceding that there would be an equal protection problem if the statute in question applied to both men and women, Harbison explained that the paternity statute applied only to suits against men alleged to be fathers of illegitimate children. "Regardless of the miracles of modern science," he explained, "within the purview of the statutes under consideration, paternity can only be accomplished by one of the male sex."

Given the increasing mobility of Tennessee's population, the Court also was faced with disputes between ex-spouses about the plans of the custodial parent to move out of the state and take the children with them. The Court charted a new legal course for Tennessee when, in *Seessel v. Seessel* (1988), it restricted the substantial discretion traditionally afforded the custodial parent to determine where the child would be raised. For the first time, the Court endorsed the use of the "best interest of the child" standard in removal cases and required that the custodial parent establish that the move would benefit the child. The Court did not, however, articulate clear guidelines for the lower courts to follow when determining whether a move would be in the best interest of the child.

The Supreme Court also grappled with a number of significant issues relating to Tennessee's criminal law, including crimes against nature, the insanity defense, entrapment, probation, and sentencing, including the death penalty. Not long after taking office, the Court was faced with the question of whether Tennessee's statute prohibiting "crimes against nature" was unconstitutionally vague. In *Young v. State* (1975), the Court reaffirmed its prior holdings that oral sex was a crime against nature and held that the statute was not impermissibly vague in violation of Article I, Section 8 of the Tennessee Constitution. Indicating its awareness that attitudes with regard to sexuality were changing, however, the Court specifically indicated that it was making no judgment about the constitutionality of the statute were it to be applied to private consensual sexual acts engaged in by adults or practices pursued in private within the framework of the marital relationship. The Court also invited the legislature to take a fresh look at the 150-year-old "crime against nature" statute. "Such a re-evaluation," Justice Henry wrote, "in light of modern mores and morality, would be in the public interest and would be of substantial interest in the administration of criminal justice."

The Court also broke new ground in *Graham v. State* (1977), in which it unanimously rejected the traditional M'Naghten Rule that defined the insanity defense in terms of whether the defendant both knew right from wrong and knew the nature and quality of his act. Viewing the M'Naghten Rule as "at variance with current medical theories of mental illness," the

Court replaced it with the rule proposed by the American Law Institute in its Model Penal Code. The new rule defined the insanity defense in terms of a mental disease or defect that deprived the defendant of the capacity to either appreciate the wrongfulness of his conduct or to conform his behavior to the law. The Court thought that the new standard was in harmony with the federal rule, as well as the rule in force in a significant number of other states, that it would be easier for juries to understand, and that, ultimately, it was "more in keeping with the demand of contemporary jurisprudence and more consonant with considerations of justice." Also, in a series of cases involving mentally ill criminal defendants, Justices Fones and Henry used their opinions to urge the General Assembly to reform Tennessee's laws relating to the criminally insane. In their view, these laws left judges and jurors with a Hobson's choice of either sending an insane person to prison, without treatment, or releasing him upon society.[8]

The Court also made new Tennessee law when in *State v. Jones* (1980) it noted that Tennessee was the only jurisdiction in the United States that did not recognize entrapment as a defense to a criminal prosecution and then proceeded to "bring our secession to a close and reconstruct our decisional law so as to bring it into harmony with that of our sister states and the federal system." Describing the Tennessee decisions as "a study in applied confusion, articulated ambivalence, and devious dicta," the Court welcomed the opportunity to "clarify, harmonize and modernize our law." After an extensive discussion of whether entrapment should be determined by use of a subjective test focusing on the accused's predisposition to commit the crime or an objective test focusing on the activities of the police that encouraged the crime, the Court adopted the subjective test as a "sound and progressive improvement in the administration of criminal justice in Tennessee."

Similarly, the judges tried to strike a balance between the rights of a rape victim and the accused rapist in deciding whether a rape victim could be compelled to submit to a psychological examination. In *Forbes v. State* (1977), the Court held that requiring such an examination in all cases would be contrary to public policy. Calling rape "the most humiliating, degrading and debasing of all crimes" and taking judicial notice that an alarming number of women do not report rapes because they know they will have to relive the trauma in public, the Court thought that a further requirement that the victim undergo a mental examination would "compound the humiliation of this traumatic experience" and "deter prosecution of this loathsome criminal act." The Court sought to balance the need to protect the victim with the rights of the accused to a fair trial, however, by according the trial judge discretion to order a psychological exam where necessary to ensure a just and orderly disposition of the case.

The essence of the criminal law, of course, is the imposition of punishment, and the Supreme Court assumed the responsibility of assuring that those convicted of crimes in Tennessee were punished in accordance with the law. In *Stiller v. State* (1974), however, the Court spoke in favor of the sensible use of probation as an alternative to prison because "our society is coming to realize that 'warehousing' criminals on an indiscriminate basis is financially, socially and morally unacceptable." The Court conferred broad discretion on the trial judge with respect to the grant or denial of probation, but held that such decisions were subject to appellate review for abuse of discretion. Then, in *Moten v. State* (1977), Justices Fones, Brock, and Henry, over the dissent of Justices Harbison and Cooper, heightened the emphasis to be placed on rehabilitation by holding that probation could not be denied for a first offender for the purpose of deterring crime. This holding prompted the legislature to amend the probation statute so that it specifically listed deterrence as a factor to be considered by the trial judge.

The Court was also concerned about the quality of the sentencing decisions that were being made in Tennessee. In 1978, Chief Justice Henry used the first State of the Judiciary message to urge the General Assembly to overhaul Tennessee's system in which the jury imposed a sentence upon the defendant. He called for a system by which the trial judge would sentence criminals in accordance with statutory guidelines that would establish a range of appropriate sentences for specified crimes and identify the factors to be considered by the judge in determining the actual sentence to be imposed. After the General Assembly responded by enacting the Sentencing Reform Act of 1982, the Court held in *State v. Moss* (1986) that, within the range of punishments specified in the statute, sentences should be considered on a case-by-case basis, with the judge exercising "guided discretion" to impose the sentence the defendant deserved, taking into account the seriousness of the offense and the statutory goals of preventing crime and promoting respect for the law by imprisoning repeat offenders, rehabilitating first-time or occasional offenders, and eliminating unjustified disparities in sentences.

No other part of the Court's work was as difficult as hearing the appeals of convicted murderers who had been sentenced to die in Tennessee's electric chair. Although bound to abide by the will of the legislature as reflected in the capital sentencing laws, the Court had the awesome responsibility of assuring that every death sentence had been imposed in accordance with law. In *Collins v. State* (1977), the Court upheld a conviction for first-degree murder, but invalidated Tennessee's death-penalty statute in accordance with United States Supreme Court decisions holding that a mandatory death penalty for first-degree murder was unconstitutional. Because of other decisions holding that jurors could not be given uncontrolled discretion to impose the death penalty, the Court invalidated prior death-penalty statutes as well. With the death penalty no longer available, Tennessee law specified that the penalty for first-degree murder was twenty years to life, as determined by the jury. The Court remanded the cases for new sentencing hearings. Then in *Miller v. State* (1979), Justices Henry, Cooper, and Brock held that Tennessee's constitutional prohibition against *ex post facto* laws precluded the imposition of a death sentence when that sentence was more severe than the maximum punishment provided by law when the offense was committed. The majority's decision conflicted with the United States Supreme Court's holding in *Dobbert v. Florida* (1977) that imposing the death penalty did not violate the federal *ex post facto* clause, which was identical to the Tennessee clause. The majority held that it could interpret the Tennessee Constitution to afford Tennesseans greater constitutional protection than was afforded by the decisions of the United States Supreme Court. Justices Harbison and Fones dissented, saying that "it is an unfortunate development in constitutional law for the Court, sua sponte, to conclude that the term *ex post facto* has a different meaning in the Constitution of Tennessee from the identical words used in the Constitution of the United States."

The Court again reviewed the constitutionality of Tennessee's death penalty in *State v. Dicks* (1981). Contending that he had not been actively involved in the felony during which the murder occurred, Dicks argued that his death sentence was grossly disproportionate to his moral guilt and, therefore, was cruel and inhuman punishment. The Court indicated it would be receptive to such an argument, but concluded that Dicks had been actively involved in the robbery during which the murder occurred. Of particular interest, however, was Justice Brock's dissent. Acknowledging that he had previously concurred in the Court's holding that the Tennessee Constitution imposed no greater restriction on the death penalty than did the United States Constitution, Justice Brock announced that he had changed his mind and now thought that the death penalty was per se cruel and unusual punishment because it was inconsistent with "the evolving standards of decency that mark the progress of a maturing society." He concluded that capital punishment "degrades and dehumanizes all who participate in its processes" and "is unnecessary to any legitimate goal of the state and is incompatible with the dignity of man and the judicial process." For as long as Justice Brock remained on the Court, there always would be at least one vote to reverse a death sentence, leaving the fate of the accused in the hands of the other justices. That one vote, however, afforded little relief to those on Tennessee's death row because the *Dicks* decision marked the first in a steady flow of death-penalty cases in which the Court affirmed the imposition of the ultimate sanction.[9]

Modernizing the Administration of Justice

With Tennessee changing economically, socially, and politically, the Court saw a need to modernize the administration of justice so that it would be able to keep pace with the greater demands being placed on the courts. Using both its constitutional authority to administer the judicial branch of the government and its influence with the General Assembly, the Court persistently worked to improve Tennessee's judicial system, to regulate the conduct of judges and lawyers, and to overhaul the procedures used to administer both civil and criminal justice.

The justices promptly made good on a campaign pledge and demonstrated their commitment to the integrity of the judiciary by adopting a new and stricter Code of Judicial Conduct. Thereafter, the Court worked persistently to persuade the legislature to create a Court of the Judiciary that would provide a forum in which charges of judicial misconduct could be adjudicated. This effort bore fruit in 1979. For its part, the Court in 1988 established the Judicial Ethics Committee and gave it authority to issue opinions that would provide guidance to the state's judges about proper judicial conduct.

The Court was also concerned about improving the efficiency with which justice was administered in Tennessee. The judges, for example, asserted the Court's inherent constitutional power to declare that the judicial system would operate as an integrated unit under its supervision. The primary purpose behind this initiative was to redress caseload imbalances, reduce docket congestion, and to otherwise enhance the orderly and efficient administration of justice within the state. When it came to improving the judicial branch of the government, however, the Supreme Court's ambitions exceeded what could be accomplished by exercising its constitutional authority to supervise the judicial branch. Thus, in 1976, various individual justices supported a call for a constitutional convention hoping that the convention would recommend, and the voters would approve, what Justice Henry called "badly needed reform in the judicial article." When the convention convened, Chief Justice Cooper spoke to the delegates and pointed out that the current system had become a hodgepodge of courts resulting in rural areas being shortchanged, forum shopping, and gross inequities in judicial workloads. He threw his support behind a proposal drafted by the Tennessee Bar Association that called for a unitary court system funded by the state, consisting of courts of general rather than specialized jurisdiction and with rule-making authority vested in the Supreme Court. The justices also favored amending the judicial article to require use of the Missouri Plan for the selection and retention of Supreme Court justices, as well as the judges serving on the intermediate appellate courts.[10]

The judicial article as was ultimately approved and submitted to the voters, however, disappointed the justices. Portions of the article met with their approval, such as the provision adopting the Missouri Plan for judicial selection and retention. The justices, however, were angered by an article providing that rules promulgated by the Court governing procedure and the administration of the judicial system would only be effective when enacted by the General Assembly and that such rules could also be repealed by statute. This "erosion" of the Court's rule-making authority, as well as the absence of a protection against reduction of judicial pay, would, in Chief Justice Henry's estimation, seriously undermine the independence of the judiciary. Henry, among others, actively campaigned against approval of the judicial article, and it was defeated with 54.4 percent of the voters opposed to its ratification. Chief Justice Henry then took his case to the General Assembly in 1979 and urged the legislature to approve pending legislation to modernize the trial court system, including the creation of a single trial court into which the circuit and chancery courts would be combined.[11] This effort, however, did not bear fruit. The justices also attended to the regulation of the legal profession. When the Court took office, lawyer discipline was administered on the local level by the various city and county bar associations. One proposal afoot was to "integrate" the bar by requiring all lawyers to join the Tennessee Bar Association and empowering it to impose discipline in accordance with Rules of Disciplinary Enforcement to be promulgated by the Court. Although many lawyers favored integration of the bar, at least as many opposed the idea. The issue came to a head in 1975 when the Tennessee Bar Association petitioned the Court to adopt new rules and to impose an annual license fee on each attorney that would be used to fund a centralized disciplinary system. At the same time, other lawyers petitioned the Court to establish an integrated bar. In *Petition of the Tennessee Bar Association* (1975), the Court asserted that it had the constitutional authority to regulate the legal profession and that the legislature could not constitutionally interfere with the Court's exercise of that authority. It then declared unconstitutional a statute providing that "no person shall be granted or denied the license or right to practice law in Tennessee because he or she is not a member of any lawful club, association or guild."[12] The Court reasoned that this statute interfered with its inherent power to regulate the practice of law. It also rebuffed claims that the Court's authority did not extend to "unification" of the bar or to the imposition of annual registration and license fees as a condition of the right to practice law.

Divided on the merits of the competing petitions, but agreeing that something had to be done to modernize the regulation of the legal profession and that it was important for the Court to present a united front, the justices charted an intermediate course all could support. Rather than take the ultimate step and unify the bar, the Court amended its Rule 42 to create a unified disciplinary system headed by a Disciplinary Board with authority to employ a chief disciplinary counsel and assistant disciplinary counsel who would investigate and, where appropriate, prosecute complaints against lawyers for violating the Code of Professional Responsibility. The new rule also provided for the establishment of committees that would adjudicate such complaints and specified the sanctions the committees could impose on wayward lawyers. Finally, the Court required all lawyers to pay an annual fee to fund the new system. The broader proposal to unify the bar was retained under advisement, but the Court indicated that it would await further study before making a final decision. There remained considerable opposition to the Court's intermediate action, but the Court firmly rebuffed several legal challenges to its authority to establish the new disciplinary system.[13]

The Court remained attentive to its responsibility to regulate the legal profession. Most noticeably, the Court responded as some Tennessee lawyers started to advertise in the wake of the U.S. Supreme Court's holding in *Bates v. State Bar of Arizona* (1977) that lawyer advertising was protected by the First Amendment. The Court did not approve of lawyers advertising. "The law is an ancient, honorable and learned profession and its practitioners are not tradesman in the marketplace," Henry wrote. "The role of the huckster, the hawkster, the haggler and the peddler ill becomes a member of a dignified profession." With that said, however, the Court, over the dissent of Justices Fones and Brock, adopted a rule that permitted lawyers to advertise over television and radio, as well as in the print media. The Court was more cautious with respect to advertisements in which a lawyer would be identified as practicing in specific areas of the law and prohibited such advertising pending further review by the Court. In 1989, in response to a decision of the United States Supreme Court holding that targeted direct-mail advertising could not be prohibited, the Court once again amended the Code of Professional Responsibility, this time to require that such mailings be prominently labeled "THIS IS AN ADVERTISEMENT."

The Court, of course, was interested in more than advertising. In 1984, for example, in response to a petition from the Tennessee Bar Association, the Court adopted an Interest on Lawyers Trust Accounts (IOLTA) program that authorized lawyers to put client trust funds that were nominal in amount or were expected to be held for a short period of time, in an interest bearing trust account with the interest payable to the Tennessee Bar Foundation. The foundation would then use the money to fund the delivery of legal services to the poor, provide financial support for law students, improve the administration of justice, and for such other purposes as might be approved by the Court. To enhance lawyer competency, the Court accepted a recommendation of the Tennessee Bar Association and required each Tennessee lawyer to annually complete at least twelve hours of approved continuing legal education programming. Then, in 1989, the Court established the Tennessee Lawyers' Fund for Client Protection for the purpose of promoting public confidence in the integrity of the legal profession by reimbursing at least a portion of losses caused by rare instances of dishonest conduct by Tennessee lawyers. To fund the program, the Court assessed each lawyer in the state an extra ten dollars per year.

The Court also sought to modernize the law governing the administration of both civil and criminal justice. Of particular importance were the Court's efforts to assure equal access to justice for all Tennesseans, its efforts to modernize the state's juvenile justice system, and its efforts to reshape the administration of justice by the further refinement of the rules of civil procedure and the adoption of new rules governing criminal procedure, appellate procedure, and the admissibility of evidence in the state's trial courts.

When the justices took office in 1974, it was well established that indigent criminal defendants were constitutionally entitled to legal representation. The challenge for the Court was to oversee Tennessee's compliance with this constitutional requirement. It adopted a new rule that required the state's trial judges to advise defendants of their right to appointment of counsel if they could not afford to hire a lawyer, to make such inquiry as necessary to confirm the defendant's inability to employ counsel, and, upon a finding of indigency, to appoint counsel from the Public Defender Service, if there was one, or to appoint a private attorney to handle the case. The rule provided for compensation of the appointed lawyers at rates set by the legislature. Aware of the burden on private practitioners of representing indigent defendants at the modest compensation permitted by the General Assembly, the Court persistently encouraged the legislators to create a statewide public defender system, which they did in 1989, and to increase compensation payable to appointed counsel.

The Supreme Court's sensitivity to the burden placed upon appointed counsel, however, did not diminish its commitment to provide indigent defendants a meaningful right to counsel. In *McKeldin v. State* (1974), for example, the Court extended the right to counsel to include representation at the preliminary hearing required by Tennessee law in criminal cases. The Court also insisted in *Baxter v. Rose* (1975) that criminal defendants receive "reasonably competent assistance of an attorney acting as a diligent conscientious advocate." All that previously had been required was that the proceeding not be a "farce or a mockery of justice." The Court also held in *State v. Wilson* (1975) that the state must provide indigent criminal defendants with a bill of exceptions at no expense so that they could have the meaningful appellate review of their convictions. Finally, the Court held in *Huskey v. State* (1988) that lawyers, as "sworn ministers of justice," were obligated to accept appointments and were not constitutionally entitled to compensation for doing so. "It is our opinion," the Court explained, "that the license to practice law carries with it as a condition and an obligation the rendition of public service, including service by appointment for indigents."

Although there was no constitutional right to counsel in civil cases, the Court nonetheless struck another blow for equal access to justice when in *Dungan v. Dungan* (1979) it afforded relief to a woman who wanted a divorce from a husband who had abandoned her, but who could neither locate the husband nor afford the cost of publishing a notice in the newspaper as was required in such cases. For her and other indigents, the publication requirement meant that the doors to the courthouse were closed. Holding that it had an affirmative constitutional duty to open the courts to *bona fide* indigents who were seeking dissolution of their marriages, the Court exercised its supervisory power over the judicial system to allow trial judges to order the court clerk, in lieu of newspaper publication, to mail the complaint by registered mail to the defendant's last-known address and to post the summons at three public places in the county.

The Court also left its mark on juvenile justice by requiring that it be administered by judges who were licensed to practice law and by modernizing the procedures to be used in juvenile cases. Of major concern to the justices was the issue of whether juvenile justice could be administered by judges who were not lawyers. The issue was important because it affected the well-being of the state's children and politically sensitive because many of those presiding over delinquency proceedings and other juvenile matters were not lawyers. In *State ex rel. Anglin v. Mitchell* (1979), the Court, in a three-to-two decision, held that a juvenile could not be constitutionally incarcerated or otherwise deprived of liberty in a proceeding conducted by a nonlawyer judge. Speaking for the Court, Justice Henry traced the "advancing standards of due process" with respect to juvenile proceedings, including the right to counsel, and concluded that this expansion of rights would be meaningless in a proceeding before a judge who lacked legal training. "We consider it beyond dispute," Henry wrote, "that the dictates of fundamental fairness, the demands of common sense, and the developing law of this modern era require that the state supply a law-trained judge in all our criminal courts of record, which necessarily includes the juvenile criminal court when conducting adjudicatory hearings in criminal cases." In a strongly worded dissent with which Justice Cooper concurred, Justice Harbison conceded that it probably would be desirable if all juvenile judges were licensed attorneys and that he would not be opposed to enactment of a statute or the amendment of the Constitution to require that all judges be lawyers. He insisted, however, that the majority had so far departed from precedent that their holding was "improper judicial legislation, no matter how well intended." Of equal importance was the Court's adoption in 1983 of the Tennessee Rules of Juvenile Procedure. The new rules applied to all cases in which children were alleged to be delinquent, unruly, neglected, or abandoned and to all cases involving the termination of parental rights, emergency temporary care, the revocation of probation of delinquent or unruly children, or the termination of home placements. The adoption of the rules was a major contribution of the Court to the improvement of juvenile justice for the benefit of the state's most vulnerable citizens.

In addition to its efforts on behalf of indigents and juveniles, the Court handed down a number of important decisions and worked cooperatively with the General Assembly to secure the adoption of rules that would significantly improve the administration of both criminal and civil justice in Tennessee. The Court's concern for procedural fairness was evident, for example, when in *State v. Mackey* (1977) it unanimously invalidated a defendant's guilty plea because the trial judge had not made any effort to determine that the plea was voluntarily and intelligently made. Of particular significance, however, was the Court's exercise of its supervisory power over the Tennessee court system to impose stricter requirements than required by the United States Supreme Court and to prescribe a comprehensive set of standards and procedures to be followed by Tennessee's trial judges to ascertain that a guilty plea was made knowingly and voluntarily and that there was a factual basis for believing that the defendant was guilty of the offense.

The Court also made a significant change in the law governing a judge's charge to a deadlocked jury after taking "a fresh look" at the "Allen" or "dynamite charge" that was used by trial judges when juries reported they were deadlocked on the question of a defendant's guilt or innocence. In effect, the charge attempted to "blast" a dissenting minority on the jury into agreement with the majority by strongly admonishing them to listen to the majority and consider whether their doubt could be reasonable if it made no impression on the minds of so many other equally honest and intelligent jurors. In use in Tennessee since 1955, the purpose of the "Allen charge" was to prevent hung juries. Writing for the Court in *Kersey v. State* (1975), Justice Henry noted mounting criticism of the "Allen charge" as undermining the integrity of the jury process by pressuring individual jurors to surrender their conscientiously held beliefs to the will of the majority on the jury. Although acknowledging that trial judges have a legitimate concern with the administration of justice and should lend guidance to the jury with instructions about the law, the Court would no longer permit them to use the "Allen charge." In the interest of uniformity, the Court prescribed a new charge to be given by all trial judges to deadlocked juries.

With respect to both criminal and civil procedure, the Court undertook major initiatives, in cooperation with the bar and the General Assembly, to comprehensively modernize Tennessee's procedural rules. In 1978, for example, the Court adopted new comprehensive Rules of Criminal Procedure as recommended by its Advisory Commission on the Rules of Criminal Procedure. The Court also approved new Rules of Appellate Procedure that were intended to eliminate rigid procedures that all too often had precluded effective appellate review. In the same spirit, the Court in 1983 mandated that all trial courts adopt and file written local rules governing the setting of cases for trial, obtaining continuances, the disposition of pretrial motions, settlement of plea bargain deadlines, and the preparation, submission, and entry of orders and judgments. The Court also supported a five-year effort that culminated in 1989 with the adoption by the Court, and with General Assembly approval, of the Tennessee Rules of Evidence. In numerous instances, the new rules made significant changes in the Tennessee law. The adoption of these various rules must be marked as one of the Court's major accomplishments in its effort to modernize the administration of justice in Tennessee.

In Retrospect

Between 1974 and 1990, the Tennessee Supreme Court experienced two "firsts"—one being the Democratic Party's use of its new method for selecting its candidates for the Court and the other being Governor Alexander's appointment of George Brown as Tennessee's first black Supreme Court justice. The Court had also compiled a remarkable record of achievement. The justices had resolved numerous important constitutional issues and several times afforded Tennesseans more constitutional protection of their personal liberties than was available under the federal Constitution. They had reshaped Tennessee's jurisprudence and the administration of justice in the state by stripping Tennessee law of its gender bias, expanding the circumstances in which individuals injured by the negligence of others would be afforded meaningful legal redress, modernizing domestic relations law and the administration of juvenile justice, regulating the conduct of Tennessee's judges and lawyers, and adopting important new rules of evidence, appellate procedure, and criminal procedure. The Court consistently worked to enhance the fairness of both the civil and criminal justice systems by promoting equal access to the system, the fair treatment of litigants, and the efficient disposition of a growing caseload. In some instances, however, a majority of the justices could not be mustered to change the law, either because they were not persuaded that the law needed change, that the Court was the appropriate body to make the change, or that the issue was properly before the Court. The justices saw eye-to-eye on many issues or were willing to compromise so the Court could speak with a unified voice, but they were independent thinkers who were willing to voice their dissent from the views of the majority. The split decisions indicate that the justices were more likely to agree about current law than about the need to change the law. They were also more likely to agree about what the law ought to be than about whether it was appropriate for the Court, rather than the General Assembly, to make the change. In this respect, one can characterize Justices Henry and Brock as most likely to press for change; Justices Harbison, Cooper, and O'Brien as more likely to question the appropriateness of a change; and Justices Fones and Drowota as about as likely to end up in one camp as the other. In the end, however, this study reveals that, no matter what their differences, each of the seven justices who served the Court between 1974 and 1990 demonstrated an abiding commitment to comply with the judicial oath of office.

ELECTING A NEW COURT, 1990

As 1990 approached, Justices Harbison, Cooper, Drowota, and O'Brien each decided to seek reelection to the Court, which, of course, meant seeking the nomination of the Democratic Party's executive committee. Justice Fones, on the other hand, announced that he would retire after seventeen years on the Court, leaving room for at least one newcomer. Unlike 1982, however, there were numerous Democratic judges and lawyers who were willing to challenge the incumbents. Court of Appeals Judge E. Riley Anderson had begun to seek support among executive committee members to become the party's nominee for the East Tennessee seat held by Justice Cooper. With the enthusiastic support of the committee's seven black members, Court of Criminal

Appeals Judge Adolpho A. Birch Jr. Tennessee's first black appellate judge, sought nomination for the at-large seat held by Justice Drowota. Court of Criminal Appeals Judge Martha (Cissy) Craig Daughtrey, Tennessee's first female appellate judge, had been actively seeking the support of executive committee members for her bid to replace Justice Harbison as the party's nominee for the Middle Tennessee seat on the Court. With Justice Fones not seeking reelection, Court of Criminal Appeals judge Lyle Reid, with strong support in rural West Tennessee, emerged as the leading contender for the nomination for the West Tennessee seat. Justice O'Brien was not opposed in his bid for renomination. The prevailing wisdom was that he could not be defeated because of the political influence of his wife, Democratic state senator Anna Belle Clement O'Brien. All of these candidates were approved as qualified by a blue-ribbon screening committee similar to that first used by the executive committee in 1974.

The executive committee first selected Justice Drowota as its candidate for the at-large seat by a margin of fifty-five to eight over Judge Birch. Birch garnered the support of the committee's black members, one of whom, Korlon Kilpatrick, urged the members not to tell black Democrats that "our only chance for a black to get on the Supreme Court is to wait for a Republican to appoint us."[14] The next vote was between Justice Harbison and Judge Daughtrey for the Middle Tennessee seat. Daughtrey was selected by a surprising fifty-to-twelve landslide. O'Brien was nominated by acclimation for the other at-large seat. Before the vote for the East Tennessee seat, Justice Cooper asked the committee members "to give me another opportunity to serve with these other nominees to bring some continuity to the court." His appeal, however, could not prevent a landslide vote of fifty-four to nine in favor of Judge Anderson. Finally, Judge Reid was selected as the party's candidate for the West Tennessee seat. Executive committee members indicated that, although they thought it was time for a changing of the guard on the Court, they did not want their votes to be seen as questioning the contributions of Justices Harbison or Cooper or as evidencing dissatisfaction with the Court. That Judge Daughtrey would now be the Democratic Party's first female candidate for the Court resulted in more attention being paid to her victory over Justice Harbison than to Judge Anderson's victory over Justice Cooper. Although acknowledging that Judge Daughtrey's gender was a plus, most saw her victory as being primarily due to her accomplishments as a lawyer and judge, the effectiveness of her face-to-face campaigning, and the view that it was time for the senior justices to step down (as had Justice Fones), and for the party to put forth younger candidates who would serve into the twenty-first century.[15]

In February 1990, Justice Harbison advised Governor Ned McWherter that he would resign from the Court effective at the end of March. Governor McWherter promptly appointed Judge Daughtrey to complete the remaining months of his term. Thus, upon taking her oath of office, Martha (Cissy) Craig Daughtrey, who as a female lawyer twenty-two years earlier could not find a Nashville law firm willing to interview her for a job, became the first woman to sit on the Tennessee Supreme Court. Daughtrey had previously served as United States attorney, assistant district attorney, and assistant professor of law at Vanderbilt. Then, in 1975, she was appointed to the Court of Criminal Appeals, where she served until her appointment to the Supreme Court. Justice Daughtrey would now run for election as an incumbent. With no Republican or independent candidates on the ballot and no organized opposition to any of the Democratic candidates the election was a mere formality.

THE JUSTICES, 1990–1998

The three returning incumbents provided the Court with substantial judicial experience. Justice Drowota and Justice O'Brien had each been judging for twenty years. Justice Daughtrey was in her fifteenth year on the bench. Justices Reid and Anderson were the newcomers, both having commenced their judicial careers in 1987. Prior to joining the Court of Appeals, the fifty-eight-year-old Anderson had practiced law in Oak Ridge. The sixty-year-old Reid had served as General Sessions Court judge and as assistant state attorney general. Then from 1963 to 1986, he had practiced law in Brownsville and served as Haywood County attorney. He was serving as Deputy Commissioner of the Department of Commerce when he was appointed to the Court of Appeals.

Justices Drowota, O'Brien, Daughtrey, Anderson, and Reid served together until 1993, when Justice Daughtrey resigned her seat on the Court to assume a judgeship on the United States Court of Appeals for the Sixth Circuit. Governor McWherter promptly appointed Judge Adolpho A. Birch Jr. of Nashville to complete her unexpired term. Having previously served as Tennessee's first black assistant district attorney and then as the state's first black General Sessions judge, its first black Criminal Court judge and as then as its first black judge of the Court of Criminal Appeals, Birch became only the second black to sit on the Supreme Court. Because of this extensive judicial experience, Governor McWherter was confident that Birch would not suffer the same fate as had George Brown in 1980. His only mistake in that regard turned out to be his assumption that Birch would stand for election as a Democratic Party candidate running against a Republican opponent.

In February 1993, Lieutenant Governor Wilder introduced legislation that would both revise Tennessee's Modified Missouri Plan and extend it to apply to Supreme Court justices. With respect to judicial selection, Wilder's bill simply undid the General Assembly's 1974 deletion of the Supreme Court from the plan. On a more innovative note, however, the bill also called for the establishment of a fifteen-member Appellate Court Evaluation Commission that would evaluate the performance of any Supreme Court justice or appellate judge who was seeking reelection. After considerable legislative debate and numerous changes, including a change in the plan's name, the General Assembly approved the Tennessee Plan in May 1994. The Tennessee Plan called for the creation of a nonpartisan Judicial Selection Commission that would, when a vacancy on the Court occurred, submit the names of three candidates to the governor, who could either appoint one of the three or reject all three and require the Selection Committee to submit three additional nominees. Once appointed to the Court, the justice would stand for a nonpartisan yes-no retention election at the next biennial August election. All justices, of course, would stand for a retention vote at the expiration of their term. As finally approved, the bill required that the Judicial Selection Commission reflect the diversity of the state's population with respect to gender and race, but not political affiliation. The statute also established the Judicial Evaluation Commission, which prepared and published an evaluation of any justice seeking retention in office for a new eight-year term. Finally, and of considerable immediate significance, the yes-no retention election was to go into effect immediately. Consequently, Justice Birch stood for a yes-no retention vote in August 1994. Sixty-six percent of the voters voted yes. Thus, Justice Birch scored two more firsts for Tennessee as he became the first black justice to be elected to the Court and the first justice to be elected pursuant to the Tennessee Plan.

When the Court reconvened in September, the justices elected Justice O'Brien to serve as chief justice. In late October, however, O'Brien announced that he was resigning from the Court, effective immediately, to work for Democratic gubernatorial candidate Phil Bredesen. The timing of Justice O'Brien's resignation permitted Governor McWherter to make one more appointment to the Court prior to the expiration of his term in mid-January. After receiving the recommendation of the Judicial Selection Commission, McWherter announced that he would appoint Court of Criminal Appeals Judge Penny White to succeed Justice O'Brien. The thirty-eight-year-old White started practicing law in Johnson City in 1981 and then was a Prettyman Fellow at Georgetown University Law Center, where she earned an LL.M. degree in 1987. Returning to Johnson City, White was elected in

1990 Circuit Court judge in the First Judicial District—the first woman to be so elected. Two years later, Governor McWherter appointed her to the Court of Criminal Appeals.

Given the ease with which Justice Birch had prevailed in his retention election in 1994, there was little reason at the beginning of 1996 to believe that Justice White's bid for retention would take a different course. A storm started to brew, however, in early June when the Court released its decision in *State v. Odom* (1996) upholding the conviction, but reversing the death sentence, of Richard Odom for raping and then stabbing to death a seventy-eight-year-old Memphis woman, Mina Ethel Johnson. In an opinion written by Chief Justice Birch, the Court unanimously rejected Odom's challenge to his conviction but unanimously agreed that Odom's death sentence had to be vacated because of errors during the sentencing phase of the trial. The Court also unanimously upheld the constitutionality of that portion of Tennessee's death-penalty statute which permits a jury to consider as an aggravating factor that "the murder was especially heinous, atrocious or cruel in that it involved torture or serious physical abuse beyond that necessary to produce death." The seeds of the storm, however, lay in a disagreement among the justices as to whether the multiple stabbings and rape during Mina Johnson's murder were sufficient to establish that her murder "involved torture or serious physical abuse beyond that necessary to produce death." With respect to this issue, Chief Justice Birch, with the concurrence of Justices White and Reid, wrote,

> We well understand that almost all murders are "heinous, atrocious or cruel" to some degree, and we have no purpose to demean or minimize the ordeal this murder victim experienced. In our view, however, rape . . . does not ordinarily constitute "torture" or "serious physical abuse" within the meaning of the statute. Were we to hold otherwise, every murder committed in the perpetration of rape would be classified as a death-eligible offense. Such a result, obviously, would not sufficiently narrow the class of perpetrators, nor would it distinguish the "worst of the worst" for whom the ultimate penalty must be reserved.

Justices Anderson and Drowota dissented from this holding, concluding that Odom had "tortured" Mina Johnson by inflicting severe physical or mental pain upon the victim while she was alive and conscious. This disagreement among the justices was quickly brought to the public's attention as Attorney General Burson publicly described the ruling as "quite simply astounding" and Republican state representative Beth Halteman Harwell declared the ruling both "unbelievable" and "just outrageous."[16] To this was quickly added the outrage of victims' rights advocates.[17]

As the storm formed, it headed directly toward Justice White, who had the misfortune of being the only judge up for election in August. John Davies, president of the Tennessee Conservative Union (TCU), joined the fray, vowing to raise forty-five thousand dollars to fund a campaign exposing what he called White's "shameful pro-criminal voting record." "We're going to beat Justice White," Davies declared. "She voted to let this guy off and she's the only one of three justices who's scheduled for election. And we can send a message to the entire Supreme Court by defeating Penny White."[18] In addition to the TCU, the opposition to Justice White's retention was spearheaded by police associations, victims' rights groups, and other politically conservative organizations. They maintained that she was unwilling to enforce the death penalty and was more concerned about the rights of criminals than those of their victims.

Although constrained by the Code of Judicial Conduct with respect to what she could say about the death penalty, Justice White's basic message was that capital punishment was permitted by law in Tennessee and that she would affirm a death penalty that was imposed in accordance with the law. "If I were interested in changing current law," she insisted, "I would run for the legislature."[19] White labeled as "totally and completely false" charges that she was a liberal who was reluctant to apply the death penalty and unconcerned about the rights of victims. Numerous lawyers and several organizations of lawyers came to White's defense. Their message was that she was an outstanding justice who was being attacked unfairly by fringe groups for an opinion she did not write, and that such efforts were a threat to the independence of the judiciary. Frequent reference was made to an analysis of White's opinions prepared by Nashville lawyer David Raybin that revealed she had affirmed 85 percent of the convictions of those criminals who sought reversal of their conviction on direct appeal and had upheld jail time in 90 percent of the cases in which a defendant had appealed a denial of probation. He also described seven cases in which he thought Justice White had demonstrated great concern for the rights of victims.[20]

The crosscurrents in this storm were complicated by a pending lawsuit that challenged the constitutionality of the Tennessee Plan and also claimed that it could not be applied to Justice White's election because she had not been evaluated by the Judicial Evaluation Commission. In a series of decisions in early July by a Special Supreme Court appointed by Governor Don Sundquist to hear the case after the regular justices had recused themselves, it was first held that the Tennessee Plan, although constitutional, could not be applied to Justice White's election and that she would stand for election in a traditional contested election, but without opposition because no one else had qualified to stand for election.[21] This outraged those who wanted to vote against her and would now have no way to do so. John Davies of the TCU, for example, fumed that the decision "has destroyed the little confidence that the public had left in our judicial system." "This is a case of judges looking out for their friends," he declared. "Quite literally the public has been raped." Davies indicated that he did not care whether court seats would be filled by popular election or pursuant to the Tennessee Plan. What was unacceptable, he said, was "a ruling where Judge White is just declared the winner without an opponent."[22] The Court, however, reversed itself and extended the qualifying deadline. This enabled the Republicans to field a candidate, lawyer John King of Knoxville, to oppose Justice White. In the end, however, in *Lillard v. Burson* (1996), United States District Judge Bernice Donald ruled that Justice White was legally entitled to stand for retention pursuant to the Tennessee Plan. When this decision was not appealed, public attention switched from the question of how Justice White would be elected back to the question of whether she should be reelected.

It did not take long for this nonpartisan retention election to take on a decidedly partisan cast. The Republican Party enthusiastically joined the campaign against Justice White. Then, Republican U.S. Senators Fred Thompson and Bill Frist and Governor Don Sundquist publicly announced their opposition to Justice White's retention. In turn, many Democrats came to White's defense. The Democratic Party organization also aided her retention bid. It sent a mass mailing to Democrats with an endorsement by former governor McWherter, who had appointed her to the bench.[23] By way of contrast with the outspoken opposition of Senators Thompson and Frist and Governor Sundquist, however, a considerable number of Democratic officeholders did not publicly defend Justice White. Of ten Democratic legislators asked by a reporter, for example, only one, state senator Joe Haynes of Nashville, was willing to publicly declare support for Justice White. Also, when Democratic vice president Al Gore was asked about his views on the matter, he responded that he would pay careful attention to former governor McWherter's opinion that Justice White had done a fine job and should be retained. He did not, however, say how he would vote. Such reserve stood in stark contrast to the public statements of Thompson, Frist, and Sundquist.

The campaign went down to the wire, both sides purchasing as much radio time as they could afford for their last-minute messages to the voters. On August 1, with only 19 percent of Tennessee's 2.8 million voters participating, 55 percent voted no. Penny White thus became the first appellate judge in Tennessee to lose a Tennessee Plan retention election. Those opposed to her retention applauded the outcome as a historic decision by which the voters had begun to reclaim the courts from "soft-on-crime judges." Justice White's supporters complained about "extremist elements" in Tennessee politics and worried about a threat to the independence of the judiciary.

Attention immediately turned to the selection of Justice White's successor. Governor Sundquist indicated that all other things being equal, he would like to appoint a female Republican from East Tennessee. Above all, however, he was looking for a judge who was not predisposed against the death penalty. After the Supreme Court ruled in *Holder v. Judicial Selection Commission* (1996) that West Tennesseans, as well as East Tennesseans, were eligible to fill the vacant seat, and the Judicial Selection Commission made its recommendations, the governor gave the nod to Circuit Court Judge Janice Holder of Memphis. The forty-seven-year-old Holder had practiced law in Memphis from 1979 to 1990, had been elected to the Circuit Court after a nonpartisan campaign, and described herself as "an independent who voted for the candidate rather than the Party." Until the fall of 1996, however, Judge Holder had consistently voted in the Democratic primaries. When asked about Judge Holder's lack of Republican credentials, Governor Sundquist indicated that her voting record was irrelevant to her performance as a judge. His choice was generally applauded.

There would be one more change in the personnel of the Court before the expiration of the Court's eight-year term. Justice Reid resigned from the Court, effective March 1, 1998, to become general counsel for Columbia HCA Healthcare Corporation. Governor Sundquist appointed Court of Criminal Appeals Judge William M. (Mickey) Barker of Chattanooga to succeed Justice Reid. Judge Barker had practiced law in Chattanooga from 1969 to 1983 and served as Circuit Court Judge from 1983 until his appointment to the Court of Criminal Appeals in 1994. Although Democrats and Republicans alike applauded Governor Sundquist's choice, it should be noted that Justice Barker had impeccable Republican credentials. If retained by the voters in the August retention election, he would become the first Republican to be elected to the Tennessee Supreme Court since Reconstruction.

In the end, the work of the Court between 1990 and 1998 was performed by nine justices, only two of whom, Drowota and Anderson, served the full term. The Court began with four white men and its first woman—all elected as Democratic Party candidates in a partisan election in which, however, they had no Republican opponents. As the end of the 1990–98 term approached, the Court was still being served by two of the original four white male Democrats, but they were now joined by a black male Democrat appointed by a Democratic governor and retained by the voters in a Tennessee Plan election, as well as a white female Independent and a white male Republican, each appointed by a Republican governor and yet to be approved by the voters. For a brief period, the Court was also served by a white female Democrat appointed by a Democratic governor and then successfully opposed by the Republicans in a highly partisan Tennessee Plan retention election. Amid all the turnover and electoral turmoil, however, these justices, like their predecessors, would leave a distinctive mark on Tennessee law and the administration of justice in the Volunteer State.

THE WORK OF THE COURT, 1990–1998

As the Court's first order of business, the justices elected Justice Reid to serve as chief justice. They also voted to retain Charles Burson as attorney general. When Burson resigned in 1997, the Court named John Knox Walkup to complete his term. As one might expect, given the continuing growth in Tennessee's population and the size of the legal profession, the Court saw an increase in the demand for its services. In 1991–92, for example, the Court received 208 direct appeals, but by 1997–98 there were 241 direct appeals, a 15.8 percent increase. The number of applications for permission to appeal to the Court similarly climbed by 28.1 percent from 885 in 1991–92 to 1,134 in 1997–98. The Court granted 87 of the petitions in 1991–92 and 93 in 1997–98, evidencing a greater selectivity in the cases it would hear as a matter of choice. In 1997–98, the Court authored 339 opinions, considerably more than the 211 opinions authored in 1991–92. This burgeoning workload of the Court was made somewhat more manageable by the General Assembly's passage, with the strong support of the justices, of the Appellate Court Improvement Act of 1992. The act reduced the number of cases that were appealable to the Court as a matter of right and permitted the Court to assign worker's compensation cases to a special three-judge appeals panel. The key to this latter reform was that only one of the three judges would be a Supreme Court justice and one of the other judges would normally author the panel's opinion. Like its predecessor, the new Court saw its role as developing Tennessee law by resolving issues of public importance, issues about which the courts of appeals could not agree, and issues not previously addressed by the courts. There were more than enough of such issues, and the justices demonstrated once again a willingness to reshape Tennessee law in light of modern circumstances. Like their predecessors, however, they were not always of one mind about what the law was, or should be, or about whether it was appropriate for the Court to make the change in question. The Court also continued to wield its constitutional authority and political influence to further modernize the judicial system and to enhance the public's confidence in the administration of justice in Tennessee.

Guardian of the Constitution

The new Court was afforded several opportunities to resolve important constitutional controversies. Among these were several disputes about restrictions on free speech and freedom of the press. Over the dissent of Justices Reid and Daughtrey, the Court held in *State v. Marshall* (1993) that Article I, Section 19 of the Tennessee Constitution, like the First Amendment of the United States Constitution as interpreted by the United States Supreme Court, afforded no protection to obscenity. Although willing to sustain the state's right to restrict the "hardcore pornography" at issue in the case, Justices Reid and Daughtrey argued that the Tennessee Constitution should be interpreted to protect all speech, only permitting restriction if necessary to further a compelling state interest and narrowly tailored to do so. Not long thereafter, in *Davis-Kidd Booksellers v. McWherter* (1993), the Court rebuffed a free-speech challenge to a statute that prohibited bookstores from displaying materials that were harmful to minors. Acknowledging that the statute could have the effect of limiting adults' access to literature that was not obscene, but would be harmful to minors because of its sexual content, the Court upheld the statute's constitutionality because, as construed by the Court, it was narrowly tailored to accomplish the state's compelling interest in protecting its youth from exposure to such harmful literature. The Court did, however, invalidate as unconstitutionally vague the statute's ban on materials that were harmful to children because of "excessive violence." In *Douglas v. State* (1996), the Court also rejected a constitutional challenge to a regulation that required dentists who were not licensed in a specialty branch of dentistry, such as orthodontics, to indicate in their advertising that they were general dentists and not specialists. Then in *State v. Smoky Mountain Secrets* (1996), it upheld a significant portion of the General Assembly's response to the Court's earlier invalidation of its first attempt to regulate the solicitation of charitable contributions by paid solicitors.

The Court also had several opportunities to further develop the law governing the validity of search warrants and warrantless searches and seizures. With respect to warrantless searches, the Court in *State v. Bartram* (1996) rejected the "angry wife" rule that required exclusion of evidence against a husband when consent was given to the search by an angry wife. Husbands now had one more reason to please their wives. The Court also had to deal with a number of cases involving arrests, searches incident to arrests, and frisks incident to investigatory stops. More often than not, the Court unanimously upheld the police intervention. If there was disagreement, however, Justices Drowota and Reid were likely to be in opposing camps, as was the case in *State v. Bridges* (1997) when each filed dissents from a majority decision holding that a stop-and-frisk was justified, but that a seizure of a pill bottle "felt" during the frisk was improper. Justice Reid agreed that the seizure incident to the frisk was improper, but dissented from the Court's holding that the investigatory stop was justified. Justice Drowota, on the other hand, concluded that both the investigatory stop and the seizure of the pill bottle were constitutionally permissible. Of greatest significance to the average citizen, however, was the Court's decision in *State v. Downey* (1997) that set forth the criteria to be used to assess the constitutionality of the sobriety roadblocks the police were using in their war against drunk driving. Although holding that the roadblock in the case before it was unconstitutional, the Court indicated it would uphold roadblocks if they were operated in accordance with predetermined operational guidelines and properly supervised to limit the discretion of the police officers manning the roadblock. Justice Drowota approved the general principles stated by the majority but dissented from the Court's holding that the roadblock in question was inadequately supervised.

The Court broke new constitutional ground when, in a case that attracted national attention, it determined the respective rights of ex-spouses to custody of preembryos they had produced and preserved in connection with their efforts, in a happier time, to have a baby by in vitro fertilization. In *Davis v. Davis* (1992), the Court, in an opinion authored by Justice Daughtrey, ultimately decided on the facts of the case before it that the ex-husband was entitled to the preembryos. The Court first held that, although the preembryos were neither persons nor property, they would nonetheless be treated with special respect because of their potential to generate human life. The Court then recognized the authority of the ex-spouses, as "gamete providers," to make decisions concerning the disposition of the preembryos. In the interest of providing guidance to couples who would use in-vitro fertilization procedures in the future, the Court indicated more generally that it would enforce agreements between the spouses about the disposition of the preembryos. As there was no such contract in the case, however, the Court had to resolve what it saw as a dispute between the ex-spouses as to whether they would become parents. The Court broke new legal ground by articulating a constitutional right of privacy that included a right to "procreational autonomy" with which the state could interfere only if there were a compelling state interest. As the Court could find no evidence that the legislature had established a state policy that would justify the state's intervention in the matter, it proceeded to resolve the competing claims to the preembryos by balancing the interest of the ex-husband in not fathering a child against the ex-wife's interest in donating the preembryos to another couple who wanted a baby. Conceding the case would be much closer if the ex-wife wanted to use the preembryos herself because she could not otherwise achieve parenthood, the Court found the balance of interest to favor the ex-husband. To provide guidance for future cases, however, the Court indicated that the party seeking to avoid procreation should prevail if the other party has a reasonable possibility of achieving pregnancy by other means. It left open, however, the possibility that the balance of interest could be struck in favor of the party seeking to become a parent if using the preembryos was the only reasonable means of having a child.

In a number of instances, the Court was required to determine whether legislation that only applied to selected counties or cities violated the Home Rule provisions in Article XI, Section 9, the "general law" requirements in Article I, Section 8, or the entitlement to equal protection of the law contained in the "law of the land" clause in Article 1, Section 8 of the Tennessee Constitution. In *Civil Service Merit Board of the City of Knoxville v. Burson* (1991), for example, the Court upheld the constitutionality of legislation establishing uniform rules for civil service boards in municipalities that were located in counties with a population in excess of three hundred thousand and did not operate under a mayor-aldermanic form of government. So limited, the statute only applied to Shelby, Davidson, and Knox Counties, but it would apply to other counties once they met the population threshold. The Court held that the General Assembly could enact such legislation because it was intended to apply generally to more than one county and there was a rational basis for the criteria used to determine the counties which would apply. In other cases, however, the Court did not hesitate to invalidate "special" legislation on the ground that there was no rational basis for the classification scheme employed by the statute.[24]

On at least two occasions, the dispute about legislative authority was of such unusual public importance that the Court exercised its power to assume jurisdiction without review by the intermediate appellate courts. In 1994, in connection with legislative efforts to put before the voters a proposal to amend the Tennessee Constitution to eliminate its ban on lotteries, the Court had to decide whether the requirement in Article I, Section 3 of the Tennessee Constitution that such proposals be approved by "two-thirds of all the members elected to each house" meant two-thirds of the total number of senators and representatives, counted together, or if a separate two-thirds affirmative vote was required in both the Senate and the House. More than two-thirds of the elected members of the General Assembly had approved the proposed amendment, but less than two-thirds of the senators had supported it. The Court's ruling in *State ex rel. Cohen v. Darnell* (1994) that both the Senate and the House had to approve the proposed amendment by a two-thirds margin brought to a close this effort to allow the people to decide whether to repeal the constitutional ban on lotteries. The Court then held in *Tennessee Municipal League v. Thompson* (1997) that an amendment to the municipal annexation statute permitting the incorporation of "tiny towns" within five miles of large cities or three miles of smaller cities was unconstitutional because the changes made in the law were more extensive than indicated by the caption of the bill. This violated Article II, Section 17 of the Tennessee Constitution that was intended to prevent surprise and fraud in the legislative process by requiring that a bill's caption alert legislators and the public to its subject matter. Although giving the General Assembly credit for acting in good faith, the justices unanimously voided the "tiny town" legislation as an unconstitutional surprise.

In terms of its impact on the state, the Supreme Court's most important decision was its holding in *Tennessee Small School Systems v. McWherter* (1993) that the General Assembly's system for funding primary and secondary education was unconstitutional because it resulted in substantial disparities in the quality of public education throughout the state. Because Tennessee had embarked on a highly publicized program to improve the quality of education by increased funding and efforts to improve teacher performance, the issue was both important and politically sensitive. Chief Justice Reid, writing for a unanimous Court, held that the mandate in Article XI, Section 12 of the Tennessee Constitution that the General Assembly "provide for the maintenance, support and eligibility standards of a system of free public schools" guaranteed to all children of the state a free public education. The Court then construed the Tennessee Constitution to confer upon all Tennesseans the right to be treated the same as all similarly situated persons and held that the General Assembly had to respect such rights in financing public schools. The Court accepted the determination of the trial judge that students similarly situated were not being afforded the same quality of education because of the disparity in funding. Rejecting considerable authority from other jurisdictions, which held that a desire for local control over school policy provided a basis for a funding system requiring significant local funding, the Court held there was no rational basis for Tennessee's current system of funding public education. Although willing to invalidate the current funding system, the Court did not provide guidance to the General Assembly about which alternative funding systems would meet its approval. Respectful of legislative prerogatives, the Court left it to the General Assembly to fix the problem. Subsequently, in *Tennessee Small School Systems v. McWherter* (1995), the Court approved the General Assembly's Basic Education Program that incrementally equalized funding over a five-year period. The Court stipulated, however, that the plan must provide for equalization of teacher's salaries.

Modernizing the Law

The 1990s Court made many changes in Tennessee's common law. The centerpiece of the Court's reshaping of common law was its decision in *McIntyre v. Balentine* (1992) to abolish contributory negligence and replace it with a "modified 49% comparative fault system" in which the jury would determine the comparative fault of the plaintiff and defendant. It would then award the plaintiff damages in proportion to the defendant's fault, but only in cases in which the plaintiff was less at fault than the defendant. This was a change that the Court had not been ready to make in 1976. Indicating its awareness that the General Assembly could have made this major change, a unanimous Court was unwilling to wait any longer for legislative action purging the law of an outmoded common-law doctrine, particularly one that had been "conceived in the judicial womb." In connection with its decision, the Court also abolished the doctrines of "last clear chance" and "remote contributory negligence." In the same spirit, the Court in *Glass v. City of Chattanooga* (1993) unanimously abolished the fellow-servant rule—a doctrine that precluded an employee who has been injured by a co-worker from recovering damages from the employer. In *Perez v. McConkey* (1994), it abolished the doctrine of implied assumption of risk, which denied all recovery to a plaintiff who knowingly assumed the risks inherent in a particular activity or proceeded to act with knowledge of a risk of injury. The Court held that these doctrines, which had been developed during the Industrial Revolution to reduce the risk of liability facing emerging enterprises, were obsolete in the 1990s when public policy favored compensating employees for on-the-job injuries and for injuries caused by the negligence of others.

With fewer affirmative defenses available, defendants were more often forced to argue that they did not owe a duty of care to the plaintiff. The Supreme Court addressed this issue in a number of cases. In *McClung v. Delta Square Limited Partnership* (1996), for example, the Court reversed the 1975 *Cornpropst* decision in which the majority, over the dissent of Justice Henry, had limited a store owner's duty to protect customers from crime to situations in which the merchant knew or should have known that criminal acts were occurring or about to occur. In *McClung*, the Court embraced Justice Henry's view that large malls and stores provided fertile ground for criminals to prey on customers and that the modern trend was to impose a broader duty upon businesses to take reasonable measures to protect their customers from foreseeable criminal attacks. It then adopted a balancing approach for the determination of whether the defendant owed the plaintiff a duty to act reasonably to prevent the crime. The question to be asked was whether the foreseeable probability and gravity of harm posed by the defendant's conduct outweighed the burden on the defendant of taking steps that would have prevented the harm.

The Court made two other significant changes in Tennessee tort law in 1992. In *Hataway v. McKinley* (1992), a lawsuit between two Tennesseans for negligence in connection with an excursion into Arkansas, the Court rejected the one-hundred-year-old rule choice of law principle *lex loci delicti* that required Tennessee courts to apply the law of the state where the negligent conduct occurred. The Court agreed with the modern view that *lex loci delicti* was outmoded in the modern industrial world in which people were more mobile and regularly conducted business across state boundary lines. Future Tennessee courts would apply the law of the state that had the most significant relationship to the occurrence and the parties.

Then, in *Hodges v. S.C. Toof & Company* (1992), a case in which a wrongfully discharged employee had been awarded $200,000 compensatory damages and $375,000 punitive damages, the Court decided that "the time has come to reexamine, and modify, the manner in which punitive damages are awarded in Tennessee." Writing for a unanimous Court, Justice Drowota first restricted the award of punitive damages to situations involving "the most egregious of wrongs" in which the defendant's conduct was intentional, fraudulent, malicious, or reckless. Because the purpose of punitive damages was to punish and deter defendants rather than compensate plaintiffs, the Court also held that the wrongful conduct had to be proven by clear and convincing evidence rather than by a preponderance of the evidence. Finally, it required a bifurcated proceeding. In the first stage, the jury would determine liability for compensatory damages, the amount of those damages, and whether punitive damages should be awarded. If the defendant was found liable for punitive damages, there would then be a separate hearing to determine the appropriate amount of the punitive damages award. As the Court readily acknowledged, it had substantially changed Tennessee law with respect to punitive damages. In doing so, the justices also had made it considerably more difficult for plaintiffs to recover such damages.

In another significant decision, *Kilpatrick v. Bryant* (1993), a divided Court denied recovery in a medical malpractice case for the "loss of a chance" for a more favorable medical outcome in a case in which the plaintiff was more likely than not to have suffered the harm even if the doctor had properly diagnosed the condition. The majority thought that permitting recovery would be an improper and revolutionary change in the law. Dissenting, Justice Daughtrey argued that the majority was ignoring the overwhelming weight of authority in other jurisdictions and had "put Tennessee seriously out of step with recent legal developments in this country and with sound public health policy."

With the state's divorce and out-of-wedlock birthrates still on the rise, the Supreme Court played a continuing leadership role in shaping the legal framework within which disputes between divorcing spouses would be resolved. Respecting the autonomy of the spouses relative to the state, the Court respectively held in *Perkinson v. Perkinson* (1991) and *Cary v. Cary* (1996) that ante-nuptial agreements, and agreements waiving the right to alimony, were not contrary to public policy and would be enforced if both parties knowingly agreed. Most of the Court's work, however, addressed problems about which the ex-spouses had not reached an agreement. Many of these disputes related to the custody and care of the children, an issue in which the state, as well as the parents, frequently claimed an interest. In *Hawk v. Hawk* (1993), the Court extended the new constitutional right of privacy to include parental decisions about the upbringing of their children. It held that Tennessee's Grandparents' Visitation Act was unconstitutional because it infringed on parental autonomy in circumstances in which there was no threat of substantial harm to the children as would implicate the state's compelling interest in protecting children from their parents. With the increase in the number of divorces and the mobility of the population, the Court similarly saw the need to provide a new legal framework for resolving disputes between divorced parents when the custodial parent wanted to move from the state over the objection of the noncustodial parent. The Court revisited these issues in *Aaby v. Strange* (1996) and conferred upon the custodial parent the autonomy to remove the children from the state unless the noncustodial parent could establish that the custodial parent's reasons for the move were vindictive.

No set of issues more divided the Court throughout the 1990s than those raised as it was recurrently asked to assure that the death penalty would only be imposed on the "worst of the worst." Throughout the eight years, Justices Drowota and Justice Reid seldom agreed on the propriety of imposing the death penalty. Justice Drowota was much more likely than Justice Reid to affirm the constitutional validity of Tennessee's death-penalty statute and its application to cases before the Court. At the beginning of the decade, Justice O'Brien consistently sided with Justice Drowota, and Justice Daughtrey consistently sided with Justice Reid, usually leaving Justice Anderson to cast the deciding vote.[25] In *State v. Black* (1991), for example, Justices Drowota, O'Brien, and Anderson held that the imposition of the death penalty by electrocution was not per se cruel and unusual punishment within the meaning of either the Eighth Amendment of the United States Constitution or Article I, Section 16 of the Tennessee Constitution. The justices also disagreed about the meaning of and the sufficiency of evidence to establish several of the aggravating factors necessary for imposition of the death penalty, whether any such insufficiency could be harmless error, and whether it is appropriate to use harmless error analysis in capital cases. Then, in *State v. Hale* (1992), Justice Anderson joined with Justices Reid and Daughtrey to invalidate a statute (popularly known as the "Scotty Trexler law") that permitted imposition of the death penalty for the killing of a child in connection with misdemeanor, rather than felony, child abuse. Justices Drowota and O'Brien dissented. The pivotal position held by Justice Anderson was also evidenced in *State v. Middlebrooks* (1992) when he first joined with Justices Drowota and O'Brien to hold, over the dissent of Justices Reid and Daughtrey, that it was constitutional to impose the death penalty for a murder committed during perpetration of a felony. He then joined with Justices Reid and Daughtrey to hold, over the dissent of Justices Drowota and O'Brien, that the death penalty in a felony murder case could only be justified if there was an aggravating factor other than the felony.

As hoped by those who had opposed Justice White's retention, Governor Sundquist's appointment of Justice Holder made a significant difference in the Court's death-penalty decisions. In a series of death-penalty cases in 1997 and 1998, she consistently joined with Justices Drowota and Anderson to constitute a three-to-two majority in favor of affirming imposition of the death penalty.[26] In the most legally significant of these decisions, *State v. Bland* (1997), the majority provided guidelines to assure that the imposition of the death penalty was not disproportionate to the punishments imposed in comparable cases. This was an issue about which Justices Drowota and Reid had persistently, and at times testily, disagreed. The majority adopted what it called the "precedent seeking" approach to comparative proportionality, held that the precedents to be compared were those in which a capital sentencing hearing was held, and identified seventeen factors for the courts to consider in its comparison of the case before it and the precedents. Underlying the votes in this case and the other death-penalty cases decided by a three-to-two margin during 1997 and 1998 was a fundamental and persistent disagreement between the majority and the dissenters about the proper legal standards and procedures to be used to assure compliance with the constitutional requirement that the death penalty be reserved for the "worst of the worst."

Modernizing the Administration of Justice

The justices were more like-minded about the Court's efforts to improve the administration of justice. One of the Court's most significant contributions to the improvement of the administration of justice involved the use of alternative methods of dispute resolution in civil matters. The Court upheld an arbitration agreement between a physician and a patient in *Buraczynski v.*

Eyring (1996); and in *Arnold v. Morgan Keegan & Company* (1996), it limited the scope of appellate review of an arbitrator's ruling under Tennessee's Uniform Arbitration Act. Of greatest significance, however, was the Court's adoption in 1995 of its Rule 31 governing the use of alternative dispute resolution (ADR) techniques to facilitate pretrial settlement of the ever-increasing number of lawsuits being filed throughout the state. The rule permitted trial judges to require use of ADR techniques and established minimum qualifications, continuing education requirements, and standards of professional conduct for lawyers and nonlawyers who would serve as dispute resolution neutrals.

Likewise, the Court sought to find the right balance between protection of the rights of the accused and the need for effective law enforcement and efficiency in the administration of criminal justice. The Court's decisions related to all phases of the criminal process. For example, the Court unanimously overruled prior authority and held in *State v. Anderson* (1996) that trial judges should use an objective test, from the perspective of the person being questioned, to determine whether the person was "in custody" and therefore entitled to the Miranda warning of the right to remain silent. Similarly, the Court sought to clarify the consequences of a judge's failure to adequately advise defendants of their rights prior to accepting a guilty plea. The Court admonished trial judges to strictly comply with the guidelines the Court had previously promulgated, but held that it would uphold a plea where there was substantial compliance with the requirements or if a substantial failure to comply with the guidelines was harmless error.[27]

The Court also was concerned about the fairness of the trial process. In its ongoing effort to purge all vestiges of racial discrimination from the administration of justice, the Court held in *State v. Ellison* (1992) that a defendant's right to equal protection of the law was violated if even a single prospective juror was peremptorily challenged in a racially discriminatory manner. It also established a framework to guide the trial judge's determination as to whether a peremptory challenge was purposely discriminatory. In *State v. Dyle* (1995), the Court adopted a new instruction to be given by the judge to the jury about eyewitness identifications. The justices wanted to assure that jurors would be cautioned about the risks associated with eyewitness testimony. Finally, in the interest of striking a balance between fairness to those seeking post-conviction relief and the need for some finality in the criminal justice process, the Court in *House v. State* (1995) articulated new standards governing when a petition for post-conviction relief could be denied because the petitioner had already received a "full and fair hearing" or had previously waived consideration of the ground on which he or she was now seeking relief.

Administratively, the Court maintained its interest in regulating the conduct of both judges and lawyers. On the judicial front, the Court revised its Code of Judicial Conduct, promulgated the criteria to be used by the Judicial Evaluation Commission for the evaluation of the state's appellate judges prior to their Tennessee Plan retention elections, and adopted a similar program for the voluntary evaluation of trial judges who were not governed by the Tennessee Plan. Turning its attention to the legal profession, the Court added public members to the Board of Professional Responsibility, required lawyers to maintain their client trust accounts in banks that would agree to report any overdraft to the Board of Professional Responsibility, and established a comprehensive program to certify Tennessee lawyers as specialists in various areas of practice. The Court also added two new rules of professional conduct for lawyers. The first prohibited lawyers from sending solicitation letters to accident victims within thirty days of their accident. The second was promulgated by the Court in cooperation with a legislative initiative to compel compliance with child support orders and prohibited lawyers from willfully refusing to comply with court orders in cases in which they were parties.

The members of the Tennessee Supreme Court chosen in the 1998 judicial election (from left): Frank F. Drowota III, Adolpho A. Birch Jr., William M. Barker, Janice M. Holder, and E. Riley Anderson, seated. Courtesy of Darrell Nelson.

Another set of administrative initiatives was undertaken in awareness that public confidence in the courts, like many other public institutions, was at an all-time low. In an effort to increase public confidence in the courts, the Court sought to purge from the administration of justice in Tennessee any remaining vestiges of racial or gender discrimination by creating a Commission on Racial and Ethnic Fairness and a Commission on Gender Fairness and beginning to implement their recommendations. Seeking even more comprehensively to improve the administration of justice, the Court appointed a blue-ribbon Commission on the Future of the Tennessee Judicial System, received its report in 1996, and began to implement its recommendations for changes intended to improve the fairness, efficiency, and consumer-friendliness of the judicial system. Finally, the Court sought to enhance the public's understanding of the administration of justice by permitting television coverage of all court proceedings and issuing press releases explaining in lay terms its more significant decisions. It also established its innovative and very well received SCALES (Supreme Court Advancing Legal Education for Students) program in which high school students across the state were afforded a firsthand opportunity to observe the Court hearing oral argument in typical cases and to engage in discussions with lawyers and judges about how the legal system works.

In Retrospect

Between 1990 and 1998, the Tennessee Supreme Court experienced a number of significant firsts—its first female justice, its first black justice to be elected to the Court, its first justice to be elected in a Tennessee Plan election, its first justice to be defeated in a Tennessee Plan election, and the first evaluation of Supreme Court justices by the new Judicial Evaluation Commission. During these years, the Court also experienced greater turnover in its personnel and more political turmoil over their selection and retention than had been experienced during the sixteen years between 1974 and 1990. Particularly visible, of course, was the controversy over the Court's decision in the *Odom* case and the resulting campaign against Justice White's retention. These events should not, however, be allowed to overshadow the major accomplishments of the Court. Most noticeably, these included its adoption of comparative fault, its recognition of a constitutional right of privacy, its insistence on equal funding for education throughout the state, its gradual clarification of the standards and procedures to be used in Tennessee to assure that imposition of the death penalty would not violate Tennessee's constitutional prohibition against cruel and inhuman punishment, its promotion of alternative dispute resolution, and its efforts to enhance the public's confidence in the judicial system. Despite a number of instances in which the justices disagreed, particularly death-penalty cases, it bears emphasis that the Court spoke unanimously on most of its most important decisions.

THE TENNESSEE PLAN ELECTION OF 1998

In 1998, Justices Drowota, Anderson, Holder, and Barker faced no organized opposition to their bids to serve another term on the Court. As expected, however, there was organized opposition to Justice Birch's retention. Pursuant to the Tennessee Plan, the Judicial Evaluation Commission published its evaluations of Drowota, Anderson, Birch, and Holder. The twelve-member commission unanimously recommended that all be retained for a new eight-year term. All the justices were rated either "good" or "excellent" by the survey respondents on a broad range of behaviors pertinent to the Tennessee Plan criteria. As intended by the Plan, the report did not address the justices' judicial philosophy or their holdings in specific cases. Because of the timing of his appointment, the commission was not required to prepare an evaluation of Justice Barker.

The campaign against Justice Birch was spearheaded by a coalition of law enforcement and victims' rights groups called Tennessee Justice. The campaign emphasized that he was the author of the *Odom* opinion and accused him of being oversolicitous of the rights of criminal defendants and insufficiently attentive to the interests of their victims. But there the resemblance between the 1996 and 1998 campaigns ended. Justice Birch was better prepared for a contested election. He had a longer judicial record to which his supporters could refer as they responded to charges that he was soft on crime. Also, some of White's most influential opponents either supported Justice Birch or at least did not publicly oppose his retention. Although Republican Party chairman Jim Burnett voiced his personal opposition to Justice Birch's retention, and the party donated thirty thousand dollars to Tennessee Justice, the party did not itself seek to mobilize votes against Birch as it had against White in 1996. Republican senator Fred Thompson announced during early voting that he had voted to retain Justice Birch. Governor Sundquist and Senator Frist, who had publicly announced their votes against White, publicly declined to say how they voted.[28]

When the votes were counted, the small number of voters who participated in the judicial election approved Justice Birch's retention by a margin of 54 to 46 percent. The other justices were all retained by a more comfortable two-to-one margin. Justice Birch put closure on this chapter of the Court's history by breathing a sigh of relief and declaring that "the people have spoken in their clear voice, saying judges should stick to justice, equal justice for all, every day, every case."[29] Given the extremely low turnout and the close margin of victory, however, one might question how clearly the voters had spoken.

Having been approved by the voters, Justices Drowota, Anderson, Birch, Holder, and Barker once again took their judicial oaths. Looming ahead was the twenty-first century, the next chapter in the Court's history. Behind them was the Court's past, the most recent part of which has been chronicled in this chapter. Of particular note were the institution of a new system for holding the justices accountable to the people, the appointment and election of the state's first black and female justices, the numerous decisions in which the Court vindicated the state's constitutional values and modernized its common law, and the many decisions and administrative initiatives by which the Court sought to modernize the administration of justice in the Volunteer State. Also noticeable, of course, were the occasional disagreements among the justices about the proper resolution of the legal issues before the Court. How, then, does one assess the performance of the Court and the individual justices who served between 1974 and 1998? In 1990, for example, some characterized the Court and some of the justices as conservative and called for a new Court that would be more liberal. Similarly, based on a statistical analysis of the justices' votes between 1989 and 1996, Professor Daniel J. Foley has characterized Justices Fones and Cooper as "leaning conservative"; Justices Harbison, Drowota, Birch, and O'Brien as "moderate"; Justice Anderson as "leaning liberal"; and Justices Reid and Daughtrey as "liberal."[30] Although these labels were used by Foley as a description of the justices' voting records, such labels can easily be turned into an evaluation, such as when Justices Reid, White, and Birch were condemned by their opponents as "extreme liberals." This overview of the work of the Court from 1974 to 1998, however, raises serious questions about whether such labeling does justice either to the collective accomplishments of the Court during these years or to the efforts of the justices to comply with their oath of office. One cannot read the opinions of the Court and not be impressed by the consistent effort of the justices to decide each case to the best of their knowledge of current law, their awareness of changing circumstances that might require modernization of the law, and their understanding of the judicial role. How well did they do? Answering this question is a daunting task, even for a legal historian. Yet, this is the question Tennesseans effectively answered when they voted yes or no in the Tennessee Plan elections held in 1996 and 1998 and will once again answer when they return to the polls in 2006. To help these voters cast more informed votes in 1998, the Judicial Evaluation Commission published its first evaluation of the justices. The Court's SCALES project was another "first" effort to enhance public understanding of the work of the Court. The Court also began issuing press releases explaining its most important decisions. To further enhance the public's understanding of the Court, the Tennessee Supreme Court Historical Society commissioned these essays, now published as the first history of the Tennessee Supreme Court. It is hoped that it will be read by many Tennesseans, will add to their understanding of the distinctive responsibilities of the justices of the Tennessee Supreme Court, and, in the end, will enable them to cast more informed votes as they play their constitutionally mandated role in the history of the Court that is yet to come.

Appendix 1

JUSTICES OF THE SUPREME COURT OF TENNESSEE, 1790–1998

Anderson, Joseph Inslee, appointed territorial judge by President Washington, February 1791 (1:XXIII); served until 1796; born Philadelphia, November 5, 1757; died April 18, 1837; brevet major in Continental army; member of U.S. Senate, 1797–1815; first comptroller of U.S. Treasury, 1815–36; member of Constitutional Convention of 1796; Anderson County named for him.

Anderson, E. Riley, born August 10, 1932, Chattanooga, Tennessee; B.S., University of Tennessee, 1955; LL.B., J.D., University of Tennessee College of Law, 1957; private law practice in Oak Ridge, 1958–87; appointed to Court of Appeals, March 2, 1987; elected August 1988; elected to Supreme Court August 1990; chief justice, October 1994 to May 1996; reelected chief justice for terms beginning July 8, 1997 and September 1998.

Andrews, George, appointed by Governor W. G. Brownlow, 1868; served two years (45:V); born in Vermont, December 28, 1826; died August 22, 1889; U.S. district attorney for East Tennessee after retirement from bench; member of Board of Trustees of University of Tennessee.

Bachman, Nathan Lynn, elected 1918 (141:V); resigned September 8, 1923 (148:V); born in Chattanooga, Tennessee, August 2, 1878; died April 23, 1937; judge of Sixth Circuit, 1912–18; appointed to U.S. Senate 1933 to fill vacancy when Senator Cordell Hull resigned to accept post of secretary of state; elected to U.S. Senate for unexpired term 1934, reelected 1936, and served until death; memorial and portrait, 174 Tenn. 707.

Barker, William M., born September 13, 1941, Chattanooga, Tennessee; B.S., University of Chattanooga, 1964; J.D., University of Cincinnati College of Law, 1967; U.S. Army Medical Service Corps, 1967–69; admitted to bar, 1967; private practice until 1983; adjunct professor, University of Chattanooga, 1984– ; Circuit Court judge, 1983–95; appointed to Court of Appeals, February 1995; elected to unexpired term 1996; appointed to Supreme Court, April 1998 to replace Lyle Reid; elected August 1998.

Beard, William Dwight, appointed 1890, vice William C. Folkes (88:VI); served until next biennial election, when defeated by Benjamin J. Lea; elected 1894, 1902, and 1910; chief justice, 1902–10; born in Princeton, Kentucky, October 25, 1835; died December 7, 1910; served as chancellor at Memphis, 1891–94; served as assistant adjutant general on staff of Gen. Joe Shelby in Confederate army; memorial and portrait, 123 Tenn. 713.

Bell, Bennett Douglas, appointed February 7, 1908, to fill vacancy occasioned by death of John S. Wilkes; elected August 1908 for unexpired term (120:III); defeated for reelection in 1910; born in Sumner County, July 4, 1852; died August 12, 1934; attorney general, Tenth Circuit; circuit judge, Tenth Circuit, 1902–8.

Birch, Adolpho A., Jr., born September 22, 1932, Washington, D.C.; B.A. and J.D., Howard University, Washington, D.C., 1956; U.S. Naval Reserve, active duty, 1956–58; private law practice, 1958–66; assistant public defender, Davidson County, 1963–66; assistant district attorney general, Davidson County, 1966–69; Davidson County General Sessions Court judge, 1969–78; Davidson County Criminal Court judge, 1978–87; teaching faculty, Nashville School of Law, 1991– ; appointed to Court of Criminal Appeals, April 1987, elected August 1988; reelected August 1990; appointed to Supreme Court, December 1993; elected August 1994; reelected August 1998; first black American to serve as chief justice, May 1996–July 1997.

Blount, Willie, appointed 1796, resigned same year (1:XXIV); born in Bertie County, North Carolina, 1767 or 1768; died September 10, 1835; private secretary to Territorial Governor William Blount, his half-brother; elected governor of Tennessee 1809–11 and 1811–13; member of Constitutional Convention, 1834; Tennessee House of Representatives, 1807.

Bright, A. D., appointed March 16, 1894, to fill vacancy occasioned by death of Benjamin J. Lea; served until September 1, 1894 (93:V); born in Hinds County, Mississippi, August 10, 1838; died September 11, 1898; captain in Confederate army; member of Commission of Referees, 1883–85.

Brock, Ray L., Jr., born September 21, 1922, McDonald, Tennessee; University of Tennessee, Knoxville; University of Colorado; LL.B., Duke

University, 1948; U.S. Army, 1943–44; practiced law in Chattanooga 1948–63 when appointed judge of Chancery Court; elected chancellor, 1964; reelected 1966; elected to Tennessee Supreme Court 1974; elected chief justice July 1, 1979; reelected to Supreme Court 1982; retired June 15, 1987.

Brown, George H., Jr., B.S., Florida A&M University, 1960; J.D., Howard University, 1967; born in 1939; private practice, 1973–80, 1980–83; the first African American appointed to the Tennessee Supreme Court, June 23, 1980, to serve until August 7, 1980, replacing Joe W. Henry, who died June 9, 1980; Circuit Court judge, Thirtieth Judicial District at Memphis, 1983– .

Brown, William Little, elected by legislature 1822 (7:VIII); resigned July 1824; born near Cheraw, South Carolina, August 9, 1789; died February 28, 1830; appointed solicitor general by Governor Willie Blount 1814; member of state senate, 1819.

Buchanan, Arthur S., appointed December 17, 1910, to fill vacancy occasioned by death of William D. Beard (123:III); elected 1912; resigned December 1917 because of ill health (138:V); born in DeSoto County, Mississippi, 1856; died December 25, 1919; member of Mississippi legislature, 1880; memorial and portrait, 142 Tenn. 712.

Burnett, Hamilton S., appointed October 3, 1947, to succeed Alex W. Chambliss, who died October 1, 1947 (185:V); elected 1948, 1950, and 1958; chief justice, 1963 until retirement, August 31, 1969; born Jefferson County, Tennessee, August 20, 1895, died May 1, 1973; circuit judge, Knox County, 1934–42; judge of Court of Appeals of Tennessee, 1942–47; memorial and portrait, 496 S.W.2d 3.

Caldwell, Waller C., elected 1886 (85:V); reelected 1894; served until 1902; born in Obion County, Tennessee, May 14, 1849; died December 23, 1924; brother-in-law of Chief Justice Grafton Green; served on Commission of Referees, 1883–86; memorial, 151 Tenn. XXXI.

Campbell, David, appointed territorial judge by President Washington in 1790, served until admission of Tennessee to the Union, 1796; served as judge of Superior Court October 11, 1797–1807 (1:XXIII); major in Continental army; member of Convention of Deputies, which led to establishment of State of Franklin, 1784–85; chief justice of State of Franklin; member of legislature of North Carolina, 1787; judge of Superior Court of North Carolina, 1787; impeached by Tennessee House of Representatives 1803 but acquitted by state senate by vote of nine to three; federal judge of Mississippi Territory, November 1, 1811, until death, November 21, 1812.

Campbell, George Washington, elected by legislature in 1809 and resigned in 1811 to accept appointment to U.S. Senate (1:XXV); born in Scotland, February 9, 1769; died February 19, 1848; member of Congress, 1803–9; member of U.S. Senate, 1811–14, 1815–18; secretary of the U.S. Treasury,

1814; U.S. minister to Russia, 1818–21; commissioner to adjudicate claims of American citizens against France, 1831; owned present site of state Capitol in Nashville, with home just across street; memorial, 27 Tenn. XIX.

Caruthers, Robert Looney, appointed 1852 to succeed Nathan Green (32:V); elected by legislature 1853; one of three judges elected in first popular election, May 25, 1854; served until resignation in 1861; born in Smith County, Tennessee, July 31, 1800; died October 2, 1882; clerk of Tennessee House of Representatives, 1823; attorney general for his district, 1827–18; brigadier general, Tennessee Militia, 1834; Wilson County representative in state legislature, 1835; he and A. O. P. Nicholson compiled Statutes of Tennessee, 1836; member of Congress, 1841–43; delegate to Peace Conference at Washington, 1861; member of Provisional Congress of Confederacy; elected governor of Tennessee, 1863, but never took office because of War between the States; professor of law, Cumberland University; memorial, 77 Tenn. 757.

Catron, John, elected 1824 to fill vacancy occasioned by resignation of William L. Brown (8:III); resigned as associate justice and elected first chief justice of Tennessee Court of Errors and Appeals December 19, 1831; served as chief justice until 1835, when he was defeated by Nathan Green for membership on the new Supreme Court created by the Constitution of 1834; appointed to U.S. Supreme Court March 3, 1837, and served until death; born in Wythe County, Virginia, 1779; died May 30, 1865; sergeant in War of 1812; served as district attorney general; memorial, 3 Wall.:IX.

Chambliss, Alexander W., appointed September 22, 1923, to succeed Nathan L. Bachman, who resigned (148:V); elected 1926, 1934, 1942; elected chief justice February 3, 1947, to succeed Grafton Green; born Greenville, South Carolina, September 10, 1864; died October 1, 1947; state senator from Hamilton County, 1899; Mayor of Chattanooga, 1901–5, 1919–23; special judge of Court of Civil Appeals, 1917–18; memorial and portrait, 185 Tenn. 703.

Chattin, Chester C., born November 2, 1907, at Winchester, Tennessee; died July 29, 1979; B.S., University of the South, 1929; LL.B., Cumberland University, 1930; commenced practice of law in Winchester in 1930; assistant district attorney, General Eighteenth Judicial Circuit, 1935, 1937, 1939–47; direct representative Franklin County, Tennessee, 1941, 1943; district attorney, General Eighteenth Judicial Circuit, 1947–58; circuit judge, Eighteenth Judicial Circuit, 1958–62; appointed to Court of Appeals by Governor Buford Ellington February 19, 1962; appointed to Supreme Court of Tennessee by Governor Frank G. Clement January 1, 1965; elected to full term 1966; memorial, 624 S.W.2d XXIX.

Claiborne, William C. C., appointed September 28, 1796; resigned 1797 (1:XXIV); born in Sussex County, Virginia, 1775; died November 23, 1817;

judge of First Circuit, 1796; member of Constitutional Convention, 1796; member of Congress, 1797–1801; governor of Mississippi Territory, 1801; commissioner to take possession of Louisiana, 1803; governor of Territory of Orleans, 1804–12; governor of state of Louisiana after admission to Union, 1812–16; elected U.S. senator from Louisiana, 1817, but died before taking seat; Claiborne County named for him.

COOK, WILLIAM LOCH, appointed April 12, 1923, to fill vacancy occasioned by resignation of D. L. Lansden (147:V); elected 1924, 1926, and 1934; born in Montgomery County, Tennessee, December 6, 1869; died March 5, 1942; Dickson County representative in state legislature, 1897; elected judge of Ninth Judicial Circuit, 1908, served until appointment to Supreme Court; memorial and portrait, 179 Tenn. 707.

COOKE, JAMES BURCH, appointed 1884 to fill vacancy occasioned by death of Robert McFarland (81:V); defeated 1886; born in Greenville, South Carolina, April 1, 1819; died April 18, 1899; McMinn County representative in state legislature, 1853; district attorney general; colonel in Confederate army.

COOKE, WILLIAM WILCOX, appointed May 27, 1815, resigned and reappointed October 21, 1815; served until death (1:XII); died July 20, 1816; compiled volume 3 (1 Cooke) of Tennessee *Reports.*

COOPER, ROBERT E., born October 14, 1920, Chattanooga, Tennessee; B.A., University of North Carolina, 1946; J.D., Vanderbilt University School of Law, 1949; chairman, Tennessee Judicial Council, 1967; assistant attorney general, Sixth Judicial Circuit, 1951–53; appointed judge of Sixth Judicial Circuit, November 1953, elected August 1954, reelected August 1958; appointed to Court of Appeals September 1960; elected August 1962, reelected August 1966; elected August 1, 1974, to Tennessee Supreme Court, reelected August 1982; retired 1990.

COOPER, WILLIAM FRIERSON, elected 1861, vice Robert L. Caruthers but did not serve because of War; elected 1878 (57:V); defeated 1886; born in Franklin, Tennessee, March 11, 1820; died May 7, 1909; law partner of Judge A. O. P. Nicholson; he and Return J. Meigs codified laws of Tennessee into Code of 1858; chancellor of Nashville District, November 20, 1872–August 1, 1878; prepared Cooper's edition of Tennessee *Reports,* 1870; complied Cooper's Tennessee Chancery *Reports.*

CRABB, HENRY, elected December 1826, served until death following year (8:III); born in Botetourt County, Virginia, 1793; died 1827; U.S. district attorney for Western District of Tennessee, 1824; Trustee of Cumberland College and University of Nashville (predecessor of George Peabody College) from 1816 to death.

CRESON, LARRY BARKLEY, born Memphis, Tennessee, January 17, 1906; died June 19, 1972; graduate of Vanderbilt University, 1928; LL.B., Vanderbilt

University, 1929; practiced in Memphis, 1930–65; judge, Chancery Court, Shelby County, 1947–54; served as lieutenant commander, Air Combat Intelligence, USNR, World War II; appointed associate justice of the Supreme Court of Tennessee by Governor Clement August 1, 1965, to succeed Justice Andrew O. Holmes, deceased; elected to full term 1966 and served until death in 1972.

DAUGHTREY, MARTHA CRAIG, born July 21, 1942, Covington, Kentucky; B.A., Vanderbilt University, 1964, Phi Beta Kappa; J.D., Vanderbilt University, 1968, Order of the Coif; adjunct professor at Vanderbilt Law School; former faculty member of New York University Appellate Judges Seminar and National Judicial College; Court of Criminal Appeals judge, 1975–90; Vanderbilt Law School faculty member 1972–75; assistant U.S. attorney in Nashville 1968–69; assistant district attorney in Nashville, 1969–72; first woman appointed to Tennessee Supreme Court, April 1990; elected August 1990, served until nomination to U.S. Court of Appeals for the 6th Circuit, commissioned November 22, 1993.

DEADERICK, JAMES W., elected 1870, 1878; retired 1886 (47:V); served as chief justice, 1876–86; born in Jonesboro, Tennessee, November 28, 1812; died October 8, 1890; represented Johnson, Carter, Sullivan, and Washington Counties in state senate, 1851; memorial, 89 Tenn. 759; presentation of portrait, 113 Tenn. 743.

DEHAVEN, DAVID WILLIAM, appointed January 21, 1935, to fill vacancy occasioned by resignation of William H. Swiggart (168:V); elected 1936, 1942; born in Oxford, Mississippi, October 26, 1872, died June 4, 1943; appointed chancellor at Memphis, May 1925, served until appointment to Supreme Court; memorial and portrait, 180 Tenn. 715.

DROWOTA, FRANK F., III, born July 7, 1938, Williamsburg, Kentucky; B.A., Vanderbilt Unversity, 1960; J.D., Vanderbilt School of Law, 1965; U.S. Navy, 1960–62; commander in Judge Advocate General Corps, U.S. Naval Reserve; practiced law in Nashville, 1965–70; appointed chancellor of Chancery Court, Davidson County, 1970; elected chancellor, 1972; appointed to Court of Appeals May 1974; elected August 1974; President Tennessee Judicial Conference, 1979–80; elected associate justice of Tennessee Supreme Court August 1980; reelected 1982, 1990, and 1998; chief justice, January 1989–September 1990.

DYER, ROSS W., appointed September 15, 1961, to succeed John E. Swepston, who retired (208:V); born in Lauderdale County, Tennessee, March 10, 1911; died April 30, 1993; chief justice, September 1, 1969–September 1, 1974; member of Limited Constitutional Convention, 1953; state senator, 1957–58; served with U.S. Army during World War II; executive assistant to the governor of Tennessee, 1959–61; memorial, 875 S.W.2d XXXVII.

EMMERSON, THOMAS, elected 1807 and served until 1809 (1:XXV); elected July 19, 1819; resigned 1822 (7:XII); born Brunswick County, Virginia, June 23, 1773; died July 22, 1837; member of the first Board of Aldermen of Knoxville; first mayor of Knoxville; judge of First Circuit, 1816–19; charter trustee of East Tennessee College (now University of Tennessee).

FELTS, SAM L., appointed February 1, 1960, to succeed A.B. Neil, who retired February 1, 1960 (204:V); elected 1960; born September 29, 1889, in Cheatham County, Tennessee; died October 15, 1977; served as second lieutenant in World War I; judge of Court of Appeals, 1937–60; retired 1964; memorial and portrait, 567 S.W.2d 3.

FENTRESS, FRANCIS, appointed January 1918 to fill vacancy occasioned by resignation of A. S. Buchanan, served until September 1, 1918 (138:V); elected chancellor at Memphis August 1910; born at Bolivar, Tennessee, November 2, 1873; died October 30, 1930.

FOLKES, WILLIAM C., elected 1886; served until 1890 (85:V); born Lynchburg, Virginia, June 8, 1845; died May 17, 1890; member of Confederate army; memorial, 88 Tenn. 795.

FONES, WILLIAM H. D., born October 6, 1917, Crockett County, Tennessee; Memphis State University, 1934–37; J.D., University of Tennessee College of Law, 1940; pilot, U.S. Army Air Force, four years, World War II, retired as lieutenant colonel, 1965; Memphis law practice, 1945 until appointed circuit judge of Shelby County, 1971; elected to unexpired term in August 1972; appointed justice of the Tennessee Supreme Court May 14, 1973; elected to full term August 1, 1974; elected to second full term August 1982; retired 1990.

FREEMAN, THOMAS J., elected 1870, 1878 (48:III); defeated 1886; born in Gibson County, Tennessee, July 19, 1827; died in Dallas, Texas, September 16, 1891; colonel in Confederate army; dean of Law Department, University of Tennessee, when first organized in 1889; memorial and portrait, 90 Tenn.745.

GAILOR, FRANK H., appointed June 7, 1943, to succeed D. W. DeHaven, who died June 4, 1943 (179:V); elected 1944, 1950; died April 8, 1954; born in Sewanee, Tennessee, May 9, 1892; combat duty with British army and later with U.S. Army during World War I; Shelby County representative in state legislature, 1921, and state senator, 1923; Shelby County attorney, 1937–42; memorial exercises, 196 Tenn. 709.

GREEN, GRAFTON, elected 1910, 1918, 1926, 1934 and 1942 (123:III); chief justice, August 12, 1923–January 27, 1947; born in Lebanon, Tennessee, August 12, 1872; died January 27, 1947; grandson of Judge Nathan Green Sr.; memorial and portrait, 184 Tenn. 706, 185 Tenn. 715, 188 Tenn. 708.

GREEN, NATHAN, elected 1831 (vice John Catron who had been elected chief justice) (10:III); defeated John Catron, December 4, 1835, for judge of new Supreme Court under Constitution of 1834; retired September 27, 1852; born in Amelia County, Virginia, May 16, 1792; died March 30, 1866; soldier in War of 1812; state senator, 1827; chancellor of East Tennessee, 1827–31; professor of Law, Cumberland University; memorials, 41 Tenn. XI, 44 Tenn. 643.

Hall, Frank P., elected 1918; nominated 1926 but died before election (141:V); born in Weakley County, Tennessee, September 15, 1870; died July 10, 1926; Weakley County representative in state legislature, 1899; member of Court of Civil Appeals, 1910–18; memorial and portrait, 154 Tenn. 707.

Harbison, William J., born September 11, 1923, Columbia, Tennessee; died November 20, 1993; B.A., Vanderbilt University, 1947; LL.B., Vanderbilt University, 1950; U.S. Army, 1943–46; special justice, Tennessee Supreme Court, 1966–67; elected August 1, 1974; reelected August 5, 1982; memorial, 892 S.W.2d XXXIX.

Harris, William R., appointed 1855, vice A. W. O. Totten, elected December 1, 1855, served until death (34:V); born in Montgomery County, North Carolina, September 26, 1803; died June 19, 1858, from explosion of Steamboat *Pennsylvania* on Mississippi River between New Orleans and Memphis; elder brother of Isham G. Harris; judge of Ninth Circuit, 1836–45; judge of Common Law and Chancery Court at Memphis, 1851–55 (succeeding William B. Turley); memorial, 37 Tenn. 729.

Harrison, Horace H., member of Court, 1868 (45:V); born in Lebanon, Tennessee, August 7, 1829; died December 20, 1885; principal clerk of state senate, 1851–52; U.S. district attorney for Middle Tennessee, 1863–66, 1872; chancellor, Nashville District, April 2, 1867, to February 3, 1868; member of Congress, 1873–75; vice president of Republican National Convention, 1876; member of state legislature, 1880–81; trustee of University of Nashville.

Hawkins, Alvin, appointed 1865; resigned 1868 (41:V); elected 1869; retired with adoption of Constitution of 1870; born in Bath County, Kentucky, December 2, 1821; died in Huntingdon, April 27, 1905; Carroll County representative in state legislature, 1853; elected to Congress 1862 but was never seated; U.S. attorney for West Tennessee during War between the States; served as governor of Tennessee, 1881–83; appointed U.S. consul general to Havana 1868 but resigned; memorial and portrait, 115 Tenn. 742.

Haywood, John, elected September 14, 1816 (vice W. W. Cooke) (4:I); served until 1826; born in Halifax County, North Carolina, 1753 (See *Green Bag* 5:123) or March 16, 1762 (see Caldwell, *Sketches of the Bench and Bar,* 33); died December 22 or 26, 1826; elected by legislature of North Carolina, judge of Superior Court, District of Davidson (now Tennessee), December 28, 1785, but declined; elected solicitor general of North Carolina, December 11, 1790; served as attorney general of North Carolina, 1791–94; Superior Court judge of North Carolina *Reports,* 1794–1806; compiled Haywood's North Carolina *Reports,* volumes 1 and 2, and Haywood's Tennessee *Reports,* volumes 3, 4, and 5 (volumes 4, 5, and 6 of Tennessee *Reports*); authored "The Christian Advocate," 1819, and "Natural and Aboriginal History of Tennessee" and "Civil and Political History of Tennessee," 1823; Haywood County named for him.

Henry, Joe W., born September 20, 1916, Lynnville (Giles County) Tennessee; died June 9, 1980; attended Middle Tennessee State University; LL.B., Cumberland University, 1938; admitted to Tennessee Bar, March 1940; began practice of Law in Pulaski, January 1, 1941; entered the U.S. Army, October 11, 1941; graduated from Infantry Officer Candidate School, served in Mediterranean Theater of Operations; discharged as a major February 1946; representative in Tennessee General Assembly, 1948–50; served as adjutant general of Tennessee January 1953–January 1959; elected to Tennessee Supreme Court August 1, 1974, took his seat September 1, 1974; memorial, 624 S.W.2d XXXV.

Holder, Janice M., born August 29, 1949, Canonsburg, Pennsylvania; attended Allegheny College, 1967–68; B.S., summa cum laude, University of Pittsburgh, 1971; J.D., Duquesne University School of Law, 1975, senior law clerk to Herbert P. Sorg, chief judge, U.S. District Court, Western District of Pennsylvania, 1975–77; practiced law 1977–90; elected Circuit Court judge for the Thirtieth Judicial District at Memphis, Division II, 1990; appointed to Supreme Court of Tennessee December 1996; elected August 1998.

Holmes, Andrew O., born Hernando, Mississippi, May 4, 1906; died July 24, 1965; B.A., Vanderbilt University, 1927; LL.B., Vanderbilt University, 1929; admitted to law practice in Tennessee 1928; practiced law in Memphis 1929–47; Tennessee House of Representatives, 1941; served three years in U.S. Navy in World War II, seventeen months as Air Combat Intelligence Officer on carrier in Pacific, separated from service as lieutenant commander 1945; appointed Circuit Court judge in Shelby County, March 1947; held that office until appointed associate justice of Supreme Court by Governor Clement February 1963 following the death of Chief Justice Alan Prewitt; memorial, 215 Tenn. 730, 436 S.W.2d 1.

Humphreys, Allison B., born June 28, 1906, Lebanon, Wilson County, Tennessee; died September 1, 1993; Castle Heights Military Academy; LL.B., Cumberland University, 1929; began practice of law in Lebanon, 1929; assistant district attorney general, Fifth Judicial Circuit, 1937–40;

circuit judge, Fifth Judicial Circuit, 1941–42; acting dean and professor of law, Cumberland University Law School, 1942–45; assistant to attorney general and reporter, 1943–52; state solicitor general, 1952–60; appointed to Court of Appeals by Governor Buford Ellington, January 22, 1960. Appointed by Governor Ellington April 27, 1967 to fill vacancy upon the death of Justice W. G. White. Elected to full term August 1968; retired 1974; memorial, 880 S.W.2d XXXI.

HUMPHREYS, PARRY W., elected 1807; served until 1809 (1:XXV); born Lexington, Kentucky; died January 19 or March 1, 1839; Tennessee House of Representatives, 1805, and state senate, 1807; judge of Fifth Circuit, 1809–13, 1818–36; member of Congress, 1813–15; unsuccessful candidate for U.S. Senate, 1817; Humphreys County named for him.

JACKSON, ANDREW, elected 1798; served until 1804 (1:XXIV); born near line between North and South Carolina, March 15, 1767; died June 8, 1845; president of the United States, 1828–36; U.S. district attorney, 1790; represented Davidson County in Constitutional Convention of 1796; member of Congress, 1796–97; U.S. senator from Tennessee, 1797–98, 1823–25; major general of Tennessee Militia, 1802; major general of U.S. Army in War of 1812, winning Battle of New Orleans, January 8, 1815; governor of Florida Territory, 1821; Jackson County and City of Jackson named for him.

LANSDEN, D. L., elected 1910, 1918 (123:III); elected chief justice, 1918 (141:V); resigned April 11, 1923; born in White County, Tennessee, May 16, 1869; died August 10, 1924; chancellor of Fourth Division, 1902–10; memorial and portrait, 150 Tenn. 704.

LEA, BENJAMIN J., elected 1890 to fill vacancy occasioned by death of William C. Folkes (89:VI); elected chief justice 1893 (92:V); born in Caswell County, North Carolina, January 1, 1833; died March 15, 1894; Haywood County representative in state legislature, 1859; colonel in Confederate army; member and speaker of state senate, 1889; attorney general and reporter, 1878–86; compiled volumes 70–84 of Tennessee *Reports;* memorial, 93 Tenn. 719.

LURTON, HORACE H., elected 1886 (85:V); elected chief justice January 17, 1893 (vice Peter Turney) (92:V); resigned 1893 to accept appointment as U.S. circuit judge of Sixth Circuit; appointed associate justice of U.S. Supreme Court December 20, 1909, and served until death (215 U.S.:III); born in Newport, Kentucky, February 26, 1844; died July 12, 1914; sergeant major in Confederate army; chancellor of Clarksville District, 1875–78; dean of Law School, Vanderbilt University, 1905–10; memorials, 130 Tenn. 717, 237 U.S.:V.

MCALISTER, WILLIAM K., appointed April 1, 1893, to fill vacancy occasioned by resignation of Horace H. Lurton (92:V); elected 1894, 1902; served until

1910; born at Nashville, July 4, 1850; died May 16, 1923; city attorney of Nashville, 1875–83; served as circuit judge of Seventh Circuit, 1886–93; law professor at Vanderbilt University from 1910 until death; memorial, 169 Tenn. 707.

McCanless, George F., born in Morristown, Tennessee, June 8, 1904; died June 4, 1992; B.A., Vanderbilt University, 1926, LL.B., 1928; admitted to the bar in 1928; practiced law in Morristown; city attorney, 1933–37; chancellor, Thirteenth Chancery Division, 1937–38; commissioner of Finance and Taxation, 1939–46; appointed attorney general and reporter by the Supreme Court September 29, 1954, to succeed the Honorable Roy H. Beeler, who died September 23; reelected to full term in 1958; again in 1966; appointed by the governor to fill vacancy on the Supreme Court occasioned by the resignation of Hamilton S. Burnett, chief justice, effective September 1, 1969; elected to unexpired term August 6, 1970; memorial, 875 S.W.2d. XXXIII.

McClain, Andrew, appointed 1869; served one and a half years (46:V); born in Smith County, Tennessee, April 6, 1826; died January 21, 1913; appointed judge of Sixth Circuit, July 16, 1864; served until 1869; appointed U.S. district attorney for Middle Tennessee by President Chester A. Arthur.

McFarland, Robert, appointed December 1871 (vice T. A. R. Nelson); elected 1872, 1878; resigned because of poor health 1882 (50:V); born Hamblen County, Tennessee, April 15, 1832; died October 2, 1884; major in Confederate army; memorial, 81 Tenn. 737.

McKinney, Colin P., elected 1918, 1926, 1934 (141:V); retired 1942; born at Ripley, Tennessee, May 23, 1873; died April 29, 1944; chancellor of Ninth Division, 1910–18; memorial and portrait, 180 Tenn. 724.

McKinney, Robert J., elected 1847; served until 1861 (28:III); member of first Court elected by popular vote, May 25, 1854; born in Ireland, February 1, 1803; died October 9, 1875; member of Constitutional Convention of 1834; member of Peace Commission to Washington, 1861.

McNairy, John, appointed territorial judge by President George Washington, 1790; served until 1796; appointed judge of Superior Court of Tennessee, 1796; served until 1797 (1:XXIII); born Guilford County, North Carolina, 1762; died November 10, 1837; member of Superior Court of North Carolina prior to 1790; represented Davidson County in Constitutional Convention of 1796; appointed U.S. district judge May 1797; served until 1834; McNairy County named for him.

Maynard, Horace, appointed by Governor W. G. Brownlow (vice Samuel Milligan); was member of Congress at time of appointment and his right to office was challenged; see *Calloway v. Strum,* 48 Tennessee (1 Heiskell), 764; born in Massachusetts August 30, 1814; died May 3, 1882; member of

Congress, 1857–63, 1865–75; attorney general of Tennessee, 1863–65; unsuccessful candidate for governor, 1874; U.S. minister to Turkey, 1875–80; U.S. postmaster general, 1880–81.

MILLIGAN, SAMUEL, appointed 1864; resigned and reappointed March 21, 1867; served until 1868 (41:V); born in Greene County, Tennessee, November 16, 1814; died April 20, 1874; representative from Greene and Washington Counties in state legislature, 1841; representative from Greene County, 1843, 1845; major in U.S. Army in Mexican War, 1847; judge of Court of Claims at Washington, 1868; memorial, 53 Tenn. 647.

NEIL, A. B., appointed March 9, 1942, to succeed W. L. Cook, deceased (178:V); elected 1942, 1950 and 1958; born Marshall County, Tennessee, February 28, 1873; died June 26, 1966; representative in Tennessee legislature 1899; judge of Davidson County Criminal Court, 1910–18; judge of Davidson County Circuit Court, 1918–42; dean of Law School, Cumberland University, 1935–40; professor of law, 1930–40; elected chief justice October 6, 1947, following death of Chief Justice Chambliss; retired February 1, 1960; memorial and portrait, 218 Tenn. 702.

NEIL, MATTHEW M., elected 1902, 1910 (109:III); elected chief justice February 17, 1913; served until 1918; born in Fayetteville, Tennessee, 1849; died June 23, 1925; judge of Court of Chancery Appeals, 1895–1902; memorial and portrait, 152 Tenn. 712.

NELSON, THOMAS A. R., elected 1870 (47:V); resigned December 1871 (50:V); born Roane County, Tennessee, March 19, 1812; died August 24, 1873; served as attorney general for First Circuit for two terms beginning 1833; judge of Knox County Criminal Court, 1844; declined appointment as commissioner to China 1851; member of Congress, 1859–61; counsel for President Andrew Johnson in impeachment trial before U.S. Senate; memorial, 53 Tenn. 653.

NICHOLSON, ALFRED O. P., elected 1870, served until death (47:V); named chief justice 1870; born in Williamson County, Tennessee, August 31, 1808; died March 23, 1876; he and Robert L. Caruthers compiled Statutes of Tennessee, 1836; Maury County representative in state legislature, 1833, 1835, 1837; member of state senate, 1843; appointed to U.S. Senate, 1840, elected 1859; appointed chancellor of Nashville Division in 1851 but resigned at end of year; declined appointment as U.S. postmaster general during administration of President Franklin Pierce; member of Constitutional Convention, 1870; memorials and portrait, 56 Tenn. 883; 113 Tenn. 734.

O'BRIEN, CHARLES H., born July 30, 1920, Orange, New Jersey; served in infantry during World War II; Korean War, G.H.Q. United Nations Command, Tokyo, Japan; LL.B., Cumberland Law School, 1947; law practice in Memphis, 1948–67; law practice in Crossville, 1967–70; member of 83d and

84th Tennessee General Assemblies; elected to Court of Criminal Appeals, 1970; reelected 1974 and 1982; appointed to Tennessee Supreme Court in 1987 by Governor Ned McWherter; elected to remainder of unexpired term August 4, 1988; reelected 1990 for eight-year term; retired 1994.

Overton, John, member of Superior Court (vice Andrew Jackson), 1804–10; elected judge of Court of Errors and Appeals, 1811; resigned April 11, 1816 (1:XXIV); born in Louisa County, Virginia, April 9, 1766; died April 12, 1833; commissioned Supervisor of Revenue at Nashville by President Washington; made original plan laying off City of Memphis, as coproprietor with Andrew Jackson and General James Winchester; compiled volumes 1 and 2 of Tennessee *Reports;* most intimate lifelong friend of Andrew Jackson; instigated movement to elect Jackson president; selected to preside over first Democratic National Convention at Baltimore, May 21–23, 1832, but was prevented from doing so by illness; Overton County named for him.

Peck, Jacob, elected 1822 (vice Emmerson) (7:VIII); served until new Court created by Constitution of 1834; born in Virginia, 1779; died June 11, 1869; state senator from Greene and Jefferson Counties, 1821; compiled volume 7 of Tennessee *Reports;* memorial, 46 Tenn. 657.

Powell, Samuel, elected 1807; served until 1809 (1:XXV); born in Montgomery County, Pennsylvania, July 10, 1776; died August 2, 1841; judge of First Circuit, 1812–13, 1819–41; member of Congress, 1815–17.

Prewitt, Alan M., elected to succeed C. P. McKinney, who retired September 1, 1942 (179:V); elected 1942, 1950, and 1958; born Grand Junction, Tennessee, February 1, 1893; died February 17, 1963; combat duty overseas in World War I; special judge, Court of Appeals, 1934; special judge of Supreme Court, 1937 and April 1941–March 1942; elected chief justice February 1, 1960, following retirement of Chief Justice A. B. Neil; memorial and portrait, 210 Tenn. 712.

Reese, William B., elected December 4, 1835, served until retirement, October 1, 1847 (17:III); born in Jefferson County, Tennessee, November 19, 1793; died July 7, 1859; first native Tennessean to serve on Supreme Bench (See *Green Bag* 5:176); chancellor of Eastern Division, 1831 (succeeding Nathan Green), until election to Supreme Court; unsuccessful candidate for U.S. Senate, 1847, defeated by John Bell, president of East Tennessee University (now University of Tennessee) from 1851 until shortly before death; memorial, 39 Tenn. 714.

Reid, Lyle, born June 17, 1930, Tennessee; B.S, 1954, J.D., 1956, University of Tennessee, Knoxville; Tennessee House of Representatives, 1967–68; U.S. Air Force, 1949–52; law clerk to Chancellor John Gray, 1957–60; General Sessions judge, 1960; assistant state attorney general, 1961–63; private law practice in Brownsville, 1963–86; Haywood County attorney, 1964–86; deputy commissioner of Department of Commerce and Insurance, 1987; appointed to the Court of Criminal Appeals, 1987; elected 1988; elected to Tennessee Supreme Court, August 1990; chief justice, 1990–94; retired March 1, 1998.

Roane, Archibald, member of first Court elected under Constitution of 1796; resigned 1801 (1:XXIII); was added to Court October 21, 1815, and served until death (1:XII); born in Lancaster County, Pennsylvania, 1759; died January 4, 1819; second governor of Tennessee, 1801–3; attorney general for Hamilton District, 1778; member of Constitutional Convention, 1796; member of state senate from Knox County, 1811; soldier in Revolutionary War; present at surrender of Cornwallis; judge of Second Circuit, 1811–15; Roane County named for him.

Shackelford, James O., appointed August 24, 1865 (41:V); chancellor of Nashville Division, February 28, 1868, to December 16, 1868.

Shields, John Knight, elected 1902, 1910 (109:III); elected chief justice 1910 (123:III); resigned February 12, 1913, upon election to U.S. Senate, January 23, 1913; member of U.S. Senate, 1913 to 1924; born in Grainger County, Tennessee, August 15, 1858; died September 30, 1934; chancellor of Twelfth Division, 1892–94.

Smith, Henry G., appointed 1867; served until 1870 (45:V); state senator, 1877; born in Connecticut, 1807; died December 31, 1878; memorial, 70 Tenn. 751.

Sneed, John L. T., elected 1870; failed renomination 1878 (47:V); born in Raleigh, North Carolina, 1820 (66:V); died July 29, 1901; captain of Volunteers in Mexican War, soldier in Confederate army; Shelby County representative in state legislature, 1845; district attorney general, Memphis, 1851–54; attorney general of Tennessee, 1854–59; compiled volumes 33–37 of Tennessee *Reports;* brigadier general in Confederate army; judge of Court of Arbitration, 1878–83; member of Commission of Referees, 1883; unsuccessful candidate for U.S. Senate, 1887; chancellor at Memphis, succeeding Judge William D. Beard, 1894.

Snodgrass, David L., elected 1886, 1894 (85:V); served as chief justice, 1894–1902; born in Sparta, Tennessee, April 6, 1851; died October 11, 1917; White County representative in state legislature, 1879; member of Commission of Referees, 1883–85; unsuccessful candidate for U.S. Senate, 1900; memorial and portrait, 138 Tenn. App. 7.

Swepston, John E., appointed April 12, 1954, to succeed Frank H. Gailor, who died April 8, 1954 (196:V); elected 1954 and 1958; retired September 15, 1961; born Crawfordsville, Arkansas, August 9, 1894; died October 24, 1961; served in U.S. Navy during World War I; chancellor, Shelby County,

1935–47; judge, Court of Appeals, 1947–54; memorial and portrait, 208 Tenn. 710.

Swiggart, William H., elected 1926, 1934 (154:V); resigned 1934, to accept position as general counsel of North Carolina and St. Louis Railway; born in Union City, Tennessee, October 12, 1888; died October 30, 1966; assistant state attorney general, 1914–26; trustee, Vanderbilt University; memorial and portrait, 221 Tenn. 748.

Tatum, Howell, appointed 1797; resigned 1798 (1:XXIV); soldier in Revolutionary War and topographical engineer in War of 1812; attorney general of Mero District, 1796–97; treasurer of Mero District, 1794–96; died in the fall of 1822.

Tomlinson, Pride, appointed February 1, 1947, to succeed Grafton Green, who died January 27, 1947 (184:VIII); elected 1948, 1950 and 1958; retired July 31, 1961; born in Maury County, Tennessee, July 16, 1890; died November 27, 1967; Maury County attorney, 1921–47; special judge, Supreme Court, January–March 1946; chairman, Tennessee Code Commission, 1945–February 1947; president, Judicial Conference, 1950–51; memorial and portrait, 220 Tenn. 738.

Totten, Archibald W. O., elected February 28, 1850 (vice William B. Turley); resigned July 17, 1855 (29:IV); born in Overton County, Tennessee, November 25, 1809; died 1867; member of first Court elected by popular vote, May 25, 1854; member of Peace Congress at Washington, 1861; memorials, 43 Tenn. 605, 44 Tenn. 649.

Turley, William B., elected December 4, 1835 (17:III); reelected 1847; resigned 1850 (29:V); born in Alexandria, Virginia, 1800; died; May 27, 1851; judge of Eleventh Circuit, 1829–35; judge of Common Law and Chancery Court at Memphis, 1850 until death; memorial, 30 Tenn. 421; memorial and portrait, 134 Tenn. III.

Turney, Peter, elected 1870, 1878, 1886 (47:V); elected chief justice, 1886; resigned after being elected governor of Tennessee, 1893; born in Jasper, Tennessee, September 27, 1827; died October 28, 1903; governor of Tennessee, 1893 to 1897; colonel in Confederate army; memorial, 111 Tenn. 747.

White, Hugh Lawson, elected 1801; resigned 1807; reappointed 1809; served until 1814; declined reappointment, 1824 (1:XXIV); born in Iredell County, North Carolina, October 30, 1773; died April 10, 1840; member of state senate, 1807–9, 1817–25; U.S. district attorney, 1808; member of U.S. Senate, 1825–40; unsuccessful candidate for president of the United States, 1836.

White, Penny J., born May 3, 1956, Kingsport, Tennessee; B.S., East Tennessee State University, 1978; J.D., University of Tennessee College of Law, 1981; LL.M., Georgetown University Law Center, 1985; elected Circuit Court judge, First Judicial District, 1990–92; appointed to Court of Criminal

Appeals 1992; appointed to Tennessee Supreme Court 1994, served until November 1996, when she did not receive a majority in a retention election; adjunct professor of law at the University of Tennessee College of Law 1987–97, returned in 2000; visiting professor at Washington and Lee University, West Virginia University, and Denver University, 1997–2000.

WHITE, WELDON B., appointed August 1, 1961 to succeed Pride Tomlinson, who retired July 31, 1961 (207:V); born in Waxahachie, Texas, July 22, 1907; died April 23, 1967; state senator, Davidson County, Tennessee, 1940–42; circuit judge, Davidson County, 1942–47; professor of law, Cumberland University, 1946–50; major, U.S. Army, World War II; memorial, 218 Tenn. 708, 445 S.W.2d 1.

WHYTE, ROBERT, appointed May 1816; served until 1834 (7:VIII); born in Scotland, January 6, 1767; died November 12, 1844; professor, William & Mary College.

WILKES, JOHN SUMMERFIELD, appointed January 16, 1893 (vice Peter Turney) (92:V); elected 1894, 1902, served until 1908; born in Maury County, Tennessee, March 2, 1841; died February 2, 1908; captain and purchasing commissary in Confederate army; state adjutant general, 1875; memorial and portrait, 119 Tenn. 745.

WILLIAMS, SAMUEL COLE, appointed 1913 (vice John K. Shields) (126:V); elected 1914; served until 1918; born in Gibson County, Tennessee, January 15, 1864; died December 14, 1947; appointed special chancellor, First Division, 1912; first dean of Lamar School of Law, Emory University, 1919–26; a founder of American Law Institute; chairman of Code Commission to compile 1932 Code of Tennessee, 1929–33; compiler of Williams Annotated Tennessee Code of 1934, 8 volumes; author of ten volumes on the History of Tennessee and of the South.

WILLIAMS, THOMAS L., appointed 1826 (vice Hugh L. White), but next legislature declined to fill vacancy; born in North Carolina, 1788; died December 2, 1856; chancellor for East Tennessee, 1836–54; member of state senate from Knox County, 1819, 1821, 1823; memorial, 36 Tenn. 709.

WRIGHT, ARCHIBALD, appointed June 19, 1858 (vice Wm. R. Harris); elected 1858 (37:V); born Maury County, Tennessee, November 29, 1809; died September 13, 1885; Giles County representative in state legislature, 1847; memorial, 82 Tenn. 723.

The above biographical sketches of the justices of the Court was prepared by Barbara Holton of the offices of Gullett, Sanford, Robinson & Martin, PLLC, Nashville, Tennessee. The material with respect to the justices prior to 1960 was taken from 176 Tenn. 869 (1941) as supplemented in 209 Tenn. 827 (1962).

Appendix 2

SUPREME COURTS OF TENNESSEE

The Court was composed of three judges, all of same rank, until 1870, when three additional judges were added, two to be from each grand division of the state with provision that the judges select the chief justice. The first vacancy occurring after January 1, 1873, was not to be filled, the Court thereafter to consist of five judges, with one as chief justice. Between 1974 and 1990 the term of the chief justice was nineteen months. As of December 11, 1997, under Supreme Court Rule 32, the term of the chief justice became four years.

1834–1847

Nathan Green
William B. Reese
William B. Turley

1847–1850

Nathan Green
William B. Turley, resigned December Term 1850
Robert J. McKinney (vice Reese)

1850–1852

Nathan Green, resigned December Term 1852
Robert J. McKinney
A. W. O. Totten (vice Turley), resigned August 20, 1855

1852–1855

Robert J. McKinney
A. W. O. Totten
R. L. Caruthers (vice Green)

1855–1858

Robert J. McKinney
R. L. Caruthers
William R. Harris (vice Totten)

1858–1861

Robert J. McKinney
R. L. Caruthers
Archibald Wright (vice Harris)

1864

At termination of War between the States,
Governor Brownlow appointed the following Court:

Samuel Milligan
James O. Shackelford
Alvin Hawkins (see 40 Tenn. III)

Samuel Milligan
James O. Shackelford
Alvin Hawkins
Horace H. Harrison
Henry G. Smith
George Andrews

James O. Shackelford
Alvin Hawkins
George Andrews
Henry G. Smith
Andrew McClain

1870–1871

Thomas A. R. Nelson (resigned December 1871)
James W. Deaderick
A. O. P. Nicholson, C.J.
Peter Turney
John L. T. Sneed
Thomas J. Freeman

1871–1876

A. O. P. Nicholson, C.J. (died March 23, 1876)
Peter Turney
Robert McFarland (vice Nelson)
James W. Deaderick
Thomas J. Freeman
John L. T. Sneed

1876–1878

Peter Turney
James W. Deaderick, C.J.
Robert McFarland
Thomas J. Freeman
John L. T. Sneed

1878–1884

James W. Deaderick, C.J.
Robert McFarland (died October 2, 1884)
William F. Cooper (vice Sneed)
Peter Turney
Thomas J. Freeman

1884–1886

James W. Deaderick, C.J.
Peter Turney
J. B. Cooke (vice McFarland)
William F. Cooper
Thomas J. Freeman

1886–1890

Peter Turney, C.J.
Waller C. Caldwell
David L. Snodgrass
Horace H. Lurton
William C. Folkes

1890–1892

Peter Turney, C.J.
Waller C. Caldwell
David L. Snodgrass
Horace H. Lurton
B. J. Lea (vice Folkes)
W. D. Beard (vice Folkes by appointment until Lea was elected to Folkes's vacancy)

1892–1893

Peter Turney, C.J.
John S. Wilkes (vice Turney, upon Turney's election as governor)
David L. Snodgrass
Horace H. Lurton, C.J. (vice Turney)
Waller C. Caldwell
Wm. K. McAlister (vice Lurton, upon Lurton's appointment as U.S. circuit judge)
B. J. Lea (C.J. vice Lurton)

1893–1894

David L. Snodgrass
Waller C. Caldwell
William K. McAlister
B. J. Lea, C.J. (died March 15, 1894)
John S. Wilkes

1894

David L. Snodgrass, C.J.
Waller C. Caldwell
William K. McAlister
John S. Wilkes
A. D. Bright (vice Lea)

1894–1902

David L. Snodgrass, C.J.
Waller C. Caldwell
William K. McAlister
John S. Wilkes
W. D. Beard (vice Bright)

1902–1908

William K. McAlister
M. M. Neil
W. D. Beard, C.J.
John S. Wilkes
John K. Shields (vice Snodgrass)

1908–1910

William K. McAlister
M. M. Neil
W. D. Beard, C.J.
Bennett D. Bell (vice Wilkes)
John K. Shields

1910

Grafton Green
W. D. Beard
M. M. Neil
D. L. Lansden
John K. Shields, C.J.

1910–1913

Grafton Green
Arthur S. Buchanan (vice Beard)
M. M. Neil
D. L. Lansden
John K. Shields, C.J. (resigned 1913)

1913–1918

Grafton Green
Arthur S. Buchanan
M. M. Neil, C.J.
D. L. Lansden
Samuel C. Williams

1918

Grafton Green
Francis Fentress (vice Buchanan)
M. M. Neil, C.J.
D. L. Lansden
Samuel C. Williams

1918–1923

Grafton Green
Frank P. Hall
C. P. McKinney
D. L. Lansden, C.J.
N. L. Bachman

1923

Grafton Green, C.J.
Frank P. Hall
C. P. McKinney
W. L. Cook (vice Lansden)
N. L. Bachman

1923–1926

Grafton Green, C.J.
Frank P. Hall (died July 1926)
C. P. McKinney
W. L. Cook
Alex W. Chambliss (vice Bachman)

1926–1935

Grafton Green, C.J.
William H. Swiggart
C. P. McKinney
W. L. Cook
Alex W. Chambliss

1935–1942

Grafton Green, C.J.
D. W. DeHaven (vice Swiggart)
C. P. McKinney
W. L. Cook
Alex W. Chambliss

1942

Grafton Green, C.J.
Alex W. Chambliss
D. W. DeHaven
A. B. Neil (vice Cook)
Alan M. Prewitt (vice McKinney)

1943–1947

Grafton Green, C.J.
Alex W. Chambliss
A. B. Neil
Alan M. Prewitt
Frank M. Gailor (vice DeHaven)

1947

Alex W. Chambliss, C.J.
A. B. Neil
Alan M. Prewitt
Frank H. Gailor
Pride Tomlinson (vice Green)

1947–1954

A. B. Neil, C.J.
Alan M. Prewitt
Frank H. Gailor
Pride Tomlinson
Hamilton S. Burnett (vice Chambliss)

1954–1960

A. B. Neil, C.J.
Alan M. Prewitt
Pride Tomlinson
Hamilton S. Burnett
John W. Swepston (vice Gailor)

1960–1961

Alan M. Prewitt, C.J.
Pride Tomlinson
Hamilton S. Burnett
John E. Swepston
Sam L. Felts (vice Neil)

1961–1962

Alan M. Prewitt, C.J.
Hamilton S. Burnett
Sam L. Felts
Weldon B. White (vice Tomlinson)
Ross W. Dyer (vice Swepston)

1962–1965

Hamilton S. Burnett, C.J
Sam L. Felts
Weldon B. White
Ross W. Dyer
Andrew O. Holmes (vice Prewitt)

1965–1967

Hamilton S. Burnett, C.J.
Sam L. Felts
Weldon B. White
Ross W. Dyer
Chester C. Chattin (vice Felts)
Larry Creson (vice Holmes)

1967–1969

Hamilton S. Burnett, C.J.
Ross W. Dyer
Chester C. Chattin (vice Felts)
Larry Creson (vice Holmes)
Allison B. Humphreys (vice White)

1969–1973

Ross W. Dyer, C.J.
Chester C. Chattin
Larry Creson (deceased June 19, 1972)
Allison B. Humphreys
George F. McCanless (vice Burnett)

1973

Ross W. Dyer, C.J.
Chester C. Chattin
Allison B. Humphreys
George F. McCanless
William H. D. Fones (vice Creson)

1974–1980

William H. D. Fones, C.J. effec. 9/01/74
Robert E. Cooper, C.J. effec. 5/01/76
Joseph W. Henry, C.J. effec. 12/01/78
Ray L. Brock, C.J. effec. 7/01/79
William J. Harbison

1980–1987

William J. Harbison, C.J. effec. 2/01/81
William H. D. Fones, C.J. effec. 9/01/82
Robert E. Cooper, C.J. effec. 5/01/84
Ray L. Brock, C.J. effec. 12/01/85
George H. Brown (appointed to replace Joseph W. Henry June 23, 1980, to August 7, 1980)
Frank F. Drowota III

1987–1990

William J. Harbison, C.J. effec. 7/01/87
Frank F. Drowota III, C.J. effec. 2/01/89
William H. D. Fones
Robert E. Cooper
Charles H. O'Brien (vice Brock)
Martha Craig Daughtrey (vice Harbison), effec. 4/90, resigned 11/93

1990–1994

Lyle Reid, C.J. 9/01/90 to 9/01/94
E. Riley Anderson, C.J. 10/27/94 to 5/15/96
Frank F. Drowota III
Charles H. O'Brien, C.J. 9/01/94 to 10/26/94
Martha Craig Daughtrey

1994–1996

Lyle Reid, C.J.
Adolpho A. Birch Jr., C.J. 5/16/96 to 7/07/97
Frank F. Drowota III
Charles H. O'Brien
E. Riley Anderson
Penny J. White (vice O'Brien)

1996–1998

Adolpho A. Birch Jr., C.J. effec. 5/01/96
E. Riley Anderson, C.J. 7/08/97 to 8/31/98
Frank F. Drowota III
Lyle Reid
Janice M. Holder (vice White)

1998–2000

E. Riley Anderson, C.J. effec. 9/01/98
Frank F. Drowota III
Adolpho A. Birch Jr.
Janice M. Holder
William M. Barker (vice Reid)

Appendix 3

TABLE OF CASES

NOTES

PREFACE

1. Walter W. Manley II, coauthor and ed., E. Canter Brown Jr., and Eric W. Rise, *The Supreme Court of Florida and Its Predecessor Courts, 1821–1917* (Gainesville, Fla., 1999).
2. Gerald T. Dunne, *The Missouri Supreme Court: From Dred Scott to Nancy Cruzan* (Columbia, Mo., 1993).
3. Russell K. Osgood, ed., *The History of the Law in Massachusetts: The Supreme Judicial Court, 1692–1992* (Boston, 1992).
4. Thomas R. Morris, *The Virginia Supreme Court: An Institutional and Political Analysis* (Charlottesville, Va., 1975); Margaret V. Nelson, *A Study of Judicial Review in Virginia, 1789–1928* (New York, 1947).
5. Charles H. Sheldon, *A Century of Judging: A Political History of the Washington Supreme Court* (Seattle, 1988).
6. G. S. Rowe, *Embattled Bench: The Pennsylvania Supreme Court and the Forging of a Democratic Society, 1684–1809* (Newark, Del., 1994).
7. *See* Michael H. Hoffheimer, "Mississippi Courts: 1790–1868," 65 *Mississippi Law Journal* 99–170 (1995); Cara Shelby, "Republican Benchmark: The Michigan Supreme Court, 1858–1875," 77 *Mid-America* 93–119 (1995).
8. Logan Scott Stafford, "The Arkansas Supreme Court and the Civil War," 7 *Journal of Southern Legal History* 37–114 (1999).
9. *See* Robert A. Kagan, Bobby D. Infelise, and Robert R. Detlefsen, "American State Supreme Court Justices, 1900–1970," *American Bar Foundation Research Journal* 371–408 (1984); Lawrence M. Friedman, Robert A. Kagan, Bliss Cartwright, and Stanton Wheeler, "State Supreme Courts: A Century of Style and Citation," 33 *Stanford Law Review* 773–818 (1981); Robert A. Heiberg, "Social Backgrounds of the Minnesota Supreme Court Justices: 1858–1968," 53 *Minnesota Law Review* 901 (1969); Francis H. Heller, "The Justices of the Kansas Supreme Court 1861–1975: A Collective Portrait," 24 *Kansas Law*

Review 521–35 (1976); Dean Jaros and Bradley C. Canon, "Dissent on State Supreme Courts: The Differential Significance of Characteristics of Judges," 15 *Midwest Journal of Political Science* 322–46 (1971).

10. Charles S. Lopeman, *The Activist Advocate: Policy Making in State Supreme Courts* (Westport, Conn., 1999); Mary Cornelia Porter and G. Alan Tarr, eds., *State Supreme Courts: Policymakers in the Federal System* (Westport, Conn., 1982).
11. Joseph R. Grodin, *In Pursuit of Justice: Reflections of a State Supreme Court Justice* (Berkeley, Calif., 1989). For a study of kinship and political connections as factors in judicial selection, *see* Donn M. Kurtz II, *Kinship and Politics: The Justices of the United States and Louisiana Supreme Courts* (Baton Rouge, La., 1997).
12. *See generally* James W. Ely Jr. and David J. Bodenhamer, "Regionalism and American Legal History: The Southern Experience," 39 *Vanderbilt Law Review* 539–67 (1986).
13. *See generally* Daniel R. Pinello, *The Impact of Judicial-Selection Method on State Supreme Court Policy: Innovation, Reaction, and Atrophy* (Westport, Conn., 1995) (comparing judicial selection and policy making in six state supreme courts).
14. G. Alan Tarr and Mary Cornelia Aldis Porter, *State Supreme Courts in State and Nation* (New Haven, Conn., 1988).
15. *See* Walter Murphy, "Lower Court Check on Supreme Court Power," 13 *American Political Science Review* 1017–31 (1959).

1. THE FORMATIVE PERIOD IN THE HISTORY OF THE SUPREME COURT OF TENNESSEE, 1796–1835

The author wishes to acknowledge with gratitude the assistance of Shirley Wilson, Linda Sellars, Cecil V. Crowson Jr., Frankie Lewis, James W. Ely Jr., Kermit Hall, David Bodenhamer, Edwin S. Gleaves, Charles Sherrill, Steve Cotham, Sam B. Smith, Ruth Warner, Ann H. Wells, and the law firm of Long Aldridge & Norman, LLP, in connection with the preparation of this chapter.

1. *See* George Dangerfield, *The Awakening of American Nationalism, 1815–1828* (New York, 1965), 4–35, 195–241, 267–301; Donald B. Dodd, comp., *Historical Statistics of the States of the United States: Two Centuries of the Census, 1790–1990* (Westport, Conn., 1993), 103; Marvin Meyers, *The Jacksonian Persuasion: Politics and Belief* (Stanford, Calif., 1960), 115–16; Charles G. Sellers Jr., *The Market Revolution: Jacksonian America, 1815–1846* (New York, 1991), 3–69, 172–201, 269–363, 396–401. Even in the slave South, there was increasing criticism of slavery, including proposals for gradual abolition. *See* St. George Tucker, *A Dissertation on Slavery: With a Proposal for the Gradual Abolition of It, in the State of Virginia* (Philadelphia: Mathew Carey, 1796), reprinted in Tucker, *View of the Constitution of the United States with Selected Writings* (Indianapolis, Ind.: Liberty Fund, 1999), 403, 415–16, 418, 434, 437, 445; Paul K.

Conkin, *Prophets of Prosperity: America's First Political Economists* (Bloomington, Ind., 1980), 161; Tipton R. Snavely, *George Tucker as Political Economist* (Charlottesville, Va., 1964), 1–6, 134–53. For the sake of convenience, the term "four decades" has been used throughout this chapter, although the actual number of years included in the period 1796–1835 is thirty-nine.

2. Conkin, *Prophets of Prosperity,* 201; Dangerfield, *American Nationalism,* 32, 195–96; George Dangerfield, *The Era of Good Feelings* (New York, 1952), 420–21; Meyers, *Jacksonian Persuasion,* 30–31, 108–9; Merrill D. Peterson, *The Great Triumvirate: Webster, Clay, and Calhoun* (New York, 1987), 47–84; Sellers, *Market Revolution,* 9, 15, 17, 84–90, 439; *see* Joyce Appleby, *Inheriting the Revolution: The First Generation of Americans* (Cambridge, Mass., 2000), 150–58; Leonard Baker, *John Marshall: A Life in Law* (New York, 1974), 396–417, 582–700; Michael F. Holt, *The Rise and Fall of the American Whig Party: Jacksonian Politics and the Onset of the Civil War* (New York, 1999), 843–46; Glyndon G. Van Deusen, *The Jacksonian Era, 1828–1848* (New York, 1959), 21, 257; Forrest McDonald, *States' Rights and the Union: Imperium in Imperio, 1776–1876* (Lawrence, Kans., 2000), 87; Lawrence H. White, ed., *Democratick Editorials: Essays in Jacksonian Political Economy by William Leggett* (Indianapolis, 1984), xiv, 191–230; cf. Richard P. McCormick, *The Second American Party System: Party Formation in the Jacksonian Era* (Chapel Hill, 1966), 353.
3. The terms "Court" and "Tennessee Court" are used throughout to refer to the Supreme Court of Tennessee, when that tribunal was known as the Superior Court of Law and Equity, 1796–1809, and as the Supreme Court of Errors and Appeals, 1810–1835.
4. U.S. House of Representatives, *Abstract of the Returns of the Fifth Census,* H. Doc. 263 (Washington, D.C., 1832), 28–29; Susanna Delfino, "Many Souths: Changing Social Contexts and the Road to Industrialization in Antebellum Tennessee," 22 *Southern Studies* 83, 86–89 (1983); Lawrence B. Goodheart, "Tennessee's Antislavery Movement Reconsidered: The Example of Elihu Embree," 41 *Tennessee Historical Quarterly,* 224–38 (1982); [Frances Wright], "A PLAN For the gradual Abolition of Slavery in the United States, without danger or loss to the Citizens of the South," *Nashville Republican,* Oct. 22, 1825; Clarence E. Carter, ed., *The Territorial Papers of the United States: The Territory South of the River Ohio, 1790–1796* (Washington, D.C., 1936), 4:404; Carroll Van West, et al., eds., *The Tennessee Encyclopedia of History and Culture* (Nashville, 1998), 122–23, 127–29, 288, 834–40, 853–54, 1084–85 (hereafter cited as *TEH&C*). For Blount, *see* William H. Masterson, *William Blount* (New York, 1969, rpt.), 123–24, 177, 349.
5. Tenn. Const. (1796) art. 5, §§ 1, 2; *see generally* Fletcher M. Green, *Constitutional Development in the South Atlantic States, 1776–1860: A Study in the Evolution of Democracy* (Chapel Hill, N.C. 1930), 83, 91, 102. The governor was authorized to fill any judicial vacancy that occurred during a legislative recess by issuing to such appointee a temporary commission that was to expire at the end of the next legislative session. Tenn. Const. (1796) art. 2, § 14.

6. Ch. 6, § 1, 1796 Tenn. Pub. Acts; ch. 1, § 1, 1796 Tenn. Pub. Acts; ch. 19, §§ 1, 2, 1806 Tenn. Pub. Acts; *see* Tenn. Const. (1796) art. 10, § 2; ch. 1, § 39, 1794 Terr. S. of River Ohio Acts.
7. Ch. 1, § 1, 1794 Terr. S. of River Ohio Acts.
8. Joseph Story, *Commentaries on Equity Jurisprudence as Administered in England and America* (Boston, 1839), 1:26, 32; R. Kent Newmyer, *Supreme Court Justice Joseph Story: Statesman of the Old Republic* (Chapel Hill, N.C., 1985), 291–95.
9. James W. Ely Jr. and Theodore Brown Jr., eds., *Legal Papers of Andrew Jackson* (Knoxville, 1987), lii–liii.
10. *Finley v. McClung* (1799), Bland Casebook, 34, Bland Papers, Maryland Historical Society, Baltimore (hereafter cited as Bland Papers); *Williams v. Henderson & Co.* (1791–1802), in Ely and Brown, *Legal Papers of Andrew Jackson,* lii–liii, 135–36.
11. *Impartial Review and Cumberland Repository,* May 12, 1808. Benton's arguments were similar to those that had been made by moderate Republicans in North Carolina in 1806. County courts, whose justices of the peace were untrained in the law and handed down unpredictable decisions, were the subject of criticism, as was holding sessions of the Superior Court only in certain district towns, thus making going to court so expensive and inconvenient for most parties as to render the judicial system for the "benefit of the few to the injury and oppression of the many." *See* Richard E. Ellis, *The Jeffersonian Crisis: Court and Politics in the Young Republic* (New York, 1971), 265.
12. *See* Ellis, *Jeffersonian Crisis,* 130, 185–86, 243 (including remarks by George Nicholson, *ca.* 1791 or 1792, on the need to establish Kentucky's Court of Appeals).
13. Ch. 49, §§ 1, 4, 7, 12, 22, 23, 25, 26, 28; ch. 126, §§ 8, 9, 1809 Tenn. Pub. Acts. For Benton's introduction of the legislation, *see Journal of the Senate, Eighth Tennessee General Assembly* (1809), 167 (hereafter cited as *Senate Journal,* followed by session year indicated parenthetically and page number). Tennessee's county courts had been formally known as courts of pleas and quarter sessions since the time when the state had been a part of North Carolina. *See* Theodore Brown Jr., "The Tennessee County Courts Under the North Carolina and Territorial Governments: The Davidson County Court of Pleas and Quarter Sessions, 1783–1796, as a Case Study," 32 *Vanderbilt Law Review* 349, 351–52 (1979). For the sake of brevity, these courts will be referred to hereinafter merely as "county courts." The legislature subsequently eliminated the requirement that one circuit judge sit with the Court. Ch. 72, § 16, 1811 Tenn. Pub. Acts. The reorganization of Tennessee's judicial system was similar to reforms adopted by Kentucky, Pennsylvania, and Massachusetts, 1791–1808, though the process was not as politicized as in those states. *See* Ellis, *Jeffersonian Crisis,* 121–229.
14. Ch. 72, §§ 4, 5, 1811 Tenn. Pub. Acts.
15. Ch. 77, § 3, 1813 Tenn. Pub. Acts; ch. 31, § 2, 1819 Tenn. Pub. Acts.

16. Ch. 13, §§ 1, 3, 4, 5, 6, 1822 Tenn. Pub. Acts; ch. 14, §§ 3, 10, 1822 Tenn. Pub. Acts.
17. Ch. 14, §§ 1, 2, 8, 1824 Tenn. Pub. Acts; ch. 31, §§ 1, 2, 1825 Tenn. Pub. Acts; *see also* ch. 53, § 1, 1831 Tenn. Pub. Acts.
18. *Porter v. Earthman,* 12 Tenn. (4 Yer.) 300, 309 (1833) (Peck, J.); *Tenn. Gazetteer,* 242.
19. Ch. 14, § 2, 1824 Tenn. Pub. Acts; ch. 79, §§ 1, 2, 1827 Tenn. Pub. Acts; ch. 46, § 1, 1829 Tenn. Pub. Acts; ch. 79, § 2, 1830 Tenn. Pub. Acts; ch. 47, §§ 5, 6, 1831 Tenn. Pub. Acts; ch. 55, §§ 1, 4, 1831 Tenn. Pub. Acts; ch. 56, 1831 Tenn. Pub. Acts; ch. 21, § 7, 1832 Tenn. Pub. Acts; ch. 1, § 1, 1833 Tenn. Pub. Acts.
20. John Overton to Gov. Joseph McMinn [1816], Letters of the Tennessee Governors: Joseph McMinn, 1815–1821, Box 1, Folder 2 (hereafter cited as McMinn Letters), Tennessee State Library and Archives, Nashville (hereafter cited as TSLA). *See* ch. 72, § 4, 1811 Tenn. Pub. Acts.
21. Ch. 79, § 2, 1827 Tenn. Pub. Acts.
22. Theodorick Bland to Sophia Bland, Sept. 7–10, 1800, Bland Papers; Ely and Brown, *Legal Papers of Andrew Jackson,* xlix, 358–59; *see, e.g.,* Jacob Yerger to Robert L. Caruthers, June 17, 1831, no. 1416, Robert Looney Caruthers Papers, Southern Historical Collection, University of North Carolina, Durham (hereafter cited as Caruthers Papers); William B. Campbell to David Campbell [July 11, 1831], Campbell Family Papers, Duke University, Durham, North Carolina.
23. Analysis by the author and in his possession (cited herein as Analysis of Reported Opinions). Most of these decisions are several printed pages in length and include analyses and citations of the law, all of which was accomplished, it should be remembered, without the benefit of modern technological research methods or clerical assistance. Excluded from the computation of the individual judges' opinions are unattributed *per curiam* opinions and short statements without any discussion of the facts or the law. For the Court's reported decisions for the terms specifically referred to in the text, *see* 12 Tenn. (4 Yer.) 127–489; 13 Tenn. (5 Yer.) 1–188; 14 Tenn. (6 Yer.) 1–264; 15 Tenn. (7 Yer.) 193–411; 16 Tenn. (8 Yer.) 1–56.
24. "Report of the Judiciary Committee, Tenn. House of Rep., Oct. 4, 1831," reprinted in *Knoxville Register,* Oct. 26, 1831, and in Robert H. White, *Messages of the Governors of Tennessee, 1821–1835* (Nashville, 1952), 2:352–54 (hereafter cited as *Messages,* followed by volume and page number).
25. Tenn. Const. (1796) art. 1, § 20; ch. 1, § 4, 1796 Tenn. Pub. Acts; ch. 28, §§ 1, 2, 1801 Tenn. Pub. Acts; ch. 7, §§ 2, 3, 1804 Tenn. Pub. Acts; ch. 5, § 1, 1806 Tenn. Pub. Acts; ch. 49, § 29, 1809 Tenn. Pub. Acts; ch. 34, § 1, 1819 Tenn. Pub. Acts; Petition of Judge Archibald Roane, Dec. 26, 1798, Legislative Papers: Petitions and Memorials, 1799–1809, TSLA; Samuel Powel to John Overton, Apr. 29, 1811, quoted in Daniel H. Calhoun, *Professional Lives in America: Structure and Aspiration, 1750–1850* (Cambridge, 1965), 71, 208;

Samuel Cole Williams, "A Remarkable Bench: Campbell, Jackson and White," 16 *Tennessee Law Review* 907, 908 (1941); Ely and Brown, *Legal Papers of Andrew Jackson,* xxv–xxvi, lix.

26. Ely and Brown, *Legal Papers of Andrew Jackson,* 378.
27. *Id.* at 384; *Messages* 1:103–4; *Knoxville Gazette,* Dec. 9, 1811, and Jan. 27, 1812; *Catalogue of the Officers and Alumni of Washington and Lee University, Lexington, Virginia, 1749–1888* (Baltimore, 1888), 52; *TEH&C,* 798.
28. Ely and Brown, *Legal Papers of Andrew Jackson,* 359, 363; *TEH&C,* 118–19.
29. *Id. at* 101, 103–4, 378, 388–89.
30. *Id.* at xxxvi–lx, 344–45.
31. *Senate Journal* 53 (1804); *Journal of the House of Representatives, Fifth Tennessee General Assembly, 2d Sess.* (1804), 54 (herafter cited as *House Journal,* followed by session year indicated parenthetically and page number). Unless otherwise indicated, the sources for this biographical profile of Judge Overton are Ely and Brown, *Legal Papers of Andrew Jackson,* 381–82, and the author's sketch of Overton in *TEH&C,* 716–17.
32. For Overton's statement, *see Davis's Executors v. Fulton,* 1 Tenn. (1 Overton) 94, 103 [1805] (date derived from 1 Tenn. (1 Overton) at ix; all dates so supplied are hereafter indicated by brackets); *see also Glasgow's Lessee v. Smith,* 1 Tenn. (1 Overton) 111, 118 [1805].
33. Inventory of Books, 1808, Box 12, Claybrooke and Overton Papers, Tennessee Historical Society, Nashville; Kenneth S. Cooper, *The Mind of John Overton* (Nashville, 1987), 4.
34. *Smith v. Craig's Lessee,* 2 Tenn. (2 Overton) at 653; John Overton to Gov. Joseph McMinn [1816], McMinn Letters; Ellis, *Jeffersonian Crisis,* 118; Analysis of Reported Decisions.
35. Ely and Brown, *Legal Papers of Andrew Jackson,* 390.
36. *Id.;* Nancy N. Scott, ed. *A Memoir of Hugh Lawson White* (Philadelphia, 1856), 8, 13–14; *TEH&C,* 1053–54. Initially a supporter of Jackson's presidency, White declined offers to join President Jackson's cabinet and eventually broke with the president. It was around White's subsequent presidential candidacy that Tennessee's infant Whig Party rallied during the presidential election of 1836. To Jackson's embarrassment, White won Tennessee's electoral votes.
37. Ch. 34, § 1, 1807 Tenn. Pub. Acts; *Senate Journal* (1807), 33, 193; *see* Robert M. McBride and Dan M. Robison, *Biographical Directory of the Tennessee General Assembly, 1796–1861* (Nashville, 1975), 1:389 (hereafter referred to as *BD—Tenn. Assembly,* followed by volume and page number). Governor Sevier appears to have issued a temporary commission to Thomas Emmerson to fill Campbell's seat, but Emmerson resigned in favor of Powel. Thomas Emmerson to the General Assembly, Oct. 10, 1807, reprinted in *Senate Journal* (1807), 45–46.
38. Ch. 49, § 23, 1809 Tenn. Pub. Acts; *Senate Journal* (1809), 186–87; *House Journal* (1811), 254; Hugh Lawson White to Gov. Willie Blount, Dec. 24, 1815, Letters of the Tennessee Governors: Willie Blount, 1798–1815, Folder 6,

TSLA; *Senate Journal* (1815), 122; *House Journal* (1815), 17, 145; Albert D. Marks, "The Supreme Court of Tennessee," 5 *Green Bag* 120 (1893).

39. Ch. 70, 1815 Tenn. Pub. Acts; ch. 65, § 1, 1817 Tenn. Pub. Acts; ch. 72, § 1, 1819 Tenn. Pub. Acts; chs. 37, 42, 65, 1821 Tenn. Pub. Acts; ch. 11, §§ 1, 2, 1823 Tenn. Pub. Acts.

40. Ch. 70, 1815 Tenn. Pub. Acts. For Haywood's interim appointment, *see* "Legislative Message of Gov. Joseph McMinn, Sept. 15, 1817," *Messages* 1:485; for his election by the General Assembly, Oct. 2, 1817, *see Senate Journal* (1817), 63; *House Journal* (1817), 82. For Whyte's interim appointment, *see* "Legislative Message of Gov. Joseph McMinn, Sept. 15, 1817," *Messages* 1:485; for his election by the General Assembly, Oct. 2, 1817, *see Senate Journal* (1817), 63; *House Journal* (1817), 82.

41. Mary U. Rothrock, "John Haywood: Historian of the Western Country," in John Haywood, *The Natural and Aboriginal History of Tennessee,* ed. Mary U. Rothrock (Jackson, Tenn., 1959), xi–xix, xvi–xvii, xxii; A. S. Colyar, "Sketch of the Author," in John Haywood, *The Civil and Political History of the State of Tennessee* (Nashville, 1915), 5 (*quoting* Judge John M. Lea); *Porter v. Earthman,* 12 Tenn. (4 Yer.) 300, 311 (1833) (Peck, J.); *Gray v. Darby's Lessee,* 8 Tenn. (Mart. & Yer.) 288, 411 (1825); *Nashville Republican,* Jan. 6, 1827; *Knoxville Register,* Jan. 3, 1827; *see* ch. 71, 1826 Priv. Acts; 16th Tenn. General Assembly, Extra Sess., Res. 56, Dec. 11, 1826; *see also* ch. 93, § 1, 1827 Tenn. Pub. Acts. Surrency erroneously states that only two of Haywood's reports are decisions of the Tennessee Court. Erwin C. Surrency, "Law Reports in the United States," 25 *American Journal of Legal History* 53–54 (1981).

42. *Houston's Lessee v. Pillow,* 9 Tenn. (1 Yer.) 435, 459–60 (1831) (Whyte, J.); *Whiteside's Administrator v. Hickman,* 10 Tenn. (2 Yer.) 318, 321–22, 332 (1830); Marks, "Supreme Court of Tennessee," 124; Andrew Jackson to Robert Whyte, Mar. 18, 1806, and Jackson to Whyte, Aug. 23, 1806, in Sam B. Smith, Harriet C. Owsley, Harold D. Moser et al., eds. *The Papers of Andrew Jackson* (Knoxville, 1980–), 2:536, 540 (hereafter cited as *Jackson Papers,* followed by volume and page number); Lewis E. Atherton, "The Problem of Credit Rating in the Ante-Bellum South," 12 *Journal of Southern History* 535–36 (1946); Enoch Mitchell, "Robert Whyte, Agrarian, Lawyer, Jurist," 10 *Tennessee Historical Quarterly* 3, 6, 8–12 (1951). Unless otherwise indicated, the source for this biographical profile of Judge Whyte is Ely and Brown, *Legal Papers of Andrew Jackson,* 391–92.

43. *Senate Journal* (1822), 207, 211; *House Journal* (1822), 161; *BD—Tenn. Assembly,* 577–78; George Andrews, Eulogy of Jacob Peck, Sept. 20, 1869, in "In Memoriam," 46 Tenn. (6 Cold.) 42 (1870). Peck recognized the inhumanity of slavery, which he once characterized as "an evil." In retirement, he became the business partner of Ezekiel Birdseye, an abolitionist businessman who settled for a time in eastern Tennessee; the two planned to establish a self-sustaining community based on the use of free labor, a project that never materialized. Jacob Peck to Gerrit Smith, Nov. 30, 1841, Letters and Papers of Gerrit Smith,

George Arents Research Library for Special Collections, Syracuse Univ., Syracuse, N.Y. (hereafter cited as Gerrit Papers); Durwood Dunn, *An Abolitionist in the Appalachian South: Ezekiel Birdseye on Slavery, Capitalism, and Separate Statehood in East Tennessee, 1841–1846* (Knoxville, 1997), 48–49, 55. For Emmerson's appointment and election, *see* Gov. Joseph McMinn to Thomas Emmerson, Jan. 20, 1819, McMinn Letters; *House Journal* (1819), 134–35.

44. Fifteenth Tenn. General Assembly, 1st sess., Resolution No. 9, reprinted in 1823 Tenn. Pub. Acts 285; *Senate Journal* (1822), 211; Edmund Dillahunty to Robert L. Caruthers, Sept. 29, 1823, Folder 1, Caruthers Papers; William L. Brown to William Carroll, Oct. 13, 1823, Letters of the Tennessee Governors: William Carroll, 1821–1827, Box 1, Folder 3 (hereafter cited as Carroll Letters), TSLA; *Messages* 2:58–59, 65–66, 69–70.
45. "Legislative Message of Gov. William Carroll, Sept. 20, 1824," *Messages* 2:65.
46. Ch. 14, §§ 1, 2, 8, 1824 Tenn. Pub. Acts.
47. *House Journal* (1824), 195; Scott, *White Memoir,* 17; Thomas L. Williams to Robert L. Caruthers, Nov. 7, 1824, Folder 1, Caruthers Papers; *see* Legislative Message of Gov. William Carroll, Sept. 17, 1827, Box 1, Folder 8, Carroll Letters.
48. Ch. 79, § 1, 1827 Tenn. Pub. Acts; *House Journal* (1831), 379.
49. John Catron to John Livingston, Dec. 24, 1851, reprinted in John Livingston, *Portraits of Eminent Americans Now Living: With Biographical and Historical Memoirs of Their Lives and Actions* (New York, 1853–54), 2:805–7, 809; *see* Walter Chandler, "The Centenary of Associate Justice John Catron of the United States Supreme Court," 15 *Tennessee Law Review* 32 (1937); Richard L. Aynes, "John Catron," in *American National Biography,* ed. John A. Garraty and Mark C. Carnes (New York, 1999), 4:579; Josephus C. Guild, *Old Times in Tennessee* (Nashville, 1878), 459; Samuel H. Laughlin, "Sketches of Notable Men," 4 *Tennessee Historical Magazine* 76; *see* "Legislative Message of Gov. Joseph McMinn, Sept. 15, 1817," *Messages* 1:485. For Catron's election to the Court, *see House Journal* (1824), 195; for his election as chief justice, *see Senate Journal* (1831), 315; *House Journal* (1831), 379.
50. 9 Tenn. (1 Yer.) 207, 212–15 (1829). The Court's decision apparently came as a surprise. *See* Edmund Dillahunty to James K. Polk, Jan. 25, 1828, Herbert Weaver et al., eds., *Correspondence of James K. Polk* (Nashville, 1969–), 1:131–32 ("We anticipate with great confidence the reversal of the [circuit court's] opinion"); Henry S. Foote, *The Bench and Bar of the South and Southwest* (St. Louis, 1876), 146–51.
51. Andrew Jackson Donelson to Andrew Jackson Donelson Jr., Sept. 27, 1856 (characterizing Catron as a notorious political "wirepuller"), reprinted in St. George L. Sioussat, ed., "Selected Letters, 1846–1856, from the Donelson Papers," 3 *Tennessee Historical Magazine* 289–90 (1917); Newmyer, *Joseph Story,* 219, 310, 313; John Catron to James K. Polk, July 23, 1844, quoted in Carl B. Swisher, *Taney Period, 1836–64,* vol. 5 of *The Oliver Wendell Holmes Devise History of the Supreme Court of the United States,* 223–24; *see* Catron to Andrew Jackson, Jan. 2, 1833, Catron Papers, TSLA; *see also* Andrew Jackson to William B.

Lewis, Dec. 18, 1844, reprinted in St. George L. Sioussat, ed., "Selected Letters, 1844–1845, from the Donelson Papers," 3 *Tennessee Historical Magazine* 146 (1917). It was Catron who wrote to president-elect Buchanan on the eve of the latter's inaugural in 1857 to apprise him of the status of the Court's deliberations in the Dred Scott case, to submit a draft paragraph about the case for use in Buchanan's inaugural address, and to ask Buchanan to intercede with Justice Robert Grier about the case. *See* John Catron to James Buchanan, Feb. 19, 1857, in John B. Moore, ed., *The Works of James Buchanan* (Philadelphia, 1910), 10:106–8; Catron to Buchanan, Feb. 23, 1857, in Philip Auchampaugh, "James Buchanan, the Court and the Dred Scott Case," 9 *Tennessee Historical Magazine* 231, 238 (1926). For Catron's editorials, *see Nashville Whig,* June 2, 16, 26, 30 and July 3, 1829; *Knoxville Register,* July 8 and 15, 1829; St. George L. Sioussat, "Some Phases of Tennessee Politics in the Jackson Period," 14 *American Historical Review* 64–65 (1909):.

Defeated in his effort to serve on the new Court, Catron was nominated to fill one of two new seats on the Supreme Court of the United States in the waning hours of Jackson's second term. Andrew Jackson to U.S. Senate, Mar. 3, 1837, in *Journal of the Executive Proceedings of the Senate of the United States of America from March 4, 1829, to March 3, 1837, Inclusive* (Washington, D.C., 1887), 4:631; *Journal of the Executive Proceedings of the Senate of the United States of America from March 4, 1837, to September 13, 1841, Inclusive* (Washington, D.C., 1887), 5:11, 21; Livingston, *Portraits* 2:809. John Niven and Charles Sellers are unfortunately incorrect in stating that it was Jackson's successor, Van Buren, who nominated Catron. *See* John Niven, *Martin Van Buren: The Romantic Age of American Politics* (New York, 1983), 435; Charles G. Sellers, *James K. Polk: Jacksonian, 1783–1843* (Princeton, 1957), 175. Catron retained his Jacksonian devotion to the Union during the Civil War, although he was forced to leave Nashville after Tennessee seceded from the Union. He returned to the city in June 1862 and resumed his circuit duties under the protection of occupying federal troops. He died in Nashville on May 30, 1865. In his will, which was executed at the time of his return to Nashville in June 1862, he provided for his wife and his slaves, kept a death-bed promise to his "friend and brother-in-law Judge [William L.] Brown" to see that his widow was respectably supported and cared for by devising to her two of his slaves and a lot in Nashville, left to his executors "a white child named Margaret Hickman owned by me and held as a slave . . . since it was born in my possession," and devised to the State of Tennessee "my portrait of Genl. Jackson by Earle (full length)." Last Will and Testament of John Catron, June 2, 1862, Davidson County Wills, Book 20, 31–36 (Reel 435), TSLA; Memoranda, 70 U.S. (3 Wall.) ix–xiv (1865); Timothy S. Huebner, *The Southern Judicial Tradition: State Judges and Sectional Distinctiveness, 1790–1890* (Athens, Ga., 1999), 66–67. The free African American barber James Thomas (d. 1913), whose shop was located on capitol hill in Nashville, claimed that Catron was his father, and the allegation has been repeated in the collateral writings of the editor of Thomas's autobiography. *See, e.g.,* Loren

Schweninger, ed., *From Tennessee Slave to St. Louis Entrepreneur: The Autobiography of James Thomas* (Columbia, Mo., 1984), 2, 60; Schweninger, "The Free-Slave Phenomenon: James P. Thomas and the Black Community in Ante-Bellum Nashville," 22 *Civil War History,* 293–307 (1976). There appears to be no surviving corroborating evidence to support the claim.

52. R. D. Cox, "History of Adverse Possession Statutes of Tennessee," 6 *Memphis State University Law Review* 673, 681 (1976). For a brief discussion of the grant system, *see* Ely and Brown, *Legal Papers of Andrew Jackson,* 34.
53. Remarks of Thomas Washington, quoted in editor's endnote to *Weatherhead v. Bledsoe's Heirs,* 2 Tenn. (2 Overton) 708, 736–37 (1815).
54. 1 Tenn. (1 Overton) 353 (1796); for the statute, *see* ch. 27, §§ 3, 4, 1715 N. Car. Laws. Overton's comments are in *Weatherhead v. Bledsoe's Heirs,* 2 Tenn. (2 Overton) 708, 724 (1815) (Overton, J.).
55. Ch. 43, § 4, 1797 Tenn. Pub. Acts; *Hampton's Lessee v. M'Ginnis,* 1 Tenn. (1 Overton) 226, 229–30 (1808); *Napier's Lessee v. Simpson,* 1 Tenn. (1 Overton) 354 (1809); *see* Cox, "Adverse Possession," 695–96; *see also Sawyer's Lessee v. Shannon,* 21 Fed. Cas. 579, 1 Tenn. (1 Overton) 465 (U.S. Cir. Ct. D. Tenn. 1809).
56. 2 Tenn. (2 Overton) 352 (1815).
57. 14 U.S. 476 (1816).
58. 8 Tenn. (Mart. & Yer.) 288, 394, 402–3, 408–11, 417 (1825). *Cf. Guion's Lessee v. Bradley Academy,* 12 Tenn. (4 Yer.) 192 (1833); *Love v. Love's Lessee,* 10 Tenn. (2 Yer.) 256 (1829). In 1819, the General Assembly had enacted legislation reflecting the view that ultimately prevailed in *Gray.* That legislation did not and could not, however, address pre-1819 disputes. Hence, the controversy continued after 1819 until the Court finally resolved the matter in *Gray.*
59. *Green v. Neal's Lessee,* 31 U.S. (6 Pet.) 291 (1832).
60. Morton J. Horwitz, *The Transformation of American Law, 1780–1860* (Cambridge, Mass., 1977), 59.
61. 3 Tenn. (Cooke) 339, 345 (1813) (Overton, J.).
62. Horwitz, *Transformation of American Law,* 61; *see Nelson v. Allen,* 9 Tenn. (1 Yer.) 325, 340 (1830) (Whyte, J.); James Kent, *Commentaries on American Law,* 3d ed. (New York, 1836), 2:335–36.
63. 3 Tenn. (Cooke) 223 (1813); for the statute, *see* ch. 31, § 11, 1809 Tenn. Pub. Acts; *see also Bristoe v. Evans,* 9 Tenn. (1 Yer.) 325 (1815) (construing ch. 24, 1813 Tenn. Pub. Acts); Horwitz, *Transformation of American Law,* 61–62; R. D. Cox, "An Exegesis of the Ejectment Statutes of Tennessee," 18 *Memphis State University Law Review* 659 n. 334 (1988).
64. 9 Tenn. (1 Yer.) 325, 346, 347 n. 1.
65. *Loftin v. Espy,* 12 Tenn. (4 Yer.) 68, 75 (1833); *Hope v. Johnson,* 10 Tenn. (2 Yer.) 111, 114 (1826) (Haywood, J.); *Harris v. Clarissa,* 14 Tenn. (6 Yer.) 153 (1834); Arthur F. Howington, *What Sayeth the Law: The Treatment of Slaves and Free Blacks in the State and Local Courts of Tennessee* (New York, 1986), 2–4, 17; Thomas D. Morris, *Southern Slavery and the Law, 1619–1860* (Chapel Hill, N.C., 1996), 404–14; *see generally* William W. Fisher III, "Ideology and Imagery in

the Law of Slavery," 68 *Chicago-Kent L. Rev.* 1051, 1054–55 (1993); Daniel J. Flanigan, "The Criminal Law of Slavery and Freedom, 1800–1868" (Ph.D. diss., Rice Univ., 1973), 10; Ariela Gross, "Pandora's Box: Slave Character on Trial in the Antebellum South," 7 *Yale J. of L. & the Humanities* 267 (1995); Charles C. Trabue, "The Voluntary Emancipation of Slaves in Tennessee as Reflected in the State's Legislation and Judicial Decisions," 4 *Tennessee Historical Magazine* 50–68 (1918).

66. *M'Cutchin v. Price,* 4 Tenn. (1 Hayw.) 149 (1817).
67. 10 Tenn. (2 Yer.) 111.
68. 14 Tenn. (6 Yer.) 78 (1834). For the statute, *see* ch. 29, 1829 Tenn. Pub. Acts; *see also Sylvia v. Covey,* 12 Tenn. (4 Yer.) 247, 248 (1833) (affording extrastatutory protection against removal and sale of slave pending determination of issue of freedom).
69. 8 Tenn. (Mart. & Yer.) 1, 6, 15–17 (1827). One of Phebe's lawyers was a former member of the Supreme Court, William L. Brown. *See also Miller v. Denman,* 16 Tenn. (8 Yer.) 156, 158 (1835); Andrew Fede, *People Without Rights: An Interpretation of the Fundamentals of the Law of Slavery in the U.S. South* (New York, 1992), 141 ("even in Tennessee, the black slave faced a presumption of slavery that derived from his black skin"). For the rebuttable nature of the presumption, *see Edwards v. M'Connel,* 3 Tenn. (Cooke) 231, 232, 238 (1813); *Ex Parte Renney v. Mayfield,* 5 Tenn. (2 Hayw.) 338, 339 (1817); *Clarissa v. Edwards,* 1 Tenn. (1 Overton) 311 (1809).
70. Ch. 7, 1777 N.C. Acts; ch. 27, § 1, 1801 Tenn. Pub. Acts; ch. 102, § 2, 1831 Tenn. Pub. Acts; Howington, *What Sayeth the Law,* 18, 20, 24, 32–33.
71. Howington, *What Sayeth the Law,* 21–22.
72. 10 Tenn. (2 Yer.) at 114 (upholding its own decree granting executor time within which to pursue legislative petition for emancipation after county court's refusal to consent). In its willingness to overlook, if not to facilitate evasion of, the technicalities of the consent statute, the Court was not entirely alone among the highest courts in the Southern states. *See* Linda O. Smiddy, "Judicial Nullification of State Statutes Restricting the Emancipation of Slaves: A Southern Court's Call for Reform," 42 *South Carolina Law Review* 589 (1991).
73. Howington, *What Sayeth the Law,* 18, *quoting Blackmore v. Negro Phill,* 15 Tenn. (7 Yer.) 297, 306 (1835) (Peck, J.).
74. 15 Tenn. (7 Yer.) at 307; *Hadley v. Latimer* and *Hadley v. Blackmore* case files, Tennessee Supreme Court Records, Middle Tenn. Box 51, TSLA. For the Court's upholding of Hadley's initial conveyance of the slaves to Latimer, *see Hadley v. Latimer,* 11 Tenn. (3 Yer.) 426 (1832).
75. Howington, *What Sayeth the Law,* 8–9, *quoting Fisher's Negroes v. Dabbs,* 14 Tenn. (6 Yer.) 78, 104 (1834) (Catron, C.J.).
76. *Id.* at 9; *see Maria v. Surbaugh,* 23 Va. (2 Rand.) 228 (1824); Morris, *Southern Slavery,* 404–12. David Brion Davis termed the issue "one of the most troublesome questions" in the law of emancipation. David Brion Davis, *The Problem of Slavery in Western Civilization* (Ithaca, N.Y., 1956), 270.

77. *Matilda v. Crenshaw* Case File, Tennessee Supreme Court Records, Box MT 34, TSLA; Notebook of Jacob Peck: Cases Heard by the Supreme Court in 1827, McClung Historical Collection, Knoxville (hereafter cited and referred to as Peck Casebook); *see Matilda v. Crenshaw,* 12 Tenn. (4 Yer.) 249, 250 (1833). Regrettably, the Peck Casebook is not paginated. The Peck Casebook is inscribed "Jacob Peck Notes Jany. 1827—Supreme Court—Nashville" but includes Judge Peck's notes on cases heard by the Court throughout 1827.
78. 12 Tenn. (4 Yer.) at 252–54.
79. *Harris v. Clarissa,* 14 Tenn. (6 Yer.) 153, 155–64 (1834); Morris, *Southern Slavery,* 414; *but see* A. E. Keir Nash, "Reason of Slavery: Understanding the Judicial Role in the Peculiar Institution," 32 *Vanderbilt Law Review* 7, 157 (1979).
80. The Court's second decision in *Clarissa,* which occurred in March 1834, came before the Constitutional Convention of 1834 convened in May of that year and well before the final draft of the proposed constitution, which included a provision establishing the Court as a distinct and equal branch of government not dependent upon the legislature, was finalized in August 1834 and subsequently submitted to the electorate for approval. *See* ch. 76, § 2, 1833 Tenn. Pub. Acts; *Journal of the Constitutional Convention* (1834), 389, 411. The state's new Constitution was not ratified by the electorate until March 1835. Jonathan M. Atkins, *Parties, Politics, and the Sectional Conflict in Tennessee, 1832–1861* (Knoxville, 1997), 4.
81. *See* Atkins, *Parties, Politics, and Conflict,* 8, table 2. In 1829, approximately 73.2 percent of the members of the General Assembly were slave owners. By 1831, the percentage had risen to 81.1 percent and by 1839 had decreased only to 80.1 percent. *Id.*
82. The special local slave courts were a continuation of the prestatehood practice under North Carolina law. Ch. 24, § 48, 1741 Laws of N.C., *as amended by* ch. 14, 1783 Laws of N.C.; Brown, "Tennessee County Courts," 349, 358–61. The slave courts were not abolished until 1854. Howington, *What Sayeth the Law,* 150.
83. Ch. 18, 1815 Tenn. Pub. Acts; ch. 35, 1819 Tenn. Pub. Acts; Howington, *What Sayeth the Law,* 148. The 1815 measure directed that when the applicable criminal statute "already prescribed a specific punishment" for the offense in question, the slave court was to "cause such punishment, and none other to be inflicted." Ch. 18, 1815 Tenn. Pub. Acts.
84. 10 Tenn. (2 Yer.) 155 [1825]; Brown, "Tennessee County Courts," 361; Howington, *What Sayeth the Law,* 141–43.
85. 10 Tenn. (2 Yer.) at 157–62; *see* Howington, *What Sayeth the Law,* 161–62.
86. For Peck's concurring opinion, *see* 10 Tenn. (2 Yer.) at 162–65. For the legislative response, *see* ch. 24, 1825 Tenn. Pub. Acts; Howington, *What Sayeth the Law,* 142–43. The General Assembly in 1831, however, restricted the right to appeal slave court convictions to those cases "where the punishment is death" and denied appeals in cases of "actual rebellion or insurrection" when proof of the same consisted of an "overt act committed, by the preparation of arms

and publicly assembling in numbers to carry the same in execution." Ch. 103, 1831 Tenn. Pub. Acts.

87. It also has been argued that it was not slaves and their interests as human beings, but actually slave owners and their pecuniary interests that were being protected by procedural safeguards such as those that were afforded in cases like *Bob.* Andrew Fede, "Toward a Solution of the Slave Law Dilemma: A Critique of Tushnet's 'The American Law of Slavery,'" 2 *Law & History Rev.* 301, 317–18 (1984). The actual, underlying, determining motivations for decisions like *Bob,* however, even were they capable of being identified with any degree of certainty, would not appear to have made any difference in terms of the procedural protections that resulted from such decisions. "Either way," Howington reminds us, "the end result was the same: the humanity of the slave was recognized and the judicial protection and trial rights of bondsmen were significantly broadened." Howington, *What Sayeth the Law,* 148–49 n. 72.
88. Howington, *What Sayeth the Law,* 163. Although the slave courts were not abolished from the Tennessee judicial system until 1854, the General Assembly significantly weakened their power in 1835 by vesting exclusive original jurisdiction over all trials of slaves for capital offenses in the circuit courts, which retained jurisdiction in such cases for the remainder of the antebellum period. Ch. 19, 1835 Tenn. Pub. Acts; Howington, *What Sayeth the Law,* 145.
89. Ch. 56, 1813 Tenn. Pub. Acts; Howington, *What Sayeth the Law,* 83–85.
90. Ch. 9, § 1, 1799 Tenn. Pub. Acts; *see* Flanigan, "Criminal Law of Slavery and Freedom," 148–56; *see also* Morris, *Southern Slavery,* 175–76. The likelihood of convicting a white defendant under the statute was significantly lessened by what has been called "the fatal weakness of the law" of slavery, the prohibition against slave testimony against white defendants. Eugene D. Genovese, *Roll, Jordan, Roll: The World the Slaves Made* (New York, 1974), 38; Howington, *What Sayeth the Law,* 84–85.
91. 9 Tenn. (1 Yer.) 141, 142 (1829).
92. Thomas D. Morris, "'Villeinage . . . as it existed in England, reflects but little light on our subject': The Problem of the 'Sources' of Southern Slave Law," 32 *American Journal of Legal History* 95, 128, 129 (1988).
93. *Neal v. Farmer,* 9 Ga. 555, 583 (1851) (Nisbet, J.).
94. *George (a Slave) v. State,* 37 Miss. 316, 319–20 (1859). Not surprisingly, Harris has been called "a warm proslavery apoligist." Morris, "'Sources' of Southern Slave Law," 125.

    More recently, *Fields* has been criticized for not having gone far enough in extending to slaves the "protections" afforded by the substantive common law of crimes. "[T]he slave's rights were irrelevant," one modern critic has contended in discussing *Fields,* "because the slave never benefitted from the full measure of protection afforded by the common law of crimes. . . . The real right that was protected was that of the owner. . . . [S]laves never benefitted from the full measure of protection that the common law [of crimes] afforded to 'real people.'" Fede, *People Without Rights,* 70, 71, 75. At least in the case of the substantive law of homicide, the views of this critic and those even of non-critics of *Fields* seem to reflect a mistaken notion that substantive criminal law provides "protection" for the victims of violent crimes. *See, e.g., id.;* Howington, *What Sayeth the Law,* 84–85; Morris, "'Sources' of Southern Slave Law," 129. Except for its possible deterrent effect, however, substantive criminal law rarely if ever provides the victims of homicide and other acts of violence with any meaningful protection in the sense of preventing such victims from becoming victims. Substantive criminal law prescribes varying degrees of punishment for what society, speaking through its legislative bodies, deems to be antisocial behavior, and the significance of *Fields* was to provide that some degree of punishment rather than none at all would be imposed for killing slaves.

95. *See* Arthur Howington, "'A Property of Special and Peculiar Value': The Tennessee Supreme Court and the Law of Manumission," 44 *Tennessee Historical Quarterly,* 302–17 (1985); *cf.* A. E. Keir Nash, "A More Equitable Past? Southern Supreme Courts and the Protection of the Antebellum Negro," 48 *North Carolina Law Review* 197, 213 (1970).

96. Carter, *Territorial Papers* 4:81, 404; *Return of the Whole Number of Persons Within the Several Districts of the United States, According to "An Act Providing for the Enumeration of the Inhabitants of the United States" Passed February the twenty eighth, one thousand eight hundred* (Washington, D.C. [1801]), Tennessee Returns, n.p.; *Aggregate amount of each Description of Persons within the United States of America, and the Territories thereof . . . 1810* (Washington, D.C., 1811), 3:77–78; Bureau of the Census, *Census for 1820* (Washington, D.C., 1821), Tennessee Returns, n.p.; *Abstract of the Returns of the Fifth Census,* 28–29; *see* Chase C. Mooney, "Some Institutional and Statistical Aspects of Slavery in Tennesse," 1 *Tennessee Historical Quarterly* 208 (1942); Caleb Perry Patterson, "The Negro in Tennessee, 1790–1865," Univ. of Texas Bulletin No. 2205 (Feb. 1, 1922), 11–12, 212. For a comparison of Tennessee's slave population (both real numbers and percentages of total population) with that of other Southern states, *see* Dodd, *Historical Statistics of the States of the United States,* 2, 8, 18, 20, 22, 35, 37, 41, 49, 51, 67, 81, 85.

97. Atkins, *Parties, Politics, and Conflict,* 8, table 2. Although it has been estimated that by 1779 approximately 10 percent of the inhabitants of the area that now comprises eastern Tennessee owned slaves, I am unaware of any statistical study of census records for the period 1790– 1830, comparable to Mooney's analysis of fifteen sample counties in Tennessee for the years 1850 and 1860, that estimates the percentage of Tennessee's total white population that were slave owners. *See* Randall M. Miller and John D. Smith, eds., *Dictionary of Afro-American Slavery* (Westport, Conn., 1997 rev. ed.) (hereafter referred to as *DAS*), 718; Mooney, "Slavery in Tennessee," 211–20. Unfortunately, even Mooney's analysis is based only upon heads of agricultural families, thus excluding consideration of slave ownership by Tennessee's urban whites and an ever-increasing number of whites in the state who were engaged in nonagricultural pursuits. *See generally* Delfino, "Many Souths," 89. In 1860, "[a]t the height of the slavocracy,"

slaves throughout the South and the District of Columbia were held by 384,884 owners, or by only approximately 3 percent of a total population in the slave states and the District of Columbia of just more than 12.3 million. Richard B. Morris, "The Measure of Bondage in the Slave States," 41 *Mississippi Valley Historical Review* 219 n. 1 (1954). It is likely, therefore, that the percentage of Tennessee's total white population that owned slaves in the 1820s and 1830s was significantly less than the percentage of Tennessee legislators who owned slaves during the same period.

98. *See Niles Weekly Register,* Jan. 7, 1832 (report, initially appearing in the *Shelbyville (Tenn.) Western Freeman* of a plot of insurrection among slaves near Fayetteville, Tennessee, to set a building afire, seize "as many guns and implements of destruction as they could procure" amid the resulting confusion, and "commence a general massacre"); *see also id.,* Feb. 27, 1836 (rumor, later determined to be false, of slave insurrection in Nashville); Chase C. Mooney, *Slavery in Tennessee* (Bloomington, Ind., 1957), 16–17 (Nashville white vigilance committee formed in response to fears aroused by circulation of abolition materials); *TEH&C,* 653 (1835 pamphlet, claiming to be the "confessions" of John Andrews Murrell of Tennessee, purporting to reveal vast conspiracy to bring about regionwide slave insurrection); William W. Freehling, *The Road to Disunion: Secessionists at Bay, 1776–1854* (New York, 1990), 112.

99. Bureau of the Census, Population Schedules of the Fourth Census of the United States, 1820: Davidson County, Tenn., 1:37, 49, (M33, Reel 122), Record Group (hereafter referred to as RG) 29, National Archives (hereafter referred to as DNA); Bureau of the Census, Schedules of Heads of Family, Fifth Census of the United States, 1830: Town of Nashville and Davidson, Franklin, and Jefferson Counties, Tenn., Scheds. 57, 277, 301, 312, (M19, Reels 174, 176, 180), RG 29, DNA; Rothrock, "Haywood," xxv–xxvi. Census entries for future Judges Catron, Crabb, and Peck for 1820 have not been located. For the generally accepted definition of large slave owner, *see DAS,* 668.

100. *DAS,* 675; Otto H. Olsen, "Historians and the Extent of Slave Ownership in the Southern United States," 18 *Civil War History* 112 n. 40 (1972). Estimates of the average investment of owning one slave vary from $750 to between $1,400 and $1,450; as Otto Olsen has noted, $750 was about four and one-half times the average annual agricultural wage in 1860. Olsen, "Historians and Slave Ownership," 112 n. 40.

101. G. Edward White, "The Appellate Opinion as Historical Source Material," 1 *Journal of Interdisciplinary History* 492–93 (1971); *see* Charles G. Sellers Jr., "The Travail of Slavery," in *The Southerner as American,* ed. Charles G. Sellers Jr. (Chapel Hill, N.C., 1960), 49; *see also* William E. Wiethoff, *A Peculiar Humanism: The Judicial Advocacy of Slavery in High Courts in the Old South, 1820–1850* (Athens, Ga., 1996), 1–12. The suggestion even has been made (and ultimately rejected) that "cunning pro-slavery" might have led to "dressing their [southern antebellum judges'] decisions in the rhetoric of humanity" in

order to make "more elusive the abolitionist's target." *See* Nash, "Reason of Slavery," 100, 121–23.

102. *Matilda v. Crenshaw,* 12 Tenn. (4 Yer.) at 254; *Loftin v. Espy, id.* at 75.

103. *Vaughan v. Phebe,* 8 Tenn. (Mart. & Yer.) at 15–17. For a characterization of Crabb's remarks as an illustration of judicial advocacy, *see* Wiethoff, *Peculiar Humanism,* 20–21.

104. *Niles Weekly Register,* Nov. 10, 1821.

105. Charles T. Cullen, "St. George Tucker and Law in Virginia, 1772–1804" (Ph.D. diss., Univ. of Virginia, 1971), 212–16, 230–31; Thomas Jefferson, *Notes on the State of Virginia* (Chapel Hill, N.C., 1955), 137, 286–87 n. 6; Laurence Shore, *Southern Capitalists: The Ideological Leadership of an Elite, 1832–1885,* (Chapel Hill, 1986) 3–4; Tucker, *Slavery,* 403, 415–16, 418, 434, 437, 445. Jefferson's *Summary View* (1774) and draft of the Declaration of Independence took the British Crown to task for having defeated colonial efforts to abolish slavery and to suppress the slave trade. Julian P. Boyd, ed. *The Papers of Thomas Jefferson* (Princeton, 1950–), 1:130, 318. One of Jefferson's drafts of Virginia's Constitution of 1776, for example, had provided that "[n]o person hereafter coming into this country shall be held in slavery under any pretext whatever." His subsequent proposal for a revision of the new state's laws included a measure that would have emancipated all slaves born after passage of the act, an effort that received notice in his *Notes on the State of Virginia,* which, after initial publication in 1785, went through many editions during and after the author's lifetime. His draft of a proposed revision of the state's Constitution in 1783 contained a provision that would have prohibited the continuation of slavery beyond the generation living on the last day of the year 1800, "all persons born after that day being hereby declared free," and, as a delegate to Congress in 1784, his proposed plan of government for the Northwest Territory included a similar provision that no slavery should exist in any of the states created out of the territory after 1800. Boyd, *Jefferson Papers* 1:353; 2:470–73; 6:298, 608. For the younger Tucker and other early-nineteenth-century antislavery political economists such as Theodore Sedgwick, Daniel Raymond, and to an extent Thomas Cooper, *see* Conkin, *Prophets of Prosperity,* 77, 105–7, 147, 161, 203, 207; Shore, *Southern Capitalists,* 31, 207 n. 27; Snavely, *George Tucker as Political Economist,* 1–6, 134–53.

106. *Fields v. State,* 9 Tenn. (1 Yer.) at 148–50 (Peck, J.).

107. Dunn, *Abolitionist in the South,* 48–49, 55; Jacob Peck to Gerrit Smith, Nov. 30, 1841, Gerrit Papers. For Smith, *see* Laurence J. Friedman, *Gregarious Saints: Self and Community in American Abolitionism, 1830–1870* (New York, 1982), 15, 96–126.

108. [John Haywood], *The Christian Advocate* (Nashville, 1819), 26–27, 50–57, 75, 101–3.

109. *Bob v. State,* 10 Tenn. (4 Yer.) at 158–59; *Hope v. Johnson,* 10 Tenn. (2 Yer.) at 114.

110. *Nashville Republican,* Oct. 22, 1825; Sellers, *Southerner as American,* 40–46, 48.

111. William Blackstone, *Commentaries on the Laws of England* (Oxford, 1766), 2:433; Maxwell Bloomfield, *American Lawyers in a Changing Society, 1776–1876* (Cambridge, 1976), 95. The Court during the period under examination was unwilling to recognize the validity of common-law marriages, which were solemnized by verbal contracts and cohabitation and were recognized under English law. *Bashaw v. State,* 9 Tenn. (1 Yer.) 160 (1829); *Grisham v. State,* 10 Tenn. (2 Yer.) 520 (1831). Most American jurisdictions recognized common-law marriages during the antebellum period. Lawrence M. Friedman, *A History of American Law* (New York, 1973), 180–81.

112. Bloomfield, *American Lawyers in a Changing Society,* 121; Nelson M. Blake, *The Road to Reno: A History of Divorce in the United States* (New York, 1962), 50–51; Linda K. Kerber, "From the Declaration of Independence to the Declaration of Sentiments: The Legal Status of Women in the Early Republic, 1776–1848," 6 *Human Rights* 115, 120 (1977). The states farther south, however, generally were reluctant to make such a shift. Blake, *Road to Reno,* 51, 54.

113. *See* Jane T. Censer, "'Smiling Through Her Tears': Ante-Bellum Southern Women and Divorce," 25 *American Journal of Legal History* 24, 25–26 (1981); Lawrence B. Goodheart, Neil Hawks, and Elizabeth Johnson, "'An Act for the Relief of Females . . .': Divorce and the Changing Legal Status of Women in Tennessee, 1796–1860," pt. 1, 44 *Tennessee Historical Quarterly* 318, 320 (1985); Kerber, "Legal Status of Women," at 119.

114. Goodheart, Hawks, and Johnson, "Act for the Relief of Females," pt. 1, at 320. North Carolina did not enact similar legislation until 1814, New York permitted divorce only on the ground of adultery, and South Carolina had no divorce statutes at all until after the Civil War. *Id.*

115. Ch. 19, 1799 Tenn. Pub. Acts §§ 1, 2, 7, 9, 10. The Court subsequently held, however, that a decree of absolute divorce could not be granted in the absence of a specific prayer for such relief in the petition. *Pillow v. Pillow,* 13 Tenn. (5 Yer.) 420 (1826). Legislation enacted in 1825 for the benefit of married women who had been abandoned by their husbands or who had been forced to leave as a result of having received personal abuse or violent and ill treatment from their husbands insulated any property obtained by a wife after such a separation either "by the labor, care and industry, of the wife" or by descent, gift, or otherwise, from the claims of the husband's creditors. Ch. 10, 1825 Tenn. Pub. Acts. From time to time, the legislature passed private relief acts for nondivorced wives that also allowed what is presumed to have been an abandoned wife, although the statutes are rarely clear on the point, to enter into and enforce contracts and to enjoy all of the other rights of a *femme sole* except that of remarrying. *E.g.,* chs. 65, 119, 197, 1822 Tenn. Priv. Acts. Tennessee was not the only jurisdiction to pass such acts, and although increasing the financial independence of wives separated from their husbands, such relief measures also helped to ease or avoid altogether

the burden to local communities of supporting such women. *See* Elizabeth B. Warbasse, "The Changing Legal Rights of Married Women, 1800–1861" (Ph.D. diss., Radcliffe College, 1960), 74–76.

116. Ch. 20, 1831 Tenn. Pub. Acts § 1. Under the provisions of the 1799 divorce statute, the Court had been authorized to exercise its discretion in awarding costs to the prevailing party or in ordering that each party pay his or her own costs. Ch. 19, 1799 Tenn. Pub. Acts § 8; *see* Goodheart, Hanks, and Johnson, "Act for the Relief of Females," pt. 1, at 324. Married women were not permitted to initiate divorce actions in their own names until 1836. Act of Feb. 19, 1836, ch. 26, 1835 Tenn. Pub. Acts § 3.

117. 2 Tenn. (2 Overton) 418 (1804).

118. 16 Tenn. (8 Yer.) 45, 52 (1835); *Wilson v. Richardson* Case File, Tennessee Supreme Court Records, Middle Tenn. Box 50A, TSLA (regrettably, this large case file is not paginated). For the more typical approach, *see Chenault v. Chenault,* 37 Tenn. (5 Sneed) 119, 120–21 (1856) (McKinney, J.). A subsequent request on Wilson's part to review and reverse the decision in *Richardson* was dismissed by the Court on procedural grounds in *Wilson v. Wilson,* 18 Tenn. (10 Yer.) 148 (1836).

For the trend, *see* Act of Feb. 19, 1836, ch. 26, § 10, 1835 Tenn. Pub. Acts; *see Lovett v. Lovett,* 11 Ala. 763 (1847); Censer, "Smiling Through Her Tears," 50; Glenda Riley, *Divorce: An American Tradition* (New York, 1991), 46–48; Marylynn Salmon, *Women and the Law of Property in Early America* (Chapel Hill, 1986), 66–80.

119. For examples of the Court's interposing of its equitable powers to protect married women in addition to the cases discussed below, *see M'Elhatton v. Howell,* 5 Tenn. (2 Hayw.) 235, 238–40 (1817); *Combs v. Young's Widow,* 12 Tenn. (4 Yer.) 180 (1833); *McKay v. Allen,* 14 Tenn. (6 Yer.) 26 (1834).

120. 12 Tenn. (4 Yer.) 313, 372 (1833); *see* Bloomfield, *American Lawyers in a Changing Society,* 95; Kerber, "Legal Status of Women," 119; Carol E. Jenson, "The Equity Jurisdiction and Married Women's Property in Ante-Bellum America: A Revisionist View," 2 *International Journal of Women's Studies* 144, 147 (1979); Riley, *Divorce,* 43. Although the focus of this discussion is on prenuptial agreements, the Court also construed Tennessee law to allow postmarital trust agreements by which a separate estate could be created for the benefit of an already married woman as a third-party beneficiary; the married woman's property interest, as so created, was also insulated from the claims of her husband's creditors. *Crenshaw v. Anthony,* 8 Tenn. (Mart. & Yer.) 97 (1827).

121. Ch. 5, 1797 Tenn. Pub. Acts; *see* James W. Ely Jr., "'There are few subjects in political economy of greater difficulty': The Poor Laws of the Antebellum South," 1985 *American Bar Foundation Research Journal,* 851–57, 860; Durwood Dunn, "Apprenticeship and Indentured Servitude in Tennessee Before the Civil War," 36 *West Tennessee Historical Society Papers* 26 (1982); William P. Quigley, "The Quicksands of The Poor Law: Poor Relief Legislation in a

Growing Nation, 1790–1820," 18 *Northern Illinois University Law Review* 15–18, 53, 57, 63–64, 68 (1997).

122. 5 Tenn. (4 Hayw.) 377 (1816); *see* Ely, "Poor Laws," 869–70. For the modification of the 1741 act, *see* ch. 29, 1822 Tenn. Pub. Acts.
123. 9 Tenn. (1 Yer.) 83 (1826); *see* Ely, "Poor Laws," 871. For further examples of the Court's treatment of apprenticeships generally, *see Stringfield v. Heiskell* 10 Tenn. (2 Yer.) 481 (1831) (holding father had no authority to bind infant son out as apprentice without his consent); *Houston v. Turk* 15 Tenn. (7 Yer.) 4 (1834); Dunn, "Apprenticeship," 25–40.
124. *Philips v. Rudle & Carmichael,* 9 Tenn. (1 Yer.) 110, 112–13 (1826); *Brumley v. Hayworth,* 11 Tenn. (3 Yer.) 335 (1832); *see* ch. 22, §§ 1, 3, 1821 Tenn. Pub. Acts.
125. For the debate, *see* James W. Ely Jr. and David J. Bodenhamer, "Regionalism and the Legal History of the South," in *Ambivalent Legacy: A Legal History of the South,* ed. James W. Ely Jr. and David J. Bodenhamer (Jackson, Miss., 1984), 7–9.
126. *Corporation of Memphis v. Overton,* 11 Tenn. (3 Yer.) 307 (1832); *Blair v. Carmichael,* 10 Tenn. (2 Yer.) 272 (1829); *Allen v. Farnsworth,* 13 Tenn. (5 Yer.) 189 (1833); *see* Horwitz, *Transformation of American Law,* 44, 47, 115–16. The Court's cases predated the decision by the Supreme Court of the United States in *Charles River Bridge v. Warren Bridge,* 36 U.S. (11 Pet.) 420 (1837), rejecting the common-law assumption that long use was sufficient to create an exclusive property interest. For the applicable statutes, *see* ch. 3, § 4, 1764 Laws of N.C.; ch. 14, 1784 Laws of N.C.; ch. 25, § 1, 1807 Tenn. Pub. Acts.
127. 1 Tenn. (1 Overton) 156 [1806] (the date is taken from *id.* at 198). For the statute, *see* ch. 23, 1777 Laws of N.C.
128. 11 Tenn. (3 Yer.) 33 (1832). For the statutory condemnation provision, *see* Ch. 23, § 2, 1777 Laws of N.C.
129. 7 Tenn. (Peck) 283, 284–85 (1823); *Johnson v. Friar,* 12 Tenn. (4 Yer.) 38 (1833); *Gordon v. Buchanan,* 13 Tenn. (5 Yer.) 71 (1833); *Turney v. Wilson,* 15 Tenn. (7 Yer.) 222, 224 (1835) ("the carrier is regarded as being in the nature of an insurer"); *Transformation of American Law,* 203–7. *Craig* actually contained dicta to the effect that certain risks could be "specially provided against in the contract, and then the carrier will not be liable for them." 7 Tenn. (Peck) at 285. No such contractual provisions appear to have been at issue in any of the Court's subsequent reported decisions on the liability of common carriers.
130. 13 Tenn. (5 Yer.) 459 (1830); Richard Maxwell Brown, "Southern Violence—Regional Problem or National Nemesis? Legal Attitudes Toward Southern Homicide in Historical Perspective," 32 *Vanderbilt Law Review* 225, 232–33 (1979).
131. 2 Tenn. (2 Overton) 475 (1806). The defendant in *Doherty,* a young girl accused of having brutally murdered her father with an axe, appears to have

rendered such a convincing performance of mental derangement that she fooled two juries and the Court's judges. *Id.* at 482.

132. 10 Tenn. (2 Yer.) 142 (1826). For the reserve provisions of the treaties, *see* Treaty with the Cherokees, July 8, 1817, art. 8 (referred to herein as the Treaty of 1817), *American State Papers, Class II, Indian Affairs,* 2:129; Treaty with the Cherokees, Feb. 27, 1819, arts. 2, 3 (referred to herein as the Treaty of 1819), *id.* at 187.

133. Ch. 142, 1826 Tenn. Priv. Acts; *see also* ch. 100, 1828 Tenn. Priv. Acts; ch. 227, 1830 Tenn. Pub. Acts. Also in anticipation of *Winton*-generated actions by Cherokee Indians holding title to land pursuant to reserves stipulated in the Treaty of 1819 against those in possession of the same property under titles issued by Tennessee, the General Assembly in 1826 passed legislation providing that citizens living in the Hiwassee District who were sued by Indian reservees or their assigns were not to be liable for the payment of either principal or interest accruing on the price of the lands at issue until the final determination of such actions, and the treasurer of East Tennessee was directed not to issue any executions or receive any money in connection with any such judgments. Ch. 33, 1826 Pub. Acts. The purpose for the statute was clear: the non-Indian defendants in such actions were not to be held liable for the payment of adverse judgments in such cases until the appellate process with respect to such judgments had been exhausted.

134. Resolutions 11, 14, and 15, reprinted in 1827 Tenn. Pub. Acts.

135. 10 Tenn. (2 Yer.) 406, 420–21 (1830); *M'Connell v. Mousepaine's Lessee, id.* at 387 (1830); *Grubbs' Lessee v. McClatchy, id.* at 431 (1830); *Morgan v. Fowler, id.* at 449 (1830).

After protracted subsequent litigation in the chancery court sitting in Kingston and several appeals to the Supreme Court, Pathkiller's lessee eventually lost at least a portion of the land in question in the Court's 1830 decision to the executors of the estate of James Blair, the keeper of a ferry on the Tennessee River at the present site of Loudon. *See Blair v. Pathkiller's Lessee,* 13 Tenn. (5 Yer.) 230 (1833); *Blair v. Pathkiller's Lessee* case file and related case files, Tennessee Supreme Court Records, East Tenn. Boxes 241, 242, and 245, TSLA. I am very much indebted to Chancellor Frank V. Williams III, Chancery Court, Ninth Judicial District, Kingston, Tennessee, for his assistance with the *Pathkiller* litigation. Pathkiller (d. 1827), principal chief of the Cherokee Nation, organized and led Cherokee warriors in battles against the Creeks, including that at Horseshoe Bend, with Jackson. *Jackson Papers* 2:439–41, 3:80.

136. At the Court's January 1830 term in Nashville, Judge Whyte had stated that it was his opinion that an 1813 statute allowing the losing party in ejectment proceedings to recover the value of improvements made by that party to the property from which he had been ejected was unconstitutional, but Judge Catron disagreed, stating that the record presented no constitutional issue. *Nelson v. Allen,* 9 Tenn. (1 Yer.) 325, 338–48 (1830).

137. Dangerfield, *Era of Good Feelings,* 175–79; Stanley J. Folmsbee, Robert E. Corlew, and Enoch Mitchell, *Tennessee: A Short History* (Knoxville, 1969), 140–41; Sellers, *Market Revolution,* 135–37.
138. 7 Tenn. (Peck) 1, 10–20 (1821). Under the Endorsement Act, judgment creditors were prohibited from executing on their judgments for a period of two years unless they agreed, by placing an endorsement upon each such judgment, to accept the state bank's depreciated paper money in satisfaction thereof. Folmsbee et al., *Tennessee,* 140–41. For the law-of-the-land provision of the Declaration of Rights, *see* Tenn. Const. (1796) art. 11, § 8.
139. John Haywood, *Opinion of Judge Haywood in the Case of Toka Will versus Matthew Nelson, Treasurer of East Tennessee, Concerning the Right of the State to dispose of the School Lands* (Knoxville, 1826), 14–15.
140. 10 Tenn. (2 Yer.) 230 (1829). For the statute at issue, *see* ch. 97, 1821 Tenn. Priv. Acts.
141. James W. Ely Jr., "The Oxymoron Reconsidered: Myth and Reality in the Origins of Substantive Due Process," 16 *Constitutional Commentary* 315, 328 (1999). *See also* William E. Nelson, "Changing Conceptions of Judicial Review: The Evolution of Constitutional Theory in the States, 1790–1860," 120 *University of Pennsylvania Law Review* 1166, 1169–70 (1972); Don E. Fehrenbacher, *Constitutions and Constitutionalism in the Slaveholding South* (Athens, Ga., 1989), 20–21; Margaret V. Nelson, *A Study of Judicial Review in Virginia, 1789–1928* (New York, 1947), 32, 53, 202–3, 205. For examples of earlier assertions by the Court of its right in theory to review legislative acts, *see Jones v. Jones,* 2 Tenn. (2 Overton) 418 (1804); *Bristoe v. Evans,* 2 Tenn. (2 Overton) 698, 702 (1815).
142. *See* Fehrenbacher, *Constitutions and Constitutionalism,* 19.
143. *See* Ely, "Myth and Reality in the Origins of Substantive Due Process," at 328, 336–37; Howard Gillman, *The Constitution Besieged: The Rise and Demise of Lochner Era Police Powers Jurisprudence* (Durham, N.C., 1993), 12, 53–54. Prior to *Townsend, Toka Will,* and *Vanzant,* the Court appears to have given a limited construction to the law-of-the-land clause. *See, e.g., M'Carrol's Lessee v. Weeks,* 6 Tenn. (3 Hayw.) 596, 602 (1814).
144. 9 Tenn. (1 Yer.) 452 (1830). For the statutes in question, *see* ch. 49, § 1, 1827 Tenn. Pub. Acts, and ch. 128, 1824 Tenn. Pub. Acts.
145. 10 Tenn. (2 Yer.) 529, 535–36, 548–49 (1831); *see also* Tenn. Const. (1796) art. 11, § 8; ch. 95, 1829 Tenn. Pub. Acts. In addition to Peck, the tribunal was comprised of Chancellor Nathan Green and Circuit Judge William Kennedy. Although not technically a decision by the Supreme Court, consideration of the special court's decision in *Cooper* is included here because one of the Supreme Court's jurists sat as a member of the tribunal; because, for all intents and purposes, the decision was by a court of last resort from which there was no right of appeal; because of its significance as a law-of-the-land decision; and because, coming as it did in the midst of the Court's vigorous exercise of its right to invalidate legislative enactments that it considered to

be unconstitutional, it is believed to have been a significant factor in the legislative effort in 1831 to abolish the Court.

146. 10 Tenn. (2 Yer.) 489 (1831). For the statute, *see* ch. 39, § 1, 1827 Tenn. Pub. Acts.

147. Act of Apr. 18, 1806, ch. 31, § 2, 2 Stat. 381 (1806).

148. For the statute authorizing the sale of school lands, *see* ch. 85, 1825 Tenn. Pub. Acts. For discussions of school lands, *see Messages* 1:213–14; Albert V. Goodpasture, "Education and Public Lands in Tennessee," 4 *American Historical Magazine* 210 (1899); Robert H. White, *Development of the Tennessee State Educational Organization, 1796–1929* (Nashville, 1929), 10–21, 164–76.

149. Haywood, *Opinion in the Case of Toka Will,* 7–20. This very rare title is among the holdings of the McClung Collection in Knoxville. For the texts of the pleadings and the record of the proceedings before the Court of Equity in *Toka Will, see* Roane County Chancery Court Record Book 1, 1824–1833, pt. 2, 448, 455–57, Chancery Court, Ninth Judicial District, Kingston, Tennessee; *see also Neddy v. State's Lessee,* 16 Tenn. (8 Yer.) 166 (1835). The petition was filed by Toka Will's agent because, according to Judge Haywood, the reservee had been "unlawfully driven from" his home of more than thirty years "by threats and violence against his person." Haywood, *Opinion in the Case of Toka Will,* 5. For initially bringing the Court of Equity's *Toka Will* case to my attention and for providing me with copies of the chancery records for the case, I am very much indebted to Chancellor Frank V. Williams III, Ninth Judicial District, Kingston, Tennessee, and to Circuit Judge Carroll L. Ross, Tenth Judicial District, Athens, Tennessee. The texts of the petition to Peck and of Peck's response are reproduced in Haywood, *Opinion in the Case of Toka Will,* 3–4; the text of the petition is reproduced in Cox, "History of Adverse Possession Statutes of Tennessee," 680.

150. Resolution 25, Jan. 14, 1830, reprinted in 1829 Tenn. Pub. Acts at 301–2.

151. 10 Tenn. (2 Yer.) 472, 477–78 (1831); *Lowry v. Francis* Case File, Tennessee Supreme Court Records, East Tenn. Box 249, TSLA ; *Knoxville Register,* Aug. 17, 1831.

152. Ch. 31, §§ 2, 9, 15, 1831 Tenn. Pub. Acts; *Messages* 1:222.

153. Circular Letter, Corresponding Committee of the Nashville Bar Association, to Wilson County, Tenn. Bar Members, June 10, 1831, with enclosure, Form Petition to Judges Whyte, Peck, and Catron (n.d.), Caruthers Papers; *see also* Jacob S. Yerger to Robert L. Caruthers, June 17, 1831, *id. See generally* James Summerville, *Colleagues on the Cumberland: A History of the Nashville Legal Profession* (Dallas, 1996), 22–23.

154. *See, e.g., Nashville Gazette,* July 28, 1831.

155. *House Journal* (1831), 22, 35, 64; *Senate Journal* (1831), 58; *Messages* 2:350–51; *Nashville Whig,* Sept. 2, 1831; John Catron to Tenn. H.R. Jud. Comm., Sept. 23, 1831, *Messages* 2:353–54.

156. Tenn. H.R. Jud. Comm. Rep., Oct. 4, 1831, *Messages* 2:352–54; "Remarks of Rep. David W. Dickinson, Tenn. H.R., Oct. 4, 1831," *Messages* 2:368–81.

157. Ch. 52, §§ 1, 2, 7, 1831 Tenn. Pub. Acts; *House Journal* (1831), 320; *Senate Journal* (1831), 288; *Messages* 2:415–17.
158. Fehrenbacher, *Constitutions and Constitutionalism,* 17. During the interim between 1831 and adoption by Tennessee of a new constitution, the Court never hesitated to declare legislative measures unconstitutional. *See, e.g., Tate's Executors v. Bell,* 12 Tenn. (4 Yer.) 167 (1833); *Smith v. Normant,* 13 Tenn. (5 Yer.) 271 (1833); *Fisher's Negroes v. Dabbs,* 14 Tenn. (6 Yer.) 78 (1834).
159. Supreme Court of Errors and Appeals Equity Min. Bk., 1812–1838, 431, Supreme Court Archives, Supreme Court of Tennessee, Knoxville, Tennessee (hereafter cited as TSCA).
160. 31 U.S. 515 (1832).
161. *Id.* at 521–26, 542–63.
162. *State v. Foreman,* 16 Tenn. (8 Yer.) 171 (1835); Tim Alan Garrison, "The Legal Ideology of Removal: The Southern State Judiciary and the Sovereignty of Native American Nations, 1776–1838" (Ph.D. diss., Univ. of Kentucky, 1997), 3, 327, 338. Catron suggested that the 1833 statutory extension of the state's jurisdiction over certain criminal offenses had resulted from *U.S. v. Bailey,* 24 Fed. Cas. 937 (U.S. Cir. Ct. E.D. Tenn. 1833) (No. 14,495), in which the federal circuit court sitting in Knoxville invalidated an act of Congress passed in 1817 by which the federal government had attempted to extend its jurisdiction over criminal offenses committed within the Cherokee Nation. 16 Tenn. (8 Yer.) at 209.
163. *State v. Foreman,* 16 Tenn. (8 Yer.) at 173–203; Tennessee Supreme Court of Errors & Appeals Equity Min. Bk., 1812–1838, 438–39, TSCA; Garrison, "Ideology of Removal," 347. In the aftermath of *Worcester,* two political factions had emerged within the Cherokee Nation, one led by Principal Chief John Ross, the organizer of the legal challenge to the Georgia statutes who favored a dual policy of resisting the southern states' aggression against the Nation while attempting to secure federal protection of the Nation's continued independence, and a rival faction referred to as the Treaty Party, which believed that the only realistic means of retaining independence was removal of the Nation to the west. Taking advantage of the Cherokees' internal dissension, federal officials began separate negotiations with the Treaty Party and its leader, Major Ridge, for removal. By late in the summer of 1834, rumors of threatened assassinations had spread throughout the Nation, and violence occasionally had erupted between the rival groups. One of the victims was John "Chief Jack" Walker Jr., one of the leaders of the removal faction. On his way home from a session of the National Council of the Eastern Cherokees at Red Clay in Tennessee on August 23, 1834, Walker was ambushed and shot by two assailants. He lingered for nearly three weeks and died on September 11, but not before reporting that he had seen James Foreman and his half-brother, Anderson Springston, fleeing from where the shots originated. An enraged President Jackson, interpreting the attack as the opening salvo in a campaign of violence against the Treaty Party, ordered a full investigation

into the incident. The investigation concluded that Foreman and Springston had been responsible for Walker's death. In October, the sheriff of McMinn County in southeastern Tennessee arrested Foreman and Springston, and both were indicted for the murder of Walker. At their arraignment before the circuit court in Athens, the defendants' lawyers challenged the constitutionality of the 1833 statute under which they had been charged. The shooting, defense counsel stated, had occurred south of the Hiwassee River, that is, "within the limits of [the] Cherokee Nation and within the jurisdiction of said nation as secured to said nation of Indians by sundry treaties between the United States of North America and said nation of Indians." Tracking Chief Justice John Marshall's analysis in *Worcester,* counsel argued that those treaties had acknowledged the Cherokee Nation to be "a sovereign and independent nation authorized to govern itself by its own laws, usages and customs free from any legislative interference by the several states." On November 6, 1834, after a three-day hearing, Circuit Judge Charles Fleming Keith concluded that "[i]t seems to the court that the law is for the Defendants." It was Keith's decision that was under review by the Court in *Foreman. See* Garrison, "Ideology of Removal," 327–39.

Judge Whyte's nonparticipation in *Foreman* remains unexplained. There is no evidence that Whyte ever resigned from the Court, but he appears to have been absent for most, if not all, of the Court's 1835 terms, most notably during that at which the significant *Foreman* case was decided.

164. 16 Tenn. (8 Yer.) at 226–38 (Green, J.).
165. *Id.* at 238–48 (Peck, J.); Garrison, "Ideology of Removal," 354, 359.
166. *Cornet v. Winton's Lessee,* 10 Tenn. (2 Yer.) at 130–32, 135; *Holland v. Pack,* 7 Tenn. (Peck) 157, 158–59, 160 (1823); *State v. Ross,* 15 Tenn. (7 Yer.) 74 (1834); *see Blair v. Pathkiller's Lessee,* 10 Tenn. (2 Yer.) at 364, 366, 369. For Catron's brief treatment in *Foreman* of the inconsistencies in his opinions, see 16 Tenn. (8 Yer.) at 223. Certainly, one of the most curious aspects about Catron's *Foreman* opinion is that he seems to have forgotten the law-of-the-land principles that he had articulated so eloquently in *Vanzant.* It is possible, of course, that he believed that the law-of-the-land protections provided by the state's Constitution simply did not apply to Cherokee Indians because they were not, paraphrasing the language used in *Ross,* "citizens." Yet the fair and equitable result that he reached in *Ross* raises the question of why he chose not to follow a similar fair-and-equitable analysis in *Foreman,* as subjecting the Cherokees to the state's criminal laws surely must have appeared even to Catron just as unfair and inequitable as, if not more so than, the practice of subjecting the Indians to the state's licensing requirements, which the Court disapproved in *Ross.*
167. *See* John Catron to Martin Van Buren, Dec. 12, 1835, Martin Van Buren Papers, Series 2 (Mf 798, Reel 14), Library of Congress; Catron to Newton Cannon, Nov. 4, 1835, *Messages* 2:4–5, 30, 36, 94–98; Niven, *Van Buren,* 394–95; Edmund C. Gass, "The Constitutional Opinions of Justice John Catron," 8 East Tennessee Historical Society *Publications* (1936), 56–57; Frank O. Gatell, "John

Catron," in *The Justices of the United States Supreme Court 1789–1969: Their Lives and Major Opinions,* ed. Leon Friedman and Fred L. Israel (New York, 1969), 742; Robert V. Remini, *Andrew Jackson and the Course of American Freedom, 1822–1832* (New York, 1981), 257–65; Michael P. Rogin, *Fathers and Children: Andrew Jackson and the Subjugation of the American Indian* (New York, 1975), 206–23. It is true that Jackson's treaty negotiator, John F. Schermerhorn, reached an agreement in March 1835 with a delegation of the pro-removal Treaty Party on the terms of a proposed removal treaty. Robert V. Remini, *Andrew Jackson & His Indian Wars* (New York, 2001), 265–68; *see* Unratified Agreement with the Cherokee, Mar. 14, 1835, reprinted in Charles J. Kappler, ed., *Indian Affairs: Laws and Treaties* (Washington, D.C., 1904), 2:1041–47. This does not mean, however, that the Cherokees had capitulated and accepted the concept of removal by March 1835. The debate over the proposed removal treaty raged on throughout the ensuing summer and autumn and culminated in the rejection of the proposal by the Cherokee Nation at its annual council at Red Clay in late October 1835. Thurman Wilkins, *Cherokee Tragedy: The Ridge Family and the Decimation of a People,* 2d rev. ed. (Norman, Okla., 1986), 264–80. At the conclusion of the October council, a joint delegation, representing both the anti-removal Ross faction and the pro-removal Treaty Party, was authorized to resume treaty negotiations with Schermerhorn. Wilkins, *Cherokee Tragedy,* 279–80. At least as late as October 1835 (the month in which the Court's *Foreman* decision was announced), therefore, the Cherokee Nation had refused to agree to removal. While the Cherokees' authorized delegation was en route to Washington in late December, however, Schermerhorn convened an unauthorized council at New Echota on December 21 for the purpose of entering into a removal treaty. The resulting Treaty of New Echota, the removal provisions of which were substantially similar to those that had been rejected two months earlier, was signed on December 29, 1835, was approved the next day by an extraordinarily small number of Cherokees attending the council, and was ratified by the United States Senate in May 1836. Wilkins, *Cherokee Tragedy,* 280–81, 285–90, 292; William G. McLoughlin, *Cherokee Renascence in the New Republic* (Princeton, 1986), 449–50; *see* Treaty with the Cherokee, Dec. 29, 1835, reprinted in Kappler, *Indian Affairs,* 2:439–48. For Catron's support of Jackson's removal policy, *see* Catron to Jackson, June 8, 1836, in John Spencer Bassett, ed., *Correspondence of Andrew Jackson,* vol. 5, 1833–1838 (Washington, D.C., 1931), 401. After his own defeat for election to the new Court in December 1835, Catron channeled his energies into a small group, including Jackson and Polk, that managed Martin Van Buren's presidential campaign in Tennessee in 1836 and, in the midst of that campaign, actually edited the Democracy's organ, the *Nashville Union.* Powell Moore, "The Revolt Against Jackson in Tennessee, 1835–1836," 2 *Journal of Southern History* 350, 352 (1936); Niven, *Van Buren,* 395; Sellers, *Polk: Jacksonian,* 175.

168. When the Court announced its decision in Knoxville in October 1835, counsel for the defendant requested and was granted a writ of error to the U.S.

Supreme Court. Foreman was allowed post a bond of five thousand dollars for his personal appearance before the Supreme Court in Washington the following January and to go free on bail in the meantime. Supreme Court of Errors & Appeals Equity Min. Bk., 1812–1838, 438–39, TSCA. A writ of error was issued to the Tennessee Court by the clerk of the Circuit Court of the United States for the Seventh Circuit and District of East Tennessee, and a citation was issued to Tennessee's newly elected Governor Cannon by Chief Justice Catron on December 9, 1835. The writ of error and citation were duly served upon Governor Cannon later that same day. The clerk of the federal Circuit Court subsequently forwarded certified copies of the writ of error and citation, dated December 18, 1835, to the office of the clerk of the Supreme Court, and those documents were received in Washington on January 1, 1836. On the same day on which copies of the writ or error and citation were received in the clerk's office in Washington, the state senate in Tennessee passed legislation authorizing the employment of counsel to represent the state in the appeal. No further record of the case in the records of the Supreme Court has been located. *State v. Foreman,* Records of the Supreme Court of the United States, Papers in Undocketed Appellate Case Files, 1791–1920, RG 267, Entry 24, DNA; *Senate Journal* (1835), 252. The other records of the Supreme Court that have been searched are Minutes of the Supreme Court of the United States, 1829–1848 (M215, Reels 2 and 3); Dockets of the Supreme Court of the United States, 1834–1860 (M216, Reel 2); and Index to the Appellate Case Files of the Supreme Court of the United States, 1792–1909 (M408, Reels 6, 16, and 17), DNA. The absence from the holdings of the National Archives and its branch facility at East Point, Georgia, of any records for the federal court sitting in Knoxville at the time has complicated the search for any indication of the ultimate disposition of the appeal of the *Foreman* decision to the Supreme Court of the United States.

In the absence of any decision by the Supreme Court of the United States reversing the Tennessee Court's decision in *Foreman,* the latter decision should have resulted in a remand of the case to the circuit court sitting in McMinn County, Tennessee, for trial. The author of the only other scholarly treatment of *Foreman* states that "there is no record of a jury trial in the McMinn County records." Garrison, "Ideology of Removal," 379 n. 80. No circuit court records for the Seventh Circuit of any kind, however, appear to survive for any period prior to the 1850s. The Treaty of New Echota, which was signed within three months after release of the Court's *Foreman* decision, included provisions for cession to the United States (and thus to the states of Tennessee and Georgia) of the remaining territory of the Cherokee Nation and removal of the Cherokees west of the Mississippi within two years after ratification of the treaty (which occurred in May 1836). *See* John R. Finger, *The Eastern Band of the Cherokee, 1819–1900* (Knoxville, 1984), 16–17. The treaty might well have rendered any prosecution of an appeal to the Supreme Court of the United States moot but should not have mooted the prosecution and trial of Foreman and

Springston. It thus is possible that a trial of Foreman and Springston was conducted and that the records of such a trial have been lost. For assistance with the McMinn County records and other information concerning *Foreman,* I am especially indebted to the Circuit Judge Carroll L. Ross, Tenth Judicial District; Rex Moses, McMinn County Historical Society; the Fisher Public Library, Athens, Tenn.; and Charles Sherrill, TSLA.

169. Garrison, "Ideology of Removal," 359 (first quotation); R. Kent Newmyer, "John Marshall and the Southern Constitutional Tradition," in *An Uncertain Tradition: Constitutionalism and the History of the South,* ed. Kermit L. Hall and James W. Ely Jr. (Athens, Ga., 1989), 105, 116 (second quotation).

2. JUDICIAL INDEPENDENCE IN AN AGE OF DEMOCRACY, SECTIONALISM, AND WAR, 1835–1865

I wish to thank Todd M. Foss, Benjamin Houston, Nancy Hunt, Monique Labat, and Aaron Rediker for their research assistance with this chapter.

1. Paul H. Bergeron, *Paths of the Past: Tennessee, 1770– 1970* (Knoxville, 1979), 33–50; Paul Bergeron, Stephen V. Ash, and Jeannette Keith, *Tennesseans and Their History* (Knoxville, 1999), 110–30.
2. Charles M. Haar, *The Golden Age of American Law,* New York: Braziller, 1965); Grant Gilmore, *The Ages of American Law* (New Haven, Conn., 1979), 19–40; Morton J. Horwitz, *The Transformation of American Law, 1780–1860* (Cambridge, Mass., 1977).
3. Tenn. Const. (1796) art. 5, §§ 1–2; Lewis L. Laska, "A Legal and Constitutional History of Tennessee, 1772–1972," 6 *Memphis State University Law Review* 603–4 (1976).
4. Laska, "Legal and Constitutional History," 604; "Report of Adam Huntsman," *Messages* 2:292–96; "Report to the Judiciary Committee of the House of Representatives, in Relation to the Supreme Court of Errors and Appeals," *Messages* 2:353–55; Timothy S. Huebner, *The Southern Judicial Tradition: State Judges and Sectional Distinctiveness, 1790–1890* (Athens, Ga., 1999), 43–44. The impeachment charges against Judges Joshua Haskell and Nathaniel W. Williams included prejudice, capriciousness, and dereliction of official duty.
5. *Public Acts Passed at the Stated Session of the Nineteenth General Assembly of the State of Tennessee, 1831* (Nashville, 1832), ch. 52; *Messages* 2:416. The state would fund the production of the reports, but the reporter's job was not a paid position. Instead of compensation, the reporter would own the copyright of the printed decisions.

   For a discussion of the larger debate during this period over judicial accountability and independence, *see* Kermit L. Hall, "The 'Route to Hell' Retraced: The Impact of Popular Election on the Southern Appellate Judiciary, 1832–1920," in *Ambivalent Legacy: A Legal History of the South,* ed. David J. Bodenhamer and James W. Ely Jr. (Jackson, Miss., 1984), 229–55; Caleb Nelson, "A Re-Evaluation of

Scholarly Explanations for the Rise of the Elective Judiciary in Antebellum America," 37 *American Journal of Legal History* 190–224 (1993).

6. "Speech of Mr. Allen of Smith, in Committee of the Whole House, upon the Following Preamble and Resolution," *Messages* 2:365; *Journal of the House of Representatives of the State of Tennessee at the Nineteenth General Assembly,* Dec. 19, 1831 (Knoxville, 1831).
7. Most states would not adopt the practice of electing their judges until the late 1840s and 1850s. *See* Kermit Hall, "The Judiciary on Trial: State Constitutional Reform and the Rise of an Elected Judiciary, 1846–1860," 45 *Historian* 337–54 (1983); Hall, "A Progressive Reform and the Decline of Popular Democratic Accountability: The Popular Election of State Supreme Court Judges, 1850–1920," *American Bar Foundation Research Journal* 345–69 (1984).
8. *Messages* 2:578. Humphreys later served as reporter of the opinions of the Tennessee Supreme Court and in 1853 received an appointment to the federal judgeship of the Tennessee District by President Franklin Pierce. Humphreys served as federal judge from 1853 until 1862, when he was impeached for his refusal to resign despite his simultaneous service as Confederate district judge. *See* Patricia E. Brake, *Justice in the Valley: A Bicentennial Perspective of the United States District Court for the Eastern District of Tennessee* (Franklin, Tenn., 1998), 30–42; Kermit L. Hall, "West H. Humphreys and the Crisis of the Union," 34 *Tennessee Historical Quarterly* 48–69 (1975).
9. *Messages* 2:558, 562. The other delegate was Willie Blount, the younger half brother of William Blount, who had served three terms as governor. *See Journal of the Convention of the State of Tennessee, Convened for the Purpose of Revising and Amending the Constitution Thereof, Held in Nashville* (Nashville, 1834), 122–23.
10. *Journal,* 172–73.
11. *Id. at* 220, 229.
12. *Id. at* 230–34, 282. Apparently the deletion of the words "and re-eligible" was subsequently interpreted by neither the legislature nor the judges themselves to mean that judges could serve only a single twelve-year term. In 1847, twelve years after the election of Judges Nathan Green and William B. Turley, the legislature reelected both men.
13. Tenn. Const. (1834) art. 6.
14. The ratification vote, held on March 5–6, 1835, was 42,666 for and 17,691 against. Joshua Caldwell, *Studies in the Constitutional History of Tennessee* (Cincinnati, 1895), 109. On other southern states, *see* Walter F. Pratt Jr., "The Struggle for Judicial Independence in Antebellum North Carolina: The Story of Two Judges," 4 *Law and History Review* 129–59 (1986).
15. *Public Acts Passed at the First Session of the Twenty-First General Assembly of the State of Tennessee, 1835–36* (Nashville, 1836), ch. 3, pp. 26–31.
16. *Public Acts Passed at the First Session of the Twenty-first General Assembly,* chaps. 51, 68, 76, pp. 159–60, 176–77, 182–83.
17. Albert D. Marks, "The Supreme Court of Tennessee," 5 *Green Bag* 171 (1893); Joshua Caldwell, *Sketches of the Bench and Bar of Tennessee* (Knoxville, 1898),

62–63; *Journal of the House of Representatives of the State of Tennessee, Twenty-first General Assembly* (Knoxville, 1836), Dec. 4, 1835.

18. Tenn. Const. (1834) art. 6.
19. Huebner, *Southern Judicial Tradition,* 41–43.
20. Powell Moore, "The Revolt Against Jackson in Tennessee, 1835–1836," 2 *Journal of Southern History* 335–59 (1936); L. Paul Gresham, "The Public Career of Hugh Lawson White," *Tennessee Historical Quarterly,* 3 (1944), 291–318; Jonathan Atkins, *Parties, Politics, and the Sectional Conflict in Tennessee, 1832–1861* (Knoxville, 1997), 26–54; James Phelan, *History of Tennessee: The Making of a State* (Boston, 1888), 378.
21. *Journal of the House of Representatives of the State of Tennessee, Twenty-first General Assembly,* Oct. 16, 1835, Dec. 4, 1835; Henry J. Abraham, *Justices, Presidents, and Senators: A History of the U.S. Supreme Court Appointments from Washington to Clinton* (New York, 1999), 76–77; *Nashville Union,* Mar. 21, 1837. Early in 1837, Congress passed a judiciary act that created two new federal circuits and added two seats to the United States Supreme Court. In addition to Catron's close ties to Jackson, the need for a westerner to ride the new circuit encompassing Tennessee, Kentucky, and Missouri made Catron a logical candidate, and the Senate confirmed his appointment by a vote of twenty-eight to fifteen.
22. *State v. Foreman,* 16 Tenn. 256 (1835).
23. 16 Tenn. 256, 262–63, 277. *See also* Jill Norgren, *The Cherokee Cases: The Confrontation of Law and Politics* (New York, 1996), 57, 87–95; *Worcester v. Georgia,* 6 Peters (31 U.S.) 515 (1832). Catron also privately endorsed Cherokee removal. "The Indian disturbances will afford the occasion for the removal of this population beyond the M'pi, including the Cherokees I hope," he wrote. (Catron to Andrew Jackson, June 8, 1836, in Bassett, *Correspondence of Andrew Jackson* 5:401.)
24. For Catron's support of Cherokee land claims, *see Cornet v. Winton's Lessee,* 10 Tenn. 143 (1826); *Blair and Johnson v. Pathkiller's Lessee,* 10 Tenn. 407 (1830); *McConnell and Mayfield v. Mousepaines's Lessee,* 10 Tenn. 438 (1830); Huebner, *Southern Judicial Tradition,* 56–58.
25. Norgren, *Cherokee Cases,* 84; James Parton, *Life of Andrew Jackson* (New York, 1861), 3:142–43; Robert Remini, *The Election of Andrew Jackson* (Philadelphia, 1963), 63–64.
26. 16 Tenn. 256, 332–33. *See also* on *State v. Foreman,* A. S. Colyar, *Life and Times of Andrew Jackson: Soldier, Statesman, President* (Nashville, 1904), 2:780–85.
27. J. Merton England, "The Free Negro in Antebellum Tennessee," 9 *Journal of Southern History* 41–42, 49–50 (1943); Caleb Perry Patterson, *The Negro in Tennessee, 1790–1865* (New York, 1968), 153–57.
28. 16 Tenn. 256, 336; Huebner, *Southern Judicial Tradition,* 62.
29. A. S. Colyar, "Biographical Sketch of Judge Nathan Green," *Proceedings of the Eleventh Annual Meeting of the Bar Association of Tennessee* (1892), 136.
30. Marks, "Supreme Court of Tennessee," 173; Colyar, "Biographical Sketch," 134.
31. Colyar, "Biographical Sketch," 140–41; Caldwell, *Bench and Bar,* 140.
32. Colyar, "Biographical Sketch," 142–43.

33. Nathan Green, *Address by Hon. Nathan Green, Judge of the Supreme Court of Tennessee, Delivered February 28, 1849, on Entering the Duties of Professor of Law in Cumberland University at Lebanon, Tennessee* (Lebanon, Tenn., 1849), 5, 9.
34. "A Tribute to the Memories of Hon. Nathan Green and Hon. A. W. O. Totten, Formerly Judges of the Supreme Bench of Tennessee," *Proceedings of the Bar of Middle Tennessee,* 44 Tenn. 643 (1867).
35. William Frierson Cooper, Letterbook, bk. 3, 195, Cooper Family Papers, Tennessee State Library and Archives, Nashville (hereafter cited as Cooper Letterbook); "Proceedings in the Supreme Court of Tennessee, at Jackson, in Memory of Hon. Nathan Green," 41 Tenn. ix (1866); "Tribute to the Memories of Hon. Nathan Green and Hon. A. W. O. Totten," 647.
36. Alex W Campbell, "Life and Character of Judge W. B. Turley," *Proceedings of the Third Annual Meeting of the Bar Association of Tennessee* (1884), 202–3; "Obituary, Judge Turley," 30 Tenn. 424 (1850); John W. Green, *Lives of the Judges of the Supreme Court of Tennessee, 1796–1947* (Knoxville, 1947), 101.
37. Campbell, "Life and Character," 204; Henry S. Foote, *The Bench and Bar of the South and Southwest* (St. Louis, 1876), 165.
38. "Obituary, Judge Turley, Supreme Court, December Term, 1850," 30 Tenn. 424.
39. Marks, "Supreme Court of Tennessee," 175; Cooper Letterbook, bk. 3, 195; Green, *Lives of the Judges,* 102.
40. "Obituary, Judge Turley," 30 Tenn. 421.
41. Campbell, "Life and Character," 209.
42. Marks, "Supreme Court of Tennessee," 176; Caldwell, *Bench and Bar,* 152–53; "Tribute of Respect to the Memory of the Hon. William B. Reese, Formerly one of the Judges of the Supreme Court of Tennessee," 39 Tenn. 714; Green, *Lives of the Judges,* 97; Samuel C. Williams, *Phases in the History of the Supreme Court of Tennessee* (Johnson City, Tenn., 1944), 49; Henry Lee Swint, "Ezekiel Birdseye and the Free State of Frankland," *Tennessee Historical Quarterly* 3 (1944), 227–28.
43. Foote, *Bench and Bar,* 166; Marks, "Supreme Court of Tennessee," 176; "Tribute of Respect," 39 Tenn. 714.
44. Cooper Letterbook, bk. 3, 195–96; Marks, "Supreme Court of Tennessee," 176; Green, *Lives of the Judges,* 97–98; "Tribute of Respect," 39 Tenn. 714.
45. Bergeron, Ash, and Keith, *Tennesseans,* 115–17; Robert E. Corlew, *Tennessee: A Short History* (Knoxville, 1990), 200–201.
46. *A Copy of the Acts of the Corporation of Nashville and Legislature of Tennessee, Authorizing the Subscription of $500,000 of Stock in the Nashville and Chattanooga Railroad Company, with the Opinion of the Supreme Court of Tennessee, Confirming Said Subscription* (Nashville, 1849); *Nichol v. Mayor and Aldermen of Nashville,* 28 Tenn. 252, 264, 270 (1848).
47. 28 Tenn. 252, 261.
48. *Woodfolk v. Nashville & Chattanooga Railroad Company,* 32 Tenn. 422, 430, 440 (1852).

49. *Louisville & Nashville Railroad Company v. County Court of Davidson,* 33 Tenn. 637, 655 (1854).
50. Corlew, *Tennessee,* 207; Bergeron, Ash, and Keith, *Tennesseans,* 116–17.
51. Bergeron, Ash, and Keith, *Tennesseans,* 125–26; William J. Novak, *The People's Welfare: Law and Regulation in Nineteenth-Century America* (Chapel Hill, N.C., 1996), 149–89.
52. Kermit L. Hall, *The Magic Mirror: Law in American History* (New York, 1989), 150–51; *State v. Paine,* 23 Tenn. 523, 533 (1843).
53. Lawrence B. Goodheart, Neil Hawks, and Elizabeth Johnson, "'An Act for the Relief of Females . . .': Divorce and the Changing Legal Status of Women in Tennessee, 1796–1860," 44 *Tennessee Historical Quarterly* 331–32 (1985).
54. *Richmond v. Richmond,* 18 Tenn. 342, 349 (1837).
55. *Payne v. Payne,* 23 Tenn. 500, 502 (1844)
56. *Chunn v. Chunn,* 19 Tenn. 131, 136 (1838); *Hawkins v. Hawkins,* 36 Tenn. 105, 106–7 (1856).
57. Goodheart, Hawks, and Johnson, "An Act for the Relief of Females," 333–34; *Richardson v. Wilson,* 8 Tenn. 67 (1835).
58. *Rutledge v. Rutledge,* 36 Tenn. 555, 558, 559 (1858); *Thompson v. Thompson,* 40 Tenn. 527, 529 (1859).
59. *Johnson v. State,* 21 Tenn. 283 (1841).
60. Hall, *Magic Mirror,* 167. *See also* Michael Grossberg, *Governing the Hearth: Law and the Family in Nineteenth-Century America* (Chapel Hill, N.C., 1985).
61. Novak, *People's Welfare,* 149–50.
62. *Dyer v. State,* 19 Tenn. 237 (1838).
63. *Sanderlin v. State,* 21 Tenn. 315, 319 (1841).
64. *State v. Eskridge,* 31 Tenn. 413 (1852); *State v. Barker,* 36 Tenn. 555 (1857).
65. *Johnson v. State,* 36 Tenn. 614, 621–22 (1857).
66. *Childress v. Mayor and Aldermen of Nashville,* 35 Tenn. 347, 357 (1855).
67. *Hollingsworth v. State,* 37 Tenn. 518, 520 (1858). On the influence of religion on nineteenth-century jurists, *see* Peter Karsten, *Heart versus Head: Judge-Made Law in Nineteenth-Century America* (Chapel Hill, N.C., 1997).
68. Corlew, *Tennessee,* 112–17; John Hope Franklin, *The Militant South, 1800–1861* (Cambridge, Mass., 1956), 43; Bertram Wyatt-Brown, *Southern Honor: Ethics and Behavior in the Old South* (New York, 1982); Edward Ayers, *Vengeance and Justice: Crime and Punishment in the 19th-Century American South* (New York, 1984).
69. *Grainger v. State,* 13 Tenn. 459 (1830); Huebner, *Southern Judicial Tradition,* 47–48.
70. *Copeland v. State,* 26 Tenn. 479, 480 (1846).
71. 42 Tenn. 479, 482, 493, 497.
72. *Morgan v. State,* 35 Tenn. 474 (1856)
73. 35 Tenn. 474, 479–80; *Mahala v. State,* 18 Tenn. 532 (1837).

74. 35 Tenn. 474, 480–81.
75. *Rippy v. State,* 39 Tenn. 217 (1858).
76. 39 Tenn., 217, 218–19.
77. 39 Tenn. 217, 219. Historians of southern law have slightly distorted the Tennessee Supreme Court's record on the issue of self-defense. One historian writes that the *Grainger* rule "swept through the South," when in fact it hardly swept through Tennessee before the Court attempted to halt its misinterpretation and misapplication. Catron clearly never intended to expand the common-law doctrine of self-defense to allow a supposed fear of bodily harm to excuse murder. *See* Richard Maxwell Brown, "Southern Violence—Regional Problem or National Nemesis? Legal Attitudes toward Southern Homicide in Historical Perspective," 32 *Vanderbilt Law Review* 232–33 (1979); Paul Finkelman, "Exploring Southern Legal History," 64 *North Carolina Law Review* 104 (1985).
78. *Aymette v. State,* 21 Tenn. 154 (1840); *Haynes v. State,* 24 Tenn. 120, 122 (1844).
79. *Senate Journal for the First Session of the Twenty-Seventh General Assembly of the State of Tennessee, which convened at Nashville on the First Monday of October,* A.D. *1847* (Nashville, 1848), Nov. 1, 1847, 165–66; Nov. 3, 1847, 179; *Messages* 4:187.
80. Williams, *Phases,* 54–55; *Senate Journal,* Nov. 4, 1847, 185–89; *Messages* 4:187–88.
81. Williams, *Phases,* 52–53; Foote, *Bench and Bar,* 210.
82. Foote, *Bench and Bar,* 210.
83. *Messages* 4:333–34.
84. *Nashville Daily Union,* Mar. 16, 1849, *Messages* 4:334–36.
85. *Nashville Daily Union,* Sept. 27, 1849, *Messages* 4:337.
86. "Report of the Committee on the Judiciary on the Subject of the Election of Judge by the People," *Messages* 4:341; Trousdale, "Legislative Message, October 22, 1849," *Messages* 4:301–2.
87. *Journal of the House of Representatives of the State of Tennessee, Twenty-eighth General Assembly, Held at Nashville, 1849–50* (Nashville, 1849), Nov. 12, 30, 1849, 269.
88. Tenn. Const. art. 11, § 3; *Messages* 4:452.
89. *Nashville Union,* July 16, 1853, July 21, 1853.
90. *Nashville Gazette,* Aug. 3, 4, 1853.
91. The total number of votes cast in the state was 118,270. Of these, 68,676 voted for the amendment. Laska, "Legal and Constitutional History," 616–17; *Messages* 4:589; *Acts of the State of Tennessee Passed at the First Session of the Thirtieth General Assembly for the Years 1853–1854* (Nashville, 1854), ch. 32, 102–5.
92. Marks, "Supreme Court of Tennessee," 175–76; *Memphis Daily Appeal,* May 29, 1851.
93. Green, *Lives of the Judges,* 112; Caldwell, *Bench and Bar,* 154–55; "Tribute to the Memories of Hon. Nathan Green and Hon. A. W. O. Totten," 649.

94. "Tribute," 44 Tenn. 643, 648. On the early history of Cumberland Law School, *see* David J. Langum and Howard P. Walthall, *From Maverick to Mainstream: Cumberland School of Law, 1847–1997* (Athens, Ga., 1998), 1–71.
95. Philip M. Hamer, *Tennessee: A History, 1673–1932* (New York, 1933), 1:512; John Trotwood Moore, *Tennessee: The Volunteer State, 1769–1923* (Chicago, 1923), 2:138; Foote, *Bench and Bar,* 167; Caldwell, *Bench and Bar,* 142; "Tribute," 44 Tenn. 643, 648. Green's son, Nathan Green II, went on to serve as law professor at Cumberland Law School, while Nathan Green Sr.'s grandson Grafton Green later served on the Tennessee Supreme Court.
96. *Senate Journal of the First Session of the Thirtieth General Assembly of The State of Tennessee, which convened at Nashville, on the first Monday in October,* A.D. *1853* (Nashville, 1854), Nov. 11, 1853, 178. Although the popular judicial election amendment had already passed, statewide elections for judges and attorneys general were not scheduled to take place until May 1854. In the meantime, elections for judicial vacancies thus proceeded as formerly, but with the following proviso passed by the legislature: "Provided that any Judges or Attorneys-General elected by this General Assembly shall not hold their offices for any longer time than the election of their successors by the people and their qualification." *See Messages* 4:602–3.
97. Green, *Lives of the Judges,* 118–24; Caldwell, *Bench and Bar,* 144–46; Andrew B. Martin, *Address Upon the Life and Character of Judge Robert L. Caruthers* (Nashville, 1883), 4–13; Moore, *Tennessee,* 87–88; "A Tribute to the Memory of Hon. R. L. Caruthers, Formerly one of the Supreme Judges of Tennessee," 77 Tenn. 757.
98. John A. Pitts, *Personal and Professional Reminiscences of an Old Lawyer* (Kingsport, Tenn., 1930), 56.
99. Warren David Broemel, "The Beginning of a Court System: A Study of Tennessee Courts," 10, Tennessee State Library and Archives.
100. Mooney, *Slavery in Tennessee,* 68–69, 101–2; Bergeron, Ash, and Keith, *Tennesseans,* 121–22.
101. Mooney, *Slavery in Tennessee,* 8–20; Hamer, *Tennessee,* 466.
102. *State v. Claiborne,* 19 Tenn. 331, 339–41 (1838).
103. Arthur Howington, "'A Property of Peculiar and Special Value': The Tennessee Supreme Court and the Law of Manumission," 44 *Tennessee Historical Quarterly* 303-3-5, 313 (1985).
104. *Elias v. Smith,* 25 Tenn. 33 (1845); Howington, "Property of Peculiar and Special Value," 304–5.
105. David M. Potter, *The Impending Crisis, 1848–1861* (New York, 1976), 104–5; Thelma Jennings, *The Nashville Convention: Southern Movement for Unity, 1848–1850* (Memphis, 1980).
106. *Bridgewater v. Pride,* 33 Tenn. 197 (1853); Charles C. Trabue, "The Voluntary Emancipation of Slaves in Tennessee as Reflected in the State's Legislation and Judicial Decisions," 4 *Tennessee Historical Magazine* 59 (1918).

107. *Lewis v. Daniel,* 29 Tenn. 314 (1849); *Boone v. Lancaster,* 33 Tenn. 576, 583 (1854); Howington, "Property of Peculiar and Special Value," 314–15; England, "Free Negro in Ante-Bellum Tennessee," 46.
108. 33 Tenn. 576.
109. 33 Tenn. 576, 583, 584–85.
110. *Nelson v. State,* 29 Tenn. 518 (1850); *State v. Caesar,* 31 N.C. 391 (1849); Thomas D. Morris, *Southern Slavery and the Law, 1619–1860* (Chapel Hill, N.C., 1996), 291–92; Timothy S. Huebner, "The Roots of Fairness: State v. Caesar and Slave Justice in Antebellum North Carolina" in *Local Matters: Race, Crime, and Justice in the Nineteenth-Century South,* ed. Christopher Waldrep and Donald G. Nieman (Athens, Ga., 2001), 29–52.
111. *Ford v. Ford,* 26 Tenn. 92, 95–96 (1846); Arthur F. Howington, "'Not in the Condition of a Horse or an Ox': *Ford v. Ford,* the Law and Testamentary Manumission, and the Tennessee Courts' Recognitions of Slave Humanity," 34 *Tennessee Historical Quarterly* 249–63 (1975).
112. *Dred Scott v. Sandford,* 60 U.S. 393 (1857); Bergeron, Ash, and Keith, *Tennesseans,* 133.
113. Bergeron, Ash, and Keith, *Tennesseans,* 134.
114. Green, *Lives of the Judges,* 109; Henderson, "Life and Character," 115; Caldwell, *Bench and Bar,* 157.
115. Green, *Lives of the Judges,* 123; Martin, "Address," 13; Caldwell, *Bench and Bar,* 144.
116. The West Tennessee seat on the Court experienced much turnover during the late antebellum period. William R. Harris replaced A. W. O. Totten in 1855, and Wright replaced Harris in 1858.
117. William M. Robinson Jr., *Justice in Grey: A History of the Judicial System of the Confederate States of America* (Cambridge, Mass., 1941), 267.
118. Corlew, *Tennessee,* 304–11; Bergeron, Ash, and Keith, *Tennesseans,* 142–44.
119. Robert McBride and Dan M. Robinson, *Biographical Directory of the Tennessee General Assembly,* vol. 1, *1796–1861,* (Nashville, 1975), 821; "Tribute," 82 Tenn. 729; L. B. McFarland, "Some Reminiscences of the Memphis Bar," *Proceedings of the Bar Association of Tennessee* (1898), 97; Green, *Lives of the Judges,* 130; Robinson, *Justice in Grey,* 267.
120. Robinson, *Justice in Grey,* 268. Many sources indicate that the Court did not meet at all from secession until the war's end. Robinson convincingly shows that this was not so.
121. Laska, "Legal and Constitutional History," 621–22.
122. Clifton R. Hall, *Andrew Johnson, Military Governor of Tennessee* (Princeton, N.J., 1916), 44–45, 131–33.
123. Laska, "Legal and Constitutional History," 623–24; Thomas B. Alexander, *Political Reconstruction in Tennessee* (New York, 1968), 18–32; *Messages* 5:389.
124. Johnson most likely appointed Russell Houston, Samuel Milligan, and Henry G. Smith to the Tennessee Supreme Court on January 25, 1865. Sources give

a variety of names and dates of service for the judges of the Court from 1865 to 1870. Johnson definitely appointed Milligan on January 25, 1865, as this is confirmed in the *Supreme Court Minutes, Middle Tennessee,* Dec. 4, 1865. Supreme Court Clerk Records, Tennessee State Library and Archives. Milligan took his oath of office two days later. Such confirmation of the appointments of Houston and Smith in manuscript sources appears unavailable, but other published sources indicate that Johnson appointed them at the same time. *See* Charles A. Miller, ed., *Official and Political Manual of the State of Tennessee* (Nashville, 1890), 181.

125. E. Merton Coulter, *William G. Brownlow: Fighting Parson of the Southern Highlands* (Knoxville, 1999); Wilson D. Miscamble, "Andrew Johnson and the Election of William G. ('Parson') Brownlow as Governor of Tennessee," 37 *Tennessee Historical Quarterly* 308–20 (1978).

126. Will T. Hale and Dixon L. Merritt, *A History of Tennessee and Tennesseans* (Chicago, 1913), 386. The *Supreme Court Minutes* kept by the Supreme Court Clerk include Milligan's official commission and oath in the minutes for December 4, 1865. Gov. Johnson had appointed him on January 25, 1865. Gov. Brownlow appointed Hawkins on May 16, 1865, and Shackelford on August 24, 1865. Both swore their oaths on September 11, 1865, at the opening of the Court's September Term. *Supreme Court Minutes,* Middle Tennessee, Dec. 4, 1865, Supreme Court Clerk Records.

127. Caldwell, *Bench and Bar,* 328–30; Green, *Lives of the Judges,* 137–40, 158–62; "A Tribute to the Memory of Hon. Alvin Hawkins, Formerly Governor and one of the Justices of the Supreme Court of Tennessee," 115 Tenn. 744, 745.

3. THE TENNESSEE SUPREME COURT DURING RECONSTRUCTION AND REDEMPTION

1. Thomas B. Alexander, *Political Reconstruction in Tennessee* (Nashville, 1950), passim. *See also* Stephen V. Ash, *Middle Tennessee Society Transformed, 1860–1870: War and Peace in the Upper South* (Baton Rouge, La., 1988).
2. Alexander, *supra* note 1 at 29–40. Lewis L. Laska, *The Tennessee State Constitution: A Reference Guide* (New York, 1990), 11–14.
3. *See* Morton J. Horwitz, *The Transformation of American Law, 1780–1860* (Cambridge, Mass., 1977) for the most complete development of this argument. *See also* Christopher L. Tomlins, *Labor, Law and Ideology in the Early American Republic* (New York, 1993) for the argument that law was the discourse that antebellum Americans used to create the facts of everyday life.
4. For the history of Tennessee after Reconstruction, *see* Roger Hart, *Redeemers, Bourbons and Populists: Tennessee, 1870–96* (Baton Rouge, La., 1976). For Tennessee during the war and Reconstruction, *see* Ash, *Middle Tennessee Society Transformed.*
5. Laska, *Tennessee State Constitution,* 7–14.

6. Sam Milligan's given name was Sam, not Samuel.
7. John W. Green, "Judges of the Reconstruction Era (1865–1878)," 17 *Tennessee Law Review* 413, 413–16 (1942).
8. *Id.* at 416–18.
9. John W. Green, "Some Judges of the Tennessee Supreme Court (1865–1878)," 17 *Tennessee Law Review* 789, 791–94 (1943).
10. *Id.* at 789.
11. John W. Green, *Lives of the Judges of the Supreme Court of Tennessee, 1796–1947* (Knoxville, 1947), 174–77.
12. John W. Green, *supra* note 7 at 420–22.
13. *Id.* at 418–20.
14. John W. Green, *supra* note 11 at 178–80.
15. *Wright and Cantrel v. Overall,* 42 Tenn. 336, 339 (1865).
16. *Id.* at 344.
17. *Wood v. Stone,* 42 Tenn. 369, 371 (1865).
18. *See Stillman v. Looney,* 43 Tenn. 20 (1866); *Gill v. Creed,* 43 Tenn. 295 (1866).
19. *Jones v. Thomas,* 45 Tenn. 465, 466, 469 (1868).
20. *Robertson v. Shores,* 47 Tenn. 164,168 (1869).
21. *Smith v. Ishenhour,* 43 Tenn. 214, 217 (1866).
22. *Armstrong v. Pearre,* 47 Tenn. 171,179 (1869).
23. *Bedford v. Williams,* 45 Tenn. 202, 209 (1867). This strange "intermediate" state had its roots in a series of testamentary manumission cases decided by the Tennessee Supreme Court in the antebellum years. The most famous is Judge Nathan Green's decision in *Ford v. Ford,* 26 Tenn. 92 (1846). For a full discussion of this unusual doctrine, *see* Arthur F. Howington, "'Not in the Condition of a Horse or an Ox': *Ford v. Ford,* the Law of Testamentary Manumission, and the Tennessee Courts's Recognition of Slave Humanity," 34 *Tennessee Historical Quarterly* 249 (1975).
24. The Court used the same reasoning to release a freedman who, as a slave, killed another slave he found in bed with his wife. *Keith v. State,* 45 Tenn. 35 (1867).
25. Robert E. Corlew, *Tennessee: A Short History* (Knoxville, 1981), 333–35.
26. Recent scholarship has confirmed this notion that Reconstruction at the local level varied significantly between areas within the same state. *See* Laura F. Edwards, *Gendered Strife and Confusion: the Political Culture of Reconstruction* (Urbana, Ill., 1997); Randolph B. Campbell, *Grass-Roots Reconstruction in Texas, 1865–1880* (Baton Rouge, La., 1997).
27. Alexander, *supra* note 1 at 213.
28. *Nashville Union and American,* Apr. 21, 1869.
29. *Nashville Banner,* Apr. 21, 1869.
30. *Daily Memphis Avalanche,* Apr. 27, 1869; *Nashville Banner,* Apr. 26, 1869.
31. Alexander, *supra* note 1 at 213–14.
32. *Id.*
33. *Nashville Banner,* June 5, 1869, excerpted items from Franklin, Athens, Shelbyville, Springfield, and Murfreesboro; *Chattanooga Daily Republican,* June 1, 1869; *Memphis Daily Appeal,* June 11, 1869.

34. *Nashville Banner,* June 15, 1869.
35. Corlew, *supra* note 26 at 343–44.
36. Alexander, *supra* note 1 at 217–22.
37. Substantive due process is the idea that the constitution so protects some rights that it can prohibit the legislature from infringing on them no matter what procedure the legislature adopts. In the nineteenth century, this doctrine was most often used to protect property rights. Thus the court drew the analogy between the right to vote and a property right. *See* James W. Ely Jr., "The Oxymoron Reconsidered: Myth and Reality in the Origins of Substantive Due Process" *Constitutional Commentary* 16 (1999) 315–45.
38. *State v. Staten,* 43 Tenn. 233, 280 (1869).
39. *Id.* at 269.
40. *Id.* at 278.
41. Corlew, *supra* note 26 at 344.
42. Hart, *supra* note 4 at 3–4.
43. Samuel C. Williams, *Phases of the History of the Supreme Court of Tennessee* (Johnson City, Tenn., 1944), 79–80.
44. Corlew, *supra* note 26 at 351.
45. Green, *supra* note 9 at 799–802; *see also* Patricia P. Clark, "A. O. P Nicholson of Tennessee: Editor, Statesman and Jurist" (Master's thesis, Univ. of Tennessee).
46. Green, *supra* note 9 at 796–99; *see also* Thomas B. Alexander, *Thomas A. R. Nelson of East Tennessee* (Nashville, 1956). Nelson is the only judge from this period whose life has attracted a full biography.
47. Green, *supra* note 9 at 802–4.
48. John W. Green, *supra* note 11 at 185–88.
49. John W. Green, *supra* note 11 at 198–201.
50. John W. Green, *supra* note 11 at 182–84.
51. Clark, *supra* note 47 at 154–55.
52. *See also Chesney v. Rodgers,* 48 Tenn. 239 (1870) where the court doubted a Union soldier's authority to confiscate horse.
53. *Gunter v. Patton,* 49 Tenn. 257, 263 (1870).
54. *Naff v. Crawford,* 48 Tenn. 111, 123 (1870).
55. *Id.* at 126–27.
56. *Sherfy v. Argenbright,* 48 Tenn. 128, 144 (1870).
57. *Lanier v. Lanier,* 52 Tenn. 462, 464 (1871)
58. 1870 Tenn. Pub. Acts ch. 30.
59. *Lonas v. State* 50 Tenn. 287, 298 (1871).
60. *Id.* at 305.
61. *Id.* at 310.
62. 1870 Tenn. Pub. Acts ch. 13, p. 28.
63. *Andrews v. State,* 50 Tenn. 165, 173. The idea that the 14th Amendment had incorporated the Bill of Rights against the states lay in the future.
64. *Id.* at 177.

65. The cropper system in the postbellum period developed as a compromise between landowners and free black laborers. Black laborers refused to work in gangs for wages; landowners refused to take the risk that harvests would cover the costs of guarantied wages. In the years immediately after the war, share agreements with white tenants imposed less work restrictions on the tenants then did share agreements with black tenants. However, as the cropper system matured, these racial distinctions died out and the share agreements became more uniform. The court's interpretation of these agreements became more important then the exact wording of the contract. *See* Donald Winters, "Postbellum Reorganization of Southern Agriculture: The Economics of Sharecropping in Tennessee," 62 *Agricultural History* 1 (1988); Harold D. Woodman, "Post–Civil War Southern Agriculture and the Law," 53 *Agricultural History* 325 (1979).
66. For instance, in Alabama lien laws early in the postbellum period gave merchants and landowners equal rights to place liens on crops, while in Tennessee only landowners could take a lien for supplies. *See* Jonathan Weiner, *Social Origins of the New South: Alabama 1860–1885* (Baton Rouge, La., 1978), 77–133. For a view of the battle over lien priorities in South Carolina, *see* Lacy Ford, "Rednecks and Merchants: Economic Development and Social tensions in the South Carolina Upcountry, 1865–1900," 71 *Journal of American History* 294–318 (1984).
67. *Philips v. Maxwell,* 60 Tenn. 25, 31 (1872).
68. 1875 Tenn. Pub. Acts ch. 116.
69. *See* Weiner, *supra* note 68 at 77–133.
70. *Singer Manufacturing Co. v. Cole,* 72 Tenn. 439, 441 (1880).
71. 1856 Tenn. Pub. Acts 1856, ch. 95 interpreted in *Horne v. Memphis and Ohio* R.R. Co. 41 Tenn. 42 (1860).
72. *Memphis & Charleston RR v. Smith,* 56 Tenn. 680, 684 (1872)
73. *See* Lawrence M. Friedman, *A History of American Law,* 2d ed. (New York, 1985), 479, in which he reports that in Illinois in 1876 railroads paid $3,654.70 for injuries to workers and $119,288.24 for injuries to animals.
74. *Hill v. Louisville and Nashville Railroad Co.,* 56 Tenn. 650, 657(1876).
75. *See Farwell v. Boston & Worcester Railroad Co.,* 45 Mass. 49 (1842)
76. *But see* Peter Karsten, *Heart versus Head: Judge-Made Law in Nineteenth Century America* (Chapel Hill, N.C., 1997) who argues that the judiciary's rulings on this issue fail to support the subsidy thesis.
77. Thomas D. Morris, *Southern Slavery and the Law, 1619–1860* (Chapel Hill, N.C., 1996), 147–58; Paul Finkelman, "Slaves as Fellow Servants: Ideology, Law, and Industrialization," 31 *American Journal of Legal History* 269–305 (1987).
78. Corlew, *supra* note 26 at 356.
79. Corlew, *supra* note 26 at 342, 356. Hart, *supra* note 4 at 35.
80. J. Mills Thornton III, "Fiscal Policy and the Failure of Radical Reconstruction in the Lower South," in *Region, Race, and Reconstruction: Essays in Honor of C. Vann Woodward,* ed. J. Morgan Kousser and James M. McPherson (New York, 1982), 349–94.

81. Hart, *supra* note 4 at 35–37.
82. *Id.* at 49–53.
83. *Lynn v. Polk,* 76 Tenn. 121, 227 (1882).
84. Robert B. Jones, *Tennessee at the Crossroads: The State Debt Controversy, 1870–1883* (Knoxville, 1977), 130–31.
85. *Id.* at 132–46.
86. *Nashville Banner, May 12, 1886.*
87. *Nashville Banner,* June 10, 1886.
88. *Id.* at 206–12. *Nashville Banner,* June 10, 1886.
89. Daniel M. Robinson, *Bob Taylor and the Agrarian Revolt in Tennessee* (Chapel Hill, N.C., 1935), 33–46.

4. THE TENNESSEE SUPREME COURT, 1886–1910

I wish to express my appreciation to David J. Bodenhamer, Jon W. Bruce, and John C. P. Goldberg for their helpful comments on earlier versions of this chapter.

1. Paul H. Bergeron, Stephen A. Ash, and Jeanette Keith, *Tennesseans and Their History* (Knoxville, 1999), 202–4; Robert E. Corlew, *Tennessee: A Short History,* 2d ed. (Knoxville, 1990), 368–70; Robert L. Hart, *Redeemers, Bourbons & Populists: Tennessee, 1870–1896* (Baton Rouge, La., 1975), 107–78.
2. Bergeron, Ash, and Keith, *Tennesseans,* 181–88.
3. Paul H. Bergeron, *Paths of the Past: Tennessee, 1770–1970* (Knoxville, 1979), 82.
4. Bergeron, Ash, and Keith, *Tennesseans,* 204–9.
5. *Id.,* 194–99; Joseph H. Cartwright, *The Triumph of Jim Crow: Tennessee Race Relations in the 1880s* (Knoxville, 1976), 161–263.
6. Karin A. Shapiro, *A New South Rebellion: The Battle Against Convict Labor in the Tennessee Coalfields, 1871–1896* (Chapel Hill, N.C., 1998); Pete Daniel, "The Tennessee Convict War," 34 *Tennessee Historical Quarterly* 273 (1975).
7. Corlew, *Tennessee,* 415.
8. *See generally* Paul E. Isaac, *Prohibition and Politics: Turbulent Decades in Tennessee, 1885–1920* (Knoxville, 1965), 61–181.
9. William R. Majors, *Change and Continuity: Tennessee Politics since the Civil War* (Macon, Ga., 1986), 35–40.
10. Tenn. Const. (1870) art. 6.
11. For biographical information about the members of the Supreme Court, *see* Joshua W. Caldwell, *Sketches of the Bench and Bar of Tennessee* (Knoxville, 1898); John W. Green, *Lives of the Judges of the Supreme Court of Tennessee, 1796–1947* (Knoxville, 1947); John W. Green, "The Supreme Court of Tennessee in 1886," 16 *Tennessee Law Review* 899 (1941); John W. Green, "Five Judges on Our Supreme Court (1894–1910)," 17 *Tennessee Law Review* 355 (1942).
12. *See* David J. Langum and Howard P. Walthall, *From Maverick to Mainstream: Cumberland School of Law, 1847–1997* (Athens, Ga., 1997), 49–195.

13. Robert H. White, *Messages of the Governors of Tennessee, 1883–1889* (Nashville, 1967), 7:466.
14. Samuel C. Williams, *Phases of the History of the Supreme Court of Tennessee* (Johnson City, Tenn., 1944), 69. For an assessment of Turney's legal and judicial work, *see Messages,* 7:452–53.
15. David M. Tucker, "Justice Horace Harmon Lurton: The Shaping of a National Progressive," 13 *American Journal of Legal History* 223, 225–27 (1969); Williams, *History of the Supreme Court of Tennessee,* 66–69.
16. Horace H. Lurton, "Is the Trust Dangerous?" *Proceedings of the Tenth Annual Meeting of the Bar Association of Tennessee* (Nashville, 1891), 144–69.
17. *Nashville Daily American,* Mar. 23, 1893.
18. Green, "Five Judges of Our Supreme Court," 361.
19. Samuel C. Williams, "History of the Courts of Chancery of Tennessee," 2 *Tennessee Law Review* 6, 22 (1923).
20. Green, *Lives of the Judges,* 252–53.
21. *Messages,* 7:59–62, 75.
22. An Act to facilitate the trial of causes in the Supreme Court, ch. 257, Laws of Tennessee, 1883; Caldwell, *Bench and Bar,* 391–93.
23. *Messages,* 7:479.
24. An Act to establish a Court of Chancery Appeals, ch. 76, Laws of Tennessee, 1895. *See* Roscoe Pound, *Organization of Courts* (Boston, 1940), 239.
25. An Act to amend chapter 76 . . . so as to increase the number of Judges . . . to change its name, to increase its jurisdiction, ch. 82, Laws of Tennessee, 1907.
26. Caldwell, *Bench and Bar,* 394–96.
27. Robert Kagan, Bliss Cartwright, Lawrence M. Friedman, and Stanton Wheeler, "The Business of State Supreme Courts, 1870–1970," 30 *Stanford Law Review* 121, 128–30 (1977).
28. Kermit L. Hall, *The Magic Mirror: Law in American History* (New York, 1988), 227–30; James W. Ely Jr., *The Chief Justiceship of Melville W. Fuller, 1888–1910* (Columbia, S.C., 1995), 42–44.
29. Pound, *Organization of Courts,* 169–70; Lawrence M. Friedman, *A History of American Law,* 2d ed. (New York, 1985), 387.
30. Lawrence M. Friedman, Robert A. Kagan, Bliss Cartwright, and Stanton Wheeler, "State Supreme Courts: A Century of Style and Citation," 33 *Stanford Law Review* 773, 786–87 (1981).
31. Morton Keller, *Affairs of State: Public Life in Late Nineteenth Century America* (Cambridge, Mass., 1977), 362–64.
32. *Illinois Central Railroad Company v. Wells,* 104 Tenn. 706, 710, 59 S.W. 1041, 1043 (1900).
33. *J.I. Case Company v. Joyce,* 89 Tenn. 337, 348–49, 16 S.W. 147, 149 (1890).
34. *Wilkins v. Chicago, St. Louis & New Orleans Railroad Company,* 110 Tenn. 422, 455–61, 75 S.W. 1026, 1034–35 (1903).
35. Friedman et al., "State Supreme Courts," 801–12.

36. *See* Charles W. McCurdy, "The 'Liberty of Contract' Regime in American Law," in *The State and Freedom of Contract,* ed. Harry N. Scheiber (Stanford, Calif., 1998), 161–97.
37. Hall, *Magic Mirror,* 242–43.
38. *Harbison v. Knoxville Iron Company,* 103 Tenn. 421, 429–30, 440, 53 S.W. 955, 960 (1899). The same analysis governed a situation in which employees were paid in orders on the company store. *Dayton Coal and Iron Company v. Barton,* 103 Tenn. 604, 53 S.W. 970 (1899).
39. *Knoxville Iron Company v. Harbison,* 183 U.S. 13 (1901).
40. Friedman, *History of American Law,* 454–57.
41. *Haworth v. Montgomery,* 91 Tenn. 16, 19, 18 S.W. 399 (1891).
42. *O'Neil v. State,* 115 Tenn. 427, 90 S.W. 627 (1905).
43. *Bailey v. Master Plumbers,* 103 Tenn. 99, 105–6, 52 S.W. 853, 854 (1899).
44. For the history of state antitrust legislation, *see* James May, "Antitrust Practice and Procedure in the Formative Era: The Constitutional and Conceptual Reach of State Antitrust Law, 1880–1918," 135 *University of Pennsylvania Law Review* 495 (1987).
45. *State v. Witherspoon,* 115 Tenn. 138, 90 S.W. 138 (1905).
46. *Standard Oil Company v. Tennessee,* 217 U.S. 413 (1910).
47. Tenn. Const. (1870) art. 1, § 21 provides: "That no man's particular services shall be demanded, or property taken, or applied to public use, without the consent of his representatives, or without just compensation being made therefor."
48. *Chicago, Burlington and Quincy Railroad Company v. Chicago,* 166 U.S. 226 (1897). *See generally* James W. Ely Jr., "The Fuller Court and Takings Jurisprudence," 2 *Journal of Supreme Court History* 120–35 (1996).
49. *Cumberland Telegraph and Telephone Company v. United States Electric Railway Company,* 93 Tenn. 492, 520–21, 29 S.W. 104, 111 (1893).
50. *Gray and Wife v. Mayor of Knoxville,* 85 Tenn. 99, 101, 1 S.W. 622 (1886).
51. *Barron v. City of Memphis,* 113 Tenn. 89, 91, 93, 80 S.W. 832, 832–33 (1904).
52. *Watauga Water Company v. Scott,* 111 Tenn. 321, 76 S.W. 888 (1903). *See also White v. Railroad,* 101 Tenn. 95, 45 S.W. 1073 (1898).
53. *Alloway v. City of Nashville,* 88 Tenn. 512, 513, 13 S.W. 123 (1890).
54. *Mann v. Russey,* 101 Tenn. 596, 598–99, 49 S.W. 835, 836 (1898).
55. *Byrd v. Byrd,* 95 Tenn. 364, 367–68, 32 S.W. 198, 199 (1895).
56. *Louisville & Nashville Terminal Company v. Lellyett,* 114 Tenn. 368, 402, 85 S.W. 881, 889 (1905).
57. *See Louisville & Nashville Terminal Company v. Lellyett,* 114 Tenn. 368, 85 S.W. 881 (1905); *Gossett v. Southern Railway Company,* 115 Tenn. 376, 89 S.W. 737 (1905).
58. *Madison v. Ducktown Sulphur, Copper & Iron Company,* 113 Tenn. 331, 366–67, 83 S.W. 658, 666–67 (1904).
59. *See Rogers v. Burnett,* 108 Tenn. 173, 65 S.W. 408 (1901).

60. For the division in the Cumberland Presbyterian Church over the proposed union and the litigation over local church property, *see* Ben M. Barrus, Milton L. Baughn, and Thomas H. Campbell, *A People Called Cumberland Presbyterians* (Memphis, 1972), 353–67; John W. Patton, "The Cumberland Church Cases," 64 *University of Pennsylvania Law Review* 66 (1915).
61. *Landrith v. Hudgins,* 121 Tenn. 556, 646, 120 S.W. 783, 806 (1908). For another case growing out of the Cumberland Presbyterian merger controversy, *see Bonham v. Harris,* 125 Tenn. 452, 145 S.W. 169 (1911).
62. *Parker v. State,* 84 Tenn. 476, 480, 1 S.W. 202, 203 (1886).
63. *McDowell v. Murfreesboro,* 103 Tenn. 726, 54 S.W. 976 (1900). *See also McKinney v. Nashville,* 96 Tenn. 79, 33 S.W. 724 (1896).
64. *Breyer v. State,* 102 Tenn. 103, 50 S.W. 769 (1898).
65. Isaac, *Prohibition and Politics,* 1–11, 32–60, 81–98.
66. *E.g., State v. Raucher,* 69 Tenn. 96 (1878); *Frost v. State,* 103 Tenn. 685, 54 S.W. 986 (1903).
67. *Webster v. State,* 110 Tenn. 491, 503–4, 82 S.W. 179, 182 (1903).
68. *See* Cassandra Tate, *Cigarette Wars: The Triumph of "The Little White Slaver"* (New York, 1999), 18–56; Rivka Widerman, "Tobacco Is a Dirty Weed. Have We Ever Liked It? A Look at Nineteenth Century Anti-Cigarette Legislation," 38 *Loyola Law Review* 387 (1992).
69. *Austin v. State,* 101 Tenn. 563, 566, 48 S.W. 305, 306 (1898). *See also Blaufield v. State,* 103 Tenn. 593, 53 S.W. 1090 (1899).
70. *Austin v. Tennessee,* 179 U.S. 343 (1900).
71. *Railway Company v. Hull,* 88 Tenn. 33, 12 S.W. 419 (1889).
72. *Trotter v. Furniture Co.,* 101 Tenn. 257, 47 S.W. 425 (1898); *Corbett v. Smith & Co.,* 101 Tenn. 368, 47 S.W. 694 (1898).
73. *E.g., Knox v. Railroad,* 101 Tenn. 375, 47 S.W. 491 (1899); *Fletcher v. Louisville & Nashville Railroad Company,* 102 Tenn. 1, 49 S.W. 739 (1899); *Louisville & Nashville Railroad Company v. Dillard,* 114 Tenn. 240, 86 S.W. 313 (1904). On the fellow-servant rule, *see* Keller, *Affairs of State,* 401–4.
74. *E.g., Railroad v. Jackson,* 106 Tenn. 438, 61 S.W. 771 (1901); *Stuber v. Louisville & Nashville Railroad Company,* 113 Tenn. 305, 87 S.W. 411 (1904).
75. *Louisville & Nashville Railroad Company v. Dillard,* 114 Tenn. 240, 86 S.W. 313 (1904).
76. *E.g., Ohio River & Charleston Railway Company v. Wilson,* 111 Tenn. 31, 76 S.W. 897 (1903).
77. *Railroad v. Crider,* 91 Tenn. 489, 496, 19 S.W. 618, 620 (1892).
78. *Cincinnati, New Orleans & Texas Railway Company v. Stonecipher,* 95 Tenn. 311, 32 S.W. 208 (1895).
79. *Adams v. Cumberland Inn Company,* 117 Tenn. 470, 101 S.W. 428 (1906).
80. Morton J. Horwitz, *The Transformation of American Law, 1780–1860* (Cambridge, Mass., 1977), 85–101. For criticism of this thesis, *see* Gary T. Schwartz, "Tort Law and the Economy in Nineteenth-Century America: A Reinterpretation," 90 *Yale Law Journal* 1717 (1981).

81. A special passenger car for women and men travelling with them was congruent with societal attitudes, and the Tennessee Supreme Court had no hesitancy in upholding the authority of railroads to furnish such accommodation. *Memphis & Charleston Railroad Company v. Benson,* 85 Tenn. 627, 4 S.W. 5 (1887).
82. Stanley J. Folmsbee, "The Origin of the First 'Jim Crow' Law," 15 *Journal of Southern History* 235 (1949); Kenneth W. Mack, "Law, Society, Identity, and the Making of the Jim Crow South: Travel and Segregation on Tennessee Railroads, 1875–1905," 24 *Law & Social Inquiry* 377 (1999).
83. Cartwright, *Triumph of Jim Crow,* 189–91.
84. *Smith v. Smith,* 100 Tenn. 494, 510, 46 S.W. 566, 570 (1898).
85. *Memphis Street Railway Company v. State,* 110 Tenn. 598, 75 S.W. 730 (1903).
86. *Railroad Gazette,* June 19, 1903.
87. *Morrison v. State,* 116 Tenn. 534, 546, 95 S.W. 494, 496–97 (1906).
88. Cartwright, *Triumph of Jim Crow,* 223–53; J. Morgan Kousser, *The Shaping of Southern Politics: Suffrage Restriction and the Establishment of the One-Party South, 1880–1910* (New Haven, Conn., 1974), 104–23.
89. *E.g., Rivers v. State,* 117 Tenn. 235, 96 S.W. 956 (1906).
90. *Ransom v. State,* 116 Tenn. 355, 96 S.W. 953 (1905).
91. Ely, *Chief Justiceship of Melville W. Fuller,* 155–60.
92. Hall, *Magic Mirror,* 150–53.
93. *Scruggs v. State,* 90 Tenn. 81, 15 S.W. 1074 (1891); *Bradshaw v. Jones,* 103 Tenn. 331, 52 S.W. 1072 (1899).
94. *Spellings v. Parks,* 104 Tenn. 351, 58 S.W. 126 (1900).
95. *Kaufman v. Fye,* 99 Tenn. 145, 42 S.W. 25 (1897).
96. *E.g., McBride v. McBride,* 111 Tenn. 616, 69 S.W. 781 (1902).
97. *McClanahan v. McClanahan,* 104 Tenn. 217, 232, 56 S.W. 858, 862 (1900).
98. Peter W. Bardaglio, *Reconstructing the Household: Families, Sex, and the Law in the Nineteenth-Century South* (Chapel Hill, N.C., 1995), 137–57.
99. *Lyle v. Lyle,* 86 Tenn. 372, 375, 6 S.W. 878, 880 (1888).
100. Lawrence M. Friedman, *Crime and Punishment in American History* (New York, 1993), 255–58.
101. *Powers v. State,* 117 Tenn. 363, 97 S.W. 815 (1906).
102. *Leach v. State,* 99 Tenn. 584, 42 S.W. 195 (1897); *Givens v. State,* 103 Tenn. 648, 55 S.W. 1107 (1899); *Holder v. State,* 119 Tenn. 178, 104 S.W. 225 (1907).
103. *State v. Foster,* 102 Tenn. 33, 38, 49 S.W. 747, 748 (1899).
104. James O. Nall, *The Tobacco Night Riders of Kentucky and Tennessee, 1905–1909* (Louisville, Ky., 1939).
105. *Gardner v. State,* 121 Tenn. 684, 712, 120 S.W. 816, 823 (1908).
106. *Rhinehart v. State,* 122 Tenn. 698, 127 S.W. 445 (1909); Christopher Waldrep, *Night Riders: Defending Community in the Black Patch, 1890–1915* (Durham, N.C., 1993), 165–66.
107. *Jamison v. State,* 117 Tenn. 58, 94 S.W. 675 (1906).
108. Friedman, *Crime and Punishment in American History,* 229–30.

109. *Edge v. State,* 117 Tenn. 405, 99 S.W. 1098 (1906).
110. *Kendall v. State,* 118 Tenn. 156, 101 S.W. 189 (1907).
111. *State v. Watkins,* 123 Tenn. 502, 130 S.W. 839 (1910).
112. *State v. Alston,* 94 Tenn. 674, 680–81, 30 S.W. 750, 751 (1895).
113. *English v. Crenshaw,* 120 Tenn. 531, 110 S.W. 210 (1908).
114. *Knoxville and Ohio Railroad Company v. Harris,* 99 Tenn. 684, 693, 43 S. W. 115, 117 (1897).
115. *In re Henderson,* 88 Tenn. 531, 539, 13 S.W. 413, 415 (1890).
116. *Id.; Davis v. State,* 92 Tenn. 634, 23 S.W. 59 (1893).
117. *Ingersoll v. Coal Creek Coal Company,* 117 Tenn. 263, 310, 98 S.W. 178, 190 (1906).
118. Ely, *Chief Justiceship of Melville W. Fuller,* passim; Keller, *Affairs of State,* 365–69.

5. A FREE AND UNTRAMMELED JUDICIARY

1. Dewey W. Grantham, *Southern Progressivism: The Reconciliation of Progress and Tradition* (Knoxville, 1983), xv–xxii; George B. Tindall, *The Emergence of the New South* (Baton Rouge, La., 1967), 5–9; William R. Majors, *The End of Arcadia: Gordon Browning and Tennessee Politics* (Memphis, 1982), 44–47.
2. *See,* for example, Carol Chomsky, "Progressive Judges in a Progressive Age: Regulatory Legislation in the Minnesota Supreme Court, 1880–1925," 11 *Law and History Review* 383–85 (Fall 1993); Paul Kens, "The Source of a Myth: Police Powers of the States and Laissez Faire Constitutionalism, 1900–1937," 35 *American Journal of Legal History* 70–73 (1991); Melvin I. Urofsky, "State Courts and Protective Legislation during the Progressive Era: A Reevaluation," 72 *Journal of American History* 63–65 (June 1985).
3. Knoxville attorney John W. Green wrote several books during the midcentury on Tennessee's bench and bar, including, *Lives of the Judges of the Supreme Court of Tennessee, 1796–1947* (Knoxville, 1947). Unless otherwise noted, the information about the judges comes from this source. In addition, brief biographical sketches of the judges of the Tennessee Supreme Court from 1790 to 1940 can be found in an appendix to volume 176 of the Tennessee *Reports.* Unfortunately, space concerns prevent more than a brief look at each of the eighteen men who sat on the high bench during these decades, and it should also be noted that a number of other jurists served on the bench during this period as "special justices." For example, the future state attorney general L. D. Smith served on the court for a period of eighteen months during the illness of his former law partner, Justice Lansden. *In Memoriam, Leonidas D'entrecasteaux Smith,* pamphlet, Tennessee State Library and Archives, Nashville; *Nashville Banner,* Sept 26, 1926, 1. However, this chapter will focus on the men who were elected or appointed to fill full terms.
4. *Nashville Banner,* Dec. 7, 1910, 1; *ibid.,* Dec. 19, 1910, 7.
5. David D. Lee, *Tennessee in Turmoil: Politics in the Volunteer State, 1920–1932* (Memphis, 1979), 47–48.

6. Samuel C. Williams, "A History of Codification in Tennessee," 10 *Tennessee Law Review* 61–78 (1932); *id.*, "The Genesis of the Tennessee Supreme Court," 6 *Tennessee Law Review* 75–85 (1928); *id.*, *Phases of the History of the Supreme Court of Tennessee* (Johnson City, Tenn., 1944); William Henry McRaven Papers, Box 18, File 10, Tennessee State Library and Archives, Nashville (hereafter cited as McRaven Papers); *Nashville Banner*, Aug. 4–7, 1914.
7. "Bachman, Nathan Lynn," Box 17, McRaven Papers; *Knoxville Journal and Tribune*, Apr. 1, 1910, 5.
8. "Alexander Wilds Chambliss," in *Biographical Directory of the Tennessee General Assembly*, vol. 3, *1901–1931*, ed. Ilene J. Cornwell (Nashville, 1988), 151–52; Box 17, McRaven Papers; *Nashville Tennessean*, Mar. 6, 1942, 1, 9; *In Memory of Mr. Justice William Loch Cook*, 79 Tenn. 707–17 (1943).
9. After his retirement, Chief Justice Neil wrote a brief autobiography about his years in Tennessee's legal community. Albert Bramlett Neil, *My Great World or Fifty Years on the Bench* (manuscript, 1964). Harry Phillips, "Remarks on Unveiling of Portraits of Judges Caruthers, Chambers, Neil, and Galbreith," MS 68-303, Tennessee State Library and Archives, Nashville, contains a brief review of Justice Neil's career; Box 18, File 6, McRaven Papers; Scrapbook 4, p. 47, Roy H. Beeler Papers, Tennessee State Library and Archives, Nashville (hereafter cited as Beeler Papers).
10. *Knoxville News-Sentinel*, Apr. 9, 1954, p. 9; *Memphis Commercial Appeal*, Apr. 9, 1954, p. 1.
11. On southerners, progressivism, and prohibition, *see* Grantham, *Southern Progressivism*, 160–61, 177. Tennessee's long struggle with prohibition is treated in Paul E. Isaac's *Prohibition and Politics: Turbulent Decades in Tennessee, 1885–1920* (Knoxville, 1965), 2–11, 79–80 and Eric Russell Lacy's, "Tennessee Teetotalism: Social Forces and the Politics of Progressivism," *Tennessee Historical Quarterly* 24 (1965): 219–22.
12. James Summerville, *The Carmack-Cooper Shooting: Tennessee Politics Turns Violent, November 9, 1908* (Jefferson, N.C., 1994), 10–12; Lacy, "Tennessee Teetotalism," 226–29. The Carmack-Cooper trial continues to attract interest by both lawyers and students of Tennessee history. *See, e.g.*, Donald F. Paine, "The Cooper Trial and Impeachment by Bad Acts," 30 *Tennessee Bar Journal* 24–26 (Nov–Dec. 1994).
13. Summerville, *Carmack-Cooper Shooting*, 12–24; Joe Michael Shahan, "Reform and Politics in Tennessee, 1906–1914" (Ph.D. diss., Vanderbilt Univ., 1981), 212–13; *Knoxville Journal and Tribune*, Mar. 31, 1910, 5, *ibid.*, Apr. 5, 1910, 5.
14. Shahan, "Reform and Politics," 217; *Knoxville Journal and Tribune*, Mar. 31, 1910; *ibid.*, Apr. 1, 1910, 5 (quote)
15. *Knoxville Journal and Tribune*, Apr. 1, 1910, 5 (quote); Shahan, "Reform and Politics," 211–14.
16. Summerville, *Carmack-Cooper Shooting*, 123. The official report of the case contains an unusual notation at the end of the opinion, as the reporter states that

the governor pardoned Colonel Cooper "while the court was still sitting." *Cooper v. State,* 123 Tenn. 37, 231, 138 S.W. 826 (1910).

17. *Nashville Banner,* Apr. 18, 1910, p. 1; *ibid.,* Apr. 27, 2, p. 11. *Knoxville Journal and Tribune,* May 19, 1910, p. 1; John K. Shields, Draft of remarks addressed "To the People of Tennessee," Senator John K. Shields Collection, MS 1708, Box 2, File 2, University of Tennessee Special Collections, Knoxville. The word "deliberate" is crossed over with a pencil in the original.
18. Shahan, "Reform and Politics," 220; *Knoxville Journal and Tribune,* May 8, 1910, 5; May 10, 1910, 4 (quote).
19. *Nashville Banner,* Apr. 25, 1910, p. 1, *ibid.,* May 18, 1910, p. 2. *Knoxville Journal and Tribune,* July 6, 1910, p. 5; *ibid.,* Aug 5, 1910, p. 1; *Memphis Commercial Appeal,* Aug. 5, 1910, p. 1; Ben W. Hooper, *The Unwanted Boy: The Autobiography of Governor Ben W. Hooper,* ed. Everett Robert Boyce (Knoxville, 1963), 56–61; Paul E. Isaac, "The Problems of a Republican Governor in a Southern State: Ben Hooper in Tennessee," 27 *Tennessee Historical Quarterly* 229–48 (1968); Verton M. Queener, "The East Tennessee Republican Party, 1900–1914," *The East Tennessee Historical Society's Publications* 22 (1950): 123 (citing *Knoxville Journal,* Aug. 6, 1910); *Nashville Tennessean,* June 4, 1910, p. 1; *ibid.,* June 5, 1910, p. 1.
20. Isaac, *Prohibition and Politics,* 186; Shahan, "Reform and Politics," 221 (*quoting* from the *Nashville Tennessean*); *Nashville Banner,* Apr. 30, 1910, p. 1; *Nashville Banner,* Apr. 28, 1910, p. 1; *ibid.,* July 16, 1910, p. 1; *ibid.,* July 27, 1910, p. 8; *ibid.,* Aug. 3, 1910, p. 3; *Knoxville Journal and Tribune,* Aug. 4, 1910, pp. 5, 7.
21. *Knoxville Journal and Tribune,* May 10, 1910, p. 4; *ibid.,* May 28, 1910, p. 5; *Nashville Tennessean,* May 28, 1910, p. 1; *Nashville Banner,* July 13, 1910, p. 2 (quote).
22. *Knoxville Journal and Tribune,* May 20, 1910, p. 6.
23. *Nashville Banner,* Aug 5, 1910, p. 1; Isaac, *Prohibition and Politics,* 188.
24. Hooper, *Unwanted Boy,* 62–74; Lacy, "Tennessee Teetotalism," 233–35; Shahan, "Reform and Politics," 228–44; J. Winfield Qualls, "Fusion Victory and the Tennessee Senatorship," 15 *West Tennessee Historical Society Papers* 81–83 (1961); *Nashville Banner,* Dec. 19, 1910, p. 7; Green, *Lives of the Judges,* 114–15.
25. *Motlow v. State,* 125 Tenn. 547, 145 S.W. 177 (1912). Justice Green dissented without comment. Four years later, Justices Neil, Green, Buchanan, and Williams wrote Governor Rye in support of Motlow's pardon application. The governor pardoned Motlow on December 8, 1915. Letter from M. M. Neil, Grafton Green, A. S. Buchanan, Samuel C. Williams to Governor Tom C. Rye, Sept. 25, 1915, Tennessee Court Actions Papers, Ser. 1, Subseries D, Box 1, File 5, Tennessee State Library and Archives, Nashville; Pardon of Lem Motlow by Governor Tom C. Rye, Dec. 8, 1915, *ibid.*
26. *Webb v. Carter,* 129 Tenn. 182, 271, 165 S.W. 426, 450 (1913).
27. *Spencer-Sturla Co. v. City of Memphis,* 155 Tenn. 70, 79, 290 S.W. 608 (1927).
28. Both the founding of Vanderbilt University and the complicated issues swirling around during the "Bishops' War" are comprehensively treated in

Paul K. Conkin's *Gone with the Ivy: A Biography of Vanderbilt University* (Knoxville, 1985), 3–18, 159–84.

29. The attorney general's office has since repudiated the *Evans* holding, saying that an income tax would be constitutional. *See* Lewis L. Laska, *The Tennessee State Constitution: A Reference Guide* (New York, 1990), 89–90.
30. *Campbell v. McIntyre,* 165 Tenn. 52, 42 S.W.2d 162, 163 (1932).
31. *State ex rel. Michael v. Witham,* 179 Tenn. 250, 252–58, 165 S.W.2d 378 (1942).
32. *Winton v. State,* 151 Tenn. 177, 194, 268 S.W. 633 (1925).
33. Edward J. Larson, *Summer for the Gods: The Scopes Trial and America's Continuing Debate Over Science and Religion* (New York: Basic Books, 1997), 170–81.
34. *Scopes v. State,* 154 Tenn. 105, 110–11, 122–25, 129, 289 S.W. 363 (1927); Robert S. Keebler, "Limitations Upon the State's Control of Public Education: A Critical Analysis of *State of Tennessee v. John Thomas Scopes,*" 6 *Tennessee Law Review* 153, 158 (1928).
35. *Rounds v. State,* 171 Tenn. 511, 517, 106 S.W.2d 212, 213–14 (1937).
36. *State of Tennessee, ex rel. v. Caldwell,* 165 Tenn. 77, 40 S.W.2d 1036 (1931); *Caldwell v. State* 164 Tenn. 325, 48 S.W.2d 162 (1932); *State ex rel. Lea v. Brown,* 166 Tenn. 669, 64 S.W.2d 841 (1933).
37. Majors, *End of Arcadia,* 108–10.
38. V. O. Key Jr., *Southern Politics in State and Nation* (New York: Alfred A. Knopf, 1949), 58–81, 539, 578; Grantham, *Southern Progressivism,* 364; Lee, *Tennessee in Turmoil,* 14–18; Majors, *End of Arcadia,* 132–34; William Miller, *Mr. Crump of Memphis* (Baton Rouge, 1964), 212, 292–93; Linda Reed, *Simple Decency and Common Sense: The Southern Conference Movement* (Bloomington, Ind., 1991), 65–76; *Nashville Tennessean,* Aug. 1, 1942, 5 (quote).
39. *Biggs v. Beeler,* 180 Tenn. 198, 173 S.W.2d 144, 147, 148–50 (1943); *Nashville Tennessean,* Feb. 2, 1943, p. 4.
40. *Memphis Press-Scimitar,* June 8, 1942, p. 6; *Nashville Tennessean,* June 11, 1943, p. 1, 14; *ibid.,* July 4, 1943, p. 1–2.
41. *Nashville Banner,* July 5, 1943, p. 4.
42. *Webb v. Carter,* 129 Tenn. 182, 204–5, 165 S.W. 426, 432 (1913).
43. *Moore v. Love,* 171 Tenn. 682, 694, 107 S.W.2d 982, (1937).
44. 1903 Tenn. Pub. Ch. 247; 173 Tenn. 889–92 (1938); Walter P. Armstrong Jr., "Regulation of the Bar in Tennessee," 53 *Tennessee Law Review* 730 (1986).
45. *In re Bowers,* 138 Tenn. 662, 666, 200 S.W. 521 (1918).
46. 1919 Tenn. Pub. Acts, ch. 154; David J. Langum and Howard P. Walthall, *From Maverick to Mainstream: Cumberland School of Law, 1847–1997* (Athens, Ga., 1997), 101–4, 137; James Summerville, *Colleagues on the Cumberland: A History of the Legal Profession in Nashville* (Nashville, 1996), 60; Henry B. Witham, "Requirements for Admission to the Bar in Tennessee," 9 *Tennessee Law Review* 35–36 (1930).
47. *In re Cameron,* 126 Tenn. 614, 658–59, 151 S.W. 64, 76 (1912); *State ex rel. Hawk et al. v. Rogers,* 136 Tenn. 578, 584, 191 S.W. 125 (1916).
48. "Charles T. Cates Jr.," in *Notable Men of Tennessee,* ed. John Allison (Atlanta, 1905), 224–25; "Frank M. Thompson," in *Tennessee: The Volunteer State,*

1769–1923, ed. John Trotwood Moore (Chicago, 1923), 3:80–83; *In Memoriam, Leonidas D'entrecasteaux Smith;* Neil, *My Great World,* 159; clipping, Scrapbook 1, Reel 3, Beeler Papers.

49. William H. Combs and William E. Cole, *Tennessee: A Political Study* (Knoxville, 1940), 144–45; Williams, *Phases,* 87. Williams, a native of East Tennessee, and the only member from that section who served on the Court from 1913 to 1919, wrote that the unnamed justice lived in what he called "the most democratic section" of the state.
50. 1935 Tenn. Pub. Acts ch. 36; "Tennessee Builds First Home for Supreme Court," *Nashville Banner Magazine,* Sept. 20, 1936, 8–9, 14; Tennessee Building Commission Minutes, Mar. 20, 1936, Supreme Court Building Records, RG 24, Box 2, File 4, Tennessee State Library and Archives, Nashville.
51. *Nashville Banner,* Dec. 4, 1937, 1–2, *Nashville Tennessean,* Dec. 4, 1937, 1.
52. Charles S. Coffey, "A Challenge and an Appeal to the Tennessee Bar," 15 *Tennessee Law Review* 698–702 (1939); "Report of the Committee on Judicial Administration and Remedial Procedure," Tennessee Bar Association Meeting, June 6, 1941, 17 *Tennessee Law Review* 100–102 (1941); 1943 Tenn. Pub. Acts ch. 130; "The Judicial Council in Tennessee," 19 *Tennessee Law Review* 65–68 (1945); "Report of the Judicial Council," 19 *Tennessee Law Review* 677–80 (1946).
53. William H. Wicker, "Constitutional Revision and the Courts," *Proceedings of the Sixth Annual Southern Institute of Local Government* (Knoxville, 1947): 12–15, 17–27; Grafton Green, "The Judiciary," 15 *Tennessee Law Review* 142–43 (1938). *See also* Wicker, "The Reorganization of Appellate Courts in Tennessee," in *Papers on Constitutional Revision* (Knoxville, 1947), 1:69–78.

6. THE TENNESSEE SUPREME COURT, 1946–1974

I would like to thank Michelle Broussard for her research on Tennessee Supreme Court justices; James Ely for reading and editing several previous drafts; Brannon Denning, Thomas Van Dervort, and Mark Byrnes for commenting on an earlier draft of this chapter; and Kermit Hall for help with locating outside sources.

1. For biographies of twentieth-century Tennessee senators, *see* William H. Frist with J. Lee Annis Jr., *Tennessee Senators, 1911–2001* (Lanham, Md., 1999).
2. For a useful history that encompasses this entire period, *see* Alpheus T. Mason, *The Supreme Court from Taft to Burger,* 3d ed. (Baton Rouge, La., 1979). For a useful interpretation of the Warren Court, *see* Alexander Bickel, *The Supreme Court and the Idea of Progress* (New York, 1970).
3. For examples of later state courts in other states that took a more activist approach, *see* Charles S. Lopeman, *The Activist Advocate: Policy Making in State Supreme Courts* (Westport, Conn., 1999).
4. *See* Ed Young, "Tennesseans on the United States Supreme Court," *Tennessee Bar Journal* 20–24 (May/June 1996).
5. Robert A. Kagan, Bliss Cartwright, Lawrence M. Friedman, and Stanton Wheeler, "The Evolution of State Supreme Courts," 67 *Michigan Law Review*

994 (May 1978), place the Tennessee Supreme Court as tied for last place with the Alabama Supreme Court among sixteen such courts surveyed in percentage of non-unanimous decisions (2.4 percent) from 1940 to 1970.

6. *Ibid.,* 992 reported that, of sixteen state courts of last resort surveyed, Tennessee tied with two others for the shortest decisions, ranked eleventh in the number of law review articles cited, and fourteenth in the number of cases cited.
7. Mary Jean Delozier, "The Tennessee Supreme Court on Religious Liberty 1900–1960" (Master's thesis, Tennessee Tech Univ., June 1966), vi.
8. *Ibid.,* 162. DeLozier was specifically writing about religious liberty, but the point she made has much wider application.

   With the advent of the Burger Court, some state supreme courts have widened individual rights by accepting arguments that their constitutions called for more expansive rights than comparable provisions in the United States Constitution. *See* Stanley H. Friedelbaum, "Independent State Grounds: Contemporary Invitations to Judicial Activism," in *State Supreme Courts: Policymakers in the Federal System,* ed. Mary Cornelia Porter and G. Alan Tarr (Westport, Conn., 1982), 23–54. I found no evidence that the Tennessee Supreme Court engaged in such decision making during the time period covered by this chapter.
9. [Delmar Karlen and Robert J. Martineau], *The Judicial System of Tennessee* (Nashville, 1966), 18.
10. For a chart of the justices who served on the Tennessee Supreme Court, *see* James Summerville, *Colleagues on the Cumberland: A History of the Nashville Legal Profession* (Nashville, 1996), 150.
11. I have gathered bibliographic information from *Blue Books,* all published at the state Capitol in Nashville, from the entire period covered in this chapter.
12. G. Alan Tarr and Mary Cornelia Aldis Porter, *State Supreme Courts in State and Nation* (New Haven, Conn., 1988), 237–28.
13. Robert Keele, "The Politics of Appellate Court Selection in Tennessee: 1961–1981," in *The Volunteer State: Readings in Tennessee Politics,* ed. Dorothy F. Olshfski and T. McN. Simpson III (N.p., 1985), 232. For further reflections on the Tennessee judicial selection process, *see* William A. Summerfield, "The Selection and Removal of Judges in Tennessee and Alternative Techniques" (Master's thesis, Middle Tennessee State Univ., 1969).
14. 31 *Tennessee Law Review* 397–404 (1963); quotation from 397. Similarly, Albert B. Neil devoted the last chapter of his autobiography to the "Rewards of Faith." *See My Great World or Fifty Years on the Bench* (Nashville, 1964), 211–17.
15. David J. Langum and Howard P. Walthall, *From Maverick to Mainstream: Cumberland School of Law, 1847–1997* (Athens, Ga., 1997), 140.
16. Lewis Laska, *A History of Legal Education in Tennessee, 1770–1970* (Ph.D. diss., George Peabody College for Teachers, 1978), 587–617.
17. In 1949 there were five part-time schools in the state. These were the YMCA School in Nashville (now the Nashville School of Law), the College of Law at Jackson, the Southern Law University and the University of Memphis both in

Memphis, and the McKenzie School in Chattanooga. *See* Elliott E. Cheatham, "The Law Schools of Tennessee, 1949," 21 *Tennessee Law Review* 283–304 at 283 (1949). Laska, *History of Legal Education in Tennessee,* at 626, notes that at an earlier time there were eleven evening law schools in the state.

18. Michael Nelson, "Foreword," *Government and Politics in Tennessee: Democracy in the Volunteer State,* ed. John R. Vile and Mark Byrnes (Nashville, 1998), ix.
19. *My Great World or Fifty Years on the Bench, supra.*
20. Clyde W. Key, Walter Chandler, & John J. Hooker, "Resolution," 441 S.W. 2d 3, 6 (1970).
21. Neil, *My Great World,* unnumbered page labeled "foreward [*sic*]."
22. *Ibid.,* 15.
23. *Ibid.,* 170, 172.
24. *Ibid.,* 173. For a similar opinion from Neil's successor as chief justice, *see* Alan M. Prewitt, "The Way of the National Chief Justices' Conference at Pasadena, California, 1959," 27 *Tennessee Law Review* 19–25 (Summer 1960). Prewitt noted, "We believe that in the fields with which we are concerned, and as to which we are entitled to speak, *the Supreme Court too often has tended to adopt the role of policy-maker, without proper judicial restraint.* We feel this is particularly the case in both of the fields we have discussed—namely the extent and extension of the federal power, and the supervision of state action by the Supreme Court by virtue of the Fourteenth Amendment" (24).
25. Neil, *My Great World,* 178–82.
26. *Ibid.,* 183, Neil thus referring to his many years as a trial judge, said, "There were probably some isolated instances in some of our courts when racial prejudice was a controlling factor, but I cannot recall any case where the verdict of the jury or judgment of the court was unfair to any Negro. On the contrary, in the Criminal Court it was extremely difficult for the State to convict in any case when the defendant proved a good character. In other cases the jury, in case of conviction, was most lenient in fixing his punishment."
27. *Ibid.,* 84.
28. *Ibid.,* 184.
29. *Ibid.,* 188.
30. Tarr and Porter, *State Supreme Courts in State and Nation,* 240.
31. Neil, *My Great World,* 139–40.
32. *Ibid.,* 159. The Court appointed George McCanless, who would later become a justice.
33. Lee Seifert Greene, David H. Grubbs, and Victor C. Hobday, *Government in Tennessee* (Knoxville, 1982), 159.
34. Kagan et al., "Evolution of State Supreme Courts" at 984. Kagan et al. at 984 identified two other kinds of courts—those in "low population states" with "no supreme court case-selection discretion, no lower appellate court, and relatively light caseloads" and "medium-sized . . . and large states with little or no supreme-court setting discretion, and heavy caseloads."
35. [Karlen and Martineau], *Judicial System of Tennessee,* 11.

36. Kagan et al., "Evolution of State Supreme Courts," 989.
37. *Ibid.,* 994. This pattern, however, was typical for Courts, like Tennessee's, with relatively high discretion over the cases it accepted and relatively light case loads.
38. [Karlen and Martineau], *Judicial System of Tennessee,* 16.
39. The author's own count of written opinions found in the *Southwest Reports* for the years 1947 through 1973 is as follows: 1947 (118); 1948 (181); 1949 (149); 1950 (179); 1951 (138); 1952 (136); 1953 (127); 1954 (147); 1955 (128); 1956 (149); 1957 (147); 1958 (101); 1959 (128); 1960 (162); 1961 (120); 1962 (135); 1963 (147); 1964 (149); 1965 (146); 1966 (147); 1967 (100); 1968 (118); 1969 (108); 1970 (81); 1971 (77); 1972 (92); 1973 (120). Kagan et al., "Evolution of State Supreme Courts" at 985 found that the mean number of published opinions of more than one page by the Tennessee Supreme Court was 132 in the period from 1945 to 1955 and 128 from 1960 to 1970.

    The justices who appear to have been the most prolific writers (in terms of the most decisions per year) were Prewitt, Gailor, Tomlinson, Burnett, Swepston, White, Creson, Dyer, McCanless, and Humphreys.

    Alan Prewitt claimed in "The Judicial Structure in Tennessee," 29 *Tennessee Law Review* 1–7 at 7 (Fall 1961), that each justice handled between 135 to 140 cases for a total of about 700 annually. Prewitt was almost surely describing the total number of certiorari petitions each justice received rather than to the total number of cases that each justice decided.
40. Green, Grubbs, and Hobday, *Government in Tennessee,* 348.
41. Looking at another court in Tennessee, Patricia E. Brake notes that "moonshine cases comprised the majority of criminal cases on the docket of the United States District Court for the Eastern District of Tennessee until the mid-twentieth century." *See Justice in the Valley* (Franklin, Tenn., 1998), 57.
42. *Lawrence v. MacFarland,* 354 S.W. 2d 78 (1962); In *Gallagher v. Butler,* 378 S.W. 2d 161 (1964), however, the Court ruled that the tax did not apply to capital gains.
43. Henry R. Glick, *State Courts in State Politics: An Investigation of the Judicial Role* (New York: Basic Books, Inc., 1971), 38–51. John T. Wold used a similar analysis to Glick's, adding a category for "Eclectic" in "Political Orientations, Social Backgrounds, and Role Perceptions of State Supreme Court Justices," 27 *Western Political Quarterly* 239–48 (1974).
44. 205 S.W. 2d 963, 966.
45. *Haynes v. Sanford,* 206 S.W. 2d 796 at 799 (1947).
46. *Phillips v. Butloroff Mfg Co. v. Carson,* 217 S.W. 2d 1,6.
47. *Manahan v. State,* 219 S.W. 2d 900 (1949). For similar cases, *see Furlotte v. State,* 350 S.W. 2d 72 (1961), where the Court suggested that a man who had threatened another in order to get information about an illicit affair he believed his wife was having, should seek a pardon from the governor and *Anderson v. State,* 383 S.W. 2d 763 (1964), where the Court recommended that the governor commute a death sentence to imprisonment for life in the case of a defendant believed to be insane and in need of medical treatment.

48. *Meadon v. City of Nashville,* 200 S.W. 2d 877 (1949).
49. Neil, *My Great World,* 220–28.
50. *Petition of Carter, Green County Sheriff,* 222 S.W. 2d 11, 12 (1949).
51. 223 S.W. 2d 913, 921.
52. *West Tennessee Flood Control & Soil C. Dist. v. Wyatt,* 247 S.W. 2d 56, 62 (1952).
53. Neil noted this in *My Great World,* 173: "[T]o say that judges can make the law at will, based alone upon sociology, and declare their decision to be 'the law of the land' is a complete abandonment of our system of constitutional government."
54. *Krohn v. Richardson-Merritt, Inc.,* 406 S.W. 2d 166, 167–68 (1966).
55. *Dennis v. Sears, Roebuck & Company,* 446 S.W. 2d 260 (1969).
56. *Davis v. Beeler,* 207 S.W. 2d 342, 348.
57. *Mascari v. Int. Bro. of Teamsters,* 215 S.W. 2d 779, 782.
58. *State ex rel. Loser v. National Optical Stores,* 225 S.W. 2d 263, 269. *Cf. Williamson v. Lee Optical,* 348 U.S. 483 (1955).
59. 237 S.W. 2d 946, 948.
60. *Phillips v. State,* 304 S.W. 2d 615 (1957).
61. *Metropolitan Life v. Northington,* 300 S.W. 2d 911, 919 (1957).
62. 335 S.W. 2d 360, 362.
63. *Ewin v. Richardson,* 399 S.W. 2d 318 (1966).
64. *Arutanoff v. Met. Government of Nashville/Davidson,* 448 S.W. 2d 408, 411 (1969).
65. *Winters v. Sawyer,* 463 S.W. 2d 705.
66. 209 S.W. 2d 273, 275 (1948).
67. *RJ Reynolds Tobacco Co. v. Carson,* 213 S.W. 2d 45, 50 (1948).
68. *McCord v. Southern Railway Co.,* 213 S.W. 2d 184, 193 (1948).
69. 302 S.W. 2d 57, 59. The Court further cited a 1923 Arkansas decision, *Pugsley v. Sellmeyer,* 250 S.W. 538, sustaining a public school regulation forbidding girls from wearing makeup.
70. *Morrison v. Hamilton County Board of Education,* 494 S.W. 2d 770, 773–74.
71. *Checker Cab v. Johnson City,* 216 S.W. 2d. 335 (1948).
72. *State v. White,* 288 S.W. 2d 438 (1956).
73. *Norris v. Bradford,* 321 S.W. 2d 543 (1958).
74. *City of Memphis v. Brannan,* 456 S.W. 2d 657.
75. *Canale v. Steveson,* 458 S.W. 2d 797, 800.
76. Thus, in his much cited decision in *Eakin v. Raub,* 12 Sargeant & Rawle 330 (1825), in which Supreme Court Justice John B. Gibson of Pennsylvania responded to Chief Justice John Marshall's early arguments for judicial review in *Marbury v. Madison,* 5 U.S. 137 (1803), even Gibson said that he believed that courts had power to declare laws invalid when they had not been properly passed by the legislature.
77. *See* Thomas D. Ungs and Frank Essex, "The Institutionalization of the Tennessee Legislature, 1968–1997," in Vile and Byrnes, *Tennessee Government and Politics.*
78. 241 S.W. 2d 583, 585.
79. 461 S.W. 2d 386, 392.
80. *Unicoi County v. Frye,* 270 S.W. 2d 381 (1954).

81. *See, e.g., Ragon v. Thrasher,* 252 S.W. 2d 31 (1952), *Crewse v. Beeler,* 212 S.W. 2d 39 (1948), and *Carter v. Beeler,* 219 S.W. 2d 195 (1949).
82. Private bills were reduced after 1955 as a result of amendments restricting such legislation. Green, Grubbs, and Hobday, *Government in Tennessee,* 86–87.
83. *Town of McMinnville v. Curtis,* 192 S.W. 2d 998.
84. *Southern v. Beeler,* 195 S.W. 2d 857.
85. *Ibid.,* 857.
86. *Bandy v. State,* 204 S.W. 2d 819, 820.
87. *Lynch v. Farris,* 227 S.W. 2d 17 (1950).
88. *Taylor Theater v. Town of Mountain City,* 227 S.W. 2d 30.
89. *Davidson County v. City of Nashville,* 228 S.W. 2d 89 (1950).
90. *Sanford v. Pearson,* 231 S.W. 2d 336.
91. *State Ex rel. Dental Examiners v. Allen,* 241 S.W. 2d 960.
92. *Wilson v. Beeler,* 245 S.W. 2d 620.
93. *Cagle v. McCanless,* 285 S.W. 2d 118 (1955).
94. 471 S.W. 2d 944, 947.
95. *Smith Amusement Co. v. Mayor of Chattanooga,* 330 S.W. 320 (1959).
96. *Jones v. Haynes,* 424 S.W. 2d 197 (1968).
97. *Frost v. Chattanooga,* 488 S.W. 2d 370 (1972).
98. *Brentwood Liquor Cor. v. Fox,* 496 S.W. 2d 454, 457 (1973).
99. *Knoxtenn Theatres v. Dance,* 208 S.W. 2d 536, 539.
100. *Frazer v. Carr,* 360 S.W. 2d 449, 452 (1962).
101. *Houck v. Mintan,* 212 S.W. 2d 891 (1948).
102. *Department of Public Welfare v. National Help 'U' Ass'n.,* 270 S.W. 2d 337 (1954).
103. *Gamble v. State,* 353 S.W. 2d 816 (1960).
104. *Pharr v. Nashville C. & St. L. Ry,* 208 S.W. 2d 1013 (1948).
105. *State ex rel. Haywood v. Superintendent, Davidson County Workhouse,* 259 S.W. 2d 159, 162 (1953).
106. Lewis Laska notes that in 1953, "Tennessee's constitution was the oldest unamended constitution in the United States." *See The Tennessee State Constitution: A Reference Guide* (New York, 1990), 144.
107. 223 S.W. 2d 912, 923.
108. Lewis Laska, "A Legal and Constitutional History of Tennessee, 1772–1972," 6 *Memphis State University Law Review* 657 (1976).
109. 454 S.W. 2d, 115, 119, 120 (1970).
110. *Southern Pacific Railway Co. v. Fower,* 497 S.W. 2d 891 (1973). For futher developments consistent with these earlier decisions, *see Snow v. City of Memphis,* 527 S.W. 2d (Tenn. 1975) as cited in Robert F. Williams, ed., *State Constitutional Law: Cases and Materials with 1990–1991 Supplement* (Washington, D.C., Oct. 1990), 453–59.
111. David M. O'Brien, *Civil Rights and Liberties,* vol. 2, *Constitutional Law and Politics,* 4th ed. (New York, 2000), 1072–73.
112. 426 S.W. 3d 503, 506.
113. *Grooms v. State,* 426 S.W. 2d 176 (1968).
114. *Smith v. State,* 385 S.W. 2d 748 (1965).

115. *See, e.g., Christin v. State,* 197 S.W. 2d 797 (1946); *Thompson v. State,* 230 S.W. 2d 977 (1950). Charges that Judge Raulston Schoolfield imposed prison sentences without jury concurrence were prominent in his Senate impeachment trial. *See* Lee S. Greene, *Lead Me On: Frank Goad Clement and Tennessee Politics* (Knoxville, 1982), 266.
116. *Bailey v. State,* 280 S.W. 2d 806 (1955).
117. *Vines v. State,* 231 S.W. 2d 332, 334 (1950).
118. By contrast, counsel had referred to the white victim as "a sweet little woman" and as "this little woman left all alone in the home to herself." *Ibid.,* 335.

 In Kenneth N. Vines, "Southern State Supreme Courts and Race Relations," 18 *Western Political Quarterly* 5 at 9–10 (1965), he notes, without citing specific cases, that the Mississippi Supreme Court kept "racial demagoguery" out as well.
119. *Manning v. State,* 257 S.W. 2d 6, 8 (1953).
120. *Bonds v. State,* 421 S.W. 2d 87 (1967).
121. *See, e.g., McKennie v. State,* 379 S.W. 2d 214 (1964).
122. *Kennedy v. State,* 210 S.W. 2d 132 (1947).
123. *See, e.g., Dylas v. State,* 296 S.W. 2d 861 (1856).
124. *Ripley v. State,* 227 S.W. 2d 26 (1950), involving judge's instructions regarding the testimony of codefendants, and *Hooper v. State,* 325 S.W. 2d 56 (1959). Tenn. Const. art. 6, § 9 prohibits judges from charging juries "with respect to matters of fact." *See* Laska, *Tennessee State Constitution,* 119.
125. *Lovell v. McCullough,* 439 S.W. 2d 105 (1969).
126. *State v. Dunn,* 453 S.W. 2d 777 (1970).
127. *See Harvey v. State,* 468 S.W. 2d 73 (1971).
128. *Franklin v. State,* 496 S.W. 2d 885 (1973).
129. Jerry K. Beatty, "State Court Evasion of United States Supreme Court Mandates During the Last Decade of the Warren Court," 6 *Valparaiso Law Review* 260–85 (Spring 1972).
130. Consistent with findings in this chapter, Vines classified the Supreme Court of Tennessee (along with those in Texas and North Carolina) in the first category. *See* "Southern State Supreme Courts and Race Relations," 18 *Western Political Quarterly* 5 at 14 (1965).
131. *Rowe Transfer & St. Co. v. International Brotherhood,* 209 S.W. 2d 35.
132. 297 S.W. 2d 72, 74 (1956).
133. 384 S.W. 2d 6, 7–8 (1964).
134. *Bowen v. State,* 488 S.W. 2d 373–75.
135. *Walker v. Dunn,* 498 S.W. 2d 102 (1972).
136. *United Artists Corp. v. Board of Censors, Memphis,* 225 S.W. 2d 550, 551–52, *quoting* from the letter issued by the Board of Censors.
137. Vines, "Southern State Supreme Courts and Race Relations," at 11 says that from 1954 to 1963, 40 percent of the Tennessee Supreme Court's decisions in civil rights cases were favorable to Blacks. This number was fairly consistent with high courts in the other peripheral southern states (North Carolina, 46.6 percent; Texas, 40 percent, and Virginia, 50 percent) except for

Florida (9.5 percent) but generally higher than such courts in the Deep South states (Alabama, 7.7 percent; Arkansas 33.3 percent; Georgia, 54.5 percent; Louisiana, 29.1 percent; Mississippi, 23.8 percent; and South Carolina, 28.6 percent). Vines, at 17, notes that southern Supreme Courts often played a role within their states in reversing judgments against African Americans that the U.S. Supreme Court played over other federal courts at the national level.

138. For a thorough account of this incident, *see* Greene, *Lead Me On,* 200–208. *See also* Janice M. McClelland, "A Structural Analysis of Desegregation: Clinton High School, 1954–1958," 56 *Tennessee Historical Quarterly* 294–309 (Winter 1977). Two years later, the school was destroyed by a bomb. *See* Greene, *Lead Me On,* 219.
139. *Roy v. Brittain,* 297 S.W. 2d 72 (1956).
140. *Davis v. Fentriss County,* 402 S.W. 2d 873, 875 (1966).
141. *Stratton v. Conway,* 301 S.W. 2d 332, 334 (1957).
142. *Tennessee Negro Funeral Directors Ass'n v. Board of Funeral Directors,* 332 S.W. 2d 195.
143. *Highlander Folk School v. State,* 208 Tenn. 234, 242 (1961). For background of the trumped up charges in this case, *see* Thomas Bledsoe, *Or We'll All Hang Separately: The Highlander Idea* (Boston, 1969), 106–30.
144. Nashville experienced a number of sit-ins in 1960. *See* Linda T. Wynn, "The Dawning of a New Day: The Nashville Sit-ins, February 13–May 10, 1960," 50 *Tennessee Historical Quarterly* 42–54 (Spring 1991) and David Halberstam, *The Children* (New York, 1998).
145. 355 S.W. 2d 102 (1962).
146. Ironically, after the adoption of the Civil Rights Act of 1964, the real violation would be that of obstructing interstate commerce. *See Heart of Atlanta Motel v. United States,* 379 U.S. 241 (1964) and *Katzenbach v. McClung,* 379 U.S. 294 (1964).
147. *McKennie v. State,* 379 S.W. 2d 214, 217 (1964).
148. 442 S.W. 2d 248, 252.
149. 192 S.W. 2d 998. The state eliminated the poll tax in 1953. *See* Green, Grubbs, and Hobday, *Government in Tennessee,* 35.
150. *Walker v. Dunn,* 498 S.W. 2d 102 (1972).
151. *Smith v. Allwright,* 321 U.S. 649 (1944).
152. *South Carolina v. Katzenbach,* 383 U.S. 301 (1966).
153. *My Great World,* 84.
154. *Ledbetter v. State,* 199 S.W. 2d 112, 113.
155. *See, e.g., Evans v. State,* 221 S.W. 2d 952 (1949).
156. 477 S.W. 2d 517, 521 (1972).
157. *Fischer v. Fischer,* 477 S.W. 2d 513, 514–15 (1972).
158. *Goins v. Coulter,* 206 S.W. 2d 379.
159. *Donnell v. Donnell,* 415 S.W. 2d 127 (1967).
160. *See Sherrill v. State,* 321 S.W. 2d 813 (1959), rejecting the testimony of boys in a "crime against nature" case; *Boulton v. State,* 377 S.W. 2d 936 (1964), also

involving the testimony of boys in a similar case; and *Scott v. State,* 338 S.W. 2d 58 (1960), and *King v. State,* 215 S.W. 2d 813 (1948), both involving the testimony of daughters against their fathers in incest cases.

161. *ICA v. Hogsett,* 486 S.W. 2d 730.
162. *Miller v. State,* 225 S.W. 2d 62.
163. *Williams v. State,* 403 S.W. 2d 319.
164. *Dupuy v. State,* 325 S.W. 2d 238 (1959).
165. *Hogan v. McDaniel,* 319 S.W. 2d 221, 224 (1958).
166. *Durrett v. Owens,* 371 S.W. 2d 433 (1963).
167. *Shousha v. Matthew Drivurself Service, Inc.,* 358 S.W. 2d 471.
168. *Langford v. Vanderbilt University,* 287 S.W. 2d 32 (1956). *Cf. Cox Broadcasting v. Cohn,* 420 U.S. 469 (1975).
169. *Martin v. Senators, Inc.,* 418 S.W. 2d 660.
170. *Arutnoff v. Mt. Gov't of Nashville/Davidson,* 448 S.W. 2d 708, 712 (1969).
171. Edward J. Larson, *Summer for the Gods: The Scopes Trial and America's Continuing Debate Over Science and Religion* (Basic Books, 1997), 253.
172. Quoted by Robert H. Birkby, in "The Supreme Court and the Bible Belt: Tennessee Reaction to the 'Schempp' Decision," in *The Impact of Supreme Court Decisions,* 2d ed., ed. Theodore L. Becker and Malcolm M. Feeley (New York, 1973), 117.
173. *My Great World,* 178–82.
174. *Carden v. Bland,* 288 S.W. 2d 718, 721–25.
175. 216 S.W. 2d 709,710.
176. *Goff v. State,* 209 S.W. 2d 13.
177. *Kirk v. Olgiati,* 308 S.W. 2d 471.
178. *York v. American Service Co.,* 319 S.W. 2d 76.
179. *Sunday School Board v. Evans,* 241 S.W. 2d 543.
180. 360 S.W. 2d 458, 467.
181 *Fort Sanders Presb. Hospital v. Health and Ed. Fac. Ed.,* 453 S.W. 2d 771, 777 (1970).
182. *Row Transfer & Storage Co. v. International Brotherhood,* 209 S.W. 2d 35 and *Ira Watson Co. v. Watson,* 215 S.W. 2d 801 (1948).
183. *Row Transfer & Storage Company v. International Brotherhood,* at 36.
184. *See Nashville Corporation v. United Steelworkers, etc.* 215 S.W. 2d 818 (1948).
185. *Lodge Mfg. Co. v. Gilbert,* 260 S.W. 2d. (1953).
186. *Cloyd v. State,* 308 S.W. 2d. 467, 469.
187. *New Fiveria Arts Theatre v. State,* 422 S.W. 2d 890, 894 (1967).
188. *Art Theater Guild, Inc. v. State,* 469 S.W. 2d 669.
189. *Cambist Films, Inc. v. State,* 495 S.W. 2d 812.
190. *Robert Arthur Management Corp. v. State,* 414 S.W. 2d 638, 639, 641, 643 (1968).
191. *Langford v. Vanderbilt University,* 287 S.W. 2d 32 (1956).
192. *Logan's Super Markets, Inc. v. McCalla,* 208 Tenn 68.
193. One of the earliest Supreme Court decisions involving the rights of criminal defendants originated in Tennessee in 1906. *See* Mark Curriden and Leroy Phillips Jr., *Contempt of Court* (New York, 1999).

194. *King v. State,* 215 S.W. 3d 813 (1948).
195. *Ellis v. State,* 364 S.W. 2d 925, 929 (1963).
196. *Templeton v. State,* 264 S.W. 2d 565 (1954).
197. *See Epps v. State,* 205 S.W. 2d 4 (1947) and *Rambo v. State,* 481 S.W. 2d 379 (1972).
198. *See Robertson v. State,* 198 S.W. 2d 633 (1947), *Morrison v. State,* 237 S.W. 2d 548 (1951); and *Reels v. State,* 355 S.W. 2d 97 (1962).
199. *Lindsey v. State,* 231 S.W. 2d 380 (1950).
200. *McDonald v. State,* 259 S.W. 2d 524 (1953).
201. *Bromley v. State,* 310 S.W. 2d 432.
202. *Worden v. State,* 273 S.W. 2d 139 (1954) and *Johnson v. State,* 208 Tenn. 620 (1961).
203. *Murphy v. State,* 254 S.W. 2d 979 (1953).
204. *Evans v. State,* 354 S.W. 2d 263 (1962).
205. *State v. Smith,* 477 S.W. 2d 6 (1972).
206. *Kaufman v. State,* 225 S.W. 2d 75 (1949). *Cf. U.S. v. Calandra,* 414 U.S. 338 (1974).
207. *Churn v. State,* 202 S.W. 2d 345.
208. *Camper v. State,* 216 S.W. 2d 19.
209. *Giles v. State,* 206 S.W. 2d 412 (1947).
210. *Beaver v. State,* 398 S.W. 2d 261, 263 (1966).
211. *Harris v. State,* 399 S.W. 2d 749, 751 (1966).
212. *Monts v. State,* 400 S.W. 2d 722, 732 (1966).
213. *See State v. Henderson,* 413 S.W. 2d 674 (1967) and *Beaver v. State,* 414 S.W. 2d 841 (1967).
214. *Shannon v. State,* 427 S.W. 2d 29 (1968).
215. *State v. Lleweln,* 286 S.W. 2d 590, 592.
216. *Edgemin v. State,* 260 S.W. 2d 263.
217. 383 S.W. 2d 41, 43.
218. *Campbell v. State,* 384 S.W. 2d 4, 6 (1964).
219. For the most thorough discussion of the King murder case, *see* Gerald Posner, *Killing the Dream* (New York: Random House, 1998). In September 1998 Attorney General Janet Reno opened a preliminary reinvestigation of this case at the request of the King family.
220. *Hanning v. State,* 201 S.W. 2d 669 (1947).
221. *James Earl Ray v. State,* 451 S.W. 2d 854, 855, 857 (1970).
222. *See, e.g., Gregg v. Georgia* 428 U.S. 153 (1976).
223. *Hunter v. State,* 440 S.W. 2d 1, 5 (1969).
224. Greene, *Lead Me On,* 170.
225. *See, e.g., Turner v. State,* 213 S.W. 2d 281 (1948); *Steele v. State,* 225 S.W. 2d 270 (1949); and *Tines v. State,* 315 S.W. 2d 111 (1958). *See also Elliott v. State,* 435 S.W. 2d 812 (1960), where such a conviction was overturned because of the state's failure to provide transcripts for appeal.
226. *State v. Bomar,* 354 S.W. 2d 763 (1962) and *State v. Bomar,* 368 S.W. 2d 748 (1963).

227. *Bowen v. State,* 488 S.W. 2d 373 and *White v. State,* 490 S.W. 2d 502.
228. *See Veach v. State,* 491 S.W. 2d 77 (1972) citing *Bell v. Burson,* 402 U.S. 535 (1971).
229. *Wagner v. Elizabethton City Board of Education,* 496 S.W. 2d 468 (1973).
230. Paul H. Bergeron, Steven V. Ash, and Jeanette Keith, *Tennesseeans and Their History* (Knoxville, 1999), 290.
231. For a good discussion of this and succeeding cases, *see* Richard C. Cortner, *The Apportionment Cases* (Knoxville, 1970). For an article focusing on *Kidd v. McCanless, see* Michael W. Catalano, "Kidd v. McCanless: The Genesis of Re-apportionment Litigation in Tennessee," 41 *Tennessee Historical Quarterly* 72–91 (1985).
232. *See* Peter Irons and Stephanie Guitton, eds., *May It Please the Court* (New York, 1991), 7–22 and corresponding tapes. For Neil's views, *see My Great World.*
233. *See Schoolfield v. Tn. Bar Assoc. of Chattanooga,* 353 S.W. 2d 401, 403 (1961).
234. 292 S.W. 2d 40, 44.
235. Summerville, *Colleagues on the Cumberland,* 77–78.
236. *State v. Bomar,* 381 S.W. 2d 297, 298 (1964).
237. *Williams v. Carr,* 404 S.W. 2d 522, 529 (1966).
238. This was a constant topic of Tennessee Bar Association proceedings, which are recorded throughout much of this time period in issues of the *Tennessee Law Review.*
239. *Petition for Rule of Court Activating, Integrating and Unifying the State Bar of Tennessee,* 282 S.W. 2d 782, 787.
240. *In re Adoption of Rule of Court,* 479 S.W. 225, 225.
241. 330 S.W. 2d 337, 342.
242. For this trial, *see* Greene, *Lead Me On,* 247–72 and *Proceedings of the High Court of Impeachment in the Case of the People of Tennessee v. Raulston Schoolfield, Judge,* comp. John W. Cooke Jr. and Fleming Hughes (Nashville, 1958).
243. 206 S.W. 2d 789.
244. *LaFaver v. Ware,* 365 S.W. 2d 55, 51 (1963).
245. Laska, *Tennessee State Constitution,* 122.
246. Keele, "Politics of Appellate Court Selection in Tennessee," 233.
247. *State v. Dunn,* 496 S.W. 2d 480, 487.
248. In a decision rendered on May 8, 1998, Davidson County Circuit Court Judge Thomas Brothers agreed that retention votes for state judges did not constitute true elections under the state constitution, but he felt bound to follow Tennessee Supreme Court rulings of 1973 and 1996 on the subject. *See* Kirk Loggins, "Judge back Hooker but sides with Court," *Tennessean,* May 10, 1998, B-1.
249. *State v. Dunn,* 494. A 1998 decision by Davidson County chancellor Ellen Hobbs Lyle agreed that the current selection method does not comport with the constitutional provision providing that judges be "elected by the qualified voters." *See* Kirk Loggins, "Ruling throws judges' election bids into turmoil," *Nashville Tennessean,* June 11, 1998, 94:1, p. 2A. The Tennessee Court of Appeals reversed. A court of special supreme court justices subsequently appointed by Governor Don Sundquist, decided that the law relating to retention elections

could not properly be challenged in this case because the incumbent candidate was not running for reelection. *See DeLaney v. Thompson,* 982 S.W. 2d 857 (1998).

250. Keele, "Politics of Appellate Court Selection in Tennessee," 236.
251. *Ibid.,* 238.
252. *Ibid.,* 239–40. In *A History of Legal Education in Tennessee,* Laska noted at 707 that Vanderbilt, one of the first private law schools to desegregate, did not have its first black graduate until 1959. Moreover, he reports, at 730, that only 1.7 percent of the Tennessee bar was female in 1955 and notes at 752 that "the growth of the female bar in Tennessee is a post-1970 phenomenon."
253. Voting was especially constricted at the beginning of the period covered by this chapter. V. O. Key estimated that, through 1946, it was rare for more than one-fourth of those of voting age to vote in a gubernatorial election. *See* Key's *Southern Politics in State and Nation* (Knoxville, 1984), 60.

7. THE TENNESSEE SUPREME COURT AND THE STRUGGLE FOR INDEPENDENCE, ACCOUNTABILITY, AND MODERNIZATION, 1974–1998

I wish to acknowledge with appreciation the research assistance of Harry Garner, Emily Urban, and Katherine Pittenger; the secretarial and editorial assistance of Pat McNeil; and the many helpful suggestions of Professor James W. Ely Jr.

1. *See* Paul H. Bergeron, Stephen V. Ash, and Jeanette Keith, *Tennesseans and Their History* (Knoxville, 1999), 319–39.
2. Developments in other states with respect to the selection of Supreme Court justices and judicial law reform initiatives are usefully discussed in G. Alan Tarr and Mary C. A. Porter, *State Supreme Courts in State and Nation* (New Haven, Conn., 1988); Daniel R. Pinello, *The Impact of Judicial Selection Method on State-Supreme-Court Policy* (Westport, Conn., 1995); and Charles S. Lopeman, *The Activist Advocate: Policy Making in State Supreme Courts* (Westport, Conn. 1999).
3. *Nashville Tennessean,* June 2, 1974, p. 2.
4. *Nashville Tennessean,* July 31, 1974, p. 1.
5. *Nashville Tennessean,* July 28, 1974, p. 13-A.
6. *Nashville Tennessean,* July 29, 1974, p. 8.
7. Justice William H. D. Fones, interview by Daniel Foley, Dec. 27, 1995 (notes on file with the *Tennessee Law Review*).
8. *See Edwards v. State,* 540 S.W.2d 641, 657 (Tenn. 1976); *State v. Stacy,* 601 S.W. 2d 696 (Tenn. 1980).
9. *See, e.g., State v. Williams,* 690 S.W.2d 517 (Tenn. 1985); *State v. Thompson,* 768 S.W.2d 239 (Tenn. 1989); *State v. Henley,* 774 S.W.2d 908 (Tenn. 1989).
10. *See generally* Lewis L. Laska, "The 1977 Limited Constitutional Convention," 61 *Tennessee Law Review* 485, 495–96, 539–63, 570 (1994).
11. Chief Justice Joseph W. Henry, "The State of the Judiciary," 91st General Assembly, Mar. 7, 1979 (on file with the author).

12. Public Acts of 1955, ch. 54, codified as TCA § 29–110.
13. *See Barger v. Brock,* 535 S.W. 337 (Tenn. 1976); Petition of Tennessee Bar Association, 539 S.W.2d 805, 808 (Tenn. 1976); and *Carden v. Fones,* 539 S.W.2d 810 (Tenn. 1976).
14. *Memphis Commercial Appeal,* Jan. 14, 1990, p. A-14.
15. Leach, "Justice Daughtrey Didn't Win Because of Gender," *Nashville Banner,* Jan. 18, 1990, p. A-13.
16. *Nashville Banner,* June 14, 1996, p. A1.
17. *Id.*
18. *Nashville Banner,* June 18, 1996, p. A1.
19. *Knoxville News-Sentinel,* July 17, 1996, p. A1.
20. Raybin, "Justice White's Opinions Show Judicial Integrity," *Nashville Banner,* July 19, 1996, p. A15. *See also* Robinson, "Penny White: Justice Isn't Soft on Crime," *Knoxville News-Sentinel,* July 29, 1996, p. A8.
21. *See State ex rel. Hooker v. Thompson,* 1996 WL 570090 (Tenn. 1996).
22. *Nashville Tennessean,* July 9, 1996, p. 1A.
23. *Nashville Banner,* July 22, 1996, p. A1.
24. *See, e.g., Hart v. City of Johnson City,* 801 S.W.2d 512 (Tenn. 1990) (statute permitting adjacent property owners to challenge annexation that was only applicable in fourteen of the state's ninety-five counties held to violate the Municipal Boundaries Clause in art. 11, § 9 of the Tennessee Constitution); *State v. Tester,* 879 S.W.2d 823 (Tenn. 1994) (no rational basis for limiting applicability of second offense DUI work release statute to counties with a population in excess of seven hundred thousand or a metropolitan form of government); and *City of Tullahoma v. Bedford County,* 938 S.W.2d 408 (Tenn. 1997) (private act of General Assembly permitting Bedford County Commission to impose a tax on solid waste water disposal is unconstitutional because it was inconsistent with general laws governing solid waste disposal throughout Tennessee).
25. *See generally* David J. Foley, "Tennessee Supreme Court: A Statistical Analysis of an Ideological Shift after the 1990 Election," 64 *Tennessee Law Review* 155, 169–75 (1996); Penny J. White, "A Survey of Tennessee Supreme Court Death Penalty Cases in the 1990s," 61 *Tennessee Law Review* 733 (1994).
26. *See* Foley, "A Move to the Right," *Knoxville News-Sentinel,* June 28, 1998, p. F1.
27. *State v. Neal,* 810 S.W.2d 131 (Tenn. 1991). *See also Johnson v. State,* 834 S.W.2d 922 (Tenn. 1992); *State v. Montgomery,* 840 S.W.2d 900 (Tenn. 1992); *Blankenship v. State,* 858 S.W.2d 897 (Tenn. 1993); *Wills v. State,* 859 S.W.2d 308 (Tenn. 1993). In *Neal, Johnson* and *Blankenship,* the Court affirmed the guilty plea; in *Montgomery* and *Wills,* the Court invalidated the plea.
28. *Memphis Commercial Appeal,* July 31, 1998, p. B4.
29. Associated Press Political Service, Aug. 7, 1998 (1998 WL 7435660).
30. Foley, *supra* note 34 at 176.

SELECT BIBLIOGRAPHY

PRIMARY SOURCES

Manuscript Collections

Bland Papers. Maryland Historical Society, Baltimore.

Beller, Roy H. Papers. Tennessee State Library and Archives, Nashville.

Bureau of Indian Affairs. Records of the Cherokee Indian Agency, East. RG 75. National Archives.

———. Records of the Office of the Secretary of War Relating to Indian Affairs, 1794–1824. RG 75. National Archives.

———. Records Relating to Indian Removal, 1817–1886. RG 75. National Archives.

Campbell Family Papers. Duke University, Durham, North Carolina.

Caruthers, Robert Looney. Papers. Southern Historical Collection. University of North Carolina, Durham.

Catron, John. Papers. Tennessee Historical Society, Nashville.

Claybrooke and Overton Papers. Tennessee Historical Society, Nashville.

Cooper, William Frierson. Letterbook. Cooper Family Papers. Tennessee State Library and Archives, Nashville.

Davidson County Wills (1865). Reel 435. Tennessee State Library and Archives, Nashville.

In Memorium, Leonidas D'entreasteaux Smith. Pamphlet. Tennessee State Library and Archives, Nashville.

Legislative Papers: Petitions and Memorials, 1799–1809. Tennessee State Library and Archives, Nashville.

Letters and Papers of Gerrit Smith. George Arents Research Library for Special Collections. Syracuse University, Syracuse, New York.

Letters of the Tennessee Governors: Joseph McMinn, 1815–1821. Tennessee State Library and Archives, Nashville.

Letters of the Tennessee Governors: William Carroll, 1821–1827. Tennessee State Library and Archives, Nashville.

Letters of the Tennessee Governors: Willie Blount, 1798–1815. Tennessee State Library and Archives, Nashville.

McRaven, William Henry. Papers. Tennessee State Library and Archives, Nashville.

Metro District Superior Court Minute and Record Books. Nashville–Davidson County Metropolitan Archives, Nashville.

Notebook of Jacob Peck: Cases Heard by the Supreme Court in 1827. McClung Historical Collection, Knoxville.

Phillips, Harry. "Remarks on Unveiling of Portraits of Judges Caruthers, Chambers, Neil, and Galbreith." MS 68-303. Tennessee State Library and Archives, Nashville.

Roane County Chancery Court Record Book 1, 1824–1833. Part 2. Chancery Court, Ninth Judicial District, Kingston, Tennessee.

Shields, John K. Collection. MS 1708. University of Tennessee Special Collections, Knoxville.

Records of the Supreme Court of the United States.Dockets of the Supreme Court of the United States, 1834–1860. M216, Reel 2. RG 267, Entry 24. National Archives.

———. Index to the Appellate Case Files of the Supreme Court of the United States, 1792–1909. M408, Reels 6, 16, and 17. RG 267, Entry 24 National Archives.

———. Minutes of the Supreme Court of the United States, 1829–1848. M215, Reels 2 and 3. RG 267, Entry 24. National Archives.

———. Papers in Undocketed Appellate Case Files of the Supreme Court of the United States, 1791–1920. Entry 24. RG 267. National Archives.

Tennessee Supreme Court of Errors and Appeals Equity Min. Bk., 1812–1838. Tennessee Supreme Court Archives. Knoxville.

Tennessee Supreme Court of Errors and Appeals Records, 1830–1835. Archives of Appalachia. East Tennessee State University, Johnson City.

Tennessee Supreme Court Records. Tennessee State Library and Archives, Nashville.

U.S. Bureau of the Census. Population Schedules of the Fourth Census of the United States, 1820: Davidson County, Tennessee. National Archives M33, Reel 122. RG 29.

———. Schedules of Heads of Family, Fifth Census of the United States, 1830; Town of Nashville and Davidson and Franklin Counties, Tennessee. Schedules 57, 277, 301, 312. National Archives M19, Reels 174-176-180. RG 29.

Van Buren, Martin. Papers. Series 2. Mf 798, Reel 14. Library of Congress.

Washington County Court Records, 1780–1965. Archives of Appalachia. East Tennessee State University, Johnson City.

Washington District Superior Court Records, 1785–1811. Archives of Appalachia. East Tennessee State University, Johnson City.

Whyte, Robert. Papers. Tennessee Historical Society, Nashville.

Newspapers

Impartial Review and Cumberland Repository
Knoxville Gazette
Knoxville Journal
Knoxville Journal and Tribune
Knoxville News-Sentinel
Knoxville Register
Memphis Commercial Appeal
Memphis Daily Appeal
Memphis Press-Scimitar
Nashville Banner
Nashville Gazette
Nashville Republican
Nashville Tennessean
Nashville Union
Nashville Whig
Niles Weekly Register

State Documents

Acts of the State of Tennessee Passed at the First Session of the Thirtieth General Assembly for the Years 1853–1854. Nashville: McKennie and Brown, 1854.

Journal of the Convention of the state of Tennessee. Convened for the purpose of revising and amending the constitution therof. Nashville: W. H. Hunt and Co., 1834.

Journal of the House of Representatives of the State of Tennessee at the Nineteenth General Assembly. Knoxville: Heiskell & Hall, 1831.

Journal of the House of Representatives of the State of Tennessee, Twenty-eighth General Assembly, Held at Nashville, 1849–50. Nashville: Watterson, 1849.

Journal of the House of Representatives of the State of Tennessee, Twenty-first General Assembly. Knoxville: Ramsey & Craighead, 1836.

Journal of the Proceedings of a Convention Began and Held at Knoxville, January 11, 1796. Knoxville: George Roulstone, 1796.

Proceedings of the High Court of Impeachment in the Case of the People of the State of Tennessee vs. Raulston Schoolfield, Judge. Compiled by John W. Cooke Jr. and Fleming Hughes. Nashville: Rich Printing, 1958.

Public Acts at the First Session of the Twenty-first General Assembly of the State of Tennessee, 1835–36. Nashville: Nye and Company, 1836.

Public Acts Passed at the Stated Session of the Nineteenth General Assembly of the State of Tennessee, 1831. Nashville: Hall & Heiskell, 1832.

Senate Journal for the First Session of the Twenty-Seventh General Assembly of the State of Tennessee, Which Convened at Nashville on the First Monday of October, A.D. 1847. Nashville: Bang and Company, 1848.

Senate Journal of the First Session of the Thirtieth General Assembly of the State of Tennessee, Which Convened at Nashville, on the First Monday in October, A.D. 1853. Nashville: Bang, Poats, and Company, 1854.

[Tennessee General Assembly.] *House Journal* (1804); *House Journal* (1811); *House Journal* (1817); *House Journal* (1819); *House Journal* (1824); *House Journal* (1831); *Senate Journal* (1807); *Senate Journal* (1809); *Senate Journal* (1815); *Senate Journal* (1817); *Senate Journal* (1822); *Senate Journal* (1831); *Senate Journal* (1832).

Contemporary Published Sources

Aggregate Amount of Each Description of Persons within the United States of America, and the Territories Thereof . . . 1810. Vol. 3. Washington, D.C.: n.p., 1811.

Bassett, John Spencer, ed. *Correspondence of Andrew Jackson.* 5 vols. Washington, D.C.: Carnegie Institute, 1931.

A Copy of the Acts of the Corporation of Nashville and Legislature of Tennessee, Authorizing the Subscription of $500.00 of Stock in the Nashville and Chattanooga Railroad Company, with the Opinion of the Supreme Court of Tennessee, Confirming Said Subscription. Nashville: W. F. Bang, 1849.

Green, Nathan. *Address by Hon. Nathan Green, Judge of the Supreme Court of Tennessee, Delivered February 28, 1849, on Entering the Duties of Professor of Law in Cumberland University at Lebanon, Tennessee.* Lebanon, Tenn.: J. T. Figures, 1849.

Haywood, John. *Opinion of Judge Haywood in the Case of Toka Will versus Matthew Nelson, Treasurer of East Tennessee, Concerning the Right of the State to Dispose of the School Lands.* Knoxville: Heiskell & Brown, 1826.

Lurton, Horace H. "Is the Trust Dangerous?" *Proceedings of the Tenth Annual Meeting of the Bar Association of Tennessee,* 144–69. Nashville, 1891.

Martin, Andrew B. *Address Upon the Life and Character of Judge Robert L. Caruthers.* Nashville: Cumberland Presbyterian Publishing House, 1883.

Pitts, John A. *Personal and Professional Reminiscences of an Old Lawyer.* Kingsport, Tenn.: Southern Publishers, 1930.

White, Robert H. [ed.] *Messages of the Governors of Tennessee.* 7 vols. Nashville: Tennessee Historical Commission, 1952–67.

SECONDARY WORKS

Books and Articles

Abernethy, Thomas P. *From Frontier to Plantation in Tennessee: A Study in Frontier Democracy.* Chapel Hill: Univ. of North Carolina Press, 1932.

Abraham, Henry J. *Justices, Presidents, and Senators: A History of the U.S. Supreme Court Appointments from Washington to Clinton.* Rev. ed. New York: Rowman and Littlefield, 1999.

Alexander, Thomas B. *Political Reconstruction in Tennessee.* Nashville: Vanderbilt Univ. Press, 1950.

———. *Thomas A. R. Nelson of East Tennessee.* Nashville: Tennessee Historical Commission, 1956.

Allison, John, ed. *Notable Men of Tennessee.* 2 vols. Atlanta: Southern Historical Association, 1905.

Appleby, Joyce. *Inheriting the Revolution: The First Generation of Americans.* Cambridge: Harvard Univ. Press, 2000.

Armstrong, Robert J. "Regulation of the Bar in Tennessee." *Tennessee Law Review* 53 (Summer 1986): 723–51.

Arroyo, Elizabeth R. "Poor Whites, Slaves, and Free Blacks in Tennessee, 1796–1861." *Tennessee Historical Quarterly* 55 (1996): 57–65.

Ash, Stephen V. *Middle Tennessee Society Transformed, 1860–1870: War and Peace in the Upper South.* Baton Rouge: Louisiana State Univ. Press, 1988.

Atherton, Lewis E. "The Problem of Credit Rating in the Ante-Bellum South." *Journal of Southern History* 12 (1946): 534–56.

Atkins, Jonathan M. *Parties, Politics, and the Sectional Conflict in Tennessee, 1832–1861.* Knoxville: Univ. of Tennessee Press, 1997.

Ayers, Edward L. *The Promise of the New South: Life After Reconstruction.* New York: Oxford Univ. Press, 1992.

———. *Vengeance and Justice: Crime and Punishment in the 19th-Century American South.* New York: Oxford Univ. Press, 1984.

Baker, Leonard. *John Marshall: A Life in Law.* New York: Macmillan, 1974.

Bardaglio, Peter W. *Reconstructing the Household: Families, Sex, and the Law in the Nineteenth-Century South.* Chapel Hill: Univ. of North Carolina Press, 1995.

Barnhart, John D. *Valley of Democracy: The Frontier versus the Plantation in the Ohio Valley, 1775–1818.* Bloomington: Indiana Univ. Press, 1953.

Barrus, Ben M., Milton L. Baughn, and Thomas H. Campbell. *A People Called Cumberland Presbyterians.* Memphis: Frontier Press, 1972.

Beatty, Jerry K. "State Court Evasion of Supreme Court Mandates During the Last Decade of the Warren Court." *Valparaiso Law Review* 6 (1972): 260–85.

Bergeron, Paul H. *Antebellum Politics in Tennessee.* Lexington: Univ. Press of Kentucky, 1982.

———. *Paths of the Past: Tennessee, 1770–1970.* Knoxville: Univ. of Tennessee Press, 1979.

———. "Tennessee's Response to the Nullification Crisis." *Journal of Southern History* 39 (1973): 23–44.

Bergeron, Paul H., Stephen A. Ash, and Jeannette Keith. *Tennesseeans and Their History.* Knoxville: Univ. of Tennessee Press, 1999.

Blake, Nelson M. *The Road to Reno: A History of Divorce in the United States.* New York: Macmillan, 1962.

Blassingame, John. *The Slave Community.* New York: Oxford Univ. Press, 1972.

Bloomfield, Maxwell. *American Lawyers in a Changing Society, 1776–1876.* Cambridge: Harvard Univ. Press, 1976.

Brake, Patricia E. *Justice in the Valley: A Bicentennial Perspective of the United States Court for the Eastern District of Tennessee.* Franklin, Tenn.: Hillsboro Press, 1998.

Brown, Richard Maxwell. "Southern Violence—Regional Problem or National Nemesis?: Legal Attitudes Toward Southern Homicide in Historical Perspective." *Vanderbilt Law Review* 32 (1979): 225–50.

Brown, Theodore, Jr. "The Tennessee County Courts Under the North Carolina and Territorial Governments: The Davidson County Court of Pleas and Quarter Sessions, 1783–1796, as a Case Study." *Vanderbilt Law Review* 32 (1979): 349–412.

Caldwell, Joshua W. *Sketches of the Bench and Bar of Tennessee.* Knoxville: Ogden Brothers, 1898.

———. *Studies in the Constitutional History of Tennessee.* Cincinnati: Robert Clarke, 1895.

Calhoun, Daniel H. *Professional Lives in America: Structure and Aspiration, 1750–1850.* Cambridge: Harvard Univ. Press, 1965.

Campbell, Alex W. "Life and Character of Judge W. B. Turley." *Proceedings of the Third Annual Meeting of the Bar Association of Tennessee* (1884): 201–13.

Cartwright, Joseph H. *The Triumph of Jim Crow: Tennessee Race Relations in the 1880s.* Knoxville: Univ. of Tennessee Press, 1976.

Catalano, Michael W. "Kidd v. McCanless: The Genesis of Reapportionment Litigation in Tennessee." *Tennessee Historical Quarterly* 41 (1985): 72–91.

Censer, Jane T. "'Smiling Through Her Tears': Ante-Bellum Southern Women and Divorce." *American Journal of Legal History* 25 (1981): 24–47.

Chomsky, Carol. "Progressive Judges in a Progressive Age: Regulatory Legislation in the Minnesota Supreme Court, 1880–1925." *Law and History Review* 11 (Fall 1993): 383–440.

Cimprich, John. *Slavery's End in Tennessee, 1861–1865.* University: Univ. of Alabama Press, 1985.

Coffey, Charles S. "A Challenge and an Appeal to the Tennessee Bar." *Tennessee Law Review* 15 (1939): 698–702.

Colyar, A. S. "Biographical Sketch of Judge Nathan Green." *Proceedings of the Eleventh Annual Meeting of the Bar Association of Tennessee* (1892): 134–43.

———. *Life and Times of Andrew Jackson: Soldier, Statesman, President.* Nashville: Marshall & Bruce, 1904.

Combs, William H., and William E. Cole. *Tennessee: A Political Study.* Knoxville: Univ. of Tennessee Press, 1940.

Conkin, Paul K. *Gone with the Ivy: A Biography of Vanderbilt University.* Knoxville: Univ. of Tennessee Press, 1985.

———. *Prophets of Prosperity: America's First Political Economists.* Bloomington: Indiana Univ. Press, 1980.

Corlew, Robert E. *Tennessee: A Short History.* 2d ed. Knoxville: Univ. of Tennessee Press, 1990.

Cornwell, Illene J. *Biographical Directory of the Tennessee General Assembly.* Vol. 3, *1901–1931.* Nashville: Tennessee Historical Commission, 1988.

Cortner, Richard C. *The Apportionment Cases.* Knoxville: Univ. of Tennessee Press, 1970.

Coulter, E. Merton. *William G. Brownlow: Fighting Parson of the Southern Highlands.* Knoxville: Univ. of Tennessee Press, 1999.

Cox, R. D. "History of Adverse Possession Statutes of Tennessee." *Memphis State University Law Review* 6 (1976): 673–99.

Dangerfield, George. *The Awakening of American Nationalism, 1815–1828.* New York: Harper & Row, 1965.

———. *The Era of Good Feelings.* New York: Harcourt, Brace & World, 1952.

Daniel, Pete. "The Tennessee Convict War." *Tennessee Historical Quarterly* 34 (1975): 273–92.

Davis, David Brion. *The Problem of Slavery in Western Civilization.* Ithaca, N.Y.: Cornell Univ. Press, 1956.

Dunn, Durwood. "Apprenticeship and Indentured Servitude in Tennessee Before the Civil War." *West Tennessee Historical Society Papers* 36 (1982): 25–40.

Ellis, Richard E. *The Jeffersonian Crisis: Court and Politics in the Young Republic.* New York: Oxford Univ. Press, 1971.

Ely, James W., Jr. *The Chief Justiceship of Melville W. Fuller, 1888–1910.* Columbia: Univ. of South Carolina Press, 1995.

———. "The Fuller Court and Takings Jurisprudence." *Journal of Supreme Court History* 2 (1996): 120–35.

———. *The Guardian of Every Other Right: A Constitutional History of Property Rights.* 2d ed. New York: Oxford Univ. Press, 1998.

———. "The Oxymoron Reconsidered: Myth and Reality in the Origins of Substantive Due Process." *Constitutional Commentary* 16 (1999): 315–45.

———. "'There are few subjects in political economy of greater difficulty': The Poor Laws of the Antebellum South." *American Bar Foundation Research Journal* (1985): 849–79.

Ely, James W., Jr., and David J. Bodenhamer. "Regionalism and the Legal History of the South." In *Ambivalent Legacy: A Legal History of the South,* edited by David J. Bodenhamer and James W. Ely Jr., 3–29. Jackson: Univ. Press of Mississippi, 1984.

———. "Regionalism and American Legal History: The Southern Experience." *Vanderbilt Law Review* 39 (1986): 539–67.

Ely, James W., Jr., and Theodore Brown Jr., eds. *Legal Papers of Andrew Jackson.* Knoxville: Univ. of Tennessee Press, 1987.

England, J. Merton. "The Free Negro in Antebellum Tennessee." *Journal of Southern History* 9 (1943): 37–58.

Fancher, Frank Trigg. *The Sparta Bar.* Milford, N.H.: Cabinet Press, 1950.

Fede, Andrew. *People Without Rights: An Interpretation of the Fundamentals of the Law of Slavery in the U.S. South.* New York: Garland, 1992.

Fehrenbacher, Don E. *Constitutions and Constitutionalism in the Slaveholding South.* Athens: Univ. of Georgia Press, 1989.

Feistman, Eugene G. "Radical Disfranchisement and the Restoration of Tennessee, 1865–1866." *Tennessee Historical Quarterly* 12 (1953): 135–51.

Fisher, William W., III. "Ideology and Imagery in the Law of Slavery." *Chicago-Kent Law Review* 68 (1993): 1051–83.

Foley, Daniel J. "Tennessee Supreme Court: A Statistical Analysis of an Ideological Shift After the 1990 Election." *Tennessee Law Review* 64 (1996): 155–93.

Folmsbee, Stanley J. "The Origin of the First 'Jim Crow' Law." *Journal of Southern History* 15 (1949): 235–47.

Foote, Henry S. *The Bench and Bar of the South and Southwest.* St. Louis: Soule, Thomas, and Wentworth, 1876.

Franklin, John Hope. *The Militant South, 1800–1861.* Cambridge: Harvard Univ. Press, 1956.

Freehling, William W. *The Road to Disunion: Secessionists at Bay, 1776–1854.* New York: Oxford Univ. Press, 1990.

Friedman, Laurence J. *Gregarious Saints: Self and Community in American Abolitionism, 1830–1870.* New York: Cambridge Univ. Press, 1982.

Friedman, Lawrence M. *Crime and Punishment in American History.* New York: Basic Books, 1993.

———. *A History of American Law.* 2d ed. New York: Simon and Schuster, 1985.

Friedman, Lawrence M., Robert A. Kagan, Bliss Cartwright, and Stanton Wheeler. "State Supreme Courts: A Century of Style and Citation." *Stanford Law Review* 33 (1981): 773–818.

Genovese, Eugene D. *Roll, Jordan, Roll: The World the Slaves Made.* New York: Pantheon Books, 1974.

Gillman, Howard. *The Constitution Beseiged: The Rise and Demise of Lochner Era Police Powers Jurisprudence.* Durham, N.C.: Duke Univ. Press, 1993.

Gilmore, Grant. *The Ages of American Law.* New Haven, Conn.: Yale Univ. Press, 1979.

Glick, Henry R. *State Courts in State Politics: An Investigation of the Judicial Role.* New York: Basic Books, 1971.

Glickstein, Jonathan A. *Concepts of Free Labor in Antebellum America.* New Haven, Conn.: Yale Univ. Press, 1991.

Goodheart, Lawrence B. "Tennessee's Antislavery Movement Reconsidered: The Example of Elihu Embree." *Tennessee Historical Quarterly* 41 (1982): 224–38.

Goodheart, Lawrence B., Neil Hawks, and Elizabeth Johnson. "'An Act for the Relief of Females . . .': Divorce and the Changing Legal Status of Women in Tennessee, 1796–1860." *Tennessee Historical Quarterly* 44 (1985): 318–39, 402–16.

Grantham, Dewey W. *Southern Progressivism: The Reconciliation of Progress and Tradition.* Knoxville: Univ. of Tennessee Press, 1983.

Green, Fletcher M. *Constitutional Development in the South Atlantic States, 1776–1860: A Study in the Evolution of Democracy.* Chapel Hill: Univ. of North Carolina Press, 1930.

Green, Grafton. "The Judiciary." *Tennessee Law Review* 15 (1938): 142–44.

Green, John W. "Five Judges of Our Supreme Court (1894–1910)." *Tennessee Law Review* 17 (1942): 355–67.

———. "Judges of the Reconstruction Era (1865–1870)." *Tennessee Law Review* 17 (1942): 413–39.

———. *Lives of the Judges of the Supreme Court of Tennessee, 1796–1947.* Knoxville: Archer & Smith, 1947.

———. "Some Judges of the Supreme Court of Tennessee (1865–78)." *Tennessee Law Review* 17 (1943): 789–804.

———. "The Supreme Court of Tennessee in 1886." *Tennessee Law Review* 16 (1941): 899–906.

Greene, Lee S. *Lead Me On: Frank Goad Clement and Tennessee Politics.* Knoxville: Univ. of Tennessee Press, 1982.

Greene, Lee S., David H. Grubbs, and Victor C. Hobday. *Government in Tennessee.* Knoxville: Univ. of Tennessee Press, 1982.

Gresham, L. Paul. "The Public Career of Hugh Lawson White." *Tennessee Historical Quarterly* 3 (1944): 291–318.

Grossberg, Michael. *Governing the Hearth: Law and the Family in Nineteenth-Century America.* Chapel Hill: Univ. of North Carolina Press, 1985.

Haar, Charles M. *The Golden Age of American Law.* New York: Braziller, 1965.

Halberstam, David. *The Children.* New York: Random House, 1998.

Hale, Will T., and Dixon L. Merrit. *A History of Tennessee and Tennesseans.* Chicago: Lewis, 1913.

Hall, Clifton R. *Andrew Johnson, Military Governor of Tennessee.* Princeton, N.J.: Princeton Univ. Press, 1916.

Hall, Kermit L. "The Judiciary on Trial: State Constitutional Reform and the Rise of an Elected Judiciary, 1846–1860." *Historian* 45 (1983): 337–54.

———. *The Magic Mirror: Law in American History.* New York: Oxford Univ. Press, 1988.

———. "Progressive Reform and the Decline of Popular Democratic Accountability: The Popular Election of State Supreme Court Judges, 1850–1920." *American Bar Foundation Research Journal* (1984): 345–69.

———. "The 'Route to Hell' Retraced: The Impact of Popular Election on the Southern Appellate Judiciary, 1832–1920." In *Ambivalent Legacy: A Legal History of the South,* edited by David J. Bodenhamer and James W. Ely Jr., 229–55. Jackson: Univ. Press of Mississippi, 1984.

———. "West H. Humphreys and the Crisis of the Union." *Tennessee Historical Quarterly* 34 (1975): 48–69.

Hall, Kermit L., and James W. Ely Jr., eds. *An Uncertain Tradition: Constitutionalism and the History of the South.* Athens: Univ. of Georgia Press, 1989.

Hamer, Philip M. *Tennessee: A History, 1673–1932.* New York: American Historical Society, 1933.

Hart, Robert L. *Redeemers, Bourbons and Populists: Tennessee, 1870–1896.* Baton Rouge: Louisiana State Univ. Press, 1975.

Henderson, W. A. "Life and Character of Judge McKinney." *Proceedings of the Third Annual Meeting of the Bar Association of Tennessee* (1884): 107–15.

Hollingsworth, Harold M. "George Andrews—Carpetbagger." *Tennessee Historical Quarterly* 28 (1969): 310–23.

Holt, Michael F. *The Rise and Fall of the American Whig Party: Jacksonian Politics and the Onset of the Civil War.* New York: Oxford Univ. Press, 1999.

Hooper, Ben W. *The Unwanted Boy: The Autobiography of Governor Ben W. Hooper.* Edited by Everett Robert Boyce. Knoxville: Univ. of Tennessee Press, 1963.

Horwitz, Morton J. *The Transformation of American Law, 1780–1860.* Cambridge: Harvard Univ. Press, 1977.

Howington, Arthur F. "'Not in the Condition of a Horse or an Ox': *Ford v. Ford,* the Law of Testamentary Manumission, and the Tennessee Court's Recognition of Slave Humanity." *Tennessee Historical Quarterly* 34 (1975): 249–63.

———. "'A Property of Peculiar and Special Value': The Tennessee Supreme Court and the Law of Manumission." *Tennessee Historical Quarterly* 44 (1985): 302–17.

———. *What Sayeth the Law: The Treatment of Slaves and Free Blacks in the State and Local Courts of Tennessee.* New York: Garland, 1986.

Huebner, Timothy S. *The Southern Judicial Tradition: State Judges and Sectional Distinctiveness, 1790–1890.* Athens: Univ. of Georgia Press, 1999.

———. "The Roots of Fairness: State v. Caesar and Slave Justice in Antebellum North Carolina." In *Local Matters: Race, Crime, and Justice in the Nineteenth-Century South,* edited by Chistopher Waldrup and Donald G. Nieman, 29–52. Athens: Univ. of Georgia Press, 2001.

Isaac, Paul E. *Prohibition and Politics: Turbulent Decades in Tennessee, 1885–1920.* Knoxville: Univ. of Tennessee Press, 1965.

———. "The Problems of a Republican Governor in a Southern State: Ben Hooper in Tennessee." *Tennessee Historical Quarterly* 27 (1968): 229–48.

Jennings, Thelma. *The Nashville Convention: Southern Movement for Unity, 1848–1850.* Memphis: Memphis State Univ. Press, 1980.

Jones, Robert B. *Tennessee at the Crossroads: The State Debt Controversy, 1870–1883.* Knoxville: Univ. of Tennessee Press, 1977.

Kagan, Robert A., Bliss Cartwright, Lawrence M. Friedman, and Stanton Wheeler. "The Business of State Supreme Courts, 1870–1970." *Stanford Law Review* 30 (1977): 121–56.

———. "The Evolution of State Supreme Courts." *Michigan Law Review* 76 (1978): 961–1005.

[Karlen, Delmar, and Robert J. Martineau.] *The Judicial System of Tennessee: A Background Survey.* Nashville: State of Tennessee, 1966.

Karsten, Peter. *Heart versus Head: Judge-Made Law in Nineteenth Century America.* Chapel Hill: Univ. of North Carolina Press, 1997.

Keebler, Robert S. "Limitations Upon the State's Control of Public Education: A Critical Analysis of *State of Tennessee v. John Thomas Scopes.*" *Tennessee Law Review* 6 (1928): 153–77.

Keller, Morton. *Affairs of State: Public Life in Late Nineteenth Century America.* Cambridge: Harvard Univ. Press, 1977.

Kens, Paul. "The Source of Myth: Police Powers of the States and Laissez Faire Constitutionalism, 1900–1937." *American Journal of Legal History* 35 (1991): 70–98.

Key, V. O., Jr. *Southern Politics in State and Nation.* New York: Alfred A. Knopf, 1949.

Kousser, J. Morgan. *The Shaping of Southern Politics: Suffrage Restriction and the Establishment of the One-Party South.* New Haven, Conn.: Yale Univ. Press, 1974.

Lacy, Eric Russell. "Tennessee Teetotalism: Social Forces and the Politics of Progressivism." *Tennessee Historical Quarterly* 24 (1965): 219–40.

Langum, David J., and Howard P. Walthall. *From Maverick to Mainstream: Cumberland School of Law, 1847–1997.* Athens: Univ. of Georgia Press, 1997.

Larson, Edward J. *Summer for the Gods: The Scopes Trial and America's Continuing Debate Over Science and Religion.* New York: Basic Books, 1997.

Laska, Lewis L. "The 1977 Limited Constitutional Convention." *Tennessee Law Review* 61 (1994): 485–572.

———. "A Legal and Constitutional History of Tennessee, 1771–1991." *Memphis State University Law Review* 6 (1976): 563–672.

———. "The Tennessee Constitution." In *Tennessee Government and Politics: Democracy in the Volunteer State,* edited John R. Vile and Mark Byrnes, 7–24. Nashville: Vanderbilt Univ. Press, 1998.

———. *The Tennessee State Constitution: A Reference Guide.* New York: Greenwood Press, 1990.

Lee, David D. *Tennessee in Turmoil: Politics in the Volunteer State, 1920–1932.* Memphis: Memphis State Univ. Press, 1979.

Mack, Kenneth W. "Law, Society, Identity, and the Making of the Jim Crow South: Travel and Segregation on Tennessee Railroads, 1875–1905." *Law and Social Inquiry* 24 (1999): 377–405.

Majors, William R. *Change and Continuity: Tennessee Politics Since the Civil War.* Macon, Ga.: Mercer Univ. Press, 1986.

———. *The End of Arcadia: Gordon Browning and Tennessee Politics.* Memphis: Memphis State Univ. Press, 1982.

Marks, Albert D. "The Supreme Court of Tennessee." *Green Bag* 5 (1893): 120–28, 171–84, 225–36.

May, James. "Antitrust Practice and Procedure in the Formative Era: The Constitutional and Conceptual Reach of State Antitrust Law, 1880–1918." *University of Pennsylvania Law Review* 135 (1987): 495–593.

McCormick, Richard P. *The Second American Party System: Party Formation in the Jacksonian Era.* Chapel Hill: Univ. of North Carolina Press, 1966.

McCurdy, Charles W. "The 'Liberty of Contract' Regime in American Law." In *The State and Freedom of Contract,* edited by Harry N. Scheiber, 160–97. Stanford, Calif.: Stanford Univ. Press, 1998.

McDonald, Forrest. *States' Rights and the Union: Imperium in Imperio, 1776–1876.* Lawrence: Univ. Press of Kansas, 2000.

McFarland, L. B. "Some Reminiscences of the Memphis Bar." *Proceedings of the Seventeenth Annual Session of the Bar Association of Tennessee* (1898): 87–105.

Meyers, Marvin. *The Jacksonian Persuasion: Politics and Belief.* Stanford, Calif.: Stanford Univ. Press, 1960.

Miller, William D. *Mr. Crump of Memphis.* Baton Rouge: Louisiana State Univ. Press, 1964.

Miscamble, Wilson D. "Andrew Johnson and the Election of William G. ('Parson') Brownlow As Governor of Tennessee." *Tennessee Historical Quarterly* 37 (1978): 308–20.

Mooney, Chase C. *Slavery in Tennessee.* Bloomington: Indiana Univ. Press, 1957.

Moore, John Trotwood. *Tennessee: The Volunteer State, 1769–1923.* Vol. 3. Chicago: S. J. Clarke, 1923.

Moore, Powell. "The Revolt Against Jackson in Tennessee, 1835–1836." *Journal of Southern History* 2 (1936): 335–59.

Morris, Thomas D. *Southern Slavery and the Law, 1619–1860.* Chapel Hill: Univ. of North Carolina Press, 1996.

———. "'Villeinage . . . as it existed in England, reflects but little light on our subject': The Problem of the 'Sources' of Southern Slave Law." *American Journal of Legal History* 32 (1988): 95–137.

Nall, James O. *The Tobacco Night of Kentucky and Tennessee, 1905–1909.* Louisville, Ky.: Standard Press, 1939.

Nash, A. E. Keir. "A More Equitable Past? Southern Supreme Courts and the Protection of the Antebellum Negro." *North Carolina Law Review* 48 (1970): 406–51.

———. "Reason of Slavery: Understanding the Judicial Role in the Peculiar Institution." *Vanderbilt Law Review* 32 (1979): 7–218.

Neil, Albert Bramlett. *My Great World or Fifty Years on the Bench.* Nashville: Privately printed, 1964.

———. "Letter of Justice A. B. Neil, June 18, 1945." *Tennessee Law Review* 19 (1945): 68–70.

Nelson, Caleb. "A Re-Evaluation of Scholarly Explanations for the Rise of the Elective Judiciary in Antebellum America." *American Journal of Legal History* 37 (1993): 190–224.

Nelson, Margaret V. *A Study of Judicial Review in Virginia, 1789–1928.* New York: Columbia Univ. Press, 1947.

Nelson, William E. "Changing Conceptions of Judicial Review: The Evolution of Constitutional Theory in the States, 1790–1860." *University of Pennsylvania Law Review* 120 (1972): 1166–85.

Newmyer, R. Kent. *Supreme Court Justice Joseph Story: Statesman of the Old Republic.* Chapel Hill: Univ. of North Carolina Press, 1985.

Norgren, Jill. *The Cherokee Cases: The Confrontation of Law and Politics.* New York: McGraw Hill, 1996.

Novak, William J. *The People's Welfare: Law and Regulation in Nineteenth-Century America.* Chapel Hill: Univ. of North Carolina Press, 1996.

Oakes, James. *The Ruling Race: A History of American Slaveholders.* New York: Alfred A. Knopf, 1982.

Olshfski, Dorothy F., and T. McN. Simpson, eds. *The Volunteer State: Readings in Tennessee Politics.* N.p.: Tennessee Political Science Association, 1985.

Parton, James. *Life of Andrew Jackson.* New York: Mason Brothers, 1861.

Patterson, Caleb Perry. *The Negro in Tennessee, 1790–1865.* New York: Negro Universities Press, 1968.

Patton, John W. "The Cumberland Church Cases." *University of Pennsylvania Law Review* 64 (1915): 66–76.

Payne, Donald F. "The Cooper Trial and Impeachment by Bad Acts." *Tennessee Bar Journal* 30 (Nov.–Dec. 1994): 24–26.

Perry, Jennings. *Democracy Begins at Home: The Tennessee Fight on the Poll Tax.* Philadelphia: J. B. Lippincott, 1944.

Phelan, James. *History of Tennessee: The Making of a State.* Boston: Houghton, Mifflin, 1888.

Potter, David M. *The Impending Crisis, 1848–1861.* New York: Harper and Row, 1976.

Pound, Roscoe. *Organization of Courts.* Boston: Little, Brown, 1940.

Qualls, J. Winfield. "Fusion Victory and the Tennessee Senatorship." *West Tennessee Historical Society Papers* 15 (1961): 72–92.

Queener, Verton M. "The East Tennessee Republican Party, 1900–1914." *East Tennessee Historical Society's Publications* 22 (1950): 94–127.

Quigley, William P. "The Quicksands of the Poor Law: Poor Relief Legislation in a Growing Nation, 1790–1820." *Northern Illinois Law Review* 18 (1997): 1–98.

Reed, Linda. *Simple Decency and Common Sense: The Southern Conference Movement.* Bloomington: Indiana Univ. Press, 1991.

Remini, Robert V. *Andrew Jackson and the Course of American Democracy, 1833–1845.* New York: Harper & Row, 1984.

———. *The Election of Andrew Jackson.* Philadelphia: Lippincott, 1963.

"Report of the Committee on Judicial Administration and Remedial Procedure." *Tennessee Law Review* 17 (1941): 100–103.

"Report of the Judicial Council." *Tennessee Law Review* 19 (1946): 677–80.

Riley, Glenda. *Divorce: An American Tradition.* New York: Oxford Univ. Press, 1991.

Robinson, Daniel M. *Bob Taylor and the Agrarian Revolt in Tennessee.* Chapel Hill: Univ. of North Carolina Press, 1935.

Robinson, William M., Jr. *Justice in Grey: A History of the Judicial System of the Confederate States of America.* Cambridge: Harvard Univ. Press, 1941.

Salmon, Marylynn. *Women and the Law of Property in Early America.* Chapel Hill: Univ. of North Carolina Press, 1986.

Schwartz, Gary T. "Tort Law and the Economy in Nineteenth-Century America: A Reinterpretation." *Yale Law Journal* 90 (1981): 1717–75.

Sellers, Charles G., Jr. *The Market Revolution: Jacksonian America, 1815–1846.* New York: Oxford Univ. Press, 1991.

Shapiro, Karin A. *A New South Rebellion: The Battle Against Convict Labor in the Tennessee Coalfields, 1871–1896.* Chapel Hill: Univ. of North Carolina Press, 1998.

Stampp, Kenneth M. *The Peculiar Institution: Slavery in the Ante-Bellum South.* New York: Knopf, 1956.

Stockard, Russell. "The Election and First Administration of Ben W. Hooper as Governor of Tennessee." *East Tennessee Historical Society Papers* 32 (1960): 38–59.

Summerville, James. *The Carmack-Cooper Shooting: Tennessee Politics Turns Violent, November 9, 1908.* Jefferson, N.C.: McFarland, 1994.

———. *Colleagues on the Cumberland: A History of the Nashville Legal Profession.* N.p.: Taylor, 1966.

Swint, Henry Lee. "Ezekiel Birdseye and the Free State of Frankland." *Tennessee Historical Quarterly* 3 (1944): 226–36.

Tate, Cassandra. *Cigarette Wars: The Triumph of "The Little White Slaver."* New York: Oxford University Press, 1999.

Tindall, George B. *The Emergence of the New South, 1913–1945.* Baton Rouge: Louisiana State Univ. Press, 1967.

Tomlins, Christopher L. *Law, Labor and Ideology in the Early American Republic.* New York: Cambridge Univ. Press, 1993.

Trabue, Charles C. "The Voluntary Emancipation of Slaves in Tennessee as Reflected in the State's Legislation and Judicial Decisions." *Tennessee Historical Magazine* 4 (1918): 50–68.

Tucker, David M. "Justice Horace Harman Lurton: The Shaping of a National Progressive." *American Journal of Legal History* 13 (1969): 223–32.

Urofsky, Melvin I. "State Courts and Protective Legislation during the Progressive Era: A Reevaluation." *Journal of American History* 72 (June 1985): 63–91.

Van West, Carol, ed. *Tennessee Encyclopedia of History and Culture.* Nashville: Tennessee Historical Society, Rutledge Hill Press, 1998.

Vile, John R., and Mark Byrnes, eds. *Tennessee Government and Politics: Democracy in the Volunteer State.* Nashville: Vanderbilt Univ. Press, 1998.

Vines, Kenneth N. "Southern State Supreme Courts and Race Relations." *Western Political Quarterly* 18 (1965): 5–18.

Waldrep, Christopher. *Night Riders: Defending Community in the Black Patch, 1890–1915.* Durham, N.C.: Duke Univ. Press, 1993.

Ward, John W. *Andrew Jackson: Symbol for an Age.* New York: Oxford Univ. Press, 1955.

White, Penny J. "A Survey of Tennessee Supreme Court Death Penalty Cases in the 1990s." *Tennessee Law Review* 61 (1994): 733–45.

Wicker, William H. "Constitutional Revision and the Courts." *Proceedings of the Sixth Annual Southern Institute of Local Government.* Knoxville: Bureau of Public Administration, 1947.

———. "The Reorganization of Appellate Courts in Tennessee." In *Papers on Constitutional Revision,* vol. 1, 69–78. Knoxville: Bureau of Public Administration, 1947.

Widerman, Rivka. "Tobacco Is a Dirty Weed. Have We Ever Liked It? A Look at Nineteenth Century Anti-Cigarette Legislation." *Loyola Law Review* 38 (1992): 387–423.

Wiethoff, William E. *A Peculiar Humanism: The Judicial Advocacy of Slavery in High Courts in the Old South, 1820–1850.* Athens: Univ. of Georgia Press, 1996.

Williams, Samuel C. "The Genesis of the Tennessee Supreme Court." *Tennessee Law Review* 6 (1928): 75–85.

———. "The Golden Era of Tennessee's Judiciary." *Tennessee Law Review* 17 (1943): 805–20.

———. "A History of Codification in Tennessee." *Tennessee Law Review* 10 (1932): 61–78.

———. "History of the Courts of Chancery of Tennessee." *Tennessee Law Review* 2 (1923): 6–23.

———. *Phases of the History of the Supreme Court of Tennessee.* Johnson City, Tenn: Watauga Press, 1944.

———. "A Remarkable Bench: Campbell, Jackson and White." *Tennessee Law Review* 16 (1941): 907–14.

Winn, Thomas H. "Liquor, Race, and Politics: Clarksville During the Progressive Period." *Tennessee Historical Quarterly* 49 (Winter 1990): 207–17.

Winters, Donald. "Postbellum Reorganization of Southern Agriculture: The Economics of Sharecropping in Tennessee." *Agricultural History* 62 (1988): 1–19.

Witham, Henry B. "Requirements of Admission to the Bar in Tennessee." *Tennessee Law Review* 9 (1930): 22–37.

Wyatt-Brown, Bertram. *Southern Honor: Ethics and Behavior in the Old South.* New York: Oxford Univ. Press, 1982.

Wynn, Linda T. "The Dawning of a New Day: The Nashville Sit-Ins, February 13–May 10, 1960." *Tennessee Historical Quarterly* 50 (1991): 42–54.

Dissertations and Theses

Cason, Palmer P. "History of Tennessee's Court System from Its Beginnings to 1834." Master's thesis, George Peabody College, 1930.

Clark, Patricia P. "A. O. P. Nicholson of Tennessee: Editor, Statesman and Jurist." Master's thesis, Univ. of Tennessee, 1965.

Cullen, Charles T. "St. George Tucker and Law in Virginia, 1772–1804." Ph.D. diss., Univ. of Virginia, 1971.

Delozier, Mary Jean. "The Tennessee Supreme Court and Religious Liberty 1900–1960." Master's thesis, Tennessee Technological Univ., June 1966.

Dickson, John L. "The Judicial History of the Cherokee Nation from 1721 to 1835." Ph.D. diss., Univ. of Oklahoma, 1964.

Flanigan, Daniel J. "The Criminal Law of Slavery and Freedom, 1800–1868." Ph.D. diss., Rice Univ., 1973.

Garrison, Tim Alan. "The Legal Ideology of Removal: The Southern State Judiciary and the Sovereignty of Native American Nations, 1776–1838." Ph.D. diss., Univ. of Kentucky, 1997.

Laska, Lewis L. "A History of Legal Education in Tennessee, 1770–1970." Ph.D. diss., George Peabody College for Teachers, 1978.

Malone, Henry T. "Cherokee Civilization in the Lower Appalachians, Especially in North Georgia Before 1830." Master's thesis, Emory Univ. 1949.

Shahan, Joe Michael. "Reform and Politics in Tennessee, 1906–1914." Ph.D. diss., Vanderbilt Univ., 1981.

Thompson, Ruth Anne. "After Suffrage: Women, Law, and Policy in Tennessee, 1920–1980." Ph.D. diss., Vanderbilt Univ., 1994.

Warbasse, Elizabeth B. "The Changing Legal Rights of Married Women, 1800–1861." Ph.D. diss., Radcliffe College, 1960.

ABOUT THE AUTHORS

PROF. R. BEN BROWN is a graduate of Vanderbilt Law School and holds a Ph.D. from the University of Michigan. Professor Brown has served on the faculty of John Marshall Law School and has presented numerous papers dealing with aspects of southern legal history. His Ph.D. dissertation is entitled "The Southern Range: A Study in Nineteenth Century Law and Society."

THEODORE BROWN JR. earned a J.D. degree at Vanderbilt Law School and is engaged in the private practice of law in Atlanta, Georgia. Long interested in the legal history of Tennessee, Brown is the co-editor, with James W. Ely Jr., of the *Legal Papers of Andrew Jackson* (1987).

PROF. JAMES W. ELY JR. holds an LL.B. degree from Harvard Law School and a Ph.D. from the University of Virginia. He is Milton R. Underwood Professor of Law and Professor of History at Vanderbilt University. Ely has published extensively in American legal and constitutional history, including *The Chief Justiceship of Melville W. Fuller, 1888–1910* (1995) and *Railroads and American Law* (2001).

PROF. TIMOTHY S. HUEBNER holds a Ph.D. from the University of Florida and is presently a member of the Department of History at Rhodes College. He has written widely on southern legal history and is the author of *The Southern Judicial Tradition: State Judges and Sectional Distinctiveness, 1790–1890* (1999).

PROF. CARL A. PIERCE earned a J.D. degree at Yale University and is a member of the law faculty at the University of Tennessee. He is the author of a wide range of articles and reviews dealing with legal history as well as the professional responsibility of lawyers, including "A Vacancy on the Supreme Court: The Politics of Judicial Appointment, 1893–94," 39 *Tennessee Law Review* 555 (1972).

PROF. RUTH THOMPSON holds a law degree from the University of Tennessee and a Ph.D. from Vanderbilt University and is presently a member of the Department of History at Georgia Southern University. Thompson has made many academic presentations dealing with aspects of Tennessee history, giving particular emphasis to the status of women. Her dissertation was entitled "After Suffrage: Women, Law and Policy in Tennessee, 1920–1980."

PROF. JOHN R. VILE earned a Ph.D. from the University of Virginia and is currently chair of the Department of Political Science at Middle Tennessee State University. Specializing in American constitutional law, Vile is the author, most recently, of *Tennessee Government and Politics: Politics in the Volunteer State* (1998) and editor of *Great American Lawyers: An Encyclopedia* (2001).

INDEX

A History of the Tennessee Supreme Court was designed and typeset on a Macintosh computer system using QuarkXPress software. The text and the chapter openings are set in New Baskerville. This book was designed by Bill Adams, typeset by Kimberly Scarbrough, and manufactured by Thomson-Shore, Inc. The paper used in this book is designed for an effective life of at least three hundred years.